ThirdPerson

ThirdPerson

Authoring and Exploring Vast Narratives

edited by Pat Harrigan and Noah Wardrip-Fruin

The MIT Press
Cambridge, Massachusetts
London, England

For information about special quantity discounts, please email ⟨special_sales@mitpress.mit.edu⟩.

This book was set in Adobe Chapparal and ITC Officina on 3B2 by Asco Typesetters, Hong Kong.

Printed and bound in the United States of America.

Library of Congress Cataloging-in-Publication Data

Third person : authoring and exploring vast narratives / edited by Pat Harrigan and Noah Wardrip-Fruin.
p.   cm.
Includes bibliographical references and index.
ISBN 978-0-262-23263-0 (hardcover : alk. paper)
1. Electronic games. 2. Mass media. 3. Popular culture. 4. Fiction.
I. Harrigan, Pat. II. Wardrip-Fruin, Noah.
GV1469.15.T48   2009
794.8—dc22   2008029409

10   9   8   7   6   5   4   3   2   1

Contents

I   Authoring

II   Exploring

Contents

Dedication

Pat dedicates his work to his grandparents, Irene and Gregory Leo

Noah dedicates his work to the friends who make these projects possible

Acknowledgments

For this third book in the trilogy, we would like to single out the following people for special thanks:

Doug Sery, Alyssa Larose, Deborah Cantor-Adams, Cindy Milstein, and everyone else at the MIT Press; those who supported this work, directly or indirectly, at the University of California at San Diego, the Minnesota Justice Foundation, and the Johnston Center for Integrative Studies at the University of Redlands; Carrie Rainey, Jennifer Mahal, Peter Darvill-Evans, April Derleth, Andrew Edlin, Melissa Kaercher, Carl McKinney, Justin Richards, Joseph Tabbi, Ben Underwood, and others who made noninstitutional contributions of time and support; our contributors; and our family and friends.

Thank you all,
Pat and Noah

Contributors

Pat Harrigan (ed.)
Noah Wardrip-Fruin (ed.)

Rafael Alvarez
Richard A. Bartle
Michael Bonesteel
Stanford Carpenter
Monte Cook
Paul Cornell
Anne Cranny-Francis
Sam Ford
Chaim Gingold
A. Scott Glancy
Richard Grossman
Matt Hills
Kenneth Hite
William H. Huber
Adriene Jenik
Henry Jenkins
David Kalat
Matthew Kirschenbaum
Norman M. Klein
Tanya Krzywinska
David Lavery
Robin D. Laws
Sarah Lewison
Henry Lowood
William E. McDonald
Matthew P. Miller
Jason Mittell
Stuart Moulthrop
Kate Orman
Sean O'Sullivan
Lance Parkin
Robert M. Price
Ren Reynolds
Trina Robbins
Ken Rolston
Dave Sim
Greg Stafford
Tamiko Thiel
John Tulloch
Walter Jon Williams

ThirdPerson

Introduction
Pat Harrigan and
Noah Wardrip-Fruin

Shall I project a world?
—Thomas Pynchon, *The Crying of Lot 49*

Our intention with *Third Person* is to bring into conversation different types of artists, scholars, and media practitioners working in areas and forms that are not often considered together. This has been our explicit aim as well with the two earlier books in this series, *First Person* and *Second Person*. *First Person*'s subject matter was largely that of digital media at the start of the new century, with a particular emphasis on its literary and ludic dimensions. It can be seen as a focused companion volume to Noah's book with Nick Montfort, *The New Media Reader*, which traced the history of ideas of digital media from the 1940s through the 1990s.

Second Person began to broaden the history and context of the work considered in *First Person*, drawing out connections between contemporary forms of digital media and nonwired interactive media such as tabletop role-playing games and improvisational theater—while considering a range of digital projects from mainstream games to cutting-edge experiments.

Third Person continues these discussions, while also branching into the parallel worlds of literary, comic book, and televisual fiction, guided by the "vastness" that—although perhaps most apparent in the newness of digital media—is a cross-media phenomenon that must be approached as such. Considered together, the three *Person* volumes provide readers with a wide-ranging overview of how fictions are constructed and maintained in different forms of media at the start of the twenty-first century as well as their debt to the character, narrative, and play strategies of earlier decades.

We would like to stress that the various nondigital media discussed in this and the earlier books should not be viewed simply as precursors of today's sexy digital matter. Massively multiplayer online games like *World of Warcraft*, for example, may have been heavily influenced by the tabletop *Dungeons & Dragons*, but *D & D* remains a viable commercial and occasionally artistic force in its own right, although one often invisible to scholars of digital media. Similarly, the long history of superhero comic books did not end when *City of Heroes* was released. As for literary and televisual forms of vast narrative, of course these continue to develop with time, as their own strong traditions of influence and refinement produce epics like George R. R. Martin's *A Song of Ice and Fire* or HBO's *The Sopranos*.

To Seek a Newer World

The rapidly expanding vastness of computational culture continually surprises us. There is an often-retold story that early in the commercial history of computing, an IBM official predicted there was only a market for five computers. Later, in the 1980s, Microsoft designed DOS for a maximum memory of 640K, less than a tenth of one percent of what a standard laptop ships with in 2008. In the 1990s, Yahoo!'s initial approach to the Web was that of a library card catalog—but the Web's size and growth proved to be such that only the warehousing and analysis of as much of its vast body as possible (the approach that catapulted Google to success) could possibly grapple with the task of finding things within it.

Today we are in the process of discovering what narrative potentials are opened by computation's vastness. Unsurprisingly, many of the initial attempts are simply in the service of traditional forms—first computer special effects, and then computer animated films, nonlinear editing systems, digital projection, and so on. In these cases, the vastness of computation is largely absent from the narrative experience it serves. But other possibilities, which employ computation at the time of audience experience, are now being explored.

Norman Klein's chapter in this volume considers how the novel might take form within our culture's most pervasive software approach to vastness: the database. His approach is interactive but nonsimulative, presenting a set of lessons learned in his experiments with reading, viewing,

Pat Harrigan and Noah Wardrip-Fruin

What do we mean by the "vast narratives" in the subtitle of this book? We don't intend, in this introduction, to offer a complete categorization or theoretical accounting of the concept of vast narratives but have made a series of editorial decisions that are guided by our view of the topic. In particular, certain types of vastness appear repeatedly in the following pages, in various combinations and configurations:

▪ **Narrative extent**   Some narrative experiences are significantly more extensive than others. As Dave Sim points out in his contribution to this volume, we can consider a work "vast" inasmuch as it exceeds the usual expectations of extent we have for a work of that form (e.g., a three-hundred-page book or a two-hour film). This is not simply the drawing out of a narrative situation; otherwise this book would have many contributions on topics such as *The Simpsons*, with its seemingly innumerable twenty-two-minute stories. Instead, this book's essayists are more likely to consider narratives such as the various seasons of HBO's *The Wire*, which depart from the tradition of the televised police procedural by dedicating hours to the narrative of a single investigation.

▪ **World and character continuity**   Sitcom characters often find themselves each week placed back in a default situation little changed from the series outset, and in 1972 Umberto Eco famously observed the same of Superman.[1] Long-running series characters like Rex Stout's Nero Wolfe frequently appear to exist in a sort of narrative limbo, where neither internal actions (i.e., the events of previous stories) nor external ones (e.g., social changes) make any impact. But other worlds and characters (even those who, like sitcom characters and Superman, may be written by many authors over long periods of time) operate within less cyclic narrative models. The often-ingenious methods of sustaining open-ended narratives are a major theme of this project.

▪ **Cross-media universes**   Though it is now typical for a blockbuster narrative (e.g., *The Da Vinci Code* or *Harry Potter*) to sprout multiple instantiations (e.g., novels, films, games, comic books, or narrated tours of real-world locations), one narrative form is generally still considered "canonical," from which the others are derived. On the other hand, some narrative "universes," such as those of *Doctor Who* and *Star Wars*, instead treat contributions from many media as authorized (often elaborately authorized) elements of a vast fictional quilt.

▪ **Procedural potential**   The computational power of computing has opened the potential of combinatorial narrative techniques to a level of vastness far exceeding paper forms such as the *Choose Your Own Adventure* books. The most commonly discussed of these operate via some form of world simulation, such as those found in video games, interactive fictions, virtual reality environments, and story-generation systems. But as a number of authors here demonstrate, procedural techniques can also produce vastness at levels ranging from textual production to overlays on the embodied world.

▪ **Multiplayer interaction**   While fan culture creates vast narrative universes around many types of media, some types of media—particularly playable media—include mechanisms in their design for incorporating the actions of certain audience members into the experiences of others. Indeed, some forms, such as tabletop role-playing games and MMOs, are specifically designed as mechanisms for playing together with others within a fictional world. In these cases, the possibilities for interpretable but unanticipated vastness far exceed anything that could be produced algorithmically.

listening, and action. Tamiko Thiel, on the other hand, gives an overview of her work in simulated worlds—but makes it clear that the rules of the simulation can be those that appropriately shape a narrative experience, rather than those that create a stable world.

Yet something like a stable world is precisely the prerequisite for the combination of collaborative play, individual character development, and narrative experience that takes place in massively multiplayer online role-playing games. The roots of these experiences, in turn, trace their history to the multiuser dungeon or domain, a form pioneered by Richard Bartle. In his chapter here, Bartle proposes a three-part typology for virtual worlds and an approach to combining the narrative strengths of two of them. Ren Reynolds takes an even wider view of such worlds, examining the narratives through which we understand them.

Matt Miller, in contrast, gets much more specific, writing as one of the creators of the massively multiplayer online game *City of Heroes*. He relates how this superhero-themed virtual world in some ways faces a narrative dilemma even more profound than that diagnosed by Umberto Eco in his reading of Superman—and resolves it. The specifics of play and fiction are also a concern of William Huber. Writing here about the single-player role-playing game *Final Fantasy X*, he concludes that critical approaches to game space are generally too simplistic to allow for effective consideration of either play or fiction.

The space of simulated worlds can also have other forms of relationships to players, their characters, and fiction. For example, the software of virtual worlds is, like any software, subject to appropriation and reuse. Henry Lowood's chapter considers how *World of Warcraft*'s space and software is used to produce "machinima" (animated films created using game engines) that tell stories of a traditional linear form —but that are frequently told as responses to the non-linear virtual world. Chaim Gingold, one of the creators of *Spore*, describes a rather different form of audience role via a history of the game, in which what the audience creates through play can be the worlds across which other players will experience narratives.

Or in another permutation of vast digital narrative, the fictional world can overlay our own world, as Adriene Jenik and Sarah Lewison discuss in their chapter on SPECFLIC. Here, digital media fictionalizes the audience's own space, creating something like a new form of cinema—but one much larger than the space of the screen and with a vast set of potential performances within its design.

The Vasty Deep

To see a world in a grain of sand,
And a heaven in a wild flower,
Hold infinity in the palm of your hand,
And eternity in an hour.
—William Blake, "Auguries of Innocence"

The traditions of literary vastness in the twentieth century are as varied as J. R. R. Tolkien's *The Lord of the Rings*, Marcel Proust's *In Search of Lost Time*, Dorothy Richardson's *Pilgrimage*, Anthony Powell's *Dance to the Music of Time*, James Joyce's *Ulysses*, and Thomas Mann's

In addition to the presence of many chapters engaging digital media in the *Person* books, this series has also been part of an experiment in digital media. Specifically, we have been undertaking an experiment in electronic publishing in collaboration with the online journal *electronic book review* (*ebr*) and The MIT Press. While The MIT Press had previously and successfully worked with authors who wished to place the complete text of a monograph online (as with William J. Mitchell's *City of Bits* in 1996), *First Person* was the first time the press had published an edited volume made up of essays that would also appear online.

The experiment was of interest to us as editors because of *ebr*'s still-unique approach to online scholarly publication. Rather than continue the practice of publishing "issues"—as a paper journal must—*ebr* is organized into thematic "threads." These threads are updated as new material for them appears. Sometimes this is many thousands of words, as when a set of new essays is made available. Sometimes it may be only a few hundred words, as when an author contributes one of the thoughtful "ripostes" for which the journal is known. All this material, as it comes online, is woven into a set of connections that run across the *ebr* database, bringing together concerns from multiple threads and also, as of version 4 of the journal's interface (which appeared shortly after the publication of *Second Person*), "enfolding" material from the wider World Wide Web of ideas.

In *First Person*, we included the initial threads of *ebr* ripostes to each chapter as part of the paper book's layout. But the online evolution of the *ebr* thread went far beyond the stubs presented on paper, with further developments ranging from a substantial new essay by Brian Kim Stefans to a provocative exchange between *First Person* author Simon Penny and digital media theorist Jan Van Looy. Ripostes also came from leading digital media figures such as Ian Bogost, Jane McGonigal, Matthew G. Kirschenbaum, Adrian Miles, and Scott Rettberg. Finally, the electronic versions of the chapters also brought in new audiences, from readers of *Slashdot* to those following other *ebr* threads.

In short, the *First Person* experiment was viewed as a success by *ebr*, the MIT Press, and us as editors. We hope it can serve as an example of how edited volumes can participate in online culture in new ways. At the very least, it is the precedent that has led us to take similar approaches with *Second Person* and *Third Person*—the outcomes of which it is too soon to report. We hope, however, that readers of this introduction will make themselves part of this experiment, beginning with a trip to ⟨http://www.electronicbookreview .com⟩.

Joseph and His Brothers. It should be noted that Tolkien was famously allergic to allegory, and would not have felt comfortable in the sort of company we have just placed him—with *Ulysses* particularly, operating as it does on multiple levels of meaning simultaneously.[2] Still, the impulse toward vastness is there in all of them. Powell and Proust documented in fine strokes decades of societal change and the fine inner workings of memory, Joyce tried to collapse all of human existence into a few complicated books, and Tolkien spent much of his life sketching out the geography, languages, history, and customs of an imaginary world. Tolkien's artistic project is far from that of literary modernism, but his technique is not miles away from, say, William Faulkner's pocket universe of Yoknapatawpha County.

Vast literary ambition is not a twentieth-century invention, of course. Well before Faulkner, Honoré de Balzac's *La Comédie humaine* tried to capture French society in an enormous story sequence. And well before Balzac, Dante invented the towering cosmological structure of his own *Commedia*, into which he placed all of God, human-kind, history, and morality, as well as half of Florence. As far back as we'd like to go, we find literary structures that either create imaginary new worlds or try to artistically systematize the existing one, often by telescoping all of human experience into a more manageable form (a tripartite afterlife, one day in Dublin, one county in Mississippi, Achilles' shield).

All that said, possibly because of our everyday lived experience, we often think of modern life as being more complex, more difficult to understand, than the lives of our forebears. But narcissism aside, major twentieth-century social and ideological changes as well as unprecedented advances in communications have presented artists with significant challenges if they are to produce meaningful work. Literary modernism, for example, was exuberant in its attempts to create new literary styles with which to interpret experience.[3]

We think of the modernists as representing a particular cultural moment in the literary life of the West. This helps greatly to enhance their reputation. Joyce is about as

revered a literary figure as the twentieth century has produced, and still *Finnegans Wake* makes us uneasy, wondering as we do whether there isn't a hint of madness about the whole project. Without the modernist imprimatur, an eccentric work such as Henry Darger's 15,145-page *The Story of the Vivian Girls, in What Is Known as the Realms of the Unreal, of the Glandeco-Angelinnian War Storm, Caused by the Child Slave Rebellion* suggests an obsessive disorder more than it does literary ambition. Dave Sim, author of the 300-issue, 6,000-page *Cerebus* graphic novel, published regularly between 1977 and 2004, is by his own admission considered an outsider in the comic book industry—primarily for his controversial opinions, but these opinions have manifested more and more directly in the *Cerebus* graphic novel itself, and changed the tenor of the work enough that his readership dropped precipitately. On the other hand, early twenty-first-century century audiences found J. K. Rowling's 1,000,000-plus-word *Harry Potter* series (approximately twice as long as *War and Peace* in English translation) more accessible and appealing than many other traditionally scoped counterparts. It remains to be seen what the reception will be—surely somewhere between Darger's and Rowling's—for Richard Grossman's 3,000,000-page novel *Breeze Avenue*, also discussed in this volume.

Relative Dimensions

As well attested to elsewhere, new technology and new viewing habits have changed some of the ways in which U.S. television shows are produced. HBO has rightly received the most attention in this regard, having produced critically well-received shows like *Oz*, *The Sopranos*, *Six Feet Under*, *The Wire*, and *Deadwood*. Many books could be, and have been, written about these shows alone, to say nothing of *Lost*, *24*, *Veronica Mars*, *Buffy the Vampire Slayer*, and many others. One of our concerns in this book is how this new crop of television dramas express themselves as vast narratives—that is, how they maintain an ongoing structure, with narrative consistency and thematic coherence, throughout large numbers of episodes and sometimes seasons.

David Lavery, in his chapter, provides a brief history of the extended narrative form on television from the 1990s through the 2000s, with a specific focus on *Lost* and the British police drama *Life on Mars*. Sean O'Sullivan, in discussing the third season of *Deadwood*, extrapolates to a narratological understanding of "third seasons" in general. Tanya Krzywinska reads the differing narrative devices of *Buffy the Vampire Slayer* and the *World of Warcraft* massively multiplayer online game against each other. Rafael Alvarez, speaking as a fiction writer, a writer for *The Wire*, and an oral historian, explores the myriad connections between his different works and how they form their own, ever-expanding narrative. Lastly, and a little surprisingly to us editors, Jason Mittell ends this book with a consideration of *The Wire*, viewing it through some of the critical ludic strategies outlined by previous contributors to *First Person* and *Second Person*.

Television also provided the starting point—and recently a new influx of energy—for the multiauthored cross-media phenomenon *Doctor Who*. Beginning on BBC television in 1963, it has since branched into all manner of other media, and the thousands of published and broadcast *Doctor Who* stories are now probably impossible to systematize into a coherent whole. Despite this, some have bravely tried, such as *Third Person* contributor Lance Parkin, in his *A History of the Universe* (1996), and its revised version *Ahistory* (2006).

Doctor Who writer Paul Cornell, speaking here in dialogue with *Doctor Who* writer Kate Orman, argues that there is no such thing as "continuity" any more in *Doctor Who*, except for reader-response-style personal preference. Other chapters in this volume suggest that issues of *Who* continuity and canonicity are controlled by whatever production team is currently maintaining the franchise. Matt Hills examines how Russell T. Davies and the current *Doctor Who* television production team address or avoid issues of continuity from earlier versions of *Doctor Who*, while John Tulloch and Anne Cranny-Francis discuss some of the contemporary political material that Davies' production team has incorporated into the new series.[4] In any case the *Doctor Who* universe, considered as a whole, is now as fractured and contradictory as anything envisioned by H. P. Lovecraft.[5] Here is a hallmark of vast narratives, also noticeable in works like *Cerebus*: their tendency to waver, sometimes drastically, from their original concept.

It is also not uncommon for vast narratives to enlarge themselves by swallowing up other material, as when novelist Michael Moorcock revised many of his earlier works (such as his "Hawkmoon" series) to include references to his ever-expanding "Eternal Champion" cycle of stories. *Doctor Who*, as with so many things, is the quintessential example of this, incorporating or referencing innumerable other vast narratives; Andy Lane's *Doctor Who* novel *All-Consuming Fire* (1994) alone references the other vast narratives of Sherlock Holmes and the Cthulhu Mythos. Elements of the television series *Twin Peaks* are referenced in Lawrence Miles's *Alien Bodies* (1997), and there is a James Bond joke common in *Who* fandom, to the effect that MI6 has a Time Lord working for it—referring to Bond's common cinematic practice of changing his appearance. Vast narratives are omnivorous; in the seventeen years Thomas Mann worked on the *Joseph* novels, the political situation in Europe and the rest of the world was drastically altered, and major events such as the rise of Nazism are referenced in disguised form in the books —something that Mann could scarcely have envisioned when he began writing *Die Geschichten Jaakobs* in 1926.

Infinite Earths

I think it's simply this: that the time has come to wave goodbye to history. Until the day the publishers allow characters to grow old, die and be replaced, there can be no real use for "continuity." Otherwise, allow characters to simply go on forever with no pretense towards real time and under the full understanding that this is an imaginary world made by generations of workers.
—Grant Morrison, in "Punching Holes through Time"

As for the vast narratives of ongoing comic book series, their efforts to remain coherent within an ever-increasing frame are, frequently, heroic. How does one, for example,

Pat Harrigan and Noah Wardrip-Fruin

deal with the fact that Spider-Man—created by Stan Lee and Steve Ditko in 1962 as a teenage character—would be in his sixties in 2008? The problem is both commercial and artistic. No one wants to see an aging superhero; the nature of the mythology is that they remain young and vital.[6] At the same time, a fictional universe in which nothing of any consequence (such as a character aging) is allowed can scarcely be considered to be a home for meaningful narrative. Many comic book fans of a certain age in fact date the decline in quality of Marvel Comics to the point when the major characters stopped aging— somewhere around 1970. Before that point, Peter Parker graduated from high school to college, Reed Richards and Sue Storm married and had a child, and there was a palpable sense that the Marvel Comics universe consisted of real people, who aged and changed in a universe of real consequences. But this couldn't continue, lest commercially successful characters grow too old, and so those characters did not appreciably advance for the next thirty-some years.

These are not incidental questions for large ongoing concerns like DC and Marvel Comics, and the companies have addressed them in various ways over the decades. DC's increasingly baroque reimaginings of its universe are well documented elsewhere.[7] Although they may seem almost incomprehensible to noncomics fans, these are all for the purpose of *simplifying* the DC universe in order to make it seem more inviting to new fans, who might otherwise be put off by decades of accreted published story lines, most of them intricately intertwined, and more often than not, out of print.

As another way of doing things, in 2000, Marvel Comics launched its "Ultimate" line of comics, which took established Marvel Comics characters and rebooted them, effectively creating a separate or subuniverse. This not incidentally allowed it to reintroduce popular heroes and villains, and rewrite popular story lines in Ultimate versions —drawing on decades of mainstream Marvel continuity, incorporating what worked and discarding what didn't. As a commercial strategy this was successful, pulling in new readers who could then follow their favorite characters

"from the beginning." Artistically, it allowed Marvel to use the story lines and other elements that had proved popular in the past. This had a twofold result: dramatically strong story lines (generally supported by strong contemporary writers and artists) with not as much junk in between; and a fun second level of enjoyment for fans familiar with the original story lines, who could appreciate how the new stories compared with the old ones.

These are not the only strategies employed. As of this writing, DC Comics has reintroduced the concept of the "multiverse" to its stories, allowing differently branded versions of DC characters to appear in nonoverlapping (and noncontradictory) story lines, considered to be happening in parallel universes. So, for instance, while Captain Marvel, Mary Marvel, and the rest of the Marvel family are well-established characters within the primary DC universe, they also appear in more cartoony, kid-friendly versions in a miniseries written and illustrated by Jeff Smith (well-known for his independent crossover hit *Bone*). Similarly, Superman and his supporting cast (Lois Lane, Lex Luthor, etc.) appear in mainstream DC comics, but also (in "timeless," "iconic" versions) in Grant Morrison and Frank Quitely's *All-Star Superman*. There is no contradiction between these various versions of characters, because they are not considered, among DC readers or creators, to be "in the same universe."

This may seem like a lot of heavy labor to justify the ontological status of imaginary stories, but the fact is that this is the inescapable result of a vast narrative spread over time that by necessity involves many of the same elements (characters particularly) in perpetual novel deployment. Sooner or later, you have to invent the ground rules for the stories you want to tell. Anthony Powell never had these sorts of problems.

In this volume, in an interview with Sam Ford, Henry Jenkins provides a lucid overview of contemporary narrative strategies in superhero comics, and Stanford Carpenter examines the shifting fortunes of one individual character, Black Lightning, as the commercial and narrative background of DC Comics changes around him. Stuart Moulthrop takes a look at Alan Moore and Dave Gibbons's seminal *Watchmen*, concluding that their narrative unfolds in important spatial, not only temporal, ways—and that this can be seen as similar to many of today's digital media narrative strategies. In a different vein, Trina Robbins discusses Tarpe Mills's syndicated comic strip *Miss Fury*, an early example of both an extended superhero story written and illustrated by a single person, and, still somewhat unusual, one created by a woman.

Epic Campaigns

A crucial consideration when editing our previous volume, *Second Person*, was to give close attention to the under-examined area of tabletop role-playing games. Generally speaking, what scholarly consideration these games have received has cast them as of historical interest, as forerun-ners of today's digital games. In his chapter here, Ken Rolston—the designer of major computer role-playing games such as the Elder Scrolls titles *Morrowind* and *Oblivion*—says that his strongest genre influences are tabletop RPGs and live-action role-playing (LARP) games. He considers nonwired RPGs to be a continuing vital force, and so do we.

One of the difficulties of studying the tabletop RPG field has been the ephemeral nature of much of the industry. With the rise of online sales, brick-and-mortar hobby stores are in perpetual danger of going out of business, but pub-lishers fare little better. If a publisher goes under, published material might remain forever out of print, and important development information might be lost for good. Even if a particular property (such as Greg Stafford's *Pendragon*, discussed in part I) finds a new home, it may be mildly or drastically revamped, and tracking these sorts of multiple iterations can be a daunting task. The recent edition of *Paranoia*, from Mongoose Publishing, is different from the original West End Games edition, and an academic writer unfamiliar with the game's complex publishing history is in danger of making significant errors.[8] Also, as Robin Laws points out in his chapter, the prevalence of nondisclosure agreements in the industry (especially in regard to licensed properties) often makes it difficult for the primary creators to even discuss their work.

Nevertheless, the main reason that tabletop games haven't received the attention they deserve is a failure of will. Academics have overcome far greater obstacles to research, as any historian of, say, the KGB can attest. Tabletop RPGs are generally considered peripheral phenomena, not artistic creations in their own right, and this more than anything has self-supportingly led to the dearth of writing on the subject.

As a step toward remedying this, we present here a handful of chapters on tabletop RPGs, including several that specifically talk about their emblematic form of vast narrative: the campaign. Stafford and A. Scott Glancy examine the specific campaign design of *Pendragon* and *Delta Green*, respectively; Laws provides an overview of the hobby market's artistic and commercial considerations; Ken Hite sketches a possible typology of RPG setting design; and Monte Cook discusses the interaction of planned material and on-the-fly improvisation that typifies an active campaign. The reader will notice many points in these chapters that are brought up in other areas of *Third Person*; writing within a vast ongoing narrative has certain similarities, whether the form is literary, televisual, digital, or otherwise.

Projecting a World

Walter Jon Williams, in his chapter here, writes of his experiences as a novelist in four different types of narrative structures. He has worked as a single author, defining a new narrative universe and writing a potentially open-ended set of stories situated within it. As a "sharecropper," he has written a sequel to a Roger Zelazny story. He has written a tie-in novel for the byzantine *Star Wars* "Expanded Universe." And he has worked as a more equal collaborator on the *Wild Cards* series of books. While these narratives are different in many ways, in each case a kind of *continuity*—which can be pushed against and played with, but must be acknowledged—is primary to the undertaking.

Continuity is a central concern for vast narratives, but one of the goals of this collection is to explore the ways in which continuity and connection need not mean consistency. This is not simply because the task of maintaining consistency is Herculean, though for large enough undertakings this is certainly the case.[9] Rather, it is because consistency is not necessarily the goal. So, for example, the totalizing ambition of the literary modernists can be seen in weirdly modified form in the works of H. P. Lovecraft, as Robert Price describes in part II of this volume. For his part, Lovecraft created what might be called an antimythology: a literary system fractured and contradictory, its parts unable to be systematized. This was a deliberate aesthetic decision by Lovecraft, reflecting his philosophical idea of "cosmic horror."

Drawing from a different Continental movement, the Fantômas stories that David Kalat discusses in his chapter make something of a fetish out of their inconsistency; they incorporate explicitly surrealist narrative techniques to produce wildly swerving narratives that aim more for immediate sensation than for controlled elaboration. Even beyond the initial novels by Marcel Allain and Pierre Souvestre, the literary history of the character Fantômas follows a similarly erratic path.

Finally, as Matt Kirschenbaum describes, we find important narrative elements even in forms for which consistency is anathema—such as in the underexplored area of tabletop wargames. A game that plays out consistently is, of course, no game at all. It is precisely the variation in the system, the wide range of possible and inconsistent narratives, and the elements of the system designed to provoke these experiences that define the form. These wargames, and the other game and playable forms discussed in *First*, *Second*, and *Third Person*, frequently produce vast narratives, but not ones marked by a formal continuity.

In short, we must move beyond understanding continuity as a defining element of vast narratives, and begin to appreciate other organizing techniques as well. Tonal and thematic shifts in the focus of *Joseph and His Brothers*, multiple reversionings of Black Lightning, and the lack of canonical integration in *Doctor Who* can be markers of a robust vast narrative as much as *The Wire*'s novelistic formalism or the medieval fatalism of *The Great Pendragon Campaign*.

I date my interest in vast narratives, rather arbitrarily, to sometime in the early 1980s, when I was eight or nine years old. Even before that time, my family had been forced to indulge my strange interests in comic books and role-playing games, among other things. But sometime in 1980 or 1981 my grandmother's favorite soap opera, *General Hospital*, began to run an unusual story arc, which veered away from the strict romantic melodrama of the soap opera formula and into the baroquely science fictional.[10]

By stages, a plot was revealed wherein the wicked millionaire Mikkos Cassadine stole the huge uncut black diamond named the "Ice Princess," and incorporated it into a weather-control device, which he then used to blackmail the city of Port Charles, *General Hospital's* principal locale. While Port Charles suffered under its unseasonable blizzard, main characters Luke and Laura, in the company of enigmatic foreigner Robert Scorpio, tracked Cassadine down to his tropical island base and, interspersed with embarrassing kissing, foiled the awful scheme. In a scene worthy of *Doctor No*, Luke battled Cassadine hand to hand, and the villain was shockingly frozen to death in his own evil machine. Some sort of countdown was stopped (the computer shutdown password was "Ice Princess"), Luke and Laura were married, and life returned to some semblance of normality.

My grandmother was nonplused. For my part, I was eager to return home from school each afternoon so I could see how the story unfolded. I recognized that this was something like the two-part stories in *Fantastic Four* and *Justice League of America*, and something like my favorite TV show, *Doctor Who*. Later *General Hospital* story lines failed to capture my interest, though I vaguely remember something about a magic sword that I liked at the time. But long before I read Dickens or Tolstoy, and well before sophisticated serialized TV like *The Wire* or *The Sopranos*, I loved watching an unfolding story, an hour every weekday, and talking it over with my grandmother, while my grandfather typed away at his book in the upstairs master bedroom and I waited for my mother to pick me up after work.

This internal semiaesthetic experience is permanently associated in my memory with those days spent as a child with my family. It is the peculiar habit of memory, as Proust knew, to embed the deepest feelings within the deeply trivial. The vast narratives of our lives, like those of fiction, are omnivorous and frequently unpredictable.
—Pat Harrigan

Notes

1. Although contemporary comic book narratives usually operate with a more complex model of narrative continuity and development. See the section "Infinite Earths" below.

2. Depending when you asked him, Powell might find the company a bit modern for his tastes as well.

3. Modernism's most recognizable stylistic innovation, the stream of consciousness, is really a lens used to scope out, or a tool used to shape, the inner life. For Joyce especially, extant literary devices just weren't up to the job, and he went about adapting them into new forms in *Ulysses*, and laboring for seventeen years on the dream language of *Finnegans Wake*—a language that may lack the linguistic rigor of Tolkien's Elvish, but more than makes up for it in allusiveness. And elusiveness.

4. Though it is beyond the scope of this volume, fan reactions to the various incarnations and forms of *Doctor Who* are as varied as *Who* itself. The new BBC Wales series produced by Davies has made *Who* more popular than it has probably ever been, but some fans still question the artistic merit of the new series (while generally still maintaining a loyalty to the franchise)—as when comedian Joshua Scrimshaw remarked to Pat that Davies had turned him into "the kind of fan I hate the most: the kind who hates his favorite show."

5. As opposed to the "Cthulhu Mythos" stories, such as those by August Derleth and Lin Carter, which have often tried to organize Lovecraft's system into a coherent myth cycle. See the section "Projecting a World" on page 7.

6. Or the fact that they are not young and vital is itself integral to the point of the story, as in Alan Moore and Dave Gibbons's *Watchmen*, Frank Miller's *The Dark Knight Returns*, or any number of stories in which a hero is unnaturally aged.

7. See, for example, ⟨http://www.io.com/~woodward/chroma/crisis.html⟩.

8. The game was originally named *Paranoia XP*, until a certain software giant objected.

9. Despite competent full-time staff dedicated to the maintenance of a consistent *Star Wars* universe, nearly every new addition to the media empire contributes new inconsistencies, and even the single-author *Harry Potter* novels contradict one another at points. Well, even Homer nodded.

10. See ⟨http://www.buckwildeweb.com/ice_princess.htm⟩.

References

Eco, Umberto (1972). "The Myth of Superman." *Diacritics* 2, no. 1 (Spring): 14–22.

Lien-Cooper, Barb (2002). "Punching Holes through Time" (interview with Grant Morrison). *Sequential Tart* 5, no. 8 (August). ⟨http://www.sequentialtart.com/archive/aug02/gmorrison2.shtml⟩.

I Authoring

Truths Universally Acknowledged: How the "Rules" of *Doctor Who* Affect the Writing

Lance Parkin

There is a case to be made that the long-running fictional series is a distinct class of art. Telling the latest in the line of continuing stories of a character like, for example, Sherlock Holmes, Superman, James Bond, or Doctor Who requires a writer to take into account a set of rules that don't apply to stand-alone stories as well as almost all of those that do. There are constraints and freedoms in telling a *Doctor Who* tale that don't apply to other science fiction stories, let alone a nongenre one. The story has to meet conditions that "make it" a *Doctor Who* story, yet coming up with a list of those necessary and sufficient conditions isn't as straightforward as it might seem.

As a series becomes a long-running one, often the involvement of the original creators diminishes, and the weight of internal history and audience expectation begins to affect the stories themselves. Fashions and tastes change, and writers have to make choices about how the series will reflect that. One common characteristic is that such series frequently transfer to other media, often surpassing the success of the original medium. The most successful of these narratives endure. Many have a "literary career" that has lasted longer and generated a larger body of work than that of any single author. It is a hundred and twenty years since the first Holmes story was published, and there was not a single year of the twentieth century without a new adaptation or story. There has been a continuous supply of Superman stories since 1938, Bond stories since 1952, and Doctor Who ones since 1963.

There has been little study of the dynamics at work in continuing narratives. Academic attention in this area has tended to focus on the social context of a character, or even on the group dynamics of their audiences. Such narratives are rarely considered on their literary merits or as a whole. There are historical, commercial, and artistic reasons for this poor reputation. Most continuing stories work within the action-adventure genre, and so have neither sought nor attained academic or critical approval. The creator of Tarzan, Edgar Rice Burroughs, made his feelings plain: "I wish you to know that I am fully aware of the attitude of many scholars and self-imagined literati toward that particular brand of deathless literature of which I am guilty" (quoted in Leavis 1932). Equally important, many continuing stories have traditionally been written by people who are poorly paid, with little artistic freedom or control over the rights. This situation has not so much changed in recent decades as completely reversed—some of the highest-paid, most powerful storytellers are those who have created (or even helped to develop) long-established continuing narratives. Even so, even decades after "the death of the author," a text written by one person is still most commonly seen as inherently more impressive and worthy of study than one that is the work of many hands.

The terminology used is often disparaging. The most popular U.S. term for ongoing narratives, "franchise," places them in the realm of burger joints and pretzel stands, rather than art or academia, and a term used by some British critics, "sharecropping," is even less flattering. I will use a less emotive term, coined in the title of the first academic analysis of *Doctor Who*: "unfolding text" (Tulloch and Alvarado 1984). I am defining an unfolding text as fiction based around a common character, set of characters, or location that has had some form of serial publication. The works that make up an unfolding text can have a single author, particularly in their early stages, but are typically written by many.

An unfolding text is often not a single series; most contain a number of distinct series, in different media, usually with different creators and even intended audiences. In the 1990s, for example, *Batman* managed to incorporate

Lance Parkin

a successful series of comics, a series of films, and an animated television series. These were effectively the stories of three separate individuals, in separate fictional universes, for separate audiences, made by separate production teams. As I will go on to illustrate, though, there is generally a tangled interrelationship between such series. The unfolding text adapts to meet the changing demands of its audience over time. Perhaps as a way to frame these disparate series, another characteristic of an unfolding text is that there is a metanarrative: a "story about the story" that combines major story lines with references to what went on behind the scenes.

I am going to concentrate on *Doctor Who*, which started as a BBC television series in 1963 (the first episode was shown the day after President John F. Kennedy was assassinated). But it has long been hard to classify *Doctor Who* as simply a television series. There are around a thousand individual stories making up the one unfolding text, told in just about all the media: television, novels, novellas, novelizations, short stories, cinema, radio, comic strips, theater, Webcasts, and even sweet cigarette cards. *Doctor Who* exists as "multimedia," but there is more to it than that. There are links between stories; there is a strong internal continuity. Beyond that, there is also a real-life production history, a social context, and the personal responses (contemporary and nostalgic) of the audience, all shaping the storytelling. *Doctor Who* is perhaps the best example of how continuing narratives change over time in a process that is analogous to natural selection: unfolding texts adopt strategies to ensure their continued survival in the face of a changing environment of artistic and commercial imperatives. But much of what I will discuss applies to all continuing narratives. Indeed, I hope to demonstrate that much of traditional literature is now actually read as franchise, and so is subject to the same processes and can be analyzed using the same methods.

Writing for a long-lived running series like *Doctor Who* throws a number of challenges that would be unfamiliar to an author of stand-alone fiction. Some of these are common to all serial storytelling; others are peculiar to *Doctor Who* itself.

It is crucial to note that someone writing for a series still has to do the vast majority of things any other storyteller must. A *Doctor Who* novelist, say, is still writing a novel, and for it to work, must create compelling characters, place them in interesting situations, structure the plot, research what needs to be researched, and compose convincing dialogue—the list is a familiar one. With that in mind, the unfolding text has much to offer an author. The writer of a new *Doctor Who* story can take for granted at the outset advantages that many authors spend a whole career searching for: there is a loyal, global audience (or guaranteed market, to put it in more crass commercial terms); the story will be almost endlessly reviewed and discussed by informed critics; and there is a degree of familiarity with the core concepts of the book and genuine devotion to some of the characters. With so much already established, the author can play with the format—indeed the audience demands it.

The *Doctor Who* novels published while the television series was off air between 1992 and 2005 had the freedom to—as Virgin Publishing, which published the first original novels, put it—tell stories "too broad and too deep for the small screen." Freed from the budgetary constraints of television, and by necessity written with a smaller, more devoted audience in mind, the *Doctor Who* novels twisted and stretched the unfolding text—both in terms of the subject areas covered by the books and the storytelling techniques that were used. At their best, the novels would take *Doctor Who* and reinterpret it, critique it within their text, deconstruct it. This, though, was simply a more concentrated version of what *Doctor Who* had been doing since its inception.

Doctor Who has an exceptionally loose format for a running series—the protagonist, the Doctor, can travel to any point in time and space in his TARDIS. The styles of stories range widely: the Doctor meeting Charles Dickens in a Victorian ghost story; a parody of reality television; a claustrophobic action-adventure story in which soldiers fight an escaped monster; or a story that explores the implications of a companion deciding to change history, so that her father didn't die when she was a baby.

Those are all examples from a single season, each by a different writer.[1] As fan, novelist, and television writer Paul Cornell (1996) put it, "The format is there's no format." Almost every television drama series has a "bible," a document for the use of the production team that spells out the characters' biographies and personalities as well as which sets are available and so on. Once a show is up and running, these might not be referred to on a day-to-day basis, but they tend to be quite hefty documents.[2] *Doctor Who*'s traditionally runs to a handful of pages. Added to this, unlike most series, *Doctor Who* producers and script editors have generally discouraged a "house style." Each television story is written by an individual author, not a story team. Consecutive stories are rarely directed by the same person. Most adventures have entirely new casts, apart from the Doctor and his companion, and only one recurring set (the interior of the TARDIS). This is in stark contrast to *Doctor Who*'s transatlantic rival *Star Trek*, which was based on the idea of boldly going "where no one has gone before," but was shot mostly on standing sets, using a set of standardized camera angles, with a large regular cast along with a small pool of writers and directors.

The *Doctor Who* television series was originally developed in 1963 with the Reithian brief to educate children. The stories alternated between what fans typically now call "pure historicals" (stories with no other science fiction element than the time-traveling regular characters), and those set on alien planets that were, in theory at least, meant to avoid "bug-eyed monsters" in favor of morality plays and science lessons.[3] The Doctor was a mysterious old man, accompanied by his kooky teenage granddaughter and a couple of schoolteachers. The Doctor never interfered, only observed, and stated he was on a "scientific expedition." *Doctor Who* on television in 2007 is a series about an immortal alien who resembles a young man, the last of a race of Time Lords, who travels the universe on a moral crusade to fight monsters, alongside a beautiful young woman with whom he shares a palpable sexual attraction. There are similarities: the Doctor still travels through time and space in a TARDIS that looks like a police box, viewers from 1963 would recognize his arch enemy, the Daleks, and perhaps

1.1 Cover of *Trading Futures* (2002). (© BBC Books)

most significantly, the series is still broadcast to a "family audience" on Saturday nights on BBC1.[4] Despite that, even discounting the advances in television production techniques, *Doctor Who* in 2007 is practically a completely different show to the one aired in 1963.

The changes were almost all gradual, building on successes, discarding those that didn't work, and trying new things—either out of necessity or because the show was so successful it knew it could experiment without alienating its audience. Sometimes, these plans were quietly forgotten; in 1965, for example, a conscious effort was made to create monsters to rival the Daleks—the Mechanoids—but despite merchandise and spin-off stories, they just didn't catch on and only made one television appearance. Two of the most iconic and enduring companions of the Doctor, the Brigadier and K9, were originally intended to appear in only one story each.

Over the decades, a hugely elaborate internal continuity built up organically, with the various writers and script editors struggling to maintain consistency, and viewers of the series gleefully writing in to point out when contradictions ("continuity errors") or other mistakes (such as scientific or historical inaccuracies) arose. So many of the things that the modern *Doctor Who* audience takes for granted were not part of the original format. Viewers now know that the Doctor is a Time Lord from Gallifrey, has two hearts, and has the ability to regenerate his body when he suffers a mortal injury (up to a maximum of twelve times; he's regenerated nine times so far), but these facts were established long after the show started, often on the spur of the moment, and all have also been explicitly contradicted at one point or another.[5]

Those are just the basics; there are whole books given over to listing or ordering the "fictional facts" of *Doctor Who*, and even books dedicated to reconciling them into some consistent form. There was a sense in the 1980s that the television series was becoming weighed down by its past, but twenty years on, prospective writers are faced with as many novels, audio plays, and comic strips each as there are television stories: around a thousand stories in total. For a *Doctor Who* story to work, it has to be in the spirit of what has gone before, but it can't simply repeat or rehash. Any format, however flexible, can only have a limited number of permutations, and it has become increasingly difficult in recent years to come up with a completely original idea for a *Doctor Who* story—even more so if you want the idea to be entertaining and workable.

But there is a more general challenge. The balance to be struck by writers of an unfolding text is between audience expectation and appealing to contemporary tastes. *Doctor Who* does not exist in a bubble; readers compare and contrast it with the other television dramas they watch or

books they read. A *Doctor Who* television episode or novel of 2007 is a product of the year 2007—its competition is what is on the other channels or bookshop shelves that day. Over the years, *Doctor Who* survived by tracking prevailing fashions and concerns. Early success generally comes from—often in quite counterintuitive or unplanned ways—appealing to the mood of the moment, but as the mood changes, an unfolding text faces the same dilemma that a long-lived rock band does: do they change their style to keep up with fashion, or do they stick to the formula that made them a long-lived rock band in the first place?

Different series adopt different strategies to survive changing times. Ian Fleming's original Bond novels were set over a relatively short period, and were rooted in the context of the early cold war, but even so Fleming felt it necessary to fiddle with the details of Bond's birth date a little in the later books to avoid Bond becoming "too old." This now appears ironic, given that the films have almost always emphasized that the different actors who have played the part since 1962 are playing the same individual. George Lazenby's Bond saw his wife killed by Blofeld, Sean Connery's Bond avenged her death, Roger Moore's Bond visited the grave, and the loss was mentioned by a friend of Timothy Dalton's Bond.[6] Playing against that, the film series has deliberately tried to remain current. Bond wears fashionable suits, he drives the latest sports cars, and the stories have featured technology or geopolitical developments that root them clearly in the year they were made: the energy crisis, the space shuttle, the war in Afghanistan, or the collapse of the Soviet Union. Meanwhile, a highly successful series of *Young Bond* children's novels started in 2005, featuring a Bond at Eton in the early 1930s, as Fleming's novels had originally described.

Logically, we are long past the point where the protagonist of all these adventures can be the same individual, but the audience understands and accepts it. This was proved by the success of *Casino Royale* (2006). The movie, an adaptation of Fleming's first novel, depicts Bond's first mission, yet it's not set in the 1950s or 1960s, and M is the "modern" version of the character, played by Judi Dench. Nor does it seek to fudge the issue: we know from dialogue that it's set explicitly after 9/11, Bond drives the latest Aston

Martin and Ford cars, and we can see from the dates on cell phones, computer records, and newspapers that it is 2006, the year the film was released. Critics have occasionally wondered whether Bond is relevant to the modern world, and—in a self-aware flourish that is characteristic of the unfolding text—this has been echoed in the movies themselves (so, for example, in *GoldenEye* (1995), the new M tells Bond to his face that he is "a sexist, misogynist dinosaur. A relic of the cold war." Naturally, the events of the movie intend to prove her and the real-life critics wrong. Bond may have his spiritual roots in the cold war, but audiences accept him as relevant to the modern world.

On the other hand, when we think of Holmes, we think of the Victorian era, and perhaps when we think of the Victorian era we quickly think of Holmes. Michael Chabon (2005) has a radical interpretation of the character:

> In 1889, J. M. Stoddart, American editor of Lippincott's Magazine, took Oscar Wilde and another writer to lunch, over which he proposed that each man write a long story for his publication. One of his lunch guests that memorable day went off and dreamed up a tale of an uncanny, bohemian, manic-depressive genius who stalks the yellow fog of London, takes cocaine and morphine to ease the torment of living in this "dreary, dismal, unprofitable world," and abates his drug habit by compulsively scheming to peel back the commonplace surface of other people's lives, betraying secret histories of violence and vice. Stoddart published Conan Doyle's second Holmes novel as *The Sign of Four*. Wilde, for his part, turned in *The Picture of Dorian Gray*.

But even that reading roots the character to his time. If someone were to write a Holmes story set in the early twenty-first century, it would seem extremely odd. More than one recent story has portrayed Holmes in the modern day, but always as a result of some form of time travel, struggling to adapt his methods to the brave new world in which he finds himself.[7] In reality, a dozen of Doyle's stories are set in the Edwardian period, not the Victorian. Sir Arthur Conan Doyle's last Holmes story was published in 1927, and in it he took the character to the eve of the First

World War. From the start, Holmes was living in a world of electric lights, the London Underground, and the telephone. Indeed, the original stories he is a man out of step with his time, ahead of the game, and using the latest developments to solve crimes (famously, he was using fingerprints before any police force in the world). But somehow when Holmes uses a telephone or jumps into a motorcar it seems anachronistic. Bond shows how the evolution of Holmes's unfolding text could have taken a different path by continuing to be set in the year of publication. Indeed, the movies starring Basil Rathbone have long been seen as the definitive film interpretation, although all but the first two were set in the period they were made, during the Second World War, with Holmes thwarting the schemes of Nazi spies. In the early twenty-first century, the unfolding text of Holmes survives, thrives even, but as a period piece. Perhaps Holmes is so central to our notion of both the Victorian era and the detective genre that it's impossible to set a story in a version of the modern day that isn't informed by him. Interestingly, modern Holmes stories frequently feature him as a young man or as ancient, playing with the iconography of the texts.

Some long-running unfolding texts find it possible to carry on regardless. P. G. Wodehouse wrote Jeeves and Wooster stories from 1917 to 1974, and even at their first appearance the gentleman's gentleman and his gentleman were already from a world that had all but disappeared in reality. Their scrapes existed in a bubble—one that often felt timeless. (It is odd to think that they are, easily, contemporaries of both Holmes and Bond.) Later stories show Jeeves and Wooster watching the Rolling Stones in concert, and getting caught up in a march organized by the Campaign for Nuclear Disarmament, although these stories are not generally popular among devotees.

The Simpsons television series has been running since 1989, and because it is a cartoon, the characters don't need to age. Even though the show has Halloween and Christmas episodes every year, even though it explicitly encompasses the George Bush, Bill Clinton, and George W. Bush presidencies, Bart Simpson is still ten years old. Originally portrayed as a "dysfunctional family," the marriage of Homer and Marge has endured for decades, and Homer must be one of the few blue-collar Americans who since the early 1980s has managed to hold on to the same job (with only temporary diversions). Characteristically, the show has frequently drawn attention to the problem without offering a solution.

Doctor Who, like Bond, can get away with endlessly recasting the lead actor. Bond's producers originally planned to explain Bond's change of appearance by saying he'd had plastic surgery, but in the end decided to make a joke of it. When a beautiful woman, whom Bond had been fighting to protect, steals his car and drives off, leaving him alone at the start of *On Her Majesty's Secret Service* (1969), Bond notes that "this never happened to the other fella." The entire audience is in on a joke that makes no sense within the narrative—they know this is the debut of a new actor, Lazenby, who replaced (briefly, as it turned out) Connery in the role. This raises an important factor: if audiences remain entertained by a running series, they will understand and forgive even the most blatant changes, perhaps particularly if they feel they are invited to laugh it off. *Doctor Who* can switch lead actors via a (surprisingly vague) science fictional explanation, and carries the strong advantage of a character who is immortal within the fiction itself and can use his time machine to make sure that when he visits "the present day," it is the year of broadcast. It allows the series to evolve and stay current.

Doctor Who's format may be extraordinarily flexible, and experimentation may be encouraged, but clearly there is some factor that makes a story a *Doctor Who* story. And there is an important corollary to this: that means that there is someone, somewhere, who has the authority to say what makes a story a *Doctor Who* story.

With *Sherlock Holmes*, there seems to be one overriding consideration, as expressed in the reviews quoted on the back of one modern collection of Holmes short stories, and that is not to deviate too far from the template established by Doyle:

An homage to the master.

The stories here remind readers of the elements of Conan Doyle's greatness: difficult puzzles, vivid but selective detail, and tight dialogue.

Uniformly faithful to the spirit of Doyle's creation. (Greenberg, Lellenberg, and Stashover 2001)

And this is a sentiment echoed in the reviews of Bond novels not written by Fleming, although note that the quotations the publisher has selected also emphasize that this is not simple pastiche:[9]

Ian Fleming's inheritance has been well and aptly bestowed…fast-moving action, a rather superior Bond-maiden, violence, knowledgeableness about guns, golf and seamanship…good dirty fun.

Gardner's James Bond captures that high old tone and discreetly updates it.

John Gardner has got the 007 formula down pat. But not too pat…he manages to create suspense and spring a few surprises.

The authority here rests with the reviewers—and the publishers that reprint what the reviewers have said. In both cases, though, new writers have been brought in to continue an unfolding text created by an author who has died (note the word "inheritance" in the first Bond review). Their job, at least in part, is to stay true to that creator—to maintain the same "tone" and "formula." In the majority of these quotations it is implicit that readers will understand what the formula is, but a couple of the reviewers summarize the formula explicitly.

In his study of *Batman*, Will Brooker (2000) suggests what might be an alternative model: that a Batman story, regardless of medium or tone, has a core set of concepts. Not all of them are used, not all of the core concepts were there at the beginning of the series, and some stories actively subvert expectations, but readers and viewers understand them as "rules," and are critical, or at least initially suspicious, when these rules are broken. This may apply more to unfolding texts that were always the work of many hands—or it may be that "written by a particular person" is one of the core concepts for some unfolding texts.

Who is to say what this core concept is? All television and film series are the work of many hands, but most U.S.

series have a clear (indeed contractually obligated) "created by" credit. Gene Roddenberry was dead before the television series *Star Trek: Deep Space Nine*, *Star Trek: Voyager*, and *Star Trek: Enterprise* were developed, but they bear the caption "based on *Star Trek*, created by Gene Roddenberry." While alive, Roddenberry exerted a degree of control over all the various *Star Trek* spin-offs, vetoing story lines, overseeing merchandise, and ordering changes so that everything conformed to his vision of the series. George Lucas, the writer-director of *Star Wars*, has even greater control. They defined the rules.

But this isn't always the case. *Doctor Who*, for example, has no "creator." *Doctor Who* was developed in-house at the BBC in 1963, with a number of writers, producers, and executives contributing vital components of the format.[10] Indeed, Nigel Kneale, a noted television playwright famous for his science-fantasy scripts, turned down the invitation to write for the series on the grounds that it was a "producer's show"—in other words, not one developed by a writer. Within a few years, the original production team and regular cast had moved on and been replaced. When David Whitaker, the first story editor, contributed a script for the 1967 series, the only credited name he would have recognized from his time on the show four years previously was Ron Grainer, who composed the theme music.

Without a creator, where does the authority to say what defines a *Doctor Who* story lie? *Doctor Who* is owned by the BBC, which began to license *Doctor Who* products within a few months of the show's premiere (unlike today, toy companies and publishers used to wait to see if the show was a hit before securing the merchandising rights). But any control the BBC has exercised over the years has been, without exception, simple brand management (e.g., it asked Virgin Books to tone down the swearing in its line of *Doctor Who New Adventures* novels). Successive television production teams have had approval of merchandising; currently, for instance, they check the plots of the books and audio plays to make sure they don't clash with the plans for the television show, and in the past they've ensured that the family show isn't associated with products that promote smoking or drinking. Yet this is brand management, not artistic control. *Doctor Who* producers come

and go, and are often brought in by the BBC precisely because they will have different thoughts and priorities than their predecessor.

Does the authority lie with the audience? *Doctor Who* is a national institution in the United Kingdom. Because it is a family show, many Britons encountered it first as a child, and then again watching it with their children. The show has been much parodied on television and in newspaper cartoons. The core concepts of the show are parts of everyday speech—the autobiography of former Prime Minister John Major (1998), to pick just one example, referred to Number Ten Downing Street as "like the TARDIS" because the building is far larger than it appears from the street and to a particular security system as "Dalek-voiced."

The audience knows that the format allows the lead actor to change, and whatever else an actor who takes on the role goes on to achieve, they will always be introduced as "former Doctor Who." There is a collective memory of the show. Former *Doctor Who* producer John Nathan-Turner complained that "the memory cheats," and it is true that nostalgia and the passing of time means that the average *Doctor Who* viewer tends to elide details from different stories, eras, or even shows.[11] People frequently appeal to *Doctor Who* message boards with a vivid childhood memory of a story, often referring to two in particular: one with a faceless man at the top of a flight of stairs, and another where paintings at a school came alive—only to be told these were actually from *Sapphire and Steel* and *The Tomorrow People*, respectively. Despite this, the British public has a good grasp on what Brooker would call the core concepts of *Doctor Who*. Audiences hold the ultimate power over a show: if they don't like the current series, they will stop watching and *Doctor Who* will be taken off the air. So that would seem to give them authority.

Unfolding texts exist in a complicated relationship with authors and readers, but there is actually a third group as well: the fans. A number of studies have been written analyzing fans and fandoms, and these have traditionally concluded that fans are superattentive readers. Not only can their expertise be called on to sort out any confusion about whether a particular episode was *Doctor Who* or *The*

Tomorrow People, they often possess a level of knowledge that to call "encyclopedic" would be to flatter encyclopedias. John Tulloch and Henry Jenkins (1995), however, analyzed fandom in their book *Science Fiction Audiences*, and found that there was a more complex relationship at work, with fandoms constituting a "powerless elite"—an organized group of superinformed people quite distinct from the mainstream audience, but with no substantive control or influence over the unfolding text itself.

In his earlier work, *Textual Poachers*, Jenkins (1992) had used the analogy of the studio as gamekeeper and the fan as poacher—*Star Trek*, say, was owned (produced, published, and trademarked) by Paramount Studios, and when fans engaged with the material, it was as if they had snuck under a metaphoric fence to exploit "gaps" in the texts. *Star Trek* fans were frequently interested in what was left unaddressed by the television series: one early series of fan fiction concentrated on Uhura, a black female character often held up as an emblem of the show's egalitarian agenda, but who was little more than a switchboard operator in practice. More notoriously, a whole genre of fan fiction, "slash," infers sexual liaisons between characters. The name comes from the punctuation in "Kirk/Spock," whose relationship was the subject of much early fan speculation, to the point where Roddenberry even took the opportunity to have Kirk mention it.[12] Since then, elements of almost every fandom have copied the *Star Trek* model to infer sexual relationships between just about any and every character on their favorite shows. Fans took pleasure in depicting what was not—and in many cases, could not be—depicted on network television. *Star Trek* fandom established the template on which all subsequent U.S. fandoms were based: conventions, organized "save our show" campaigns, fanzines, fan fiction, art, and so on. *Star Trek* fans were early adopters of the Internet, using it to create a social network and debate the show.[13]

As a British phenomenon, *Doctor Who* fandom developed at first in a way that avoided many trappings of the *Star Trek* template. There are UK *Doctor Who* conventions, but they often have the air of British trick-or-treaters: many of the participants seem more than a little self-conscious, if not actively reluctant to be there. Instead of

1.2 Cover of *The Infinity Doctors* (1998). (© BBC Books)

communal celebration, *Doctor Who* fandom has always taken a rather discursive approach, with more than a whiff of a university common room. The advent of cheap photocopying in the late 1970s, just as an organized *Doctor Who* fandom was forming, meant that groups of fans could start putting together fanzines. The show's two decades of history provided almost endless things to write about: simple summaries of stories as well as lists of companions and monsters quickly gave way to discussions of the relative merits of "eras" of the show, easily marked out by the reigns of the lead actors. (*Doctor Who* fandom, right from the beginning, emphasized the making of the show as much as the show itself.) Fans quickly learned that stories could also be divided up into the reigns of producers—and swiftly factionalized into those who liked Barry Letts's vision and those who preferred that of his successor, Philip Hinchcliffe (no fans worth their salt, at that point, rated the then-current producer, Graham Williams). Even now, *Star Trek* fans are more likely to debate the merits of individual characters ("Who's the best Captain: Kirk or Picard?" or "Who's strongest: Data or Worf?") or immerse themselves in the fictional world than delve too deeply into the production of the show. Most *Doctor Who* fans are not only aware when there was a change of script editor but they also will have a well-established view on their relative merits.[14]

A number of the fan contributors to Tulloch and Jenkins's book told the authors that their model was already outdated. Kate Orman, described as "of the *Doctor Who* fan club of Australasia," is quoted in 1993 as suggesting the following: "After reading the manuscript of this book, her feeling is that the current fans are 'more po-mo,' more diverse, more ironic, more able to laugh at themselves than those a decade earlier" (Tulloch and Jenkins 1995, xi).

But the authors missed out on the most significant development. In 1993, Orman's first *Doctor Who* novel, *The Left-Handed Hummingbird*, was published. She quickly became a stalwart of the range, writing, among other things, the novel that saw the departure of Ace, the last television companion, and Orman was one of the first people that the BBC contacted to write for its new range of novels in 1997. The power relationship had shifted, decisively, to the fans.

At one end of the process, studios have realized that having a small number of devoted fans can prove more lucrative than having a mass audience; fans tend to be completists and early adopters, and with conventions, fan groups, and particularly the Internet, it is extremely easy—and cheap—to advertise to them. A modestly successful show (even shows that were failures when broadcast, such as Joss Whedon's *Firefly*) can justify lavish DVD box sets, high-end replica props, glossy official magazines, and ranges of novels. These are often produced *by* fans of the show as well as being *for* those fans. More to the point, the pro-

duction teams of long-running shows are frequently now themselves (as they are inevitably described in interviews) "self-confessed fans." Fans reading an Internet interview or attending a convention want reassurance that the producer "understands the show" (usually a thinly veiled euphemism for that fandom's specific preferences).

So when the television series *Buffy the Vampire Slayer* started in 1997, it consciously sought to create a fandom for itself, and become a cult hit in a way that the original *Buffy* movie had failed to do. Whereas *Star Trek* fans poached subversive readings, spun romantic relationships out of sideways glances, and inferred queer readings, *Buffy* spoon-fed its audience by giving them a parade of increasingly unlikely characters pairing off or coming out as gay. It openly asked "fannish" questions within the text, and subverted its own format. U.S. television in the 1990s allowed far more to be seen than television in the 1960s (*Buffy* often dressed up in analogy what other teen soaps simply depicted), leaving fewer "gaps" in the text for fans to exploit than something like *Star Trek*. The show was created by Joss Whedon, a third-generation television writer and "comics geek," and successfully gained the attention of members of existing fandoms. It helped that the show was well written, witty, and generally well performed, but to extend Jenkins's analogy, *Buffy* fans weren't cheeky young poachers so much as grown-ups paying to go on a corporate shoot.

Doctor Who's relationship with its fans is different and more complex. It's a British show, and noticeably grew up with its audience. While it was smart and self-aware right from the first episode, it was clearly aimed at a younger audience in the 1960s than in the 1980s. The production team was conscious of this; a behind-the-scenes guide from the 1970s noted that some of the children who had watched the early episodes "were now old enough to have children of their own" (Dicks and Hulke 1976). As these original viewers grew up, particularly when they started going to college in the mid-1970s, fandom started to coalesce—a process helped along by a surge in the current show's popularity, the *Star Wars* phenomenon, and a growth in an undergraduate culture exemplified by the appeal of *Monty Python*. During his time as script editor on the show (1979–1980), Douglas Adams was able to plot a course for the show that managed to appeal to longtime fans of the show while pitching it at almost the exact midpoint between *Star Wars* and *Python*.

As the BBC is not a commercial organization, it was often almost constitutionally unable to build on the success of the show; a twentieth-anniversary celebration that attracted fifty thousand people was never repeated (internally, the BBC described it as "a disaster" because far more people showed up than it had been expecting), and it canceled *Doctor Who* in 1985, just as the show was starting to take off in North America. Adams, who had long ago left the production team by that point, wrote to the BBC pointing out that taking foreign sales and merchandise into account, *Doctor Who* made seven times as much as it cost to produce, and was told, "Our accountants don't think that way" (Brown and Cybermark Services 1998).

In the 1990s, the BBC started to realize the value of the *Doctor Who* brand, and as with their U.S. counterparts, it recruited fans to exploit the franchise. The striking fact about the 2005 television series, the first for over fifteen years, was that the writers were all fans who had contributed at least a short story, novel, or audio adventure in the absence of the television show.

When the television series was off the air, fans of the series had the greatest incentive to write stories in other media. When the television series returned, there was an existing pool of many dozens of such authors to choose from—all aware of how *Doctor Who* had evolved while away from television, and many with an extensive track record in writing for television—so it was natural enough that executive producer Russell T. Davies would look there for his writers. With over forty years of history and so many previous stories, has it now reached the point where only fans have the understanding to write an effective *Doctor Who* story? It would seem so—not because people like Cornell are masters of the arcane facts of old episodes but because as writers, they can see old episodes in terms of storytelling strategies that succeeded or failed. Cornell's first script was exactly the "time travel paradox" story that was often resisted by previous production teams, which were more interested in action-adventure stories than more cere-

bral science fiction concepts, but Cornell understood that the new show's emphasis on character-led stories allowed him room to tell his story. A newcomer to the show might not be so confident.

Doctor Who is a highly developed example of an unfolding text, and perhaps has the most highly developed (and influential) fandom, but it's by no means unique. It is tempting to see this as a phenomenon of the multimedia age, helped along by technological advances like home video, desktop publishing (to print fanzines), and the Internet. There were unfolding texts in the first half of the twentieth century, though: Holmes, Tarzan, Superman, Jeeves and Wooster, but also descendants of Holmes like Father Brown, Campion, and Agatha Christie's detectives Hercule Poirot and Miss Marple. Even in the late twentieth century, ongoing novel series like Patrick O'Brien's Aubrey/Maturin series or Terry Pratchett's *Discworld* novels established themselves as unfolding texts in one medium, by one author.

Throughout history there have been unfolding texts; Robin Hood, King Arthur, and the classical myths, for example, have all the characteristics of an unfolding text: widely understood core concepts and characters, and stories told in every available medium that have grown organically over huge timescales and have been adapted for successive generations.

The greatest unfolding text of all, at least in Western culture, is that of the Bible myths; it is perhaps a little much to equate the Christian priesthood with the *Doctor Who* Appreciation Society, yet considered purely as literature, the difference may genuinely only be one of scale, and many an Anglican vicar might identify with the idea of being part of a powerless elite.[15] The sort of person who becomes a fan nowadays—typically they are, or will be, tertiary educated, male, and bookish—may well have become a monk in former times. The British science fiction magazine *Interzone* used to, rather snobbishly, dismiss unfolding texts as "spinoffery" and tended not to review them. If the analogy holds, had there been a like-minded Christian fanzine, it would no doubt have felt *The Divine Comedy*, *Paradise Lost*, *The Last Supper*, and Chartres Cathedral as beneath its notice.

So the unfolding text has always been with us. I think there is another, more modern phenomenon that has started to change the way traditional literature is treated. There have long been uniform editions of authors' books, and authors like Laurence Sterne and Dickens were "merchandising" their own work centuries before Lucas approved his first Darth Vader pencil case. Now something new is happening: audiences and publishers are treating traditional forms of literature as if they were unfolding texts. The works of Jane Austen do not share any characters or specific settings. Since the highly successful 1995 television adaptation of *Pride and Prejudice*, though, there has been a marked shift in the way Austen's works are seen. One BBC executive has an amusing anecdote about meeting a U.S. counterpart who congratulated her on *Pride and Prejudice*, but complained that there had never been a second series. Details of that adaptation are now established parts of the story, particularly a memorable scene where Colin Firth's Darcy emerges dripping from a morning swim. The pond is marked for special attention on the tourist maps at Lyme Hall, where it was filmed. It's not a unique case; the adaptations of a story often contain innovations that become iconic, but with Austen, it has reached the point where the tour guide of the Austen museum in Bath can unself-consciously say the line, "For those who have seen or read *Pride and Prejudice*." There is now an Austen industry— quite apart from the DVDs and souvenirs, every Austen novel now has literally dozens of sequels, prequels, and other spin-offs.[16] That there is a market for these is evidence enough that there is a sizable Austen fandom. There is even a movie, *Becoming Jane* (2007), based around an Austen metanarrative: it takes a scrap of biographical information about Austen and weaves it into a story in which Austen herself is cast as a typical Austen heroine.

The unfolding text, then, is one of the most prevalent modes of storytelling in our modern culture—one that has been easy to dismiss as a commercial, rather than artistic, endeavor, but that is built around an extremely sophisticated relationship between author, reader, and fan. Traditional criticism would see *Star Wars* as "six films" or *Doctor Who* as "a television series," but those are the tip of the ice-

berg, and there are aspects of both narratives that every member of the audience understands, yet which are literally incomprehensible without "meta" knowledge. Everyone of a certain age (and their parents) knows what an Ewok is, but the word Ewok is never used in *Return of the Jedi* (1983), the movie in which they appear; the information was transmitted via the spin-off toys, comics, cartoons, and books. We are so used to this sort of in-joke that we don't see how prevalent it is. Movie stardom is itself based on a "meta" principle—somehow, Tom Hanks, Julia Roberts, Arnold Schwarzenegger, and Jack Nicholson are all playing characters, but at the same time also adding their own unique screen personae to the equation.

Traditional critical analysis often seeks to decouple the metanarrative from the individual stories; reviews frequently state that they seek to judge one installment on "its own merits," or see it as cause for criticism (rather than celebration) that a film will appeal to fans or that it only makes sense as part of the whole. To do so misses the point—and appeal—of the unfolding text: that each new *Doctor Who* story or Bond film is inevitably part of something much larger and more enduring, something greater than the sum of its parts. This privileges the returning audience (particularly the fans) for an unfolding text. In turn, this means that unfolding texts tend to be "critic proof"— a state of affairs that critics themselves often bemoan. The solution, it would seem, would be the creation of a better critical apparatus for unfolding texts.

Notes

1. The 2005 television series. The stories are "The Unquiet Dead" by Mark Gatiss, "Bad Wolf" by Russell T. Davies, "Dalek" by Rob Shearman, and "Father's Day" by Paul Cornell, respectively.

2. I worked on the soap opera *Emmerdale*, which had a 103-page bible drawn up in 1990, but by 2002, when I was researching a book that celebrated the show's thirtieth anniversary, the last copy languished on the script editor's shelf, and it took a little while even to find it.

3. The term *pure historical* was common in 1980s' analysis of the show, and is well understood by most *Doctor Who* fans, but has been challenged more recently; many historical stories had a science fiction idea at their heart. In "The Aztecs" (1964), for example, one of the Doctor's companions wants to change history so that the Aztecs become less violent and won't be wiped out by the conquistadors. Yet *The First Doctor Handbook* reprints memos that make it clear that

the production team in the 1960s drew a clear distinction between "past" and "future" stories.

4. In 1963, police boxes were everyday items. In 2007, most Britons shown a picture of a police box would almost certainly say it looked like the TARDIS, not that the TARDIS looked like a police box.

5. We learn that he's a Time Lord in "The War Games" (1969), that he has two hearts in "Spearhead from Space" (1970), and that he can regenerate in "The Tenth Planet" (1966), although it's not called regeneration until "Planet of the Spiders" (1974), and the limit is established in "The Deadly Assassin" (1976).

6. In the films *On Her Majesty's Secret Service* (1969), *Diamonds Are Forever* (1971), *For Your Eyes Only* (1981), and *Licence to Kill* (1989), respectively.

7. See, for example, *The Return of Sherlock Holmes* (1987) and *Sherlock Holmes in San Francisco* (1991).

8. For example, Michael Chabon's *The Final Solution* (2005) and Kelly Hale's *Erasing Sherlock* (2006).

9. The quotations are from the first paperback editions of Robert Markham's (Kingsley Amis) *Colonel Sun* and John Gardner's *Icebreaker*.

10. The best account of the process is in Howe, Stammers, and Walker (1994).

11. For example, only the Fourth Doctor, Tom Baker, wore a long scarf, but the scarf is seen as shorthand for the character, as are tuxedos for Bond.

12. "I would dislike being thought of as so foolish that I would select a love partner who came into sexual heat only once every seven years" (Roddenberry 1979, 19).

13. There were long-established virtual communities of *Star Trek* fans when *Star Trek: The Next Generation* debuted in 1987, a good five to ten years before most people even knew there was such a thing as email. The movie *Star Trek: Generations* (1994) was the first to have its own dedicated Web site.

14. The script editor tends to be a fairly obscure job on most British television shows, but on *Doctor Who*, perhaps because the job entailed reconciling the imagination of the scripts with the prosaic demands of making the episodes on limited resources, it required a huge amount of work and knowledge—and the script editor was quickly established as second in command to the producer.

15. The number regularly attending church every Sunday in Britain in 2006 was 7 percent of the Christian population (see ⟨http://news.bbc.co.uk/2/hi/uk_news/3725801.stm⟩), so around 2.1 million people; the number of people watching *Doctor Who* weekly averaged out at 7.95 million.

16. As of this writing, Amazon.co.uk lists twenty sequels to *Pride and Prejudice* currently in print.

References

Brooker, Will (2000). *Batman Unmasked: Analyzing a Cultural Icon*. London: Continuum.

Brown, Anthony (ed.), and Cybermark Services (1998). *In-Vision #81: The Mark of the Rani* (November).

Chabon, Michael (2005). "Inventing Sherlock Holmes." *New York Review of Books* 52, no. 2 (February 10).

Cornell, Paul (ed.) (1996). *Licence Denied: Rumblings from the Doctor Who Underground*. London: Virgin.

Dicks, Terrance, and Malcolm Hulke (1976). *The Making of Doctor Who*. London: W. H. Allen.

Greenberg, Martin H., Jon L. Lellenberg, and Daniel Stashover (eds.) (2001). *Murder in Baker Street: New Tales of Sherlock Holmes*. New York: Carroll and Graf.

Howe, David J., Mark Stammers, and Stephen James Walker (1994). *Doctor Who—The Handbook: The First Doctor*. London: Virgin.

Jenkins, Henry (1992). *Textual Poachers*. London: Routledge.

Leavis, Q. D. (1932). *Fiction and the Reading Public*. New York: Random House.

Major, John (1998). *John Major: The Autobiography*. New York: HarperCollins.

Roddenberry, Gene (1979). *Star Trek: The Motion Picture*. New York: Simon and Schuster.

Tulloch, John, and Manuel Alvarado (1984). *Doctor Who: The Unfolding Text*. London: Macmillan.

Tulloch, John, and Henry Jenkins (1995). *Science Fiction Audiences: Watching Doctor Who and Star Trek*. London: Routledge.

In What Universe?
Walter Jon Williams

The writers of science fiction and fantasy are required to make decisions about their work that are unique to their genre, and these decisions are almost entirely concerned with the setting. Other branches of literature are set either in the present or some version of the accepted historical past—settings to which fantastic literature is not restricted. When a writer sets out to compose a science fiction or fantasy piece, the author not only has to work out such commonplace details as character and plot but also must, quite literally, decide in what universe the story takes place.

Fantastic literature not only doesn't share a common setting with other genres of fiction, it normally doesn't share settings with other works within the genre. An author will engage in "worldbuilding," ideally a careful and meticulous construction of a fictional reality in which the writer does not live. Within science fiction, the difference between the fictional world and that of our commonly understood reality can be temporal or technological—the work might take place in a future setting in which travel between the stars is common, human beings have cybernetic enhancements implanted in their brains, or Earth has suffered some kind of catastrophe resulting in a massive population decline followed by a renewal of barbarism...or all three at once.

With genre fantasy, by contrast, the differences are temporal or metaphysical. The setting could be as simple as our present-day world, different only in that "magic works," as in, for example, the Harry Potter novels. These sorts of fantasies have a long history, and include fairy tales, classic ghost stories, and *Dracula*.

The working out of a coherent fantasy world different from our own, however, is a more recent development. This innovation initially seemed to require some literary device to explain the existence of fictional worlds to an audience unused to the concept. Both C. S. Lewis's fantasy world of Narnia and the Zimiamvia of his contemporary E. R. Eddison were reached via some form of gateway from our own world, while works as wildly different in tone as J. R. R. Tolkien's *Lord of the Rings* and Robert E. Howard's stories of Conan the Barbarian were both supposed to be set in the dim, mythical past of our own Earth. More recent fantasy writers, with an audience more accustomed to genre tropes, have dispensed with this sort of framing device entirely, and the story takes place in its own world, with its own maps and history, and no explanation is required.

As an example of worldbuilding, consider my own open-ended series *Dread Empire's Fall*, starting with *The Praxis* (2002), and continuing through *Conventions of War* (2005). Briefly stated, the series was set centuries after Earth and its inhabitants were conquered by imperialist aliens called the Shaa, who subjected humanity and various alien races to thousands of years of brutal, if inefficient, tyranny devoted to their absolute law, called the Praxis. The series begins with the death of the last Shaa, and follows the subject races as they explore the ramifications of their new-found freedom.

The decisions I had to make included the following:

Aliens: What did the various species of the Praxis look like? How did their behavior and customs differ from those of humanity? What were their special needs?

I needed to work out not only the answers to these questions but also the secondary and tertiary implications of these answers. For example, having decided that one of the alien species tended to be belligerent, I decided that this was a consequence of their being carnivorous as well as naturally aggressive hunters. Having decided that their preferred diet was raw meat served warm at body temperature, it was easy enough to conclude that their dining facilities were kept separate from those of other species.

Politics: How is the empire of the Shaa governed? How were the decisions of the rulers enforced? How are the various bureaucratic departments organized? How do the police and judiciary function? Is there is a criminal underclass, and if so, how does it relate to the authorities?

I decided that the Shaa empire was a fundamentalist tyranny, though one based on adherence to a political philosophy rather than a religion. On a day-to-day basis, the empire was ruled by an aristocracy of collaborators known as the Peers, who reported to the Shaa and took orders from them. The various alien underspecies were largely segregated from one another, so as reduce the chance of their uniting against their rulers. The enforcement of the laws was ruthless, especially in the case of the political police, the Legion of Diligence. Because of the rigid nature of the laws and society, a thriving criminal underclass evolved, supplying the population with the pleasures and vices denied them by the regulations.

Technology: How do the species of the Praxis travel from place to place? What comforts equip their homes? What is their primary energy source?

I decided that much of their energy came from the generation and use of antimatter, which made certain other decisions easy. It permitted the series spaceships to be powered by matter-antimatter reactions, and it meant that warships' primary weapons would consist of antimatter missiles, and their secondary weapons of antiproton beams.

This decision in turn dictated a great many others, including the appearance of the warships, the tactics used by the war fleets, and the methods by which the war fleets impose their will on the populations of planets.

Along the way, I had to decide what buildings looked like and how they differed from our own, what forms of electronic communication were available, and what sorts of weapons were available to the general population.

Interstellar travel: As our current understanding of nature tells us that it's impossible to exceed the speed of light, science fiction writers tend to generate a lot of hand-waving pseudoscience to explain how their vehicles get from star to star before their crews die of old age. I decided to avoid both the hand waving and the pseudoscience, and have my characters travel from star to star through wormholes, which (assuming they exist at all) would indeed provide instantaneous transport from point to point throughout the universe.

Though the wormholes themselves provided instantaneous travel, ships still needed to travel to or from the wormholes by more conventional means. Voyages took weeks or months, rather than years. The pace of travel was similar to that of Earth's age of sail, where a voyage between Britain and India could take six months. This had large implications for the story in terms of trade, the movement of populations, and getting information from one place to another. That travelers would live on ships for months at a time also told me what the interiors of interstellar ships looked like.

Because I have no scientific background to speak of, I consulted with scientists on the subjects of wormholes and antimatter. I made files of the names of characters and planets, jargon and slang, alien plants, animals, and foodstuffs. I drew maps of wormhole networks. I created titles and bureaucracies. I had to decide what all these things looked like, tasted like, and smelled like. And on top of that I had to do the sorts of things that other writers do. I had to decide who my characters were, what they looked like, and what they wanted from life. I had to devise character arcs and character interactions. Because the series was intended to be an epic that ran for many books, all the characters came with family, friends, enemies, and relationships already in place, and due attention had to be paid to all the secondary and tertiary characters. The size of my files increased. Also, I had to pay attention to structuring the series. While the series was theoretically open-ended, the publisher had bought three books only. I accordingly constructed a plot arc that would take up three books, and would resolve itself at the end of the third, though with enough subplots and complications left over to continue the series if both I and the publisher desired. The three books are thus best viewed as a continuous narrative broken into three volumes, with "pauses"—I will not say "resolutions"—at the end of the first and second books.

I also buried in the narrative elements what I thought of as "time bombs"—the seeds for new narratives, which could be detonated whenever I needed new stories. For instance, I made it clear that the empire supported itself by taxing trade, rather than taxing wealth per se. Under the pressures of an interstellar war, this policy was reversed, which inevitably would result in the rise of a large, wealthy commercial class. The rise of this class and the reaction of the traditional aristocracy could be used as the seed for further conflict.

In another case, one of my characters—the unstable and occasionally homicidal Caroline Sula—won an urban guerrilla conflict by arming the urban proletariat. The consequences of a heavily armed underclass with military experience, with allegiance not to the social order but to a rogue character, would be explored in future volumes.

And then, after all that, I had to write the thing, which took over three years of my life. As the early books of the series were published before I finished the final volume, I was unable to return to the earlier work to revise plot elements that proved inconvenient. I was stuck with everything I'd put in the earlier work—the inconvenience that attends any long series.

The careful working out of a self-consistent future history with its technologies and their implications is a sufficiently challenging task that many writers find it convenient to return to the same background again and again, such as Frank Herbert's *Dune*, with its many sequels, or Robert A. Heinlein's "Future History" of stories and novels, beginning with "Life-Line" (1939) and continuing through *To Sail beyond the Sunset* (1987).

Many of these invented universes proved enormously popular with the reading public, and commercial publishers were not slow to perceive the opportunity that lay within that popularity. When the author was unavailable or not inclined to write further installments in the series, other writers were commissioned to pen "authorized" sequels. The background of Isaac Asimov's popular robot stories, for example, provided the framework for the *Robot City* novels of the late 1980s.

This is a practice known in the industry as "sharecropping," and as with sharecropping in the agricultural sector, the greatest benefit is gained by the owner of the (in this case literary) property, and much less by the workers toiling on that property. Typically, the original creator is given a large advance, usually with the expectation of doing little or no work on the project. The sharecropper receives a much smaller share of the money. (I have, for instance, turned down a number of offers to sharecrop novels in part because the advance offered was far less than I could have earned elsewhere.) The sharecropper is often a new writer

whose profile would be raised by having his or her name associated with that of a best-selling author—the *Robot City* novels, for example, were written by Michael Kube-McDowell and William F. Wu, both relative newcomers.

Sharecropping is a practice with a venerable history. Many of the works of Alexandre Dumas père, as an example, were written in large part by his stable of collaborators —this includes all three Musketeers books as well as *The Count of Monte Cristo*. Unlike modern sharecroppers, however, Dumas's collaborators were rarely, if ever, credited for their work. The French tradition of sharecropping has continued with books written in the settings of the popular science fiction writer "Jimmy Guieu" (Henri René Guieu, 1926–2000).

For authors whose popularity does not fade with death, sharecropping has become commonplace. *Gone with the Wind* has had both authorized and unauthorized posthumous sequels, and contemporary writers have provided posthumous prequels or sequels to *The Big Sleep*, *Jane Eyre*, and *Pride and Prejudice* as well as Roger Zelazny's *Amber* series and Asimov's *Foundation* books.

The biggest sharecropping success is doubtless the *Dune* prequels written by creator Herbert's son Brian in collaboration with Kevin J. Anderson. These have appeared on lists of best sellers, and their authors claim these prequels' success has resulted in increased popularity for the original *Dune* books.

The politics of the genre seem to require that the publicity for sharecropped works state that the writers are "honoring" the creator with their works. Perhaps they are sincere, and perhaps some creators are capable of feeling honored when derivative works are placed at their feet. There remains the suspicion that everyone is in it for the money.

Still, I have to admit that in my own brief experience with sharecropping, I hoped I was doing honor to the original work. In any case, my sequel (the novella *Elegy for Angels and Dogs* (1990), a sequel to Zelazny's novella *The Graveyard Heart* (1964), succeeded in bringing back into print a worthy story that had been unavailable for over twenty years. At any rate Roger, a generous man, seemed to take no offense.

Sharecropping remains a purely mercenary activity—few claim that the original works are improved by the appearance of sequels by other hands—and whether a work continues to be sharecropped depends entirely on whether the derivative works make a sufficient profit for the publisher and the creator (or his or her estate).

For the actual author of such works, however, one thing is depressingly familiar: in addition to the low advances and demanding deadlines, the author doesn't own the products of his or her labor. Sharecropped novels almost always fall under the category of "works made for hire."

Works made for hire are those made under an employer-employee agreement, with the author agreeing that the copyright belongs to the employer. Except in European countries that follow the law of moral right (*droit morale*), the employer is not even legally obligated to identify the actual creator.

Works made for hire include media tie-in novels, novels written under a "house name" owned by the publisher (such as the ghostwriters working for the Stratemeyer Syndicate, producing books about Nancy Drew, the Hardy Boys, and Tom Swift), books allegedly written by celebrities (such as William Shatner) but actually written by someone else, film novelizations, and ghostwritten autobiographies of celebrities, captains of industry, sports figures, and military heroes.

For decades, works made for hire were considered bottom-of-the-barrel employment in the writers' community. The money was insignificant and the prestige nonexistent, and many writers worked under pseudonyms to disguise their involvement.

On the other hand, the work was considered easy. On a tie-in work, the characters and setting are created before the writer begins his or her labor. On a film novelization, all that's required is to turn an already-written screenplay into a novel by the addition of description to the dialogue—though sometimes this can reach high levels of absurdity, as in, say, *Francis Ford Coppola presents Bram Stoker's Dracula, by Fred Saberhagen* (1992).

This changed as media tie-in works began to achieve higher levels of commercial success than had ever been anticipated. With the rise of cable television and its need for twenty-four-hour programming, many series went into infinite rerun. Popular television series such as *Star Trek* became nothing short of hour-long advertisements for *Trek* fiction. In 1984, the nineteenth *Star Trek* novel, *Tears of the Singers*, by Melinda M. Snodgrass, reached the *New York Times* best-seller list—the first tie-in novel to do so.

This was combined with a change in the way media titles were financed. Traditionally, authors of tie-ins were paid a (small) flat fee for their work, with no royalties. David G. Hartwell, the creator of the *Star Trek* line for Pocket Books, persuaded his superiors of the advantages of offering a small royalty of 2 percent, one-fourth the normal royalty for a paperback book—this coupled with an even smaller fee. Hartwell told me that he intended to save his employers money, and perhaps he did, but in the case of successful tie-in lines, with books regularly appearing on best-seller lists, Hartwell inadvertently created a class of authors who were earning a good living indeed.

Prestige, as is often the case, followed the money. Critically successful authors, such as Joe Haldeman, John M. Ford, and Greg Bear, were found writing tie-in novels. For the most part, authors no longer tried to disguise their authorship of tie-ins.

Enough money was involved so that in 1998, when Bantam Books, which had the license for *Star Wars* books from Lucasfilm, tried to reverse Hartwell's innovation by eliminating the royalty in exchange for a larger advance, the Science Fiction Writers of America began a well-organized protest that included a full-page newspaper advertisement in the form of an open letter addressed to George Lucas.

It is impossible to prove that the protest had any effect, but nevertheless Bantam lost the *Star Wars* license shortly thereafter. The license went to Ballantine, which offered its authors a royalty of 1 percent, with 0.5 percent on foreign editions. Quite possibly the SFWA protest was responsible for any royalty being retained at all.

Though most tie-in writers view their work as mercenary activity, some do it for love, out of devotion to the original source material, and a desire to contribute to its ongoing success.

My single tie-in book was in the *Star Wars* line, after the shift to Ballantine. I decided that a large advance, a couple million new readers, and a virtually guaranteed spot on the *New York Times* best-seller list were artistically justifiable reasons for my joining the *Star Wars* list. Little did I realize at the time how complex the *Star Wars* universe had become in the years since the release of the original films.

The ink was barely dry on the contract before *Star Wars* reference material began arriving from Ballantine. *The Star Wars Encyclopedia*, *The Essential Guide to Planets and Moons*, *The Essential Guide to Weapons and Technology*, and *The Essential Guide to Alien Species*. The *Essential Guides* to droids, vehicles, and time lines. All the recent *Star Wars* novels. And a 166-page bible for the *New Jedi Order*, the series of novels to which mine had been attached.

Colossal as this infodump was, it wasn't nearly enough. The original stories, characters, and background of the *Star Wars* films have been augmented by hundreds of books and comics, board, role-playing, and electronic games, toys, radio and television series, holiday specials, fake documentaries focusing on *Star Wars* characters, and short films—all of which is known to its devotees as the "Expanded Universe."

The relationship of all this to the films, and the elements of the Expanded Universe to each other, is complex. The Expanded Universe is nearly thirty years old, and has included significant changes in the characters and settings of the films. Sometimes, the later films have introduced elements that contradict the Expanded Universe or even the earlier films. The efforts to resolve these paradoxes approach the complexity of biblical exegesis. Anything with Lucas's name attached is considered canonical, even if it contradicts well-established elements of the Expanded Universe. The novels are less canonical than the films, but more canonical than the comic books. It takes more than a dozen *Essential Guides* to keep it all straight.

My own work would be the fifteenth volume in a twenty-book epic series called *New Jedi Order*, the broad outlines of which had been decided before I ever joined the project. As the Expanded Universe had continued the time line for more than twenty-five years after the events of the original film, the familiar characters of the films had aged and changed. The Empire of Darth Vader had been vanquished, leaving the New Republic in control of most of the galaxy. Han Solo and Princess Leia had married, and pro-

duced three children who were having adventures of their own. Luke Skywalker had reestablished the Jedi Order, married a character who hadn't existed in the films, and had conceived a son. The Wookie, Chewbacca, had been killed.

My story had not been plotted ahead of time. I was required to introduce several plot elements or "beats"—I got to kill off a couple major characters, always a pleasure, and end with a space battle, which would be fun—but what happened between the beats was up to me. It was like being recruited to write one section of *War and Peace*, covering the lives of Andrei, Natasha, Pierre, Sonya, the czar, and the Emperor Napoléon from March 1810 to September 1811.

While nondisclosure agreements prevent me from quoting from the series bible, I can report that it included background on the *Star Wars* universe, information about major characters, the Jedi Knights, the government, and the military, a list of major worlds, and a discussion of the Hero's Journey as defined by Joseph Campbell. It also had a great many pages concerning the Yuuzhan Vong, the alien invader species who were our heroes' antagonists. Tie-in novels are said to be easier than the original ones because the characters and settings are already established. As far as my *Star Wars* book went, it would have been a lot less work to have invented it all myself.

The deadlines were tight. My outline for the novel required approval from Lucasfilm—an approval that took several months. As I suspected I knew which of my ideas Lucasfilm would approve and which it might stick at, I began work early, writing the parts I thought would meet its consent. It was lucky that I did, since by the time Lucasfilm finally accepted my revised outline I had only four months to complete the novel.

I am not a particularly fast writer. I achieve volume by dogged persistence, not through the gift of celerity. I normally take nine to twelve months to write a book, and especially lengthy or knotty ones have taken up to two years. My deadline was forcing me to write at more than twice my normal rate.

Writing quickly has its hazards. Professionals are generally experienced enough to avoid incoherence, but are often so caught up in the tempo of writing that they use too many words and write too many scenes. Fast writing frequently has a gushy quality, and books written quickly often have far too many pages. It is one of the paradoxes of the craft that lean writing generally takes more time than wordy writing—it takes *time* to choose the best word of those available, craft phrases, avoid redundancy, and eliminate unnecessary scenes. As Blaise Pascal wrote to a friend, "I have made this letter longer than usual, only because I have not had the time to make it shorter."

I wanted to avoid this prolixity if I could, and so I deliberately adopted a minimalist prose style. I avoided long descriptions, partly on the theory that the fans knew better than I what most of this stuff looked like. For those four months I ate, slept, and breathed *Star Wars*, and in the end produced a work called *Destiny's Road*.

To my surprise I enjoyed myself. I'd taken on the job because I wanted a large advance and an expanded readership, not because I'd always had a secret longing to write about Princess Leia. But in the end I found myself caught up in intricacy of the Extended Universe. I also developed a theory about why media tie-in fiction is so popular.

I've written for television and the screen, and for a writer whose characters have strong inner lives, the lesson of screenwriting that was the most difficult to absorb was that screen characters *have* no inner lives. Their lives are entirely on the screen; they are defined completely by action. You can't show their innermost thoughts and feelings, except insofar as they choose to share these with other characters or (via some clumsy device such as voice-over narration or soliloquy) the audience.

What tie-in fiction provides for the fan is exactly that inner life that's missing from the characters on screen. Readers share the hopes, fears, frustrations, and torments of the characters, and can grow to understand those characters much better than they could sympathize with a celluloid image on screen.

For instance, I wrote these lines from the point of view of Han Solo:

He glanced at the empty copilot's chair—Chewbacca's, now Leia's—and found himself wishing he was in the second laser cockpit, with Chewbacca in the pilot's seat.

But Chewie was gone, the first of the deaths that had struck him to the heart. Chewbacca dead, his younger son Anakin killed, his older son Jacen missing, presumed dead by everyone except Leia...death had been haunting his footsteps, on the verge of claiming everyone around him.

There is no way even a good actor could transmit these thoughts to an audience without a voice-over or dialogue—and it would have to be a fairly lengthy piece of dialogue, because it wouldn't contain just these thoughts alone, it would have to lead up to them. But in fiction, Han's state of mind can be relayed to the reader in a single paragraph.

After turning in the manuscript to *Destiny's Road*, I heard nothing from my editor or Lucasfilm for months, except for a request to change the title. "Road" was judged not to be science fictiony enough of a word. I replied that *Destiny's Hyperspace Bypass* was probably too prolix, and would *Destiny's Way* do? Apparently it would, and *Destiny's Way* was the title of the book that appeared in 2002.

After months had passed, long enough so that I'd forgotten most of what I knew about *Star Wars* and its Expanded Universe, I received eighty-five pages of requested changes from Lucasfilm. I was staggered. I'd never gotten anything like eighty-five pages of changes from anyone.

Most of these were of the "change this character's eye color from green to brown" variety, but some would have required rewrites amounting to hundreds of manuscript pages. Fortunately for me the publisher's production schedule didn't permit time for this, and the book that was finally published was substantially the book I'd submitted, including a couple glaring mistakes in continuity that someone, somewhere, should have caught.

From what I gather from other writers in the series, my experience was not uncommon.

In any case, I acquired many new readers and a place on the *New York* and London *Times* best-seller lists, so my objectives in undertaking the project were accomplished.

A relatively unexplored category of fiction in which some of the work is done for the author is the shared-world novel. The first of these that I can find, *The Floating*

Admiral, dates from 1931, with the authors' credit line of my 1980 Charter edition reading, "A Novel by Agatha Christie, Dorothy L. Sayers, G. K. Chesterton, and Certain Other Members of the Detection Club." In fact there are no less than thirteen authors, all writing a single chapter of a mystery novel set in a common setting and using common characters.

This was such a sufficiently difficult trick that no one tried it again for nearly fifty years, until the appearance of *Thieves' World* (1979), edited by Robert Lynn Asprin and Lynn Abbey, and featuring stories by such well-known science fiction and fantasy writers as C. J. Cherryh, Gordon R. Dickson, John Brunner, Poul Anderson, and Marion Zimmer Bradley. These stories all shared a common background, set in the fantasy world of Sanctuary. The writers were encouraged not only to use the common background but to write stories involving one another's characters.

Though many of the best-known authors dropped out early, the series was popular enough to continue through fourteen anthologies, seven novels, a comic book series, role-playing games, and a MUD. In addition, some of the writers wrote novels about their characters outside the *Thieves' World* setting.

The success of *Thieves' World* inspired other shared-world series, including *Liavek*, edited by Will Shetterly and Emma Bull; *Merovingen Nights*, edited by Cherryh; *Wild Cards*, edited by George R. R. Martin (often with Snodgrass as coeditor); *The Man-Kzin Wars*, set in the "Known Space" universe of Larry Niven; *Heroes in Hell*, edited by Janet Morris; and *Naked Came the Manatee*, a collaborative novel by humorist Dave Barry, mystery writer Carl Hiaasen, and eleven other writers known collectively as the "South Florida Bunch of Wackos."

My own experience with shared-world series is principally with *Wild Cards*, which has so far run to fourteen anthologies, three novels, a role-playing game, a comic book series, and a graphic novel. At least three more anthologies are planned. It is the most successful shared-world series outside of *Thieves' World*.

The arrangements between the authors and editors of a shared-world series vary from one series to the next. *Wild Cards* was able to learn from the mistakes of *Thieves' World*,

the creators of which freely shared their experience with editor Martin, and therefore *Wild Cards* was responsible for certain advances in the form.

Wild Cards is set in a contemporary United States, in which certain individuals are granted comic-book-style superpowers as a result of the release of an alien virus over New York City in 1947. The series is therefore set in an alternate present resembling our own, but different in certain respects—not only have superheroes existed since 1947, but Fidel Castro became a pitching coach for the Dodgers (which remained in Brooklyn), and therefore left Cuba to the mercies of the Batista regime and the Mafia; Frank Zappa became a U.S. general; and the loss of China to the Communists was blamed, by the House Un-American Activities Committee, on a progressive superhero group known as the Four Aces.

Martin and Snodgrass invented certain important elements of the common background, and the authors collaboratively created the rest. Monies derived from the series went not only directly to the editors and writers but also into the "Wild Cards Consortium," in which the creators were awarded "points" (shares). Points were awarded for contributing a story, editing a volume, or giving permission for another author to use one's character. At regular intervals, monies in the consortium were divided between the creators, with the greatest share going to those with the largest number of points.

While authors were always at liberty to forbid other writers from using their characters, the consortium gave them a financial incentive to allow such use. Creators were not only permitted to veto other writers' use of their characters but also were allowed to comment on and even alter others' interpretations of their characters.

For instance, in the sixth *Wild Cards* volume, *Ace in the Hole*, I used one of Martin's characters, the obese Hiram Worcester, known in the superhero world as "Fatman." George rewrote all of Hiram's dialogue, saying I hadn't got the voice right, and changed some minor elements of my interpretation.

The *Wild Cards* anthologies were not merely collections of stories with a common setting—each volume had its own arc to which each story was expected to contribute.

Every third anthology was a "mosaic" novel, in which the contributors braided their stories together into a single narrative that was intended to read like a novel.

Some character arcs continued for the entire series. In the first volume, my character Golden Boy was disgraced by testifying against his friends before the House Un-American Activities Committee. His attempts to redeem himself led to his involvement in the 1988 presidential campaign, where he supported the candidate Gregg Hartmann, the revelation of whose secret life as a sadistic manipulator and killer called Puppetman contributed to Golden Boy's ongoing trauma—itself not yet resolved.

Hartmann himself, created by writer Steve Leigh, provides another example of a multivolume arc. Ostensibly a liberal Democratic senator from New York, Hartmann's secret life and ultimate disgrace were played out over seven volumes. A crucial story in that arc, "Puppets" in *Aces Abroad* (1988), was written by Victor Milán, not by Hartmann's creator, and supplied new insights into the character. This is a sterling example of the strength of the shared-world concept, where writers other than the creator can offer a new vision of an established character or situation.

The ambitious goals of the series required considerable editorial discipline. The series began in the mid-1980s, before the Internet, and the collaboration required a good deal of mailing pages back and forth between the various collaborators. The advent of email made the work easier, but no less necessary.

Maintaining continuity remains an ongoing problem, particularly for a series like *Wild Cards* that has been playing out for twenty years. The latest *Wild Cards* series, for which contracts were signed in 2006, attempts to solve this problem by jettisoning the earlier characters and plotlines, and starting over with a new generation of heroes.

Unlike tie-in or sharecropped novels, few authors participate in shared worlds for the money alone. Although *Wild Cards*, for instance, paid better than the science fiction magazines for a story of similar length, and though the consortium occasionally distributed extra income from comic books and role-playing games, this benefit was balanced by the extra work required along with the fact that a story so

dependent on other stories will almost certainly never win awards or be reprinted outside its original context. (My own story "Witness," introducing Golden Boy, being the sole exception, as it was nominated for a Nebula award and reprinted in numerous anthologies.)

Authors with established careers could earn more money working on their solo projects—a factor that no doubt contributed to the best-known writers in shared worlds such as *Thieves' World* and *Heroes in Hell* dropping out of the project after the first volumes. For the most part, authors participate in shared worlds for the fun of working on a project alongside their friends.

The heyday of the shared-world experiment was the 1980s. Though *Thieves' World* and *Wild Cards* have both survived to the present, the other series have not. The period of formal experimentation within the shared-world milieu is over, and so is the novelty. From this point, success will depend on whether any shared-world project can offer the reader as much pleasure as a work by a single author.

Perhaps, in the end, a single creator is best.

References

Asprin, Robert, Poul Anderson, Lynn Abbey, Marion Zimmer Bradley, John Brunner, Christine Dewees, Joe Haldeman, and Andrew Offutt (1979). *Thieves' World*, edited by Robert Aspirin and Lynn Abbey. New York: Ace.

Christie, Agatha, et al. (1980). *The Floating Admiral*. New York: Charter.

Martin, George R. R., Edward Bryant, Michael Cassult, Gail Gerstner-Miller, Leanne C. Harper, Stephen Leigh, Victor Milán, John J. Miller, Lewis Shiner, Walton Simons, and Melinda M. Snodgrass (1988). *Wild Cards: Aces Abroad*, edited by George R. R. Martin. New York: Bantam.

Martin, George R. R., Edward Bryant, Leanne C. Harper, Stephen Leigh, Victor Milán, John J. Miller, Lewis Shiner, Melinda M. Snodgrass, Howard Waldrop, Walter Jon Williams, and Roger Zelazny (1987). *Wild Cards*, edited by George R. R. Martin. New York: Bantam.

Martin, George R. R., Edward Bryant, Leanne C. Harper, Victor Milán, John J. Miller, Lewis Shiner, Melinda M. Snodgrass, Howard Waldrop, and Walter Jon Williams (1990). *Wild Cards: Ace in the Hole*, edited by George R. R. Martin. New York: Bantam.

Williams, Walter Jon (2002). *Destiny's Way*. New York: Del Rey.

Williams, Walter Jon (2003). *The Praxis*. New York: HarperTorch.

Williams, Walter Jon (2005). *Conventions of War*. New York: Eos.

Two Interviews about *Doctor Who*

Paul Cornell and Kate Orman

On the Different *Doctor Who* Media

Paul Cornell: All of the different *Who* media I've worked in have been nurturing, and to some extent they've all learned from each other. The editor of the Virgin line of *Doctor Who* books (1991–1997), Peter Darvill-Evans, had decided to take over from the television show and had to find a way to do that. This provided an example to everyone who came after. Peter had things he wanted to bring to *Doctor Who*, mostly literary science fiction, which hadn't ever really been part of the *Who* mix. But he also wanted to continue what had been done on television. To accomplish both goals, he brought in *Doctor Who* fan writers, reached out to the fan audience, and carved out a niche. He narrowcast it. And because of his example, bringing in new writers and nurturing them has been something that all later forms of *Who* have done.

A form has evolved for *Doctor Who* editorial structures that has even to some extent carried over into Russell T. Davies's new series, which is also nurturing. Peter prepared a new writer's bible for the Virgin novel line every year. Gary Russell has a set of guidelines available for the Big Finish Productions audio dramas. When I started writing for BBC Books' *Doctor Who* line (1996–2005), they were in the middle of a hefty great story arc, so there were regular updates of where the arc was and where it was going. For the new *Who* television series (2005–), Davies prepared an initial writer's document, which was basically a four-sentence summary of each plot he wanted for the first series.

In general, all of these different editorial lines developed a little cadre of writers that the editors liked, and

they formed an ongoing committee under a central authority. Virgin had an office consisting of two or three people, Peter and Rebecca Levene notably, and the committee was composed of Peter, Kate Orman, Gareth Roberts, Jim Mortimore, and some others, like Justin Richards, who came up through the slush pile at Virgin and finally took over at BBC Books. At BBC Books, the committee became a kind of rotating circus between Justin, Steven Cole, Lawrence Miles, Peter Angelides, and Lance Parkin.

Big Finish actually has employees; Simon Guerrier (formerly along with Ian Farrington) runs the Bernice Summerfield range of audios. They also have an interesting rotating editorial structure on the *Short Trips* story collections: a subeditor commissions the stories for a collection, overseen by the editor of that particular story range. Ultimately Nick Briggs (formerly it was Russell) has the final authority to say no, don't do that, do this—but the editor of an individual book has lots and lots of autonomy, which is an interesting set of water wings.

Kate Orman: For Virgin and the BBC line, major events such as the departure or arrival of a companion were decided on by the editors, and there was a fair bit of planning of story arcs, so an author was quite likely to be handed an "assignment" for their book. I needed to deepen the rift between the Doctor, Benny, and Ace in *The Left-Handed Hummingbird*. I pitched *Set Piece* specifically as Ace's leaving story.

Our contracts specified that other authors in the range could use our creations, but generally we asked each others' permission before running riot. Relations between the writers were on the whole pretty friendly, although the editors did sometimes catch us having a go at each other. I'm ashamed to admit that Rebecca Levene had me cut a rude remark about *Timewyrm: Genesys* from *Set Piece*.

Cornell: A good example of one of Peter's incredibly brave decisions at Virgin was to create the new line of Bernice Summerfield books. Bernice was a character I created early on in the Virgin run of books, for the

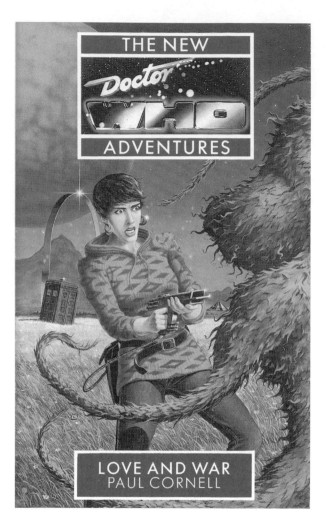

3.1 Cover of Paul Cornell's *Love and War* (1992). (Lee Sullivan)

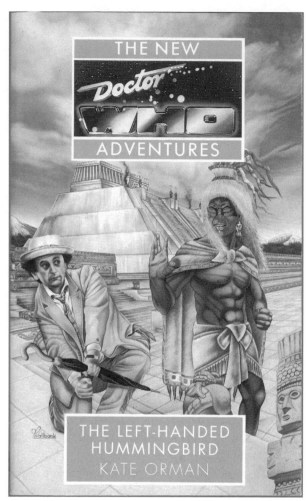

3.2 Cover of Kate Orman's *The Left-Handed Hummingbird* (1993). (Pete Wallbank)

novel *Love and War*, and she became a popular companion of the Doctor's.

When Peter heard that the success of the *Doctor Who* books at Virgin had prompted the BBC to pull the line back in-house and make a bit of money out of it, he could have decided to simply publish books with the *Doctor Who* logo on the cover right up to the deadline and then stop. But instead he decided that Virgin would pull the *Doctor Who* logo off the books early and slowly remove the *Doctor Who* content from the books as well. This was to see if he had managed to build up a strong

literary science fiction line at Virgin, and a fanbase of people who were reading for the new stuff, as opposed to the BBC-oriented stuff. And to his amazement, he found that there *was* an audience out there for non-*Who* material.

Since Bernice had never really gone away in the *Doctor Who* books—she kept on popping up at intervals even after she left as a companion—Peter decided to make her a central character. He removed the logo six months before he had to and zoomed straight on into the Bernice format. I remember the initial meeting for the format very well. It was Dave Stone, Justin Richards, Matt Jones, and myself. We were writing the first four books in the Bernice line—that was all Peter commissioned at first. He already had the basic shape of the story arc he wanted, which included breaking up Bernice and her fiancée Jason; I really objected to it at the time, but in retrospect, that's drama. So Dave, Justin, Matt, and I worked out the kind of plot we'd be writing for those first four books, and then Peter kept having further small meetings, commissioning two or three books, or five or six. I think he got about three years out of them in the end—far more than anyone thought he would.

If you talk to anybody who was involved in the Virgin days, I think they'll mention three things. They'll mention how great Peter was, and what an inspirational figure. They'll mention the huge parties of New Adventures writers that he used to hold upstairs at a bar in London, where we'd actually get to meet our peer group as well as sit and worship at the feet of Terrance Dicks. And they'll also mention that we had an unwritten law, which was that we didn't criticize the Virgin range or each other in public. That law held throughout the whole span of the New Adventures, and that was the crucial thing the BBC didn't put in place when it started its own range of books. Mind you, there could have been a sense of camaraderie there, but if there was, I wasn't there to witness it. I'm sure BBC Books loyalists will tell you their own stories of having fun, but I wasn't there to talk about it.

That being said, I did write a few books for the BBC line, such as *The Shadows of Avalon*. Also, the BBC online drama *Scream of the Shalka*, starring Richard E. Grant as the Ninth Doctor, was supposed to be the beginning of the new official BBC *Doctor Who*. As it turned out, we turned out to be the final straw for those within the BBC who were pushing for a live-action show. They said, if we don't get one now, this is what we've got: a niche online animated version. Now, it was less niche than virtually anything else BBC Interactive was doing, and it had many more viewers than anything else, but it still

had nothing compared to what a televised *Doctor Who* could have. So I'm quite proud that we might have been the tiny pebble that started the avalanche of Davies new series going. I really like *Shalka*, but I'm really glad we got televised *Doctor Who* instead.

Continuity and Canonicity in *Doctor Who*

Orman: I've been reading a lot of ancient mythology recently, and man, do the Greeks and Mesopotamians contradict themselves a lot. A huge, sprawling, inconsistent narrative seems to be a feature of modern mythology, too.

Cornell: There is, with some caveats, no such thing as a *Doctor Who* canon. Sherlock Holmes fans only consider those things canonical that Sir Arthur Conan Doyle wrote; despite the fact that Doyle contradicted himself all over the place, they at least have a logical basis for their canon. But *Who* doesn't.[1]

Orman: If the *Who* novels of the 1990s and early 2000s were like the television show with the paperweight taken off, then the new series is a bit like the novels with *their* paperweight taken off. Many of the same features are there—story arcs, emphasis on characters, mythological resonances, an exploration of the meaning of the Doctor. Each stage of *Who* is like a development of the last.[2]

That said, I can't see any reason why the new show has to take any particular note of "facts" established in the novels, which perhaps only a few hundred audience members would remember anyway. To me, that's not disrespectful or invalidating in any way.

Each of these is a separate line, with separate ownership and copyright issues—so while there's a fair bit of cross talk between them, with authors bringing their concepts and characters along, there's no need for each line to try to strictly stay in sync with the others. I doubt even the readers and listeners can keep up with so much material, let alone the makers.

Still, it can seem disrespectful for one line to deliberately contradict another. There was a bit of a hue and cry when the comic strip in *Doctor Who Magazine* decided to give Ace a different departure from the one I'd written in *Set Piece*. *Doctor Who Monthly* needed to make it clear that its strip wasn't trying to stay in sync with Virgin, but book fans interpreted the move as deliberately dissing the novels. Back in those days, though, there wasn't nearly as much product; if something like that happened now, it might get lost in the vast outpouring—not to mention being totally overshadowed by the show itself.

So from an authorial point of view, it always comes back to, "What can I use, what should I try not to contradict?" A practical definition of "continuity" or "canon."

Cornell: And when the new series of *Doctor Who* came along, it also addressed the concept of a canon as a matter of practicality. Inevitably, when a new television show began, it was always going to be simply about what was currently on television, because not enough of the audience would remember anything else—and so what is on television starts to count more than what is not. In the new series, however, there have still been (in a quiet, unobtrusive way that no uninformed viewer would ever notice) a number of references to nontelevision stuff, and Davies has never rolled over continuity from other media just for the hell of it or to make a point.[3] He has occasionally done so because it would get in the way of storytelling. But the relationship is still kind of ghostly and complicated: the memories of those fifteen years worth of nontelevised *Doctor Who* do still hang around, despite the fact that we've had the juggernaut of a new show coming along and saying, simply because the horrible force of practicality, that television is the only thing that counts.

Any authority that the original series might have is superseded by the new version, although Davies's new show has taken a great deal of care not to roughly impinge its authority on the old version. Big Finish Productions, for example, is still allowed to produce audio *Doctor Who* dramas starring previous Doctors, although nobody else is on a professional basis.

This is possible because *Doctor Who* has only the barest hint of a continuity compared to other shows.

Star Trek took great pains with continuity after the original series had ended. But *Doctor Who* never had much textual authority in the first place—there are, for instance, three different versions of the sinking of Atlantis, two of which were broadcast within two years of each other. If the same actor is able to turn around and say a line that contradicts something he himself said the year before, it doesn't establish much textual authority over what comes after.

Of course, there is a strain of *Doctor Who* fandom (we call it "trad") that thinks anything new should only conform to what's already been done. I've written trad myself, because sometimes it's fun. But the show itself does not offer any kind of crushing authority that stops fan fiction, Big Finish, and new series-style elaboration from happening.

Writing for *Doctor Who*

Orman: The most powerful influence on my own *Who* novels were the other *Who* novels. I often tell the tale of the shock I got reading Paul's landmark *Timewyrm: Revelation*, arguably the first real *novel* in the Virgin range. It was rich with surrealism, mythology, literary references, poetry…. I remember thinking, "You can *do* this?"

I don't think I ever had a deliberate project to redefine the television *Who*; that was just part of the general project of the New Adventures, to tell stories "too broad and deep for the small screen." For some authors (and many readers preferred this approach) that meant telling a television story writ large. The rest of us got carried away! We had so many advantages that the television show lacked: an unlimited "budget" for special effects, of course, but also plenty of room to develop the characters, especially the Doctor. Thinking about what the Doctor *meant* became important to many of the novels, starting with the mythological connotations in *Revelation*. Writers like Ben Aaronovitch also injected a large amount of science fiction into the Doctor's character—by which I mean the sort of thing you find in science fiction novels, rather than the broader space opera of something like *Star Trek*.

In the novels we were picking up and developing each others' ideas, something the television show had little opportunity to do. In fact, the story arc was not yet a commonplace part of television, so each story stood alone—although this was already changing in the show's last years on the box.

Paul and I were very much on the same wavelength, so we had a ball plotting *Return of the Living Dad* and *Human Nature* together. The same was true for Jon Blum and I when we collaborated on our first couple of *Who* novels for the Beeb, *Vampire Science* and *Seeing I.* We agreed so much that it was easy to come up with both the story line, and write and edit each other's prose.

By contrast, Jon's and my third novel, *Unnatural History*, was an absolute cow to write. We'd just gotten married, and were still learning how to live together without murdering each other; plus I spent most of 1998 sick as a dog, probably thanks to the contamination of Sydney's water supply that made life so difficult for everyone that year.

Looking back, I think I was also starting to get a bit fed up with writing *Who* novels; by that point, I'd been trying to write something original, with no success at all, for a few years. I suspect the fact that I had to collaborate was also starting to feel like a straitjacket—I couldn't just scribble anything I pleased any more. The next *Who* novel we did, *The Year of Intelligent Tigers*, was coplotted, but written by me with Jon's help, rather than entirely cowritten. Similarly, I fended Jon off from *Blue Box*—you can tell, because he's scrupulous about plotting, and that book could've benefited from more Blum. By contrast, *Fallen Gods* was very much Jon's book, and in my view contains some of the best writing to bear our names.

Cornell: Various authors have had different points of view on what the Doctor means: who the Doctor is, or who the Doctors are. Robert Holmes famously thought he was always the same guy. I think that isn't true. Part of the attraction of the show is that the Doctor is different from actor to actor. There are a few central

3.3 Cover of Paul Cornell's *Human Nature* (1995). (Bill Donohoe)

elements of his character, but they contradict each other a little. Dicks's famous definition—he's never cruel or cowardly, he's a man of peace even in a time of war, and so on—holds pretty well, and we fetishized it a bit in the New Adventures, and made it into a kind of *Batman*-esque mission statement. But the kind of story you can tell really depends on which Doctor you're writing for. There are genres within *Doctor Who* (even, say, two or three different genres within something as long lasting as Tom Baker's time on the show), and they're dependent on which Doctor you're writing for.

P. Cornell and K. Orman

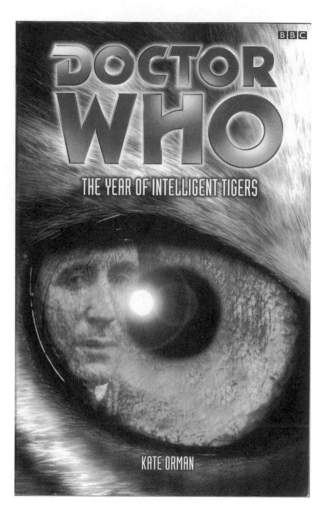

3.4 Cover of Kate Orman's *The Year of Intelligent Tigers* (2001). (© BBC Books)

For instance, the First and Second Doctor novels that don't confine the action to small sets, lots of corridors, and bases under siege actually lose some of the character of their Doctors, and don't somehow feel right. It's hard to come up with (although various authors have tried) what William Hartnell's Doctor would say to a vast Technicolor, CGI alien in front of him— because we just never saw him do that. Now that's the conservative fan in me speaking! But it's extraordinary that television production circumstances from 1963 can affect texts written over forty years later.

When writing contemporary *Doctor Who*, there are two or three different approaches, some of which have been inherited from fan fiction. As a text, *Who* has never had one single authority to lay down what's included and what's not, like *Star Trek* had with Paramount and Gene Roddenberry. So it has tended to contradict itself all over the place, and that contradiction has been a useful breeding place for fiction, especially fan fiction. I started my career in fan fiction, as did virtually all of my peers, and from a fan fiction point of view—we're used to thinking of their stories as part of a vast ongoing narrative. We used to refer to the "gaps" in *Doctor Who*: unclear or contradictory elements from *Doctor Who* episodes, or other things that begged to be further explained. People would write cute little continuity stories, usually with a twist at the end, that filled in one of those gaps. The shape of the gap defines the character of the Doctor as well: the absence when he's not there.

Also, there's the fact that there are almost no relationships in old *Doctor Who*—certainly no romantic relationships. So increasingly in the 1990s and the 2000s, before the new series came along, writers, especially women, would write fan fiction that filled in those romantic relationships.[4] So fan writers could be seen as building up the walls of *Doctor Who*, adding supports of our own, adding bits we thought should be there. From a more professional point of view, of course, character is always a good place to start. I find that I want to tell stories about how a particular character would act in a particular situation.

Many of the New Adventures writers, myself included, made a point of trying to advance the form of *Doctor Who*. We did an awful lot of this sort of thing, competing with each other to come out with different versions of *Doctor Who* that were still *Doctor Who*. My Big Finish audio drama *Circular Time* is probably, with one caveat that I'll mention later, the last of this sort of thing I'll do: it's four individual twenty-five-minute stories, which is something the audio format hadn't done yet.[5] I wanted to do something different for each of those four stories, so they each hit on one of the various genres of *Doctor Who*: a historical story, a story set on an alien planet, the new *Who* genre of exploring human relationships on earth, and also a continuity-heavy filling-the-gaps story in the old fan fiction style.[6]

Final Thoughts on the Current *Doctor Who*

Orman: Purely from the point of view of a former *Who* novelist, the new show is a mixed blessing. It's such a hot property for the BBC that the current line of *Doctor Who* books is being carefully produced in-house—the days of farming the books out to any old hack, like me, are over! What's more, the books are now being written very much for the new family audience, rather than an aging collection of adult fans—for me personally, that makes them less appealing, both to read and write. So there's this incredibly exciting new version of the show, but as a scribbler, I'm locked out of it.

There is a certain advantage to this, though—I'm just another member of the audience now, which means the show can take me by surprise. I can simply enjoy it. I can even write a little fan fiction, with no official constraints whatsoever.

Cornell: For me, it was a pleasure to go back and do a Big Finish audio again. I wrote it in a nostalgic way: I keep writing good-byes to the show, because one of the things that *Doctor Who* means to me is nostalgia, and because it always seems to be something receding. It means memories of my own childhood and family. Even "Father's Day," from the new television series, is about my dad. I can't help but look backward when I write *Doctor Who*. I don't think I'll ever write a *Doctor Who* book again, mainly because I've done everything I can do in prose for *Doctor Who*. I'll come back to the television show as long as they keep asking me, and maybe after my latest story for Big Finish (a story called *100*, which is the one-hundredth Big Finish release) I've now said good-bye to the audios as well, because again, I've done my last thing. But if I come up with another idea for how to do something different, which can't be done on the television show, I might write another audio. You never know.

From Peter Darvill-Evans's Author Guidelines for Virgin Publishing's Line of *Doctor Who* New Adventures (1993)

Recommendations

There's a lot of humor in *Doctor Who*. Much of it stems from the character of the Doctor—his alienness, his bizarre Britishness, and his knowledge of past and future.

Make full use of companion characters. Use them as narrative viewpoints—they are privy to some of the Doctor's thoughts, but not his innermost secrets. They are Watsons to his Holmes.

Happy endings are fine, tragic endings are inappropriate, and perhaps the best resolutions could be described as bittersweet: the Doctor defeats the baddie, but at the cost of some innocent lives; or the Doctor saves the innocents, but in doing so has to let the baddie escape. In recent years, the character of the Doctor has become appreciably darker: his humor now comes in flashes, between periods of morose introspection. He's feeling the weight of his responsibilities, particularly toward Earth: he's interfered so many times that he's on a treadmill, having to interfere more and more frequently to maintain the time-line that he has, in large part, forged for the planet.

If you're familiar with the TV stories, remember that they were constrained by low budgets. You have no similar restrictions: your stories can contain the most spectacular scenes you can imagine. Think big.

Settings

If I have to read another submission that begins, "The space station hung silently in space," I'll scream. At all costs avoid *Who* clichés, such as the TARDIS materializing in the cargo hold of a rickety old spaceship. The TV stories were very constricted in terms of setting, but some budgetary limit has no meaning in an original novel. Be imaginative but believable. And beware of using settings that have been very popular in the past. Victorian and present-day England, for example, have been used frequently. A story set there would have to be exceptionally good, and feature some original ideas, for me to consider publishing it.

From Justin Richards's Author Guidelines for BBC Books' line of *Doctor Who* (2002) (© BBC Books)

Doctor Who Continuity

Please keep to the character of the Doctor as depicted in the TV series. You should not use characters from Virgin's New Adventures series (Roz, Cwej, Benny, Kadiatu, etc.) or the Big Finish audio series (Evelyn, Erimem, Bev Tarrant, etc.). If you are reusing former companions from TV, they should also remain true to their TV personae. Bear in mind that the reader may not necessarily know the TV series and may never have read another *Doctor Who* novel before. You will need to bring out your players' characters, without inserting long character sketches.

If in Doubt . . .

We often receive inquiries asking, "Is it OK for me to . . . ?" In general, if you feel you have to ask, it probably isn't something we want to see. New incarnations of the Master (or the Doctor!), adventures set before "An Unearthly Child," the later lives of companions (or indeed, their deaths), *Blake's 7* crossovers, multiple Doctor stories, the Valeyard, more adventures for K9 and Company, new (or non-TV/BBC Books) companions, Time Lord mythology or history, virtually any sequel to a televised adventure—these are just a few of the things we don't want to see, and in general they'll lead to an automatic rejection. That doesn't mean we will never publish a book featuring any of the above—just that, if we do, it will almost certainly be specially commissioned from a previously published author. For unsolicited proposals, we prefer to see wholly original submissions— you stand a much better chance of impressing us with your inventiveness and imagination that way!

Notes

1. *Cornell*: A lot of fans have had a vast ongoing argument about this—and many of them have come to the conclusion that canon is simply a matter of personal choice: you decide what goes in and what doesn't. I find it can be an index of what a person is like, those things they decide to include. Because sometimes they don't even include certain bits of the television show! I've recently written a long blog post on exactly this subject (see 〈http://paulcornell.blogspot.com/2007/02/canonicity-in-doctor-who.html〉).

2. *Orman*: It'd be risible to compare the novels, which sold in the thousands, to the new show, viewed by millions, if Davies hadn't written one of the books and *Human Nature* hadn't been adapted for the 2007 series.

3. *Cornell*: Such as the Daleks' name for the Doctor: "The Oncoming Storm." That's a phrase from my novel *Love and War*. And of course, I adapted my novel *Human Nature* as a two-part story for Series Three.

4. *Cornell*: Some stories are also done specifically as exercises. This happens a lot in the world of female fan fiction. A writer is given two particular characters and depicts a meeting between them, or something like that.

5. *Cornell*: There's an amazing tension within *Doctor Who*, between the conservative fan base and the driven extremity of the authors. I think one feeds the other in a strange sort of way; we want to do new and different things because *Who* on television always did new and different things, and always contradicted itself.

6. *Cornell*: For any other television show, human relationships on earth are the bread and butter, but for *Doctor Who* it's a new genre.

On Writing *Cerebus*
Dave Sim

The scope of the *Cerebus* project tends to overpower perception despite the best efforts to try to convey that scope. Even in the comic book field, *Cerebus* is usually contextualized with much shorter works and found wanting. Overpowered perception retreats to the familiar, and the knee-jerk response to contemplating a six-thousand-page graphic novel is to heap praise on a hundred-page graphic novel. The unconscious impulse is to make *Cerebus* not exist and replace it with something whose parameters are more easily perceived. Why? You tell me, and then we'll both know.

Having completed work on *Cerebus* in December 2003, I have the negligible advantage of a little over three years of overview to bring to the question of its nature. To hint at the thesis: an actual overview will not be possible until I'm dead. If, as an example, I live to be 78 years old, it can be said that I spent a third of my life writing and drawing *Cerebus*. If I live to be 104, I spent a quarter of my life doing so. If I die in two years, I will have spent half my life doing so.

The core thesis in contemplating *Cerebus*'s vast narrative really centers on context, or more precisely, the extent to which context is a more nebulous thing than is popularly conceived in the generally accepted context (that is, context within context) of the generally accepted parameters of narrative. (That is, a movie is ninety minutes long, a book is roughly two hundred pages, and a play runs two hours with an intermission.).[1]

The most common questions center on the variance: "What was it like writing and drawing something that long?" "What was it like to be finished?"

The request is for an appropriate simile that can only be imperfect: "It was like going through public school, senior public school, and high school twice." But of course, the fact that I started my schooling at the age of five and started *Cerebus* when I was twenty-one years old makes that analogy specious at best. Its only advantage is that it invokes

the questioner's own experience, his inner awareness of how long a period public schooling takes up—and then undermines itself by needing to be doubled.

The average mind can't actively grasp going through public schooling twice except as an immense (and terrifying) abstraction. And it must be remembered that doing *Cerebus* was the only thing I have done for twenty-six years, so I have nothing to compare it to either. The context of the book is so firmly wedded to the context of my life that there's no way for me to stand back far enough to find something to which I can compare it. Everything else—my four-year marriage, various relationships, friendships, hobbies, and interests—has all been of a shorter duration, and so exists only as fragmentary elements within my life and the context of the *Cerebus* experiment.

And of course, the still-larger questions implied ("What effect did that have on your life?") remain unanswerable because there is no "control group." There is no Dave Sim who *didn't do Cerebus*, whose life we can examine and compare to the life of the Dave Sim who *did do Cerebus*. Am I this way because I wrote and drew a comic book for twenty-six years, or did I write and draw a comic book for twenty-six years because I'm this way? There are probably as many gradations of responses to that as there are people who are aware of me and the project.

Perception breaks down. What people want to hear is that I lost my mind under the terrible weight of having to juggle six thousand pages of narrative—that it involved exploring boundaries the human mind was never meant to explore, and my hair turned white overnight when it all sunk in. A lot of that is a defense mechanism for smaller ambitions. Most people would still be doing victory laps if they ever wrote a book that was one hundred pages long, and came and went from the bookstores without notice, so the idea that someone embarked on a twenty-six-year project that was four times the size of its nearest competitor causes a different kind of perception meltdown—that the outside boundaries of ambition and execution are to work on something for two or three years. To have something exist that dwarfs that boundary compounds the near-universal sense of fatalism and defeatism, and raises issues of mortality: "I've just been wasting my life watching

4.1 *High Society*, page 209.

television and have nothing to show for it." As long as no one attempts a twenty-six-year project, then no one is a failure. If someone attempts it and succeeds, that makes everyone else a failure in some sense.

Another common, and somewhat more answerable question is, "How did you do it?" This one is easier.

Basically it was a matter of macrocosm and microcosm. I wrote twenty-page stories and then a sixty-page story before I decided to fill a big block of the six thousand pages with a five-hundred-page story: *High Society*. I thought I could tell the story of the world in five hundred pages, but I only got about halfway through the material that I

wanted to cover, so that established for me the limit of what could be conveyed in five hundred comic book pages. So next I allocated a thousand pages to the other half of the story I had tried to tell in five hundred, and I managed to get it all in about twelve hundred pages, so that gave me a clearer idea of how much story I could communicate.

At that point, I switched from my ambition of wanting to tell a series of Russian-style novels in comic book form to trying to write one Russian-style novel over the course of six thousand pages. Let's say that *The Brothers Karamazov* is five hundred pages. What I decided was that you have to do ten comic book pages to communicate what you can communicate in one page of a Russian novel.

A picture may have the value of a number of words, but I think one thousand is an inaccurate rate of exchange. I can get more across in one thousand words than I can in one picture when it comes to evocation, getting under the reader's skin, and having the slow dawning of insight come crawling across their scalps. A comic book is sort of halfway between a movie and a novel, and combines the greatest weaknesses of each, while also having its own strengths, but my net conclusion was: if you want to actually do a graphic *novel* and not just a big fat comic book, the ratio is pretty much one to ten in terms of the page count.

If you do a two-hundred-page graphic novel, what you have done is the equivalent of a twenty-page short story. Now, there are great twenty-page short stories, like Shirley Jackson's "The Lottery," one of the most widely admired short stories in the world, the top of its class. But no one would compare "The Lottery" to a novel of any length, and then maintain (with a straight face) that they weren't comparing apples and oranges (or more proportionally, cranberries).

Take a book like *Watchmen*. It might be called "base nine": nine panels to the page, and most of those panels have at least one word balloon in them. Will Eisner's *A Contract with God* is base two: two panels a page, with the average caption or word balloon containing maybe a dozen to two dozen words. I can read *A Contract with God* in its entirety in about twenty to thirty minutes. And I do, often—there are few better ways in the graphic novel field to spend twenty to thirty minutes. These base figures aren't a measure of quality but a ranking according to structure, like "time" in music.[2]

Most of *Cerebus* was base six: six panels to the page, with an average of one to two word balloons per panel; the reading time would be comparable. When I went lower than base six, I'd compensate with more word balloons to offset the fewer number of panels. I'd have longer stretches of "off the map" variations because the canvas was six thousand pages, as opposed to, say, *Watchmen*'s four hundred or so. And part of *Cerebus*'s ratio did include the long blocks of text in *Jaka's Story*, the text pieces in *Reads*, and so on, counterbalancing many long stretches of reasonably wordless comic page narrative.

You organize a six-thousand-page graphic novel the same way you organize a six-hundred-page prose novel: you sketch out the overall parameters, touchstone moments, plot the outline, characters, themes, and narrative tones, and then having macromanaged the overall project, you begin to micromanage the component parts.

Cerebus campaigns to become prime minister, so you allocate issues 37, 38, 39, 40, 41, and 42—120 pages—to the campaign trail. You have election night in issue 43 in mind, and tinker with it at the periphery of your thoughts, and if a good line or approach pops into your mind you write it down, but your focus is on the campaign. What's funny about a political campaign? What can you laugh at and get the reader to laugh at, and what can you laugh with and get them to laugh with? What's dramatic about a political campaign, and how do you communicate that?

What's a strong image? The candidate so far away on the stage that you can't hear what his is saying. All you can hear is the guy next to you, commenting on it. OK, that's good. Is that one or two pages? Put it down, and if it starts getting some momentum to it and you have a good punch line, but it needs some buildup and room to breathe, you expand it to two pages. Tighten up the phrasing during penciling, read it and reread it, pick at it, take words out, put words in, or try different words that might be funnier. When it works you start lettering it.

All you have to do is a page a day, so if you have two pages tightened up, you've got the creative side of the next few days taken care of (say, Tuesday and Wednesday). OK, while you're doing purely technical things, like tightening things up in pencil or filling in solid blacks, you start thinking, all right, what about Thursday? What can I do on Thursday that's really funny or dramatic?

And the same thing holds for the next sequence. Cerebus becomes prime minister. OK, let's do Richard Nixon's *My Six Crises*. What are six good crises for Cerebus to go through? Write those down, and then revisit them over the four or five months it takes until it's time to do the pages leading into that part—the last two campaign issues, election night and the deciding vote. Same thing holds true for the next story line. I'm not going to get into the religious part of the story, so that's the next book. What's a good way to start? Get little mental snapshots of what the next book is going to start like, the pacing, the tone, and so forth. That's a year away, or a year and a half away, so you start solving a lot of the problems unconsciously while you're micromanaging the story line you're working on now.

So the net effect is that as you go along, things get easier. By the time I was in the middle of *Church and State*, I had a pretty good idea that the next one would be a love story: *Jaka's Story*. In the middle of *Church and State*, I still had two and a half years of micromanaging to tell that part of the story—six hundred pages. So that means I had two and a half years to get the rough shape of *Jaka's Story* straight in my mind. Ask any writer how much better a book he would write if he had two and a half years to get the rough shape of it in his mind before he put word one down on paper. It was living in the lap of literary luxury.

All that mattered then was a good work ethic. Early on, I treated it as a job. Unless there was a good reason, I worked every day just as if I were working in a factory or an office. I had found that most creative works flame out because of bad work habits. My job was to give the audience the best twenty pages I could every month. Of course, their opinion of the best twenty pages and my own varied a lot. I was the only one who could see the larger picture, and knew that something that looked like a waste of ten

4.2 *Jaka's Story*, page 115.

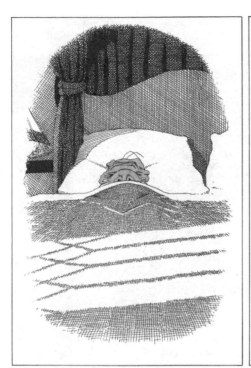

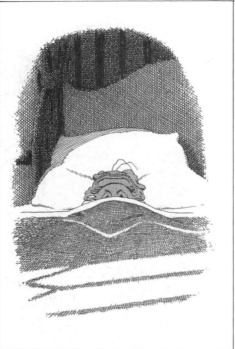

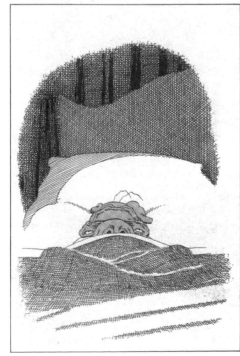

4.3 *The Last Day*, page 180.

pages at the time looked like a good creative choice when seen in the context of the twelve-hundred-page *Church and State* than it did as half of a monthly twenty-page comic book.[3]

Speaking as both a writer and an artist, I think the writer has far more artillery for communication than does the artist, so the drawing side of things tends to be more charismatic but less communicative. The artist will always be seen as more important than the writer in the comic book field ("Good art can save a bad story, but even the best story can't be saved by bad art"), so you have to play to that, and think in terms of visually interesting layouts as well as narrative tricks like jump-cutting, rendering sound as image through lettering, differently shaped panels, and the layering of visuals to create illusions of narrative and pictorial depth.

But it's still trickery, whereas a perfectly composed page by Dostoyevsky contains no trickery. That's what makes it the best. You don't read a good page of *The Idiot* and think, Oh hey, that was a clever way of doing that. If you're remarking on the cleverness of the effect, you've already pulled out of the story to a degree, which is the opposite of what the author is trying to do.

The problem in comics is that if you don't do a certain number of visual tricks, you just end up with bland visuals, and that raises the question, Why bother to draw this if you bring that little to it? Or put another way, if you think the visuals have to be this bland in order not to overpower the words, why not just photocopy one head four hundred times and paste different word balloons over each one?

I don't think we have an answer right now because we're just beginning to explore the medium outside the superhero context, so there are only a handful of, for example, historical graphic novels, all of which take different approaches to relating history in comics form. All we know is that there exists at least a handful of ways of doing historical narrative in comics form. Assuming the medium continues to exist and people continue to work in it, somewhere two hundred years from now we are apt to have a thousand historical graphic novels, and by examining all of them we can maybe draw some conclusions about

what works and what doesn't work, and decide there are two or three basic structures. But I'm pretty confident that the conclusion is going to be that there is a one-to-ten ratio or thereabouts.[4] So that will tell us a lot of what we're trying not to know right now: a 200-page graphic "novel" contains the same amount of information as a 20-page magazine article on a given subject. Which means historical graphic novels are all just magazine articles in a different form that take a lot longer to produce than magazine articles, and the graphic novel equivalent of, say, *The Rise and Fall of the Roman Empire* is just completely out of graphic narrative range, in the same way that you couldn't make a viable movie out of it that did justice to the historical work itself.

Of course as the only person who has done a 6,000-page graphic novel, I'm the only one who could be comfortable holding that opinion. Virtually everyone else would have to admit that they had worked for decades in order to produce the equivalent of a half-dozen magazine articles. I can certainly understand why they would be loath to think that. After all, within my own frames of reference, I had to work for 26 years to produce one 600-page-equivalent of a prose novel. Not the happiest conclusion to come to, but I think it's an accurate one.

Notes

1. To my mind, the closest analogue to *Cerebus* is probably Lynne Johnstone's *For Better or for Worse* because it's also done in comic form, and it's also a rare instance where comics characters actually age and change. A lot of people will tend to roll their eyes at that because *For Better or for Worse* is not seen as a particularly sophisticated (as opposed to populist) strip, and certainly if you were to read the entire history of the strip it would far more resemble a soap opera than it would a novel, but in terms of large narratives it does strive for realism and the sense of being a document of actual lives, as opposed to the latest try at breathing life into an old trademark.

2. David Lapham's *Stray Bullets* is the best example of base eight. Chris Ware's work occasionally goes all the way off the map, up to base thirty-two or base sixty-four, depending how drastically he chooses to subdivide his pages.

3. I tended to think of it as "value for the money." When I started mapping the story in longer arcs, so that a whole issue might end up having light pages in terms of literary density, I expanded the letters pages to bring the "total package" literary density up higher.

4. I don't think it changes my basic point, but Japanese manga such as *Lone Wolf and Cub* does seem to have a different literary density. The idea is that you're supposed to read manga very, very quickly, making the experience, even more so than usual, partway

between reading a book and watching a movie: flip flip flip flip. In this case the ratio goes up considerably; you might have to do as many as fifty pages of manga-style narrative in order to equal what a page of text communicates. I'm not going to make any friends in the manga or graphic novel communities, but those are the opinions I hold.

References

Sim, Dave. *Cerebus* (containing the volumes *Cerebus* [1987], *High Society* [1986], and *Church and State I* [1987]). Kitchener, ON: Aardvark-Vanaheim.

Sim, Dave, and Gerhard. *Cerebus* (containing the volumes *Church and State II* [1988], *Jaka's Story* [1986], *Melmoth* [1991], *Flight* [1993], *Women* [1994], *Reads* [1995], *Minds* [1996], *Guys* [1997], *Rick's Story* [1998], *Going Home* [1998], *Form and Void* [2001], *Latter Days* [2001], and *The Last Day* [2004]). Kitchener, ON: Aardvark-Vanaheim.

The Archdiocese of Narrative

Rafael Alvarez

In my Father's house, there are many mansions.
—The Gospel of John

The Wire and the Cable Ship

In 2003, I joined the writing staff of the HBO crime drama *The Wire*, the much-lauded story of left behinds in the United States filmed in my own backyard. I'd made it all the way to Hollywood without having to leave East Baltimore.

It was never my intention to leave the Holy Land (Alvarez 1997) of my childhood—the narrow, concrete back yards of trash cans and rosebushes, retired shipyard workers listening to the ball game on the radio. The only other destination I truly desired was the shelves of bookstores and libraries around the world.

But once I accepted an invitation to the dance, the Tinseltown cha-cha began having its way with me.

The initial come-on came in 1996 from David Simon, who sat next to me in the newsroom of the *Baltimore Sun* when we were kid reporters on the city desk. Simon's book, *Homicide: A Year on the Killing Streets*, had been developed into a dramatic series for NBC by Baltimore native Barry Levinson and was a cult favorite.

"I can help if you wanna give it a try," said Simon, who'd risen through the ranks of the show's writing staff after leaving the paper. "It's easier than reporting and pays a lot better."

I didn't own a television, having gotten rid of it when the kids were little in favor of Chinese checkers, crayons, and copy paper brought home from work. My children were not pleased: "Dad," they whined, "kids need TV!" As though it were air.

Simon gave me a pile of *Homicide* scripts and videos of the show. I bought a television and a cheap VCR player in a Tom Waits suburb of Baltimore called Glen Burnie, and

sat down to read the scripts while screening the accompanying episodes, looking up now and then to see how the words translated into image.

And then I sat down to abuse the tab key on an old IBM personal computer—one of those "towers" from the mid-1990s—to build a script like a set of monkey bars in which a lot of the pieces don't fit and others are missing. I'd never done it before, and had never wanted to.

When I give readings, people frequently ask me to explain the difference between writing fiction and writing for television. To begin with, there is the constricting, Rubik's Cube nature of a one-hour episodic script, especially a network teleplay in which the drama must be manipulated to hover at the edge of each commercial break, and do it so compellingly that it often feels false.

The biggest way the genres vary, and the part that disappoints me most, is how useless the camera renders description, how moot the precision and rhythm of the language I'd worked on for so long—the way sunlight looks on the side of a building, and how that light strikes the same building different at 10:00 a.m. versus 4:00 p.m. Screenwriting sums it all up in a single direction, one that no one has better sustained throughout an entire film than the great Terence Malick in *Days of Heaven*. Magic hour.

Scribbling quotes in a reporter's notebook for so many years, however—listening for lyricism instead of looking for it—proved to be great preparation for screenwriting. When my characters speak, no matter what ridiculous situation they might be in on a cartoonish show like the *The Black Donnellys*, they tend to sound like real people. Or at least what passes for real in Baltimore.

With no small amount of cynicism, it comes down to this for me: spend half a lifetime in letters and you're lucky you win a hundred readers who can discern your work stripped of your byline. But go and get that same name attached to the credits of something that airs on television a half-dozen times, and then you get invited to write for books like this one. Which, by the way, falls into the category of writing that pays the least.

I knew very little of this when I sat down in fall 1996 to write my "spec" script—a tryout, an audition, if you can bounce, then bounce high—for *Homicide*. My idea was to tell a story about the kinds of killings that don't get much attention in the ballistic age: someone using their bare hands in intimate slaughter, preferably between best friends.

I named one of the homicidal, glue-sniffing goofs Butchie. I can't remember who Butchie beat to death, but he did it by the railroad tracks at the end of Foster Avenue, around the corner from my grandfather's Macon Street row house, the place where I heard my first stories at the kitchen table: Spain's Civil War, sailing ships, and the men who went ashore in Baltimore and sometimes made their way to that kitchen table with stories of their own.

With Simon's support and fine-tuning (from him I learned that dialogue, however clever, cannot twist the actor's tongue), the script was good enough to freelance an episode for *Homicide*'s fifth season. Producer Jimmy Yoshimura assigned the idea to me; he wanted a murder pivoting on AIDS and an urban legend that held that drinking bleach could cleanse the victim of the virus.

The episode, "All Is Bright," aired on December 12, 1997, and actually retained some of the scenes and dialogue I had written. I was especially pleased that my suggestion for music to accompany a key scene—Suzanne Vega's "Blood Makes Noise"—was used. Simon's bosses, though, didn't think the work quite good enough, and it was back to the city desk for me.

Five years later, I had left the newspaper to go to sea. For $7.80 an hour plus health insurance, I washed dishes and mopped decks on the *Global Link*, a Tyco cable layer that docked near the Port Covington printing plant of the *Baltimore Sun*. In port—stretched out in my rack reading *Half a Life* by V. S. Naipaul—I'd look out the porthole and see the giant logo of the paper where I'd learned to write twenty years earlier. And I did not miss it a bit.

At the same time, Simon had sold a pilot called *The Wire* to HBO and was preparing for the show's inaugural season. I was invited to write a script that first year: "One Arrest," which aired July 14, 2002, as I tossed bags of garbage into an incinerator aboard a British cable ship, the *Atlantic Guardian* (Alvarez 2003b), off the coast of the Virgin Islands.

"Sure you wrote a TV show," my shipmate on the incinerator detail laughed. "How about you throw me another bag of garbage."

The next year, *The Wire* moved to those same docks where the cable ships tied up, its plot anchored deep in the long, slow death of a well-paid working class protected by organized labor. I joined the staff full time.

At the same time, I scrambled to complete a book manuscript much larger and more difficult than anticipated when, broke and waiting for a ship, I had accepted the job over summer 2001: a history of the Archdiocese of Baltimore commissioned by Cardinal William H. Keeler.

Overbooked as usual—like the small-time home improvement who promises to renovate a half-dozen kitchens and as many bathrooms just so he can make ends meet with the down payments—I began taking my lime, clamshell Mac iBook to the set of *The Wire*. I'd sit in a canvas Hollywood deck chair behind whatever director was working that episode and bang out boilerplate on parish after parish, hammering four hundred years of Catholic history on both sides of the Chesapeake Bay into a manageable text. My goal was to leaven the history, well documented by scholars, with first-person remembrances of as many everyday Baltimore Catholics as possible.

Every now and then I'd look up to make sure the actors were saying their lines as written—my primary chore as the staff writer on the set. One day, Simon asked that I not take the laptop to filming. He claimed not to care much about it, but Nina Noble, his fellow producer and the show's wrist slapper in chief, did not like my attention so flagrantly divided. (Sort of like a short-order cook scanning the sports page while flipping eggs. The mug who owns the joint knows the quality of the food isn't suffering, he just doesn't like it.)

So I began printing out pages of the archdiocese manuscript, shoving them in my pocket and taking them to the set, editing as many paragraphs as possible while making sure that the British-born Dominic West didn't lapse from Balti-moron cockney into Limey cockney in his portrayal of Detective Jimmy McNulty.

On both the *Global Link* and the *Atlantic Guardian*, I'd welded together a few Catholic chapters, and between ships and scripts I took the manuscript to ball games, holidays by the sea, and out of town assignations that would serve as first drafts for short fictions (Alvarez 2000).

In the end, my experience on *The Wire*, working alongside the 150 or so people it takes to get a U.S. television show on the air, informed my Catholic history as my knowledge of Catholic Baltimore would inform *The Wire*. As a manager, Simon plays to people's strengths, and early on I was assigned to write the Catholic scenes. The first task was to create a pastor for Saint Casimir, the southeast Baltimore church where my parents were married in 1953, and the place where fictional waterfront union leader Frank Sobotka went fishing for the political favors on which season two would pivot.

Virginia-based actor Tel Monks won the role of the Reverend Jerome Lewandowski and wanted to know why I'd created a priest from Poland, which was the accent he'd been working on.

"Not a Polish priest from Poland," I laughed, channeling the spirit of my Polish grandmother, Anna Potter Jones. "A Polack from East Bawlmer."

As this was something not to be found in the Laurence Olivier repertoire, we hopped in my car and headed to the far reaches of East Baltimore, over the county line into Dundalk, where my ex-wife had been raised among Polish, Italian, and Southern steelworkers both white and black. We went down Route 40 to a stainless steel diner owned by a Greek who'd launched himself in the United States with a hot dog cart.

I scanned the joint, found my mark, and led Monks to a booth behind a middle-aged woman who looked like Divine, except that she wasn't a man and this wasn't a movie. It was just a heavyset woman on her lunch break, legs spread to get as close to the plate as possible.

I sat Monks with his back to the woman, plopped down across from him, and gave him direction: "Just listen to what she says and how she says it. Somewhere between bites of that open-faced turkey sandwich she's destroying is the voice of your Polish priest." (This is what passes for a day of work in television land.)

Monks nodded, intrigued that I'd so quickly navigated a route to the soul of his character. I've known people like this my entire life; I was related to them, and carried them inside of me. But Monks's time in Baltimore was brief, and his task of nailing the echt of the locals and how they

spoke was nothing a day player could prepare for. His performance bore this out.

A few weeks later, *The Wire* filmed on board the SS. *John W. Brown*, one of two Liberty ships still operational out of the 2,710 built in Baltimore and other port cities around the country to ferry military freight in World War II. In this episode, detectives Bunk Moreland and Lester Freamon board the *Brown*, rechristened the *Atlantic Light*, to interview sailors about the deaths of fourteen Eastern European women found asphyxiated in a shipping container on the piers.

As we filmed, the volunteers who keep the *Brown* afloat sat in the galley, taking it all in. Hanging with them between shots, I mentioned that my father's old tugboat buddy, the souse-making and cabin-cruiser-building Chester Rakowski, had done some welding on the *Brown*. The men just nodded. But when I mentioned the Catholic history project, a quiet man in the corner spoke up.

He said his name was Jay Tinker, a volunteer deckhand on the *Brown* and a devout Catholic. Soon, Tinker was sitting for a portrait in the ship's chapel and telling of his devotion to the rosary, the Eucharist—from the Greek, meaning Thanksgiving—and his work with the Knights of Columbus.

What was the result of so much research seemingly at odds with itself?

5.1 Practicing Catholic Jay Tinker aboard the *SS John W. Brown*, the set for "Collateral Damage," episode 115, season two, *The Wire*. (Kirsten Beckerman)

A People's History of the Archdiocese of Baltimore, published in 2006 by Editions du Signe of Strasbourg, France.

And the preservation of a way of life all but lost. The stevedoring season of *The Wire* not only captured the culture of labor along an urban waterfront for the small number of folks who'd lived it—many of whom made cameos and were interviewed at length before the first camera rolled—the artifice of television also made it real for millions who'd never seen anything like it.

Crimson Hexagons and the Meandering Mississippi

How vast is the universe of storytelling when glimpsed through the prism of a library! How boundless when that library is harnessed to television!

Imagine that the fabled sorcerer Jorge Luis Borges—author of "The Library of Babel"—was head honcho of his own network, able to fling moving pictures through all the cathode tubes of Earth for our enjoyment. Borges, of course, would "broadcast" in the original sense of the word, the farm term for sowing seed over a wide area, scattering by hand. Not always in a row, for the best narratives, like time itself, are not linear.

"I, who imagined paradise as a kind of library," declares Borges on the Argentinean postage stamp honoring him on his death in 1986. His would be a curious paradise marked by a crimson hexagon wherein lies a book holding the truths of all other books; the librarian who is capable of divining its contents on a par with the divine (Borges 1999).

In the golden age of television (how strange the honorific "golden" applied to a genre's infancy), literature was the primary source for small screen drama. This was back before Hollywood was being run by the fourth generation of kids raised on the medium. Way, way, way back...when young people still dreamed of writing the Great American Novel.[1]

Consider an extraordinary episode of *The Outer Limits* from 1963 called "The Man Who Was Never Born." Directed by Leonard Horn and wrapped in the soft lighting of Conrad Hall, the episode was written by Anthony Lawrence, who—in the potluck so peculiar to Hollywood—would go on to write a television movie about Liberace.

In the story, a young and earnest Martin Landau gives a time-traveling astronaut from Earth a short tour of the future, an AD 2148 glimpse of what remains of the great human civilization.

"Come," says Landau, human and monstrously deformed, his face a bloom of boils and blisters created by the same corrupted microbe that destroyed the race. "I will show you all that's left of moments, men, and places."

And he takes the astronaut to a deserted library where the architecture is futuristic and spare, and the books are old and leather bound. Had the show been filmed in Technicolor, you might have seen a crimson hexagon shimmering beyond the stacks.

"Here lies the protected history of man," says Landau, acting out the essence of each immortal tome. "The cherished words and pictures of all he has known and loved. The noble Hamlet; Anna Karenina putting on her gloves on a snowy evening; Gatsby in white flannels; Moby Dick and Mark Twain's whole meandering Mississippi."

Stung, the astronaut grabs Herman Melville from a shelf and reads a random passage aloud: "Hope proves a man deathless."

"There is no hope here," says the mutant Landau.

"There has to be."

"There is no future. Only a safe and dear host of memories."

Holy host, as my old editor Cardinal Keeler might say; host from the Latin *hostia* for victim. And memories like ghosts who sacrificed their lives to create them.

Whether writer or waitress (and so very often both at once), we pay for our stories with our lives.

To this day I can see Gilbert Lukowski, a long-dead stevedore from a long-gone Baltimore, standing in front of the waterfront saloon where he grew up, just across the cobblestones from the pier used by NBC to film *Homicide*.

Lukowski, a tough guy with a strong sense of himself, the brother of my father's best friend from the tugboats, called me up on the city desk one day to say that he wanted to read his obituary before he died (Alvarez 1999). To that end, to see the memories for which he'd traded his life in nine-point type across the local page, Gilbert gave me a time machine tour of the once-rough and now-gilded neighborhood of his Great Depression youth.

With tears in his eyes, a man who'd never backed down from anything stared at his mother's house at 1718 Thames Street and spoke as though talking to himself.

"Nobody remembers," he said, "but I think about it every day."

From Borges to Hollywood science fiction to tears in a longshoreman's jaded eyes, every permutation of narrative: high, low, and vast.

David Simon's Books on Film

My writing career has followed two parallel and simultaneous paths: the stuff I do for money, which can be just about anything, although I once drew the line at dialogue for a particularly violent video game; and the prose over which I labor because I am moved to bring it into the world.

The writing I care least about, television, pays the most—enough to dream the kind of dreams not every writer dares: to be left alone to write as one pleases whether anyone cares or not.

The work dearest to my heart, fiction about life on the untethered planet of Baltimore, pays the least—less even than the odd piece of journalism I bang out when the subject demands, like a short sketch of the woman who took dictation from F. Scott Fitzgerald for *The Last Tycoon* (Alvarez 2006).

On season two of *The Wire*, all of the important things—money, subject matter, and a cumulative importance greater than the subject itself—came together in a way I've not experienced since.

Like me, I don't believe Simon ever desired to tell stories on television. I've heard him say he envisioned a long career not just in newspapers but specifically at the *Baltimore Sun*, and one big enough to include leaves of absence to write the books he believed in. And then, always, a faithful return to the paper.

For generations, this privilege was granted to ambitious writers at the *Washington Post* and the *New York Times*, but was not looked on kindly by newsroom management on Calvert Street in Baltimore in the mid-1990s.

At the *Sun*, founded in 1837 by A. S. Abell and controlled by his descendants for the next 150 years (Williams 1987), corporate buyouts began after the Times Mirror Company bought the paper for $600 million in 1986. The pace of early retirement picked up when the Tribune Company swallowed the Times Mirror Company whole in 2000 for $8.3 billion.

Simon exited in 1995, leaving a job he might admit to loving more than any before or since; his departure was part of a hemorrhage of talent that claimed dozens of *Sun* reporters (Smolkin 2004) who might have stayed had the culture been more sympathetic to the quirks of the individual, once a hallmark of the best newsrooms, however parochial.

Finding a new home at HBO after his second adapted-for-television book—*The Corner*—won the cable network a pair of Emmys in 2000, Simon began using screenplays to write the books he would have tackled as a journalist.

Thus, the five seasons of *The Wire*, an open-ended narrative as vast as the history of North America from the time the first slave ship landed, break down along these stated themes:[2]

1. The failed war on drugs

2. The death of the working class

3. The hollow promise of reform

4. The failure of public education in the American city

5. The media and its consumers as complicit in all of the above

I wrote one episode in each of the first three years—"One Arrest," "Backwash," and "Homecoming"—before moving to Los Angeles to find work during *The Wire*'s nearly two-year hiatus between seasons three and four.

Each episode was integral to the one before and after it, just as each season built on and advanced those on either side. Simon's sociological arguments provided a sweeping outline, driven always by the crime story percolating beneath it, for even HBO, after all, is television. More so than on any other show I have yet to work for, I was permitted to draw between those lines with freedom.

The colors I chose came from the bottomless Crabtown quarry I've mined since selling my first story to the weekly *City Squeeze* (Alvarez 1977)—the precursor to Baltimore's *City Paper*; it was an overview of an International Longshoremen's Association strike not unlike the labor strife covered by *The Wire* nearly thirty years later.[3]

When it was my turn to bring a script full of dockworkers to life in "Backwash," I conjured the Italian knife grinders who once roamed the alleys of Baltimore to sharpen kitchen utensils, repairing everything from loose handles on stew pots to umbrellas. Their stories had come my way through a family of local knife grinders named Vidi, via an anecdote from the incomparable composer and Baltimore native Frank Zappa.

In a key scene from "Backwash" (season two, episode seven), dock chief Sobotka—deluded by his quixotic "all's well that ends well" scheme to bring more work to the port—is getting bad news from a lobbyist (hired with money from stolen cargo) about the state's reluctance to dredge the harbor. When Frank rails about robots taking jobs that should be the birthright of many generations of Sobotkas to come, the lobbyist argues that education—and not nepotistic craft guilds—are the only way to survive in the United States.

The Italian lobbyist, played by Keith Flippen, says how his grandfather pushed a stone grinding-wheel up and down the alleys, and demanded that his son graduate high school. And that man demanded that his son go to any college that would take him. And *that* guy—the lobbyist whose grandfather pushed the grinding wheel—raised a boy who went to Princeton.

All because when I got the chance to interview one of my adolescent heroes—guitarist Zappa, who'd been born right down the street from the *Baltimore Sun* at Mercy Hospital—he told me that one of his earliest memories before the family moved to California was watching the knife grinder man come down the alley (Alvarez 1986).

The cherry on top was the last shot in the scene, which was something so parochial and so brief that perhaps only a dozen people caught it the first time around. When the lobbyist leaves Sobotka's shack on the pier, the angry union boss hurls a dart at a board on the wall. In the center of

5.2 David Simon (left) and Rafael Alvarez in front of Baltimore Harbor tugs at the corner of South Broadway and Thames Street, fall 1997. Publicity photo for reading to benefit the Mother Seton Academy middle school. (Jim Burger)

that board was a photo of Robert Irsay, the man who moved Baltimore's beloved Colts to Indianapolis in 1984—a civic crime that continued to cause nausea as late as 2007 when the blue horseshoes won Super Bowl XLI.

This is the nature of a real Baltimore story, as infinite as love lost, as faithful as grudges held: nothing goes to waste.

The Card Catalog as Schindler's List

I have knelt by the side of the bed and prayed for my characters, so that they might choose to do what they were fated and not be coerced into what I think is best. I wish for them what the sages who constructed the kabbalah maintain: the universe in its entirety—*olam mullay*—spinning within each and every one of us. Thus, the most poetic of wisdoms: one who saves a single life has saved the world.

But what of the Samaritan who rescues that beaten high school copy of *Heart of Darkness* from the nickel-and-dime bin at a suburban yard sale?

I would argue that if the cosmos exists in each of us, then an infinite library lies between the lines of each story told: by mouth, in the hieroglyphics of ink on paper, and in the rivers of light pushing pictures across silver screens.

A library to dwarf the lost palace of papyrus of ancient Alexandria; bigger by fourscore than the one that Thomas Jefferson launched; stacks on stacks of shelves beyond anything in the hexagonal rooms of Borges's Library of Babel.

Once, when teaching fiction workshops with George Minot at an East Baltimore gin mill known as Miss Bonnie's Elvis Bar, George declared, "Only two things last: love and stories" (quoted in Alvarez 1994).

Radiation has a half-life, but turn your back on narrative for five minutes—particularly if left in the hands of a confidant—and it starts to rise and twist like pizza dough in a monster movie. Writers may tear off a piece to bake a cupcake here and a loaf of raisin bread there, temporarily containing it with shape and heat, but the dough keeps growing.

As does my ongoing soap opera of the luckless lovers Orlo and Leini, in which the couple's ritualistic assignations paint a history of twentieth-century Baltimore.

My Italian, legally blind grandmother loved her "stories," and would put on her thick eyeglasses from the Wilmer Clinic at Hopkins and sit an inch or two away from the screen to follow *As the World Turns*. At the typewriter, I summon her voice, hear her tell a lady friend at the huckster's produce truck in the alley that she was going inside: it was time for her stories.

We lost Grandmom during summer 1976, not long after I graduated high school and went to sea for the first time, not to learn how to splice line, but how to braid sentences. Thirty years later, I have placed her—Frances Prato Alvarez, and the life she carried with grace and humility for seventy years—at Leini's side, the Greek beauty's best friend.

A key motivation for the Orlo and Leini stories is the altar they provide to display all of not just who my grandmother was but also what she meant to me: the blindness, the siblings who didn't care quite as much as they could have, the hardheaded husband who came from the West Virginia of Spain to make a home with her in the East Baltimore house where I live today, a sanctuary to which she allowed Leini to invite Orlo when no one was home.

And while the Baltimore of my stories will always be the Baltimore laid out on street maps and in the morning paper, I have set my grandmother—known in the tales as Francesca Bombacci Boulossa—on a broad stage she would not have recognized.

Think of nonfiction, the facts and anecdotes of my grandmother's temporal life, as a gallon of clear water. Think of fiction, the long summer nights that Francesca sat with Leini as clouds sailed past half a moon above the Patapsco, as a single drop of blood.

In the diffusion, see scarlet pass to vermilion to pink to mauve to wisps too subtle to name as Leini gives Francesca the dignity of being able to write her name at a church carnival on the other side of town (Alvarez n.d.).

I did not dream up the scene in which Leini teaches Francesca how to escape the humiliation of making an *X* in place of her signature. It arrived one afternoon as my then-teenage daughter Amelia conducted an oral history with my father. There was something she'd wanted, money for something, and I told her I'd give it to her if she talked to my father about his life as I took notes.

I'd interviewed my Dad many times—he was always cooperative, as thorough as possible—but somehow the story of how he'd taught his mother to sign her name when he was fifteen never came up.

"We traced it over and over," he said.

"Like learning a dance step," said Amelia.

And I had a new Orlo and Leini story, yet one more in a sweep of narrative that I have come to see as a mural.

The tales were written out of order, beginning with Orlo's death in 1988 before jumping around between 1922—when the thirteen-year-old Leini discovered she'd been traded to a barren couple in the United States for fourteen sewing machines (Alvarez 2004b)—on through Leini's own passing in the early 1990s.

Each story is grounded in a different part of Baltimore; each new panel, like episodes of *The Wire* rippling into the seasons not yet filmed, invigorates the ones around it. Sometimes a newly imagined Orlo and Leini tale will fit tongue-and-groove with those already in place; at other times they explore a patch of white.

As I concentrate smaller amounts of information into each telling, reducing a relationship of some sixty years down to the sharing of an orange on a city bench, the panorama

5.3 Minas Konsolas's mural of Leini. (Eric Mithen)

becomes exponentially larger, each tile amplifying not only what has come before it but also what's been left unsaid.

A few years ago, the metaphor became literal (interpretation is the impregnation through which literature procreates) when artist Minas Konsolas was asked to contribute an image for a wall of Greek themes behind Saint Nicholas Orthodox Church a couple blocks from my house. On the wall that faces Oldham Street, Minas chose to portray Leini in the prime of her beauty, the apex of her suffering. She now broods over passersby just a few blocks from the row house on Ponca Street where she lived all of her adult life, across from the public transit bus yard and a few blocks from her friend Francesca.

For years, Leini took those municipal buses to meet Orlo with a basket of food on her lap. Though she never

ventured far beyond the city, the stories documenting her journeys have traveled the globe. Each year, out of my own pocket (again, the writing I care most about remains the least rewarded), I get together with a friend who works in design and my artist son Jake to produce a thousand copies of whatever story is keeping me up at night.

And then I throw them to the wind, giving away copies at readings, coffee shops, and gas stations on cross-country trips, or to friends willing to slip a couple copies in their luggage when they travel overseas. In this way, tales of Orlo and Leini's heroic adultery have been left for wayfarers to find in Budapest, Borges's Buenos Aires, and Beijing, where copies were left in crevices of the Great Wall.

Perhaps the stories aren't any more accessible than Leini's inscrutable gaze is to those who see her face as they walk along Oldham Street. I like to imagine people—old men and little kids, folks who don't speak English—happening on the ten-foot visage and imagining her story anew. Leini alive!

"Very alive," said Konsolas, who immigrated to Baltimore from Greece as a young man. "Her story stirred up things inside of me, things I went through myself. As I read her story, I found myself putting in my own conversations."

It's hard to imagine that the street drunks with their Mad Dog and junkies scoring methadone from the Johns Hopkins Bayview campus up the road give a shit about the woman on the wall. But perhaps, in the proper narcotized haze, pupils rolling back as their heads find the curb, the lost soul's eyes meet Leini's for the only exchange that matters in this world: "I know how you feel."

A mural no frame can hold.

Endvast

Notes

1. For my money, Thomas Wolfe's *Look Homeward Angel* is as close as anyone is likely to come to claiming the prize, especially now that the middle class no longer discusses books at barbecues. God love you, Thomas, it's the only book that ever made me cry.

2. David Simon, email message to author, March 10, 2007.

3. Lukowski handed me that story, which was a scoop since International Longshoremen's Association officials were refusing to talk to reporters from the *Baltimore Sun*. When I asked why he'd agreed to talk to me, he barked: "Who's your father?" That family favor helped me jump from the *Baltimore Sun* circulation department, where I

dispatched trucks while writing for *City Paper*, to the daily's sports department in 1978.

References: Literature

Alvarez, Rafael (1977). "Longshoremen Are Unsuremen." *City Squeeze* (Baltimore), November.

Alvarez, Rafael (1986). "I Never Set Out to Be Weird." *Baltimore Sun Magazine*, October 12.

Alvarez, Rafael (1992). "Cannery Rows." *Baltimore Sun Magazine*, February 16.

Alvarez, Rafael (1994). "The Annunciation," In *Mondo Elvis*, edited by Lucinda Ebersole and Richard Peabody. New York: St. Martin's Press.

Alvarez, Rafael (1997). *The Fountain of Highlandtown*. Baltimore: Woodholme House Publishers.

Alvarez, Rafael (1999). "Tales of Old Fells Point." *Hometown Boy: The Hoodie Patrol and Other Curiosities of Baltimore*. Baltimore: Baltimore Sun.

Alvarez, Rafael (2000). *Orlo and Leini*. Baltimore: Woodholme House.

Alvarez, Rafael (2003a). "Orlo and Leini Meet the Invisible Man." *Crabtown Stories*. Baltimore: Macon Street Books.

Alvarez, Rafael (2003b). "Shore Leave: A Night to Remember." *Professional Mariner* 71 (April–May).

Alvarez, Rafael (2004a). "Divorce." *Style Magazine* (Baltimore), September–October.

Alvarez, Rafael (2004b). "How Leini Landed in America." *Urbanite* (Baltimore), May 2004.

Alvarez, Rafael (2004c). *The Wire: Truth Be Told*. New York: Pocket Books.

Alvarez, Rafael (2006). "Recalling Fitzgerald's Life, Death." *Baltimore Sun*, December 21, op-ed.

Alvarez, Rafael (n.d.). "Fourteen Holy Martyrs." Unpublished short story.

Borges, Jorge Luis (1999). "The Library of Babel." In *Collected Fictions*, translated by Andrew Hurley. New York: Penguin Putnam.

Smolkin, Rachel (2004). "Uncertain Times." *American Journalism Review* 26, December.

Williams, Harold A. (1987). *The Baltimore Sun, 1837 to 1987*. Baltimore: Johns Hopkins University Press.

References: Television

"The Man Who Was Never Born" (1963). *The Outer Limits*, first broadcast October 28, ABC. Directed by Leonard Horn and written by Anthony Lawrence.

"Backwash" (2003). *The Wire*, first broadcast July 13 on HBO. Created by David Simon and written by Rafael Alvarez.

The Black Donnellys (2007). First broadcast on NBC. Created by Paul Haggis and Bobby Moresco, and written and produced by Rafael Alvarez.

Intellectual Property Development in the Adventure Games Industry: A Practitioner's View

Robin D. Laws

Operating below the radar of mainstream pop culture, but saturated even more thoroughly in certain distinctive tropes and images, is the adventure games industry, also known as hobby gaming. This catchall term refers to a constellation of related products, aimed at seriously dedicated game fans whose tastes in narrative entertainment run toward the fantastic modes of the action-adventure genre. The most notable of these are the fantasy, science fiction, and superhero subgenres. Though first devised in the late 1970s by executives at the game publishing firm TSR, Inc., to apply a positive marketing tag to the then-controversial category of role-playing games, the term adventure gaming now encompasses an entire marketplace of products including other genres of games played around a gaming table, such as collectible card games, miniatures games, and a variety of board games geared to a complexity-seeking, fantasy-friendly audience.

Though each of these various subcategories offers its own distinct play experience, appealing to the various gamer tastes, their audiences overlap to some extent, bound together by a common allegiance to geek culture. All of these game forms either directly engage in (as in the case of role-playing games) or easily support the formation of large narratives. Most such games take place in an imaginary world, alternately known as a setting. Many feature a handful of iconic characters.

To practitioners in the field, including myself, the setting plus characters and other intangible elements such as emotional tone and visual style are collectively referred to as an intellectual property. An intellectual property can be seen as a large narrative or at least forms the foundation for such. These large narratives may be created by the gamers themselves as they run individual role-playing games, or consumed in a more traditional passive mode in the form of ancillary media spin-offs, including novels, computer games, television shows, and movies.

The growth of the adventure gaming hobby has led to a degree of corporate consolidation. Wizards of the Coast, the publisher of *Magic: The Gathering*, grew large enough to acquire TSR, the owner of *Dungeons & Dragons*, and was itself later acquired by the publicly traded toy giant Hasbro. Even so, adventure gaming is, to a degree no longer possible in larger sectors of the entertainment industry, dominated by entrepreneurs and creators. Role-playing games in particular have low development and production costs compared to other mass media entertainment forms, and thus provide a relatively cheap way of introducing a property to the fans who serve as early adopters for fantastic genre properties. The threads of development, however, can originate from any stop along the continuum of product categories. Once a product becomes popular in its original category, it is typically spun off into as many others as the vagaries of licensing allow.

To use myself as an example, I've written novels based on a miniatures game (*Honour of the Grave*, *Sacred Flesh*, and *Liar's Peak*, based on *Warhammer*) and a massively multiplayer computer game: *Freedom Phalanx*, a tie-in with *City of Heroes*. Another similar credit is *Cathedral of Thorns*, an online fiction serial to expand the world of the *Dreamblade* collectible miniatures game. I've designed multiple original role-playing games, including *Feng Shui* and *The Esoterrorists*, developing their intellectual properties as part of the manuscript. I've contributed to computer game adaptations of a role-playing game (*King of Dragon Pass*) and a collectible card game, providing additional dialogue for an early *Magic: The Gathering* computer game. Other role-playing designs of mine were adapted from a computer game (*Rune*), a series of influential fantasy stories (*The Dying Earth*), and *HeroQuest*, a preexisting fantasy world first devised for another role-playing game called *RuneQuest*.

The cross-pollination of intellectual properties developed for the adventure gaming industry has traditionally occurred on an after-the-fact basis. Role-playing game books typically include large sections of text, supplemented by illustrations, detailing their settings. These instructions for the game master effectively serve the purpose of so-called setting bibles, which can also be used to provide information to novelists, screenwriters, and other creators assigned to adapt the property to other media.

The term *bible* originates in television and is also employed in the computer game industry. In the former case, it is a document meant to convey the characters and conventions of a series to studio executives and the writers assigned to various episodes. In computer gaming, a bible usually includes inspirational production sketches and a description of the setting, which maintains a consistency of depiction within a team of game developers.

Recent trends in the adventure gaming sector have reduced the appeal of the role-playing game as a vehicle for launching intellectual properties. In 2000, Wizards of the Coast, in conjunction with the release of a major revamp of the game, began to allow other publishers to produce books compatible with *Dungeons & Dragons* according to the terms of the so-called d20 License. This initiative triggered one of the boom-bust cycles to which the sector is prone. Until approximately 2003, the market rewarded publishers that produced supplemental material for *Dungeons & Dragons* over those that attempted to launch stand-alone role-playing games. New and old publishers alike rushed to meet the demand for books tailored to the stock fantasy setting of *Dungeons & Dragons*, leaving by the wayside the presentation of unique new intellectual properties. In 2003, Wizards of the Coast issued a partial revision of its previous new edition, rendering somewhat obsolete the vast quantity of books sold in the previous few years. Shortly thereafter, the demand for role-playing products by publishers other than Wizards of the Coast dropped significantly, and remains soft as of this writing.

Yet publishers of other adventure gaming products continue to see the value of creating distinctive worlds, characters, and properties suitable for export to other media. Lacking a viable role-playing game market, some have turned to creators with role-playing game and fiction experience to create or flesh out setting bibles for their new intellectual properties. Writers who work on game fiction during a property's developmental stages may also act as de facto consultants, helping to hash out issues arising from the adaptation of the setting from the game medium to the short story or novel form. For example, designers of board, card, or miniatures games may create the game around a central activity without having to worry about the traditional building blocks of character motivation. Fiction writers may find themselves quizzing the intellectual property creators on questions like, "What do these characters want? How do they get it? How do they spend their time?"

Let's say you're working with a game where its various creatures, represented by cards or other playing pieces, fight to control a particular territory on a map. The game designer may answer those questions of motivation and character in a narrow way that suits their immediate purposes: the creatures want to control that territory because they're acting out of a vaguely defined, inherent instinct. That's all the designer needs to make their game premise work. The fiction author looking at that premise immediately spots a problem: if the characters act without conscious volition, they're deprived of the choices essential to drama, even in its pulpiest form. Also, the world as currently envisioned supports only one story: creatures battling to control a location. That concept provides an obvious premise for a first story or novel set in this world, but no grounds for variation if further episodes or sequels are called for. The designer and author may then collaborate to invest the characters with the potential to make choices and undergo changes, and widen the setting to support more than one basic plotline.

Whether the large narratives of adventure gaming become a subject of concentrated academic study will be a matter of its perceived cultural relevance over time. If it does so, it will most likely be as an antecedent to computer games, whose burgeoning significance as a pop culture medium recalls the film industry of the early twentieth century. Adventure gaming is a relatively small industry, remaining vulnerable to the business vagaries of one or two market leaders. Although I'm personally optimistic about its survival, many equally informed observers believe that it will eventually wind up on the ash heap of pop culture history. Nevertheless, the computer gaming industry, which it played a vital role in inspiring, now earns revenues eclipsing Hollywood's, and as a media form will be to the twenty-first century what film was to the twentieth.

These hypothetical future researchers into the methods of production of adventure gaming (or computer gaming for that matter) will face a few hurdles unseen in English literature or even film studies departments. As a matter of course, the creative participants—or anyone else viewing bible material in its early, developmental stages—are required to sign nondisclosure agreements. The details of these imaginary worlds as they're created are treated as proprietary commercial secrets. The creators agree not to reveal them on pain of litigation.

You'll note, therefore, an unfortunate scarcity of specific examples in this chapter.

The use of nondisclosure agreements can be seen as a ritual gesture, a signifier of the importance of the project and creative relationship to come. The adventure hobby industry has yet to see a case of nondisclosure agreement violation lead to lawsuits or scandal. That said, the nondisclosure agreements also indicate the tone of the activity. Intellectual property development is as much a business-minded act as it is a creative one. Discussions with the property's lead developer often oscillate, sometimes in the same sentence, between commercial and purely creative considerations. Certain elements are inserted because the lead developer finds them inherently fun and interesting. Others identify perceived tastes and attempt to cater to them. The classic split between instinct and intellect that governs any creative endeavor manifests itself as a balance between personal expression and market satisfaction.

As collaborative efforts, game settings raise questions of authorship familiar to students of film studies. The identity of the primary author varies by project. The designer of the original game may be the setting's sole author, but this is the exception to the rule. Unlike the traditional publishing industry, it is rare for an outside writer to successfully pitch a game to a preexisting publisher, deliver a manuscript, and see it published more or less as is. More often, creator-entrepreneurs hatch an idea and publish it through their existing companies, or found companies to bring particular games to market. The entrepreneur who signs the checks may sketch out a series of basic concepts, determine an overall tone, and then farm out the job of creating the details to other writers, who are either employees or work as independent contractors. It is not uncommon for would-be designers who start companies to publish their own games to find themselves preoccupied with business matters, forcing them to rely on collaborators to do the creative work that inspired them to set up shop in the first place. Creator-entrepreneurs, whether distanced from the detail of setting creation by choice or necessity, can be counted on to exercise their power by requesting changes to material that fails to square with their original vision.

With fantastic properties in increasing demand in the larger movie, television, and computer game fields, portability between media is almost invariably a crucial stated concern during setting development. A tension may arise between the immediate needs of the setting to dovetail with game play and the hypothetical but attractive possibility of future lucrative media tie-ins.

Complexity levels—the largeness of the narrative—are one such point of tension. Gamers love detail. Role-playing groups in particular demand a wide set of possible narratives in which to engage their characters. Settings often include, for example, large numbers of competing organizations to which the characters might belong. The conflicts between these organizations pose a huge number of possible story lines. Nearly any hobby game requires a huge slate of creatures and characters. Miniatures manufacturers need many different types of figures, as visually distinct as possible, to sell to their customers. Trading card games likewise require multiple cohorts of fantastic beings, which offer infinite variations on a series of themes corresponding to the game's card suits.

Traditional mass entertainment media thrive on simplicity. Rather than count on the fanatic devotion—and repeat purchases—of a small coterie of extremely dedicated audience members who are heavily invested, emotionally and financially, in their products, they strive to appeal to a broad audience. Adapting a game property to a mass form is a matter of boiling it down from a large narrative into a tightly focused one.

To cite an example, in 1995, I created a setting inspired by Hong Kong action movies that was used as the basis of the collectible card game *Shadowfist* and the role-playing game *Feng Shui*. While creating the world, its portability to other media, especially movies, was uppermost in my mind. Nonetheless, when a producer expressed interest in the game as a movie property and I set about writing a screenplay, I bumped head-on into the inherent conflict between the largeness of game narrative and the singularity of focus required by mass media storytelling.

As is common for gaming settings, *Shadowfist* included a number of competing organizations, each with its own distinctive characters, creatures, and themes, and put them at odds with one another by giving them all a common goal. In this case, the organizations of the world are embroiled in a massive, time-spanning battle for control of history, which they win or lose by seizing control of magically powerful places. By hobby gaming standards, this is a simple, bare-bones concept.

By movie standards, it turned out to be painfully unwieldy, requiring large passages of expository dialogue, even after many of the setting's organizations and signature characters were left out of the mix. The central conceit, which gave the characters an overarching motivation to justify their actions in both collectible card game and role-playing game expressions of the setting, seemed bizarre and abstract in the context of a traditional narrative.

Exposition is always a thorny matter for the genre writer, especially so in visual media like film or comic books. Even in fiction, where passages of explanatory text are more acceptable and easily woven into the narration, it must be doled out in small doses.

Yet hobby game setting material, whether published as a role-playing game, descriptive material supporting a collectible card game, miniatures, or a board game, is typically all exposition and no story. It provides a foundation for narrative by establishing an attractive imaginary world rife with possibility, but relies on the players themselves to generate the narrative during play.

This process is most visible in a role-playing game, where each player takes on the persona of a particular character he or she has created. Players supply the characters' motivations and make decisions for them. The game master supplies a situation, including supporting characters and various obstacles the player characters must overcome, weaving them together into what one hopes is a satisfying narrative. (Sometimes game masters rely on preexisting adventures or scenarios, which lay out a likely narrative for the player characters to complete, but even here the published product merely supplies a more fleshed-out blueprint for the story line, and it is in the interactions of players and the game master that the actual story finally appears.)

Traditional narrative springs from character, and is expressed through the actions that the protagonists undertake in furtherance of their goals. The central characters in a role-playing game experience are created not by the game designers but by the participants themselves. Writers assigned to adapting a property from one traditional medium to another already have their protagonists in place. They know who they are, and can be assured that they are the heart of the property and its popularity. Whenever a movie studio decides to make a film about Batman, Tarzan, or James Bond, it knows who those characters are and, one hopes, understands their appeal.

Game properties either have no set central characters, as is often the case with a role-playing or board game, or include a large number of lightly sketched characters. This latter instance pertains most frequently to collectible card games and miniatures, where characters are playing pieces (cards or figures) to which the players form an ill-defined attachment.

This attachment, since it either springs directly from the gamer's creativity or is projected on to a loosely sketched character, may create a stronger bond between audience member and media property than in a similar traditional narrative. Unlike practitioners of other media, the role-playing game designer is not the primary author of the final work. The designer collaborates with the game master and players, who create the large narratives based on the game books provided by the designer. This collaboration takes place indirectly, separated by time and space. Designers receive, at best, a secondhand impression of the narratives that unfold, all of them different, in the many groups playing their games. Knowledge of this end use comes second hand, either in the form of personal conversations at game conventions or via Internet response. Moreover, it is fragmentary: I might learn that you enjoyed a given prewritten scenario or hear you describe a particularly enjoyable moment from a game. The effect is like hearing someone recount a scene from a movie you haven't seen. Role-playing narratives are so large that the game authors don't get to see them. The games themselves are building blocks for gamer creativity.

Educated guesswork, therefore, plays a considerable role in role-playing game design. The designer attempts to assemble the set of tools to best facilitate an entertaining and unique narrative for game masters and players.

Role-playing games invariably draw on well-known genres.[1] As in any media, genre provides audience members with a sense of aesthetic comfort—they're signing on for an experience like other pleasurable ones they've had in the past. The comfort zone extended by a genre becomes even more essential in role-playing gaming, serving as an easy and shared stepping-off point for gamer creativity. Knowing a genre's archetypes allows players to conceptualize the characters they want to portray, and alerts them in advance to the sorts of images and story obstacles they're apt to encounter.

Yet if a new game is too familiar, if it fails to offer any crucial points of distinction between itself and other games, it will not be adopted by sizable numbers of players. They'll already have invested considerable effort in mastering the rules of similar games, and have developed attachments to characters and situations in the large narratives they developed with those games. On the other hand, a game that departs too radically from the touchstones of the familiar will be rejected because the effort of coming to terms with its characters, tropes, images, and structures seems too great. Key to the process of role-playing game design, then, is striking a balance between originality and familiarity.

Role-playing games occupy a peculiar position in their tiny niche of a marketplace. In most outward aspects, they function like other narrative entertainment products, such as novels, computer games, and movies. But because they allow their users to fashion theoretically boundless large narratives, they are not consumed once or twice and then put aside for new works. Instead, they engender a consumer loyalty similar to that found in the field of packaged goods, like breakfast cereals or toothpaste. The role-playing gamer, when in need of a new game product at all, seeks out another iteration—a sourcebook or adventure—of the game he's already playing.

This decision making resembles that we use when buying packaged goods. We buy the same toothpaste we always buy, or rotate our breakfast cereal purchases between a small number of brands that we already know we like. In the packaged goods sector, such a dynamic means that top brands are rarely displaced by their competitors. Enduring top brands are, with a few notable exceptions, the earliest well-executed example of their category. Where packaged goods sort themselves into categories according to function —this product cleans your teeth, and this one keeps you smelling good—role-playing games find their niches by genre. One way to find the balance point between originality and accessibility is to identify a preexisting action-adventure subgenre, and then turn it into a role-playing game before anyone else does. The original fantasy role-playing game, *Dungeon & Dragons*, is still the leader in that genre. The first superhero game to solve the problems of its genre and establish a sizable fan base was *Champions*; it has weathered the many vagaries of the industry to retain its dominance in that genre today.

Feng Shui, for example, was the first role-playing game to base itself on the new breed of Hong Kong action movies that had its heyday in the late 1980s and early 1990s. It took these films as inspiration, but then added elements to make the game more amenable to the large narratives of role-playing. A science-fantasy plot device allowed characters from the distinct main time periods of Hong Kong action cinema to interact. This allowed the addition of fantasy and science fiction elements to the modern-day shoot-'em-up ethos of John Woo. It expanded the number of potential character types available to the players. It added an element of distinctiveness, creating a setting of its own that could then be marketed as its own intellectual property. At the time of its publication, Hong Kong movies were only dimly appearing on the Western pop culture radar screen, so elements were added to reference more accessible Hollywood action flicks. The game book was produced to match the state of the art then prevalent: it was a thick, lavishly produced book presenting a complete set of rules and large passages of setting material.

My latest game, *The Esoterrorists*, published in late 2006, reflects changed publishing conditions, and with it, a different set of design objectives. A slump in demand for role-playing games through the traditional supply chain, with brick-and-mortar stores as its end point, coupled with increased opportunities for print-on-demand books and electronic publications, have steered the market away from big fat game books like *Feng Shui* and toward shorter books featuring more narrowly tailored games.

The Esoterrorists finds its point of uniqueness by centering itself on a single technique. Its publisher, Simon Rogers of Pelgrane Press, challenged me to create an investigative game that circumvented a traditional problem of mystery role-playing: what happens when the players are meant to discover a crucial piece of information before the plot can move forward, but then fail the skill rolls that allow them to find it? *The Esoterrorists* removes chance operations from the information-gathering process, so that the players always find the clues they need, assuming they have the right skills and look in the proper place for them. It's not about whether you get the clues but instead how you interpret them.

Everything about the game, including its relatively low page count, exists to highlight this one rules concept. The setting is one of occult investigation by government agents. To keep the focus on the rules conceit, it is sketchily depicted and hardly diverges from other settings of its type. This allows game masters to flesh out the setting as they go, as a television series of occult investigation would do. Even so, the setting does have a unique hook: that the occult bad guys subvert and manipulate public opinion, with the intention of making the world seem more disturbing and surreal. When successful, their efforts soften the boundaries between our reality and the alien dimension of the Outer Dark, which in turn allows them to work sinister

magic more easily. This fuses the traditional supernatural mystery game with the topical procedural of television drama, where true crime stories are promoted as being "ripped from the headlines."

The purpose of this fusion is twofold. First, it intensifies the horror, rendering it more believable by juxtaposing it with real-life story elements not usually referenced in the genre. Second, it allows the author to indulge his penchant for satire and social commentary. Although we've only just begun exploring media tie-in possibilities, we hope that these two innovative elements will give the property life outside its central rules conceit.

The intense emotional connection that role-playing gamers feel to a property, because they have collaborated in the authorship of their experience of it, is difficult, if not impossible, to adapt into ancillary media. Fiction and to a lesser extent comic books provide a relatively low-cost way for game publishers to increase their audience's emotional connection to their worlds. Here traditional narratives can supplement the large narrative, creating the iconic characters that the games themselves lack.

A prime example of this phenomenon can be found in the *Dungeons & Dragons* tie-in novels, whose spotlight characters Elminster the Sage (created by Ed Greenwood) and Drizzt Do'Urden (created by R. A. Salvatore) have become enduringly popular in their own right. Over the years, the more successful *Dungeons & Dragons* novel lines have performed the leap game that publishers most hope for, capturing not just the core gamer audience but also additional readers who are only dimly aware of the setting's role-playing game origins.

The writer faces another set of challenges when working from a so-called bible to create an adapted work. Because they are internal documents, bibles may or may not receive the sustained editing attention given to a game product created for direct audience consumption. Often they are created early in the game creation process and then not updated as development on the core product continues. As this happens, the property's developers and managers evolve an understanding of the material that differs from the bible. Because this occurs as part of an organic, ongoing process—generally conducted under the intense time pressures associated with the production of any entertainment product—the divergence between the original document and the managers' current intentions may be invisible to them. As an outside author called on to create an adaptation, it is all too easy to seize on a now-irrelevant reference and invest it with an importance it no longer warrants.

The first few adaptations from game to traditional media tend to establish a template for later efforts. The adapting writer may be in a position to lobby for changes to the primary game material that allow for easier portability into fiction or drama. The actions of characters in board, miniatures, and card games are typically abstract. Designers need consider only what happens to them within the confines and victory conditions of the games themselves. The adapting authors must be able to consider anything the characters do, and how to dovetail these with the structural demands of popular fiction.

In short, games and their ancillary media offer a wide range of unorthodox narrative challenges to their writers and designers—challenges that have yet to be codified into a set vocabulary, either from the practitioner's or critic's point of view. We practitioners are still feeling our way through it. Our talent base is too small, our form too nascent, to have spawned the profusion of how-to texts and course curricula now surrounding the film industry. Operating largely beneath academic radar we have so far mostly escaped containment within any aesthetic framework— unless you count a few overly literal attempts by gamers themselves, such as those created by designer/critic Ron Edwards and his so-called Forge movement.

The analytic part of me sees our field as rife with opportunity for further study, while the practitioner, naturally, views this prospect with suspicion and unease.

Note

1. These almost always include elements of the fantastic, from magic powers and mythical creatures, to superpowers or science fiction gadgets and weaponry. Other genres become commercially viable only with these elements added. For example, the field for many years lacked a successful Western game, despite the early appearance of *Boot Hill*, published by the industry leader TSR. Only in 1996 did designer Shane Hensley and his publishing company, Pinnacle Entertainment Group, succeed in launching a popular Western game, *Deadlands*, by adding elements of horror and fantasy to the six-guns and silver mines.

References

Champions. George MacDonald, Steve Peterson, Bruce Harlick, and Ray Greer; Hero Games. 2002.

Dungeons & Dragons. Gary Gygax and Dave Arneson; TSR, Inc. 1974.

The Esoterrorists. Robin D. Laws; Pelgrane Press. 2006.

Feng Shui. Robin D. Laws; Daedelus Entertainment. 1996.

Magic: The Gathering. Richard Garfield; Wizards of the Coast. 1993.

Shadowfist. Robin D. Laws and Jose Garcia; Z-Man Games. 1995.

Multicampaign Setting Design for Role-Playing Games
Kenneth Hite

Narrative construction in role-playing games is primarily the task of the players, usually with the game master taking a leading role. Although many published game lines feature a strong, even overpowering narrative (called the "metaplot" in the role-playing game community) as part of their background, the specific narrative of any given campaign is constructed by the players.[1] A "campaign" is a series of adventures or scenarios, usually featuring the same players and player characters, and usually using the same rules system (Masters 1994). Like many serial narrative art forms, role-playing campaigns may never end (or may end abruptly for nonnarrative reasons, such as the game master moving out of town), may be deliberately aimed (by players, game masters, or designers) toward a specific climax, or may develop an emergent story line as they continue. A campaign usually takes place in the same "game world" or "world," which is the setting (including the physical locations, nonplayer characters, and ongoing situations) of the campaign narrative (ibid).[2]

Although the players (including, or especially, the game master) determine the narrative of the individual campaign, the designers often create its game world, or at least the broad outlines thereof. This creation, with a few exceptions, is designed to support multiple campaigns. It is thus this artifact, the designer's creation, that is the most dependably "vast" of a role-playing game's narrative elements. The characters may begin (and remain) inconsequential people with petty desires (as in the standard *Dungeons & Dragons* campaign, which starts characters off at relatively weak and ineffectual power levels), and the plot may merely reflect quotidian serial monster slaying rather than any grand story arc, but a setting designed for multiple campaigns must almost inherently support a vast narrative, if only

implicitly. Sometimes this vast narrative is built into the setting as a metaplot; at other times it is designed by the players or emerges from their play. At still other times, of course, the players ignore it, whether it is a design feature or merely a potential use of a setting.

For the most part, any given published role-playing game setting must support any number of campaigns taking place in any number of versions of the "standard" setting, or even in a wide variety of divergent game worlds. As role-playing game and setting designer Rebecca Borgstrom (2007, 57) points out: "The setting that one group plays in is not the setting that another group plays in. In effect, role-playing games in their static published form do not describe a specific fictional world or story. They describe a large multidimensional space of fictional worlds and stories organized by unifying data."

Some role-playing game texts provide more or less unification, more or less organization, or more or fewer data, but all of them at least implicitly provide such a "multidimensional space," suitable for multiple campaigns and multiple play groups. The general term used by role-playing game designers for such a space—the one they design, as distinct from the ones constructed by the players either using the designers' material or from whole cloth—is "setting" or occasionally "universe."[3] This chapter attempts to set out some guidelines to such multicampaign setting (or universe) design from a number of perspectives, including the historical, the utilitarian, and the modal, and concludes with some notes on the relatively unexplored and underemphasized question of formal campaign structures and their relevance to setting design.

Historical Patterns

The vast majority of setting design advice presented in role-playing game books is actually either:

- Game world design advice, as exemplified in Richard Baker's *World Builder's Guidebook* (1996) for *Advanced Dungeons & Dragons* (2nd ed.)

- Campaign design advice, often focusing less on setting per se than on questions of play balance or genre emulation, as in my own *GURPS Horror* (2002)

• Adventure setting design advice (as opposed to campaign setting or game world design advice), as in the *World Builder's Handbook* (1989) for *MegaTraveller*, which provides guidelines for individual planet design, but not for universes or campaign backgrounds, or in D. Vincent Baker's *Dogs in the Vineyard* (2004), which provides narrative (rather than physical) templates for adventure settings

Some books for some game lines (especially "universal" systems encouraging multigenre play) combine all of the above, such as Jon F. Zeigler and James L. Cambias's *GURPS Space* (2006) or Steven S. Long's *Fantasy Hero* (2003). Most significantly, all three sorts of setting design advice can be found in any iteration of the *Dungeon Master's Guide* for the various editions of *Dungeons & Dragons*.[4]

In principle, the advice in such large-scope setting design guides could be used to construct universes (as opposed to single-campaign game worlds). Because a given game master or play group only needs one campaign at a time, however, such multicampaign universe construction has most often been the purview of the game designer. The canonical example of such a universe (and one of the earliest to be published) is the "World of Greyhawk," which provides an interesting case of the potential for interpenetration between the game world, game rules, and multicampaign setting. It began as *Dungeons & Dragons* codesigner Gary Gygax's original home game world, became the title of a rules supplement with minimal setting material (*Supplement I: Greyhawk* [1975]), served as the default background for a series of individual adventures, and saw publication as a full-scale setting product intended for multiple campaigns (*World of Greyhawk* [1980]). Throughout this process, characters, monsters, concepts, and gods from Gygax's game world became game elements in the ostensibly setting-free *Dungeons & Dragons* rules.

The designers of the superhero role-playing game *Champions* (1981) and the science fiction role-playing game *Traveller* (1977) engaged in similar "setting accretion," until the "*Champions* Universe" and the *Traveller* Imperium settings became cemented into the rules.[5] Setting accretion does not always result in successful setting design, however. After

nine years of such ad hoc development, the *Traveller* Imperium became too stultified for frontier adventures, free traders, scouts, and many other supposed features of the setting. In an attempt to correct the problem, the designers rebooted the setting twice, in *MegaTraveller* (1987) and *Traveller: The New Era* (1993), explaining in the latter book: "The Third Imperium had been frozen at its borders for centuries, hemmed in by its neighbors. Perhaps it was this lack of frontiers that made it stagnant and hollow" (11).

Other designers such as Greg Stafford (*RuneQuest* [1978]) began with a more developed setting in mind, designing the rules and writing the game text from the start to privilege campaigns transpiring in the "official" game world. The first such role-playing game, M. A. R. Barker's *Empire of the Petal Throne* (1975), was a fantasy game set on the planet Tékumel. Like Greyhawk, it was the author's home game world, repurposed as a multicampaign setting. Unlike Greyhawk, it was extremely complex and detailed from the outset. In 1976, the Judges Guild published the first independent multicampaign setting, Bob Bledsaw and Bill Owen's *The City-State of the Invincible Overlord*. It contained no rules, but was designed for use with *Dungeons & Dragons*.

Besides those settings created by the game master or a game designer, there are preexisting ones from history or fiction, or both. Darryl Hanny and Frank Chadwick's *En Garde!* (1975) is set in a seventeenth-century Paris vaguely based on Alexandre Dumas's Musketeers novels, and Brian Blume and Gygax's *Boot Hill* (1975) is set in the semilegendary U.S. West. Designers also often deliberately pastiche historical or fictional settings in role-playing games; examples include *Seventh Sea* (1999), based on seventeenth-century Europe and the Caribbean, and *Dogs in the Vineyard* (2004), closely adapted from the religious and geographic environment of nineteenth-century Mormon Utah. Other games have taken settings from specific fictional works, beginning with James F. Dunnigan's *Dallas* (1980), the first role-playing game to use a licensed setting. A number of role-playing games have used J. R. R. Tolkien's Middle-earth, Robert E. Howard's Hyborian Age, or the "universes" of *Star Wars*, Marvel Comics, or *Star Trek*. With such preexisting settings, the designer's task is frequently that of organization, presentation, and selection as well as the creation of additional setting material to serve the needs of role-players as opposed to readers or viewers.

Utilitarian Goals

The published multicampaign setting ideally serves the purposes and meets the goals of three major parties: the designer, whose concerns are primarily artistic; the publisher, whose concerns are primarily commercial; and the gamer, game master, or play group who will set their own campaign there and make the setting their game world, whose concerns are primarily practical. Each party has a set of complementary goals that can mesh with those of the other parties, but often conflicts with them.

What I call artistic goals center on the personal vision of the designer. Creativity and originality go hand in hand, and both open the way for the designer's personality (and therefore beliefs) to emerge in the final setting. Most designers value the originality of a concept or treatment: hacking out the hundredth variation on Middle-earth challenges nobody. Likewise, many designers prefer the opportunity for individual creation rather than adaptation from some other property, although in my personal case I also value the chance to adapt an interesting setting (such as H. P. Lovecraft's cosmos) and would rather not do any design work on a setting I find bland regardless of its pedigree. And in some cases (as in other fiction), designers wish to use a setting to convey a personal message. The goals of Jonathan Swift in his *Gulliver's Travels* and Ray Winninger in his *Underground* (1993), a satirical role-playing game of superheroics and political activism set in a dark, future United States, are not too far apart. A message need not be political or satirical; the world of Glorantha (the setting of *RuneQuest*) is designed in large part to demonstrate Stafford's conceptions of myth.

In this triad of ideal role types, publishers share the designer's goal set to some extent, preferring a distinctive setting (and hence, one more easily and effectively marketed as well as controlled) to one with no particularly noticeable creativity or originality behind it. Yet publishers also prefer games with mass appeal to those so quirky (or with such strongly presented messages) as to turn away

customers. Obviously, publishers can and do overcome this preference for a sufficiently intriguing setting; despite its immensely arcane nature and staggering complexity, Tékumel has been the setting for four separate role-playing games in thirty years.[6] But this is almost always an example of a publisher thinking like a designer. Such decisions rarely pay off commercially, and at best only secure a small cult audience for a given publisher. Along the same line as mass appeal, commercial concerns tend to drive broader settings—those that support a wide range of character powers, types, and abilities. Long-term campaigns (in games with rules for increasing player character power over time) work best if characters don't outgrow the setting's challenges, and if settings aren't too deadly for beginning player characters at first. Likewise, customers with specific tastes in character types will tend to avoid settings where such characters are impractical.

Still other criteria suit the practical needs of gamers, although some similarities to the publisher's goals exist. For example, just as a publisher prefers a well-known setting that appeals to a wide range of customers, the user needs a setting to be accessible, meaning that stories in that setting should be easy for game masters and players to imagine and grasp.

Accessibility and mass appeal go hand in hand almost by definition. Along this same axis, gamers will often play several campaigns in the same setting, so for them the setting should ideally have sufficient depth that the same game group can retain interest in it, finding new challenges over multiple campaigns. Such depth might come in a number of ways. The designer might spread diversely challenging geographic areas (as in the Forgotten Realms for *Dungeons & Dragons*) across the setting. She might deepen the setting historically, presenting different subsettings separated in time, as in my *Star Trek Roleplaying Game* (2002) from Decipher, or the four "eras" Chaosium has developed for *Call of Cthulhu* (1981).[7] A designer (or publisher) will occasionally set numerous different game lines in the same universe (as White Wolf Publishing does with its *World of Darkness*).

Such diversity within a setting also enables a different player goal: modularity. Many game masters and player groups (especially of self-proclaimed universal systems such as *GURPS* [1986] or the *Hero System* [1990]) only use pieces of a given setting, alter settings over time, combine published settings, or cobble them together with ones of their own design. For example, the *Eberron Campaign Setting* (2004, 7) is specifically designed with such use in mind: "We envisioned a different kind of campaign setting…from which DMs [dungeon masters] and players could loot material for whatever campaign world they play in." A setting that is too unified, too all of a piece, to allow such alteration is a setting less than ideal from a gaming end user perspective.

Of course, these parties and their utilitarian goals represent ideal types. In actuality the roles of all three parties can overlap, as we have seen with *Greyhawk*, for which setting Gygax was the designer, publisher, *and* game master. Many game masters extensively modify a published setting to their own taste (taking on the designer role), and the designer-publisher is a commonplace figure in the role-playing game industry.[8] The goals of the three parties are likewise not exclusive. Many game masters, for instance, prefer to play in a world showing a strong designer's stamp or use a game world that other players will already be familiar with. Many designers seek the widest possible appeal for their work, even if it means producing a less personal document.

Probably the most succinct, unified, cross-role set of design goals for a role-playing game setting are the "Five Fs" developed by veteran role-playing game writer S. John Ross in the 1990s:[9]

- *Fantasy*   This is not a reference to genre but rather to the player's ability (not necessarily the character's ability) to fulfill wishes or fantasies, usually of power over one's environment.

- *Friends*   Since most role-playing game play groups have multiple players (and since multiple-player gaming is more fun), a successful role-playing game setting should allow for multiple characters of roughly equal status to engage in adventures together.

- *Familiarity*   The players should be able to understand the setting and its common assumptions. This privileges

settings based on popular culture stalwarts such as *Star Trek*, or settings based on widely read but not particularly differentiated genres such as vampire fiction; in other words, settings with mass appeal or at least a mass knowledge base.

- *Freedom*   The player characters should not be tied to any given hierarchy or agenda but instead be able to wander about the setting having adventures on their own and at their own whim. Hence, even military role-playing games such as Joe F. Martin's *Recon* (1982) usually cast the player characters as "detached units" or special forces.

- *Fuzziness, or fudge factor*   The setting should feature some element that allows the game master (and possibly the players) to insert events, change tacks, or present story elements at need or whim. In fantasy role-playing games, for example, this is usually done with magic, arbitrary gods, and/or "unmapped" areas of the setting. In science fiction role-playing games, fuzziness comes from omnipotent alien races, enigmatic precursor artifacts, *Star Wars*–style psionics, or *Star Trek*–style "technobabble."

In theory, then, a game designer could create an ideal setting maximizing all of Ross's Five Fs or fulfilling all the design goals listed above. Yet in practice, not only do many of the above goals clash but modal constraints on the setting often prevent such open-ended design as well.

Modal Constraints

Setting design must also fit within those constraints that arise from the various modes of play encouraged by the game rules and those that previous design decisions impose, which in turn also encourage specific modes of play. These modes may derive from the types of scenarios or adventures supported by the rules (or previous iterations of the setting), other features of the stories that the game facilitates, or the genre or source material from which the game takes its inspiration.

For example, the rules and rules text of *Dungeons & Dragons* encourage and privilege repeated combat encounters, usually in the context of a "dungeon crawl," meaning a geographically constrained location full of monsters and treasure. The mode of dungeon crawling thus constrains *Dungeons & Dragons* settings; such settings need plentiful ruins, evil temples, and so forth. Hence Eberron, the "different kind of campaign setting" developed after a lengthy setting search, still offers as a paradigmatic adventure in that setting "colossal ruins...towering keeps...a hidden desert shrine...a ruined castle...and finally...a dungeon" (*Eberron* 2004, 9).

Default characters can constrain setting as much as default adventures. On its front and back covers, John Tynes and Greg Stolze's *Unknown Armies* (2002) bills itself as a "game of power and consequences," and asks "what will you risk to change the world?" The characters are therefore all assumed to be risk takers, gamblers with the consequences, people "turning away from the everyday to scratch deeper" (ibid., 30). Mirroring the player characters, every non-player character or "cabal" in the setting is also part of the "occult underground."[10] The protagonists' nature constrains the nature of their antagonists, and hence the population of the setting.

The types of stories that the designers wish to enable also constrain the setting for *Unknown Armies*. A game about risk requires consequences, which implies opponents or obstacles of sufficient power and ability to defeat the player characters. The primary non-player characters cannot be normal, complacent folk (otherwise the game would be about predation or power fantasy) but fellow risk takers and gamblers, "fervent, fixated, and highly motivated" rivals who create competition, and provide drama (ibid., 84).

Such story-driven modal constraints can be second-order effects of the utilitarian goals mentioned earlier. Designers will naturally constrain settings to match the stories they feel their game tells best, or those that best highlight their own creativity or message. Publishers, likewise, will seek to emphasize stories with mass appeal or wide ranges of character power.

A story with mass appeal comes with its own constraints. The various *Star Trek* role-playing games all assumed that player characters began as a Federation starship crew (similar to the protagonists of the various *Star Trek* series), although some offered optional or divergent starting points. Their settings were likewise constrained by the preexisting material—television episodes, films, and "reference manuals"—describing the *Star Trek* universe. For the setting of the Arthurian role-playing game *King Arthur Pendragon* (1985), designer Stafford had more options—the Arthurian canon is larger, less well defined, and not subject to vetoes by Paramount—but was still constrained not just by the source material but also by potential players' assumptions about the source material.[11]

Genre concerns also constrain setting design. Both the horror and science fiction genres assume a certain vastness of scope, in time, space, or both, to achieve the "Gothic sublime" or the science-fictional "sense of wonder." More specifically, for example, horror games must have horrific settings. Descriptions of the World of Darkness, the setting for most White Wolf games, have always been explicit about the degree to which the setting is constrained by genre and mood: "The world of Vampires is not our world. It is a Gothic-Punk vision of our world—monolithic, majestic, and very twisted. The entire society is corrupt and the mortals are helpless to do anything about it" (*Vampire: The Masquerade* 1991, 167).

Another case of genre-driven setting design is the *Dungeons & Dragons* setting Ravenloft, which began as the background country Barovia in a single adventure not part of a given universe (*I6: Ravenloft* [1983], 1) but intended instead as "a classic gothic horror story." With the adventure an unexpected success, TSR designers expanded the setting, naming it Ravenloft after the original adventure, and presenting it as a "demiplane of dread" tangent to all *Dungeons & Dragons* universes. Ravenloft eventually spawned its own subsetting, "Gothic Earth," based on historical Earth in the nineteenth century (*Masque of the Red Death* [1994]). In its newest version, *Expedition to Castle Ravenloft* (2006), Ravenloft/Barovia is once more a standalone one-adventure background, though with suggested connections to the Eberron and Forgotten Realms settings. Throughout its history, Ravenloft's many designers have constantly worked to evoke the mood of Gothic horror, in some cases changing the *Dungeons & Dragons* core rules to make stories in the setting more horrifying. Many elements of the setting (such as the omnipresent fog) are taken from Gothic horror films and novels, and its major non-player characters such as Count Vlad Drakov and Rudolph von Richten are mostly (fairly obvious) genre pastiches.

As the Ravenloft setting expanded, the designers wished to add other sorts of horrors to the setting, and decided that the demiplane contained a number of "domains," each with its own Dark Lord and horror-setting flavor. Thus, Ravenloft became a multigenre (or perhaps multi-subgenre) setting. This can be a fairly elegant or at least simple method of multicampaign setting design, at one stroke addressing mass appeal and breadth while providing potentially infinite creativity, modularity, and accessibility. Such games as *Lords of Creation* (1983), *Rifts* (1990), and *Torg* (1990) each addressed that design method differently. *Lords of Creation* assumed the characters were potential gods capable of entering any sort of world; *Rifts* and *Torg* both posited catastrophes that smashed parallel worlds of varying sorts together. *Torg* even provided rules for modeling a genre within a world as the player characters traveled between them.

Rifts and the "Infinite Worlds" setting from *GURPS Time Travel* (1991) also came out of publisher goals, specifically to capitalize on a multigenre universal game engine by offering a potential common setting for all of the various games.[12] Thus, players of fantasy games, for example, could have their characters meet horror monsters or use science-fictional weapons, with such cross-genre play leading (hopefully) to cross-genre sales.

In the case of *GURPS* (and less prolifically, the *Hero System*), the intentionally generic and universal nature of the game's sourcebooks meant that designers needed to open up campaign and setting design, in large part, to the players, if only to avoid stepping on customers' toes by closing off alternatives. *GURPS* books presented a number of settings, both original and licensed, but the major "genre books" such as *GURPS Space* (1988), *GURPS Cyberpunk* (1990), and *GURPS Supers* (1989) had to address questions of campaign design, and implicitly at least, setting design and formal campaign structure.

Formal Structures

A multicampaign setting usually provides at least minimal guidance to game masters for constructing at least one potential campaign using that setting. Such advice is almost always aimed at either the practical questions of running and maintaining a campaign, or general questions of genre emulation, theme, and mood.[13] A significant fraction of such books, however, offer guidance for the overall "narrative structure … why the characters are working together and what their goals are" (*Unknown Armies* 2002, 267). The third edition of *GURPS Horror* (2002) offers five such narrative structures ("escape," "gauntlet," "nemesis," "picaresque," and "quest"), although it emphasizes the goals over the character backstory.[14] The *Eberron Campaign Setting* (2004) addresses the character backstory ("Creating a Party") and goals or story aims ("Plot Themes") separately, but clearly links them conceptually.[15]

Few such texts complete this implicit process by offering would-be game masters a structural, formal look at how "standard campaign types" might run under the game rules. The *Dungeon Master's Guide II* (2005) divides campaigns into two narrative types: "episodic" and "continuity." In the first type, the adventures are unrelated, with only the player characters' presence in common. In the second, "one adventure leads to another, creating an overall story arc that builds over time" (ibid., 75). Most published campaigns (e.g., Larry DiTillio's *Masks of Nyarlathotep* [1984]) are, perforce, continuity campaigns, although most published multiple-campaign settings (e.g., Monte Cook's *Ptolus* [2006]) support either type. In *GURPS Fantasy* (2004, 15–16), William H. Stoddard offers a location-based set of formal campaign structures: "point campaigns" in which "all the adventures take place in a single location," "area campaigns" that wander all over the place, "arc campaigns" that travel over a predefined course (such as the traditional quest), and "base and mission campaigns" in which adventures take place at a number of different points, but the heroes have a single location as their home base.

These types, and the general theory of formal campaign structure, remain relatively undeveloped and underexamined. One could postulate a third narrative type alongside episodic and continuity: "organic," in which any given adventure changes or sets up future adventures (or casts new light on previous ones), but no overall story arc ever develops. One could, on the other hand, refine the *Dungeon Master's Guide II* narrative types along two axes: "cohesion" (how many elements aside from the player characters the adventure has in common with the others) and "progress" (how much directed change occurs over time in the campaign). (Thus a continuity campaign becomes cohesive/progressive.) One could create a second sort of dichotomy: between campaigns driven by player choice (e.g., "We elves hate the Dark Lord and want to kill him") and those driven by game master fiat (e.g., "Your mission, Jim, should you accept it, is to kill the Dark Lord").[16]

Rules, genre, play conventions, and any of the other constraints mentioned above may make a given setting more or less amenable to any of those campaign types. As indicated above, a setting based on *Mission: Impossible* or the James Bond stories will wind up supporting game-master-driven, "base and mission" campaign structures to an overwhelming degree, if only to replicate the feel of the source material. Narratives produced by such campaign structures depend on the game master for vastness, which seemingly emerges more easily if the players aim for continuity over episodic play. A setting based on traditional fantasy literature, on the other hand, will better support "quest" narrative structures, and arc or "area" campaigns, themselves more amenable to vast narratives even with seemingly episodic adventures: vastness in space enables vastness in scope.

Or take a highly creative, idiosyncratic, personal setting. It likely requires "point campaigns" (as only a small fraction of the setting will be at all accessible to beginning players), mostly driven by game master fiat (as players will not be familiar enough with the world to drive their own stories). The "nemesis" and "escape" narrative structures will be strongest in such a setting, as both require intensive design of only one story element (the nemesis or the prison). If such a setting is to produce a vast narrative, it is usually up to the designer to provide it, either as a metaplot or a published campaign. More familiar, accessible settings will allow

game masters to run area campaigns or use picaresque narrative structures. Extremely familiar settings allow player-driven campaigns of any type or structure.

It is incumbent on the designer of the multicampaign setting to know how her setting will deform under any such pressures, and ensure that the campaign type or types that the designer intends the game to support are possible, encouraged, and fun in her setting. No game and no setting can possibly balance all of these concerns. But many games and virtually all setting books can do better at both balancing setting design questions and clearly offering potential players opportunities for the sorts of stories—vast or otherwise—that the setting is intended to support.

Notes

1. Some games in the new wave of "indie" role-playing game designs remove much of this narrative agency from the players (including the game master), as the designer's goal in such cases is to present a "narrativist" game that explores individual reactions to a predestined story arc. Paradigmatic examples of such designs include *My Life with Master* (2003), *The Mountain Witch* (2005), and *Contenders* (2006). For the most part, such games and designs remain outside both the mainstream of the hobby and the purview of this chapter. I will note that all three have strongly impressionistic settings.

2. A game world can be a literal world (such as a planet or single fantasy world), or a smaller region like a continent or city. Or it can be a solar system, an entire galaxy, a group of dimensions, or a multiverse comprising many parallel worlds or alternate histories. The term is usually the same.

3. Some designers also use the term world, although this article restricts world to the game world of an individual campaign or play group.

4. For example, the sections (among others) headed "The Campaign," "Conducting the Game," and "Random Dungeon Generation" in the *Advanced Dungeons & Dragons* (1st ed.) and *Dungeon Master's Guide* (1979), or the sections (among others) headed "World-Building," "Characters and the World around Them," and "Adventures" in *Dungeons & Dragons* (version 3.5) and *Dungeon Master's Guide* (2003).

5. The strong desire of superhero role-playing game fans to play in other published superhero settings (such as the DC or Marvel Comics universes) mitigated total setting accretion, as did Hero Games' use of the *Champions* core rules engine (the Hero System) to power other games such as *Danger International* (1985) and *Justice, Inc.* (1984).

6. *Empire of the Petal Throne* (1975) published by TSR, *Swords and Glory* (1983–1984) published by Gamescience, *Gardasiyal* (1994) published by Theater of the Mind Enterprises, and *Tékumel* (2005) by Guardians of Order.

7. The *Star Trek Roleplaying Game: Narrator's Guide* (2002) provides guidance for games set during the events of the original *Star Trek* series, *Star Trek: The Next Generation, Star Trek: Deep Space Nine, Star Trek: Voyager,* or *Star Trek: Enterprise.* Chaosium has at one time or another supported four setting eras for *Call of Cthulhu*: the 1920s (contemporary with the Lovecraft tales on which the game is based), the modern era, the 1890s, and the Dark Ages.

8. In addition to Gygax, prominent examples include Stafford (*RuneQuest* [1978] and *King Arthur Pendragon* [1985]), Steve Jackson (*GURPS Fantasy* [1986]), and Mark Rein-Hagen (*Vampire: The Masquerade* [1991]).

9. I constructed this list based on a number of personal communications from Ross between 1997 and 2000. During the writing of this article, no copy was available, although in June 2008, Ross published a modified version as "Five Elements of Commercial Appeal in RPG Design," on his Web page at: ⟨http://www.io.com/~sjohn/five-elements.htm⟩.

10. The arguable exception, the Sleeper cabal, represents the house in this gamble. The Sleeper cabal exists to stop player characters from breaking the setting: "They want magick to stay underground, so they cull punks" (*Unknown Armies* 2002, 84).

11. For example, the setting of *Pendragon* (1985) featured both medieval-style knights out of Sir Thomas Malory's epic and Dark Ages Saxons out of Geoffrey of Monmouth's history.

12. A version of the Infinite Worlds setting, slightly expanded and redesigned by David Pulver, appears in the *GURPS* 4th edition core rules (*GURPS Basic Set: Campaigns* 2004) and, further expanded by myself, *GURPS Infinite Worlds* (2005).

13. For a somewhat stereotypical example of this dichotomy, contrast the almost entirely mechanical discussion of "Maintaining a Campaign" (*Dungeon Master's Guide* 2003) with the almost entirely thematic discussion of "Storytelling" (*Vampire: The Requiem* 2004). *Vampire: The Requiem* does, however, also offer an outline of campaign plot structure and a few sample narrative structures.

14. Like many *GURPS* genre books, *GURPS Horror* (2002) offers an extensive litany of nonformal, nonstructural campaign types demarcated by style, genre and subgenre, and a grab bag of general "design parameters" such as scale, scope, austerity, and boundaries.

15. Even more radically, the *Requiem Chronicler's Guide* (2006) offers a number of different, irreconcilable narrative structures, many of which involve serious changes to the background setting, rules, or play style of *Vampire: The Requiem* games.

16. For many of the insights in this section, I am indebted to a July 2006 online discussion with, among others, William H. Stoddard, Phil Masters, Steve Dempsey, Arref Mak, Malcolm Sheppard, and Wren Thornton.

References: Literature

Borgstrom, Rebecca (2007). "Structure and Meaning in Role-Playing Game Design." In *Second Person*, edited by Pat Harrigan and Noah Wardrip-Fruin, 57–66. Cambridge, MA: MIT Press.

Masters, Phil (1994). "On the Vocabulary of Role-Playing." *Interactive Fantasy* 2:57–74. ⟨http://www.philm.demon.co.uk/Miscellaneous/Vocabulary.html⟩.

References: Games

Advanced Dungeons & Dragons. 1st ed. Gary Gygax; TSR, Inc. 1977–1979.

Advanced Dungeons & Dragons. 2nd ed. David "Zeb" Cook; TSR, Inc. 1989.

Boot Hill. Brian Blume and Gary Gygax; TSR, Inc. 1975.

Call of Cthulhu. Sandy Petersen; Chaosium. 1981.

Champions. George MacDonald and Steve Peterson; Hero Games. 1981.

The City-State of the Invincible Overlord. Bob Bledsaw and Bill Owen; Judges Guild. 1976.

Contenders. Joe J. Prince; Prince of Darkness Games. 2006.

Dallas. James F. Dunnigan; Simulations Publications, Inc. 1980.

Danger, International. L. Douglas Garrett, George MacDonald, Steve Peterson; Hero Games. 1985.

Dogs in the Vineyard. D. Vincent Baker; Lumpley Games. 2004.

Dungeon Master's Guide. Gary Gygax; TSR, Inc. 1979.

Dungeon Master's Guide. Monte Cook; revision by David Noonan and Rich Redman; Wizards of the Coast. 2003.

Dungeon Master's Guide II. Jesse Decker et al.; Wizards of the Coast. 2005.

Dungeons & Dragons. Version 3.5. Monte Cook, Jonathan Tweet, and Skip Williams; revision by Andy Collins et al.; Wizards of the Coast. 2003.

Eberron Campaign Setting. Keith Baker, Bill Slavicsek, James Wyatt; Wizards of the Coast. 2004.

Empire of the Petal Throne. M. A. R. Barker; TSR, Inc. 1975.

En Garde! Darryl Hanny and Frank Chadwick; Game Designers' Workshop. 1975.

Expedition to Castle Ravenloft. Bruce R. Cordell and James Wyatt; Wizards of the Coast. 2006.

Fantasy Hero. 5th ed. Steven S. Long; Hero Games. 2003.

Forgotten Realms Campaign Set. Ed Greenwood and Jeff Grubb; TSR, Inc. 1987.

Gardasiyal. M. A. R. Barker and Neil R. Cauley; Theater of the Mind Enterprises. 1994.

GURPS. 1st ed. Steve Jackson; Steve Jackson Games. 1986.

GURPS Basic Set: Campaigns. 4th ede. Steve Jackson, Sean Punch, and David Pulver; Steve Jackson Games. 2004.

GURPS Cyberpunk. Loyd Blankenship; Steve Jackson Games. 1990.

GURPS Fantasy. 1st ed. Steve Jackson; Steve Jackson Games. 1986.

GURPS Fantasy. 3rd ed. William H. Stoddard; Steve Jackson Games. 2004.

GURPS Horror. 3rd ed. Kenneth Hite; Steve Jackson Games. 2002.

GURPS Infinite Worlds. Kenneth Hite, Steve Jackson, and John M. Ford; Steve Jackson Games. 2005.

GURPS Space. 1st ed. William A. Barton and Steve Jackson; Steve Jackson Games. 1988.

GURPS Space. 4th ed. Jon F. Zeigler and James L. Cambias; Steve Jackson Games. 2006.

GURPS Supers. 1st ed. Loyd Blankenship; Steve Jackson Games. 1989.

GURPS Time Travel. Steve Jackson and John M. Ford; Steve Jackson Games. 1991.

Hero System. 1st ed. George MacDonald, Steve Peterson, and Rob Bell; Hero Games/Iron Crown Enterprises. 1990.

I6: Ravenloft. Tracy Hickman and Laura Hickman; TSR, Inc. 1983.

Justice, Inc. Aaron Allston, Steve Peterson, Michael A. Stackpole; Hero Games. 1984.

King Arthur Pendragon. Greg Stafford; Chaosium. 1985.

Lords of Creation. Tom Moldvay; Avalon Hill. 1983.

Masks of Nyarlathotep. Larry DiTillio; Chaosium. 1984.

Masque of the Red Death. William W. Connors et al.; TSR, Inc. 1994.

MegaTraveller. Marc W. Miller, Frank Chadwick, Joe D. Fugate Sr., and Gary L. Thomas; GDW, Inc. 1987.

The Mountain Witch. Timothy Kleinert; Timfire Publishing. 2005.

My Life with Master. Paul Czege; Half Meme Press. 2003.

Ptolus. Monte Cook; Malhavoc Press. 2006.

Recon. Joe F. Martin; RPG, Inc. 1982.

Requiem Chronicler's Guide. Will Hindmarch et al.; White Wolf Publishing. 2006.

Rifts. Kevin Siembieda; Palladium Books. 1990.

RuneQuest. Steve Perrin, Ray Turney, and Greg Stafford; Chaosium. 1978.

Seventh Sea. Jennifer Wick, John Wick, and Kevin Wilson; Alderac Entertainment Group. 1999.

Star Trek Roleplaying Game. Matthew Colville, Kenneth Hite, Ross A. Isaacs, Steven S. Long, Don Mappin, Christian Moore, and Owen Seyler; Decipher, Inc. 2002.

Star Trek Roleplaying Game: Narrator's Guide. Matthew Colville, Kenneth Hite, Ross A. Isaacs, Don Mappin, Christian Moore, and Owen Seyler; Decipher, Inc. 2002.

Supplement I: Greyhawk. Gary Gygax and Rob Kuntz; TSR, Inc. 1975.

Swords and Glory. M. A. R. Barker; Gamescience. 1983–1984.

Tékumel: Empire of the Petal Throne. Patrick Brady, Joe Saul, and Edwin Voskamp; Guardians of Order. 2005.

Torg. Greg Gorden et al.; West End Games. 1990.

Traveller. Marc W. Miller; Game Designers' Workshop. 1977.

Traveller: The New Era. Frank Chadwick and Dave Nilsen; GDW, Inc. 1993.

Underground. Ray Winninger; Mayfair Games. 1993.

Unknown Armies. 2nd ed. John Tynes and Greg Stolze; Atlas Games. 2002.

Vampire: The Masquerade. Mark Rein-Hagen et al.; White Wolf Publishing. 1991.

Vampire: The Requiem. Justin Achilli et al.; White Wolf Publishing. 2004.

World Builder's Guidebook. Richard L. Baker; TSR, Inc. 1996.

World Builder's Handbook. Joe D. Fugate Sr., J. Andrew Keith, and Gary L. Thomas; Digest Group Publications. 1989.

The World of Darkness. Bill Bridges et al.; White Wolf Publishing. 2004.

World of Greyhawk. Gary Gygax; TSR, Inc. 1980.

Multicampaign Setting Design

World without End: The *Delta Green* Open Campaign Setting

A. Scott Glancy

As a vast narrative, the *Delta Green* campaign setting for the *Call of Cthulhu* role-playing game was two steps ahead of most fiction even before the first line of the *Delta Green* sourcebook (1997) was written. The first is that *Delta Green* is a role-playing game, and the second is that its narrative exists within an even broader narrative that weaves its way through not just role-playing games but also novels, television series, film, computer games, and many other forms of media.

As a role-playing game, *Delta Green*'s narrative differs from the traditional narratives of literature, theater, and film because it offers only plot without characters to drive the story forward. It's up to the role-players to provide the characters. Role-playing game settings are narratives not built around any specific protagonist, yet capable of accommodating multiple protagonists. Thus, role-playing games, particularly the classic paper-and-dice ones, are by their very nature vast narratives.

Computer games are limited by the amount of code that the creators have dedicated to their virtual worlds. As long as the players play long enough, they will find the edges of that digital world. This is not so with classic paper-and-dice role-playing games. Generally speaking, it is impossible to stray off the map because any reasonably talented Keeper (or referee or Dungeon Master) is going to improvise more world for the players to explore. This can range from inventing an oasis beyond the impassable desert that the players just passed through, to improvising a romance between one of the players and the maid at the local hotel.

As a storytelling form, role-playing games are collaborative, unpredictable, and open-ended. I believe much of the inspiration for the design and playing of role-playing games comes from the fans' desire to create more stories set in their favorite fictional worlds. But instead of simply sitting at a typewriter in solitude, role-players create their fiction through the collaborative process of role-playing. The referee provides the basic plot and setting, and the players supply the characters, whose personalities and actions move the plot forward, sometimes changing it in dramatic ways.

Delta Green is no exception to this collaborative storytelling. The same *Delta Green* scenario can lead to the neat dispatch of supernatural evil or the end of human civilization. The variety of ways that a team of characters can succeed or fail is infinite. This is because all but the barest elements of plot and character are driven by an infinite number of players with infinitely varied tastes, tendencies, and agendas—and also by dice, which adds an element of random direction that keeps *Delta Green* decidedly away from the predictability of traditional narrative.

The second advantage *Delta Green* had on its way to becoming a vast narrative is that its role-playing game setting is based on one of the greatest vast narratives in modern fiction: the Cthulhu Mythos of H. P. Lovecraft.[1] But even before *Delta Green* burst on to the scene, the Cthulhu Mythos had been greatly enriched by the *Call of Cthulhu* role-playing game. Beginning in the early 1980s, new writers began expanding the Cthulhu Mythos through the publication of material for the role-playing game. These were not new short stories or novellas but role-playing game scenarios and campaigns. New creatures were created, previously unnamed monsters were christened, new eldritch tomes were described, and new spells, cults, and sects were invented. Just as the Lovecraft Circle (and the later "New" Lovecraft Circle) expanded the original narrative, the Cthulhu Mythos was expanded once again by role-playing game writers like Sandy Petersen, Larry DiTillio, and Keith Herber.

It is interesting to note that Lovecraft's stories strongly lend themselves to adaptation as role-playing game scenarios. Lovecraft preferred the use of the first-person narrative, frequently presented in the form of a rambling confession or journal entry. More often than not, the narrator did not devote much time to self-description, leaving such details

8.1 Cover of Pagan Publishing's role-playing game sourcebook *Delta Green: Countdown*.

vague enough that the narrator paled in significance when compared to the situation he found himself in. In this way, the stories were much like the blueprints for role-playing game scenarios: filled with plot, location, and atmosphere, but lacking a central protagonist. With only one exception, no protagonist appears more than once in any Lovecraft story. The one thing that remains constant from story to story is the cosmic horror of Lovecraft's nihilistic and hostile universe.

The *Call of Cthulhu* role-playing game always garnered high praise from players and critics alike. It was called "the thinking man's role-playing game." Unlike *Dungeons & Dragons*, the *Call of Cthulhu* game mechanics didn't allow for game experience to translate into greater levels of physical survivability. Sure, your character's skills and abilities improved, but the character always remained a fragile human being who was as likely to die from a gunshot wound on day one as he or she was to survive several long campaigns. Because of this fragility, violence was always a last resort in *Call of Cthulhu*, especially since many of the supernatural horrors that the players faced were immune to physical violence. Furthermore, *Call of Cthulhu* was a game of supernatural horror set in "the real world." Those players who came over from *Dungeons & Dragons* to *Call of Cthulhu* were usually in for a rude shock when they found they couldn't just kick in the cultists' front door, blow their heads off, and take all their stuff. The police in the game were just as unlikely as those in the real world to accept homicidal violence as the way to solve a supernatural problem. So the lethality of violence and its legal consequences conspired to encourage the players to use their heads to solve the supernatural problem, rather than their fists.

If there was ever one thing that was missing from the *Call of Cthulhu* role-playing game, it was a central organizing reason for why the group of player characters came together to investigate and defeat the threat of the Cthulhu Mythos. Certainly, once player characters had encountered the horrors of the Mythos, they would be motivated to keep striving to delay the inevitable return of the Great Old Ones. Saving the world becomes a full-time job. But what was missing was a reusable reason why characters of diverse backgrounds would start working together. Why is

the professional stage magician working with the professor of archaeology, the cub reporter, and the private investigator? Who brought them together? How do they receive the information that leads them to their next adventure?

Both Chaosium and Pagan Publishing published some early experiments in creating a private foundation or society to support a group of investigators. The Theron Marks Society and *The Golden Dawn* sourcebook were both designed to provide that kind of structure. The Theron Marks Society, which first appeared in Chaosium's publication *Terror from the Stars*, was a wholly fictional institution set in the Roaring Twenties and comprised of Cthulhu Mythos investigators who operated the society as a kind of clearinghouse for leads on new investigations as well as a recruiting ground for adding new player characters when the inevitable casualties occurred. *The Golden Dawn* was a fictionalized version of the real-life society of occult enthusiasts that operated in Victorian London. In this fictional Golden Dawn, investigators were members of the society, and could use the society's contacts and resources, but the Golden Dawn was not reimagined as a kind of gaslight era *Ghostbusters*. Both these experiments tried to create a mechanism whereby the investigators could reasonably pick up new adventure hooks and replace casualties. At the same time, neither society had any official power or even credibility, thereby preserving one of the standards of the *Call of Cthulhu* standards—the authorities are not going to help.

The primary challenge to any group of *Call of Cthulhu* players is the fact that they don't have the power of the civil authorities to back them up during their investigations. Traditionally, convincing the authorities to act against a supernatural threat is only slightly less difficult than keeping the authorities from having you committed once you start ranting about ghosts, ghouls, and ancient alien gods. If the investigators had the powers of the police or the military, much of the challenge of the role-playing game would be lost. They could sit in their office, behind their polished oak desk, and dispatch armies of flatfoots and doughboys to stamp out whatever problems their investigations uncovered. Such authority also insulates the players from the consequences of any illegal actions they take, especially the use of violence. Giving the player characters too much government authority could easily lead to the players always taking the lazy way out, and simply applying more and more force to resolve any scenario.

John Tynes originally conceived of *Delta Green* as a way to find a balance between organization and authority. He published the first *Delta Green* material just a few months before *The X-Files* premiered on network television, and at exactly the same time that I was sending Pagan Publishing similar material for publication in *The Unspeakable Oath*—Pagan Publishing's quarterly journal for the game *Call of Cthulhu*. My concept was for an agency that began with the federal raid on Innsmouth (from the Lovecraft story "The Shadow over Innsmouth") and evolved through the World War II era Office of Strategic Services and the cold war alphabet soup of spy agencies. My agency's agenda would be murky as to whether it was trying to destroy the Mythos or control it. My agency, in turn, could be made up of mysterious patrons, competitors, or even adversaries of any group of players, sometimes helping and at other times hindering the investigation. Although I thought that "The Shadow over Innsmouth" conclusively demonstrated that the U.S. government knew about some aspects of the Cthulhu Mythos, I couldn't imagine a way for the players to be part of my agency and yet not break the mood of the game.

Tynes found the way. He brought the players inside the agency, and preserved the challenge that comes with having limited resources and authority by having Delta Green be disbanded due to a supernatural Bay of Pigs–level catastrophe in its past. Instead of an official government agency, Delta Green would be a conspiracy of people working within the government. Delta Green would be a cabal of officials who were "in the know" about the Mythos, and despite being officially decommissioned, were soldiering on, fighting the good fight against a threat so monstrous that it was official policy to pretend it didn't exist. This created a group with a long history, a secret membership, institutional memory, a dedicated mission, and the ability to recruit new members, but most important, not too much power. The investigators in *Call of Cthulhu* have always been the underdogs, striving against impossible odds to save the world. The ability to pick up the phone and call in Delta Force or

a B-52 strike would have unbalanced the game and broken the mood.

There were two rules we tried to follow when writing the *Delta Green* source materials. The first was to root the game material in the published fiction, particularly the work of Lovecraft and the members of the First Lovecraft Circle—the classics, if you will. *Delta Green* exists only because Lovecraft himself gave us the opening with "The Shadow over Innsmouth." That short story firmly established that the U.S. government—both its law enforcement and military agencies—were aware of the Deep One colony and the Esoteric Order of Dagon cult. We just extrapolated the history of Delta Green from there, using the real histories of the Office of Naval Intelligence, the OSS, and the CIA as guides. Majestic-12, Delta Green's long-time competitor and nemesis, was inspired by the Lovecraft story "The Whisperer in Darkness." In that story, it is established that humans have been helping the dangerous and enigmatic alien Mi-go for centuries. We just married that idea to the modern conspiracy theories that put the U.S. government in collusion with the alien visitors, so that instead of little gray aliens, it was the Fungi from Yuggoth who were trading technological trinkets to the government in exchange for protection and test subjects. The Fate—the occult underground of New York City—was created by carefully mining stories like "The Horror at Red Hook" and poems like "Nyarlathotep." PISCES, the United Kingdom's version of Delta Green (and Majestic-12 for that matter) came from Ramsey Campbell's stories "The Moon-Lens" and "The Insects from Shaggai," which we tweaked to create a kind of *Invasion of the Body Snatchers* style of play. All these ideas were born out of material that already existed as part of the Cthulhu Mythos.

The second rule we followed was to include as much historical fact as possible. In this we were trying to mimic Lovecraft himself, who mixed his fiction with enough historical facts that it often became a matter of debate among his readers as to what was historical fact and what elements Lovecraft had created. Because Delta Green was set in the real world with an added layer of supernatural, it was critical for the suspension of disbelief that the real world elements hold up to scrutiny. Many of Delta Green's nemeses are deeply rooted in historical facts. The Nazi Karotechia is based on a number of Nazi programs that pursued elements of the occult in order to advance Nazi intelligence gathering and propaganda. Majestic-12 is based on several conspiracy theories surrounding UFO lore, principally the well-publicized Roswell Incident, but also incorporated a number dubious and historical research programs that were conducted during the cold war, especially the MKULTRA mind control experiments. The Skoptsi Cult is lifted right out of history, using an extinct Christian ecstatic cult (which really did practice castration as an extreme form of celibacy) on which we grafted some Cthulhu Mythos connections. The prime rule we followed about this was that the Mythos could not change the outcomes of historical events. If there was a Nazi organization trying to use Mythos magic to change the outcome of World War II, then obviously it failed. The Mythos could be an element of history or even drive it, but it would never displace recorded history.

Because of this connection to history, and because Delta Green was envisioned to have a history that stretched back before the Great Depression, the setting could accommodate many different time periods, not just the modern era. Players could have adventures in the "good old days" of World War II, back when the enemy was easy to identify, resources were practically unlimited, and the action could take the players anywhere in the world. Following close on the heels of World War II, the cold war era, particularly during the 1950s and 1960s, provides a global theater of operations for Delta Green agents. With more than seven decades of the twentieth century to work with, scenarios could be set on any stage that the Keeper could envision. Granted, the first three decades of the twentieth century pass before Delta Green comes into existence, but the classic era *Call of Cthulhu* game already covered these decades very well.

Since the Cthulhu Mythos presents not merely a global problem but one of genuinely cosmic proportions, there is no spot on earth, or anywhere in the universe for that matter, where a scenario cannot be set. Throw in the well-established Lovecraftian concept of dimensional gates, and there really is no time or place that a scenario cannot take

place. Just because a group of players starts off in the modern era doesn't mean that it cannot travel (unusually involuntarily) to anywhere in time and space for the purposes of a scenario. So because *Delta Green* was built on to the Cthulhu Mythos, scenarios and stories can be set even beyond the limits of the organization's history.

During the designing of the *Delta Green* vast narrative it was decided that we would publish more open-ended source material than scenarios. Source material is usually built around an enemy of Delta Green with a particular agenda or set of goals, much like a traditional role-playing game scenario is set up, only without the framework of scenes and set pieces designed to channel the players through to a resolution of the scenario. The reason for emphasizing open-ended source material over scenarios is that we were trying to encourage Keepers to design their own scenarios without pinning them down with too much canon. That is always a danger with creating a role-playing game background. You want to create a rich environment, but you don't want to fill in so many details that there is nothing new for the players and Keepers to create with their own games.

One of the most successful role-playing games of the 1990s was White Wolf's *Vampire: The Masquerade*. This role-playing game created its own vast narrative—a secret world of supernatural forces that exist just below the surface of known history. While this vast narrative did provide a wide, varied, and endlessly unfolding world for the players to explore, all too often that world was already populated by interesting non-player characters with a myriad of agendas and motives, who were already having adventures. The scenarios (and in my opinion, the game mechanics) too often cast the players in the roles of supporting characters in those epic struggles between titanic figures. This situation always felt like the equivalent of being reduced to the role of sidekick to the real protagonists. No one wants to have to play one of Doc Savage's sidekicks or one of the "red shirts" from *Star Trek*. People play role-playing games to be the heroes, to take center stage, to feel as if they are changing the course of events, rather than being swept along by them.

In order to avoid hemming in our players, we tried to imply more in the source material than we stated outright.

8.2 Cover of John Tynes's *Delta Green* novel *The Rules of Engagement*.

For instance, we left many of the details concerning how the Delta Green conspiracy was organized and funded as well as how it communicated with its members quite vague. This gave the Keepers and players around the world a lot of room to experiment. Linked by the Internet, the fans of *Delta Green* created a mythology around a named yet otherwise anonymous Delta Green agent code-named Agent Andrea. Her code name is mentioned only once in the *Delta Green* sourcebook while describing A Cell, the leadership cell of Delta Green. The other two members of the leadership cell are described in great detail, and somehow the players just couldn't leave that gap in the story alone. They had to

fill it. Over time, Agent Andrea became Delta Green's Lord High Executioner. She's the woman behind the bullet you never hear. She's the one who put the heart attack powder in your drink. She's the one who shows up when Delta Green agents have been naughty and deserve a lump of coal in their stocking. Of course, none of this is canon, but its ubiquity on the Internet and among players means that Agent Andrea has appeared in hundreds of *Delta Green* games around the world.

This open-endedness has led many fans to deluge us with requests for clarification and questions about what was and was not considered canon for *Delta Green*. We always tried to steer clear of definitive answers because we felt that the canon of the game didn't matter as much as what the players accomplished in their own games with their Keeper—telling their version of Delta Green's battle against the Mythos. Naturally, we want to suggest new ideas and expand our vast narrative with new non-player characters and organizations to help as well as hinder the players, but these elements should only be added if they enrich the environment, rather than cluttering it up. To that end, we have tried not to add too many "mytharc" style adversaries to the *Delta Green* universe.

I'm borrowing the term *mytharc* from series television. Chris Carter, the creator of *The X-Files*, used the term to describe those episodes of the series that concentrated on the theme of government knowledge of and complicity in alien abductions. This theme was introduced in the first episode and continued until the last episode of the series, nine years later. Interspersed throughout the series were the Monster of the Week episodes, involving a case the protagonists would solve or resolve that was completely self-contained. Joss Whedon also described his television series *Buffy the Vampire Slayer* and *Angel* in similar terms. There were plenty of Monsters of the Week around which individual episodes revolved, but each season of the show was organized by a "season arc." The season arc provided the structured plot into which the season's Big Bad, or main adversary, could be worked. The writers would often add an additional bit of misdirection by introducing a Little Bad early in the season to get the audience's attention and make the later appearance of the Big Bad more of a surprise.

The reason that I give these two examples is to show how mytharc adversaries can be fumbled in the execution of a vast narrative. In my opinion *The X-Files* fumbled. *The X-Files* mytharc was teased and teased for at least five seasons before the plotline was apparently resolved with the destruction of all the members of the Syndicate of alien invasion collaborators. Later there was an attempt to resurrect the impending alien colonization plotline, but it limped along poorly. The writing was inconsistent and contradictory, and gave the impression that the writers weren't working from any kind of a series bible. In fairness, the greatest hurtle for the Syndicate as a mytharc adversary is that the conflict was drawn out over nine seasons. It was bound to fail to hold the audience's attention for that long. It is the same problem that series television has when the sexual tension between the lead characters is resolved: suddenly their relationship becomes much less interesting. *Moonlighting* is the classic example of this sort of disaster. In *The X-Files*, once the mystery of the collaborators and the colonists was revealed and explained, the mytharc became less compelling. This led the writers to feel that they had to resolve the Syndicate plotline, but that resolution crippled the show by removing the adversaries that had long acted as the center of gravity of the entire series.

In *Buffy the Vampire Slayer*, the mytharc element was the Hellmouth, the mystical vortex of evil buried under the town of Sunnydale that ensured that the town would always be infested with all manner of supernatural vermin. The Hellmouth was introduced in episode one and not resolved until the last episode of the final season. It was the reason why evil people and horrible things keep converging on the protagonists, but the Hellmouth itself was not an actor. It was an environmental factor; it was the backdrop. Like the Syndicate mytharc in *The X-Files*, you could not resolve the Hellmouth without permanently and radically changing the nature of the show. But unlike the Syndicate mytharc, the Hellmouth was not the Big Bad. The Hellmouth was generating the plot insofar as its presence allowed for just about any supernatural plot that the

writers could imagine. But the Hellmouth was not an actor in the plot, like the Syndicate was for *The X-Files*. Every season the writers for *Buffy the Vampire Slayer* generated a seasonal villain—a Big Bad—to be defeated over the course of the season. Each season provided the viewer with a satisfactory ending, but never removed the Hellmouth from the story. It would always be there next season to draw in some new evildoers to keep the protagonists busy.

Delta Green's mytharc is the Cthulhu Mythos. It has always been there, and it will always be there, just out of sight and threatening the future of humankind. It acts like the Hellmouth did in *Buffy*; it can be held at bay but never destroyed, and it is the source of most of the threats that arise. Threats like Majestic-12, the Nazi Karotechia, or even Steven Alziz and Club Apocalypse can, in the long run, be destroyed, dealt with, or disbanded by the actions of the players as agents of Delta Green. Ultimately, it makes no difference to the vast narrative since the Cthulhu Mythos remains. The Mythos remains because it is an ordering principal of Lovecraft's fictional universe. It exists like the laws of gravity and thermodynamics. So no matter how many times the agents put down a cult, cabal, or conspiracy, there will always be another bunch waiting in the wings.

Over the years, I have occasionally heard players who did not enjoy playing *Call of Cthulhu* complain that the game is essentially "unwinnable" because the players can't actually kill Cthulhu and the rest of the Great Old Ones. This kind of complaint is the product of too much *Dungeons & Dragons*. That system only measures success by the number of monsters killed and the amount of treasure acquired. *Delta Green* and *Call of Cthulhu* measure success using different criteria. The game mechanics of *Call of Cthulhu* emphasizes the gain and loss of Sanity points. Sanity points represent the mental health of the characters. Seeing horrible monsters, witnessing ghastly murders, and using inhuman magic erodes the characters' Sanity points; saving lives, defeating monsters, and foiling the plans of adversaries gains Sanity points. Adversaries do not have to be killed to be defeated. Players are often rewarded with Sanity points so long as they learn what their adversary's malevolent goals are and by making sure they do not accomplish those goals. The players ensure that a human sacrifice does not happen; they make sure that the book the cultists seek is destroyed; they prevent the summoning of an alien god. Any of those can add up to a victory for the players. Naturally the reverse is true, in that the failure to prevent horrible things from happening means that the players will lose Sanity points, in the end facing mental breakdowns and permanent insanity.

This brings us back to the necessity of using Big Bads, Little Bads, and Monsters of the Week to ensure that measurable and satisfying progress in a campaign setting can be achieved, and yet the campaign setting won't be exhausted. The Keeper does not want to constantly come up with reasons why ultimate victory over the Karotechia slips away every time the players have them checkmated. Then it becomes like something out of Sax Rohmer's Fu Manchu novels: Fu Manchu achieves more and more ridiculous escapes from certain death to ensure that he will return to battle Neyland Smith again. Of course, these were Sax Rohmer Fu Manchu novels, not his Nayland Smith novels. The villain there was always more compelling than the hero in that series (unlike Sir Arthur Conan Doyle's Sherlock Holmes and his nemesis Professor Moriarty, I might add). If the players in a role-playing game campaign start to think that their characters are more disposable than the villain, they are going to feel marginalized. After all, whose story is this—theirs or a non-player character's? The fastest way to alienate a group of players is to give them the impression that they are not the center of the story. If they are not the ones driving the action forward, then what's the point in playing a role-playing game? They might as well be watching a movie if they cannot affect the pacing, action, and outcome of a story.

Delta Green was created by Tynes, but Dennis Detwiller and myself added a great deal of material to the vast narrative. After the first sourcebook was published, we quickly followed it with a collection of short fiction set in the *Delta Green* vast narrative universe. An expanded sourcebook called *Delta Green: Countdown* (1999), a second collection of short stories, and two *Delta Green* novels followed. *Delta*

8.3 Cover of Dennis Detwiller's *Delta Green* novel *Denied to the Enemy*.

Green fans have now begun building on this vast narrative themselves, submitting new material to Pagan Publishing and *Call of Cthulhu* journals like the UK's *The Black Seal* and Germany's *Worlds of Cthulhu*. Other fans have created Web sites where they publish their own scenarios and source material. A *Delta Green* mailing list exists where fans exchange ideas, swap stories, and bring new conspiracy theories, spy technologies, weapons, and even bizarre news of the world to the attention of their fellow gamers. Fan fiction is also being generated and published online. So perhaps *Delta Green*'s fans are setting the stage for another Lovecraft Circle, where new authors will create new fiction to fascinate another generation of Lovecraft fans.

From the Final Transmission of Major General Reginald Fairfield, U.S. Army (Retired), as Found in the Pagan Publishing Sourcebook *Delta Green*

Evil never dies. Darkness never retreats. In the cracks and crevices of our society there are monsters undreamed of by the rank and file of humanity. I've been there. I've seen them. They exist in the spaces between things, in the folds of existence where we can't find them. Sometimes they cross over, sometimes they manifest, and all hell breaks loose. Only this is not hell, nor heaven. This is like nothing anyone has ever understood. This is pure evil, pure destruction. This is the apocalypse, and I've been fighting it tooth and nail since 1961. They made me retire in 1970 when Cambodia blew up in their faces and they blamed us, but I didn't stop then and I'm not stopping now. They think I gave it all up that day in the Pentagon when they told me the choice—the only choice—I would be allowed. I took, and then, like most of us, I made the decision to continue the fight. They thought we were washed up. They know nothing.

Note

1. For a compact and detailed history of the Cthulhu Mythos, see Robert M. Price's chapter "With Strange Aeons: H. P. Lovecraft's Cthulhu Mythos as One Vast Narrative," in part II of this volume.

References: Literature

Detwiller, Dennis (2003). *Delta Green: Denied to the Enemy*. Seattle: Armitage House.

Kruger, Bob, and John Tynes (eds.) (1998). *Delta Green: Alien Intelligence*. Seattle: Armitage House.

Kruger, Bob, and John Tynes (eds.) (1999). *Delta Green: Dark Theatres*. Seattle: Armitage House.

Tynes, John (2000). *Delta Green: The Rules of Engagement*. Seattle: Armitage House.

References: Games

Delta Green. Dennis Detwiller, A. Scott Glancy, and John Tynes; Pagan Publishing. 1997.

Delta Green: Countdown. Dennis Detwiller, A. Scott Glancy, and John Tynes; Pagan Publishing. 1999.

Delta Green: Eyes Only. Dennis Detwiller and A. Scott Glancy with Shane Ivey; Arc Dream/Pagan Publishing. 2007.

None of this fan-generated material harms the *Delta Green* vast narrative because it can be used or ignored by Keepers and players as they see fit, with no regard to the "official canon." Sure, there is an official canon that exists in the published role-playing game books and fiction, but *Delta Green* games are run on thousands of tabletops spread across the world. The official canon published by Pagan Publishing exists as an outline, a skeleton that will be fleshed out by our customers. Each gaming group's vision of the *Delta Green* narrative is different from the others, tailored by the group's Keeper to ensure that their players have the most fun possible. The only wrong way for a Keeper to run his or her game is if the players aren't having any fun.

As long as fans are generating new material, there is always a chance that one of them will generate the next big idea to be incorporated into the canon of the vast narrative. In this way, *Delta Green* is part of the long tradition of the Cthulhu Mythos, with generations of writers, amateurs, and professionals alike building on the work of those who have come before.

La Vie d'Arthur, Conflict, and Cooperation in *The Great Pendragon Campaign*

Greg Stafford

I have always loved knights, even before I knew what they were. As a boy I traded all my plastic toy cowboys for knights. I remember clearly looking at photos of castles in 1955, when I was seven years old, and marveling at the heights of the walls and wondering why they never had roofs. I was an advanced and voracious reader. *Otto of the Silver Hand*, illustrated by Howard Pyle, was my first book about knights, and provided sufficient insight into medieval courage and cruelty to set me on the right track. I remember quite consciously deciding, "I will learn more about this."

I've made similar decisions in my life. One was to start a game company to publish fantasy games, of which there were none at the time. No fantasy games, and no publishers of them. In 1975 I founded The Chaosium, later Chaosium, Inc., which became the premier "art house" of role-playing games during the height of that fashion in gaming. We didn't know much about efficient business practices but we sure knew how to make great role-playing games, as everyone agrees.

In 1985, Chaosium published my personal masterpiece of role-playing, *King Arthur Pendragon*. It was the culmination of thirty years of Arthurian study and ten years of designing games. My intent was to bring my understanding of both the Arthurian stories and the Middle Ages into a role-playing experience, expressed through a simple game system.

Both the game and its construction manifest the essential themes of conflict and cooperation, the struggle between idealism and reality, and the meaningfulness of tragedy.

The first problem was to decide what to include. Arthurian stories have been told and retold for almost fifteen hundred years, with their popularity rising and falling as custom and fashion dictate. Naturally, storytelling styles have changed depending on the audience and the media through which it has been presented. The variety is vast.

The Dark Age oral tales are savage and wild, full of fairy tale elements and pagan motifs. Fragments of these are preserved in the Welsh sources such as *The Mabinogion*, but also in folktales, fairy lore, and local legends. They are stories told around fires in the Welsh mountains and on the Breton coasts by the defeated descendants of a great and successful post-Roman warrior lord named Arthur. They are nurturing tales of the hero who had brought peace and victory to their grandfathers, and full of hope and the dream that he will come again.

Centuries later, Breton raconteurs became famous storytellers across Europe as they bore their oral tales to medieval courts. Lords and ladies marveled to hear about the great king and his brotherhood that could never be broken except by treachery. Adapted to the time, British warriors became knights, post-Roman chiefs became kings, and legendary Welsh heroes became medieval champions.

Literature changed the stories. We credit King Henry II and his marvelous Queen Eleanor with the popularization of Arthurian literature. It was good propaganda for him. Henry, like Arthur, ruled over a conglomeration of peoples united under a wise and powerful king. The stories of King Arthur united them as well, in all languages. From his court came the first written Latin version of King Arthur's history, Geoffrey of Monmouth's *Historia Regnum Britanniae* (c. 1138; English version, c. 1517), which was so powerful that every story afterward was influenced by it. From the first written French stories, compiled by Chrétien de Troyes, came the first written notices of Lancelot du Lac and the Holy Grail (c. 1170 to c. 1190). Shortly after Henry came the first written English version, Layamon's *Brut* (c. 1215). There followed several centuries of scribal literary expansion, developing themes, and accreting stories.

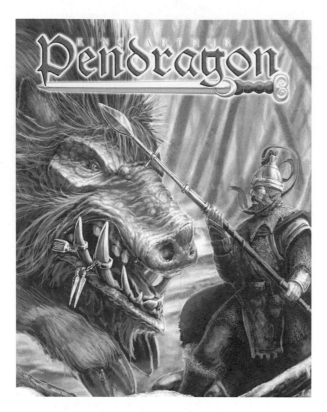

9.1 Cover of *King Arthur Pendragon* (5th ed.).

Medieval versions culminate with the masterpiece *Le Mort d'Arthur* in 1485 by Sir Thomas Malory (2000). His tale of the downfall of the greatest king in the world echoes the downfall of the chivalrous traditions of his own world, where gunpowder and the Wars of the Roses ended centuries of knighthood and chivalry, and the printed word ended scribal copying.

Modern literary versions added to the corpus with materials on new subjects. T. H. White's *The Once and Future King* is the first source to present anything of Arthur's childhood, while Marion Zimmer Bradley's *Mists of Avalon* adds a layer of feminist understanding to this often hypermasculine legend.

Modern media impacted it too. Comics are significant, with *Prince Valiant* influencing almost everyone with Arthurian interests for its seventy-year (and still going) run. It puts the tales in a broad medieval setting, vastly expanding the scope of the stories to include Byzantium,

Scandinavia, and even the New World. And of course there are the movies, from the silent *Parsifal* in 1904, to *Knights of the Round Table* (1953) with Robert Taylor and Ava Gardner, to the musical *Camelot* (1967). The nature of most films is that they familiarize, but generally lack depth. They usually concentrate on the love story, and frequently serve to bastardize and cheapen the glorious tales. An exception is John Boorman's *Excalibur* (1981).

These sources I mention in particular because each of them presented something of value to my understanding of the King Arthur story, and I wished to include those all in my game. The real problem then became how to unite this vast body of work. The key is in systemization: presenting materials so their common points are brought to the fore, rather than their differences.

The unifying solution is the game itself. To be effective, the rules need to be simple enough that they can be learned and used easily, without reference to any outside charts, tables, or books. They need to address the points of significance. They should be an invisible vehicle for mythical exploration.

Pendragon has a single system that uses one game mechanic for all of its resolutions. The skills that are important (Falconry, Flirting, Sword, etc.) have a number between one and twenty, where a higher number is a better skill. Players roll a twenty-sided die to determine success. Some rolls are simple, unopposed ("Do you find the villain's tracks?"), and if the number rolled is less than the skill value, it is a success. Some rolls are opposed: both opponents roll a twenty-sided die and whoever rolls higher, but still lower than his or her skill, wins.

But this opposition system is not applied to just physical conflicts, like sword fights or scaling a castle wall. The Arthurian legends are about people—how they feel, how they act, and what moves them. So this resolution system is also used for interpersonal, emotional conflicts.

I wanted the game to concentrate on the human experience, through the medium of the Middle Ages and its greatest legendary hero. The immense power of the Arthurian legend lies in deep human experiences. By drawing on these, the game obtains complexity and meaningful depth. The game text never advertises those things; it expresses them through play. The fields of the human conflict are the terrain of play as much as the tournament or battlefields.

One primary conflict in all human experience is between practicality and idealism. Therein lays the core of the Arthurian legend. All of the heroes are knights; likewise in *King Arthur Pendragon*, all of the player characters are knights. But the real issue is, *What kind of knight are you?* And this comes down to behavior.

Thus I introduced Personality Traits. These are statistics for how your character behaves in play. Just as the Sword statistic tells how good you are at sword fighting, so the Merciful Trait tells how merciful you are. I began with Christianity's seven deadly sins, added virtues important for chivalrous behavior (Valor, for instance), and set them against their opposites, the vices. Thus each of the Personality Traits is a balance of virtue and vice, whose total equals twenty points. If your Merciful Trait equals fourteen, then your Cruelty equals six.

These traits then characterize behavior, personal qualities, and emotions. These are the things that test virtue versus practicality. They record virtue. They record whether your knight is a practical, historical type of figure or an idealistic, legendary one.

The game is about conflict. The conflict of practicality versus idealism, as stated. Virtue versus vice.

But medieval nobles also engaged in real, fatal battle and warfare. *Pendragon* is as deadly as those nobles' lives were. It is brutal. It is easy to die, and characters often do, especially when motivated by their virtues to "do the right thing" in a dangerous situation. In fact, death is one thing everyone can be sure of. In the published campaign, everyone will die at the end, when the heroes and villains face off at the Battle of Camlann. Mortality is an integral part of the game, as it is of the legend.

This deadliness dovetails into another unique feature of the game—the dynastic segment. Missing from every other role-playing game was one universal reality of life: family. This primary drive of humanity is critical to the Arthurian legend. So in the game, characters seek wives and raise children who will inherit their goods as well as characteristics—indeed, carry on their history. The knight dies, and his son takes up the mantle.

I relate a moment of frisson when this dynastic drive paid off for me as the designer. I was playing this with my high-school-aged son and his friends, and they had had characters die, and also knew that their young sons were getting ready for play. Every time they went to Camelot I would say, "There is the High King, the greatest king in the world on his throne. Beside him, on his left, Queen Guenever, the most beautiful woman in the world. And on his right, the empty throne for his son." After a dozen visits, one of the boys heard this yet again and said, "Oh, that poor son of a bitch." And I felt the shock of that realization pass around the circle of players: these young men on the threshold of adulthood, as they looked at each other and felt the tragedy of heirlessness. What a glorious moment. They understood the tragedy of the King Arthur story. They recognized that the greatness of King Arthur would be just a transitory moment. Without an heir, it would not pass on.

In addition to conflict and death, the King Arthur stories are also about cooperation. The Round Table is an organization that unites individuals from the far corners of Arthur's realm. A role-playing game unites multiple players with different styles of play. Some enjoy the theaterlike aspect of role-playing, some appreciate the tactical challenges, and some just like to get together with friends. Furthermore, the characters vary widely in their objectives. Some are religious, others are chivalrous and mannerly, while still others are simply soldiers following orders.

The unifying facet that ties all of the parts of the game together is Glory. Glory is the currency of the game. Everything that a knight character does is to acquire Glory. Winning fights gets Glory. Having land gets Glory. Being chivalrous or religious gets Glory. Marrying gets Glory. Having office gets Glory. (I will not dwell on the irony that Glory will not provide or raise sons.)

When the core game was first released, several friends of mine who played in my campaign commented that they loved it, but that they thought the weakness was that I was the only person who could properly run a campaign. I reminded them of two things: first, I wasn't the only King Arthur fan in gaming; and second, that one need not have the knowledge I had to run a game, any more than a person had to know what J. R. R. Tolkien knew in order to run a game set in Third Age Middle Earth. Nonetheless, I always wanted to publish a guide for an intense, deep Arthurian campaign that took advantage of my knowledge without forcing people to spend thirty years accumulating it.

Thus I was thrilled when Stewart Weick of White Wolf Games asked me if I would do a revised edition, and also if I wanted to publish a campaign for it. Stewart was on a mission to acquire excellent games in these circumstances and rerelease them. He was a fan of the game for decades, and had acquired the rights to publish *Pendragon*.

The offer was like having a second chance to enter the Grail Castle! The result was *The Great Pendragon Campaign* (2006), which was completed in 2005 and released a year later. There, at last, I managed to pour my fifty years of Arthurian knowledge and thirty years of gaming into the next step of my masterpiece.

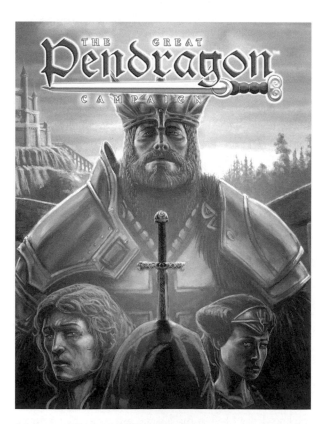

9.2 Cover of *The Great Pendragon Campaign*.

The Great Pendragon Campaign is a year-by-year guideline to the eighty-one-year-long reign of King Arthur. It takes that immense list of material from centuries of storytelling and systematizes it into a harmonious whole. It proves that the source is less important than the presentation. I've asked, and people can't tell whether a story is from the wild Welsh, medieval literature, movies, or history.

Each year is revealed through the same format. It starts in court, where everyone gathers for the Pentecost feast and tournament. News comes first from gossip, which everyone hears, and some of which is wrong. Officers of the court (Kay the Steward, Griflet the Marshall, etc.) present official information. Then insider information may be discovered through Intrigue.

The format then presents the actual events of the realm—who is rebelling, what foreigner is attacking, and so on. These are the wars of the realm, and well-known adventures that the players may participate in. Hence player knights may rescue King Arthur when he is kidnapped, witness the first appearance of Lancelot at court, and be ordered to stand guard when the queen is to be burned at the stake. Finally, it gives over a hundred original adventures and quests that may be sought. These are extraordinary events, which extraordinary individuals may seek to undertake. Often, however, the knights have their own agendas that they wish to pursue, and they provide original stories. For instance, a knight may decide to do deeds to be worthy of a rich wife, seek revenge for the death of a family member, or even decide he must leave the country for a few years because he is embarrassed or ashamed of some mistake he has committed at court.

Almost everyone knows the core facts of the story. They know Lancelot is going to betray his lord by bedding the queen. They know the Grail will appear sometime, and that Mordred is going to plot treason. They don't know *when* these will occur, and it is fun for them to be in adventures that will later become important for the Grail Quest or meet Mordred before he goes bad.

The chronology also includes many obscure facets of Arthurian lore, just to keep the superficially knowledgeable players off balance. For example, in the earliest phase they meet King Uther's son, Madoc. He's an *extremely* obscure figure, appearing only by name in an obscure Welsh poem as the father of a prophetic eagle who had been a man and who scolds Arthur. Later on, the court is blessed with the presence of two sons of King Arthur, out of three possible who are named in Welsh legend. These aren't found in the normal medieval version, which only knows of Mordred. Apparently the lack of any sons except the misbegotten incestuous one sufficiently emphasized the theme of familial heirs. But I was seeking to surprise the players, and so one day Sir Borre and Loholt, two bastard sons of King Arthur, show up at court.

Also, players have personal impact. Some of the legendary history is immutable—the Grail Quest is nearly impossible to accomplish, and the Round Table is going to fall. Yet not everything is so determined. Just as it is delightful to surprise players with the sons of King Arthur, it is even more so when they perform deeds attributed to known heroes—*they* have rescued King Arthur. They can complete tales that are unfinished in the literature—*they* capture the Questing Beast or slay the gigantic Troit Boar. *They* rescue Lancelot. *They* may change the stories. One time a player knight even killed Sir Agravain!

I wanted this epic to be soaked in medieval beliefs, so other medieval sources contribute to the story as well. Local folklore knows of dozens of dragons, ghosts, mysterious black dogs, and giants who inhabit the countryside. Each of those is a potential adventure, as are the strange tunnels under Richmond Castle, the bottomless Hell Kettles of Darlington, or the Rollright Stones that march to the nearby river each midsummer to drink. British fairy lore in general adds another layer of adventure. In the wilds lurk malevolent things like the bloodthirsty redcap, spriggans who shrink from giant size to sprite size as they are hurt, or the afanc, an enormous beaverlike creature who eats herds of cattle. Knights can enter the glittering realm of King Oberon, whose magical court rivals that of King Arthur, and whose lords and ladies are as much of a challenge as the deadly fiends of the dark, Unseelie Court.

The campaign is long—it covers eighty-one game years. This is the longest campaign in gaming thus far, in terms of in-game chronology. This passage of time serves several purposes, the first of which is to address the problem of

creeping escalation. This is the tendency for characters to become more and more powerful, often at the expense of the setting. For instance, the game master may allow only one magic sword, one magic shield, one fairy horse, one ring of strength, and so on, but they always remain and tend to accumulate in the hands of individuals. That individual then becomes too powerful for normal settings, or else more powerful than the other characters and thus dominates the action.

To help compensate for this I created an ongoing escalation for the whole campaign world. Players now have to work to keep up with the campaign, rather than pulling out ahead of it in terms of personal power. I combined a historical progression of arms, armor, and customs in the game. Given this, everyone has a chance to get better armor, a more powerful horse, and fancier equipment. It is done through campaign time. Roughly, each fifteen years of the campaign is the equivalent of a century of medieval history. An arms race goes on where armor improves to make them nearly impervious, to be trumped by larger horses capable of doing more damage, canceled by improved armor, and so on. At the start, then, knights have only Norman chain mail and chargers, while at the end they are trooping around in full plate armor astride huge destriers. Customs change too, from the harsh Dark Ages of King Uther to periods of Romance and Tourney.

History combines with legend in that many historical events are mirrored in the campaign. Arthur introduces many methods to address the problems of the decentralized Anarchy Period, just as William the Conqueror did. In 1086, for instance, William had his nobles swear the famous Sarum Oath. This pledged them directly to him rather than to their traditional barons. Arthur offers the same type of oath, so that the knights can afterward call themselves Arthur's Men. Other parallels exist: Sir Borre, Arthur's pompous son, dies in exactly the manner that King Richard does. Cambria is conquered in the same manner that Wales was. Grinding wars in France and Ireland offer a chance for battle at any time.

The pleasant surprise is that all these sources combine. Systemizing them and using the game as the filter through which these are revealed unites legend, folklore, literature, and history into a seamless tale where knightly characters act, and players play.

Pendragon has been criticized for its deadliness. It is easy to die (indeed, it is guaranteed that by the end of the campaign, *everyone* will die). But I didn't want it to be a game styled on a television series where the story always ends with a neat little plot resolution. It has been pointed out that the Arthurian characters always do succeed, but that the Arthurian stories are *not* always full of success. It is easy, with the focus on Lancelot, Gawaine, and Percivale, to overlook the knights who preceded them and failed. We never read the tales of those knights who tried but did not succeed, and are freed from the dungeon by Lancelot. No story tells about the dozen knights whose rusting shields mark their graves by the chapel freed of an invisible demon by Gawaine, or reveals the trials of the men who are now corpses hanging in the trees over the ground that is later sanctified by Percivale's victory. Yet those many failures are, nonetheless, there. And the player knights may be the victims of those stories of failure.

Without prospect of failure there is no challenge. The Arthurian story is one of great challenges, so there must also be the opportunity for great failure. Hence the death rate. Furthermore, that deadliness is a reflection of the feudal reality that is contrasted with the legendary ideal.

All this reinforces my key point: this is *not* about being one of the Round Table knights; *it is about earning one's way to becoming a great character.*

So characters start off as ordinary knights. They fight and sometimes die. They struggle and sometimes fail. They must pick and choose their battles, and sometimes suffer the shame of running away. They can always come back— in one game three generations of characters visited the Castle of the Stork before finding the key to success.

Most important here is that because failure looms, success is deeply appreciated. Successful knights are highly esteemed. Some player knights do become members of the Round Table and are greatly admired. No such emotions would fill and motivate the game if everyone simply began there. The game has *meaning.*

One deep meaning of the game is the presence of tragedy. The Round Table is the perfect brotherhood that can only be defeated by treachery from within. After the membership dares to attempt perfection in finding the Holy Grail, the flaws of its hubris come to the fore. The dream of perfection will come to its tragic conclusion. Love will *not* conquer all. Equality and idealism are not enough. It must end.

And so must the campaign. Eighty-one years of glory— likely to have been expressed in over a hundred sessions of gaming—draw to a close. I was worried the first time I came to that moment. That's a lot of time and emotion invested by players, and sometimes players feel a strong sense of sadness when their characters die. I thought that the Battle of Camlann might result in massive depression among the friends who'd spent so much time together.

It proved to be otherwise. Sure, part of it was probably relief at just being finished at last, but it was much, much more. And yes, there is always one who is left alive at the end, to cast the sword into the waters, and see the Once and Future King off to the Isle of Apples. The players vied to be that one.

But the largest emotional expression was in the game terms—the knights were going forth to fight for king and justice, as they had done so many times before. Even more than duty, though, was a sustained conflagration of exhilaration, occasioned by the opportunity for a good and meaningful death. The meaning was in doing duty, as I said, but also in the sense that this tragic conclusion was necessary for the ideas and ideals to be immortalized. Every player participated with tremendous gusto and delight as their characters, one by one, fell silent forever.

This, indeed, is the purpose of role-playing games: to provide a vicarious experience. It might be for entertainment, education, or even to find meaning. I have found that a sustained experience provides a deeper experience, and that a game with meaningful content, structured to express that meaning, provides me—as creator, game master, and player—with the most satisfying experience of all. When we experience the realities of conflict and cooperation in this surrogate reality, we find satisfaction beyond just entertainment. We participate in the tragedy, triumph, and immortality of legend. It is everyone's story. And in the end, we are richer for it.

Some Samples of Sources

Here are several samples from the different literatures to illustrate the different styles from different ages. In the *Pendragon* game, these kinds of examples are inserted in the margins or in boxes to the side.

Celtic Arthur

From *The Mabinogion*, published by Lady Charlotte Guest (1906) in 1849, but containing stories that are much, much older, here is an excerpt from "Kilhwch and Olwen," a tale in which King Arthur and his companions seek to secure a bride for the king's cousin.

This is the earliest appearance of two of King Arthur's companions from the literature who remained with him throughout the centuries of his epic, though transformed by later stories. In particular Kai, who becomes Sir Kay, turns into quite a different character. Here we see him as the right-hand man of his king, as he will be in almost all subsequent tales. But here, typical of the times, he is also a supernatural hero.

> Thereupon Kai rose up. Kai had this peculiarity, that his breath lasted nine nights and nine days under water, and he could exist nine nights and nine days without sleep. A wound from Kai's sword no physician could heal. Very subtle was Kai. When it pleased him he could render himself as tall as the highest tree in the forest. And he had another peculiarity—so great was the heat of his nature that when it rained hardest, whatever he carried remained dry for a handbreadth above and a handbreadth below his hand; and when his companions were coldest, it was to them as fuel with which to light their fire.
>
> And Arthur called Bedwyr, who never shrank from any enterprise upon which Kai was bound. None was equal to him in swiftness throughout this island except Arthur and Drych Ail Kibddar. And although he was one-handed, three warriors could not shed blood faster than he on the field of battle. Another property he had; his lance would produce a wound equal to those of nine opposing lances.

Historical Arthur

Geoffrey of Monmouth compiled this first complete history of Britain—*Historia Regum Britanniae*, or the *History of the Kings of Britain*, circa 1138—drawing on written sources, oral legends, and his own imagination. Written in Latin, this is a formal document with a minimum of the fantastic elements of the Welsh predecessors and also lacking the romantic element of subsequent legends.

The description of this military expedition is fairly typical of the book. Here we find the first mention of Arthur's marvelous sword, and also of the magical Isle of Avalon.

> At these words, all of them, encouraged with the benediction of the holy prelate, instantly armed themselves, and prepared to obey his orders. Also Arthur himself, having put on a coat of mail suitable to the grandeur of so powerful a king, placed a golden helmet upon his head, on which was engraven the figure of a dragon; and on his shoulders his shield called Pridwen; upon which the picture of the blessed Mary, mother of God, was painted, in order to put him frequently in mind of her. Then girding on his Caliburn, which was an excellent sword made on the isle of Avallon, he graced his right hand with his lance, named Ron, which was hard, broad, and fit for slaughter.
>
> After this, having placed his men in order, he boldly attacked the Saxons, who were drawn out in the shape of a wedge, as their manner was. And they, notwithstanding that the Britons fought with great eagerness, made a noble defense all that day; but at length, towards sunset, climbed up the next mountain, which served them for a camp: for they desired no larger extent of ground, since they confided very much in their numbers.
>
> The next morning Arthur, with his army, went up the mountain, but lost many of his men in the ascent, by the advantage which the Saxons had in their station on the top, from whence they could pour down upon him with much greater speed than he was able to advance against them. Notwithstanding, after a very hard struggle, the Britons gained the summit of the hill, and quickly came to a close engagement with the enemy, who again gave them a warm reception, and made a vigorous defense. In this manner was a great part of that day also spent; whereupon Arthur, provoked to see the little advantage he had yet gained, and that victory still continued in suspense, drew out his Caliburn, and calling upon the name of the blessed Virgin, rushed forward with great fury into the thickest of the enemy's ranks; of whom (such was the merit of his prayers) not one escaped alive that felt the fury of his sword; neither did

he give over the fury of his assault until he had, with his Caliburn alone, killed four hundred and seventy men.

The Britons, seeing this, followed their leader in great multitudes, and made slaughter on all sides; so that Colgrin, and Baldulph his brother, and many thousands more, fell before them. But Cheldric, in this imminent danger of his men, betook himself to flight.

Early Romance

Chrétien de Troyes was a clerk who composed a series of entertaining stories for the court of Marie of France—*Yvain, le Chevalier au Lion*, or *Yvain or, the Knight with the Lion*, circa 1150. These introduced Lancelot du Lac, the Holy Grail, and the customs of chivalric romance to the literature. The customs in these tales are those of high chivalry, with an emphasis on jousting and fine manners rather than war.

Here we see Sir Kay, fallen from his great heroic state in the Celtic stories, to be an ill-tempered steward, far less competent but still loyal to Arthur. The king's party has traveled to a marvelous spring to witness the adventure there, unaware that one of their number has become the guardian.

And it was my lord Kay's desire to request the first encounter. For whatever the outcome might be, he always wished to begin the fight and joust the first, or else he would be much incensed. Before all the rest, he requested the King to allow him to do battle first. The King says: "Kay, since it is your wish, and since you are the first to make the request, the favor ought not to be denied."

Kay thanks him first, then mounts his steed. If now my lord Yvain can inflict a mild disgrace upon him, he will be very glad to do so; for he recognizes him by his arms. Each grasping his shield by the straps, they rush together. Spurring their steeds, they lower the lances, which they hold tightly gripped. Then they thrust them forward a little, so that they grasped them by the leather-wrapped handles, and so that when they came together they were able to deal such cruel blows that both lances broke in splinters clear to the handle of the shaft. My lord Yvain gave him such a mighty blow that Kay took a somersault from out of his saddle and struck with his helmet on the ground.

My lord Yvain has no desire to inflict upon him further harm, but simply dismounts and takes his horse. This pleased them all, and many said: "Ah, ah, see how you

prostrate lie, who but now held others up to scorn! And yet it is only right to pardon you this time; for it never happened to you before."

Thereupon my lord Yvain approached the King, leading the horse in his hand by the bridle, and wishing to make it over to him. "Sire," says he, "now take this steed, for I should do wrong to keep back anything of yours."

"And who are you?" the King replies; "I should never know you, unless I heard your name, or saw you without your arms." Then my lord told him who he was, and Kay was overcome with shame, mortified, humbled, and discomfited, for having said that he had run away. But the others were greatly pleased, and made much of the honor he had won. Even the King was greatly gratified, and my lord Gawain a hundred times more than any one else. For he loved his company more than that of any other knight he knew.

Late Romance

Sir Thomas Malory was a knight who lived and fought in the Wars of the Roses and compiled perhaps the greatest rendition of the story of King Arthur while in prison toward the end of his colorful, adventurous life—*Le Morte d'Arthur*, circa 1470. He used many written sources as well as creating original material.

Here, in "The Death of Arthur," King Arthur lies mortally wounded on the field, with only two wounded old men left from his once-great brotherhood of knights. Even here at the end of the era we find virtue being tested. Myself, I am touched to find Sir Bedivere there at the end, just as loyal and true as he had been as Bedwyr in the Celtic tales from centuries earlier.

"Therefore by my rede," said Sir Lucan, "it is best that we bring you to some town."

"I would it were so," said the king, "But I may not stand, mine head works so. Ah Sir Lancelot," said King Arthur, "this day have I sore missed thee: alas, that ever I was against thee, for now have I my death, whereof Sir Gawaine me warned in my dream."

Then Sir Lucan took up the king the one part, and Sir Bedivere the other part, and in the lifting the king swooned; and Sir Lucan fell in a swoon with the lift, that the part of his guts fell out of his body, and therewith the noble knight's heart brast. And when the king awoke, he beheld Sir Lucan, how he lay foaming at the mouth, and part of his guts lay at his feet.

"Alas," said the king, "this is to me a full heavy sight, to see this noble duke so die for my sake, for he would have holpen me, that had more need of help than I. Alas, he would not complain him, his heart was so set to help me: now Jesu have mercy upon his soul!" Then Sir Bedivere wept for the death of his brother. "Leave this mourning and weeping," said the king, "for all this will not avail me, for wit thou well and I might live myself, the death of Sir Lucan would grieve me evermore; but my time hieth fast," said the king. "Therefore," said Arthur unto Sir Bedivere, "take thou Excalibur, my good sword, and go with it to yonder water side, and when thou comest there I charge thee throw my sword in that water, and come again and tell me what thou there seest."

"My lord," said Bedivere, "your commandment shall be done, and lightly bring you word again."

So Sir Bedivere departed, and by the way he beheld that noble sword, that the pommel and the haft was all of precious stones; and then he said to himself: If I throw this rich sword in the water, thereof shall never come good, but harm and loss. And then Sir Bedivere hid Excalibur under a tree. And so, as soon as he might, he came again unto the king, and said he had been at the water, and had thrown the sword in the water.

"What saw thou there?" said the king.

"Sir," he said, "I saw nothing but waves and winds."

"That is untruly said of thee," said the king, "therefore go thou lightly again, and do my commandment; as thou art to me lief and dear, spare not, but throw it in."

Then Sir Bedivere returned again, and took the sword in his hand; and then him thought sin and shame to throw away that noble sword, and so eft he hid the sword, and returned again, and told to the king that he had been at the water, and done his commandment.

"What saw thou there?" said the king. "Sir," he said, "I saw nothing but the waters wap and waves wan."

"Ah, traitor untrue," said King Arthur, "now hast thou betrayed me twice. Who would have weened that, thou that hast been to me so lief and dear? and thou art named a noble knight, and would betray me for the richness of the sword. But now go again lightly, for thy long tarrying putteth me in great jeopardy of my life, for I have taken cold. And but if thou do now as I bid thee, if ever I may see thee, I shall slay thee with mine own hands; for thou wouldst for my rich sword see me dead."

Then Sir Bedivere departed, and went to the sword, and lightly took it up, and went to the water side; and there he bound the girdle about the hilts, and then he threw the sword as far into the water as he might; and there came an arm and an hand above the water and met it, and caught it, and so shook it thrice and brandished, and then vanished away the hand with the sword in the water. So Sir Bedivere came again to the king, and told him what he saw.

"Alas," said the king, "help me hence, for I dread me I have tarried over long." Then Sir Bedivere took the king on his back, and so went with him to that water side. And when they were at the water side, even fast by the bank hoved a little barge with many fair ladies in it, and among them all was a queen, and all they had black hoods, and all they wept and shrieked when they saw King Arthur.

"Now put me into the barge," said the king. And so he did softly; and there received him three queens with great mourning; and so they set them down, and in one of their laps King Arthur laid his head.

And then that queen said, "Ah, dear brother, why have ye tarried so long from me? alas, this wound on your head hath caught over-much cold." And so then they rowed from the land, and Sir Bedivere beheld all those ladies go from him.

Then Sir Bedivere cried, "Ah my lord Arthur, what shall become of me, now ye go from me and leave me here alone among mine enemies?"

"Comfort thyself," said the king, "and do as well as thou mayst, for in me is no trust for to trust in; for I will into the vale of Avilion to heal me of my grievous wound: and if thou hear never more of me, pray for my soul."

But ever the queens and ladies wept and shrieked, that it was pity to hear. And as soon as Sir Bedivere had lost the sight of the barge, he wept and wailed, and so took the forest; and so he went all that night, and in the morning he was ware betwixt two holts hoar, of a chapel and an hermitage.

References: Literature

Chrétien de Troyes (1985). *Yvain, le Chevalier au Lion*, translated by William S. Kibler. New York: Garland.

Geoffrey of Monmouth (c. 1517). *Historia Regum Britanniae*. Paris: Io. Badius Ascensius.

Guest, Charlotte, Lady (trans.) (1906). *The Mabinogion*. New York: E. P. Dutton and Company.

Mallory, Thomas, Sir (2000). *Le Morte d'Arthur*, edited by John Matthews. London: Cassell.

References: Games

The Great Pendragon Campaign. Greg Stafford; Arthaus. 2006.

King Arthur Pendragon. Greg Stafford; Chaosium. 1985.

King Arthur Pendragon. 5th ed. Greg Stafford; White Wolf. 2005.

The Game Master and the Role-Playing Game Campaign
Monte Cook

Six people sit around a table. A few hours ago, someone might have eaten dinner there, but now the table is covered in stacks of rule books, strangely shaped dice, and miniature figurines of orcs, warriors with swords and axes, and strangely garbed sorcerers. A single player, calling him- or herself the game master (GM), consults maps drawn on graph paper and handwritten notes before providing the other players with an imaginative description of a locale in a fictional world. The six of them engage, collectively, in creating a narrative as engrossing as (or perhaps more than) any novel, movie, or television show.

Traditional role-playing games—called pen-and-paper RPGs to distinguish themselves from computer versions— have been around for more than thirty years, and much of their success can be attributed to the hard work and creative talent of the game masters that both create and manage the game into ongoing series called campaigns.

Creating and maintaining a role-playing game campaign involves a style of narrative structure that differs from any other type of creative enterprise. Among such endeavors it is unique and requires highly specialized skills. At the heart of every role-playing game campaign lays a story. It can be simple or astonishingly complex, but it usually falls somewhere in between. The game master is the steward of that story, and the campaign is a story told in many parts, over the course of many sessions of the game. Of the various comparable narrative forms—books, movies, and comics— only role-playing games require the direct involvement of the creator in the experience of the ongoing narrative.

Storytelling in RPG Campaign Form
The game master works with the players to create a story. Before they can do that, they need an outline, to which only the game master is privy. The GM plans out where the campaign will start, and where it will hopefully go. This outline is typically simplistic, since so many of the details will actually be filled in as the GM goes along. It's more like a travel itinerary than an outline, really. All the GM really knows is the general "stops" along the way—the destinations—but not necessarily how they will get there.

The GM might, for example, plan on an adventure dealing with goblins to start with and then at some point after that an urban adventure dealing with thieves in a city. Next on his or her plan is an adventure with a dragon in the mountains and finally a trip to another plane of existence. Any one of these stops might be a published adventure that the GM has purchased to integrate into the campaign. For example, the urban adventure might be an adventure—or "module"—for which the GM knows that all he or she has to do to start it is to get the player characters (PCs) into a city. In fact, often these points on the planned campaign path are location specific, so the GM knows that to move the plot along, he or she simply has to entice the characters, controlled by their players to reach a specific location.

Presumably, the GM plans for one point in the campaign outline to lead to the next to maintain an ongoing narrative. Thus, something happens in the adventure with the dragon that leads the PCs to travel to another plane of existence. But of course, things in the game might not turn out that way, and the GM may have to modify the narrative to keep them going. In all but the most rigid campaign structures are malleable points for keeping the story moving. Good GMs know that campaigns take on a life of their own.

While most creative endeavors focusing on story creation dwell heavily on an exciting climax, like many comic book or serialized television writers, most GMs do not even plan for an "end" to the campaign. Mostly, this is because if the campaign ends, the fun ends. Most players like the continuity of playing the same character over time and don't want to see things draw to a close (in the same way in which fans of a book or movie thirst for sequels to see more of their favorite characters).

The end to most campaigns comes when real-world concerns intervene, not when the story comes to a logical conclusion. A player moves away, the group gets an interest in another game or genre, or someone else decides to take on the role of the GM for a while—these are the things that end campaigns. In such a situation, the GM must wrap things up, often without a lot of forewarning. In such a case, the GM typically picks one possible short-term conclusion or some goal that can be achieved in the time remaining, and attempts to guide the campaign to that point. Some campaigns get no satisfactory conclusion at all, and the story is left unresolved.

With so much unresolved to start with and no planned ending, it would seem that role-playing game campaigns are not a good medium for telling a satisfying story. From a conventional point of view, that might be true. Few role-playing games produce stories that would make compelling narratives for a broad audience (at least not without heavy editing after the fact). The tales that come out of a campaign are likely only interesting to the people who participated in it. In a role-playing game, however, the participants are also the audience, or at least the only audience that matters. Their investment and interest in the story is the metric by which the campaign must be judged, not by an outsider who can only be told the story in a conventional way, with no direct relationship to the characters or events.

Serving as the Game Master

Being the game master in a role-playing game is by itself a daunting task. Equal parts mathematician, epic novelist, and improvisational actor, the GM performs many different kinds of tasks in the game. First and foremost, the GM creates the background for the story. Like a fantasy novelist, he or she invents a world or setting in which a story will occur. Entire books can be (and have been) written on the topic of world building. It is a huge undertaking, and perhaps one of the very heights of creative endeavor.

Of course, a GM can opt to purchase an "off-the-shelf" setting, such as *Ptolus: Monte Cook's City by the Spire* (2006), or base the game world on one already well established in fiction (Middle-earth or Camelot). A GM can even use the real world. Whichever it is, mastering that setting and its wealth of information is always a challenge. A GM likely pours a great deal of creativity into even a setting he or

10.1 Cover of *Ptolus: Monte Cook's City by the Spire*.

she did not create, either because the source material or his or her knowledge of it is incomplete.

A GM has to know a setting well enough that when a player asks a question, there is a ready answer. If the GM created the setting, he or she likely either knows the answer or feels comfortable making one up. But even if the setting is not the GM's own creation, the GM still has to come up with an answer on the spot. Either way, an accurate or at least consistent answer is vital to the game, because the players make decisions for their characters based on their knowledge of the world. If the information they receive does not make sense in the context at hand, they cannot make meaningful decisions. In other words, if the name of the mayor of the fictional hamlet of Edlesburg was "William" two game sessions ago, it had better be "William" today as well. And more important, if the river separating Edlesburg from the wilds of the Shadow Woods could not be forded previously, no one should be able cross it today, unless there is a ready and (at least eventually) apparent reason why things have changed. Maintaining consistency is one of the GM's most critical tasks. The game, on its most fundamental level, cannot function without some manner of consistency that the players can observe and thus act on.

The GM also creates and controls all the minor characters of the story. Similar to a novelist or screenwriter, the game master invents a host of characters that fill out the minor roles of the story or simply act as "extras" without lines at all. Not only does the GM flesh out these characters he or she also he controls them in the same way that the players control their own characters. But where a player will control only one character, a GM will have dozens or even hundreds of non-player characters (NPCs) on stage at any one time. Their actions in the game as well as their dialogue are the GM's purview; usually they simply react to the actions of the player characters, but sometimes they react to one another as well. These NPCs might be endangered townsfolk screaming for help, a grateful authority figure offering a reward, dangerous brigands threatening everyone around them, and even animals, rampaging monsters, or unknowable alien beings who act in unpredictable ways. Each have their (or its) own motivation, personality, and purpose in the story. Some work with the player characters, and some work against them; some ally with each other, and some operate at cross-purposes. All the while, the GM monitors, maintains, and portrays each and every one of them.

Lastly, of course, the GM manages the action of the story as he or she determines the success or failure of the deeds of the characters in the game. A campaign is an ongoing series of such sessions, requiring adjudication during the session, careful planning in between them, and narrative management at all times.

Perhaps the most obvious of a GM's duties is adjudicating the success or failure of all the characters' actions during a session. This is in-game management. When explaining the GM's job to a new player, a veteran role-player often starts

by describing the role of a judge, adjudicator, or referee, because this is the primary way in which the GM interacts with the players, and it sets the GM apart from them. While the GM's duty of controlling NPCs and managing events resembles the players' role of controlling their characters' actions, the GM alone possesses the authority to rule whether an action succeeds or fails.

Simply put, one can reduce a role-playing game to a session of questions and answers, with the players doing the asking and the game master doing the answering. The players ask, in essence, "What do we experience?" and the game master tells them. The players then provide a response, but it comes down to another question: "Do we succeed?" And the game master answers. Of course, the rules of the game and the all-important die rolls supply the metric for success or failure. In the role as the arbiter and referee, the GM does not necessarily create the rules, but he or she does enforce and occasionally interpret them. This is why most people refer to the GM's task as "running the game."

Managing a Campaign

It is, however, the out-of-game campaign management that is the most specialized of the GM's required tasks. In addition to creating the world, the side characters, and the foes, the GM conceives a story line for the campaign. Events do not simply end at the close of the session; they continue on to the next. The plot, too extensive to be completed in one session, keeps moving along as well. What this means is that a GM plans out a story line in advance, knowing full well that the story will be "told" episodically. While each session has its own beginning, middle, and end, the story line contains many sessions—sometimes dozens, and sometimes hundreds.

World creation and plot planning occur mainly before the campaign ever starts, but the management of the campaign happens between each of the sessions. When a game session ends, the GM is usually left with numerous dangling plot threads as well as a number of unresolved issues; it is almost impossible to wrap up all the consequences of the PCs' actions by the end of a session. Nor is it desirable to do so. Dangling plot threads and unresolved issues become story fodder for the next session. They provide the GM with material to work with "off stage" to connect the recent session with the next one. The break between sessions allows the GM to shape the world and story in response to the player characters' actions.

Reaction to player actions is vital to a role-playing campaign; it is part of what separates playing a game from reading a book or watching a movie. The players must feel that their characters' choices affect the world around them in some way. For instance, choosing to follow the cultists of the dark god to their secret temple provokes a reaction from the cult. Destroying the prison walls and freeing the convicts within results in an influx of criminals into the surrounding area. Routing the rampaging orc army brings peace to the land.

A wise GM can predict with a great deal of accuracy what choices the players will make for their characters and will prepare for the likely outcome ahead of time. The GM knows that the PCs looking for the secret temple will probably follow the cultists. The GM knows that if the PCs have a huge conflict within the prison, it is likely that the walls will be destroyed. He knows that the PCs will do everything they can to stop the orcs. The GM knows these things because the GM knows the players, because he or she has thought through the actions of the scenario ahead of time, and because he or she is subtly guiding them along a preplanned path. Sometimes, though, a turn of events in the game session may surprise the game master, requiring that both plans and setting are altered to accommodate the unfolding story's new direction.

Fluidity of the Game

In a role-playing game, these surprises can come from two different sources. First and foremost, the players can choose an unexpected path. In a story line involving a quest to protect some valuable jewels, the players might decide to have their characters steal the jewels for themselves. Or they might choose to forget all about the jewels and explore the wilderness instead. What's more, the GM may plan to have thieves steal the jewels right out from under the PCs' noses, but find that the players come up with a foolproof means of safeguarding them that the GM never considered.

The strength of a role-playing game is that the players have no limitations on what they can attempt. The GM creates a story, but the players do not have to participate in a prescribed way. They do not have to be a part of it at all if they wish—they can do something completely different. Most games operate with a sort of inherent unspoken agreement that the players will attempt to stay within the bounds of the story that the GM originally planned, but it may not always be clear to them exactly what that plan was. That unspoken agreement also compels the GM to provide the players with a story line that interests them; if their characters wander off to do something else, this may indicate that the GM's plan was not to the players' liking. In such a case, the GM may want to alter it as a part of his or her campaign management.

Second, however, the randomness inherent in the game can surprise both the game master and the players during a session. A routine encounter can go horribly awry because of a poor die roll. Or thanks to some amazingly good die rolls, a player character may accomplish something that should have been impossible—or at least impossible to predict. Some role-playing enthusiasts criticize this element of the games and attempt to minimize it (or even eliminate it through GM fiat), usually in the name of storytelling. Yet it is this very element that makes a role-playing game a *game*. Both the GM and the players may assume that they will succeed in overcoming some terrorists plotting to detonate a bomb under a stadium. But the possibility that they might fail is inherent within the game and provides real tension. Poor decisions and die rolls might result in the stadium's destruction. After this unexpected event occurs, the GM must rework the story line to accommodate it. The GM changes his or her setting to reflect the fact that the stadium is gone and determine how the people in the world—from the authorities to the main populace to the villains who perpetrated the vile act—are going to react. The game master must continually ask him- or herself "Well then, what happens *now*?"

From Session to Session

As part of campaign management, the game master must look at the events of the previous session from every possible angle to determine what is likely to happen in the next one. This involves a sort of out-of-game role-playing exercise on the GM's part. The GM takes on the role of all the people (or creatures) who might be affected by events of the previous session and determine their reaction. This might be as simple as deciding that the ogre in the dungeon heard a ruckus when the characters encountered a manticore in the next room and will come to investigate. It might be as complex as figuring out how various organizations will change to fill the vacuum left after the evil empire that controlled the galaxy collapses. Each session presents the GM with a new set of paradigms that he or she must use to plan for and guide the next session, all the while keeping the overall campaign story line in mind.

Sometimes the GM needs to come up with the means to guide a wandering campaign back to the original plot outline so that the story can continue, while at other times he or she must change the story to fit the events of a game session. Consider the following extremely simplistic example. A game master wishes to create a role-playing campaign story arc that involves a villainous noble who desires to assassinate a king and usurp the throne. He plans for the PCs to discover a series of clues to lead them ultimately into a confrontation with the villain and allow them to save the king. The PCs follow the first clue, but they make some mistakes and fail to follow it correctly to the second clue. Now the GM must present them with different clues to get them back on track. Later, the PCs get into combat with an NPC who is supposed to provide them with the third clue after they capture her. But in the course of events, she dies before she can give them the information. This time, the GM changes how the characters can discover the information and allows things to continue. All this time, the GM must continually keep in mind his setting and the NPCs who live there. Are the PCs taking too long to discover the noble's plot? If so, the villain might make his move against the king before the PCs are ready. What effect will this have on the plot? Perhaps rather than ending with the player characters saving the king, this campaign will conclude with them avenging the king and putting his rightful heir on the throne instead.

The session-based structure of a role-playing game campaign presents unique considerations for a GM to manage. If it were continuous and ongoing—which is to say, one long game session—there would be little time or opportunity for the GM to modify the story to react to player character actions. In creating a computer role-playing game, for example, the designers have to anticipate all player actions ahead of time and build in contingencies for those actions. Consequently, any action that the designers did not anticipate cannot happen in the game. Those actions are simply impossible within the framework of the programming. If, on the other hand, a role-playing game were purely episodic, with each session existing in a vacuum, there could be no continuing plots. Story lines could not extend across multiple sessions.

Flexibility in Action

Campaigns, then, are serialized, like some television series and most comic books. Like those media, the plot has been planned from the beginning. But in a role-playing game campaign, the game master has to be flexible enough to continually modify that story line as each game session is played out and the actions of the player characters change things. As stated previously, it is like a travel itinerary. The GM knows that he or she needs things to start at point A and continue to point B, and to observe ahead of time what direction point B lies from point A, but it is not until the players are involved that the GM will know the actual road choices (or to carry the analogy further, even the mode of travel that will be used), the timing of the trip, or the detours and stops along the way. The trick is, while managing a campaign, to cope with the changes needed to accommodate the players' actions while still getting the plotline to the proverbial point B.

Although they face their own challenges, the television series scriptwriter does not have to react to the unplanned actions of his or her characters. The comic book writer does not suddenly have to accommodate the failure of characters when he or she had assumed these characters would succeed (or vice versa). Creating a role-playing campaign is actually an ongoing process. The world-building and plot-planning creative work that the game master did at the beginning has to be modified continually. Unlike a fictional setting of a novel or movie, the setting of the game needs to be flexible—the GM has to be able to stick a dangerous set of troll-filled caves in a mountainous region that (in his or her original plan) had no such caves, if the story suddenly needs them for some reason. While writing *The Fellowship of the Ring*, J. R. R. Tolkien (1965) did not have to alter the location of Rivendell in the middle of the action because Frodo and the other hobbits went the wrong way. A GM, however, might have to make such a change to make things work in a role-playing game.

Alternatively, the GM may never have given the aforementioned mountainous region much advance thought, knowing that it would be better to provide such details only when the player characters approached the area. Only as the characters draw near to the peaks does the GM populate them with troll-filled caves, friendly villages of gnomes, or whatever the campaign now calls for. This can be a wise approach for the experienced GM. Rather than risk having to redo a lot of advance work, the GM details only the areas that the PCs are likely to deal with in the campaign's early sessions and keeps the rest of the campaign (both the setting and plot) sketchy and general. Of course, this results in a game where the world is being created just over the horizon from the player characters' perspective; an area really has no substance or life until just before they arrive there. The GM does not have to reveal that this is what's happening, though. The players do not need to know. In fact, it is crucial that they do not. This would imply that their actions have no consequence—that the game master can merely rearrange the world to suit his or her ultimate goals no matter what the players do. Certainly the game master could do just that, but the need for a cooperative storytelling experience is what sets role-playing campaigns apart from other types of narrative.

This delicate balance is why some GMs prefer to detail the world more concretely from the beginning; this creative groundwork makes it easier to portray the setting realistically to the players, even if it forces the GM to change some things later on. If the players realize that the GM is creating things as they go along, the setting loses all verisimilitude. For an optimal game experience, the players do not want to believe that the world revolves around their characters' choices. They want to embrace the fiction that the game setting is a "real" place and their characters are merely some of the people who live there. Allowing the players to think that the world exists only for their benefit diminishes the escapist nature of the hobby and, even more, lessens the triumph of their successes. If the dragon they slew was put there for them to slay, the experience is not as satisfying. Of course, this is all a self-deception—the dragon was there for them to slay no matter how one looks at it. But while the game continues, this fact need not—*should* not—be made unavoidably obvious.

Assisting the Game Master

Even though the job of a game master is challenging, lots of resources exist to make it less taxing and help improve a GM's performance, and thus the overall game experience. Some companies base their entire product lines around making the GM's task easier.

Creating products to help GMs requires a careful understanding of what they need and what they don't. A book like *Ptolus: Monte Cook's City by the Spire*, which attempts to be both a milieu in which GMs can set their campaigns and a detailed campaign guide in and of itself, is more like a toolbox for building a narrative than an independent narrative. It is basically a travel guidebook to a place that does not exist. Its purpose is to allow the GM who purchases it to become a tour guide for that imaginary place.

Ptolus provides the game master with a setting that is extremely intricate. It gives the GM general setting details, specific locations within that setting (with descriptions and maps), and premade NPCs. It also gives the game master complete scenarios and adventure locations—enough that a GM can run an entire campaign and never need to create one entirely on their own. Neither of these things makes *Ptolus* unique, however. There are dozens of complete campaign settings and hundreds of designed scenarios that GMs can buy. Where *Ptolus* attempts to shine is in how it addresses the specific needs of a GM running a campaign. For example, there are various types of encounter that occur in virtually every campaign, but that GMs commonly do not prepare for: "random person on the street" encounters, "rumor-spewing shopkeeper" encounters, and so on. *Ptolus* provides such encounters, written up and ready for GMs to use. These are virtually without context, and intentionally so. They are meant to be springboards to new adventures or experiences, not to tie into what is going on in the campaign at the moment. They also help maintain the illusion that there is a whole world of events going on around the PCs that does not involve the PCs (until the PCs get involved, that is).

There are other approaches to designing a product to help a GM running a campaign as well. There are general sources of game master advice, like the first chapter of the *Dungeon Master's Guide* (2000) or the book *Game Mastering Secrets* (2003), screens for displaying handy charts, and of course the aforementioned premade campaign settings and adventure scenarios, but those that deal specifically with the challenges of handling campaign play are actually somewhat rare. Some of these come in the form of record-keeping tools like *Campaign Planner Deluxe* (2005), a set of premade forms and record sheets to help organize notes (and remind the GM of what he or she needs to create to be ready). Managing an ongoing campaign requires the GM to think through the ramifications that certain events will have on the game world. What would happen if a war broke out between two neighboring kingdoms in the setting that the GM has crafted, for example? What would be the immediate and long-term effects of such a conflict? And how would this war affect the player characters? Game products like *Cry Havoc* (2003), *Requiem for a God* (2002), and *When the Sky Falls* (2003)—so-called event books—present single monumental events (a war, the death of a god, and the fall of a massive meteor, respectively) that can happen in a fantasy campaign. They do not provide the GM with an entire campaign or even a single scenario; instead, these books present tools for incorporating a single event into a campaign, and advice for crafting the implications and ramifications of doing so.

Today GMs also learn by examining what other GMs do in their campaigns. Rather than learning from reading fiction or watching movies—which are really different types of creative endeavors that lack many of the challenges of running a campaign—GMs can read online "campaign logs" written by other GMs. These accounts of different campaigns are almost always written in a standard narrative format, making them read, at first blush, like standard fiction. Yet informed and insightful readers know that what they are reading is really a transcript of a campaign. They can see how unexpected events or surprising player choices arose, and how the GM reacted to them. These opportunities to learn by example may well be the most valuable tool available to teach GMs how to properly handle the monumental task of managing a role-playing game campaign.

Creating and maintaining a role-playing campaign is a little like writing an ongoing episodic story like a comic book or television show—but one in which the writer is not in control of the main characters. It is as much about reacting to what the characters do as it is about planning story arcs. It is about managing an entire world and determining how its inhabitants respond to the actions of the characters while maintaining the desired story arc. It is about giving the players what they want and providing the story line what it needs to continue. It is the very heart of the role-playing game hobby.

References: Literature

ENWorld Story Hours. ⟨http://www.enworld.org/forumdisplay.php?f=14⟩.

Infiniti Campaign Log. ⟨http://p222.ezboard.com/fokayyourturnfrm17.showMessage?topicID=2086.topic⟩.

Praemal Chronicles. ⟨http://praemal.blogspot.com⟩.

Tolkien, J. R. R. (1965). *The Fellowship of the Ring*. New York: Random House.

References: Games

Campaign Planner Deluxe. Philip J. Reed; Ronin Arts. 2005.

Cry Havoc. Skip Williams; Malhavoc Press. 2003.

Dungeon Master's Guide. Monte Cook, Jonathan Tweet, and Skip Williams; Wizards of the Coast. 2000.

Game Mastering Secrets. Aaron Rosenberg; Grey Ghost Games. 2003.

Ptolus: Monte Cook's City by the Spire. Monte Cook; Malhavoc Press. 2006.

Requiem for a God. Monte Cook; Malhavoc Press. 2002.

When the Sky Falls. Bruce R. Cordell; Malhavoc Press. 2003.

Alice and Dorothy Play Together

Richard A. Bartle

Curiouser and curiouser!
—Lewis Carroll, *Alice's Adventures in Wonderland* (1865)

We will go to the Emerald City and ask the Great Oz
how to get back to Kansas again.
—L. Frank Baum, *The Wonderful Wizard of Oz* (1900)

According to the conventions of fiction, it would seem that
when a young girl finds herself unexpectedly in a strange
and wonderful place, she has two ways to proceed. She can,
as Dorothy did, set out to follow a predetermined path; or
she can, as Alice did, go where fortune takes her.

The same two options are available to players of virtual
worlds.[1] When they begin, they can either follow the yellow
brick road laid out before them or simply wander as they
will. The advantage of the former is that they know where
they're going; the advantage of the latter is that they'll see
things that can't be seen from the well-trodden trail.

The journeys of Alice and Dorothy both occur at two
different conceptual levels: literally, in the imaginary
worlds of Wonderland and Oz; figuratively, in the self-
understanding of the protagonists. The former are metaphors for the latter—they're *hero's journeys* (Campbell
1949). Thus, when Dorothy sets out along the yellow brick
road, she is traveling not so much to find the Great Oz as
to find herself. Alice's outing in Wonderland is far less
directed, but it nevertheless holds that same promise of
personal growth.[2]

Virtual world designers, through their creations, necessarily affect their players.[3] Rather than merely *suggesting* a
hero's journey, however, virtual worlds are unique among
fictional constructs in that they enable players actually to
undertake their own, personal hero's journey directly.
Designers, in the shaping of their virtual worlds, have immense influence on how players do this. Should they foster

an environment in which the path to self-understanding is
set out from the beginning (a Dorothy world) or should
they encourage players to find their own way (an Alice
world)? And why is the distinction an issue anyway?

To answer these questions, it's instructive to take a brief
look at how they came to be in competition.

Designers of early virtual worlds took the Alice approach, at least at the level of giving players goals: their
aim was to provide what might today be called a *sandbox*—an open-ended world in which players can explore
both their environment and themselves.[4] Although there
was a given overall objective (to acquire, through action,
sufficient points to reach some "you have won" total), quite
how this was to be achieved, well, that was up to the individual. The fun was in the journey, not in the arrival.

A decade or so later, in 1989, there was a sudden shift
in attitudes. A fresh kind of virtual world came along: the
social world. Previously, almost all virtual worlds had been
couched in terms of being *games*; with *TinyMUD* (1989),
the game aspect was explicitly and entirely removed. Not
only did the players have no set paths to follow but the virtual world itself offered none: it was a playground, rather
than a game. There was therefore never any pretense that
such worlds might be anything other than adjuncts to reality.[5] Their players had much the same view as Wendy in
Peter Pan (Barrie 1911), for whom Neverland was an extension of her own imagination; thus, we might call these newcomers Wendy worlds.[6]

In reaction to this antigame swing, further virtual worlds
were developed (primarily in Scandinavia) that were even
more gamelike than their predecessors.[7] They structured
and formalized playing styles, chiefly by using ideas imported from tabletop role-playing games such as *Advanced
Dungeons & Dragons* (2003). In *MUD1* (1978), if you
wanted to be a mage, a thief, or a warrior, you merely had
to act like one (use a lot of magic, sneak around stealing
things, or hit things with swords); in *DikuMUD* (1990), if
you wanted to be a mage, a thief, or a warrior, you chose
the character class Mage, Thief, or Warrior. You couldn't
even *occasionally* sneak around and steal things as a mage
or warrior, because only predefined thieves could do that.
You no longer had to find your own way; you chose which

track to run on, and then set out to follow it. Newbies in particular liked this Dorothy way of doing things.[8] And because the socially oriented players who had always railed against it had by now left for the *TinyMUD* derivatives, it rapidly established itself as the dominant form.[9]

In the original, Alice worlds, designers provided a fixed overall goal, but the player roles were left undetermined. The 1989 schism led to gamelike Dorothy worlds, in which the player roles were also preordained, and to the social Wendy worlds, in which the player roles *and* the overall reason for playing were both left unstated. Alice worlds were no longer created; new worlds were either Dorothy or Wendy worlds, depending on the players' preferences.

This partitioning gave designers new energy and focus. They were able to add more of what their particular player base wanted, because each was no longer constrained by the needs of the other. Thus, the gap between them widened, until it became the gulf it is today.[10]

Yes, we do still have this divide. The vast majority of virtual worlds, whether commercial or hobbyist, are gamelike (Dorothy) worlds, with the leading title at the moment being *World of Warcraft* (2004) at close to 8,500,000 players. There are also social (Wendy) worlds of some significance, however—the most important of which is *Second Life* (2003) with its 450,000 or so users.[11] The players of those few balanced (Alice) worlds that remain usually consider them to be game-related, while nevertheless recognizing that they're somehow different than Dorothy worlds; the closest that we have to one in terms of the large-scale graphic worlds of today is probably *Ultima Online* (1997), which still has over 100,000 players even as it enters its second decade.[12]

Now it's easy to look at this history, and suppose that Dorothy and Wendy worlds are the future, with Alice worlds as mere relics of the past. It's easy, but it's unwise. Here's why: Dorothy and Wendy worlds were each deliberately established to reject the tenets of the other, but some of those tenets are actually relevant to both. Yet because of their opposing views, they can't simply expropriate the ideas they need—the contextual differences are too great. Dorothy and Wendy can't play together.

Both, though, *can* play with Alice.

As its title suggests, this chapter is concerned with just one of the two options available: how concepts from (balanced) Alice worlds can help (gamelike) Dorothy worlds. This isn't because they can't help the (social) Wendy worlds but rather because the Dorothy worlds' needs are currently more pressing. In particular, a big problem that Dorothy worlds have right now is that the kind of content they need is expensive to create. Alice worlds, which also have gamelike content, are significantly less costly.[13] Shortly, we will see why.

Furthermore, although the Dorothy style has been dominant for over fifteen years, there remains among game world designers a lingering suspicion that by dropping the Alice perspective, they were somehow losing something important. Dorothy emphasizes *game* over Alice's *world*; Dorothy *sets* a narrative, whereas Alice's narrative *emerges*; Dorothy's certainty appeals to *newbies*; Alice's freedom appeals to *oldbies*. Surely there's some room for maneuver here?

As a result, there is an ongoing dialectic among designers as to which way is ultimately the better one. Although in the past this has been merely an academic exercise (people play Dorothy worlds in droves, so why change anything?), of late, as the expense of competing with *World of Warcraft* on its own terms has become apparent, the issue has begun to assume some urgency. Yet how can prospective players be persuaded to risk engaging in an Alice world when some competing game will always be happy to offer them the assurances of Dorothy?

The answer, I propose, is that it really doesn't matter. A virtual world can cater to the needs of both Alice and Dorothy *at the same time*.

On Story

What is a story?

Well, it's anything running the gamut of narrative, with individual events (real or imaginary) at one end and full-blown novels at the other. Games have a story, even abstract ones like *Tetris* (1985): tell someone about how you were close to filling up the box, how only one tile shape and color would do, and how wow, it came, and you only *just* slotted it in, whereupon it triggered off a chain reaction that collapsed the whole pile into practically nothing—

Table 11.1

	Backstory	Story	History
Individual	Your character's family was slaughtered by lizard people	You must defeat the ogres to gain the respect of the villagers	That time you were accused of robbery when it was an accident
Group	Mages cannot wear mail because iron interferes with their spells	It will take our combined effort to stand up to the powerful dragon	Raising the money for a guild-hall took weeks, but brought us together
World	Following the Gold War, the world settled into an uneasy peace	A conspiracy to resurrect the Golden Gods in more terrible form	This drought came because players burst a dam to destroy Goldfort

that's a story.[14] Yes, it's the story of how you played the game, and it may not be all that compelling, but it's still a story.

Although this broad range of narrative is almost a continuum, it's not quite: there are some step changes within it. Interaction is one of the key ones. All stories are interactive, in that they're written for an audience (even if it's an audience of one—the writer), but some are more interactive than others. If you watch a movie, your behavior in the audience does not affect what you see, although it may affect the experience of others in the audience; if you watch a play, the actors can pick up on audience reactions and make subtle adjustments to their performance. Similarly, if you play a game with more than one player, you're interacting not only with the designer but also (and more immediately) with the other players; moreover, you're doing this as an audience to both the designer's story and one another's emerging personal histories (which are themselves a form of story). Virtual worlds, with many, many players, are highly interactive—so much so that tracking all the overlapping stories going on within them is next to impossible.

Nevertheless, it is possible to describe the *kind* of stories that virtual worlds exhibit. They essentially come in three forms:

- *Backstory* Describing the initial setup[15]

- *Story* Describing the plot actively being followed

- *History* Describing events that have happened since the backstory ended

These stories can involve any number of players, from one to all of them. To simplify, let's say that they'll concern either:

- *Individuals* For example, your personal struggle to reconcile your desire to help others with the dark magic you must practice to deliver this help

- *Groups* The orcs' attempts, say, to gain self-esteem through honest industry in response to the shame they feel following their defeat in a major war

- *World* For instance, the comet will strike the planet unless the players can deflect it

This gives us a handy grid.

The backstory serves two purposes: to add context, and to provide fictional cover for otherwise troubling decisions. As an example of the latter, a designer may decide that if healing-oriented characters were to be allowed to wield swords, it would make them too powerful. The designer therefore decrees that healers can't use swords. Although this makes sense in terms of the gameplay, it makes no sense within the game fiction. Why *shouldn't* a healer use a sword? The designer thus adds some backstory to explain that healers are sponsored by the god of life, for whom blood is the symbol of the god of life's divinity. If healers shed the blood of others, the god of life will not grant them healing powers. Healers, then, must use blunt weapons such as maces and war hammers, or offend their deity and lose their healing powers. This justification after the fact becomes part of the world's lore, and may then be used as a springboard to generate new story ideas independently (perhaps the elimination of a cult of vampire worshippers who are affecting the ability of healers to function in some part of the world).

History, although often confused with the backstory, is apart from it. It begins when the backstory ends, being the retelling of causally related events such that they form a narrative. It emerges from action and interaction, rather than being fixed as flavor text. Best of all, it comes almost for free: so long as players have interesting things to do in virtual worlds, they have interesting things to relate to other players. They collate these into anecdotes (i.e., story form) and so build on the backstory to provide an ongoing, living history.

The story (in this context) means a predetermined plot that is being followed by the players, groups, or world. In general, world-level stories take so much effort to implement that they pretty well have to be linear in nature, which leads to all kinds of problems to do with players' feelings of impotence in the face of unavoidable impending doom (Bartle 2003). Group-level stories, again, tend to be linear, but are less epic; there are usually several different ways to thread through them, and failure is a viable ending. Individual-level stories are multiple and overlapping, as with soap operas, such that by the time you're done with one quest, you're already engaged with another.

In all virtual worlds (Alice, Dorothy, and Wendy), history invariably arises from player action, whether as individuals, groups, or an agglomeration. Also in all such worlds, the players concerned will write the individual backstories (when they are written at all).[16] Beyond that, though, the backstory as well as the story can be created either by players or the virtual world's designers, and it's here that the difference between traditions is laid bare:

- Dorothy worlds have their backstories and stories created by their designers

- Alice worlds have their backstories created by their designers, but their stories created by their players

- Wendy worlds have their backstories and stories created entirely by their players

Creating a story is expensive because so much of it is needed and so much of it can't be reused from other stories.[17] As a general rule, the greater the number of players who are affected by a story, the more expensive it becomes to create. Virtual worlds wouldn't need instances if there were enough story experiences—what designers call *content*—to go around, but there aren't enough and so instances have to substitute.[18]

Alice worlds don't provide a story; what they offer is the mechanism for a story to arise within a framework that is explained by the backstory and realized as the game world. Dorothy worlds do supply a story, but at the cost of employing designers to create it. Wendy worlds provide neither story nor backstory; as with Alice worlds, they do supply the mechanism for a story to arise, but they place the entire burden of narrative context on the players. In other words, if you want a story in a Wendy world, you have to write it yourself.[19]

Wendy worlds have no formal game content and do little to promote any personal hero's journey. Because of this, they take no further part in this chapter's analysis. Alice and Dorothy worlds do both strive to give their players the chance to *be* or *become* who they really *are*, but differ in their philosophies as to how best to promote this. Alice worlds give players the freedom to find their own way, yet suffer because newbies can't easily inform their choices. Dorothy worlds explain what the main choices are and offer direction, but prevent players from finding what might be their ideal were it to lie somewhere in between the prescribed paths.

So we have Dorothy worlds and Alice worlds, both of which want to give the players a narrative experience that equates to their participation in a hero's journey, but disagreeing on how best to do this. Their designers share the opinion that while they own a backstory, the history is emergent from player activity; however they diverge when it comes to plot. Because, on the grand scale, an overall narrative is extremely difficult to keep on track (let alone sufficiently compelling to engage the majority of players), the main unit of story for virtual worlds is the quest. The two conventions handle these somewhat differently.

On Quests

In both Dorothy and Alice worlds, players have things they want to do, which they express in terms of goals. In practice, there's the overall "game" goal that is ostensibly driving their play, and then there are the smaller (personal and group) goals that are steps along the way. These intermediate goals lead to self-contained mininarratives that players call *quests*. Their opposite—playing without aiming to solve any specific goal (simply killing monsters for points, say)—is *grinding*. Players like quests, but they don't like grinding. Quests that involve much repeated action with little narrative connection to a goal are often regarded as a form of grinding, too, as in a "prove your ability by killing ten lesser Xs and five X mages" template (which when achieved, inevitably leads to "prove your further ability by killing fifteen greater Xs and ten X arch mages").

So where do quests come from?

There are three main sources:

- Handcrafted quests, created by game designers

- Automatic quests, created by a program code that has been specified by the virtual world's designers

- Emergent quests, created by the players

Dorothy worlds always have the first one, frequently have the second one, and only have the third one by accident. Alice worlds only have the third one.

In terms of players' shared experience, handcrafted quests are usually the best, so long as the designers know what they're doing in terms of storytelling (Sheldon 2004). Automatic quest generation (in which the designers try to generate story content procedurally, typically because they don't have enough resources to handcraft it all) is universally dismal.[20] Emergent quests, wherein players give themselves or each other things to do, are, at least in Dorothy worlds, often tantamount to grinding (e.g., killing 362 voidcallers over the course of six hours to obtain the pattern required to make Robes of Arcana).[21]

It doesn't have to be this way!

Let's look closer at what's going on.

In Dorothy worlds, quests are the molecules of a preconstructed narrative. The designers determine how these are put together, and their constituents—the "atoms"—are not directly accessible to players. For example, a quest may involve the killing of a wizard to obtain a potion required by a witch; although there is some freedom in how they go about killing the wizard, there is no possibility that the potion can be acquired any other way (e.g., made by a player or bought from the wizard) and no way of addressing the witch's stated need except by performing the quest (e.g., there is never anything other than that *one potion* that will do). That said, the way they *are* put together is sufficient to sustain anything from fifteen minutes to six hours of usually entertaining gameplay for one or more players, albeit they're expensive to create.

Alice worlds don't have formal quests. Their granularity of story is much finer—they deal only with the atoms, leaving the players themselves to build the molecules. Players have goals not because the game gives them those goals but because the world does.[22] In an Alice world, the witch mourns her lost youth; the potion may restore her looks, but so might an apple that has been dunked in the fountain of eternal youth; and the attentions of a toyboy satyr may make her decide she's fine as she is anyway. Solutions to dramatic tensions are resolved through the combination by the players of small narrative units, rather than by tackling a handcrafted but larger unit provided by the designers.

While Alice worlds don't have formal quests, they do have narrative possibilities. To create these, designers anticipate what players will want to do and add obstacles; this creates a narrative tension. The designers also provide the means for players to circumvent those obstacles; these narrative fragments offer plot, the following through of which by player action leads to history (in its retelling). The crucial thing to note about stories in Alice worlds is that over time, these atoms of narrative accrue until eventually they reach a critical mass such that when the designer adds a new obstacle, the means to avoid or evade it may well be *already in place*.

For example, the designer may decide to add a complex of rooms far underground, accessible only through a deep shaft. The first solution that players will think of is to use magic to float down, so the designer adds a series of jagged rocks sticking out that will impale players even if they are in some kind of slow fall. In a barn nearby, however, the designer places a length of rope; now the players can construct the narrative molecule: "go to the barn, obtain the rope, come back to the shaft, and use the rope to get down." So far, so good, but now suppose that some players have teleport stones. You leave one in a location and you can teleport to it if you carry its mate. This system may originally have been introduced as a mechanism for allowing players to get back to town quickly after a long session out in the wilderness, yet it now offers a solution to the shaft puzzle: drop a teleport stone down the shaft, and then teleport to the bottom once it lands. Thus, although the designer added a solution (the rope), another solution already existed.

Virtual worlds that have this critical mass of narrative atoms are said to be *rich*. All Alice worlds are rich to some degree. Dorothy worlds tend not to be, on account of how their story is put together at the molecular (quest) level, so there are fewer possibilities for quest/quest interaction; also, richness leaves them more open to exploits.[23] They do have the potential for richness, though, primarily in crafting. For example, you may know how to make a number of potions, some of which are directly useful to you and others, of which you can sell some for profit. Off you go to collect the plants, salves, and other things you need to make the potions. There's no formal quest to "make twenty potions of healing"; it's something you decided to do to satisfy a goal that you created from nowhere. There may be several different ways to obtain the ingredients you wanted, although probably not enough to qualify as being rich (could you grow your own bloodweed or do you have to pick it from the wild?). The point is, though, that it's not a molecular quest, it's a quest you made yourself that is achievable using only the atomic actions you can perform —it's *emergent*.

The question arises, Is this grinding? If it is, players won't be too happy about doing it. It would certainly be grinding if you had to make a hundred expensive yet useless potions in order to gain the expertise you needed to make that one potion you *really* wanted, but assuming that there's a reasonable return for the investment of your time,

you probably wouldn't have this point of view. After all, if it were likely to feel like grinding, you wouldn't have begun it in the first place.

In Alice worlds, the richer the world is, the less the grind. You don't do a quest because some quest giver adds it to your quest list; you do it because it's *your* goal you want to satisfy. Non-player characters are then obstacles to overcome or circumvent, not mere dispensers of mininarratives. Players make their *own* stories, rather then following those of the designers.

Is that a good or bad thing?

On Structure

Needless to say, Alice worlds regard this as a good thing. Their philosophy is one of freedom: the world is structured, but the game is unstructured. Players do whatever they find to be the most fun; they determine their own path to self-understanding.

Dorothy worlds, on the other hand, consider it a bad thing. Their philosophy is one of structured play. Too few players know or are prepared to discover what they find to be the most fun; they prefer to be given direction that is appropriate to their basic preferences.

Each of these philosophies is apt, but only for some of the time. Dorothy's philosophy means choosing the narrative path you wish to take before you take it, which sounds attractive at first yet suffers because people change as they play (Bartle 2003, 2005); what's right now may—indeed, probably *will*—be wrong later. Alice's philosophy means changing the narrative path as you follow it, which sounds unattractive at first yet comes into its own when people take the wrong direction at the start or find that the path doesn't go where they thought it went.

Put this way, it can be seen that these philosophies are not irreconcilable. You ought to be able to start to play by following Dorothy's example, but have the option of switching to Alice's when it seems right. So why don't we have virtual worlds that allow you to do this?

The main reason is that game at the literal level has become detached as a metaphor from the journey that gives it its meaning. Although most designers have a solid understanding of *what* they're designing, too few have a grasp of *why* they're designing it. It's as if they're creating a cookbook filled with increasingly difficult-to-make dishes, neglecting to consider whether the results might actually be edible or not. Yes, you do learn to cook, but it would be better if you'd learned to cook things you could eat.

How do Dorothy worlds provide players a narrative path? Through quests delivered at appropriate points, so the players feel as if they're achieving things as they're lead inexorably toward the final level? Well yes, but a series of quests to add experience points to a character doesn't say a great deal about the advancement of the player as a *person*. There's a disconnection between the narrative and the purpose of the narrative. The purpose of the narrative is, in fact, defined by an entirely different system: the available character classes (and to some extent, races). These prime players have atomic actions they can use to overcome the obstacles that the quests put before them. You don't progress on your hero's journey because you completed a quest; you progress because you completed it as a heat-of-the-battle sword swinger, a long-range missile thrower, a sneaky backstabber, or whatever; you completed it according to your *role*—these are, after all, role-playing games.

It's within the narrow band of their role that players' personal journeys take place. The quest-determined game narrative is supposed to be reflective of this journey, but this is too infrequently the case. Quests are there to give players something to do; they should be there as waypoints.

There is some flexibility here. If there are enough quests, players can pick and choose those that suit them best, carving out their own narrative in a way that mirrors their further understanding of their character. Quests, as I keep saying, are expensive to create, though. There may also be some discretion in the rigidity to which players are held to their character classes; adjustment might be possible as specializations kick in at higher character levels. Yet on the whole in Dorothy worlds, it's still the case that if you play as a fighter, you're not going to be able to cast druid spells, and that if you play as a druid, you won't be as good in a toe-to-toe tussle as a fighter. This means they're fine if you pick a role for which you are well matched, but a pain if you choose a wrong one.

Alice worlds have a much closer bond between character activity and players' self-exploration. Eschewing formal quests, players can only do things that they themselves want to do, in a manner of their own choosing. This lack of structure is alarming for many players, however; they just want to play a game, not undergo some mystical transformation of the soul.[24] Dumping them in a world and telling them to get on with it requires too much effort on their part. They sense the difference between a game world (Dorothy) and a world that's a place to game (Alice). When they start, they want the former, not the latter.

The hero's journey demands a connection between the advancement of the protagonist (i.e., the character) and the advancement of the reader (i.e., the player). Dorothy worlds have an accessible advancement of the character (through quests), an accessible advancement of the player (through character classes), and yet a poor connection between the two (the quests don't promote the players' self-exploration).[25] Alice worlds have an inaccessible advancement of the character (make-your-own quests), an inaccessible advancement of the player (be your own person), and yet a strong connection between the two (you do what you most need to do right now).

Dorothy's structure gives it accessibility, but it drives a wedge between the player and the character. Alice's lack of structure keeps the player and the character in step, but is hard to get into. If Dorothy worlds could have more flexible classes, that would allow players to adjust their playing styles in response to the quests presented to them; if Alice worlds could have quests that looked like quests, that would allow players to engage with the world while finding the solutions that worked best for them.

Actually, Alice worlds *could* have quests. So why don't they have them?

Actually, Dorothy worlds *could* have flexible classes. So why don't they have them?

The answer is partly doctrinal and partly practical.

Alice worlds are *about* freedom. If you offer any restrictions, you're cutting back on freedom. Character classes are restrictions and therefore they have no place in Alice worlds. Also, from a practical point of view, as soon as you have classes you have issues of balance. Some classes will inevitably have an easier time of it than others, so players will either gravitate toward the same few classes or they'll quit in frustration.

Dorothy worlds are *about* structure. A game with no rules is no game at all.[26] If you remove too much structure, you remove the game. Classes are structure, and removing them takes away an interesting decision (i.e., a piece of gameplay) and diminishes them as a game.[27] Also, from a practical point of view, if you don't have classes then players will max their characters out in every direction so they become invincible machines that can fight, heal, and lob fireballs with impunity.[28]

Looking first at the practical issues, the concern of both games is that players will wind up being clones of each other. But the reasons for such anxiety are largely historical and no longer apply. Alice games came from an era when not only was player *versus* player combat the norm but so was permadeath.[29] In other words, if one class had *any* tangible advantage over another, you *had* to play it, or else you'd be attacked and lose your character permanently. Today's virtual worlds are tame by these standards, and there is no longer such great pressure to play one class rather than another.[30]

Dorothy worlds' worries about maxed-out characters are also less justified than they were, because the tabletop role-playing games they drew the ideas from in the first place have advanced since the 1980s. Whereas before it was a case of "if we let mages wear armor, they'll be unstoppable!" nowadays even *Advanced Dungeons & Dragons* has arcane spell failure for armor types worn by multiclass characters.[31] The backstory has been adapted not to prevent mages from ever wearing armor but rather to allow players to choose whether their character should spend the next few encounters as a mage or a fighter. In tabletop role-playing games, players can play maxed-out characters without causing imbalance, because although they're multiclass as a general concept, they can only be effectively one class at any one time while playing.[32] This could easily be done in Dorothy worlds, too.

Turning now to the philosophical objections that Alice and Dorothy have for each other's methodologies, all it takes to reconcile the two is a little more open-mindedness.

They're currently set up as if the opposing point of view were so bad that it must not be allowed to taint the purity of the "true vision," yet this hardly reflects the actual relationship between the two: unlike the case with Dorothy and Wendy worlds, players can happily play both an Alice or Dorothy world without any feelings of "betraying the cause." Alice worlds' conviction that freedom of expression through play is all, and therefore constraint on such expression is heinous, has a certain charming contrariness about it. To be true to itself, shouldn't it allow players the freedom to play in a constrained fashion, just so long as they can always stray back into less structured territory if they wish?

Likewise, Dorothy worlds' belief that players should be educated rather than self-taught in the ways of self-fulfillment—even when much of the education involves what amounts to private study—is also overly dogmatic. For any path to become well trodden, someone has to find the path in the first place. Where is the harm in allowing players to wander if they can always come back safely to the highway?

All it would take to do this is a class system built from smaller bricks that players can customize as they see fit—skill based or gear based, say.[33] Players who want to be a generic mage begin by choosing the generic mage template, and there they are, ready to play; players who want to be a mage specializing in necromancy, demonology, conjuration, or whatever can take the basic template and tinker with the starting parameters a bit; players who want to be a mage who can pick locks and backstab enemies can build their own combination mage/rogue class from scratch (or download one that someone else has put on the Internet). As characters advance, players can either choose their own advances (Alice style) or go with the ones the game recommends (Dorothy style). The result: both camps are happy.

So Alice and Dorothy can play together. Now, at last, we can examine why they'd want to do that.

On Emergence

Alice worlds are unstructured. This makes them relatively cheap to implement, but acquiring newbies is relatively expensive.

Dorothy worlds are structured. This makes them relatively expensive to implement, but acquiring newbies is relatively cheap.

If we can get the lack of structure of Alice worlds to provide the structure of Dorothy worlds, we end up with a hybrid that is relatively cheap to implement and for which acquiring newbies is *also* relatively cheap. We get the best of both—*if* it can be done.

It can be.

Alice gives the world, but needs the game; Dorothy gives the game, but needs the world. In theory, then, if we construct an Alice experience so that it can generate what a Dorothy experience needs, the Dorothy experience can in turn generate what the Alice experience needs. We can achieve this by designing for the Alice world concept of *richness*. Having sufficient interactions between objects, player characters, non-player characters, monsters, and locations will lead to a critical mass situation, in which these interactions themselves give rise to the goals that players tackle as quests. Furthermore, they'll add tension and conflict, making for narrative in their resolution. In a rich world, goals come as a side effect of that richness—just as they do in the real world, which manages to be pleasingly interesting for individuals without the clumsy attention of any designer.[34]

Here's an example of how an emergent goal can appear.

When I start to play, all I know is that if I kill things I'll get better at it. So when I appear in the world surrounded by low-level wildlife, I set about obliterating them. At this point, I have no quest, I'm just grinding. The creatures behave differently, depending on their type, which holds my interest for a while. After a few minutes, I'm killing bears because, basically, there are bears here and I get points for killing them. I notice at this point that the bears are so big, even an inexperienced character like mine can skin them, so OK, I'll take those bear skins. The meat looks a bit tough, though, so I'll leave that. After a while longer, I have a stack of bear skins and decide to sell them, except no one wants bear skins. What use are bear skins? What people want are coats to keep out the cold. So I take a bear skin and try to make a coat, and mess up, but I take another, and clean it up better and sew it better, and after a few more attempts

I wind up with a coat. Now I have something other people want. I get some coins in exchange for the coat. I make some more coats, I get some more coins, and then I decide that really I'd rather be killing bears, so I hire some nonplayer characters to make the coats and go back into the woods. After some more of this, however, I get bored of killing bears and it starts to feel like work rather than play. I therefore put up a notice offering money to people who bring bear pelts to my workshop. The next newbie who comes along no longer has to grind: they can see there's coin to be made from killing bears, so that's what they do. Their quest to kill bears has arisen entirely from my actions. It's an emergent consequence of the richness of the virtual world.

That's an example showing how goals can arise through economics. Yet this kind of quest can feel rather grindy after a while, and the interaction between competing enterprises can affect how worthwhile their quests are. If everyone sets up a bear skin coat cottage industry, the result will be either too few bears or too many coats. Nevertheless, all is not lost, as changes in circumstances can lead to tension between rival producers, which ultimately leads to politics. Your low-cost coats are putting the coat makers of my village out of business, so if you want to sell the coats here, you'll have to pay a tariff.

Political quests are far more interesting, far less grindful, and altogether more compelling than other quests. They vary, too; that blow-up-the-bridge-to-ruin-your-trade quest is a one-off. The situation won't be as it is in some worlds, where you rest after having just killed a major figure, then stand up and see someone else killing him again right before your eyes while his recently dead form is still lying there.[35]

It's not just the quests that change but also the way you solve them. That harpoon launcher you built to shoot down dragons might be just the thing to take a rope across a ravine. The bowl you use to teleport objects to your vault may be able to do the same thing to incoming fireballs.[36] The metal balls you fling with your sling could be scattered around you before you sleep, to alert you if anyone tries to sneak up and slit your throat. Also, it's not just objects that interact but their uses as well; when things have multiple applications, there are multiple interactions, and therefore multiple (potentially conflicting) goals will arise from them.

Traditionally, this kind of world was the exclusive preserve of the Alice approach. Predetermined quests were seen as overconstraining, straitjacketing players into doing things they didn't want to do. Designers wanted their players to have the freedom to *live* the world, not just to *play* it. Unfortunately, while this is fine for players who have grown into their character, it's not much good for newbies, who as far as they are concerned, *do* just want to play it.

Why should it be Alice only, though? There's no reason why the Dorothy worlds couldn't employ this system. Players of such games may crave direction, but that doesn't mean the direction has to be set out by the game designer through quests; it could be set out through opportunities for players to create their own quests. Also, just because this produces a good many quests, high in context and strongly related to each other, that doesn't mean there's *no* room for handmade quests. Designers can, if they wish, prebuild quest chains of their own, to keep the narrative pace and hint at a backstory so as to make the world feel more alive. The thing is, they don't have to create anywhere near as many of these quests as they would have done without the Alice quests in support, and although making a world rich enough for a critical mass is not free, it's a lot less expensive than one in which all the quests are lovingly crafted by storytellers who can't code or coders who can't storytell.[37]

In this suggested approach, the designer constructs a world with no story line, but with a lush capacity for interaction. This results in a framework for the creation of a story by the players themselves. The designer doesn't determine what particular stories become manifest but does determine what kind of stories *can* become manifest—what quests can emerge.

Is this possible? Can a world really be complex enough that players give themselves their goals, rather than relying on the designer to do it for them?

Well, yes, it can; we're seeing the beginnings of it now, with the impressive *EVE Online* (2003) at the forefront. *EVE* manages to sustain a player-driven, emergent quest system while still feeling as if it were a game. OK, so it's not exactly newbie friendly, but it nevertheless shows that what once was the sole preserve of Alice can now be shared with Dorothy to the benefit of both. It may seem like a paradox, but the result of adding more content aimed at players who don't want directed play really *can* help those who do.

Conclusion

Historically, there have been three philosophies for designing virtual worlds: Alice worlds, Dorothy worlds, and Wendy worlds. Alice worlds offer freedom to play in a game context, Dorothy worlds offer structured play in a game context, and Wendy worlds offer freedom to play in a nongame context.[38] Although the underlying philosophy of Alice worlds is compatible with both Wendy (freedom) and Dorothy (game) worlds, the relationship between Alice and Dorothy worlds is of particular interest because players regard them as close in a way they don't regard Alice and Wendy worlds. In other words, the strength of the game conceit is stronger than that of the freedom conceit.

Alice and Dorothy worlds each have a problem not shared by the other: Alice worlds can't attract newbies, and Dorothy worlds are expensive to create. The roots of these difficulties lie in the way they construct narrative: Alice does so at the atomic level, which gives players rich possibilities for creating a new story, albeit too rich for most newbie tastes; and Dorothy does so at the molecular level, providing narrative in bite-size chunks that newbies find tasty, albeit too chunky to suit an educated palate. By combining the two, the result is a world with a range of granularities of narrative, laid out before the players in such a way that it's natural that they'll choose whichever possibility best suits their mood at the time.

Most players would start off in Dorothy mode and then switch to Alice mode as they progressed. It doesn't have to be like that, though: some could play the whole time in one mode and never change to the other—and it *wouldn't matter*. The important thing is that you finish a journey you made on your own terms, whatever those terms may be. By combining the merits of Alice and Dorothy, more people will be able to do so than ever before.

Alice and Dorothy *can* play together, and their games will be better as a result.

Notes

1. What I'm calling virtual worlds here are also known as MMORPGs, MMOGs, MUDs, and several dozen other acronyms or terms, none of which has really stuck, and all of which mean different things to different people. What *I* mean by virtual worlds is exemplified by *World of Warcraft* (2004), *Second Life* (2003), *EverQuest* (1999), *Ultima Online* (1997), *DikuMUD* (1990), *LambdaMOO* (1990), and *MUD1* (1978). For a slightly more formal definition, see Bartle (2003).

2. Quite literally, after she downs the contents of the bottle marked "drink me."

3. For example, the player of a paladin may feel genuine outrage that the population of a helpful, peaceful village has been slaughtered by legions of undead. It's a real-world emotional effect that has resulted from game world actions.

4. Such early virtual worlds include *MUD1*, *Shades* (1985), *Gods* (1985), *Federation II* (1985), *MirrorWorld* (1986), and their ilk.

5. In gamelike worlds, there is a conceit that they are somehow separate from reality, which corresponds to the *magic circle* (Huizinga 1938) maintained by players of regular games: spaces in which the normal rules of the real world don't, by consensus of the players, apply.

6. Wendy's first words in Neverland are satisfyingly consistent with the aims of many players in social virtual worlds:

> I wish I had a pretty house,
> The littlest ever seen,
> With funny little red walls
> And roof of mossy green. (Barrie 1911)

7. In particular, Sweden's *LPMUD* (1989) and Denmark's *DikuMUD*.

8. Newbies always get their way (Bartle 2004).

9. *TinyMUD* itself gave rise to three major code-base families: MOOs, MUSHes, and MUCKs. MOOs primarily remain nongame in their outlook; MUSHes and MUCKs are mostly focused on strong role-playing, valuing the emotional development of player characters based on their interaction. Because the form of role-playing used in these games came from face-to-face games developed in the United States (particularly *Advanced Dungeons & Dragons* [2003]), for a while it was known as "American role-playing," whereas the type pioneered in virtual worlds up until then was "British role-playing." Rather than get dangerously stereotypical about it, however, I shall refer to them as "Dorothy" and "Alice" role-playing instead. That said, social psychologists might like to note that Alice was British and Dorothy was American, and that one early British virtual world, *Shades*, actually featured Alice as a major non-player character.

10. Prior to the split, virtual worlds were generically referred to as MUDs (after *MUD1*). After it, there were sporadic attempts by the players of social worlds to distance these from the *MUD1* tradition, using new terms to assert their newfound independence. The only one of these that gained much currency was MU*, but there was never any grand consensus as to whether it referred to all virtual worlds or just the social ones. The *, by the way, is there because it's the wildcard symbol in Unix; MU* reads pretty much as "multi-user whatever."

11. Although this figure might seem small alongside that of *World of Warcraft*, it's respectable when compared to the gamelike worlds in the chasing pack—any with over one hundred thousand players is, traditionally, regarded as a success. For a highly approximate idea of the relative sizes of user bases, see Woodcock (2003–).

12. It has been known for some time why this dichotomy exists (Bartle 1996). In a nutshell: people play virtual worlds for different reasons; players with different reasons for playing interact with each other in predictable ways; some of these interactions feed back on each other to favor one style of play over another; and once the interplayer dynamics pan out, there are four basically stable configurations that can result. The stable configurations are:

- *Achiever heavy* These tend to be the gamelike, Dorothy worlds, such as *World of Warcraft*
- *Socializer heavy* These tend to be the social, Wendy worlds, such as *Second Life*
- *Balanced* These tend to be the sandbox, Alice worlds, such as *Ultima Online*
- *Empty* The player base remains stable, but pretty well zero

The strongest of these configurations is the third, as it requires a relatively small stream of newbies to sustain it. It is difficult to set up, though; most attempts will collapse to either the first or second configuration instead.

13. For Wendy worlds, it's even less as it's done freely by the players, but this is at the expense of the game element that the developers of Dorothy worlds specifically want.

14. It's an ongoing debate as to whether they *are* stories, though (Frasca 2003).

15. This is often called the *fiction* when applied to virtual worlds.

16. Virtual worlds with a strong role-playing element may enforce consistency with the fiction, though; for example, you can't claim you're an elf from another dimension in a science fiction space opera game.

17. Art and animation assets are even more expensive to create, but they do have the benefit of being reusable. Occasionally, quests *will* have a unique requirement—for example, they may give a special ax as a reward that can't be obtained elsewhere, but most of the time they can use what already exists. Voice assets lie somewhere in between: generic grunts and groans come from the central pool, but if you want the final boss to taunt the players verbally, well, someone actually has to voice act those lines.

18. Instances are self-contained subworlds for a limited number of player characters to enter as a group, and are created on the fly every time a group enters them.

19. The same applies to games—for instance, *Tringo* (2004), which began in *Second Life*. Creating a non-Wendy virtual world within a Wendy virtual world—while possible—is, however, a rather more daunting exercise.

20. There are artificial intelligence techniques to make the content narratively and emotionally meaningful (Bartle 2002), but the effort involved in implementing them is on a par with that of handcrafting the quests in the first place.

21. This is required to make something that warlocks need in *World of Warcraft*. It provides a steady income once you have it, and therefore the obtaining of such a pattern is the kind of goal that a

player may devise independently of the game's quest system. Just for you, I decided to obtain one as an exercise. I was *so* disappointed when it was finally dropped—I was hoping to get to four hundred to impress you even more with my dedication to duty.

22. Indeed, the grains are so fine that it's debatable whether they can indeed be called particles of narrative at all; it may be that only at the molecular level do they become serviceable as story components. I tend toward this view myself, on the grounds that if any action or event whatsoever can be considered a narrative particle, then it dilutes the concept so much as to render it vacuous. Lee Sheldon, however, argues that it's foolish to talk about things that comprise elements of narrative without accepting that they themselves must be units of narrative. Don't worry, though, we haven't come to blows over this issue.

23. An *exploit* is an unforeseen action of which the designers disapprove. For example, to encourage newbies to learn the combat system, the designers may have a town council pay a bounty for rat pelts; they would consequently be alarmed were players to set up rat farms to breed the little critters so they could hand in pelts by the cartload. If, on the other hand, the designers approve of some unforeseen action, this makes it a *feature* rather than an exploit.

24. Actually, they do want to undergo such a transformation, it's just that they don't know they do.

25. To be clear on what I mean here: I'm saying that character classes make player advancement *comprehensible* to a player, not that they are the *mechanism* for advancement. If you pick a character class of Mage, then you have in your head some stereotypical notion of what a mage is, thereby giving you a target to work toward; you have a much clearer understanding of what you will become through play than if there were no character classes.

26. Yes, I'm aware of *Nomic* (Suber 1990; see also ⟨http://www .earlham.edu/~peters/nomic.htm⟩).

27. "Gameplay is a series of interesting choices," observed Sid Meier. I'm not sure if he actually said that or if he responded to an interview question, "What makes a good game?" with the answer, "Interesting choices." The quote is now stuck to his name, though, so whether he said it or not, he said it.

28. These used to be called *tanks* or *tank mages*. Nowadays, both terms have become rather more specific in use (the actual details vary from virtual world to virtual world).

29. Permadeath—permanent death—is the regime whereby when your character is killed in the virtual world, it's obliterated. You have to start from scratch; there's no resurrection. Although real life seems to work this way (religious arguments aside), this attention to detail is not universally popular among players, and most early (Alice) virtual worlds watered it down in some way. Even so, their solutions would be seen as barbaric by today's standards (e.g., if you're killed in a fight you didn't start, you only lose *half* your experience points).

30. Even if that class has been designed to be easy—for example, paladins in *World of Warcraft*.

31. In version 3.5, this is 35 percent for full plate plus 50 percent for a tower shield.

32. Although the d20 system (the one used by *Advanced Dungeons & Dragons* from the third edition onward) has classes as its main mechanism for determining character roles, most other modern role-playing systems use a skill-based approach instead. This allows for a much finer character customization than does d20, which many role-players find superior. That said, the historical momentum propelling d20 is so great that its dominance is roughly the same as that enjoyed by Microsoft in the personal computer world.

33. In a skill-based system, the ability to perform certain actions is conditional on the character having the requisite "skill." For example, unless you have the skill "wield sword," you can't use a sword in combat. Skills can usually be improved either through use or by payment for "training," and there's usually a maximum number of skills you can have at any one time. A gear-based system uses equipment to determine what you can do. For instance, you can wield a sword merely by having it with you, but you can only carry a certain amount of equipment, so if you take the sword then you may have to leave your magely staff or your armor behind. Gear-based systems sometimes link the gear to character level, and sometimes have crude incompatibilities (e.g., you can't carry your holy symbol and a longbow at the same time).

34. People who religiously believe that there is a deity (or are deities) giving them quests, ancient Greece style, may wish to differ here.

35. Yes, Hogger, bane of my *World of Warcraft* life at level nine, this is *you* I'm talking about.

36. Of course, you wouldn't want anything *in* your vault at the time, but that may be a price worth paying. Such are the decisions that the richness of the environment creates.

37. Multiclass storytellers/coders are rare, but they make excellent designers.

38. The fourth combination—structured play in a nongame context —sounds to me like a hellish prison, but I'm open to being persuaded otherwise.

References: Literature

Barrie, James Matthew (1911). *Peter and Wendy*. London: Hodder and Stoughton. ⟨http://www.gutenberg.org/dirs/etext91/peter16 .txt⟩.

Bartle, Richard A. (1996). "Hearts, Clubs, Diamonds, Spades: Players Who Suit MUDs." *Journal of MUD Research* 1, no. 1. ⟨http://www .brandeis.edu/pubs/jove/HTML/v1/bartle.html⟩.

Bartle, Richard A. (2002). *Mobile AI*. Online: Skotos. ⟨http://www .skotos.net/articles/⟩.

Bartle, Richard A. (2003). *Designing Virtual Worlds*. Indianapolis, IN: New Riders.

Bartle, Richard A. (2004). *Newbie Induction: How Poor Design Triumphs in Virtual Worlds*. ITU Copenhagen: Other Players conference proceedings. ⟨http://www.itu.dk/op/papers/bartle.pdf⟩.

Bartle, Richard A. (2005). "Virtual Worlds: Why People Play." In *Massively Multiplayer Game Development*, edited by Thor Alexander, 2:3– 18. Hingham, MA: Charles River Media.

Baum, L. Frank (1900). *The Wonderful Wizard of Oz*. Chicago: George M. Hill. ⟨http://www.gutenberg.org/dirs/etext93/wizoz10h.htm⟩.

Campbell, Joseph (1949). *The Hero with a Thousand Faces*. Princeton, NJ: Princeton University Press.

Carroll, Lewis (1865). *Alice's Adventures in Wonderland*. London: Macmillan. ⟨http://www.gutenberg.org/dirs/etext97/alice30h.htm⟩.

Frasca, Gonzalo (2003). "Ludologists Love Stories Too: Notes from a Debate That Never Took Place." Level Up conference proceedings, University of Utrecht. ⟨http://ludology.org/articles/Frasca _LevelUp2003.pdf⟩.

Huizinga, Johan (1938). *Homo Ludens*. Haarlem, Netherlands: H. D. Tjeenk Willink and Zoon.

Sheldon, Lee (2004). *Character Development and Storytelling for Games*. Boston: Thomson Course Technology.

Suber, Peter (1990). *The Paradox of Self-Amendment: A Study of Law, Logic, Omnipotence, and Change*. New York: Peter Lang Publishing.

Woodcock, Bruce (2003–). MMOGchart. ⟨http://www.mmogchart .com/⟩.

References: Games

Advanced Dungeons & Dragons, v3.5. Monte Cook, Skip Williams, and Jonathan Tweet; Wizards of the Coast. 2003.

DikuMUD. Katja Nyboe, Tom Madsen, Hans Henrik Staerfeldt, Michael Seifert, and Sebastian Hammer; University of Copenhagen. 1990.

EVE Online. Kjartan Pierre Emilsson; CCP Games. 2003.

EverQuest. Steve Clover, Brad McQuaid, and Bill Trost; 989 Studios. 1999.

Federation II. Alan Lenton. 1985.

Gods. Ben Laurie. 1985.

LambdaMOO. Pavel Curtis. 1990.

LPMUD. Lars Pensjö; University of Gothenburg. 1989.

MirrorWorld. Pip Cordrey, Nat Billington, Lorenzo Wood, Patrick Bossert, Tim Rogers, and Piers de Lavison. 1986.

MUD1. Roy Trubshaw and Richard Bartle; University of Essex. 1978.

Second Life. Linden Lab. 2003.

Shades. Neil Newell. 1985.

Tetris. Alexey Pazhitnov; Spectrum Holobyte. 1985.

TinyMUD. Jim Aspnes; Carnegie Mellon University. 1989.

Tringo. Nathan Keir. 2004.

Ultima Online. Raph Koster et al.; Origin Systems. 1997.

World of Warcraft. Rob Pardo; Blizzard Entertainment. 2004.

My Story Never Ends
Ken Rolston

What are the specifics of writing a long-form narrative for a game? I've done it many times, and I'm ashamed to say I don't know much about it.

It's not that I don't have lots of rules. I've got vast directories full of rules. But every rule is obscured with fine distinctions, obscure references, and cagey reservations, and distinguished by the frequency with which I've ignored any given rule in a successful project. And the success of *Morrowind* (2002) and *Oblivion* (2006) is directly proportional to the resistance and contradiction I've enjoyed from smart, experienced, and contrary colleagues during production, so my confidence in the utility of those rules is somewhat shaky.

The following notions, however, are never far from my mind when I'm working on a vast narrative:

- In games, stories suck, so focus on the other elements of narrative: setting and theme

- Uncovering the fog of war without getting killed is the hero's plot

- Free-form presentation of narrative content lets the players feel they are telling their own stories

Focus on Setting and Theme

Linear forms like novels, films, and plays tell stories better than games. Vast narrative games like *Morrowind* and *Oblivion*, on the other hand, let readers explore the setting and theme at their own pace, according to impulse and whim. That's a variety of narrative experience more compelling and immersive than the linear forms can offer.

Vast narrative games like *Morrowind* and *Oblivion* come out of the paper-and-pen role-playing hobby tradition of elaborate preparation and presentation of the campaign setting and theme. In *Dungeons & Dragons* and its cousins, the unit of narrative construction is the campaign pack. Paper-and-pen role-playing creators publish their entire settings. Novelists, playwrights, and filmmakers, on the other hand,

publish only a small fraction of the setting and theme work they do to create their narrative products.

My tastes and ambitions for vast narrative settings are formed by many influences: William Shakespeare, Patrick O'Brian, *Glorantha*, live-action role-playing games (LARPs), and *The West Wing*, to mention a few. The strongest genre influences are the vast published and widely available literatures of paper-and-pencil role-playing games, and the modest unpublished and obscure literatures of live-action role-playing games). Since I personally contributed as a longtime writer for and critic of paper-and-pencil RPGs and their campaign settings and scenario supplements, I am intimately familiar with their virtues and liabilities. Concerning the more intimate interactions of setting and theme with plot and character, however, I am more profoundly influenced by experiences playing in and developing for live-action role-playing games. I've been fortunate to serve as an apprentice and general dogsbody to brilliant LARP designers and presenters (most of whom have enjoyed considerable success in paper-and-pencil role-playing game publishing as well). Deep study and practical experience with LARP design, presentation, and gaming experience is profoundly recommended for those who want to develop vast narratives in computer games.

My ideal model of setting and theme presentation is the juvenile illustrated book genre that features lost civilizations like the Egyptians, the Romans, the Aztecs, and the Vikings. Richly illustrated, presented in digestible snips and fragments, these books appeal to the intellectual appetites of their target market: a menu of gourmet fare including war, magic, gods, exotic customs, alien cultural notions, morbid burial customs, lurid rituals, violence, and epic architecture, all colored by the titillating melancholy of the tragic fall of a civilization in a distant past.

In both *Morrowind* and *Oblivion*, the leading character is the landscape, and the supporting characters are the culture and history of the land. In *Oblivion*, however, we made a conscious decision to present more elaborate narrative rigging than we did in *Morrowind*, and concerned ourselves less with exotic cultures and obscure histories. Compared with *Morrowind*, *Oblivion* greatly improved the quality and presentation of plots and characters in individual quests.

Given the critical and market success of *Oblivion*, perhaps that was a wise decision.

Unfortunately, *Morrowind* was far superior in its sense of place, richness of theme and culture, and coherence and integration of characters and plots with history, cultures, and landscapes. *Morrowind* is to *Oblivion* as the novel *Moby-Dick* is to the movie *Titanic*. *Oblivion* is slick, entertaining, and satisfying. *Morrowind* is rough going, often slow paced, wordy, and exhausting, but deep and textured in its visual and literary narrative.

If *Morrowind* had been presented with the improved interface, gameplay, and faster pacing of *Oblivion*, would it be a superior game? I'd like to think so—*Morrowind* remains my personal favorite—but I don't know. In other media, like books, comics, and even films, there are a lot more data points for comparison, and competition clearly favors more elaborately developed vast settings like George R. R. Martin's *A Song of Ice and Fire* series, the *Sandman* comics, and the *Aliens* films. When it becomes possible for a gamer to choose in a game store from among fifteen recent releases of *Oblivion*-size open-world computer role-playing games (CRPG), then the markets and critics might begin to more effectively weigh as well as compare their narrative qualities.

The Explorer-Hero

I'm told that Ernest Hemingway said that every true story ends in death. Well, that isn't how it works in vast narrative CRPGs.

The only real end to the story is when the user has completely exhausted the content: has delved every dungeon, murdered every harmless woodland creature and gone through its pockets, has opened every chest, broken every vase, and completed every quest. The only real end to the story is when there are no more places to visit—no section of the map not wiped clean of the fog of war.

And even then, strictly speaking, it still isn't the end, because the user can *replay* the game, and explore the dialogue and plot branches that he or she has missed. It's not like a book or novel, where the text is the same on the rereading or reviewing. The CRPG is actually a different text on the

second reading. (Not that I've ever been tempted to replay *Fable* as a bad guy or a Bioware game as a good guy, but I hear that some find such endeavors rewarding.)

The hero's story is, "Hey, look! I'm not dead yet! I got a lot of living to do!"

I've completed quests, sure, and even completed some elaborate multiple-episode sequences of world-saving tasks for epic main quests. The larger and more free-form the CRPG, the less important the main quest is—and the more likely that shrewd players will put off embarking on the main quest until they've sucked the goodness out of all the faction sequences, side quests, free-form exploration, and other treats and inducements of the vast setting. I imagine many abandon the game, wearied but satisfied, long before they get to the final episode of the main quest.

Exploring has more genuine suspense than following quest stages. There are so many directions to turn, so many people to talk to, so many holes to crawl into, and so many creatures and malefactors to chase after and righteously (or foully) slaughter. By contrast, the characters crafted for me are distinctly ill fitting, uncomfortable, and unlike my personal dreams of wish fulfillment. And I am forever running up against the boundaries of the plots I'm served, and disappointed in the choices of dialogue lines I'm picking from as well as the avenues of inquiry I'm offered. I'm always conscious of the ways the characters and plots limit me—but in the choices of where to go and what to do when I'm exploring, the boundaries are less chafing and frustrating.

Free-Form Gameplay

I hate getting quests. I hate the toil of completing quests. I hate the formal and predictable resolution of quests. At best, I feel a Puritan sense of rectitude for laboring dutifully, of doing my duty to uncover the fog of narrative war.

Of course, I make games for a living, and I've played games to death, so I'm more jaded and calloused than my audience. And I know that the very thing I despise—the explicit expression of the game's narrative as a sequence of procedures I have to complete to receive my reward of cheese—is exactly what many people want. Many industry professionals tell me how much more they liked the heavy-handed narrative interface of quest stages and quest targets of *Oblivion*, to the more subtle and open-ended questline presentation of *Morrowind*. And I admit, I'm grateful for the throbbing icons on *Fable*'s maps that tell me which way to go to get to the rich content.

But I prefer finding things to do and deciding myself to do them, rather than looking for quest givers to tell me what to do.

At present, my colleagues and I at Big Huge Games are outlining the content of a new vast narrative. We've planned the main quests and the side quests, and now we're planning the free-form quests. And we keep finding it hard to say exactly what a free-form quest is. I'm perfectly content to define the form by example—to draft lots and lots of free-form quest ideas, while blandly ignoring the fact that the examples don't seem to have any single formal element in common. But for the purposes of milestone delivery and task tracking, we've settled on a practical definition. A free-form quest:

- Does *not* have a quest giver

- Does not even tell you that you're on a quest until you complete it and get your reward

This definition does avoid the most chafing strictures of conventional quest presentation. Admittedly, with this definition, the distinction between a formal quest and a free-form one is just a matter of presentation.

For instance, here's a quest that can be presented either as a conventional formal quest or a free-form quest (by the above definition).

COLONEL MUSTARD HAS LOST HIS KNIFE IN THE PARLOR

Conventional Quest Presentation:

1. Talk to Colonel Mustard. He tells you he's lost his knife. (DING: You get a journal entry telling you that Colonel Mustard wants his knife and will reward you if you bring it to him.)

2. There're only so many rooms, and only one object in each room, so you search all the rooms and find the knife. (DING: You get a journal telling you you've found

the knife and that now you should return it to Colonel Mustard for your reward.)

3. You talk again to Colonel Mustard, give him his knife, and in return are given a nice piece of pipe. (DING: Quest complete!)

Free-Form Quest Presentation:

1. You find a knife in the parlor. (DING: You get a journal telling you you've found a knife. This journal offers only redundant information. You *know* you found a knife: you picked it up. The only new information is that the game thought it was worthwhile *telling* you that you'd found a knife; so you, reasonably enough, suspect that the knife is important in some way, and that there's something meaningful and game worthy you can do with it.)

2. Next time you talk to someone, you find that you have a new topic: "Knife." Select the topic during dialogue, and you find yourself asking, "Did you lose a knife?" (Now you can guess that what you are doing is trying to return a lost knife to somebody, although you can't be sure, because some wicked, devious designer may just be *tricking* you into mentioning the knife to everyone—because it's a *murder* weapon, and your possession of the knife will be taken as evidence of your guilt in a crime…har-har-har.)

3. Sooner or later you talk to Colonel Mustard, and he's so grateful you returned his knife, he gives you a nice pipe. (DING: Quest complete!)

Now, you could present this free-form quest with no DINGs at all, and then it would be completely free of any of the conventional trappings of quest procedures. Still, most players would recognize the steps of their activities as quest stages, regardless of the trappings. On the point of presentation, the free-form version feels less to me like a homework assignment, and I think a generous leavening of such questlike free-form quests will make our vast narrative more fun to navigate.

When I extol the design virtues of free-form gaming to my colleagues, however, I am not just talking about a more delicate presentation of the formal trappings of quest procedures. I'm also talking about activities that are not presented to the gamer in any way as quests: activities that are not formally recognized by the game or are recognized only in passing, without any hint of power-gaming reward.

One example of such a free-form activity is searching for the complete suit of clothing and accessories that makes you look fabulous. It was a revelation to me when I saw all the Internet postings of *Daggerfall* characters posed in elegant green velvet garments, with harmoniously colored shields and weapons—all selected to complement to best advantage, for instance, the Argonian lizardman's lurid green, scaly skin. The game doesn't care how you dress, but the user does, and the user cares particularly when he or she can post his or her own elegant sartorial splendor online.

Another example is posing your character with all the admiring women in *Morrowind*. Taking and presenting screenshots from gameplay is a fine free-form activity in itself, but the head-tracking feature of the game causes nearby non-player characters (NPCs) to turn to look at you with love in their eyes. Pose your hero center screen, staring out of the game at the viewer, watch the head of the handsome woman at your side swing to gaze at you earnestly, grab a screenshot, and you are fulfilling the dream fantasy of a lifetime.

Consider the screenshot in the nearby sidebar of NPC Fasile Charascel, a Fighters Guild of Balmora member, admiring John Walker, the game persona of my friend Chris Riemer. And read the email he shared with me. Admittedly, Chris brings a lot of his own interior landscape to the game experience, but that's the point of free-form gameplay: understanding the impulses and sensibilities that the user brings to the experience, and presenting a setting rich and open enough to stimulate his reactions and responses. Note also Chris's implicit plea in his email for more believable, and more gratifying, persistence of memory and recognition from game characters. If he only knew how much that would cost in design time and assets—well, he probably wouldn't be any more forgiving. Users are not interested in excuses. They just want what they want.

Admiring Glances

From: Chris Riemer [mail to: DELETED]

Sent: Friday, February 28, 2003 7:14 PM

To: Ken Rolston

Subject: Love that Fasile

I don't know . . .

Is it the color of her eyes? Is it that sultry turn of her head? The bangs? Maybe it's those lace-up, bondage, fuck-me boots she always wears.

Despite that dumb-ass way she has of standing in my path whenever I want to climb the stairs, she really does it for me.

So, whenever I come back to the guild in Balmora, I always slip her a compliment. Nothing dirty, something nice I tell her how her cuirass accents her form, you know? Something like that. Sometimes, she smiles and winks. But other times, she just spits right in my eye. Broads . . .

But I figure, once you've won 'em over—I mean, once they like you as well as they possibly can—it should be harder to piss 'em off. Shouldn't it?

Even if I'm a little clumsy with words, shouldn't the people who already like me cut me some fuckin' slack? I figure that having brought Fasile to the hundred out of the hundred level, I should be able to admire the shit out of her without having her think less of me. You know what I'm saying?

Just my thoughts, anyway . . .

12.1 Admiring glances.

Yet another example is the quest to tidy up taverns. Chris saw a liquor flask lying on the floor of a rough gin mill in *Morrowind*. Being a compulsive neatnik, he picked up the liquor flask and placed it on a nearby table. Alas, we betrayed this earnest user, because the liquor flask was marked as owned, and therefore taking it (i.e., picking it up) was an act of theft. So for this good deed, the hero was "rewarded" by the strident and disdainful attentions of the local guard, who accosted him with "Halt! Thief!" Here the designer's ability to envision the free-form impulses of the user failed completely. We never designed *Morrowind* with compulsive cleaners in mind. And now I dream of a future vast narrative game in which I tidy up a disordered display of merchandise, and the NPC merchant, perceiving my intent, thanks me graciously for my thoughtfulness.

The common feature of these and other examples of completely free-form activities is that they express the deeply felt impulses of the user, and they represent free and imaginative avenues for exploration. The challenges of designing for such free-form gameplay are threefold:

- Creating systems and settings that reward unstructured playfulness and self-expression

- Anticipating and avoiding inappropriate game responses to playfulness and self-expression (like imagining that someone would want to tidy up a littered barroom)

- Observing and understanding users along with their impulses for wish fulfillment, and introducing activities and tokens to the setting that stimulate those impulses

Unfortunately, I am profoundly ignorant of the many ways users use, or would *like* to use, the games I develop. I try to listen to what users say they want, but rarely are they as vivid and charming in capturing as well as communicating their responses and reactions as Chris. What I'd *like* to do is spend lots of time watching people play. And I'd *like* to have handy bulletin boards where users post the sorts of free-form activities they *try* to do in games, and how they are pleased or disappointed in their attempts. There's a topic for an academic study: what free-form activities have users attempted in games ... and which outcomes were fun, and which ones sucked?

"I'm Not Dead Yet!"

In the editors' solicitation for the *Third Person* project, they cited the following: "Alan Moore, in his introduction to Frank Miller's *The Dark Knight Returns*, makes the case that good stories need a definitive conclusion."

As usual, distinctive exceptions to profound wisdoms are often instructive.

Only stories that *end* need a definite climax.

And the most delicious, most revolutionary narrative feature of stories in tabletop role-playing games and large, single-player simulated worlds is that for their heroes—for the player characters—their stories never end.

In tabletop dice-and-dungeons gaming and free-form, open-ended computer games, stories that end are *bad* stories. Any opportunity to end the story should be avoided assiduously.

The most common anecdote I hear from players of *Morrowind* and *Oblivion* are their proud assertions that they had played for hours and hours and hours, and they hadn't even started the main quest yet. These heroes realized that the moment they stepped on to the road to dramatic resolution, they were on the road to death—death not in the sense of I'm-dead-so-it's-time-to-reload, but in the sense of the necessarily anticlimactic death of their epic narrative.

Before paper-and-pencil tabletop role-playing games like *Dungeons & Dragons*, games were always defined in terms of how they ended. That meant that you were mostly interested in winning, because that was the only real good ending.

But with the birth of the campaign player character, the story became primarily about surviving to the *next* story.

U.S.-style computer role-playing games rooted in the tabletop role-playing games inspired by the *Dungeons & Dragons* experience are shaped by the fundamentally open-ended nature of the *Dungeons & Dragons* campaign player character's story: "I'm not dead yet." That is the most important thing about the *Dungeons & Dragons* character's story: the character is still alive; he or she has not died. Everything else is of less significance. The character's story is the never-ending potential for exploration and advancement implicit in the character not being dead yet.

References: Games

The Elder Scrolls III: Morrowind. Bethesda Softworks/ZeniMax, Ubisoft. 2002.

The Elder Scrolls IV: Oblivion. Bethesda Softworks/ZeniMax; 2K Games. 2006.

Storytelling in a Multiplayer Environment

Matthew P. Miller

Our largest challenge when creating *City of Heroes* (2004) was figuring out how to tell the stories of thousands of individual characters who existed in a single interactive world. We wanted players to have unique experiences as they played through the game, so that when a group of players got together, they could talk about the exploits of their hero, and it wouldn't be identical to everyone else in the room.

Since we were setting out to emulate the storytelling of comic books, we had it easy, knowing exactly what kinds of stories to tell. We wanted characters to be superheroic, and had no problem crafting narratives about rescuing people, stopping criminal activity, and taking down arch villains. Our largest problem was conveying these stories to the players.

The characters in *City of Heroes* gain experience as they play through the game; this experience directly translates into a level for the character. The original launch of *City of Heroes* had the level maximum set to 40. We needed some way to differentiate the stories of a level 4 hero from that of a level 34 hero, and we did this by creating Stature Levels. Stature Levels were narrow bands that contained the stories for those bands. So Stature Level 1 consisted of levels 1 to 4. This meant that in order to experience any of the stories of Stature Level 1, the character needed to be of level 1 to 4. Once the character graduated to level 5, he or she would graduate to Stature Level 2, which ran from levels 5 to 14, and contained all new stories and missions for the characters to interact with. After Stature Level 2, every Stature Level was broken down into five-level increments, all the way to Stature Level 7, which was 35 to 40.

The initial story line of the game was designed to teach you the controls and how to play your hero. This tutorial could have been simply instructions about what keys to press and how to operate your powers in combat, but we took the extra step and wove a heroic story line into it. Your character is fresh off the tram in Paragon City, the City of Heroes, and finds him- or herself in the midst of a crisis right away.

A police officer greets you immediately and tells you that there is some kind of weird alien disease outbreak going on, driving the normal citizens crazy and hostile. The police officer explains how the movement controls work and that the character should visit the doctor at the hospital for more information about the disease. When the player visits the doctor in the hospital, he or she gets more information about the infected citizens (i.e., they progress their story line) and instructions about how to use the hospital should their character be defeated during gameplay (i.e., they receive more instruction about how to play the game).

We continue to weave the story and instructions throughout the tutorial, introducing combat and power-ups in a logical thematic way. In the end, the characters get the information needed to stop the plague and then find themselves whisked off to Paragon City proper, where the player now knows the basic controls, and the character already feels like a hero for stopping an alien plague.

During development we had to ballpark, and sometimes flat-out guess at, how much time the players were going to spend doing story-based missions or simply "patrolling the streets" looking to stop random crimes. The formulas we devised would tell us how much content we would need to write to make sure that the players would get a mostly unique experience. We wanted to heighten their individuality within the huge framework of a massively multiplayer online game. At the same time, we needed to be conscious of how much work we were making for ourselves and schedule enough content that the designers could accomplish it all in time for our beta test dates.

Next, we had to figure out how we were going to get the stories into the hands of the players. Our first thought was that City Hall would be filled with "mission terminals" where heroes could walk up and get their next mission, then fly off to save the day. But one of the rules this violated

13.1 Fresh off the tram in *City of Heroes*.

was that it wasn't much like a comic book, and it really made the game feel as if you were playing a game. The mission terminals were eventually replaced with "contacts." Contacts are actual non-player characters (NPCs) who interact with the player characters (PCs) and give them their missions through intelligent dialogue. Each NPC was to have its own voice along with a "story arc" that involved their background and specialty. The contact who was the leader of the Neighborhood Watch, for example, would assign you to take down a protection racket, while a scientist contact would have you investigating the stolen bodies from the morgue that keep showing up at crime scenes with cybernetics attached to them. These contacts would also draw missions from a common pool of missions shared by all of them within the Stature Level.

We realized late in the process that we simply didn't have enough manpower to have each contact have their own story arc, leaving us with two choices: cutting the number of contacts in the game to around five per Stature Level, or "genericizing" the story arcs so that multiple contacts could all hand out the same one. We didn't like the first option because we feared that a large amount of players would end up swarming all over the contacts to get the next mission, since there were fewer contacts in the world. That didn't feel right. We eventually settled on the second option. This made it possible for us to accomplish the goal of getting enough content done in time for us to make our dates.

One of the holdovers from the earlier design of *City of Heroes* was your hero's origin. Your origin was similar to "race" in fantasy games. Certain origins would give you certain advantages and disadvantages. Mutants would utilize endurance better, while technology-based heroes would deal more damage. The problem with this is these choices were all arbitrary. There was no basis in comic book lore that technology heroes did more damage—that was just something we made up. You couldn't make an intelligent decision on your character's origin in a superhero game like you could when picking a race in a fantasy game. In a fantasy game, you could reasonably assume that dwarves are stout, elves are smart and good at magic, and humans are the jacks-of-all-trades. We didn't have that luxury in *City of Heroes*, so the bonuses inherent to your character's origin were scrapped. We kept the idea of origins around, since we really felt it helped define your character in your own head, if nothing else, so we needed to find some ways to use your origin in gameplay.

This resulted in your initial contact being chosen for you, based on your character's origin. Each origin starts the game with a different contact, and the story that the contact gives out is somewhat tied to the type of character you wanted to be, so a character with a "science" origin would get stories based on scientific breakthroughs and stopping science-based abominations. When you completed everything that a contact had to offer, that contact would introduce you to the same type of contact in the next Stature Level. So the science contact in Stature Level 1 would introduce you to a science contact in Stature Level 2. This was done by way of a logical dialogue telling the player that the contact has a friend they'd like the hero to meet.

We then had the problem of forcing a certain story path on to a character, simply because they chose an origin. For the player, this was an uninformed decision. After all, you can't be expected to know what kind of enemies you are going to fight as the result of a given origin. We needed to present players with the opportunity to "jump tracks" and get the stories offered to another origin. So beginning at Stature Level 2, we made the contacts offer "friend introductions"; these were introductions to new contacts within the same Stature Level. Since we had five story tracks in each Stature Level, we could even offer the players a choice as to which contact they would get. The science contact may tell the player that they have a couple of friends they could introduce them to—a "technology story" one and a "mutant story" one. Now the player can jump tracks laterally and start on the story lines of another origin.

All of this, when played in concert, gives the players the feeling that they are a special piece of a large puzzle. Each

origin has its own story track, which traces through all forty levels of the game, and players get to experience their own part in it. Their characters will develop relationships with NPCs that grow as they do more tasks for the NPCs, and hopefully the players will bond with their particular virtual entities.

Now that we had a way to intelligently get the missions to the players, in a manner that fit both the comic book and game motifs that we were looking for, we needed to make sure that those missions would be fun and interesting. This presented several challenges. First we had to ask ourselves, "What makes a hero?" Performing deeds of heroism includes everything from stopping crime, rescuing people in need, and defeating overwhelming odds.

In a massively multiplayer online game, we are faced with a unique challenge: we can't let the players dramatically alter the landscape of the game. If we allow errant energy blasts to blow away parts of buildings on the streets, within hours the entire city will look like the aftermath of a nuclear holocaust. We needed to limit the interactivity that the players had with the environment as well as work within our given framework for stories. When we started out we had ambitious story lines—ones where things would happen like, "The player encounters a dead body on the street, and on it they find a clue." This works great in a single-player game where you can guarantee that the only person finding the body is the person who needs to find it. But in a multiplayer game like *City of Heroes*, we couldn't have a dead body only show up on one person's screen and not another, and if it showed up for you, yet it wasn't important for a mission you were doing, you would be confused by its presence. So story arcs such as this needed to be cut out.

Additionally, we were limited in the types of missions we could write. The mission editor had limited functionality, but it at least allowed us to put in objective objects (things that needed to be clicked on to end the mission) or dictate entities that needed to be defeated to complete the task at hand. Using this basic framework, we were able to invent a variety of missions where you could search for clues, recover stolen goods, or defeat a boss and his or her henchmen in order to complete the mission.

Matthew P. Miller

Soon after we started, we also developed the ability to put a timer on a mission. We could then include certain time-critical elements, which made things a lot more exciting. In the previous types of missions there was no possibility of failure; things would exist in their current state until you succeeded in completing them. With a timer, we could force a failure when the clock counted down to zero. This allowed us to include elements like time bombs—for instance, the player had to find all four of the time bombs in twenty minutes or the building would be destroyed.

In actuality, though, the building wouldn't be "destroyed"; you would just get kicked out of the mission. The outside facade of the building would remain unmarred and thus there were really no consequences for your actions. Sure, in theory you let the building get destroyed, but since you never saw it, you could easily tell yourself that it never happened. To combat this, we added a unique piece of technology: the random fame string.

The random fame string allowed us to put words in the mouths of the population. After a mission, you could walk down the street and hear a passing citizen make remarks like, "Wow, it's Awesome Guy! I heard he rescued the mayor the other day!" With this little piece of dialogue, we now made it feel like Awesome Guy was making a difference in the everyday lives of the citizens of Paragon City. One of the best parts of this was that the random fame string could also be used when a player failed a timed mission, meaning that the character would hear remarks such as, "It's a darn shame you couldn't have disarmed all those bombs earlier, Awesome Guy. My sister's going to be in the hospital for a couple of weeks at least." Now we get some consequences for actions. There's a price for failure now: being jeered by the general populace. While not as dramatic as watching the building explode around you, the emotional impact can be greater, especially when you are reminded that your virtual failure has cost the lives of many virtual citizens.

City of Heroes launched in late April 2004 to critical acclaim; we quickly approached two hundred thousand users, and the success led our publisher, NCsoft, to ask for a sequel, naturally titled *City of Villains* (2005). Ever since we first announced *City of Heroes*, players had wanted to know if they would be able to play the bad guys as well, and this often-requested feature was crafted into a full-fledged stand-alone game. *City of Villains* was a more ambitious attempt at storytelling than *City of Heroes*; since comic book bad guys have never really gotten the spotlight, we had a more or less blank canvas to work with. We wanted to recreate comic book villainy, but in the comics you don't usually see how the arch villain crafts his or her master plan —you just see the master plan in action. This allowed us a lot more creative freedom about how to construct missions and story lines from the villains' side of the equation.

We quickly realized that comic book heroes were different from comic book villains. Heroes, it turns out, are largely reactive. Their stories hinge on something else happening that sets them in motion. They stop the crimes in progress, rescue those in need of rescue, and so forth. Villains, however, are proactive. They make their own stories, crafting the crimes, kidnapping innocents, and all in all giving a hero something to do. We had to tell stories from a different perspective. Of course, this led to technical challenges as well. We needed new objectives (kidnapping instead of rescuing, planting bombs instead of disarming them, and so on), while remaining within the technical constraints of the basic system.

Still, we were able to get a lot of new technology for *City of Villains*, which helped us with the storytelling. Cut scenes could occur with a mission, so the control could be wrested away from the players, giving them a little action narrative that they wouldn't normally be privy to.

In one particular mission, we use this technique to great effect. The player is told in the mission briefing that they can expect minimal resistance, with no heroes involved. When the player arrives on the scene, though, a cutscene plays, showing him or her that Luminary, a major hero character, awaits in the final room. Even though PCs don't know that Luminary awaits them, the *players* can mentally prepare themselves for a large fight at the end of the mission.

A big challenge to the mission writers was to define what it means to be a villain—and so, what it means to be evil. There is minor evil, which is simply stealing things of value or engaging in other petty crimes. There is psychotic evil, such as kidnapping or the wanton destruction of property. Then there is megalomania or world conquering (world destroying). We made a conscious decision to avoid any of the really recognizable evils: murder, assassination, or rape. Anything that was Evil with a capital *E* was off-limits. Yes, virtual people might die as a consequence of the actions you take, but you would never be asked to personally perform an act of murder.

We also needed to give characters motivations for actually performing the tasks we set them to. One of our writers has a whiteboard in his cubicle that reads, "Heroes have morals…Villains have work ethic," which sums up the basic motivations of most villains. If there is one thing that villains can't be accused of, it's being lazy. Most have plans within plans, elaborate schemes that might rely on luck to pull off, and a driving goal of getting the job done, no matter what the cost.

One of the things we wanted to do with *City of Villains* was to take the opportunity to tie an overarching story line into the entire game. We wanted a story that could encompass thousands of villains, and yet make each one feel special and unique, so we developed the idea of the "Destined One." Lord Recluse, the leader of Arachnos (the main villain organization in *City of Villains*), heard from his mystical seers that in the future, one of his most trusted underlings would rise up and defeat him. This underling could be any one of several thousand possible people, all of whom were currently incarcerated in Paragon City's prison, the Ziggurat.

Your character is one of those prisoners. *City of Villains* begins with a tutorial much like that of *City of Heroes*. But instead of stopping a riot of plague-infested citizens, you participate in a massive jailbreak, orchestrated by Arachnos. You find your cell door open; the criminals have taken over the prison. You make your way outside (learning about the game mechanics as you do so) and eventually on to an Arachnos helicopter, where you are taken to the headquarters of the Arachnos organization, the Rogue Isles. Here, Arachnos can keep tabs on your activities; since the Destined One is said to defeat Lord Recluse, they want to ensure that you are not him, or if you are, to groom you to replace him as the leader of the organization.

Everyone in Arachnos knows of the Destined One program, and a lot of the foot soldiers see potential Destined Ones as snotty, privileged kids who didn't have to work for their favor with Arachnos. And as a matter of fact, if an Arachnos soldier can take down a Destined One, well, that would definitely show the superiors that he or she has the right stuff.

This line of thought made it conceivable that at any time, anyone in the Rogue Isles (the playing area of *City of Villains*) could be hostile to you. Even though you are working for Arachnos, there are several soldiers in the mix looking to make a name for themselves—so watch yourself. Being the Destined One has its perks, but it also comes with a big target on your back.

A key element to our big story lines was the use of in-game events to kick off or reinforce the stories. In our first update, we included a new zone called the Shadow Shard. This was a zone for high-level characters, and had a bizarre population of aberrations that looked radically different than any of the other enemies you fought in the game.

In the weeks leading up to the release of the Shadow Shard, we staged an "invasion" of sorts, where these radical aberrations broke through to our world and terrorized the game world, affecting all the players. This allowed even our low-level heroes to feel that they were participating in a world event, during which they could stave off alien invaders. The invasion scaled up over the weeks, with more and more Shadow Shard natives showing up on the streets of Paragon City. It became evident that the fabric of the universe separating the Shadow Shard from the real world was becoming increasingly tenuous. Eventually we released the update and the players could then access the Shadow Shard, since the barrier between our world and that one had weakened to the point where back and forth travel was now possible.

Once in the Shadow Shard, players performed missions to uncover the reason for all this. Throughout the story arcs presented by the contacts there, players discovered that this dimension was artificially created, as a prison for a malefic deity named Rularuu.

We also introduced a world-spanning event, in which a villain group (the fascist "5th Column," a group very familiar

Matthew P. Miller

to the players) was wiped out to the last person by a new group of villains calling itself "the Council." These combats took place in the game itself, and players could participate, picking a side and throwing down.

Since the impact of these events is so great, we couldn't have the players actually affect the outcome (we had to begin work on the outcome months before the players were actually able to play in the events). If we had prepared for separate outcomes, we would essentially have been throwing half of our work away (the half that the players prevented from happening).

We did, however, include one instance where the players hand control over when a particular outcome took place. We were changing an NPC., Sister Psyche, from one model to another, and wanted an in-story reason as to why this character was suddenly changing her look and even her race. We developed a story line in which Sister Psyche was betrayed by Malaise, her apprentice. Players could run through this story line once with each of their characters, and when enough characters had completed the story, we put the results into motion. Sister Psyche was changed, Malaise went missing, and that story line was no longer available to players.

Although this seemed perfectly reasonable to us (the story had played itself out, and there was no reason to leave the original story arc in the game), we had many complaints on our forums from players who really liked that story and wanted to run it again with other characters. The amount of negative feedback we received (from the simple removal of one story arc among hundreds) has made us think twice about doing something like this in the future.

We also have several ongoing events in the game, which are permanent parts of the zones they occupy, and each of which tell a story. The Ghost of Scrapyarder event in Sharkhead Isle from *City of Villains* is a good example. Scrapyarder was the leader of the dockworkers, and was killed by Captain Mako, an Arachnos lieutenant. He has lived on in spirit form and shows up often, leading a massive mob of dockworkers to strike out against Arachnos or any of their precious Destined Ones. This is represented in the game by the giant Ghost of Scrapyard, which appears and moves through the zone with his entourage. Players will

see the throng of workers and understand that Scrapyard is in the zone; calls for assistance in taking him down go out over the various in-game communication methods.

Overall, we have tried in *City of Heroes* and *City of Villains* to give each player a unique story, while making sure that the game also supports larger overarching story lines. Through the use of dialogue and scripted events, we have set up a living world that convincingly models a major eastern seaboard metropolis and an archipelago of islands ruled by a mad overlord.

References: Games

City of Heroes. Cryptic Studios; NCsoft. 2004.
City of Villains. Cryptic Studios; NCsoft. 2005.

A Brief History of *Spore*

Chaim Gingold

Spore (2008) grew from Will Wright's fascination with the vastness of the universe, and the probability that it contains life. Wright linked Drake's equation, which computes the probability of life occurring in the universe, with the long zoom of Charles and Ray Eames's *Powers of Ten* (1977) film.[1] Each term in Drake's equation corresponds to a different scale of the universe, and a different zoom of the Eames's film. "Spore" stood for the spread of life through the universe: minute seeds of life hopping from one planet to another, as either bacteria riding comets (as in the panspermia theory) or intelligent beings on spaceships.

Early *Spore* prototypes and design concepts focused on simulating the movement as well as evolution of alien creatures, fluids, the birth of stars, galaxies, nebulae, and the spread of intelligent and nonintelligent life in media as small as a bread crumb, and as large as a galaxy. There was a galactic potter's wheel, where you could try your hand at forming a stable spiral-armed galaxy. A blind watchmaker interface allowed you to guide the evolution of novel life-forms. You could sculpt huge piles of gas into stars that were just right for life. Will's idea, at this point, was that players were to directly experience the difficulty and frustration of making life in the universe, and appreciate the improbability that life exists at all.

I initially joined the project in this early prototyping phase, when *Spore* was no more than a handful of people, and felt less like a game development project and more of an awesome research and simulation endeavor. To me, the project was an intellectual love letter to all of existence, a depiction of the entire universe as a complex of interlocking self-similar systems. Patterns emerged—everything, from disease to culture to space travel, could be represented through some combination of cellular automata, agents, and networks. This was my summer dream job: make toys about anything in the universe, using everything I knew about interactive graphics and simulation, for the greatest simulation connoisseur in the world.

Of course, this isn't quite the *Spore* everyone knows. There are two explanations for this; one is commercial, and the other philosophical.

The Sims (2000), Wright's previous game to *The Sims Online* (2002), was in production during *Spore's* initial concept development). It was one of the best-selling games ever, and one of the most lucrative franchises in Electronic Arts' stable. *The Sims* was popular precisely because of how easily people could connect to it: you played with human beings living in suburban dollhouses. *Spore*, by contrast, looked like it could become an awe-inspiring existential crisis in a box, a toy universe so vast that it would take your breath away, not to mention your sense of self, time, and space—an acid trip on a compact disc, guaranteed to explode your brain, much like Stanley Kubrick's film *2001: A Space Odyssey* had blown a much younger Will's mind. Who was the target audience for *Spore*? Was it bigger than the market for *SimEarth* (1990) and *SimLife* (1992)? What changes would we have to make to appeal to players of *The Sims*?

The second, philosophical explanation was also the design challenge: What would players identify and empathize with in *Spore*? Where were their characters? What would players do? Would anyone want to play a complicated game/art/science experiment? The entire universe is a vast, heavy thing, and it wasn't clear that people would be able to pick it up, and if they did, that it wouldn't burn a hole through their hand—or head, for that matter.

I returned to the Georgia Institute of Technology to finish my master's degree, and said good-bye to Walnut Creek, California, and my fellow universe prototypers: Will Wright, Jason Shankel, Ed Goldman, and Kees van Prooijen. I hadn't spent much time working with most of them, since they had all been sucked into the massive *The Sims Online* development team, including Ocean Quigley, who I wouldn't meet until I returned in a little over a year.

When I came back, the team had roughly doubled in size, with some additions that put a new creative spin on *Spore*. Chris Trottier, a game designer who had spent years working on *The Sims*, had joined the project. Working with Will, Chris sought answers to some of life's and *Spore's* big questions: Who am I? What am I doing here? Why do I care?

New ideas were thrown into the design blender. Players would move through a sequential narrative, progressing through a handful of phases, corresponding to the evolution of life: creature, tribe, city, civilization, and finally outer space. Players were given a definite identity and point of view in each phase, structuring their motivations and activities. In the creature game, for example, players would control an individual creature as well as guide the species' evolution. Each phase corresponded, to some extent, to an existing game genre. As players progressed through *Spore*, their perspective and emotional investment would telescope, from individual creatures to tribes to civilizations. We would still blow peoples' minds, but in a more structured, easier to understand sort of way.

John Cimino, an artist and animator trained in the Disney tradition, had come on to the project, and started drawing pictures of strange yet adorable life-forms. It was said that John's cube was haunted by the ghost of Jim Henson. Chris asked for pictures of aliens wearing sneakers. The "cute" team was born, balancing out the project's already well-developed "science" team. Over the next four years, these two teams grew and battled over *Spore's* heart and sensibility, generating a dynamic balance that ensured *Spore* didn't become another *SimEarth* or *The Jetsons* but something in between, epic yet accessible.

14.1 Flash illustration of early John Cimino creature concepts.

Player creativity became an integral part of the project. When I came back, *Spore* had a primitive creature editor. You could draw creature skeletons, which would rattle to life and walk around. It was magic. Brad Smith, who interned the summer after I did, wrote *Spore's* first creature editor, and Kees had written the logic to make whatever the player designed walk around.

The editor was clumsy, but it signified a new design direction: *Spore* was a game about enabling player creativity, and sharing those creations. *The Sims* had a sprawling online community that trafficked in player-created stories, objects, and houses. Will wanted to build this kind of experience directly into the game, and worked it into *Spore's* existing themes of evolution and exploration. By directing their creatures' evolution, players would contribute valuable material to the *Spore* gene pool, creating aliens and civilizations for other players to discover.

Players would design all kinds of things, like creatures, buildings, tools, vehicles, or whatever, which would then be transparently pollinated from game to game. Thanks to the effort of other players, an infinite number of alien civilizations would await your discovery. The problem was going to be sorting through all this content and figuring out what to put on players' machines. You need a darn good librarian to recommend books to you if there are millions of books out there and everyone has a private press.

The other big problem was helping players to make good creations. Three-dimensional modeling software is not for everyone, and not everyone is a Pablo Picasso. John, Brad, and I spent the next several years designing and prototyping the fundamental features that became *Spore's* entire suite of editors.

The reverberating vastness of *Spore's* original concept became structured into a gentler, more appealing experience through four design principles that I'll discuss below. Instead of making *Spore* an abstract and intellectual game for astrobiologists and rocket scientists, it mutated into something more down-to-earth. You could explain the concept to almost anybody: make your own creature, take over the planet, and explore space, where you'll meet space aliens made by other players. Who wouldn't want to do that? In retrospect, the original inchoate vastness of *Spore* needed to

14.2 Will Wright often creates boxes for games early in development, as a design exercise. This is the box front and back for *Spore*'s early design concept.

be folded into a user-friendly conformation—one that would invite ordinary people to pick it up and play.

Story

Spore's early concept had no structured sense of time or sequence. Would players begin by forming a stable galaxy, stars, and planets, and then set to creating life? Or perhaps they would evolve life on a planet, hit it with some asteroids, and try to get panspermia to happen? Like a universe before a creation myth, *Spore* had no obvious beginning, middle, or end. Deciding that the game would move through a handful of stages—from cells to creatures, up through civilizations and then into space explorations— was crucial to getting the game concept to gel at a high level.

Structured narratives are unusual for Maxis games, but *Spore*'s vast scope required a skeletal structure to hang the game on. Besides, what story could be more appropriate than the evolution of life and development of civilization? The story allowed both the developers and players to locate themselves in a narrative about the growth and expansion of life. It became possible to inhabit one phase of the game, and think about where you were coming from and where you were going. As developers, we could divide our efforts and think about how the design grew out of the previous level, through this one and into the next phase of the game. Even with this high-level linear structure, *Spore* was still a monster project in terms of its scope. And of course, by dividing our production effort into level-based teams, we

14.3 Untextured Maya render of a creature created with *Spore*.

set up any kind of interlevel design trade-off and coordination to be an organizational hassle.

Point of View

Who am I? What am I doing here? What is expected of me? Why do I care? The problem is an awesome philosophical one: Who am I in this vast universe? What has meaning to me? How do I relate to the world, not through the conduit of an individual human being, but to *life*, sprawled across billions of years? If we had made *Spore* into a God game, like *SimEarth*, *SimCity*, or *The Sims*, what would the player become emotionally invested in? *The Sims* invites players into its world through its characters, who inhabit places we recognize and do things we care about, like eating, making love, working, and having fun. Sims face familiar problems: unrequited love, expensive but desirable consumer goods, and work/life balance. Biological diversity, evolutionary dead ends, atmospheric composition, and arms races might be real-world problems, but they aren't issues that people easily relate to.

We placed a thread of life, billions of years long, into the player's hands. Starting with a single cell, players are responsible for guiding an individual creature through its life. Sex, violence, and food are the creature's primary concerns, which anyone can relate to. When a single generation ends, time telescopes, and the player shifts into the role of an in-telligent designer of sorts, directing the genetic pathway of the species. The player's point of view oscillates between individual creatures and the entire species. We found that players have no trouble emotionally investing themselves into this situation, even if they don't immediately and intellectually grasp that their "self," the creature they play, is a new individual each generation. As the game progresses, the player's identity expands, from individuals to tribes, and then to civilizations. Once they've blasted off into space, players are again responsible for just one character, a cosmos-cruising astronaut.

Then, there is the problem of aliens. Popular alien narratives focus on the friction of human/alien contact. E. T. entered a human world of suspicious and hostile adults. Familiar with *War of the Worlds*, the suspicious adults knew what to expect. But the really interesting design question about first contact that *Spore* poses is not the traditional one. Earthlings always identify with the home team, whether that's humans fighting off space invaders or a family going about its life in a Sims subdivision. The monster sales of *The Sims* demonstrate that earthling gamers overwhelmingly prefer to play with virtual human beings to the aliens, elves, and robots who populate most game worlds. The path to the mass market's empathy—and dollars, it seems—is paved with asphalt, and goes directly to a suburban home populated by likable folks such as you and me. *Spore*'s dilemma was simple: people readily identify with people, but could we get them to do the same with aliens?

Creativity

Of course, these aren't any old aliens we ask players to invest in; they're your creation, your aliens. Once you start customizing, and design your creature, emotional investment is generated. It's magic. Even the ugly ones are loved by their parents. Many games thrive on the interest generated by players' creative investment. Console role-playing games, for example, get this effect when players invest time in equipping and naming characters. I've always felt more attached to my characters as I fuss over their outfits and equipment. Creative interaction seems to always generate emotional involvement and attachment. Psychologically, it

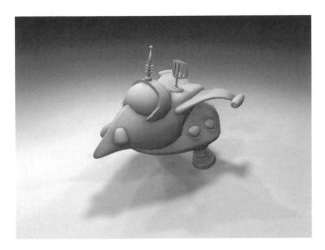

14.4 Untextured Maya render of a vehicle created with *Spore*.

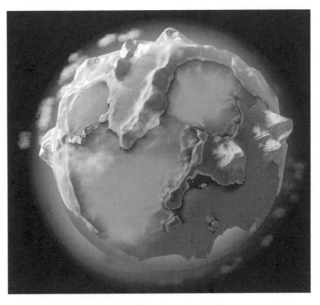

14.5 *Spore* development screenshot of a toylike *Spore* planet.

would seem that part of this stems from the sunk-cost fallacy: we become attached to the things that we've invested time and energy into. Of course, it's not just the hundreds of hours invested in a *World of Warcraft* character along with their relationships and possessions that generate attachment; it's the sense that our fabrications are extensions of ourselves. As recipients of our attention and creative energy, our handiworks are reflections of who we are; they are tangible manifestations of our personalities. It's no wonder we become attached to what we make, and take the success or failure of our own work and ideas very personally.

Spore neatly solves the alien attachment problem by asking the player to design them. If a player makes a creature, and it's appealing, they'll be quite invested in it. Reflecting on the success of *The Sims Exchange*, where players shared stories, characters, houses, and objects for *The Sims*, Will realized that shared creativity would give *Spore* a broader appeal. Why not build creative exchange into the game, rather than as a Web site that orbits it? Player-created assets are constantly being uploaded and downloaded by *Spore*, with enough material to fill a galaxy. There's nothing like taking home your latest finger painting and having mom hang it on the fridge for everyone to see. Sharing not only fills up the galaxy with cool stuff but also allows the

entire world to see your fridge, motivating you to continue creating.

A lot of deep magic must work properly for something like *Spore*'s creature creator to function properly. It must be natural to use, easily producing satisfying results for anyone, from beginners to advanced users. And these aliens, lumps of polygons that no animator has ever seen before, must be brought to life. These are rather complicated endeavors, from design, aesthetic, and technical points of view, but the player should never notice any of it. The game design implications are also challenging—the game must be playable and interesting, regardless of the creatures dropped into it.

Appeal

Disney animators understand that appeal doesn't just mean cute and cuddly characters but "anything that a person likes to see, a quality of charm, pleasing design, simplicity, communication, and magnetism" (Thomas and Johnston 1995, 68).

Spore began life as an intellectual and scientific project. The team faced the challenge of maintaining the gravitas and realism of Will's vision, while making the game as accessible and appealing as possible.

The decision to incorporate the character design aesthetic of an animator marked a turning point in the visual sensibility of the project. The genetic building blocks of *Spore*'s life-forms, the creature parts, adopted the appeal and personality of John's creature designs. And imagining how Pixar might visually treat a film about bacteria, we put eyes on our single-celled organisms. Our planets transformed into expansive landscapes, but retained a toylike sensibility. We made the galaxy more colorful. The entire team became vigilant, seeking opportunities to inject charm and wit into the project, producing the dry goofball humor that characterizes Maxis games.

Not that there was a mad rush for cartoony style, humor, and anthropomorphism. Each art review and design meeting had the potential to shift the balance of power between the "cute" and "science" teams; this is how we caricatured the opposed design sensibilities and their proponents. *Spore*'s style was a compromise worked out over many years between a scientific, realistic, and weighty aesthetic, and something popular, appealing, and full of personality.

By taking on these new design directions, the name *Spore* took on new meanings. In one sense, a spore is the germ of life, a basic reproductive element containing multiform organisms. Capable of withstanding extended hostile conditions, a spore can travel through the vast emptiness of space on a comet or asteroid, and bring the seed of life to a new world. We turned it into the genesis of *Spore*'s galactic narrative, marking the start of the player's cosmic journey.

In another sense, the kaleidoscopic possibilities contained within a single spore are akin to *Spore* itself and its enabling of player creativity. A vast galaxy of strange and wonderful aliens, civilizations, and planets await us, all unfolding from one tiny little seed. And like panspermic spores, which hop from planet to planet, pollinating the universe with life, player creations will migrate between worlds, traveling not on comets or asteroids, but on the Internet, from computer to computer.

We're trying to perform a scale inversion of cosmic proportions. We're attempting to turn everything inside out:

transform the huge, frightening, and awesome universe into something smooth, small, and delicate. *Spore* is like a fragile seedling that a child will hold and be charmed by. It is a smooth round seed, a game, that contains the vastness of the universe, the massive stampede of life, and the incomprehensible magnitude of evolution.

Note

1. This film was prefigured by Kees Boeke's book *Cosmic View: The Universe in 40 Jumps* (New York: John Day Company, Inc., 1957).

Reference: Literature

Thomas, Frank, and Ollie Johnston (1995). *The Illusion of Life*. New York: Hyperion.

Reference: Film

Powers of Ten. Charles and Ray Eames. 1977.

References: Games

SimEarth. Will Wright; Maxis. 1990.

SimLife. Will Wright; Maxis. 1992.

The Sims. Will Wright; Maxis/Electronic Arts. 2000.

The Sims Online. Will Wright; Maxis/Electronic Arts. 2002.

Spore. Electronic Arts. 2008.

Spaces Between: Traveling through Bleeds, Apertures, and Wormholes inside the Database Novel

Norman M. Klein

In 2002, in the novella for *Bleeding Through*, I wrote: "We're a civilization of layers. We no longer think in montage and collage; we multi-task in layers more and more. We are more identified with the author than the narrative—just think about watching the director's commentary on a DVD. People are developing the techniques to respond to changing visual codes."[1]

Five years later, at the time of this writing, my response to these changing visual codes has deepened. It has altered how I structure essays, novels—all my writing, particularly my next database novel, titled *The Imaginary Twentieth Century* (Klein, Bistis, and Kratky 2007).[2] What have these past five years taught me, specifically about data narrative?

The Reader/Viewer

In media (games, interfaces, electronics at home and outside—cell phones), the role of the reader has altered noticeably during this decade. So many new platforms have become comfortable to the public: blogs, wikis, my-spacing, you-tubing, i-pods, and recently, i-phones.

After two corrosive generations of digital media altering our lives at home, codes even for what a story contains have noticeably shifted. At the heart of this change is home entertainment replacing what used to be called urban culture. The infrastructure for public culture in cities is vanishing rather quickly, particularly bookstores and live theater. That is simply a fact, not a gloomy prediction.

Museums have finally turned into cultural tourism, an extension of home entertainment. Pedestrian life in cities continues to be increasingly dominated by cultural tourism as well—by what I call scripted spaces. (By scripted spaces, I mean staged environments where viewers can navigate through a "story" where they are the central characters. Thus, themed, scripted spaces can be on a city street, or inside a game; or at a casino.)

This reconfiguring of the viewer has massive consequences. It has altered our national politics so thoroughly that our republic has, at last, outgrown the "vision of the Founding Fathers." As I often say, half joking, the Enlightenment (1750–1960) has finally ended—quietly, under the radar, like lost mail.

As I also point out, we have become tourists in our own cities, and through the impact of global entertainment, become tourists in our own bodies as well (Klein 2006, chapter 2). We visit ourselves as avatars; we replace notions of the unconscious with good medication. We pharmacologically study our bodies as if they were lopsided chemistry sets with faulty wiring. The era of nano logic means that we are to be steadily invaded in almost microscopic ways (medically, pharmacologically, surgically; and then through branding, theming, etc.). It is hardly a surprise, then, that the viewer is increasingly a central character in media stories (games, immersive special effects films, themed environments, etc.).

Horizontal Tuning

Remember the horizontal and vertical dials on old televisions? Foreheads would bulge. The Rockies would jitter and shrink. I, for one, did not realize that this was a sign of things to come. Those television analog controls have become infinitely, digitally, more horizontal than ever before—and even more jittery.

In response, our sense of space within narratives (games, films, hypertext literature) has morphed. We literally morph many spaces into one—time into space—as if we were copying how the global economy morphs labor markets, national boundaries.

It is the ultimate synchronic mode of spatial design. Paradoxes dissolve under its effect. So when you build a media narrative, paradoxes must be carefully brought back into its navigation, almost like reintroducing an extinct species into a lake.

Clearly, our civilization is a comic tragedy, a mess as contrary as any imaginable. And our republic is fiercely in paradox—under assault, clearly in decline. All this hardly suggests the end of "contradiction," but indeed, this global economy pretends to be too horizontal, too much about consumerism for older forms of the dialectic (Marx for one, Freud for another, balance of powers in our national government for another).

We now imagine applying all this to a database novel. We need media stories where the paradoxes are inserted carefully. We cannot return to the media enthusiasms of the 1990s, no more obsession with design, new software, and CG polish, with the avoidance of paradoxes. We need to get truly beyond the 1990s' media exceptionalism, to generate digital stories that are more uneasy, less about the new "flash," the new gamer tropes.

And that does mean neo-noir. We also must not confuse late cyberpunk with fierce critique. Giddy apocalypses in graphic novels are simply heir to H. Rider Haggard adventures and Jules Verne "voyages extraordinaires." I love these malist fantasies; I am a noiraholic. As long as there is a corpse in low-key lighting, I am hypnotized. But that should never dominate the work. Our praxis should not echo noir fiction, 1920s graphic design, or noir cinema from 1925 to 1965. We should give up on polish, and not congratulate the Internet for wikis and folksonomy. That would be like sponsoring the horizontal economy without paradox.

And finally, we should never assume that modernism (1860–1960) solved how best to tell a digital story. That "nix" has to include forms that feature the "self-reflexive" viewer, as in plays by Luigi Pirandello or Bertolt Brecht, a John Cage event; or a Surrealist manifestation. No knee-jerk retro neo modernism. For media narratives, I have lost my faith in chance techniques, in hypertext, in neo-minimalism, in clicking and clacking to your own adventure…

The Space Between

But then what is left to work with? A great deal, I believe. To set the mood, I'll begin with three possible backgrounds, then introduce seven tools for media narratives (not games, but other modes). I will conclude with a fragment from an essay on database novels written thirty years from now.

I'll keep the pace brisk, as if we were out of time, but truthfully more because it is still historically early. Global warming aside, we are in an era that lies "in between," like Europe in the early 1840s, the United States in the late 1930s, or England in 1910. We can smell the gunpowder, but don't quite believe it. And we are certainly tired of old avant-garde bluster. We should not trust noir cuteness, second-life jingoism, glib fatalism, Manichaean abjection. We might easily be entering a golden age, quite by accident, and only culturally. Our political condition remains desperate, comical. Italy, Spain, England, and France, however, all had their golden ages while their population suffered severe declines. Yet how do we honestly manage that—in narrative? Between mass marketing and academic oligarchies, where is a truly honest place to start, to tell a story? The subject here is database, interface, digital archive.

The Virtues of Decline

Media culture may not have the patience to take the slow, ungainly steps needed to rediscover what literature and theater once delivered—in print media, for metropolises circa 1900. Yet the potential emerging out of digital archiving remains vast—for groundbreaking modes of storytelling. To realize that potential, to keep an innocent eye, many established story codes will have to be scrapped (for the most part, as far as digital media story goes). That includes film grammar, the three-act screenplay, the well-made play, melodrama, Joseph Campbell tapes. However, we must construct a history of older forms, invent points of origin.

For example, the United States and western Europe today remind me of Spain in the seventeenth century. While the population of Spain dropped by two-thirds, extraordinary picaro novels appeared—very raw.[3] They amounted to the birth of the modern novel in many ways, if you extend their influence into England by 1720. (There is so much else to add, of course: Spanish theater, the (pre)existential theater of Pedro Calderón de la Barca, the scripted phantasmagoria of Spanish Baroque painting as the response in Spain and the Spanish Americas to Baroque architecture from Rome.)

But in the boneyard that was the Spanish empire, alternatives emerged. The former Spanish Netherlands flourished, even in the midst of collapse around it (religious wars, etc.). Similarly, in the United States today, I can see exceptional growth. Consider the bizarre economic bloc where I live: California/Pacific Rim/East Asia/El Norte–America. I can already see Asia literally ending at the San Pedro Harbor in Los Angeles. The blurring of borders from Latin America is so advanced that cities utterly unlike Mexico are evolving in this Latino-identified, emerging LA.

What kind of database novels should respond to this economy—to its widening paradoxes? Advanced suburbanism remakes enclaves within the inner city. Consumerati move into these enclaves, next to paupers from literally another world. The children of immigrants are beginning to restructure the politics and material culture in LA. Eventually, all classes and ethnic groups will become immigrants.

Much of this paradox remains unnoticed in computer-driven story, in gaming, second lives, and so on. Most of the contrariness that makes LA remarkable is still hidden—beneath Google Earth. Its human scale, its neighborhoods beyond the fancy shopping, are not sexy enough to remember. Only the big bang version of LA survives: *True Crime* rapper video games, and spinouts from Hollywood s/fx movies.

But in a more casual form, like a novelistic database, the scale can be much more intimate, and also much more detailed. Database novels do not have to blow up the universe to get to act three. They can hover uneasily on a human scale, even look unfinished, like an anthropology, more than interior decorating for the end of the world.

Unfinished, however, is too often considered a sin. Less "visual excitement" (less metallic, plasmic, or holographic) runs against the grain of media marketing. Too often digital imaging means high finish. An unearthly shine, like a well-oiled haircut, passes for cheerful, upbeat. But truthfully, how often is high finish just a futile attempt at dignity, a way to sell rather than speak—that big smile during a low-grade nervous breakdown?[4]

Truth is: we fall asleep on our monitors. Many U.S. media artists are utterly "afflicted" by overwork, barely above water. They remain cheerfully haunted. Despite their/our best intentions (myself included), we still may be a culture better at forgetting than responding. And the support system for media experiment—for discovery through unfinish—remains uneven.

That said, I'll run through my list of tools for database novels:

- New points of origin: the book as Renaissance computer
- The aperture
- Bleeds
- The space between
- Wormholes
- Streaming or gliding
- The picaresque

New Points of Origin: The Book as Renaissance Computer

New software is often shiny more than "new." Clearly, some origins for new digital story are five hundred years old. In doing research for *The Vatican to Vegas* (2004), I discovered that book design by 1550 was clearly responding to a new software—to perspective. This software helped the commercial classes, military engineering, seafaring, mathematics, very much like the computer today.

By 1550, new designs for the index, appendix, footnotes and after-notes all enabled the book to contain, like a computer today, data essential to the commercial classes, in particular.[5] So I structured my "history of special effects" as if the book itself were a Renaissance computer—or a Baroque computer, circa 1650, or its descendant by 1850.[6]

Similarly, when I worked on *Bleeding Through* (Klein, Kratky, and Comella 2003), it became apparent that novels in the eighteenth century also tended toward data,[7] as did stream-of-consciousness fiction in the early twentieth century.[8]

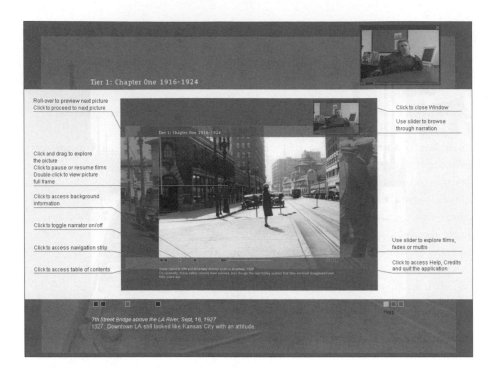

15.1 Reader's interface for *Bleeding Through*.

The Aperture

For the database novel, since it often relies on historic archives, these old forms offer "new" tools. Clearly, the act of reading a novel has always been interactive anyway—mentally interactive, that is. Absences set up within the narrative set the reader to work—"inventing," filling in the blanks. No mode of hypertext can equal the evocative power of the reader mentally filling in the blanks.

Folklore is obviously interactive in that way, since the characters are structuralist.[9] That is, the characters are ciphers, blanks for the reader to fill in. No wonder that small children expect their fairy tales to be read to them in precisely the same way each time, with the same text exactly. They need familiar absences in order to mentally enter, to use the hollow structured character as a vessel, an avatar.

All media relies on absences to tell story. These absences are the essence of each: Literature is blind; therefore, is visually imagined. Cinema is autistic, sees as a machine, not a character; therefore requires film grammar to heighten the

absences. And so on. But in that case, what is absence within the computer? What blindness or deafness can be turned into a mental interactive story?

It is impossible for any story to be nonlinear. Even graphic animation begins and ends (Oskar Fischinger, et al.). Similarly, the computer program is a code so linear that even a straight line is less perfect. Chance techniques are merely wider algorithms. Minimalism is essentially more polish, another feature.

The computer program is an almost cosmological form of cubist collage. So what possible absence can a computer program "honestly" generate, without adding finish, removing paradox, putting more grease in your hair?

For *Bleeding Through*, I decided that holes within the stream of plot points were the easiest tool for absence—not unlike holes in games; also in literary fiction, in music; a figure/ground ambiguity in the plot itself. The non-heroine, Molly, was an old woman who might have murdered her second husband. But that was too many years back. You looked into Molly's face for clues, some twitch at least. Nothing. She behaved with a gentle absence, an absentmindedness in her manner. No criminal secrets lined her face. No dead husbands rotted in her basement. There were no transitive clues anywhere, except the viewer filling in the blanks, building a fictional case, a story.

Thus, to make the absences in the novel stand out, the role of the viewer was repositioned. The reader is asked to identify as the maker or the engineer, rather than with character. The planned mental echo, enough to surprise, enough to immerse, was crucial to a database novel. Over a thousand images and film assets would stream with absences, like bubbles in a polymer wrap. Or like a stream of consciousness novel—where action itself is almost deleted by the character's state of mind. Molly's life was filled with secrets and simultaneous distractions.[10] She was a Molly who never bloomed. She hated the creaking of her bed overheard in the street. She never lets the viewer listen in.

Most important: this is an authored story, where the viewer is the maker, not the author. The viewer is invited to guess, through the research provided.

Before long, the viewer also drifts through Molly's streets. The neighbor gradually becomes more interested in just inventing a crime or being immersed in what crime leaves out. Thus, by the third tier (after chapter 12), the viewer knows more than Molly, who selectively forgets anyway. But more in what sense? Molly clearly inhabits her own experience.

The viewer now meets characters Molly should have known, but didn't. We travel thoroughly within a three-mile radius of her house. We discover that in classic noir films, more people have been murdered within those three miles than anywhere else in the world. So where do you put the camera? Molly hated crime stories. Even film and photography partially erase Molly and her city. The more photographic the image, the more apertures it suggests.

In *Bleeding Through*, the width of the aperture was controlled by key words. The effect may seem random, but actually it was planned. To repeat: in a database novel, apertures must be authored. They might *suggest* chance, but that is purely another fiction inside a fact. Chance is an assigned absence.

Baudelaire was a magnificent guide here. His theory of correspondence proved essential.[11] Only one aspect of this theory worked best—not the moment in his 1857 poem "Correspondences" *when* Baudelaire evokes synesthesia but more broadly *how* he achieves this effect.[12] How does he get the reader to smell and hear while reading? He orbits around this question throughout his poetry. Correspondence turns data into sensory fiction. It makes "living pillars...whisper in confusion."[13]

We apply correspondence to a stream of photos. The moments when the photos appear do not precisely match what the video narrator is telling us about Molly (I speak in a video insert while the images stream). The photos do not simply illustrate the city or her story; they correspond, which is quite a different matter. Correspondence does not match like a documentary film. It leaves holes. The assets in *Bleeding Through* were carefully mismatched. They left room for mental leaps and sutures.

But the aperture cannot be too wide. If the gap is too wide, no mental leap can bridge it. Apertures should generally avoid purely surrealist automatism as well as chance techniques—not just a throw of the dice or the *I Ching*. They are "figure-grounded" ambiguity for the viewer. They echo (silently) Molly's world in Los Angeles, from 1920 to 1986.

Like keyholes, apertures help us enter downtown, but not as cinema—not movie drama nor documentary—as a third form. This third form evokes story around the unreliability of film. Its aperture plays against mental pictures that the viewer already has of Los Angeles (mostly from movies). It is a vivid antimovie or antitour of a city.

Bleeds

The interface is an engine that generates gaps. Its navigation moves these gaps along. But how do these gaps help reveal character, setting, the conclusion? How do they fit well in the story?

The width and paradox of the gap are its aperture. These apertures must be vivid enough to feel immersive—more like metonym than metaphor. For the philosopher Roman Jakobson (1956), these apertures operate like a

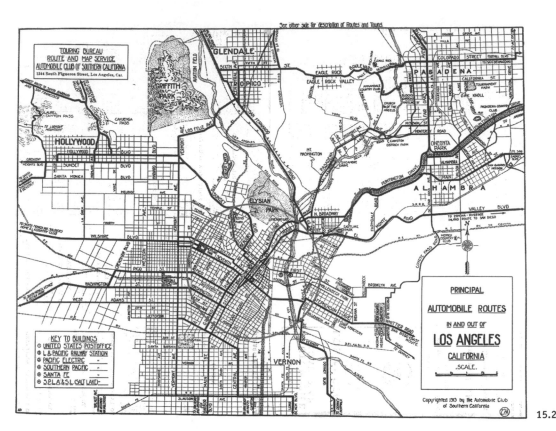

15.2

15.2–15.4 The murder capital of noir.

brilliantly engineered language disorder. For an instant, the reader cannot select. Meaning is impaired, like a charming aphasia: the visual mind cannot transfer the words back to speech. Momentarily, the hierarchy within language is suppressed. To restore contiguity, the reader substitutes, fills the gap. In a computer interface, the design gaps force substitutions so vivid that the viewer literally enters the space that moves the story along—not symbolically, but as an act of navigation.

For *Bleeding Through*, Rosemary and Andreas devoted long weekends in LA to matching old photos to streets today—exactly. The past was black and white. The present was in color. Then, by simply "bleeding" (dissolving) the present slowly through the past, the color erased what was. The gap between color and black and white generated an aperture similar to how memory distracts, or even erases.

Thus, Molly's odd memory, the erasure of city (the history of forgetting), and the unreliability of the photograph all coexisted in the same space. The interface reinforced a central idea that reappears throughout the novel. It sharpened that idea, gave it spatial simultaneity, through metonymy.

The Space Between

My newest database novel is also centered around a woman's life, but with a different working principle. Titled *The Imaginary Twentieth Century*, it reveals how the twentieth century was imagined before it took place. In 1901, if legends are to be believed, a young woman named Carrie was seduced by four men, each with their own version of the twentieth century. How they all wound up there (Scheherazade in reverse), and where they went afterward, is the engine. The archive includes twenty-two hundred illustra-

Tier 1: Chapter Six 1959-61

Tearing down houses on the Bunker Hill, 1960
Jack watching his options go down.

15.3

Tier 2: 1959-61 (Chapter Six)

Man Slai
in Row O
Cutting L

A 33-year-old wom
and killed her husb
urday during an
over which of their
should mow the lay
her sister victor
Beach, 33, of 3337 Hu
North Hollywood. H
Charlene, who held
towel to his head a
shot him, was book
murder charge.
She told police th
husband w e f e
Beach's daughter by
ous marriage, Sandr
in another room. The

Dead body in the car trunk
Fifty Ways to Murder a Man. The scene a foreplay.

15.4

15.2–15.4 (continued)

Tier 1: Chapter Four 1936

Main Street, Los Angeles, 1941

15.5

15.6

15.5–15.6 Main Street bleeds through.

15.7

The Imaginary Twentieth Century

Tier I: 1893-1901

Chapter One
Carrie's view of the Hall of Machines; her perverse husband.
Why all plans are ultimately accidental.

Chapter Two
In the caves of the Peloponnesus, a first warning goes unnoticed.
Inventors "fart in the wind" at the International Science and Crafts Movement.
Carrie meets her first suitor.

Chapter Three
After her nervous collapse, Carrie soaks in unusual cures at the Zuckerkandl spa.
Her body is jolted with electricity, rattled by machines, boiled like a trout (dressed
in parsley). And evangelized into the goddess Isis. What ensues.

Chapter Four
1901, where one of the suitors declares: "By backward steps I move."
An Arabian Nights in reverse.

Click to access the manual

Move the mouse over the side bar to scroll to the next tier

Click to access the chapters of the tier

15.8

15.7–15.10 Main screen and interface elements for *The Imaginary Twentieth Century*.

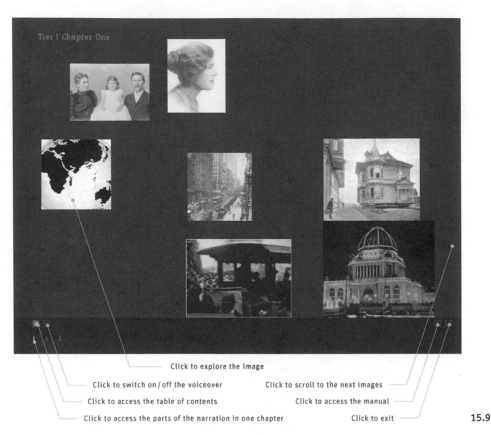

Tier I Chapter One

Click to explore the image

Click to switch on / off the voiceover   Click to scroll to the next images

Click to access the table of contents   Click to access the manual

Click to access the parts of the narration in one chapter   Click to exit   **15.9**

15.7–15.10 (continued)

tions, photos, film clips, as well as a stochastic sound engine. In all of these, there are gaps carefully assembled, between imagining the future, confronting the present, and watching the future unfold. The engine is a vast misremembering of the future, like an endless plastic surgery that never quite looks like the original.

The period 1893–1925 (mostly until 1913) was stricken by a sense of "space between"—neither/nor. The full impact of industrial design came later. The world wars were only imagined. The fears of socialist revolution and feminism had not recharted human history. Even telephones, cars, airplanes, and recorded sound were all phantoms compared to what happened after 1915 or so.

The interface, the voice-over audios, the constructing of the spaces between images—all must deliver apertures like spaces between. These had to resemble fin de siècle print—

its unusual page layouts—but the blanks between pictures are everywhere, as spatial infinity, as abstraction. They were everywhere on the streets as well—as ads on windows, kiosks. Collages were simply an artist's answer: spaces between, time overlapping.

Carrie's story takes seven chapters essentially, in two tiers. Each of her suitors imagined a different future.

• The first is the moon as Africa (Verne and others as imperialist fabulators)

• The second was the dense megacity, the metropolis—how to escape above or below the crowd

• The third was the anarchist rumblings of apocalypse and change—the world war that was coming, feminist movements, the social revolutions soon to come

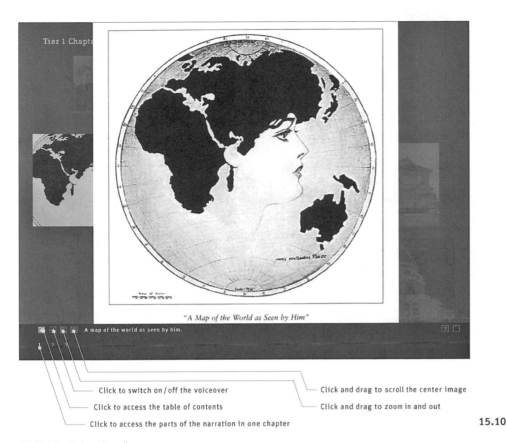

"A Map of the World as Seen by Him"

A map of the world as seen by him.

Click to switch on / off the voiceover

Click to access the table of contents

Click to access the parts of the narration in one chapter

Click and drag to scroll the center image

Click and drag to zoom in and out

15.10

15.7–15.10 (continued)

- The fourth world is about building a body that was rebuilt for the future—a body without fatigue

Each of the four worlds has a gigantic chapter of its own in tier three (with up to four hundred images apiece).

And finally, in tier four, Carrie sees what the imaginary future may actually look like in 1924–1925. The story ends, then retells itself for generations, in a vast archive assembled by the secretary of Carrie's uncle.

Each character, each technological point of view, each city in the story/archive, must jibe somehow, add to the comic tragedy. Each must reveal its misremembering of the future. In our story, the new century is both a ghost and a noisy, crowded machine. It is industrial vision in a world dominated still by agriculture. It is industrial archaeology,

industrial photography—in Chicago, New York, Paris, London, Berlin, Berne, Greek hill towns, Los Angeles.

This is fundamentally a novel about seduction—sexual, futuristic, apocalyptic, utopian. The promises never quite add up. It is like plastic surgery failing to look like the original, no matter how many operations it takes. This imagined century delivers other than what it promises. It even delivers Carrie's legend, known finally even to Marcel Duchamp. He dedicates *The Bridge Stripp'd Bare*, his Great Glass, to Carrie's legend. That legend becomes another space between in her life.

Even data fields are spaces between. They cannot generate conclusions and second acts in the same way as a novel or a film. Nor should they. So the apertures become essential, to allow the viewer to mentally set the speed, determine the rhythm, enter the shocks.

15.11

15.12

15.11–15.13 Images from the database for *The Imaginary Twentieth Century*.

15.13

15.11–15.13 (continued)

Wormholes

The wormhole is a theoretical shortcut inside an interface. We know about wormholes among stars. Wormhole physics, like computer graphics, is a visualized subjunctive geometry. It is a map of a phenomenon that seems unfindable, except mathematically, except as echo.

The computer cannot help but evolve wormholes. Its theoretical space always becomes a topos, or a chronotope; or a topology. Simply put, that spiraling milky way of visual data becomes a sleight of hand, a brilliant architecture. Part of this effect is design. The computer program turns mathematical code into user-friendly visual icons and navigation. The wormhole is another space between,

quite suitable to science fiction, time travel, being trapped in the wrong body, misremembering the future. The space between imaginary, geometric worlds, and action itself. Shall we ride the circle or cross the isthmus of the wheel?

Each one of the suitors' worlds has its wormhole effects, ways to transverse or simply dissolve into a labyrinth no wider than you prefer.

Computer wormholes are another aphasic visual effect, another metonymic trick on the eye. Their gaps are so slim, they are endless (but never infinite). The geometry of a program allows you to imagine the four worlds, spaced

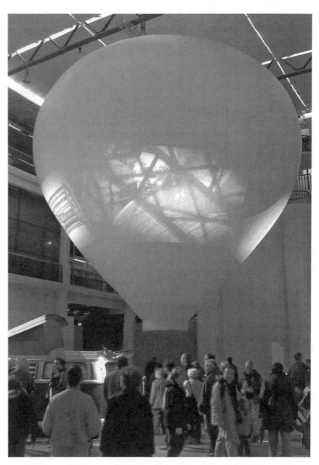

15.14

15.14–15.15 *The Imaginary Twentieth Century* as installed at the ZKM Center for Art and Media in Karlsruhe, Germany (October 2007).

Norman M. Klein

15.15

15.14–15.15 (continued)

between gaps set up by the narrator. You can reverse these gaps like a sock, turn Africa into the moon, flip the skyscraper upside down, become the body without fatigue.

Streaming or Gliding: The Animation of the Interface

In *Bleeding Through*, the images stream from left to right. In *The Imaginary Twentieth Century*, they glide, not stream, because the complexity of nineteenth-century illustrations were much more architectonic—they had to be seen at once—for the mental gaps to emerge.

Sliding resembles a stream of consciousness novel. Molly is a Molly Who Never Blooms.

Gliding suits a more episodic mode of storytelling. The viewer can move in up to four directions, or seem to.

The viewer animates the archive in order to locate apertures that express the paradoxes, the contrary facts that are also fictions, the spaces between.

The Picaresque

This baroque mode of storytelling relies on episodic breaks, relatively flat eccentric characters, and wandering through

the labyrinth of the world. Inside this world, space and time misbehave, as if you were inside the daydream of a careless god. You witness the decline of the future, along with its greatest promise. You are an epic failure in a world of utopian misunderstanding.

I am quite convinced that the picaresque is an ideal form inside a database novel. Thus, by way of picaresque, I can invoke Cervantes, Grimmelshausen, Fielding, Twain, Potocki, Pynchon, hundreds of graphic novels, video games, Philip K. Dick and science fiction of alternative worlds.

The picaresque story is often driven by a hidden archive, secret knowledge, a trace memory that never quite answers its questions. It is an oracle with a touch of senility.

The viewer navigates through these archives like an erroring knight more than knight errant. The wormholes, the spaces between, the misrememberings, the magic that is mostly legend all conspire, but with little purpose. The guidance mechanism broke last winter. But something is still running, like a waiter in a bombed-out restaurant.

The picaresque lost its appeal in the mid-nineteenth century. Only in the past fifty years, from Latin American magic realism to Pynchon to science fiction, has it achieved a comeback, of sorts.

Most of all, the picaresque is a pilgrimage through decline. Americans are particularly fascinated by picaresque now because it fits into folklore special effects, escapes into one volcano or another. Americans want to learn more clearly where their decline will lead. They want to see their alienation humanized as a dark joke.

The Imaginary Twentieth Century is a picaresque, perhaps as Duchamp, Twain, Musil, Wilde, Bierce, Woolf, and Kafka might have assembled it, might have assembled its aperture. On their behalf, and for all the picaresque that these relentless databases may bring, I offer these two experimental novels—one on stream of consciousness, the other as a picaresque. I manage better when the subject is about loss, selective memory, gaps. I am convinced that the computer is a broken necklace that continues to metastasize. It strangles us with user-friendly data. Unless we humanize its savage, comic aspects, our stories will remain as thin as bumper stickers.

For the as-yet-unknown master novelist reading this, I offer my unrestricted support. That is the purpose of this chapter: to leave an aperture where newly engaged work can follow.

Notes

1. Norman M. Klein, printed novella for *Bleeding Through—Layers of Los Angeles, 1920–1986*. The database novel—a book and DVD-ROM box set—was codirected by Norman M. Klein, Rosemary Comella, and Andreas Kratky (Karlsruhe and Los Angeles: Zentrum fur Kunst und Media [ZKM], and Labyrinth at the Annenburg Center, University of Southern California, 2003). The database novel was first exhibited in 2002, at the Future Cinema exhibition by ZKM, then published in March 2003.

2. As codirectors, while all three of us collaborated on every element of this book and DVD-ROM set, I was essentially the novelist, Bistis was the curator, and Kratky was the designer. The project opened at an exhibition on October 19, 2007, at the Zentrum fur Kunst und Media in Karlsruhe, Germany.

3. Picaro novels are baroque tale of a rogue, usually told in the first person. The form began in sixteenth-century Spain (e.g., *Lazarillo de Tormes* [1554]). In France, it takes on the spirit of more sensual escapade (with Alain-René Lesage, also borrowing from François Rabelais). In England, beginning with Daniel Defoe, it was widely studied by the likes of Henry Fielding and Tobias Smollett. Brief philosophical picaresque modes included works by Jonathan Swift, Voltaire, and Samuel Johnson. The moralism of the nineteenth-century novel shifts the picaresque toward the bildungsroman

(Goethe, Thomas Mann). The modernists' fascination with the picaresque turned into structuralist and antistructuralist episodic literature, and cinema. The 1920s Soviet fascination with the picaresque, especially Viktor Shklovsky's work, included an interest in Laurence Sterne. Picaro played a crucial role in Latin American fiction, from Borges onward. Among the critics today reviving the long tradition of scholarship about the picaresque is Ulrich Wicks.

4. In *Freud in Coney Island* (2006), I compare the stillness of U.S. mass culture, in the face of the crises since 2000, to medication and a low-grade nervous breakdown. But the high slickness of computer design, Hollywood blockbusters, of cable talk news all reinforce this cheerful fatalism, so much like the spirit of picaresque in deckling civilization gone by.

5. The first anthology to directly use the term was Rhodes (2000). I first became obsessed with this parallel when researching the histories of emblem books, memory theaters, cabinets of curiosity. By 1995, when I visited the campus at Microsoft, I found a library of these baroque books, and elaborate interest among the Microsoft teams in the antique book as computer. That probably alerted me to this most of all.

6. *Baroque computer* suggests many historical links to technologies that enter the industrial era as well, by way of the Jacquard loom, clockwork and automatons, and optical lantern effects. As Siegfried Zielinski said in 2007 at the Pervasive Animation conference held at the Tate Modern in London, "The movie was industrialized in 1895, but not invented." Encyclopedic Enlightenment models of the book evolved by 1850. By that I mean the evolving dictionaries and industrial manuals of the mid-nineteenth century the positivist structuralist model for the scientific book, heir to Diderot's *Grand Encyclopédie*.

7. This was very much a model I could share in the design of *Bleeding Through* as well, since the producer, Professor Marsha Kinder, began as an eighteenth-century scholar, and both designers, Andreas Kratky and Rosemary Comella, had strong backgrounds in literature.

What particularly fascinates me about the eighteenth-century English novel is its casual, conversational mode of departure—similar to what Barthes (1972) means by "the world as object in itself." A seemingly careless ease of discovery enriches newer forms (the novel) in their earlier stages of development. One can see much the same in Hollywood cinema from 1921 to 1960, and in practically every world cinema imaginable. That disregard must take hold in the media design of database novels as well. We should all become Fielding and Sterne, learning how to infuse the computer novel with "the gentle art of conversation," with rigor that grows out of careless associative discovery.

8. To what degree is a streaming point of view something else when assets dominate, such as photos. The archival spirit of W. G. Sebald's novels suggests the problem—how the outside and the intimate are an aperture, a streaming of gaps, misremembering, and the ruins of action. This is an apt description of database fiction.

9. By structuralist interactive folklore I mean the gaps that have been studied within the structure of myth and folklore, particularly in 1920s Soviet structuralist linguistics and the work of Claude Lévi-Strauss. This is true even in the design of dolls taken from fairy tales (i.e., the Big Bad Wolf with Little Red Riding Hood inside his dress —gaps for children to mentally fill in, quite literally). The Transformer, the Barbie outfits, and hundreds of examples from simulation games build through inversion.

10. *Simultaneous distractions* is a term I use in *The History of Forgetting* (Klein 1997). A mental image (imago) so fierce that any image resembling it gets distracted. That is, even if an image stands directly in front of you, it is erased, forgotten. A recent famous example is how 9/11 resembled the movie *Independence Day*—at first. Then an inversion of imago erased the movie. The gaps of mental imagos can be carefully widened or shrank—aperture—in computer storytelling as well.

11. This is usually associated with his poem "Correspondences," but it is essential to his theory of modernity as well, of the gap (aperture) between codes of the eternal and the transient (fashion). Baudelaire left these apertures in his poetry to enhance the feeling of the moment, of its dreamy precision and paradox.

12. Synesthesia became an essential goal in Symbolist art, in Rimbaud, later in Kandinsky; and earlier, in Baudelaire. The key for our purposes here: to erase one sense through another generates a sensory aperture. This thrill is extremely powerful. One can also bring McLuhan (and then French poststructural theory) into the discussion, around the trade-off when one medium substitutes for another (the wheel for the road, the telephone for the zone of hearing around you, etc.).

13. Also, how "infinite things sing the ecstasies of the mind and senses" (Baudelaire 1857), or in French, "Qui chantent les transports de l'esprit et des sens." The verb *transporter* has a triple nuance: to convey, to transfer, to enrapture. It is a process of correspondence in itself. Baudelaire relentlessly selected verbs with multiple mental actions, with seasoning.

Or what Henry James meant by fragrant, as in one of his many quotations: "Their fragrant faces against one's cheek, everything fell to the ground but their incapacity and their beauty" (*Turn of the Screw*, chapter 8). Or in the following from *The Golden Bowl* (II:2): "She should find him walking up and down the drawing-room in the warm, fragrant air to which the open windows and the abundant flowers contributed; slowly and vaguely moving there and looking very slight and young."

References

Barthes, Roland (1972). *Critical Essays*. Evanston, IL: Northwestern University Press.

Jakobson, Roman (1956). "The Metaphoric and Metonymic Poles." ⟨http://social.chass.ncsu.edu/wyrick/debclass/Jakob.htm⟩.

Klein, Norman M. (1997). *The History of Forgetting: Los Angeles and the Erasure of Memory*. London: Verso.

Klein, Norman M. (2004). *The Vatican to Vegas: The History of Special Effects*. New York: The New Press.

Klein, Norman M. (2006). *Freud in Coney Island and Other Tales*. Los Angeles: Seismicity/Otis Press.

Klein, Norman M., Margo Bistis, and Andreas Kratky (2007). *The Imaginary Twentieth Century*. ⟨http://interactive.usc.edu/projects// 20050813-the_imagin.php⟩.

Klein, Norman M., Andreas Kratky, and Rosemary Comella (2003). *Bleeding Through—Layers of Los Angeles, 1920–1986*. Ostfildern, Germany: Hatje Cantz Verlag.

Rhodes, Neil (ed.) (2000). *The Renaissance Computer: Knowledge and Technology in the First Age of Print*. London: Routledge.

Where Stones Can Speak: Dramatic Encounters in Interactive 3-D Virtual Reality

Tamiko Thiel

How can a virtual reality representation of an actual site compete with the richness of actually "being there"? If a site no longer exists, how can a simulation "bring the stones to speak," imbuing empty form with an aura evocative of the fascination of the original? If a virtual world depicts a place that never existed, how can it compete with the kinesthetic, full body, sensory experience of exploring a real place?

Even in the "real" world, in order to experience the true genius loci of a site it is not enough to visit it in person. Culture is not like stones; it is the events that the stones have witnessed. Even if a site's form and setting are truly impressive, if we don't experience or can't imagine the culture that filled it with life, it appears like an elaborate stage set without the accompanying play. ("Mommy, I'm tired of Rome, can't we go to Disneyland instead?") Guided tours, books and films, memorial plaques, and a well-rounded education are all aids we use to bring mute stones to speak.

In my "site-specific" interactive virtual worlds I embed layers of cultural, social, and political references into a dramatic, first-person encounter with the spatial qualities of the site itself. Going far beyond a passive viewing of material in a "virtual museum," users actively engage with the web of meaning spun by the genius loci of the site. This dramatic encounter creates in users a more personal, emotional relationship to the subject matter, making it more memorable and meaningful. Especially schoolchildren, enchanted by the gamelike quality of interactive spaces, open themselves in surprising measure to political and social content far outside of their usual spheres of interest.

These worlds do not rely on realism to convince. Realism is a false target that distracts from the true goals of an artwork: aesthetic and dramatic coherence. This chapter focuses on the generalized theory of dramatic structure I have developed in order to design such spaces—a theory that shifts emphasis from the classic *character-centered narrative* viewpoint to a *first-person experiential* one. To develop this theory I draw on narrative and drama theory, but also architecture and music. This chapter examines correspondences that have been useful for me as a practicing artist searching for new ways to think, and I beg leniency for the superficiality with which I touch on each of these vast topics.

As examples I use my large, interactive narrative 3-D spaces for which I prefer the now almost archaic term virtual reality because it expresses the fusion I seek between fantasy and reality.[1] It is the age-old human drive, as Margaret Wertheim (1999) discusses in her book *Pearly Gates of Cyberspace*, to transcend restrictions of space and time, using culture to extend and enrich physical space with metaphysical meaning. As we will see, this technology is also particularly suited to provoke a Brechtian internal dialogue in users as they seek to collate their experiences and impressions of a virtual world into a coherent narrative whole.

Project Descriptions

This chapter refers to two kinds of projects, each with different structural requirements. *Starbright World* was a networked multiuser virtual play space meant to foster communication and play among seriously ill children in hospitals. The other works discussed here (*Beyond Manzanar*, *The Travels of Mariko Horo*, and *Virtuelle Mauer/ ReConstructing the Wall*) are all single-user installations in which the goal is a dramatic encounter between the user and the spatial environment of the virtual world itself. Any "occupants" of the space must be carefully considered so as to add to rather than distract from this encounter. The following brief descriptions lay the basis for a more detailed discussion of dramatic method later on.

16.1 Children playing in *Starbright World*, Mount Sinai Hospital, 1995.

16.2 *Starbright World* screenshot, Mount Sinai Hospital, 1995.

Starbright World Networked Multiuser 3-D Virtual Reality Play Space (1995–1997)

Starbright World, commissioned in 1994 by the Starbright Foundation under its then-chair, film director Steven Spielberg, was a virtual play space where seriously ill children in hospitals across the United States could meet and play online via the private Starbright Network.[2] Using technology that was essentially the same as today's *Second Life*, children sat at personal computers in the hospital playrooms, viewing the virtual world on a monitor, and moving through the world with a mouse or cursor keys. They saw each other in the virtual world as "avatars" (graphic characters), and could communicate via text, audio, and video chat.

Worlds, Inc., a pioneer in bringing personal computer–based, interactive networked, real-time 3-D technology to the commercial market, received the commission to build *Starbright World*, and hired me as creative director and producer. I developed the initial concept for the world in discussions with doctors and child psychologists, and managed the team that built the virtual world in close collaboration with Spielberg.

This 3-D version of *Starbright World* ran at several children's hospitals in the United States between 1995 and 1997, but during that time the interactive 3-D technology remained unstable. Additionally, as I recommended in my concept study, the Starbright Foundation wanted to go beyond a simple playground concept to develop a true online community, but this meant the children needed access to the system at home as well as in hospitals. These two considerations led Starbright in 1997 to replace the 3-D version of *Starbright World* with a multimedia Web site that was more stable and accessible for an average family.[3] It was the right decision for the needs of the children, but it meant the end of an early experiment in online 3-D community.

Beyond Manzanar Interactive Virtual Reality Installation (2000)

The Manzanar Internment Camp in eastern California was the first of over ten internment camps built by the U.S.

16.3 *Beyond Manzanar,* installation view.

government during World War II to imprison Japanese Americans on a false pretext of military necessity.[4] In collaboration with theater director and poet Zara Houshmand, we created the installation *Beyond Manzanar* to compare and contrast this U.S. immigrant experience with that of Iranian Americans, who were the target of similar calls for internment during the Iranian hostage crisis in 1979–1980.[5] A year after this artwork was completed, the terrorist attacks of September 11, 2001, triggered a new wave of mass detentions on the basis of ethnicity, belying the common contention that "it could never happen again."

Users explore the internment camp not in the omnipotent role of a guard or "white visitor" but in the role of an internee. Entering the barracks leads into internal spaces that speak of the immigrants' American dream, contrasting with the external bombardment of media stereotypes demonizing an entire group as the "face of the enemy." The landscape of Manzanar, a dry desert hell to the Japanese internees yet to Iranian eyes poignantly evocative of the landscapes of Iran, forms a poetic bridge between these two diverse ethnic groups.

The Travels of Mariko Horo Interactive Virtual Reality Installation (2006)

The Travels of Mariko Horo is a reverse Marco Polo fantasy (Polo and Latham 1958), imagining the fictitious Mariko Horo as a Japanese time traveler searching for the western paradise of Buddhist mythology, the Isles of the Blest floating in the western seas.[6] Mistaking Venice for

16.4 *The Travels of Mariko Horo,* installation view, 2006. (Peter Graf)

the entire Western world, she builds an exotic, fantastic Occident visually inspired by Byzantine icons and Dante's cosmology, but structured according to Buddhist concepts.

Users experience the Western world through Mariko's eyes, exploring a lonely, abandoned archipelago at the farthest ends of the earth. The virtual world, however, is a non-Cartesian space in which vast universes can be hidden in small, drab buildings: a pavilion transports users to a piazza filled with jeweled palaces; and a small temple can open into heavens filled with angelic hosts or hells of shrieking fire. Trapped in an eternal cycle of death and rebirth, users see that their actions have consequences, letting loose evil into the world or transforming it into a paradise.

Virtuelle Mauer/ReConstructing the Wall Interactive Virtual Reality Installation (2008)

In the early morning hours of August 13, 1961, the East German government sealed off the entire western half of Berlin to block a massive population drain to the West. *Virtuelle Mauer/ReConstructing the Wall*, by the artist team T+T (led by myself and the Berlin architect Teresa Reuter), deals with the Berlin Wall and its effect on the neighborhoods it divided.[7] We rebuilt a section of the wall and its accompanying death strip, plus the immediate neighborhoods in East and West Berlin. As in *Beyond Manzanar*, the exterior spaces defined by the wall are the stage for an even more important inner life of memories and hopes, divergent fears and expectations that arose on opposite sides of the divide. The user is not the guard with the gun and

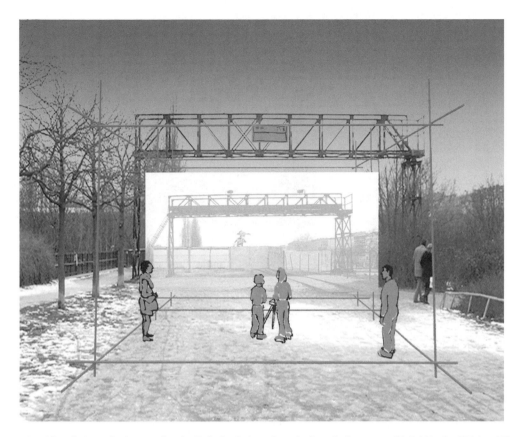

16.5 *Virtuelle Mauer/ReConstructing the Wall*, simulation of on-site installation, 2005. (T+T / Tamiko Thiel and Teresa Reuter)

license to kill but the resident whose neighborhood ends abruptly at a military border in the middle of the street. *Virtuelle Mauer* premiered on August 13, 2008, at the Museum for Communication in Berlin. In 2009, the twentieth anniversary of the fall of the wall, it will be shown both as an indoor installation in museums and galleries, as well as outdoors on the former site of the Berlin Wall.

User Interface

Although I call my works virtual reality, I use no helmets or stereo effects. As enthralling as such "full immersion" technology can be, it also severely limits the audience I can reach. *Starbright World*'s audience of seriously ill children, for instance, already spent too much time alone, physically attached to machines (dialysis, intravenous, etc.) and

fighting nausea from their medications. The isolating, uncomfortable, often nausea-inducing stereo virtual reality helmet was the last thing they wanted to use for fun. The children used normal keyboards and mice to navigate through the virtual world, typing into text windows to chat, and clicking on icons to initiate audio conferencing and videoconferencing.

The primary content of *Starbright World*, as in any online multiuser world, is the interactions between users, and encouraging play between children was also the therapeutic intent of the virtual world. Child life specialists lured children out of their beds by putting the Starbright personal computers in playrooms where they would sit together with other children to collaboratively explore the virtual world. We provided collaborative activities such as mazes with portals that required two avatars to open and the "Build-Your-Own Zone," where children could construct their own environments (buildings, gardens, racetracks, mazes, etc.). My dream was that the world would become a stage set for the theatrical narrative "make-believe" games that are the basic component of child's play, but unfortunately we were before our time. Years after the 3-D *Starbright World* went off-line, the 3-D virtual world *Second Life*, using now-matured technology, has been able to achieve what we hoped to provide for the children back in the mid-1990s: the ability to create their own world in a large online community.

In contrast to *Starbright World*, all the other works discussed in this chapter are single-user off-line installations meant to be meditative, contemplative experiences that allow users to form their own internal narrative based on their encounters with the virtual world. The works are shown as large (three by four meters, or nine by twelve feet), single-screen projections. Even without stereo, if a life-size image fills most of the peripheral visual field, the body responds to the image as a space rather than an image, reacting kinesthetically to movement through that space even when the conscious mind knows it is "merely" an illusion. The large-screen format also allows small groups to explore the piece together, and thus discover and discuss aspects that each person might have missed alone.

In order to reach the widest possible audience, the interface is kept to a simple joystick, with which one user at a time can steer their viewpoint through the virtual world. Users "walk" up to objects and into buildings, where proximity sensors then react to the user's presence and trigger the next part of the dramaturgy. This simplicity allows me to show my works in relatively low-tech venues, thereby reaching people who would never buy computer games—and perhaps would never touch a computer at all. With *Beyond Manzanar*, for instance, an important target audience was former internees of the Manzanar Internment Camp, the youngest of whom were born in 1945.

16.6 *Beyond Manzanar* installation with user, 2000.

User as Dramaturgic Linchpin

When I started building first-person interactive worlds, I realized a profound perspective shift was needed in order to apply classical narrative theory to these works. Classical narrative and drama theories focus primarily on characters, and the tensions between them in their roles as protagonist and antagonist, love interest, and so on. The audience is expected to emotionally project itself into the drama, identifying with the characters and their conflicts. This classical model translates well into character-based games, in which users' characters are the protagonists who "develop" martially, economically, socially, and so forth, as they progress through different levels of the game. Games give users clear measures of this development in points, more weapons, and the like. As users invest time in developing their characters, they become emotionally engaged; if their characters die, they suffer concrete feelings of loss as their investments of time and energy are wiped out instantly. Even in games such as *Myst*, *World of Warcraft*, or my own *Starbright World*, in which the virtual world itself is an important and finely detailed part of the game, the virtual environment is still essentially a backdrop for the tasks and actions of the users and their goals. Without these tasks and goals, the game would lose its point; the virtual world might be beautiful, but it would be empty of meaning.

In my virtual reality installations, however, the entire point is the encounter between the virtual world and the user, and the goal is for the user to understand the special qualities of the site itself—its genius loci. How can this encounter be itself dramatic and meaningful? How can the path become the goal?

Conventional wisdom holds that drama is almost impossible without characters, and research in interactive drama often centers on developing better autonomous characters rather than on investigating the dramatic potential of the first-person interactive viewpoint itself. Yet anyone who has climbed a mountain or watched a sunset knows that drama can come from a personal encounter with an environment, and its effects on one's body and mood. In such situations, an additional "character" who emotes about the beauty of the sunset is not only unnecessary but in fact extremely annoying.

The combination of first-person viewpoint and interactivity in virtual worlds allows designers to create spaces in which stories are *experienced* rather than being narrated or depicted. To construct my artworks, I have therefore developed a *first-person experiential* model of dramatic structure that focuses directly on the interactions between the virtual world and the user, rather than on a projected sympathy with the characters or narrators. To sum up the key concepts:

- It is not the users' characters who are the protagonists, it is the users themselves. "Character development" happens not within characters but *within the users themselves* in the course of their explorations of the virtual world.

- This means focusing on the *internal emotional states* that users should feel at specific points in their explorations: curiosity, trepidation, delight, fear, surprise, frustration, relief, and exaltation.

- I "choreograph" these different emotional states together into sequences to create a dramatic structure for the virtual world, and define meaningful pathways with-

in this structure. If the pathways are hyperlinked and/or looping rather than linear, this choreography becomes *episodic* with multiple dramatic arcs, rather than a classical drama with a single, all-encompassing arc.

- To convey a sense of *completeness*, the scenes in a virtual world must provide a balance of positive and negative, beauty and terror, drama and calm. Only beauty and joy are saccharine; only darkness and fear are depressing. The scenes with different emotional moods must fit together in a *cohesive* whole, with *constraints* on user movement concentrating the dramatic action and guiding users through the world.

I will give an example of such choreography later in this chapter, but first I will discuss how space and sequences of spaces can affect our emotional state, and thereby our behavior and perceptions (i.e., how space creates "emotional affect")—and I define a character-independent concept of dramatic structure.[8] Much of my thinking on this topic comes from the work of my father, Philip Thiel, who has examined the first-person user experience in detail in the context of architecture and urban planning. I refer to just a few of his concepts here, but his influence underlies this entire chapter.

The Anatomy of Space

A small space can feel cozy and protecting, or confining and claustrophobic. A large space can seem expansive and liberating, or overwhelming and terrifying. In order to be able to talk about the emotional qualities of space, and how to construct spaces to evoke specific emotional reactions in users, let us first look at a few of Philip Thiel's concepts of the "anatomy of space."[9]

First-Person Experiential Viewpoint: The "Forward Isovist"

Thiel always deals with space in terms of the first-person experiential perspective of a person moving through that space. At any given time, a person is situated at a specific point in space, and can influence or react to the volume of space contained in their *forward isovist*. This is the space they can see in front of them and in which they can move

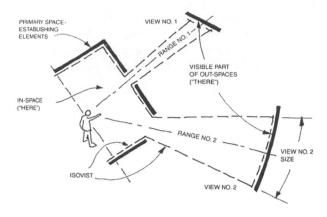

16.7 The "forward isovist." (Philip Thiel)

without encountering an obstacle, plus more distant spaces visible through openings, such as windows or doors. (If the person turns, perhaps in response to something heard from behind, their forward isovist turns with them.) In my virtual worlds, location-specific proximity sensors that react to the users' presence trigger most of the interactions, and I lure users through the work mainly with visual cues. Therefore the forward isovist is the primary spatial field that concerns me when designing user interactions with the virtual world.

Space, Place, and Occasion

Any given *scene* can be dissected into the components of space, place, and occasion:

- *Space*   The physical volumes of the space itself, delineated by solid *surfaces* that block passage and sight, *screens* that block passage but not sight, and *objects* that users can go around. A specific space can be defined by attributes of size, shape, proportion, complexity, and degree of enclosure.

- *Place*   The physical characteristics of the surfaces, screens, and objects (furnishings), plus light, sound, olfactory, and thermal effects that make this *space* particular and unique. These characteristics suggest but don't necessarily determine the emotional relationship the user might have to the place, for instance, a prosperous

and tidy village square, or a dismal, garbage-strewn slum lot.

- *Occasion*   What people are doing in this place at a specific time—partying or rioting, children playing or soldiers shooting, and so on. Designers can provoke strong emotions in the user in a single place by having a happy occasion turn into a violent one, such as by having a party scene turn into a riot scene.

If the virtual world is without "animate" occupants, the role of music, sound, and lighting expands beyond a background function indicating place, to a foreground function also indicating occasion. For example, a darkened room with dirgelike music and sounds of weeping suggests an emotionally negative occasion, such as a death in the family, whereas the same place brightly lit with festive music and happy voices indicates an emotionally positive occasion, such as a party. Occasion is time based, and the context of what occurred beforehand and the users' anticipations of what could come afterward strongly affect the emotional tone as well. As in film, music can be used to create a mood and imply a coming occasion that belies the emotional mood created by the place: when dark, threatening music is played in a bright, pleasant room, we become tense and expect an unpleasant surprise.

- *Scene*   A given space detailed as a particular place during a particular occasion. Note that even if the space and place remain the same, if the occasion changes, then the scene has changed too.

Examples of Emotional Effects of Space on the User

The place together with the occasion help set the emotional tone of each scene.[10] As the user, however, your emotional reactions to a space are dependent on your situational context and freedom of movement. The same space can feel safe if you can leave at will, and threatening if you are trapped. In *Beyond Manzanar*, for instance, the stunning beauty of the mountain backdrop defines the largest space. If you are in the middle of the camp you do not see the fence, and it seems that you can just walk away into the

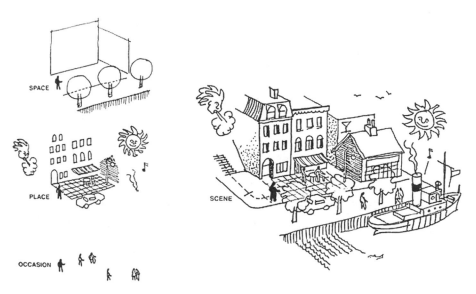

16.8 Space / Place / Occasion / Scene. (Philip Thiel)

16.9 *Beyond Manzanar,* 2000: View in the middle of camp...

16.10 ...and near the fence.

16.11 *Beyond Manzanar*: Camp with headlines.

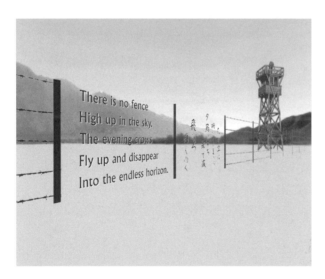

16.12 *Beyond Manzanar*: Fence poem.

16.13 *Beyond Manzanar*: Japanese American dream/Barracks life.

mountains. Emotionally, you are a visitor, perhaps disturbed by the implications of the camp but not personally involved. If you go toward the perimeter, though, the barbed wire fence springs into view, and you realize you are not in the omnipotent role of a guard or white visitor who can leave at will but are imprisoned here in the role of an internee.[11]

Virtual reality lends itself to the visualization of figures of speech, which can insert a "narrative voice" into the borderline between place and occasion. In the sky above the internment camp, headlines of the war and anti-Japanese signs fade in and out, literally "filling the air with fear." They underscore that you are confined not only by the barbed wire but also by a wall of hate and media hysteria.

As a countering voice, when the barbed wire fence blocks your path, you see that it contains poems of exile and imprisonment, inner thoughts of internees entangled in the barbed wire.

Playing with the contradictions between the signals given by place and occasion can also provoke strong emotions in users. You are inside one of the seedy tar paper barracks, and can see the barbed wire fence and watch-towers outside, but on the walls are happy family photos: the Jive Bombers jazz band and kids playing baseball. The

16.14 *Beyond Manzanar*: Iranian American dream...

16.16 *Beyond Manzanar*: Landscape framed by Japanese garden...

16.15 ...and the Iranian American media nightmare.

16.17 ...and same view framed by internment camp.

16.18 *Beyond Manzanar*: Landscape framed by Iranian garden ...

16.19 ... and framed by internment camp.

music in this scene is a lively, happy tune, yet if you listen more closely to the music you realize you are hearing the Jive Bombers' ironic theme song, "Don't Fence Me In."

Unrestricted as it is by the "rules" of conventional Cartesian space, virtual reality can employ the user's own movements as triggers to change the world in ways that drive the spatial narrative forward. A space when entered does not have to have the same size—or content—as the space when seen from outside. At one point in *Beyond Manzanar*, when you enter a barrack, the space within transforms into a much longer sequence of rooms, each representing different experiences within the immigrant American dream. In the Iranian American dream scene the room is decorated like a family living room, with carpets on the floor and framed family photos on the wall. If you approach the photos too closely, however, the walls turn transparent. You find you are surrounded by media images of "evil Iranians" and are no longer on the ground, but are suspended in the air over the Manzanar Internment Camp—threatened with the same fate that befell Japanese Americans decades before. Your own movements change this room from a secure and comfortable place, to one that provokes feelings of insecurity, vertigo, and fear.

This ability to radically alter the place is one of the most powerful tools of virtual reality. At two different points in *Beyond Manzanar*, users can enter a barrack and exit into paradise gardens that were not there before. These scenes play on the gardens actually built by Japanese American internees inside the barbed wire fence at Manzanar, and echo the paradise gardens that Iranians have coaxed out of their own deserts since time immemorial. To emphasize the emotional contrast between the prison camp and the paradise garden, we linked the scenes with the user's own actions: when you go too far into the Japanese garden, it vanishes around you, and you fall back into the prison camp. If you leave the security of the Iranian garden, you trigger a war. This framing of the Manzanar landscape, sometimes with the prison camp, sometimes with a paradise garden, underscores how your emotional relationship to a space strongly depends on your situational context.

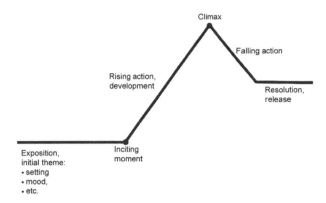

16.20 Pyramid of dramatic structure, after Freytag.

All these techniques create moments of Brechtian estrangement for the user, as Matthew Smith (2007) lucidly analyzes in his discussion of "Beyond Manzanar" in *The Total Work of Art*. They form an important part of the dramatic tension between the work and the user, provoking an internal dialogue that fuels the user's personal "character development" as he or she traverses the virtual world and make sense of its multiple meanings. Although at the time of this writing the final form of *Virtuelle Mauer/ReConstructing the Wall* is not determined, we will employ similar techniques to create dramatic tension in this work, contrasting the normalcy of daily life along the Berlin Wall with the military incision the wall made into a placid residential area, and the grimness of its death strip with the bucolic idylls that grew up in its shadow. In both of these works the point of dramatic confrontation is within the virtual world itself, between the cultural and social devices that the residents used to create a positive and protected personal space, and the grim realities of the negative external space.

In *Starbright World*, on the other hand, the point of dramatic confrontation was not *within* the virtual world but actually between it and the realities of hospital life for seriously ill children. These children had enough life-and-death drama in their own lives; what they needed from us was a fantasy space where, like the internees in the gardens of Manzanar, they could for a while escape the prison of their own conditions. For the design team, that meant having to tone down our impulses to build drama into the system, and focus instead on the psychological needs of the children, designing the virtual world to be a therapeutic counter to their "everyday" life.

We therefore designed a wide variety of environments to fit the children's varying emotional needs. To counteract the children's restricted, bedridden reality, we gave them a seemingly vast virtual world in which they felt they had total freedom of movement. Rather than a single large "playground," we created several smaller spaces that visually gave the sense of openness but were actually quite bounded. These spaces were linked together via magic portals (a rainbow, a cave entrance, etc.) that caused the current scene to be turned off and the next one to be turned on, giving the sense of a continuous world. We created a tropical oasis with a waterfall and pool as a sunny and positive environment for a child who wanted cheering up, a dark labyrinth of caves for a bored child who was up for more of a thrill, a serene sky world for a child looking for peace and calm, and the bright, cluttered game cloud and building zone for the restless child who wanted stimulation. Children could go to a space that fit their mood and expect to meet other children in similar emotional states.[12]

A Generalized Theory of Dramatic Structure

How can these various components of an interactive virtual world be fit together into a dramatically and emotionally meaningful whole? As Wassily Kandinsky looked to music for a model of how to create meaning in paintings without figurative references, I looked to music to understand how to free dramatic structure from a dependence on characters. Although some music uses leitmotifs that refer to specific "story characters," and there are cultural conventions in which certain keys are perceived as "happy" or "sad," these are clearly not the sole source of emotional meaning for the listener. How can music evoke powerful emotional reactions and the feeling of deep meaning even without explicit references to the human world?

The music theorist Leonard B. Meyer (1956), in his book *Emotion and Meaning in Music*, proposed that music

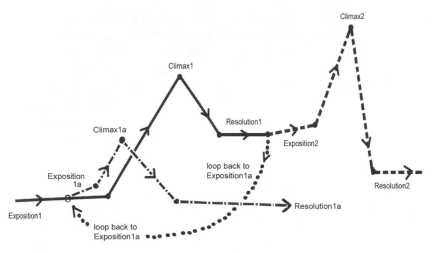

16.21 Pyramid for a hyperlinked, looping structure.

16.22 *Travels of Mariko Horo*: Mariko's house, interior.

16.23 *Travels of Mariko Horo*: Mariko's house, view toward gondola dock.

evokes emotional responses in listeners largely by purely structural means:

- Music always operates within a well-defined but culturally specific *structure*

- Within this structure, music *arouses expectations* of what the work is about and how it will develop

- *Music plays with these expectations* to create suspense and tension: fulfilling them, disappointing them, surprising them, leading them on, and so forth

- Finally, music creates meaning by *resolving the tensions* thus created, concluding with culturally based conventions that indicate the piece has come to an end

How can we apply these abstract musical concepts to a different medium—that of interactive 3-D virtual reality? Here I am indebted to the seminal work by Brenda Laurel

(1993), *Computers as Theatre*, in which she showed how the classical drama theory concept of dramatic arc can be applied to interactions with computers. If we extend this analysis to other time-based arts, looking at how they engage with the attention and emotions of the audience, we see that they all use these same basic techniques. In the following section, I use Gustav Freytag's pyramid (see Laurel 1993) as a general framework to compare dramatic structure for interactive virtual worlds, classical narrative drama, and various forms of music.[13] For a hyperlinked, looping dramatic structure, we concatenate and superimpose multiple pyramids in various ways.

- *Exposition/initial theme*   The first scene that users encounter sets their initial expectations: "What type of world is this? What could happen to me here?" This is analogous to introducing the main character and primary conflict in a narrative, or introducing the primary

16.24 *Travels of Mariko Horo*: Gondola to the pagoda.

theme in a musical work. Even if the work is looping and hyperlinked, with no real beginning or end, users will perceive the first scene they happen to see as an initial theme when they construct their own internal narrative. Users will employ common nonlinear narrative conventions such as flashbacks or "waking from a dream" to order scenes as necessary to "make sense."

- *Inciting moment* The "inciting moment" that ends the exposition is analogous to the act of "crossing the threshold" or "accepting the challenge" in Joseph Campbell's theory (1968) of the Monomyth, the point at which the narrative leaves the familiar and embarks on an adventure. In a virtual world, I often implement this literally, so that crossing the threshold to a portal changes the world around the user.

- *Rising action/development* In interactive worlds, the narrative is driven by users' actions or explorations. In their explorations users may discover unexpected aspects of the world, which change their understanding of what the world is about and their expectations of what could happen in the future. Designers can play with the sequence of scenes or moods within scenes to provoke emotional reactions in the users. If the previous scene had a positive atmosphere, the next one could be negative; if the first scene is a normal everyday world, the next one could be fantastical. This is analogous to how new characters and plot complications are introduced into a narrative, or to the introduction of a secondary theme or dissonance in a musical structure.

- *Climax* I define climax in an interactive world as the scene in which users experience an emotional high

16.25 *Travels of Mariko Horo*: In the underwater realm.

point, a point of maximum visual and acoustic turbulence, whether of positive or negative emotions. In a classical narrative, the turning point marks a distinct change in the protagonist's affairs to a situation that is much better (comedy) or far worse (tragedy); in music this could be the point of maximum dissonance, maximum or minimum tempo, loudness, and so on.

- *Falling action followed by resolution/release*   The climax is followed by a pronounced reduction of emotional arousal in the falling action phase, with a return to a state of "normalcy" or relative calm. The falling action phase, or alternately a jump directly from climax to resolution, is necessary for users to perceive the climax as a high point, as our bodies adapt to and finally ignore a continuing stimulus, even one at a high level. Classical narrative drama often aims for a grand resolution in which the hidden connections between various subplots

are revealed, the fates of the major characters are explained, and the various threads of the story are all tied together. In a virtual reality installation, however, users can enter and leave the exhibition space at any time. There is no real beginning, and especially in a looping structure there is no real end. How can we create a sense of emotional conclusion for users?

Here it is useful to look at episodic or serial narratives, which are experienced by the audience as subplots in a larger narrative, each with its own climax and falling action. There is no complete resolution of the drama, but rather a release of the built-up emotional tension to create a calm point of lowest emotional turbulence, after which the story continues into the next dramatic arc. Western music uses an analogous device, reducing or resolving dissonance by returning to the original or a harmonically related key. Another form of resolution for

16.26 *Travels of Mariko Horo*: Saints and the heavenly king.

music pieces is a strong change in tempo, either slowing to a stop or driving to a frenzy that then suddenly ends. In all cases, the works create emotional turmoil that is then soothed or released.

• *Restart*   After a dramatic arc ends, an interactive world must provide some incentive to continue—an indication that new experiences may come if the user sallies forth again. Perhaps the world has changed, or perhaps there are other paths not taken that are waiting to be explored. For myself, the rewards of a world that can be repeatedly visited and explored in depth outweigh the lessening of the dramatic climax. This means, however, that I must provide enough content in each scene to reward users for multiple visits. Most important, rather than giving users a fragmentary experience of a work of unknowable extent, I want to give them episodic experiences that are clearly part of a larger dra-

matic narrative—a small but emotionally significant difference.

Example: Choreography of Scenes in *The Travels of Mariko Horo*

To create a dramatic choreography of scenes in an interactive world, designers need to be aware of the basic emotional mood of each scene, whether neutral, negative, or positive, and how that basic mood is modulated by what could come before or after. Designers should concatenate sequences of scenes as composers arrange phrases within a piece of music, complementing or alternating emotional states, building suspense or releasing it dramatically. Neutral spaces can function as resting points, a place of calm or the lowest dramatic turbulence, which provide resolution or release within the dramatic arc. In works that loop, these function as restarting points for users' explorations.

16.27 *Travels of Mariko Horo*: The court of final judgment.

In *The Travels of Mariko Horo*, the logic of completeness, of a balance of positive and negative spaces, meant that once I decided to build heaven I also had to build hell. I used the Buddhist concept of rebirth to structure the multiple paths through these spaces into cycles that consciously disturb the linearity of the Christian cosmos and provide multiple dramatic arcs that give users a feeling of closure at the end of each cycle.

Introduction/initial Theme

Scene 1: Mariko's House Interior   You can walk into the installation at any point in the work, so there is no true initial scene. You always return to Mariko's house after rebirth, however, so this is a common starting point for many of the choreographies. If you have no experience with Japanese culture, the interior may be exotic, but as a stable, recurring environment it becomes familiar, and of all the scenes is relatively realistic and commonplace. The scene may feel slightly claustrophobic, but otherwise calm and neutral.

Scene 2: View outside of Mariko's House   The screens open automatically, and you see a herd of dolphins playing around the house—depicted in a stylized fairy tale aesthetic. Outside, a gondola is waiting for you at the foot of some steps. In the distance you see low islands in the lagoon and a few buildings. The mood is still calm and fairly neutral. There may be a slight negative feeling of loneliness, balanced with a positive feeling of curiosity.

Inciting Moment

Scene 3: Into the Gondola and Under Way in the Lagoon   When you step into the gondola, golden sea horses inflate to full size, sparking a brief feeling of surprise.

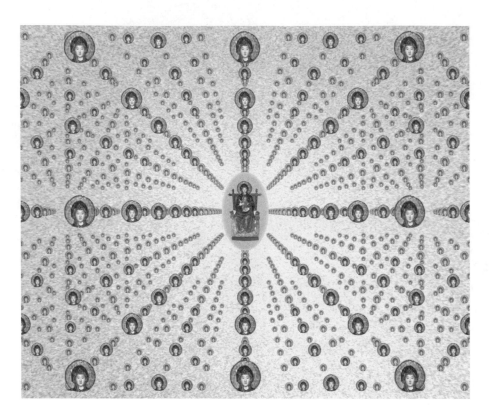

16.28 *Travels of Mariko Horo*: Crystalline heaven. In heaven, the music becomes soothing, peaceful; the air is filled with the thousandfold countenance of the goddess of mercy. You feel sudden relief and a sense of tranquillity. Here a Christian cosmos would end, but Mariko's cosmos is structured according to Buddhist concepts. Only the enlightened who are free of desire escape the cycles of death and rebirth. Those who are restless and continue to explore will fall back to earth.

Any subsequent motions with the joystick cause the sea horses to pull the gondola through the water. We have clearly crossed a threshold into the fantastic, but the world still feels fairly neutral, tinged with positive feelings of delight at the movement of the gondola, and perhaps a touch of negative feelings of loneliness and uncertainty as to what will happen next.

Rising Action/Development

Scene 4: Pagoda Portal to the Underwater Realm If you dock on the island of the pagoda and enter the building, the ground opens under your feet, provoking a transitory negative feeling of alarm, followed by positive feelings of surprise, delight, and curiosity as you fall into a fantastic

underwater realm with lacy white buildings. You may recognize Venice's Piazza San Marco, or depending on your cultural background, you could have associations with Alice's descent into Wonderland or the Palace of the Dragon King from the Japanese fairy tale "Urashimataro." Even if the scene awakens no specific associations, the mood is of positive fairy tale expectations.

Scene 5: In the Palace of the Heavenly King There are many buildings here, but I will detail only one path: when you enter the building with the most extravagant façade (the Basilica San Marco), it transforms from lacy white to bejeweled gold; the space fills with clouds of angels singing sacred music. You also see men with halos like saints, but red, demonic faces and large, staring blue eyes. Even

16.29 *Travels of Mariko Horo*: Hell. In hell, the negative stress of the previous scene is driven to a peak. Your already-beleaguered senses are additionally assaulted by shrieking flames and roaring gunfire as you find yourself in a video game war zone of ruins. Luckily, in the circular structure of Mariko's Buddhist cosmology, you can even escape from hell. If you try to raise yourself, if you really want to, you can return to the mortal world.

those who do not recognize the references to *oni* and *tengu* —ogres and goblins frequently representing foreigners in Japanese mythology—might find the figures puzzling and somewhat disturbing. The mood is a mix of positive delight at the beauty of the building and negative apprehension at the peculiar men. If you then approach a large seated figure, half hidden by the intricate facade of the building itself, the saints immediately surround you, and the music strikes a loud chord.

Climax

Scene 6: The Court of Final Judgment   You are transported up to the Court of Final Judgment. Here presides the Byzantine icon of Christ from Venice's Basilica San

Marco—but his red skin, huge, staring blue eyes, and eight arms give him the aspect of a fierce Buddhist heavenly king. He sits in judgment surrounded by heavenly hosts, and the music is loud with wild, clashing cymbals, while the flames of hell lick at your feet. Clouds of the saved rise upward; clouds of the damned fall into the hellfires. The scene has a dramatic beauty but your senses are overloaded; you are startled, confused, and apprehensive about what will happen next.

Resolution

Scene 7: Heaven or Hell   Your own movements now determine where you go next: to heaven or hell.

16.30 *Travels of Mariko Horo*: Reborn in Mariko's house.

Scene 8: Rebirth in Mariko's House

Whether you have been in heaven or hell, you are reborn in Mariko's house. It is familiar; you have awoken from a dream and returned to real life. You may feel regret at losing heaven or relief at escaping hell, but for now you are at a neutral point, a release from the tensions of your journey and the stress of the unfamiliar.

Scene 9: Garden or Ruin

From outside, however, you hear strange music. The sliding screens open, revealing a changed world. Depending on your past actions, you have changed the world for better or worse. Positive delight or negative dismay replaces the quiet neutrality of your rebirth. You have returned to the beginning, but the world is different, and you embark again into the unknown, in delighted anticipation or worried apprehension.

Overview

If we graph the positive and negative levels of arousal versus time, scene by scene, it could look as shown in figure 16.33.

If Mariko's world consisted only of the fantastic underwater realm, without a "normal" world as reference, after a time your initial surprise and delight would fade, and the dreamlike character of the world would seem normal and mundane. Without the dramaturgic tensions of the Last Judgment scene, the fall from heaven, and the possibility of descent into hell, the world would lose its edge and its dramatic arc would be much flatter. Your encounters with the sometimes-unsettling imagery and experiences in the piece are more intense as well as memorable because you are not a passive viewer but an active—if sometimes unwilling—initiator, triggering them with your own decisions and movements.

16.31 *Travels of Mariko Horo*: The world after heaven.

Conclusion

Interactive virtual reality can provide a site-specific experience that goes far beyond real life, enhancing exterior form with interior spaces carrying cultural and emotional meaning. Spaces and sequences of spaces can tell stories, if the designer understands the expressive qualities of space and how to use sequence to create dramatic structure for the user experience. The designer must understand the emotional effect of each of the virtual spaces on the user, and organize these scenes into phrases or movements, sequences of scenes that play with users' expectations to create the classic buildup, climax, and resolution of dramatic narrative. The interactive first-person viewpoint puts users in the role of protagonist, allowing them to drive the narrative forward with their own movements and actions, thereby giving them a sense of participation in and responsibility for the events that happen to them in the course of their explorations. Thus the encounter becomes an actively lived experience rather than a passively absorbed lecture.

Space, place, and occasion do not have to be logical, and in fact their affective power is enhanced when used to express verbal metaphors visually and spatially. Internal states of being can be built directly into the 3-D form, as when entering a room is "retreating into one's memories," or when archival newspaper headlines float in the sky to express "air thick with fear." These effects of Brechtian estrangement are powerful stimulants to users' internal dialogue, which is the true source of their character development as protagonists of the interactive experience. Designers should not restrict themselves to replicating real space but instead should use the transformative powers of interactive virtual reality, opening up worlds of imagination and memory in which the user is an active participant in a dialogue with the genius loci of the site—where stones can speak.

16.32 *Travels of Mariko Horo*: The world after hell.

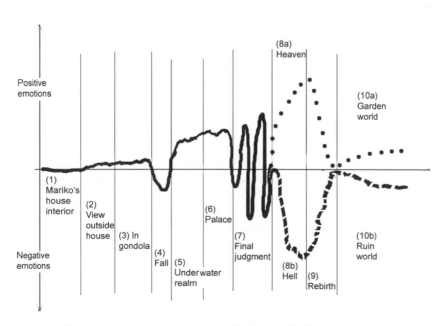

16.33 Graph of emotional arousal versus time in *The Travels of Mariko Horo*.

Notes

1. See my online portfolio, available at ⟨http://www.mission-base
.com/tamiko⟩.

2. The 3-D version of *Starbright World* is available at ⟨http://www
.mission-base.com/tamiko/starbright⟩. More information on the
Starbright Foundation is available at ⟨http://www.starbright.org⟩.

3. The current *Starbright World* is available at ⟨http://www.starlight
.org/site/c.fuLQK6MMIpG/b.1090027/k.A0FF/Starbright_World
.htm⟩.

4. *Korematsu v. United States*, 323 U.S. 214, 65 S.Ct. 193, 89 L.Ed.
194 (1944), ⟨http://bss.sfsu.edu/internment/Congressional
%20Records/19850219.html#n13⟩.

5. *Beyond Manzanar* is available at ⟨http://www.mission-base.com/
manzanar⟩.

6. *Travels of Mariko Horo* is available at ⟨http://www.mission-base
.com/tamiko/mariko-horo⟩.

7. *Virtuelle Mauer* is available at ⟨http://www.virtuelle-mauer-berlin
.de⟩.

8. See Antonio R. Damasio and the discussion of emotional affect
at ⟨http://www.affectivedesign.org/archives/30⟩.

9. The exploration here is drastically simplified; for a full discussion,
see Thiel (1997).

10. All images in this section are by Tamiko Thiel and Zara
Houshmand.

11. For a detailed discussion of these techniques as applied to *Beyond Manzanar*, see my paper for the conference COSIGN2001 Semiotics of Computer Games available at ⟨http://www.cosignconference
.org/cosign2001/papers/Thiel.pdf⟩.

12. See the "Images" link available at ⟨http://www.mission-base
.com/tamiko/starbright.⟩

13. Many thanks to Betsy Marvit, Steve Le Blanc, Dietmar Elflein,
and Marlena Corcoran for their clarifying discussions on this topic.

References

Campbell, Joseph (1968). *The Hero with a Thousand Faces*. Princeton,
NJ: Princeton University Press.

Laurel, Brenda (1993). *Computers as Theatre*. Reading, MA: Addison-
Wesley Publishing Company.

Meyer, Leonard B. (1956). *Emotion and Meaning in Music*. Chicago:
University of Chicago Press.

Polo, Marco, and Ronald Latham (trans.) (1958). *Marco Polo: The
Travels*. London: Penguin Books.

Smith, Matthew Wilson (2007). *The Total Work of Art: From Bayreuth
to Cyberspace*. New York: Routledge.

Thiel, Philip (1997). *People, Paths, Purposes: Notes for a Participatory Envirotecture*. Seattle: University of Washington Press.

Wertheim, Margaret (1999). *The Pearly Gates of Cyberspace: A History
of Space from Dante to the Internet*. New York: Doubleday.

Moving in Place: The Question of Distributed Social Cinema

Adriene Jenik and Sarah Lewison

SPECFLIC is an ongoing creative research project in performative and "playable" media. It proposes a new form of storytelling: distributed social cinema. This form seeks to integrate our mobile communication gadgets (cell phones, laptops, pagers, mp3 players, etc.)—normally thought of as distractions from the story—into the story itself, thereby creating "layers" and "zones" through which the audience experiences a multimodal story event.

Each event is formed from a template of the following elements: an iconic public building or space, a research-based narrative vision of that place in 2030, an ensemble of talented performers, prerecorded and live aural and visual media, and assorted experimental communications applications. SPECFLIC events combine high- and low-tech elements and devices, making it clear that neither the "future" nor the "past" are unique periods of time, but instead are constructed through both history and imagination. Rather than offering this story to a hushed audience in a darkened room, the project casts the story on to its public—implicating each audience member within a shared future.

As of this writing, two versions of the project have been realized. SPECFLIC 1.0 was presented at the California Institute for Telecommunications and Information Technology on the University of California at San Diego campus in October 2005. Its story focused on the near future of the public educational and research institution. SPECFLIC 2.0 took place in August 2006 at the Martin Luther King Jr. branch of the San Jose Public Library.[1] Its story was centered on the near future of books, the written word, and the public library.

The exchange below, between the director, Adriene Jenik, and critical observer/participant Sarah Lewison, was conducted shortly after SPECFLIC 2.0, and focuses primarily on this event.

Lewison: I think the events demonstrated unique possibilities for encounters in a crowd. SPECFLIC occupies an interesting ground in that the event is orchestrated to acknowledge and accommodate prior conditions in the urban landscape. These have to do with the mediation of the space itself through spatial and urban planning, and the placement of media displays within these spaces in forms characteristic of advertising. They also have to include the personal media devices people carry for entertainment and communication that effect an alienation of individuals from their physical environment and each other. The SPECFLIC events gather these factors together within a common story to produce new vectors of exchange and feedback. The project nods to the distribution of electronic media throughout the landscape and elicits participation from the spectator, which is more than symbolic, but is essential to its content.

Jenik: The layers of SPECFLIC 2.0 extended in concentric circles beyond a large dual projection of a live "gateway" character, the InfoSpherian, whose presence dominated the space most proximal to both entrances to the library building. As the audience moved away from her spectral voice-image and around the building, they encountered the elevated rear-projected "library story" with its related sound track. Live performers moved about, some in relation to a grid of images and text that formed a flashing visual border, and some seeming to emerge from the audience itself. Piles of books formed convenient stools, an incognito Sony engineer solicited comments on a future book form, and portions of text were served straight into patrons' pockets.[2]

Lewison: You sometimes describe this as a "cinema of distraction." By incorporating the media devices and data

17.1 SPECFLIC 2.0 audience members peruse Sony e-Book Readers featuring texts related to the project. (Chris O'Neal)

of spectators into the performance, you demonstrate how these gadgets, often experienced as intrusive, can bear on the proceedings as a redistribution of speech. This proposes a social media environment with political potential, where people hold the means to question and even reconceptualize their own institutions. This is a welcome alternative to the proliferation of an individually tailored personal media that reinforce perceptions of individual control of a personalized environment. To what degree do these mediations reinforce and police some social behaviors over others? How do we even define or evaluate social interaction in a society that is so designed and mediated by technological interventions?

Jenik: We, as a species, have developed in relationship to the technologies we create. Each added technology

extends our understanding of our humanness. Our memories, our voices and visions, our productive capacities, are extended beyond their previous limits, and this, of course, creates a greater sense of both agency and control. I am driven to create work that enacts these dual tensions. It is the urgency of this historical moment and my own awareness of my position as a woman in a "bleeding-edge" technology research institution that give rise to this work, which "holds up a mirror" to our culture as well as the ways contemporary society is transformed by our use of these new, mobile, and distributed technologies.[3]

Lewison: I think the media that extends our capacities to communicate and preserve information also becomes a substitute for memory itself, at least short-term visual memory—allowing it to atrophy while the transitory, habitual experience of the built environment becomes amplified. As people travel rapidly through an environment, they retreat somewhat by using devices that ameliorate the boredom of the landscape speeding by. In public conveyances, individuals also use electronics to avoid the anxiety of social contact. In both cases, one could suggest that people go somewhere else. This isn't a new phenomenon; in *The Railway Journey*, Wolfgang Schivelbusch (1977) cites how the 1830s saw a massive increase in the publication of materials for train consumption by particularly the middle classes. Watching movies on the plane, or talking on the cell while driving, is certainly analogous. What I think has changed is that the practice of using media to retreat from or augment the immediate environment has extended into new situations, into public spaces that are in fact quite stimulating, such as plazas, malls, and the like. The tendency is to individually modulate privacy and distance in the most public spaces. Everyone is a little bit of the flaneur.

It is this play-off between different kinds of mobility and identity—real, imagined, and illusory—that seems pertinent in the formulations you bring together in SPECFLIC. There's a certain optimism embedded in art projects that endeavor to mediate the urban landscape with communicative technologies. It is hoped that people will recognize their own concerns within the project, and that they will take advantage of their access to some kind of exchange. By inviting the intervention of these gadgets, one complicates the dynamics of spectatorship and also storytelling. Spectators are brought into active roles as interpreters of the messages producing the story. With SPECFLIC, the metaphor of social agency and mobility in relation to access to information is literally situated to highlight the intersections of public and private interests as well as technologies that control both information and physical space.

The InfoSpherian has three InfoFaces, which she alternates throughout her performance: Flo, Core, and Hypertia. Each subcharacter is represented through changes in voice and screenic image triggered through a performer-controlled Max MSP/Jitter interface. Transitions between subcharacters are marked through a combination of the interface program, and simple gesture and costume elements assigned to each subcharacter (i.e., Flo wears opaque glasses, while Hypertia dons a translucent veil, and Core's raw image exists in greater proximity to the audience).

The InfoSpherian enters the frame, puts on her glasses, and settles in as Flo.

Flo

Wednesday, August 9, 2030

Bienvenidos, senyores y senyoras.
Yo soy el InfoSpherian.

You are here at the gateway to the Universal Knowledge Repository known as the InfoSphere.

This is the story of a future library where books as we now know them have been all but abolished by a benevolent technocracy that has rationalized them as an inefficient means of disseminating information. The book is too static a form. The new time demands the dynamism of easily replaceable code. The book object itself has been relegated to the status of artifactual curiosity, accessible and of interest only to a few. This is not an entirely cheerful prognosis and not a generous one toward "old" technologies. The scenarios of the future you call up are ones where techno-determinism challenges our contemporary sense of civil liberties, privacy, and also tactility. But then these same media are used within the performance as tools for the production of resistant speech.

Jenik: As a creative researcher, I am daily confronted with the exciting openness and expansive potentials of these new network communications tools, and in equal measures made anxious by the degree of control they afford. Regarding the "old" and "new" media, works of literature often inspire my creative projects. In 1998, I began reading a significant amount of speculative fiction. A subset of the science fiction genre, speculative fiction is commonly understood to include works that take place in a near future (e.g., a human lifetime), and focus their speculations on sociocultural shifts, rather than fantastic world visions. *Dhalgren* (Delany 1974), *Brown Girl in the Ring* (Hopkinson 1998), *The Three Stigmata of Palmer Eldritch* (Dick 1965), *The Handmaid's Tale* (Atwood 1985), and *Boxy an Star* (King 1999), though vastly different in voice and tone, would all be included in my speculative fiction reader. In particular, the novel *The Parable of the Sower* by Octavia Butler (1993) had a profound effect on my adopted Southern California consciousness.

A poetic diary entry begins this story of a teenage empath, Lauren Olamina, as she survives a horrible yet recognizable 2025. Pulling the threads of her story line from contemporary lifestyle configurations, Butler gradually reveals a postapocalyptic scenario that emerges over time, via the daily corrosion of future creep. To create Lauren's Los Angeles, Butler combines her visions of the future of gated communities, pharmaceutical abuse, globalized capital, private utilities, miscegenation, and immersive screen entertainment, alongside the shifting dynamic of family and community loyalties. Butler's book suggested that I, too, might be able to pull on the threads of the life I lead, and play out the possibilities inherent in its values and structures.

Lewison: There is a lot of significance to the locations in which you situate projects: the research institution and the library, so far. These were, in both cases, mammoth-scaled publicly funded buildings that symbolically represent pressing, even dire questions about the destiny of public information and public space in an era of increasing privatization. Please explain how these spaces are factored intentionally into the narrative.

Jenik: SPECFLIC presents a new use or a reactivation of a familiar public space. The library presents a unique opportunity in this regard because of its rich social history, resonance within individual personal memories, and generally being identified as undergoing a transformation largely brought on by its encounter with "the digital."

In California, the Martin Luther King Jr. branch of the San Jose Public Library is the result of a partnership between the local public library system and the research library of San Jose State University. Its new building is centrally located at an important intersection of downtown, providing a public gateway to the university. Eight stories high, with extensive special collections and a wonderful children's reading room, exhibit space and an extensive integration of information technology resources, the library is a library of the future already in its "look and feel" as well as its usage patterns. In developing SPECFLIC 2.0, I leaned on the library's strengths: a centrally located public building, identifiable from afar, and perceived as open to the public.

For SPECFLIC 2.0, I projected a huge (forty by fifty feet) dynamic grid on the towering cement facade of the building visible to the casual viewer from a half mile down San Fernando Road. Meanwhile, on the street level, the giant floating head of the InfoSpherian addressed passersby. As city-goers streamed by, and noticed the crowd and light, they were transformed into audience members, and led by a series of book arrows around the building to the inner courtyard, where additional elements are accessed. Ringed with benches and bounded by grass, it was a safe space to wander around and consider the story away from the noise and danger of vehicular traffic.

Lewison: Large-scale projections facing urban streets are usually intended to mobilize consumer subjectivities. In this case, projections on the street fronting the library mobilized people to bodily move into the main space for the event. The San Jose Martin Luther King Jr. Library is an architectural gem on a scale that suggests the financial heyday of a century ago, when robber barons built civic monuments in their names. As an event, SPECFLIC's spatial mappings dissipate this sense of the monumental and turn it toward the civic. The use of the building and its plazas for a range of interactions produced an immersive and permeable space that was not only about the scale or meaning of the building, or the spectacle of the projections or sound, but about the assembly of elements for a discursive arena.

If the spatiality constructs this possibility, the notion of "distribution" you cite to describe the use of personal media devices is also operative here in the sense of space and cognition within an environment. The carnivalesque atmosphere of multiple attractions physically and cognitively broke the large site up into more discrete parts, to be explored and comprehended incrementally in semi-personalized narratives. Pathways are about attention as well as the movement of the body. The mobility of the spectator means that the comprehension is uneven too, so it is inevitable that the story will be understood variably, which seems like part of the charm; you might need to ask someone else what they experienced. Everyone has a somewhat individual experience, but there still is the physical reality of people being together, comparing, checking each other out, a theater for a multitude, and an idealized space for a projection into a future.

Like a two-way mirror formulation, the projections and performances held on both faces of the Martin Luther King Jr. Library suggestively interpolated additional points of narrative contact between the building and its aspirations, and the city's history. San Jose was renovated over the last thirty years at great expense, mostly through private investment. Although it is the oldest established city in California, San Jose shows no signs of age. The historic district is a reconstruction; distinctive activity zones define the downtown, such as corporate, recreation, government, entertainment, transportation, and education. In this downtown there are no wild lots, unfenced spatial mysteries, cacophonies of signage, or confusion about where a pedestrian should walk. The library, with its repository of resources and adjacency to San Jose State University, however, is probably one of the richest sites in the city for lines of flight and escape, or deep burrowing into a past. With the library as a centerpiece and subject, SPECFLIC emphasizes the library as a portal, or as an ideal democratic object rather than as the triumph of civic rationality.

As a meditation on technocracies, the story of the future at the core of SPECFLIC becomes extended here as it passes beyond the urban divisions: street, avenue, zone classification, and neighborhood. The layout and demographics of the city is part of the story of who habituates the library, and who paid for it. In the crowd at the event, too, there were people entering from different milieus; the locals you refer to, who habitually cut around the library and through the campus to reach the outlying working-class neighborhoods, mingled with the festivalgoers who flew in from around the world. One wonders how these differentials played out. By incorporating the interactive performative elements, you invite strangers in a crowd to see and hear each other, and to question: *Where are you coming from? Where are they going? Are they carrying books?* You constructed an alternate world, a plausible future, and placed characters within it who perform the roles of implementing and policing this world with consistent rules that people found they had to respond to.

Jenik: With each SPECFLIC, what I call the "base story" emerges from my initial research. At times, this is combined with what I know of the limitations of the site (i.e., the audience must remain outside the building for the event). As I continue to develop the base story, characters appear—sometimes in relationship to a particular visual or performative gesture, in response to the space, or as I imagine a particular performer's talents, or the affordances of a particular media form.

SPECFLIC 2.0's base story reads as follows:

2030. The public library has been incrementally transformed into the universal knowledge repository known as the InfoSphere. The InfoSphere is a generally accessible, multilingual digital archive that expands exponentially on an hourly basis. The public accesses the InfoSphere independently of the library building, and the role of the library and librarians has shifted to accommodate these changes: local public libraries now assist people in locating the bits they need in this overwhelming data flow. InfoSpherians also issue the reading licenses necessary to access various tiers of knowledge and enforce information access filters.

Now that book objects are commonly understood as an inefficient way to access, store, distribute, and further utilize knowledge, they have fallen out of daily use by the public. With the advent of e-books, books themselves became more a state of mind, and since the Great Silverfish Attack of 2012, book objects have become relics of history needing preservation for the ages.

In 2030, there still exist people who have passionate memories of "book culture" and argue its importance even in its increasingly anachronistic state, so even as the library functions are no longer localized, the library building still exists. But instead of the bustling lending library and information technology access site we know today, it has been transformed into a museum for book objects. The entirety of the libraries book holdings have been designated a "special collection," which can only be accessed via an on-site InfoSpherian.

The InfoSpherian is the 2030 equivalent to the information or reference desk librarian. She is stationed within the library building, which is now closed to the public, and is accessible as a video projection. If one wants to see a book in its object form, one can request it from the InfoSpherian. You must be patient. It may take some time. (Jenik 2006)

It was important that the InfoSpherian character inhabit the functions of the library that emerge as relevant in 2030. I was considering, in the age of the Internet as well as increasingly available and distributed information access, what is the role of the librarian? My answer took into account both what librarians them-selves are proposing (as information exponentially increases, so too do the needs of the public to organize and navigate through this data terrain), but other roles that might be foisted on them, or that they might begrudgingly take on as they strive for continued rele-vance. So the InfoSpherian oversees the issuing and en-forcement of reading licenses to the reading public. Here, I've envisioned the regularization of digital rights management and the movement of public libraries away from their historical role in defending "free open access to knowledge." The realities of current and future digital publishing access means that many libraries are in the process of instituting tiered access: some library patrons will pay higher access fees to access certain types of journals. Playing out these scenarios within the atmo-sphere of Homeland Security concerns and changes in intellectual property law resulted in the Infospherian's admonitions from the Software Protection Authority.[4]

A MESSAGE FROM THE Software Protection Authority:
Intellectual works are property.
This property is protected with the full force of civil and criminal law.

A MESSAGE FROM THE Software Protection Authority:
Prevent reading piracy, control access to your reading material at all times.

A MESSAGE FROM THE Software Protection Authority:
Friends do not ask friends to access their reading material.

A MESSAGE FROM THE Software Protection Authority:
Check your lending rights before you loan. Don't Pass the Book! (Jenik and Pilar 2006)

In between her exchanges with the public, the Info-Spherian takes breaks (during which she plays clips from the selected media archive). She periodically exhib-

17.2 Praba Pilar as the InfoSpherian in SPECFLIC 2.0. (Chris O'Neal)

its a library museum "artifact" (like bookmarks and reading glasses), explaining its use in the past. The InfoSpherian announces "It's story time" and proceeds to read a Vietnamese children's text to her assembled audience. The InfoSpherian was developed with perfor-mance artist Praba Pilar, who so deftly inhabited her role that audience members asked me how long I took to program her.[5]

The only other people who inhabit the library build-ing are library functionaries known as the Searcher and the Stacker. They are the workers who retrieve and re-place the books that the public requests. Since there are not many requests, they are not busy, but gracefully and purposefully "perform" their activities. Their exaggerated gestures make us feel as if what they are doing is impor-tant, but their languid movement tells a story of another time, when people wandered haphazardly through the library stacks looking for a book.

Lewison: These were films depicting a man and woman working, separately, inside the library. They could be seen selecting and flipping through books, moving through the stacks, and up and down the staircases. They were rarely in the same frame or on the same floor. I read them through a lens of romantic suspense, as if they knew that what they were seeking in the library and books was, in fact, each other. The warmly colored wooden interior features of the library contrasted against the steel and glass of the exterior, creating an illusion that the library had turned inside out and was revealing its innards on the surface of its architectural skin. One spectator said it was like the building was a container of its own memories, collecting the data of life by day and recapitulating the drama by night.[6]

Jenik: These characters were inspired by another text: the short story "The Library of Babel" by Jorge Luis Borges (1962). Here, among the description of the library as labyrinth, he writes, "There are official searchers, inquisitors. I have seen them in the performance of their function: they always arrive extremely tired from their journeys; they speak of a broken stairway which almost killed them; they talk with the librarian of galleries and stairs; sometimes they pick up the nearest volume and leaf through it, looking for infamous words. Obviously, no one expects to discover anything."

These characters could be seen enacting their cryptic yet familiar movements from rear projections that emanated from the third and fourth floors of the library. As one moved away from the building toward the edges of the courtyard, the projections revealed the interior life of the library. Though prerecorded, the ambient story was structured and finally edited in full knowledge of its spatial placement: one could follow both characters in their movements from one floor to another, from one area of the library to another, with the Stacker subtly following the Searcher. Their occasional encounters formed the dramatic tension within this silent twenty-five-minute cinematic loop.

The Searcher and the Stacker were played by actors Allison Janney and Richard Jenik, respectively, who also appeared in SPECFLIC 1.0. Shot on location with a high-resolution camera that enabled the audience to read the titles on the spines of the shelved books, the projections transform the library itself into a character in the story.[7] This spatialized film loop exists as a kind of elegy to the libraries' past, remembered for its beauty and expansiveness; it is a reliquary of knowledge within which one could (and still can!) be absorbed, which one can physically inhabit, where one can find sanctuary.

Other peripheral characters were created in collaboration with the participating performers, who are artists and writers in their own right. On meeting talented young poet-performer Melissa Lozano, I proposed that she work with me to develop and perform the FoolBook, a character who exists in the periphery of the spectacle, wandering the library grounds. Dressed as a distressed temp worker, she represents, through voice and gesture, those library patrons who view the library not just as a place to gather knowledge but also as a public place of dignity in which they are welcome. The distributed knowledge economy literally casts out such a figure. A cross between a raven, a Mayan curandera, and a homeless person, The FoolBook hovers over this future, distributing wordless books and mumbling her incantation.

I've been here before
I have lived here before
I have prayed in circles around legends crafted
I have lived here
I have eaten here
I have loved here
I have broken sanity here
I have erased here
I have had my back towards here
I sexed here
I prayed here
I ate here
I laughed here
I battled here

17.4 The Chief Attention Authority makes note of reading violations in SPECFLIC 2.0. (Chris O'Neal)

17.3 Melissa Lozano performs as the FoolBook in SPECFLIC 2.0. (Chris O'Neal)

I worried here
I stared off here
I sang here
Everything unfinished here
I borrowed here
I forgot here
Here I recall here
I burnt here
I shed here
I flew here
I walked here
I listened here
I delivered here
I came back here
I've been here before. (Lozano 2006)

Palettes of decommissioned library books were transformed into functional stools and tables by San Jose–based sculptor Gustavo Rodriguez. Arranged around the InfoSpherian in a "storytelling" half circle, the furniture framed the audience members as future library patrons, and added a layer of contemplation and reflection on the future of these book objects.

SPECFLIC 2.0 also featured several projections of an experimental public display form created specifically for use in SPECFLIC by information technology developer Andrew Collins. The Sousveillance Grid allowed audience members equipped with cell phone cameras to capture a picture at the live event and send it to a server that immediately displays these pictures in a dynamic, constantly updating 3 × 2-foot grid projection. Posting instructions occasionally flash across the display, and audience members help each other post their photos. The grid also has a limited short message service character caption area that can be annotated by assigned SPECFLIC crew members. In SPECFLIC 2.0, the Sousveillance Grid served as a dynamic "most wanted" poster, with the uniformed Attention Authorities and audience members alike using their cell phones to "snapCapture" the likeness of those suspected of reading license violations. Elaborate code violations were assigned by the

17.5 Media and performance artist Nao Bustamante (as La Curandera) and two student Remotes perform a technical check of their "reality fly-through" GPS video stream in SPECFLIC 1.0. (Mulloy Morrow)

17.6 The Remotes and La Curandera surveil the audience in SPECFLIC 1.0. (Mulloy Morrow)

Chief Attention Authority Officer and then posted to the Sousveillance Grid picture by the chief's deputies.[8]

The Poetxt Team was formed to serve up more poetic fragments, creating an enigmatic reflection on the themes of the event through word-image associations.[9]

Lewison: Like the exemplary play of children, this ironic enforcement of your bureaucratic regime through the detection of "reading license violations" was done with the utmost seriousness. This made a game out of the LED flashing "orange alert" signs that serve darker purposes—to notify drivers of emergencies or enlist them in the apprehension of suspected criminals.

Like these grim fixtures on the interstate, the Sousveillance Grid directly addressed viewers, and situated them in a locative closed circuit where safety is hypothetically predicated on observing and reporting on the other. The locative specificity is important: the figure of the spectator is digitally captured and transmitted only to appear as an image in the absolute space of the library grounds again, exactly where the figure is. The line between privacy and publicity is certainly muddled, but in this formulation the dispersed subject is fixed in situ, their "crime of possession" is erased and their reputation comically salvaged by poetry. One is ultimately enlisted in a dialogue about proprietary boundaries, or is it a new form of gossip?

Jenik: The collective surveillance here disguised as a playful game within the SPECFLIC story world came to life as other peripheral characters like the BlackMarket Bookseller, instigating microexchange encounters: opening a trench coat to flash layers of anarchist texts offered to the audience in trade. Because of the size of the audience (more than six hundred over the course of the evening) and the diversity (children, grandparents, library patrons, and digerati mingled together), some characters seemed to arise from within the crowd. This was the case with a phalanx of bicycle-riding demonstrators who shouted "Technology ruins our soil!" and "Technology causes birth defects" while circling the building and the assembled crowd. During both versions of SPECFLIC, the boundaries between the audience and the performer blurred and shifted throughout the course of the evening, creating a disquieting space in which one could imagine existing alongside others within this future, with its residue lingering beyond the event.

Additionally, for SPECFLIC 2.0, I invited local science fiction author Rudy Rucker (2006) to develop a short message service–generated story that could be delivered directly to audience members via their mobile phones. Rucker responded by writing a twenty-five message "koan" that echoed and punctuated the event, provoking the audience members to notice the unfolding particulars of their surrounding environment (see sidebar).

SPECFLIC Messages Show Version

August 9, 2030
First thot best thot.

Where r u?

Woman books on ground.
Big face on wall. Shhh!

Seek n stack.

I see green man?
Where r u?

Marry me. I have read license.

Stack words in phone.
Library hush.

I seek u.

Hear my voice.
Words suck.

Saucer wisdom.
Book road to past.

Where r u?

In the saucer.
In the words.

Who talking?

Is my baby?
Pregnant with book.

Big face little face.

Where r u?

On the wall.
In the book.
Loud library.
Key me.

License to read.
Word talking.

Bark bite word.
B'ware police dog.

Where r u?

Behind u.
In ur phone.

Who r u?

Read my book.
Numbers suck.
Dark to see.

Where r u?

On fone.
In the word.

Kiss me by book.
Give me word.
Write smile on face.

See u on wall?
Hear u on speaker?

I m pregnant too.

Work sucks.
Party yes.

You stack, I seek.
Stomach of words.

Remember me?

Where r u?

MATHEMATICIANS IN LOVE

Copyright © Rudy Rucker 2006

In order to collect the cell phone numbers of the audience, I developed the idea of the "reading license" station. Encountered at the entrance to the courtyard, this station initiates the audience into the intellectual property themes and parameters invoked in the story. To gain a reading license, the audience members provided us with "digital IDs" (in the form of their cell phone numbers), which we input temporarily into our system in order to serve up Rucker's poem. The process allowed for a performance of future bureaucracies, including a cryptic access-level assessment, even as it provided the audience members with a small material souvenir of the event.

17.7 Members of grassroots radio collective Radioactive Radio transmitting a live audio stream of SPECFLIC 1.0. (Mulloy Morrow)

Additional media and performance layers were created through live "sound track" mixing and the use of spatialized audio. The sound artist collective Neighborhood Public Radio recorded interviews with digital luminaries and others assembled for the ISEA 2006 symposium.[10] The collective asked a variety of people to speculate about the future of the book, the public library, and the written form, and compiled the responses on a compact disc. The compact disc and selected music were then mixed, live, by a local disc jockey, forming a sound track for the outer edges of the event.[11] As one moved closer to the building and the glowing image of the InfoSpherian, one became enveloped in her atmosphere and voice; as one moved further away, ones attention shifted: to the library story emanating from the third and fourth floors, the background music and interviews, and more peripherally the additional event performers and modules.

Lewison: This description suggests a return to the theme of distraction. Rather than reinforcing a mediated totality, SPECFLIC problematizes the integration of attention and explores its inversion. The plethora of elements brought to bear on this story capitalizes on the narrative productivity of this contemporary condition. You implicitly point to a circuit of attention that moves between the embodied locus of an individual and the messages, desires, needs, and connections that pass through the portable communication devices that an individual carries along. In SPECFLIC, you call attention to how these devices remove the person from full presence in a situation. But you incorporate these same devices to produce new attention to the circumstance—a kind of counterattention.

Distraction was a notable condition for Walter Benjamin (1968) and Siegfried Kracauer (1995), who both perceived, in the competition of spectacle for the popular imagination, the possibility of ruptures from which clear-sightedness and dissent might emerge. Distraction is about differentials of attention and circuits of cognition, and the gaps in circuits of attention where there is the potential for something else.

In this era, we find that the messages of mass culture these earlier writers described are often filtered and tailored for, and by, the individual recipient. While these appear to be distractions, the experience from the subject position is carefully orchestrated to enable a seamless experience as a discrete consumer of all good things that the world has to offer. The implications raised are familiar: people are oblivious of their surroundings, and yet they are centered and individuated—shall we say calmed—through the cultivation of these familiar remote connections.

This self-centeredness colludes with Freud's observations about our narcissistic tendency to decipher personal messages from the random signs we see. One wonders if the problem with mediascapes modeled for a neoliberal constitution is not that they are distracting but as buffers against the violence of the moment and integrators of consumerist subjectivities, they don't allow for distraction.

In exploring the definitions for a cinema that examines the processes inherent in late capitalism, Sharon Bhagwan (2003) describes distraction etymologically, as a "pulling away" from an ideal, but with no particular direction. She finds, in maneuvers that split and otherwise divert or trick attention, "a filmic logic of distraction…that is linked to the dispersed spectator in a globalized mediatized landscape." Distraction is a splitting of attention between physical location and the imperatives of the communicating device. In SPECFLIC, the aim is to see how diverse communications can spin their contingencies into a story line further extended through public encounters.

The many elements enlisted recall the "cinema of attractions" that Tom Gunning (1990) portrays as characteristic of film's first ten years. Screenings were uniquely accompanied by voice-over, live music, outspoken audiences, and technical transparency, all contributing to a temporal and sensory experience that Gunning depicts as exceeding the narrative content of the film. As a contemporary experiment in a cinema of excess, SPECFLIC conjures additional repositories of information through the incorporation of connected devices, personal information acquisition, and human interactivity. This excessive quality points backward at the way economies, bodies, and networks of information are concealed by the way contemporary connectivity organizes a flow between radically discontinuous spatial activities. SPECFLIC offers an interruption analogous to bumping into someone on the street.

At this cinema, you will not only *not* be quiet, you will have to talk. This leads to another criteria outlined by Gunning for a cinema of attractions, which is the direct gaze of the performer at the spectator. In film it is only illusory, as the actor gazes at the camera, not the spectator. But this eye-line acknowledgment disappears in narrative film, along with the presence of the spectator. In SPECFLIC 2.0, the InfoSpherian engaged with viewers in a way that compelled the spectators' presence. People lined up to ask her questions of the library.[12] On the projection screen they saw her attentively listening to their requests. While her answers varied, they were clearly responses to the individual queries. The maneuver is slyly political and extremely social, through the presence of the witnessing third parties—other spectators who participate in the exchange. In these forms of direct address, the presence and position of the spectator is acknowledged and grounded on the site and within the narrative. The spectator, sited and cited as a consumer of the spectacle, is also recognized, grounded,

and implicated as a part of a network of transmissions that add up to a story.

(Infospherian)

Mercoledì il 9 agosto. 2030

Bienvenidos, senyores y senyoras.

Now that we enjoy the Universal Knowledge Repository, known as the InfoSphere, we have no real need for the fixed book form.

Our speedy, efficient access to information represents a decades-long digitization project that doesn't end here.

No.

The InfoSphere is constantly growing and expanding, far beyond what we could ever have imagined.

END. (Jenik and Pilar 2006)

Notes

1. Presented as part of the ISEA 2006/San Jose ZeroOne Festival of Art and Technology.

2. A prerelease prototype of the Sony e-book reader was demonstrated at SPECFLIC 2.0 through placing project-related texts and visuals on its crisp small screen. In terms of placing text into pockets, repurposing information technology developer Ganapathy Chockalingam's mass text distribution application "Call 2 Communicate" was originally developed as an emergency notification system.

3. In the case of SPECFLIC, it is a fun-house mirror.

4. A number of articles proved invaluable as starting points for research into these key areas. Most helpful were Bailey (2006) and Sandler (2005).

5. This query assumed that she was an artificially intelligent response system. To me, this response revealed the ways in which we already live in the future.

6. Thanks to new media artist Paula Levine, who shared this observation with me in conversation.

7. Cinematographer John Pirozzi shot on location at the San Jose Public Library.

8. Public media advocate Martha Wallner played the chief—with great zeal.

9. The Poetxt Team was composed of a group of local English honors high school students, led by ZeroOne education fellow Gina Campanella. Perhaps more successful was the University of California at San Diego upper-division speculative fiction class members who, under the tutelage of writer Anna Joy Springer, contributed to SPECFLIC 1.0's cell phone photo grid.

10. For more information on Neighborhood Public Radio, see ⟨http://www.conceptualart.org/npr/⟩. Special Thanks to Michael Trigilio and Lee Montgomery for their contributions.

11. The disc jockey was Basura, aka Michael Boada.

12. Some of the questions included: "Where do humans come from?" "What is the state of censorship in the United States in the early twenty-first century?" "Will there be a fourth Iraq war?" "What are the borders of Lebanon?" "What is a clitoris?" and "When will machines overpower humans?"

References

Atwood, Margaret (1985). *The Handmaid's Tale*. London: Cape.

Bailey, Charles W., Jr. (2006). "Strong Copyright + DRM + Weak Net Neutrality = Digital Dystopia?" *Information Technology and Libraries* 25, no. 3.

Benjamin, Walter (1968). "The Work of Art in the Age of Mechanical Reproduction." In *Illuminations*, edited and with an introduction by Hannah Arendt. New York: Schocken Books.

Bhagwan, Sharon (2003). "Filming Local, Thinking Global." Paper presented at the University of California at Los Angeles International Institute Global Fellows Program, October 23, 2003. ⟨http://www .international.ucla.edu/globalfellows/article.asp?parentid=5041⟩.

Borges, Jorge Luis (1962). "The Library of Babel." In *Labyrinths: Selected Stories and Other Writings*, edited by Donald A. Yates and James E. Irby. New York: New Directions.

Butler, Octavia (1993). *The Parable of the Sower*. New York: Four Walls Eight Windows.

Delany, Samuel R. (1974). *Dhalgren*. Boston: Gregg Press.

Dick, Philip K. (1965). *The Three Stigmata of Palmer Eldritch*. New York: Doubleday.

Gunning, Tom (1990). "The Cinema of Attractions: Early Film, Its Spectator, and the Avant-Garde." In *Early Cinema: Space, Frame, Narrative*, edited by Thomas Elsaesser. London: BFI.

Hopkinson, Nalo (1998). *Brown Girl in the Ring*. New York: Warner.

Jenik, Adriene (2006). "SPECFLIC 2.0 Base Story."

Jenik, Adriene, and Praba Pilar, with contributions by Ricardo Dominguez (2006). Script for "The Infospherian," SPECFLIC 2.0.

King, Daren (1999). *Boxy an Star*. London: Abacus.

Kracauer, Siegfried (1995). "Cult of Distraction: On Berlin's Picture Palaces." In *The Mass Ornament: Weimar Essays*, translated and edited by Thomas Y. Levin. Cambridge, MA: Harvard University Press.

Lozano, Melissa (2006). "FoolBook Incantation," SPECFLIC 2.0.

Rucker, Rudy (2006). "SPECFLIC 2.0 Koan for SMS."

Sandler, Mark (2005). "Disruptive Beneficence: The Google Print Program and the Future of Libraries." *Internet Reference Services Quarterly* 10, no. 3–4.

Schivelbusch, Wolfgang (1977). *The Railway Journey: Trains and Travel in the 19th Century*, translated from the German by Anselm Hollo. New York: Urizen Books.

Breeze Avenue Working Paper

Richard Grossman

Introduction

Breeze Avenue can best be described as a massive, highly integrated cyberspatial literary form that disgorges music, architecture, art, dance, video, and a large variety of books in prose and verse. Sections of the work draw on information from geology, screenwriting, software development, astronomy, politics, architecture, graphic and product design, meteorology, metaphysics, linguistics, literary and social theory, material science, acoustics, musical instrumentation and composition, computer animation, cryptology, deaf theater, sleep theory, mathematics, choreography, photography, engineering, archaeology, business practice, zoology, quantum mechanics, lexicography, and Vedic, Greek, Egyptian, Chinese, and Hebrew studies. Documents are produced in Latin, Yiddish, Orkhon, Hebrew, Fraser, Sanskrit, Chinese, Hieroglyphs, American Sign Language and Sutton Signwriting, various forms of numeric and symbolic notation, and English.

The complete work contains thirty-seven "elements" or distinct groups of texts. Its first manifestation will be as a one-volume 3,000,000-page book available for reading at ⟨http://www.breezeavenue.com⟩. This book will appear in beta version in late 2008 or early 2009. Once thoroughly vetted, *Breeze Avenue* will appear in printed form. Installed in the Reading Room in a location yet to be determined, the set will consist of four thousand case-bound volumes, each consisting of 750 pages, that will be displayed on shelves surrounding a central reading area. Ultimately, a 4,500-page seven-volume work titled *The American Letters Trilogy* will be published that comprises two novels printed in the 1990s (*The Alphabet Man* and *The Book of Lazarus*) and an abridged version of this work.

The thirty-seven elements adopt different approaches to expression and in some cases are constructed on technical principles from the past (such as, for example, ancient literatures, Japanese travelogues, Renaissance sonnets, and neo-classic verse essays). Others are based on sophisticated methods of computation, process, and organization that are unique in their formulations, and far removed from anything that has ever been written.

Many elements consist of subelements and sub-subelements of various lengths, some of which carry titles. For instance, there are a number of individual essays called Tractates, which are subelements of the element called Tractates and Recantations. One of Tractates' sub-subelements is titled Branded for Life. There are, as a rough estimate, one million unique subelements and sub-subelements.

The Web site will permit readers to interact with, purchase, and be included in the work. As currently planned, the only printed sets of *Breeze Avenue* will be the Reading Room copy, a proof copy, and five editions offered for sale as individual volumes. Thirteen books of various kinds, all derived from elements, and eight forms of art will also be available for purchase.

Breeze Avenue is open-ended. The work will alter over time, and other elements will ultimately be added. Following is an abbreviated description of the formal aspects of the project. This is an evolving technical paper—presented here as a chapter—that discusses the contours of the elements in order of size. Its function has been to coordinate the activities of participants so that everyone is afforded a broad, current, and precise view of the whole. As a result, it stresses the mathematical and organizational.

There is no attempt, however, to discuss the more important matter of literary content in any depth (which in itself would form a document many times longer and more complex than the one here), nor does it contain a detailed description of the future Web site, which will be innovative in its own right, nor does it describe the trilogy. A sample of various subelement pages, showing stars, clouds, birds, and so forth, as well as a few short texts will be available for viewing at ⟨http://www.richardgrossman.com⟩.

Annual Cloud Narrative

A camera installed on top of a Minneapolis office building was programmed—with the necessary computer control, backup, weather protection, and transmission equipment—to take 1,000 evenly spaced exposures each day for a year of a section of northern daylight sky (that is, on summer

Table 18.1 Summary Listing

Title	Page Count
Annual Cloud Narrative	365,000
Bonsai Poem	300,000
The Star Canticles	280,000
Aviary Poem	275,000
Visionary Sonnets	255,000
The *Breezagon*	245,000
The *Clown-illon*	216,000
The Pythagorean Super Bowl Party	210,000
Beelines	185,000
The Fabric of Reality	150,000
The Closed-Captioned Chinese Chapbook	140,000
The Brain Opera	135,000
Tocharian Letters	111,793
Squeezeborough	62,000
The Gallery of the Purchasers	40,000
Spam from God	27,000
Madhouse Filibuster	1,000
Appendixes	472
The Interstate Bingo	170
Animal Poems	606
Reggie and Boomer Books	333
Grossman's *Trip to the Far North*	270
Grossman's *Glossary of Every Humorous Word in the English Language*	115
Tycoon Boy	61
Tractates and Recantations	50
Pop-Up Torah	40
The Goldberg Variations on a Treatment	33

Table 18.1 (continued)

Title	Page Count
The *Chuckiad*	30
Scrabble Poems	36
Grossman's *Essay on Man*	20
Tomb of the Corporate Raider	15
Front Matter	8
Foreword	3
Acknowledgments	2
"Everglades"	1
Intercalarian Commentaries	0

days the interval between exposures is greater than on winter days). The photographed sky was located precisely above the 45th parallel, thereby creating the greatest possible tension between balance and dynamism in the interplay of forces of light and dark.

The 365,000 photos—whether showing rain and snow, various cloud formations or azure—run singly, chronologically, and relatively uniformly through *Breeze Avenue*. The photography ran from June 13, 2006, to June 12, 2007, and was successfully completed.

The date and time of each cloud image appear as an appendage to the page number in the running head. For example, if a photo taken on October 16, 2006, at 3:41:23 in the afternoon were to appear on page 1,763,495 of *Breeze Avenue*, the page number would read 176349510166154123.

There are two other manifestations of the narrative, aside from its appearance in the larger work:

• A series of 719 on-demand *Cloud Minute Books* are being produced for sale in editions of five (with an additional artist's proof). The title of each edition is a particular minute—for example, *10:17*—and an edition is published of chronologically ordered images for every minute in the day that produces a minimum of 197 Central Standard Time photos annually. This is the break point where a smaller number of cloud images would produce duplicate a.m. and p.m. titles. If on a given day two cloud photos are taken within a minute's interval, only the first appears in a minute book. The date appears underneath each image.

• As a separate project, editioned *Annual Cloud Screens* are being created and sold. These are flat-panel displays —each driven by a flash chip—that play back cloud images at the time their photos were taken. To clarify, assume that a cloud screen were operating in Los Angeles on January 23, 2009. On January 23, 2007, the first Minneapolis photo was taken at 7:39 a.m. Central Standard Time. Therefore at 7:39 a.m. Pacific Standard Time, the Los Angeles screen would light up, and the first image would appear and remain on screen until the Minneapolis camera had taken the next shot. Cloud photos follow in sequence throughout the day. At sunset, the screen would go dark until the following Minneapolis sunrise.

Photos of the camera setup (which is fairly complex given Minnesota weather) and the site, the engineering and software specifications, and additional meteorologic and archival information appear in the *Appendixes* (see page 204). A short video of the cameras operating in a snowstorm will be available for viewing and free download in the Web site's media room.

Bonsai Poem

The "generative poem," precisely 3,000 characters in length and written in irregularly rhymed hexameter couplets, describes a bonsai pine's enslavement and torture at the hands of humans. The poem has a dry, precise, agonized feel.

The "generated poem," created by algorithmic means, comprises 4,500,000,000 characters and is 3,000,000 pages in length—the same length as *Breeze Avenue*. The poem builds organically ("grows") and does not come together as the generative poem until the final two pages of the larger work, where it appears entire. Precisely 10 percent of the poem, or 300,000 pages, are distributed fairly evenly throughout.

The first and last twenty pages of *Breeze Avenue* are *Bonsai* pages. Pages are always placed in the same position in the larger work as in the poem (like the sequences in

The Fabric of Reality and *The Pythagorean Super Bowl Party* described below). For example, page 409,789 of the *Bonsai Poem*, if it is printed, must appear on page 409,789 of *Breeze Avenue*.

The math behind the poem is included in the *Appendixes*, and the 3,000,000-page poem is used as the basis for a screen-based artwork, where *Bonsai* scrolls from beginning to end over a period of eighty-five years.

The Star Canticles

Imagine that the earth were transformed into a modified IBM Selectric II typeball. On such a ball the *A* might cover a portion of Central Africa and the *B* lie over Japan. One could utilize this apparatus to type out poetry in a font of stars as the ball subtends sections of night sky. Synthetic firmaments, encoding underlying text, could consequently be assembled like pieces of a puzzle.

Astronomical software has been developed specifically for *Breeze Avenue* that tracks the motion of every visible star in the universe and projects it forward for one hundred million years. (The number of stars shown is slightly greater than those that would be visible using binoculars when the sky is perfectly clear.) Twenty couplets, each a hymn to God, are typed out at fifty-thousand-year intervals ("epochs") using these star fonts. Each poetic line is then size adjusted to fit precisely on three pages, so that six pages of stars surround a central page containing the couplet in white letters on a black background. These subelements occupy 280,000 pages of the larger work.

Three additional projects emanate from this element:

• A series of on-demand *Canticle Books* are being produced for sale as unique objects, with one book for each canticle within each epoch. Each book is 120 pages (twenty canticles times 6 pages, with the central poetry page being eliminated), and there are a total of forty thousand books offered (twenty canticles times two thousand epochs). The title of each book is the dated canticle.

• *Annual Star Screens*, approximately eight feet high by five feet wide, are being created for each of the twenty canticles in editions of five plus one artist's proof. Each screen shows its couplet evolving through one hundred million years in a year's time. As with the other screens, this larger screen is driven by flash technology.

- Plans are being developed where a musical composition that sets the *Canticles* will be performed, as synthetically created universes evolve on a large screen or dome.

The method of creating artificial heavens out of literal meanings and then moving them forward has been patented. Software and hardware specifications and the original canticles as a group appear in the *Appendixes*.

Aviary Poem

In contradistinction to the *Bonsai Poem* (above), the *Aviary Poem*, about the life cycle of a tree, is extremely short:

seed
weed
sprig
sapling
tree
timber!
log
coal
cinder

This text is used as the basis of a hypothetical language construct where nine talking birds of different species are each taught one of these poem words. Once trained, they are installed together in a fictional aviary. There, if a bird says any of the words (its original word or ones learned from other birds), it receives a treat.

The element displays scenarios where the birds, in order to garner food, say words in random sequences. Grids of photographs, taken by Grant Mudford, document possible narrative-poetic realities where the birds as a group construct chronological speech chains. In each grid, the last bird in the sequence is the first to have uttered all nine words, having thereby re-created the entire poem in its head.

Three- and four-page subelement groupings describe the results of mythical aviary contests. Each first page is a photo of the "winning" bird who first completes the poem, the second is a nine by nine number matrix that provides the time that the winning bird said each of its nine words

(day, month, one-digit year, hour on the twenty-four-hour clock, and minute: for example, August 9, 2005, at 3:54 p.m. would be represented as 090851554), and the third page, and if necessary a fourth, is a sequence of bird photos and times, showing the history of when each bird first said a word. The minimum number of these images is seventeen (each bird says its initial word, and then one bird mimics all the other birds before any other bird utters a second word), and the maximum is seventy-three (each bird says eight words, and then one bird wins).

Note that each bird is taught the same first word in every contest, and that a bird may say a second word (as long as another bird has already said it) before a third bird says its first word. All contests begin on January 1, 1996, and end on or before December 31, 2005. Within that period, a program delineates stochastic events in which birds execute poetry tasks.

The original poem appears in the *Appendixes*, along with a procedural description and relevant statistics. Unique artworks of various contests are being created for sale.

Visionary Sonnets

A hundred-poem sonnet sequence dealing with aging, death, and man's relationship with God has been written in Shakespearean form, and is being changed letter by letter into eye charts. The final line of each chart is so small that it is difficult for presbyopics to decipher without magnification. Ironically, this creates difficulties for the very people for whom the poetry is primarily intended: older individuals.

In order to create this element, software strips all punctuation and line and page breaks from titles and texts, and runs them through the eye chart template. One chart picks up where the last leaves off. If a sonnet ends in the middle of a chart, the program inserts the first letter of the Roman numeral title of the next sonnet in the next available eye chart position and continues. At the end of the hundredth sonnet, the process begins again at the next position, so that the sonnet cycle "cycles" through charts. Each subelement is a single page.

The generative poems, which will also be published as a stand-alone volume of sonnets, appear together in the *Appendixes*.

The *Breezagon*

The *Breezagon* is a regular tricontagon (a thirty-sided poly-hedron) that constructs, exhibits, and markets one hundred million "branded consumer objects" in the form of triptychs derived from elements.

All triptychs are unique, although identically priced. Each of the triptych "panels" is a copy of a page (12.75 × 9 inches) in a printed volume, minus its page number. Within constraints established by the governing program, all images are assembled at random, although no more than one ele-ment can appear in any given triptych. There are a quasi-infinite number of legitimate triptych possibilities, and objects for sale are culled from this data pool.

One "enters the *Breezagon*" from the ⟨http://www .breezeavenue.com⟩ home page. On the destination page, two buttons under the polyhedron are labeled "Spin" and "Stop." There are thirty windows in total, stacked at the right and left margins, each containing eight zeroes.

When one clicks Spin, the *Breezagon* moves at a high rate of angular momentum, appearing to be circular. As it revolves, the numbers in the windows, like slot machine symbols, blur until Stop is clicked. The *Breezagon* abruptly ceases moving, and eight-digit numbers register in all thirty windows. Zeroes to the left of the integers are permitted, but no number can appear that is used in the *Breeze Avenue* text (see below) or that has already been attached to a pur-chased print. These numbers in fact are randomly assigned image references that serve to track a product through a supply chain. No image is ever reintroduced, and merchan-dise that is not acquired on the first go-around is perma-nently consigned to the dustbin. Consequently, not only every object but also every possible sales transaction is unique.

Web site software compiles objects only as a buffer. In other words, enough images are assembled and available to fill up all possible spinning *Breezagons*. When the *Breezagon* stops spinning, the top thirty triptychs in the buffer are taken off the front of the image chain and downloaded to that particular computer, and the server back builds thirty more. The images are then sequenced on the client machine to form a slideshow. At any point, the viewer can transfer a particular image to a shopping cart. Images remain in the shopping cart until purchased or discarded. Objects are in-expensive and shipped unframed in tubes to buyers.

Each triptych has the look of art, but is not aesthetic in a sophisticated sense, except insofar as the concept itself and individual panels are artful. It is merely a simulacrum— although it functions quite well in that capacity. This element embodies the marketing and dispersion of veri-similitudes. The following are the elements used in panels:

Table 18.2

Element	Inclusions
Annual Cloud Narrative	All cloud pages
Star Canticles	All star pages
Aviary Poem	All bird strips (third panels) that fill a page
Visionary Sonnets	All eye charts
The *Clown-illon*	All car pages
The *Pythagorean Super Bowl Party*	All pi-chart pages
Beelines	All pages
The Fabric of Reality	All pages
The Closed-Captioned Chinese Chapbook	All non-English text pages
Brain Opera	All pages
Tocharian Letters	Orkhon letters
Squeezeborough	All pages
Spam from God	All spam pages
Grossman's *Glossary*	Illustration pages
Goldberg Variations on a Treatment	Only pages in Latin and Yiddish
Scrabble Poems	All *Scrabble* board pages
Grossman's *Essay on Man*	Frontispiece drawings
The Tomb of the Corporate Raider	All hieroglyph pages

For book purposes, *Breezagon* single-page subelements containing ten horizontal rows of numbered triptychs are set against a black background. Triptychs that appear in *Breeze Avenue* will not be available for sale. Inventory numbers, although determined randomly, are given in ascending order from beginning to end of *Breeze Avenue*. The number of the top-row triptych, preceded by the letter *B*, displaces the page number in the running head.

A technical description of the construction, organization, and operation of the *Breezagon* appears in the *Appendixes*.

The *Clown-illon*

The Car-illon System is a musical instrument, invented by the author primarily for use in *Breeze Avenue*, consisting of a sixty-one-note keyboard strapped to the back of the front seat of a sedan, "the harpsicar." A pianist sits in the middle of the rear seat and plays while the vehicle is in motion.

The other components of the instrument are roof-mounted speakers, one placed on each of twelve other sedans of the same make. Each of these "chromatic cars" plays all the octaves of a particular note. Thus the instrument consists of thirteen "well-tempered" automobiles. When the car-illonist presses a key on the Car-illon, the appropriate note is activated on the roof of the appropriate car. It is possible for the cars to play other sounds, rather than notes of a scale, depending on the wishes of those using the instrument. Additionally, means other than a keyboard can be used to generate music from the harpsicar or chromatic cars.

The textual presentation of this instrument is the video documentation of a *Clown-illon* performance, broken into stills. Opposite the recto pages of stills are verso pages of the scores of the music being played. Score highlighting is determined by dividing a USB file into time intervals that are equal to the time-lapse of a single still (one-thirtieth of a second). The program divides the music by those time values and then colors the scored notes that are sounded within each interval. These are correlated with the video. The correlation is proximate, given the ad libitum nature of human performance.

The *Clown-illon* element documents a one-hour performance of the Car-illon System in which all of those participating, including the musicians, will either behave as or be professional clowns. During the performance, the clowns get out of the cars, run around doing clownish things, switch vehicles, and proceed. A siren sounds when the *Clown-illon* comes to a temporary halt. This particular performance is slotted to be part of a larger event, probably an important parade. The program will feature a wide variety of music. Subelements of various lengths (always an even number of pages) form a "processional" of cars, clowns, and music that wind through the books.

The Car-illon System has been patented and trademarked, and will be made available for other commercial and performance uses. It debuted as the opening event at Spoleto Festival 2006, with Car-illon music specially composed by Philip Glass. Other forms and adaptations of the instrument are being developed for performance—for example, a Boat-illon and a Ramp-illon (cars stacked vertically in parking structures).

Engineering drawings of the instrument and a performance archive appear in the *Appendixes*. Car-illon music will be available for listening on the Web site, as will performance videos.

The *Pythagorean Super Bowl Party*

This element is the mathematical deconstruction of a short story, a humorous conversation on the nature of poetry, metaphysics, mathematics, and the afterlife, conducted at a Super Bowl party among Michelangelo Goldberg (the protagonist of *The Interstate Bingo*, the third novel of *The American Letters Trilogy*, discussed below), Pythagoras, and a number of other Greek philosophers. The method is as follows:

First, the irrational number pi is run out—at 6,664 integers per page—to create 3,000,000 pages of digits. There are approximately 20,000,000,000 integers in this sequence.

Then each word in the short story is given a number equal to the number of letters it contains without punctuation, or if it contains more than nine letters, then the number of letters it contains minus ten. Thus the short story is converted into a numeric sequence as well.

A software program takes the digits derived from the story and forms them into thirteen-number chains: the first thirteen numbers, representing the first thirteen words in the story, form the first sequence, the second through the fourteenth form the second sequence, the third through the fifteenth form the third, and so on. The computer then randomly searches all thirteen-number sequences in the pi matrix in order to seek matches with all of the thirteen-number sequences in the story (thirteen is the longest chain that actually produces a match.). When such a match occurs, the two sets of integers, for the purposes of the program operation, are removed from their respective data pools. The computer then creates twelve-number sequences and tries to match these, then eleven-number sequences, and so on, until all number sequences in the text are ultimately matched (this happens in a two-number sequence).

Assume that a pi sequence matches a ten-number short story sequence on the 2,000,000th page of pi numbers. Then that page of pi numbers will appear on page 2,000,000 of *Breeze Avenue*, with the ten-number sequence highlighted in blue. The following page will provide the captured language in the form of a "pi chart." This is a circular graph, divided evenly by the sequence count, containing all the matched words in identical blue "pi–wedges." As words are removed from the story, disjunctive language occurs in pi-wedge sequences with greater frequency.

If two highlighted pi sequences appear on the same page, then two pi-chart pages follow that page. If a highlighted sequence crosses a page break, then the two pi pages appear in order followed by one pi-chart page. Once all the Pythagorean subelements are determined, the computer inserts single pages of nonhighlighted pi matrices without attached charts until the number of pages in the element totals 210,000.

Mandated pi and pi-chart pages infrequently will disrupt the flow of consecutive pages within *The Gallery of the Purchasers* and *The Madhouse Filibuster* elements (see below). Pages of these elements displaced by this forced imposition shift forward. If the imposition of mandated pi pages cause "volume breaks" in an element within the printed set (the truncation of a subelement at the end of a volume), the database program makes corrections by removing the pages of optional elements from the truncated volume and adding them to the subsequent volume.

Both the original short story and a detailed description of the algorithm, geometry, procedure, and logic appear in the *Appendixes*.

Beelines

Vertical strips of modular choreographic notation, executed by Toni Intravaia, describing a large variety of bee "dances" are placed in horizontal rows to form chorus lines of hymenopterous activity. Subelements of five to sixty-five pages create variable-length "beelines."

A detailed explanation of the notation and pertinent entomological information appear in the *Appendixes*.

The Fabric of Reality

The Vedic "Hymn of Creation," the most ancient extant poem of metaphysical speculation, has been translated from Sanskrit into a bitstream and then converted into an analogous pattern of icons (whose static structure was developed by the artist John M. Miller). This is then used to generate a two-dimensional diptych of omnipresent holiness.

These static icons are small squares fitted within a narrow white grid. An undivided icon represents a "0" in the bitstream, and an icon divided in half vertically into separate colors represents a "1." All the 0s are different random colors, as are the left halves of all the 1s. These are drawn from a data pool of approximately 1,000,000 palette choices. The right halves of the 1s share an identical base color (which in the case of the Reading Room edition is sky blue).

The bitsteam of the Vedic poem is 7,272 icons in length, in the form of a vertical rectangle 72 icons wide by 101 icons high. *The Fabric of Reality* subelements run through the work in facing sub-subelements. Subelement diptychs are spaced approximately thirty-eight pages apart.

The first verso sub-subelement in the first volume is a straight transcription of the poem in the form of a loop, beginning at a random icon and then moving like written text through the rectangle in lines from left to right. The first icon at the random point represents the first number in the bitstream, and therefore the last icon in the loop occupies the position to the left of the first icon. In the second verso sub-subelement, the entire poem shifts fifteen positions to the right for every page between that sub-subelement and the preceding one. Icons that change from 0s to 1s as a result of the poem shift change into divided icons with base-color right halves, retaining their random colors on the left. Those 1s that change into 0s become solid-colored squares with their original random colors. This constant shifting by fifteen positions continues with each subsequent page of the 3,000,000. When a loop has been completed, all random colors change at the same time (whether that page is exhibited or not), again randomly, and maintain their new colors through the next loop of the poem. The base color also changes at this point.

The same formula applies to all recto pages, except that these pages shift sixteen positions rather than fifteen positions for every page in the larger text. Whatever diptychs appear in the book reflect this uniform progression of the fabric, with recto pages moving ahead at a slightly faster rate than verso pages.

Thus, the "reality of the fabric" appears to be governed by forces that are molded by particular rules and boundaries whereas the energy of *The Fabric of Reality* is in fact driven by a deep form of linguistic and reverential meaning that is quintessentially boundless.

Vertical screens showing *Fabric of Reality* diptychs, with variable rates of progression, icon size, and colors, will be produced in multiples. Screens, by their nature, sometimes seem to exhibit waveforms and at other times particle forms.

Actual cloth fabric, made in India, will be used on *Breeze Avenue* book covers. All the covers of a printed set utilize the same individual base color.

The Sanskrit text, binary code, English poem translation, and an explanation of the mathematical, scientific, and visual logic that drives the icon activity appear in the *Appendixes*.

The Closed-Captioned Chinese Chapbook

Four deaf actors individually and separately sign fifteen single-page English-language poems ("a poem portrayal") in highly differentiated styles and forms, and on diverse subjects. The actors are not permitted to consult with one another. The signing of each poem is video recorded.

This recorded sign language is then translated by another participant into Sutton Signwriting iconography, a computer font. The iconographer works with both a video editor and a director (who is a professional in deaf theater) so that the icons are synchronized with footage. The iconographer is not permitted to communicate directly with the actors. The Sutton Signwriting is then back translated into English by an "interpreter"—someone who has an understanding of Sutton equivalent to the iconographer's. The interpreter creates separate prose sequences of the icons that because of the ideographic nature of Sutton, are similar in feel to literal translations of Chinese texts. The interpreter is not given access to the videos but only to the iconography.

Finally, these back translations are used as the source for the creation of fifteen Tang-era-style Chinese-language poems that—while based on the interpreter's prose—can stand alone as works of art. The Chinese translator is not given access to the original English verse. This translator must conflate the four prose versions that result from the iconographic interpretation of each actor in order to compose each poem.

Prior to the videotaping sessions, the author and the theatrical director divide each English poem into "meme blocks." These are contiguous word groupings that allow for optimum effectiveness in the subsequent signing process. For example, the first sentence in the first of the fifteen poems, "Aubade," is "The sprinkler had run all night in the rain," and might consist of three meme blocks: "The sprinkler," "had run all night," and "in the rain."

Each of the actors meets with the poet and the director to clarify authorial intentions, and then the poems are signed and filmed "block by block." Each signed meme block of each actor in turn generates a series of "meme chains." These are the subelements that appear in the book.

All meme chains are fourteen consecutive pages in length:

Table 18.3

Meme Block	Actor 1	Actor 2	Artor 3	Actor 4	Icon 1	Icon 2	Icon 3	Icon 4	Prose 1	Prose 2	Prose 3	Prose 4	Chinese Symbol

The meme block page shows the original English poem, with the meme block highlighted in orange. The actor 1 page generates the icon 1 page, which generates the prose 1 page, as explained above. Actor pages are the individual video stills of the edited recordings of the meme block. Each icon page shows the iconographic text of the corresponding actor's signing of the entire poem, with the relevant meme block icon(s) highlighted in yellow. Each prose page is the interpreter's translation of the complete iconographic text of a poem portrayal with the meme block passage highlighted in red. The final page contains the complete Chinese poem with those ideograms highlighted in purple that include verbal information contained in the meme block. It is possible, of course, for the highlighted ideogram(s) to be duplicated in another series of meme chains. This would occur if the meaning inherent in the Chinese symbol encompasses more than one meme block. The relationship between meme blocks and ideograms is determined by the Chinese translator once he has completed his translations.

The number of meme chains generated per meme block is determined by the number of video stills it takes for the recorded segment of the lengthiest portrayal of the block to elapse. Portrayals are reprised at the rate of four stills per second.

For example, assuming that the longest portrayal of "had run all night" is by actor 1 and takes 2.7 seconds, then there would be twelve chains in this particular block (the first still, four times 2.5 stills for every time an intermediate still is captured, and a final still). If actors 2, 3, and 4 take 2.2 seconds, 1 second even, and 1.6 seconds, respectively, to sign the same block, the portrayal sequences (pages 2–5 in the table above) of the chains would be as follows, where *A* is a video still of an actor based on the quarter-second division, and *B* is a black page.

Pages 6–14 of each meme chain remain black until each generative actor has completed his portrayal of the meme block. In the chain where his portrayal is completed, the corresponding icon and prose passage pages "light up," in the sense that the black page is replaced by one containing the generated information, highlighted within the text as a whole, as explained above. These texts with the translated,

Table 18.4

Chain number	Actor 1	Actor 2	Actor 3	Actor 4
Meme chain 1	A	A	A	A
Meme chain 2	A	A	A	A
Meme chain 3	A	A	A	A
Meme chain 4	A	A	A	A
Meme chain 5	A	A	A	A
Meme chain 6	A	A	B	A
Meme chain 7	A	A	B	A
Meme chain 8	A	A	B	A
Meme chain 9	A	A	B	B
Meme chain 10	A	A	B	B
Meme chain 11	A	B	B	B
Meme chain 12	A	B	B	B

highlighted meme appear in all subsequent chains of the meme block. In the chain where the last actor finishes his meme portrayal, the Chinese poem lights up and the symbol, which results from all the previous activity along the chain, is highlighted. The meme is now fully executed and complete.

With the next meme block the process recommences. When the last chain of the final meme of a poem is finished, the element moves to the first meme block of the next poem, until all fifteen poems have been translated. These fourteen-page subelements appear individually and are distributed in order through *Breeze Avenue*.

Note that actor pages are replaced by black pages once their portrayals are completed whereas icon, prose, and Chinese pages further along the chain go active just before the actor pages go black. Consequently, there is a constant "chromosomal movement" of black and active pages shifting laterally along the chains as they build information toward the creation of poetic meanings.

The team of actors, director, videographer, editor, iconographer, and poet writing in Chinese attempt to evidence depth and elegance in each of the derivative forms, while losing as little information as possible throughout the process. In other words, everyone is engaged in literary activity.

Sixty poem-portrayal videos of the actors signing each poem are viewable in the ⟨http://www.breezeavenue.com⟩ media room.

The Brain Opera

This is an original opera derived from brain voltage and imagistic measurements of people when talking in their sleep and when awake, respectively. These measurements are collected by a sleep clinic, in collaboration with a PET scanning facility, using procedures set up specifically for that purpose.

The encephalographic waveform data are mathematically converted into music, while sleep speech is used to create a libretto based on the electric patterns in sleepers' voices.

Subelements are constructed of encephalograms of sleepers' brain wave activity, oscilloscope readings of derived tones along with voice electric analysis, PET scans of sleepers when awake, photos of sleepers while speaking, and a musical score using nonstandard notation.

The resultant opera will be available for listening on the Web site. A description of the activities of the sleep clinic, the monitoring equipment and output, and the means of musical composition appears in the *Appendixes*.

Tocharian Letters

Michelangelo Goldberg (of *The Interstate Bingo*, discussed below) receives a series of increasingly hysterical pen pal letters from the assistant treasurer of the Poetry Society of Tocharia, a lost Indo-European people hidden in the wilds of Asia.

This correspondence—to maintain the civilization's secrecy—is supposedly encoded into two alphabets: one for outgoing letters from Asia (Orkhon, a runic form of ancient Mongolian purportedly utilized by Tocharians), and the other for Goldberg's responses (a modern script, Fraser, invented to embody Lisu, a contemporary language of neighboring Yunnan). There is, however, no actual cryptographic key, and in fact there is no Goldberg side to the correspondence.

The arrays of letters are random single-page subelements spread evenly through the larger work. There are 40,993 Orkhon letters (the number of English characters in the Tocharian text) and 41,056 Fraser letters (a random number).

The Tocharian side of the correspondence appears in the *Appendixes*.

Squeezeborough

This element presents a reification of suburban paranoia (one's home is one's enemy) through the creation of a mythical community development in which the houses squeeze their inhabitants through the movement of interior walls. Renderings of nightmarish cookie cutter dwellings, presented as properties for sale, appear throughout.

Single-page subelements depicting the homes are produced by a combination of hand drawing by commercial illustrator Jan Boer and image manipulation, where software inserts variable architectural features into twenty-four basic models. A floor plan appears below each drawing as well as the model name of each home (always a wordplay on the squeezing concept), the type of squeeze performed, and data such as footage, number of bedrooms, baths, and so forth.

A humorous text praising Squeezeborough and the benefits of constraint, and a description of the procedure followed in creating house models appear in the *Appendixes*.

The Gallery of the Purchasers

The Gallery of the Purchasers element is a lengthy series of head shots of individuals who have purchased a volume from one of the five for-sale editions of *Breeze Avenue*, with each individual's name and occupation appearing in large lettering on the subsequent page. This element will be included in all future manifestations of the work in perpetuity. Consequently, it "immortalizes" an extensive group of literate readers at a particular time, eventually functioning in a manner similar to ancient tomb paintings.

The publication of *Breeze Avenue* is the installation of the volumes in the Reading Room, and consequently none of the four thousand volumes comes to a buyer through a retailer. Ownership is not possible unless one agrees to

Breeze Avenue Working Paper

appear in *Breeze Avenue*. To do so, one must participate in *The Gallery of the Purchasers* project.

A *Be in Breeze Avenue* icon on the Web site causes an image of the "current available volume" to appear. These volumes are sold one at a time in chronological order, with the exceptions of *The Madhouse Filibuster* and *The Gallery of the Purchasers* volumes (see below). Once all available first edition books have been sold, the computer will offer the first book of the second edition and proceed from there. Individuals can page through the available volume on the Web site before deciding whether or not to purchase, which involves making a payment of a given amount, and submitting a head shot in the specified form along with one's name and occupation for acceptance. If the submission is refused, the purchase money is credited back, and that particular book takes its place at the front of the line and is exhibited on the Web site before any other book is sold. No book is made available except the one offered on the Web page, although private transactions conducted by the author or his representatives will take place. These are true art books, printed on archival paper and beautifully bound. Each volume is signed and dedicated by the author to the buyer.

Only one book is allowed per customer, although books with others' pictures may be purchased as gifts. Once a submission is accepted, the purchaser's or gift recipient's photo and particulars are immediately uploaded into the cyberbook in order of acceptance. Forty thousand consecutive gray pages carrying the words "Page of an Unknown Purchaser" will eventually be replaced by this method (twenty thousand pages of purchasers alternating with twenty thousand pages of names and occupations). These occupy fifty-four volumes. Consecutive paging may only be interrupted by the mandated placements of *Pythagorean Super Bowl* subelements.

After all the editions have sold out, *The Gallery of the Purchasers* volumes in the Reading Room set will be reprinted. For-sale editions of these volumes will be offered on the Web site, however, as soon as each individual book is complete.

The names of all purchasers and their occupations will be listed in alphabetical order in the *Appendixes*, with the page numbers of their photos.

Spam from God

The generative prose of this element is a fable about a wealthy heroin addict who receives a divine message encoded in spam. As a result of circumstances surrounding this epiphany, the junkie is driven into an alternate reality that promises salvation, but as a consequence of moral weakness leads to a bizarre and nasty turn of events.

Massive amounts of spam are being solicited from "spam dumps"—the refuse of various data-center firewalls—and voluntary submissions. This accumulation is edited to remove uninteresting material, leaving only the "juicier cuts."

The prose fable contains twenty-seven thousand characters, and once an equal number of pages of spam have been gleaned from the Web site, the material is spread in single-page subelements of purified spam language throughout the work. Within each spam page is a four-letter insert: "sp_m," where the placeholder is filled with consecutive characters, ex-punctuation, of the generative story. This marker is difficult to locate, as there are no paragraph breaks or color highlighting to assist the reader in wading through the junk.

The original fable and a description of the spam-collection procedure appear in the *Appendixes*.

Madhouse Filibuster

The fictional premise of this element is that the inmates of mental institutions nationwide have banded together in the public rooms of their asylums in order to filibuster for "amnesty." Their arguments take the form of complaints about their treatment. In the course of presenting their cases, and given that they are insane, with radically heterodox points of view, they attack each other at the same time that they argue for release.

This element, a compilation of a large number of filibusters, is created using the following method:

A satellite Web site, ⟨http://www.madhousefilibuster.com⟩, is established where the project is described and contextualized. A list of twenty propositional sentences are initially posted by the author under pseudonyms. Examples would be: "The drinking water is infested with Martians," or "The coffee cups in the cafeteria contain Department of

Defense microdevices." Certain words or phrases within these sentences are color highlighted. In the latter sentence, they would be "coffee cups in the cafeteria," "Department of Defense," and "microdevices."

A participant may revise any sentence on this list, including sentences added by others, by changing one (but only one) of these highlighted phrases, thereby creating his own personal topic. The participant is then asked to write a "bonkers" text espousing the position taken in the sentence he created, as against the proposition(s) of any previous sentence(s). Long, eloquent rants are encouraged. Participants can access prior filibusters (and optional author profile pages, which provide personal information and email links) by clicking on sentences in the list in order to aid in the determination of their own topics and speeches and to figure out whom to attack. Checking off on a computer-generated release, the participant submits his filibuster. If accepted, his sentence is added to the master list and his filibuster is immediately uploaded to the Web site.

Individuals may create as many filibusters as they wish. Each filibuster must begin with the participant's actual name in bold preceded by the words "The honorable" and followed by a colon. Participants are encouraged to strike back at those who have attacked their previous submissions by submitting additional filibusters, railing at their "fellow inmates" by name and concocting egregious stories of their opponent's insane behaviors. Note that profile pages allow for networking and the development of group strategies. (People can gang up to battle each other.)

The element, consisting of the best submitted filibusters, is intended to occupy one thousand consecutive pages (interrupted only by *Super Bowl* pages, as explained above).

Appendixes

The *Appendixes*, functioning in certain ways as appended information and in others as the source of seminal text (this does not actually count as an element), are dispersed evenly throughout the volumes. Provided are supplemental and exegetical glosses, technical, archival, mathematical, and production material, legal documents, various forms of imagery, operational descriptions, and translations. Changes in the *Appendixes* information are updated immediately to the Web site and reprinted at later dates in the relevant books.

The *Appendixes* page numbers are given in Roman numerals. In many cases it is difficult to distinguish *Appendixes* from non-*Appendixes* text without these Roman-numeric designations in the running heads.

There is only one *Appendix* for any given element, when required. Subsidiary texts ("sections") within an element's *Appendix* are alphabetically subtitled. The *Appendix*, for example, of *The Brain Opera* has sections A, B, C, and D describing the operations of the sleep clinic, the nature of the polysomnographic and tomographic output, the type of rigs used to monitor sleepers, and the compositional method, respectively. Each section forms an independent subelement. The *Appendixes* sections are spread evenly and randomly through the volumes. These are important tools for understanding the various elements and are incorporated in the research mechanisms of the Web site.

One Appendix relates to *Breeze Avenue* as a whole and comprises three sections, as follows:

The first section is *this* document, titled *The Working Paper*, which is an evolving text. Initiated in February 2003, it is the principal source of information on the organizational, nonliterary contours of *Breeze Avenue*.

The second section contains computer, Web site, and graphic design specifications as well as archives covering the overall project.

The third section provides written and photographic (ex post facto) documentation of the *Breeze Avenue* Reading Room. A brief description of the books and room is as follows:

Breeze Avenue volumes are covered in cloth from India, in a design based on *The Fabric of Reality*. Each is 12.75 inches high by 9 inches wide by 2.25 inches thick. The books are printed on archival paper and bound to lie flat when open. There is no dust jacket and the four thousand volumes contain no front or back matters since these are internalized within the texts. "Breeze Avenue" appears on all the front covers, and volume numbers appear on the spines. Attendants and readers wear gloves when handling the books.

Occupying six rows of shelves, with heights of 14 inches, the books require a room with a perimeter of approximately 140 feet. Rows of rectangular library tables with chairs are placed in a central reading area. Computers are made available with Web site information that aids in the navigation and understanding of the printed work.

The Interstate Bingo

The American Letters Trilogy comprises *The Alphabet Man*, *The Book of Lazarus*, and *Breeze Avenue* (abridged). The subjects of these three works are the spiritual states of three poets who live in their own hellish, purgatorial, and heavenly worlds, respectively. All three are unique in their formal qualities, and a multitude of poetic devices are amalgamated into the trilogy's prose structures. The trilogy is intended to be a *Divine Comedy* of U.S. life. *The Interstate Bingo* is the novel from which *Breeze Avenue* arises in its extended form.

The protagonist, a degenerate *Scrabble* player/poet, Michelangelo Goldberg, presents himself as the *Breeze Avenue* author. Goldberg gives away a fortune in order to move to Venice Beach, California, and find God. He becomes entangled in the death of a young autistic woman who works at the beach as a clown, blowing up balloons for children. This, among other situations, forces him into a spiritual reappraisal, disclosing a heavenly realm—an interior world that is ultimately expressed as a radical revision in the nature of fiction through the embodiments of *Breeze Avenue* itself.

Each of the three novels ends with a poem. The one that concludes *The Interstate Bingo* is titled "Breeze Avenue." The individual words of this poem, highlighted in red, are disseminated in order within the novel text, fitting naturally within the narrative.

Animal Poems

This actually comprises two elements: *The Animals* and *Fifty Animals*.

The Animals, a five-hundred-poem pastoral consisting of conversations between a shepherd and his flock of two hundred different creatures, was published in hardcover in 1983, and reissued in 1990 in paperback. Over twenty thousand *Animals* books have been donated to charities, especially to those that comfort the dying and help preserve the environment.

Three hundred of these poems are discussions on philosophical and social issues conducted between the shepherd and the flock, such as "Abandonment," "Absence," "Accomplishment," "Activity," "Addiction," and "Adventure" (to name those that are first in alphabetical order). In the other poems, each animal tells its own story. The flock spans the breadth of species from amoeba to whale. Included in the book are front and back illustrations by Nicolas Africano.

The second element, *Fifty Animals*, is intended to educate readers on the techniques, meanings, and motivations of poetry. Fifty poems from *The Animals* are discussed from the author's point of view.

The poetry in both elements, along with an attached commentary in the latter, is spread evenly through the volumes as subelements, but also duplicated in a consolidated form in the *Appendixes*. The two books are being published separately. *Fifty Animals* is being sold not only as a literary work but also as a textbook.

Reggie and Boomer Books

Michelangelo Goldberg writes two illustrated novels, set in the 1980s, under the pseudonym of Lucky Laureltree. These novels, describing the escapades of a beach-obsessed corporate planner, a Rastafarian drug transshipper, and an Italian dwarf, take the form of old-fashioned "boy books for men" (such as the Hardy Boys).

In the first novel, *Reggie and Boomer Go to the Beach*, the threesome fly a shipment of cocaine from Peru to South Florida, sell it to a Bronx street gang, and use the proceeds to acquire a pharmaceutical company. In *Reggie and Boomer Go to the Circus*, they create a rock band in order to found a fascist religion and invent a potent psychedelic concoction, Battle Brew, in a futile attempt to corner the domestic cola market.

Each novel, illustrated by Mark Zingarelli, forms a separate element. Each is being published separately.

Grossman's *Trip to the Far North*

This is a tongue-in-cheek photo journal of "haiku moments," with an accompanying prose narrative, describing a walking pilgrimage from Torrance to Malibu, California, and mimicking the arduous seventeenth-century journey of the Japanese poet Basho to the wilds of Japan. The *Trip to the Far North* is a discombobulated effort to discover the soul of the United States. The journal is divided into individual subelements, named after locales along the route.

The book is being published separately.

Grossman's *Glossary of Every Humorous Word in the English Language*

The *Glossary of Every Humorous Word in the English Language* is the outcome of a fourteen-year project of reading dictionaries entry by entry, including the *Oxford English Dictionary*. This element is illustrated with twenty-seven drawings by Pierre Le-Tan.

Each letter of the alphabet forms a separate subelement.

The glossary without any illustration is currently being offered in a series of sixteen-page pamphlets by Buk-America. It will eventually be published separately as a complete illustrated work.

Tycoon Boy

A collection of poetry about the humiliation, desperation, and satisfaction of working at the highest levels of a corporation is written from the point of view of a young businessman, the "son of the boss." These poems have the style and feel of homework exercises. Each appears as a separate subelement.

The book, originally published in 1977, is being reissued, and the poems as a group appear in the *Appendixes*.

Tractates and Recantations

This work is a combination of alternating subelements: a series of cultural monographs (Tractates) in sentence-length paragraphs that proceed from unusual premises and adopt surprising conclusions; and pusillanimous, absurd academic essays (Recantations) written by pseudonymous professors. The latter claim to be important scholarly contributions, when in fact each is a contemptible form of intellectual retreat.

Each essay is a separate sub-subelement.

Pop-Up Torah

A clear, synthetic corundum "Torah Ball," five inches in diameter, is being incised with the Ten Commandments and inserted in a kilometer-deep shaft in a mountain located outside of Nathrop, Colorado. After approximately twenty million years, as a result of forces of erosion that have been carefully calculated, the ball will emerge from and roll down the crumbling mountain, thus re-creating a "Mount Sinai experience" well after the human race has been driven to extinction. Corundum is almost as erosion resistant as diamond.

This is an undivided element consisting of photo and textual documentation of the ball, the landscape, the mountain site, and the drilling process.

An edition of Torah Balls is being created for sale.

The Goldberg Variations on a Treatment

Michelangelo Goldberg acquires a screen treatment from his twin brother, a film producer, and then writes a humorous commentary in Latin (generated from hell, where Catholics reside) and an equal-length commentary in Yiddish (generated from heaven, where Jews reside). The screen treatment and commentaries occur in linked form: a page of English, a page of Latin, and a page of Yiddish. This is an integral element.

Translations of the Latin and Yiddish texts appear in the *Appendixes*.

The *Chuckiad*

This is an autobiographical prose-poem epic, consisting of thirty one-page "Chuckichapters," about a minor character in *The Interstate Bingo* novel. Chucky leads a dissolute life as a male prostitute, television writer, bank robber, and clown, then goes mad, commits suicide, and ascends to heaven, where he guides the sun through the sky.

Each *Chuckiad* page is a separate subelement.

Scrabble Poems

Eighteen poems that take the form of a *Scrabble* matrix are fashioned by laying down words in order on a board, according to the rules of the game. The subject of each poem is the wind. These works exhibit the greatest possible literary value and balance (no short words near the end) while achieving the highest possible counts. Each poem uses every tile in the bag.

Grossman's *Essay on Man*

This is an extended poem in heroic couplets, an imitation of Alexander Pope's great work, describing the current debased state of mankind, lamenting the virtual extinction of poetry, and suggesting possibilities of redemption.

Included are four frontispiece images executed in eighteenth-century style, one for each of the poem's epistles. Each epistle forms a separate subelement.

The Tomb of the Corporate Raider

This integral element is a hieroglyph text consisting of a prayer for offerings, a set of instructions to a son, and an autobiography of a rapacious tycoon, a Jewish convert to the religion of ancient Egypt, Ramses Kaplan, who in a fit of architectural self-glorification erects a pyramid in Sedona, Arizona, to house his mummified corpse.

Translations of the Egyptian texts into English are placed in the *Appendixes*.

Front Matter

A title page, two pages of frontispiece photographs, three pages of dedicatory poems, and a page of epigraphs appear as an element near, but not at, the beginning of the work.

Foreword

A three-page foreword, written by a character in *The Interstate Bingo*, averring that the author of *Breeze Avenue* is Michelangelo Goldberg, appears near the middle of the work.

Acknowledgments

This is a standard acknowledgment section of contributors and former publishers. It appears near, but not at, the end of *Breeze Avenue*.

"Everglades"

A poem.

Intercalarian Commentaries

This is an element that is beyond the grasp of almost all readers.

Written by a hysterical lesbian couple who appear in *The Interstate Bingo*, the *Intercalarian Commentaries* attempts to discover its own "true author," by means of a séance. The element includes a radio talk show, a column to the lovelorn, "The Intercalarian Commentaries for Dummies," a "nameless autobiography," and a philosophical treatise on excrement, among other things.

The *Intercalarian Commentaries* are cut into the running text of the *Bonsai Poem*, replacing individual lines. Given that the latter runs for three hundred thousand pages, discovering where lines exist is equivalent to finding needles in haystacks. Furthermore, the text is "shuffled," in that the contributions of the women, of equal length, alternate letter by letter, thereby creating indecipherable nonsense.

This element is impossible to find, and once found, is impossible to decipher short of amassing and decoding it with the aid of programming. Once decoded, it is so obnoxious and aggressive (continually attacking and insulting the reader) that there are few individuals likely to finish it.

The stated purpose of the fictional authors is to denigrate, humiliate, disgust, and crush the reader in order to get him to stop reading and go away.

II Exploring

The Long Arm of Fantômas

David Kalat

Once upon a time there was a painter named René Magritte, and he lived in a rancid hellhole called Europe. No use denying it: as far as Europe is concerned, 1943 was one crummy vintage. For many already under the yoke of fascism, cringing under the barrage of firebombs and fearing the future, the world had already come to an ignominious end.

Magritte was a surrealist—one of the best, in fact. Surrealism was an art movement that emerged in response to the unutterable horrors of the previous world war to accuse the evil soul of man with images wrought from nightmares.

Magritte long strived to expose the truth of a harsh universe through the use of dreamy visions; witnessing his world succumb to fascism and war only brought urgency to his long-standing mission. He did not often indulge in overtly political work, and indeed his paintings endure today for this very timelessness. But in 1943, as he sat in Belgium and watched his continent plow itself under, he felt a yearning need to disgorge his anger and frustration on to the canvas. Thus, Magritte painted a picture that was to become one of his most recognized and celebrated: *The Backfire* (Whitfield 1992, 25; Torczyner 1979, 12; Meuris 1992, 44–45).

This is its English title. Magritte abhorred the notion of giving his art blandly descriptive titles—for him, titles were meant as "protection." Protection, that is, from others —art critics, journalists, and philistines—who might reduce the power of his images to mere words. For Magritte, pictures had potency that words could only envy. His work was those pictures, not their names (Torczyner 1979, 60).

But *The Backfire* is not entirely Magritte's art. Sure, he painted it, he signed his name at the bottom, and it is celebrated as his work. But it is a copy of another's painting— a copy so close that were it to be done today in our contemporary climate regarding intellectual property rights, Magritte would likely have been sued for plagiarism.

This was the point, in fact. Magritte wanted the world to recognize his theft; it would have pointless otherwise. The meaning is in the thievery. Hence its name—no, not *The Backfire*, rather its original French-language title: *Le Retour de Flamme*. This translates more accurately as "The Flame Returns."[1] Some destructive, primal force has returned; it threatens our end.

The picture depicts a masked villain astride a helpless city: a rather on-the-nose metaphor for the dark times of the day, and the globe-spanning influence of supercriminals like Adolf Hitler. Not that it looked anything like Hitler, mind you, but to viewers in 1943 there was no question it portrayed a villain. Magritte counted on instant audience recognition of the central figure: this is not just *any* master criminal, it is *the* master criminal, Fantômas! So Magritte copied stroke for stroke one of the most famous book covers in publishing history.

> "Fantômas."
> "What did you say?"
> "I said: Fantômas."
> "And what does that mean?"
> "Nothing—everything!"
> "But what is it?"
> "No one—and yet, yes, it is someone!"
> "And what does this person do?"
> "Spreads terror!"
> —Marcel Allain and Pierre Souvestre, *Fantômas*, 1911

Dateline: Paris, the dawn of the twentieth century. A youth with moxie, let's call him Marcel Allain, is job hunting. He approaches Pierre Souvestre for a posting. Souvestre recently abandoned his law practice to pursue, oddly enough, automotive journalism. To convince Souvestre to hire him, Allain cranks out an impromptu article lauding the merits of some new kind of truck he knows nothing about (Ashbery 1986, 2–3). And so it came to pass that Allain and Souvestre became partners in crime, so to speak, co-writing serialized detective thrillers starring one of the twentieth century's most enduring and influential pop pulp figures.

211

The Long Arm of Fantômas

19.1 Cover of the novel *Le Rour*.

19.2 Cover of the novel *Fantômas*.

Here's how it happened: Come 1909, Allain and Souvestre are responsible for the car rag *L'Auto*, the *Car Talk* guys of turn-of-the-century France. An advertiser pulls out at the last minute, and they are stuck with a few blank pages. To fill the empty space, they hastily write a serialized story called *Le Rour* (slang for "Wheels"). It turns out to be so popular that they write a parody of it, *Le Four* (slang for "Failure"). That parody catches the eye of an influential publisher (Ashbery 1986, 3; Walz 2000, 49).

Enter Arthème Fayard. His fame and fortune came from reprinting nineteenth-century novels in cheap editions

adorned with lurid covers painted by in-house graphic designer Gino Starace. Fayard asks Allain and Souvestre to pen a series of detective novels. The two authors start brainstorming names—how's about Fantomus, they propose? Fayard, distracted and inattentive, misspells the name as he hastily scribbles it down: Fantômas (Walz 2000, 50). A legend is born.

Fayard ran his empire the way that Henry Ford ran his car company: as a ruthlessly efficient assembly line. Thus, authors Allain and Souvestre were obliged to pen not one suspense thriller but dozens. In order to feed their hungry

readership, Allain and Souvestre cranked out a new Fantômas book every month for thirty-two consecutive
months—each a bestseller.

Turn-of-the-century French readers could not get
enough of their pulp villains and larger-than-life heroes.

> His boundless shadow extends
> Over Paris and distant coasts.
> What then is this gray-eyed ghost
> Whose silence surges within?
> Might it be you, Fantômas,
> Lurking upon the rooftops?
> —Robert Desnos, "The Lament of Fantômas," 1933

In the years leading up to the First World War, French
bookshelves were stacked high with the exploits of Fantômas and his ken. Why did French pulp literature become
fixated on supercriminals and ace detectives? This lurid pop
fiction was the ebullient expression of a culture throwing
off the yoke of the past in favor of a rough-and-tumble
new world. Good-bye feudal certainties; hello Age of Doubt.

The attempts of some scholars to explain it away as a
mere reaction to the popularity of Sir Arthur Conan Doyle's
Sherlock Holmes come up wanting. Holmes may be a main-
stay in English-language pulp fiction, but Holmes-like characters had been a part of the French pulp landscape well
before Doyle published *A Study in Scarlet* in 1887.

The earliest such character was actually the honest-to-
goodness real-life Eugène François Vidocq, exhibit A in the
"Truth Is Stranger Than Fiction" file. Vidocq was a notorious brigand. For years he killed, maimed, stole, and bucked
authority at every turn. He stole to pay for his insatiable
hunger for prostitutes, and took up with politically powerful women under assumed identities in between cycles of
arrest and escape. Eventually, he switched teams and
offered his services to the cops, repaying his debt to society
not by rotting in jail or swinging from the gallows but by
helping put others there. In 1812, he established the Sûreté
National, the world's first plainclothes civil police force. As
the first director of the Sûreté, Vidocq brought his skills as
a thief and crook to bear on catching thieves and crooks,
and indeed hired a couple of dozen former ne'er-do-wells as

his detectives. Historians consider him to be the father of
modern criminal investigation.[2]

Vidocq lived his colorful life from 1775 to 1857. In
1866, writer Emile Gaboriau crafted a fictionalized version
of Vidocq, renamed Lecoq, for a series of books. A good
twenty years before Holmes took up his deerstalker cap
and pipe, here was a detective's detective, using keen powers
of observation and reason to unravel complex criminal
plots.

Vidocq inspired real-life criminals as well as fictional
detectives. In 1835, serial killer Pierre-Francois Lacenaire
was arrested and tried. The flamboyant murderer explained
that he had carefully read the exploits of Vidocq and
learned the art of arch villainy from the master. Lacenaire
set his sights on becoming "the scourge of society"; he was
executed for his crimes.[3]

Then there was the case of Adam Worth, the so-called
Napoleon of Crime. Based in the United States, his empire
of crime covered London, Paris, New York, and South
Africa—the very same network later established by his fictional heir, Fantômas. Worth was a master thief, not a
killer, but detectives from all over the globe stalked him for
years. As a thief, he was second to none. Worth was so notorious in his day that William Pinkerton hunted him for
decades, finally catching his prey in 1899 (Macintyre 1997).

Catching is perhaps the wrong word. Pinkerton, mind
you, was a peerless detective whose agency employed more
gumshoes than the U.S. Army did soldiers. His father, Pinkerton's National Detective Agency founder Allan Pinkerton,
had foiled an assassination plot against Abraham Lincoln in
1861. The Pinkerton agency handled the president's security
throughout the Civil War. Sadly for Lincoln, their contract
expired at the end of the war, and the army didn't do as
good of a job of defeating would-be assassins.

Meanwhile, Pinkerton's Detective Agency got a new, even
bigger government gig. In 1871, Congress authorized the
Department of Justice to establish a national institution
dedicated to enforcing federal laws and investigating federal
crimes. But it didn't pony up enough cash to actually do
this, so the department outsourced it to Pinkerton—the
Federal Bureau of Investigation would eventually evolve out

213

The Long Arm of Fantômas

of Pinkerton's force in 1908 (Churchill 2004; Kerr 2000). In short, Pinkerton was the real deal as far as U.S. law enforcement went, but he only got his man when Worth surrendered himself and volunteered to change sides. They remained friendly for the rest of their lives, and Worth contributed greatly to improving Pinkerton's understanding of criminal methods (Macintyre 1997).

Doyle fictionalized Worth into the pages of his Holmes tales, rechristened as Professor Moriarty (Macintyre 1997, x–xi). The world hungered for fictional criminals—to take people's minds off the real ones.

Nineteenth-century Europe was reeling under rising crime rates, a consequence of the industrial age. France responded to the crisis by improving its police force, institutionalizing hardheaded ratiocination of the Holmesian stripe. By the end of the century, the combined forces of improved public education and better policing had driven France's crime rate to the lowest levels in Europe—and in so doing, created much of the market for pulp fiction. There were more potential readers, and they had come of age in a society at war with crime, obsessed with detective work, and surrounded by colorful characters like Vidocq, Worth, Pinkerton, and Lacenaire, all living XXL-sized lives.

Before Gaboriau's Lecoq, thus, came author Pierre Alexis Ponson du Terrail and his character Rocambole, first seen in a newspaper serial in 1857. Like Vidocq, Rocambole was a villain-cum-hero whose criminal talents would be put to use for socially redeeming purposes, but he was not so much a detective as a pulp adventurer. Ponson du Terrail's epic tales are key literary precursors to contemporary comic book superheroes, setting the standard by which the rest of the genre would be judged. As a sign of respect, the genre of French pulp heroes is sometimes called *rocambolesque* (Ashbery 1986, 4; Lofficier and Lofficier 2003, 231–233).

In 1905, Marcel Leblanc published the first *Arsène Lupin* story, setting in motion a cycle that would continue through twenty novels of his own, five more authorized sequels, and nearly countless film versions in France, the United States, Japan, and beyond. Lupin, the gentleman burglar, is the world's greatest thief and a master of disguise. For Lupin to steal, say, England's Crown Jewels or the *Mona Lisa* would be child's play. But he does not steal

simply to slake his greed; he is a modern-day Robin Hood, whose crimes punish the wicked.

If Lupin could steal anything, Leblanc started to think he could too. Almost right off the bat, Leblanc pitted his Lupin against the legendary Holmes. Doyle complained that no one was allowed to simply pilfer his character like that without permission (Lofficier and Lofficier 2003, 29; Leblanc 1906–1908). So Leblanc went back and reissued *Sherlock Holmes Arrives Too Late* under the (only slightly) less inflammatory title *Herlock Sholmes Arrives Too Late*.

Around the same time, Gaston Leroux (the author of *The Phantom of the Opera*) concocted his own Herlock Sholmesian pastiche, Rouletabille. In the first novel of this series, Leroux unmasks his own detective: Rouletabille is a fictional alter ego put up by journalist Joseph Josephin, who turns out to be the lost son of supercriminal Ballmeyer—and to top it all off, Ballmeyer is posing as Detective Larsan of the Sûreté, and it is up to Rouletabille to defeat him. Make a note of this: such intermixing of identities, the blending of villains, heroes/detectives, and thieves, will return shortly.

On the face of it, Allain and Souvestre invented a character to take his place alongside the Lupins and Rouletabilles, the Rocamboles and Lecoqs. Meet Fantômas, the Lord of Terror. A black-clad faceless figure capable of limitless disguise and prone to outlandish acts of terrorism, Fantômas's evil is the stuff of legend; no one is quite sure if he even really exists. That is, no one save master sleuth Juve and his headstrong associate, brash young reporter Jerome Fandor.

Ah, but it is here in the trinity of Juve/Fandor/Fantômas that the genius of Allain and Souvestre is revealed. The books chronicle the ongoing adventures of this brilliant mastermind of baroque crimes that border on works of antisocial art. In jail for his crimes, Fantômas convinces a theater troupe to stage a dramatic reenactment of his trial, just so he can secretly switch places with the actor playing him and have that poor thespian hang in his place—the ultimate method actor! Fantômas plots to kill a prominent doctor, but knows that the police have been tipped off, so he builds an exact duplicate of the man's study, mounts it on mechanized joists so that it can brought in and out of play, and kills the doctor on cue while the cops stupidly lie in wait in the fake room. Fantômas frames a poor artist for murder, pays off the prison guards to kill the guy and make it look like a suicide, steals his corpse, and then makes gloves out of the corpse's hands so he can commit other crimes leaving only the fingerprints of a man known to be dead. Blood rains down on a church congregation because one of Fantômas's victims has been substituted for the gong of the church bell. Plumbers fixing a leak cause blood to shower out of a wall that has been packed with the corpses of Fantômas's victims. Houses are blown up, innocent young girls are shot to death, people are buried alive, and the question rings, "Who is Fantômas?" The only answer, "The Lord of Terror!"

> "You know what Fantômas is?" he asked.
> "Why…"
> "The most redoubtable brigand that ever lived—and a genius into the bargain, the genius of Evil. He is all-daring, all-powerful, his cunning is limitless…"
> —Marcel Allain, *Juve in the Dock*, 1926

Yet unlike Lupin, there can be no audience sympathy for Fantômas. He does not even register as an antihero, for to do so would require him to appear as an actual character rather than a cipher. It is not for nothing that his creators introduce him in book one, page one, with the words "Nobody—and yet it is somebody!" The tension between Fantômas's being and nothingness enlivens the whole saga.

Think Batman, and then think what would happen if Batman had no Bruce Wayne. Fantômas is a fictional identity, a mask, a brand name for crime. But Allain and Souvestre never allow Fantômas to remove that mask, to reveal the man beneath. We get snippets of his backstory: we meet his lover, his daughter, and his son, we visit his hometown, and we even learn his real name, but none of these fragments adds up to anything substantial. At the end of the thirty-two-book cycle, Fantômas remains as much a mystery as at the start.

Fantômas only occasionally appears as "Fantômas" in the books—that is, identified as such, wearing his Fantômas costume of black tights and a black hood. Most of the time, the reader is not even aware of his presence in the story, save as an ominous shadow in the margins. Fantômas assumes various fake identities, several per book, and functions "as" these other characters until unmasked toward the end. Thus, the burden of audience identification falls to his opponents, Juve and Fandor.

Juve (named after Javert, from Victor Hugo's *Les Miserables*) (Steele 2006, 13) is an obsessed policeman whose single-minded fixation on Fantômas anticipates the likes of Fox Mulder. Never in the series do we find Juve investigating anything else, and he eagerly follows his prey around the world (who was signing off on this man's expense vouchers?). His Fantômania is total: the world around him starts to doubt his sanity or integrity. Perhaps there is no Fantômas, and it is merely a myth concocted by Juve to brush off too many unsolved case files? Or perhaps Juve himself is Fantômas, using the resources of his office at the Sûreté to build a secret empire of crime? Over the course of the series, Juve will be often arrested as Fantômas, even accepted as Fantômas by the criminal's own gang. And in book thirty-two, *The End of Fantômas*, we discover that Juve and Fantômas may even be brothers.

Which brings us to Fandor, reporter for *La Capitale*. The similarity between the names Fandor and Fantômas is no accident; Fandor is every bit as made-up of an identity as Fantômas is. Fandor was once Charles Rambert, possibly Fantômas's own son, framed by the crook in book one. To give the poor kid a new lease on life unburdened by these false accusations, Juve helps him concoct a new identity as Fandor. Every bit as obsessed as Juve, and for more personal reasons, Fandor is a crack reporter single-mindedly dedicated to cracking the Fantômas story—the Lois Lane to a criminal Superman.

Like Juve, Fandor successfully impersonates Fantômas at times, and is occasionally mistaken for being Fantômas. In later books, he falls head over heels for Hélène, daughter of Fantômas. He even marries her—and the reader is expected to forget that they are most likely half siblings. Or perhaps the suggestion of incest is just one more taboo, to be nonchalantly disregarded. The crisscrossing of identities is absolute: anyone can literally be anyone else. Consider this: In *The Long Arm of Fantômas* (1911)—book six, for those of you keeping score—our multitasking supervillain has managed to pass himself off as FBI agent Tom Bob. In

215

The Long Arm of Fantômas

this guise, Fantômas moves freely in the world of law enforcement, ostensibly on hand in Paris to lead the hunt against the genius of crime. Meanwhile, Fandor puts on the legendary black cloak and mask to disguise himself as Fantômas for a masquerade ball. No less than three Fantômases (Fantômi?) put in an appearance at this soiree—the real deal, Fandor's fake, and a third just for compositional balance. All this while Juve languishes in prison, suspected of being the real Fantômas.

Things take a weirder turn yet in the later chapter of the saga, *The Hanged Man of London*, in which Juve conspires to help Fantômas escape from prison. In *The Lord of Terror*, Allain's (1925) solo novel, Fandor himself suspects Juve of being Fantômas.

It is as if there is a little Fantômas in all of us. Fantômas surrounds us and penetrates us, binding the universe together. May the Fantômas be with you.

> Fantômas!…Juve!…Fandor! The three names are mutually complementary; you cannot mention one without mentioning the others.
> —Marcel Allain, *The Lord of Terror*, 1925

If your head is starting to warp, take comfort—this is the appeal of *Fantômas*.

The loopy quality of the writing is due in no small part to the grueling schedule under which Allain and Souvestre worked. The coauthors took turns writing chapters, each one setting up an impossible situation designed to challenge the other to ever-greater heights of invention (Walz 2000, 52–53). The surrealists would later term this technique "the exquisite corpse." The bizarre narrative convolutions and erratic prose that resulted from this approach turned the *Fantômas* cycle into the literary equivalent of the delirium tremens. It was good for public safety that they came out but once a month, because reading too much *Fantômas* at a time can induce a dangerous form of intoxication. Literature as mind-altering drugs—there should have been laws against driving under the influence of *Fantômas*.

> It was Fandor that summoned us here—and it is Lady Beltham we find!…It was for him to fire at Fantômas—and it is Lady Beltham who falls under

> his fire!…She is struck by a bullet—and she never bleeds!…Everything points to her having taken poison—and it is a tooth she has in her hand!
> —Marcel Allain, *Fantômas Captured*, 1926

The flu epidemic of 1914 claimed Souvestre's life. Showing a talent for self-reinvention worthy of his creation, Allain married the widow Souvestre and took over the *Fantômas* franchise. Writing alone, Allain generated five new *Fantômas* novels for Jazz Age audiences and a further three stories serialized in French newspapers.

But by then, Allain was self-consciously competing with a *Fantômas* industry spiraling out of his control.

The film business of the 1910s differs from ours today in some respects but not in this one: what sells in one media must be made into a movie. The vultures descended, a bidding war was fought and won, and Gaumont Studios started cranking out *Fantômas* films almost as prolific as the novels, directed by the legendary Louis Feuillade, the granddaddy of the suspense thriller. Any self-respecting movie buff needs to know and venerate the name of Feuillade, for he is the Big Bang that set into orbit Fritz Lang, Alfred Hitchcock, and really everyone else of consequence.

Like that familiar poster of fish crawling out of the slime, evolving into apes, upright human-apes, and finally humans with briefcases and umbrellas, we can chart the progress of Feuillade's influence. Sequences from Feuillade's serial *Les Vampires* (1915) were adopted and adapted by Lang for his *Dr. Mabuse der Spieler* (1922), which Lang then reworked as *Spies* in 1926, from which Hitchcock borrowed scenes and ideas for use in his thriller *The 39 Steps* (1935). Lang then reconstitutes *The 39 Steps* in his own idiom as *The Ministry of Fear* (1944). Claude Chabrol comes along in 1957, and writes the first serious study of Hitchcock, dedicates himself to trying to revive *Dr. Mabuse* in his own Lang-inspired films, and ultimately gets a gig remaking Feuillade's films; we've come full circle without ever venturing far from what Feuillade cooked up in the earliest days of movies. French film auteur Alain Resnais says simply, "He is one of my gods" (Berman 1995).

During his brief but monumentally prolific career, Feuillade generated no fewer than eight hundred motion pic tures for Gaumont Studios, at the rate of about eighty per year. His métier was cliff-hanger serials: *Fantômas* (1913–1914), *Les Vampires*, and *Judex* (1917) chief among them.

Objectively speaking, Feuillade's technique is literally primitive. D. W. Griffith and Thomas Ince, Lang and F. W. Murnaus, Sergei Eisenstein and Lev Kuleshov, among others, had yet to develop the cinematic language we know today; Feuillade had only limited tools at his disposal. That Feuillade's films, manufactured at the dawn of the medium, can enthrall and enrapture modern audiences speaks to something else in their construction: Feuillade's simple, un-adorned camera work and blandly realistic production de-sign gives way to dreamscapes, irrationality, and illogic that intrudes casually into the frame. The world is not as it seems; horror can break through the surface of our reality without notice.

Feuillade's films were postmodern masterpieces. He un-derstood the inherent menace of new technology, pervasive-ness of evil, and untrustworthiness of appearances. But it is not the case that Feuillade's films were ahead of their time. Watching many silent films of that era gives one the im-pression of looking through a window into the past, toward a vision of a simpler and more innocent age. Feuillade's films offer a glimpse into some alternate dimension, to a time and place that never existed.

> Perhaps the most beautiful scene in *Fantômas* isn't the struggle with the boa constrictor and the latter's death pangs, nor the gunfight among the wine barrels, nor the masked criminal slipping into a cistern, but simply that in which a policeman is expertly unscrewing the grill of a ventilator duct, holding on to the fastened side of the plaque and experiencing from time to time the resis-tance of the screws, then carefully placing them beside the piece of metal once it has been fully removed. In this marvelous poetic anthology, each of us has at our disposal beforehand an image that is destined to thrill us. And for each of us it can never be the same one.
> —Francis Lacassin, *Louis Feuillade*, 1995

Consider this scene from Feuillade's *The Dead Man Who Killed* [*Le Mort qui tue*] (1913), adapted from the novel *Mes-sengers of Evil*: Fantômas believes he has beaten his oppo-

nents and is dining out in triumph, when Juve and Fandor corner him. They grab his arms, slap on handcuffs, and begin to march him off to jail. Suddenly, Fantômas races away, leaving a befuddled Juve and Fandor helplessly hold-ing a pair of false arms.

But how come Fantômas just happened to have a spare set of fake arms with him at the time? If you need to ask questions like these, the magic of *Fantômas* will elude you. If you embrace such narrative non sequiturs, meet the surrealists.

> From an imaginative standpoint, *Fantômas* is one of the richest works that exist.
> —Guillaume Appollinaire, "Fantômas," 1914

André Breton (1924) once said that the "simplest surrealist act" would be to fire a gun into a crowd of strangers. This statement has been misunderstood as often as it has been quoted. Breton's seeming advocacy of indiscriminate murder and motiveless crime illustrates a key surrealist principle: a desire to challenge the social norms as directly and provoca-tively as possible. The seductive transgressions of *Fantômas* became a cause célèbre among the surrealists: here was something gleefully, unabashedly celebrating lawbreaking, and the crowd was going wild (Walz 2000, 70–75). Main-stream society couldn't get enough of this terrorist and his unpunished violations of the established order. No apologies asked or given, the *Fantômas* phenomenon idolized every-thing it shouldn't. This was surrealism come to life.

Allain and Souvestre probably never knew that their writing method was a surrealist game; they were just trying to keep food on the table the best way they knew how. But the surrealists saw *Fantômas* for what it was and rallied in support. Max Jacob and Appollinaire founded the Societé des Amis de Fantômas. Jacob wrote a few Fantômas poems in 1916, and Appollinaire reviewed the *Fantômas* novels positively for the literary journal *Mercure de France*.

Blaise Cendrars, who also wrote a Fantômas poem, called the series "the modern *Aeneid*."[4] The ultimate Fantômas poem came from the pen of Desnos, whose "Lament of Fantômas" was performed in France and Belgium in fall 1933 as a promotional gimmick for the latest book by Allain (then writing solo), *Could It Be Fantômas?* Directed by Antonin Artaud with music by Kurt Weill, this ambitious road show featured hundreds of performers from cabaret artists to clowns, from accordion players to opera singers and whistlers.

Of all the surrealists taken with the genius of crime, few were touched as deeply as Magritte. In fact, Magritte's work during the 1920s is sometimes called the "époque de *Fantômas*" (Meuris 1992, 44–48; Torczyner 1979, 138). His paintings during this period are chockablock with mysterious and threatening imagery inspired by Feuillade's films. *The Murderer Threatened* (*L'Assassin Menacé*) (1926), for example, could almost be a promotional still from the set of *The Dead Man Who Killed*, and this is but one of at least six Fantômas-related canvases.

Come 1943, and Magritte made the connection explicit. He re-created Gino Starace's legendary *Fantômas* book cover almost stroke for stroke (replacing Fantômas's dagger with a more surrealist rose—in the right hands, a flower can be as deadly as a blade).

In 1928, Magritte wrote the following for the magazine *Distances*:

A THEATRICAL EVENT: Juve has been on the trail of Fantômas for quite some time. He crawls along the broken cobblestones of a mysterious passage. To guide himself he gropes along the walls with his fingers. Suddenly, a whiff of hot air hits him in the face. He comes nearer.... His eyes adjust to the darkness. Juve distinguishes a door with loose boards a few feet in front of him. He undoes his overcoat in order to wrap it around his left arm, and gets his revolver ready. As soon as he has cleared the door, Juve realizes that his precautions were unnecessary: Fantômas is close by, sleeping deeply. In a matter of seconds Juve has tied up the sleeper. Fantômas continues to dream—one of his disguises, perhaps, as usual. Juve, in the highest of spirits, pronounces some regrettable words. They cause the prisoner to start. He wakes up, and once awake, Fantômas is no longer Juve's captive. Juve has failed again. One means remains for him to achieve his end: Juve will have to get into one of Fantômas' dreams. He will have to take part as one of its characters. (Gablik 1976)

The world of Fantômas is a dreamscape, and to participate one must become a dreamer oneself. In 1946, filmmaker Bob Clampett directed just such a breathless chase, with hunter pursuing hunted into his own dreamscape. The film: the Warner Brothers cartoon *The Big Snooze*, starring Bugs Bunny and Elmer Fudd.

I can't help but throw out the notion that in his heyday Daffy Duck would have made a superb Fantômas, with Bugs Bunny as Juve...and Elmer Fudd as Fandor.
—Edward Gorey, introduction to *The Silent Executioner*, 1987

Feuillade's silent masterpieces were the first and best of Fantômas's excursions into cinema, but there would be competition. Hollywood's remake factory (just as busy in the 1920s as today) took first crack with a serial that included a young Boris Karloff in the cast. This lackluster production misfired and was abandoned before all twenty of its intended episodes were made (Kohl 2000, 70–72). It was a sorry blot on the record of its director, Edward Sedgewick, who would collect more sorry blots in his tenure in Hollywood: he presided over the evisceration of Buster Keaton's career with such ignoble clunkers as *What! No Beer?* in 1933.

Fantômas returned to his native France for a 1932 talkie, *Fantômas*, written and directed by Hungarian filmmaker Pál Fejös. The cast included Jean Galland as Fantômas and Thomy Bourdelle as Juve (later that year, Bourdelle joined the cast of Lang's French-language version of the *Fantômas*-inspired *The Testament of Dr. Mabuse*). The story oddly mixed "old dark house" clichés with a racing theme, borrowed inelegantly from Allain and Souvestre's early car-related thrillers like *Le Rour* (1909).[5] Intended to launch a new cycle of *Fantômas* films, with a cliff-hanger ending enticing viewers back for more, it was a creative dead end. Even Allain took to the press to attack the film as misguided and disappointing (Walz 2000).

Setting aside the 1937 short film *Mr. Fantômas Chapter 280,000* by surrealist Ernest Moerman, Fantômas laid low through the war years until a 1947 revival. Director Jean Sacha was one of many postwar French filmmakers trying

19.3 Belgian poster for the film *Fantômas* (1947).

to reconnect with the virtues of France's silent era. Star Simone Signoret (1976, 97) remembered the project in her memoirs as "a modernist version, with helicopters, electronic gadgets, and death rays." A sequel followed in 1949, *Fantômas vs. Fantômas*, directed by Robert Vernay. Both films are now obscure.

> Men hunt him down, women look him up.
> —Advertising tagline for *Fantômas* film, 1964

The horrors of World War II served up examples of true-life master criminals that put pulp fiction to shame. The sinister apparition of Fantômas clambering across the rooftops of Paris, so nightmarish in an innocent past, was now tame and quaint.

If you can't beat 'em, join 'em: enter French *farciste* André Hunebelle in the 1960s to revamp *Fantômas* for a pop art counterculture. Embracing the lighthearted fantasy now evident in the source material, he turned out a trilogy of "detective comedies" that fused the best parts of television's *Batman* and *The Avengers*, the James Bond cycle, and the *Pink Panther* films—yet did so, pointedly, *before* these other referents.

The core of *Fantômas* had always been about shattering social taboos, unmasking the hidden menace in deceptive appearances, and how (no matter what *they* tell you) crime often *does* pay. The guilty evade punishment, innocent people may be executed, and the forces of authority and the forces of evil may switch places when you're not looking. In short, ideas that still held relevance in the 1960s.

Fantômas 1964 à la Hunebelle touches those ideas only in passing, while embracing escapism for its own sake. With lavish budgets and a clever cast, Hunebelle created colorful, lush, campy comic thrillers. They received spotty distribution in the United States, if at all—but were deservedly popular in France (Lellis 1973).

Comedian Louis De Funes stars as Inspector Juve, now depicted as an arrogant fool rather than the expert detective of old-school *Fantômas*. Opposite De Funes's Inspector Clouseau act is Jean Marais pulling double duty as both Fantômas and Fandor, both played straight. The curious juxtaposition of serious thrills and slapstick farce produces a heady blend of comedy and horror distinctive to these three films (*Fantômas* [1964], *Fantômas se Déchaîne* [*Fantômas Strikes Back*] [1965], and *Fantômas contre Scotland Yard* [*Fantômas vs. Scotland Yard*] [1967]).

In the first film of the series, Hunebelle digs right in to the identity confusion inherent in the material. Simply by casting Marais as both Fantômas and Fandor hints at some deeper, more personal link between these two. Fandor comes to believe that Juve has invented the myth of Fantômas to justify the high rate of unsolved crimes in Paris. Fandor invents a phony "interview" with Fantômas, illustrated by a photo of Fandor in a Fantômas costume. The real Fantômas, angry at people taking his name in vain, starts committing crimes disguised as Fandor. Juve then

19.4 Page from a Mexican *Fantômas* comic book.

19.5 Half sheet for *Fantômas* (1964).

concludes that Fandor equals Fantômas, until the villain switches to committing crimes in a Juve mask! Both Juve and Fandor are arrested by a police force convinced they are Fantômas, who helpfully pops by to help *them* escape.

Around about the same time that Hunebelle was revamping *Fantômas* as a pop art icon, a Mexican publishing company started running comic book adaptations of the original Allain and Souvestre novels. Gradually, the comic book Fantômas took on the charismatic characteristics of Lupin, the gentleman thief. The wellspring of material from the classic novels ran dry, and the writers were obliged to invent new scenarios—in which Fantômas became at worst an art thief and at best a champion to underdogs every-

where (Walz 2000). The comic book Fantômas wore an elegant tuxedo and a paper-thin white mask—not far from the costumes of such Mexican superheroes as Superargo or Santo. Like Batman, this version of Fantômas had a secret lair and wild gadgets. Backed up by a team of bikini-clad assistants, the Lupinized Fantômas of the comics became a dashing rogue, an unquestioned hero of his adventures.

It took the combined forces of the French New Wave and the residual elements of the surrealist movement to forcibly wrench Fantômas back to his gnarly roots.

Chabrol is one of the unsung heroes of film—an heir to the legacies of Lang and Hitchcock—toiling away in France on a prolific output of psychological thrillers that has continued virtually uninterrupted since the late 1950s. His films blend sharp-eyed satire with horror, black comedies of the blackest kind. And he loves his *Fantômas*.

There are few contemporary filmmakers who understand Feuillade as well as Chabrol does, so it was apt that he was chosen (along with the equally gifted pioneer Jean Luis Buñuel) to remake Feuillade's thrillers in color for a 1980 made-for-television miniseries. Taking the first four novels as the source text, Chabrol and Buñuel alternated directing episodes much as Allain and Souvestre had swapped the writing of individual chapters. Helmut Berger starred as the steely-eyed Fantômas in this punchy gem. It was as if Feuillade had traveled forward in time sixty-odd years and kept on truckin'.

Were Juve and Fandor among the dead?
—Marcel Allain and Pierre Souvestre, *The Silent Executioner*, 1911

Like a virulent disease, *Fantômas* mutated to keep up with the times. Every few years, a new artist or creative team would embrace the Lord of Terror as their own, remaking the character to suit their own aesthetic inclinations and the needs of their audience. Unlike other enduring pop cultural mainstays, the story of Fantômas is not a long cycle of continuity and intertwining mythology; each new manifestation of Fantômas is a fresh reboot.

He could be a ruthless murderer or a Mexican superhero; a surrealist icon or a pop art comedian; a sinister figure of the silent screen or a superstar of dime store novels. He might even cease being Fantômas altogether. In the late 1920s and early 1930s, Allain spun off some new Fantômesque alternates: Tigris, Fatala, and Miss Teria. Together, these accounted for nearly sixty additional novels on top of the already-massive *Fantômas* canon.

In 1962, Italian artists Angela Giussani and Giuliana Giussani launched the comic book chronicles of Diabolik, an antihero fusion of Fantômas and Lupin. Diabolik in turn inspired his own rip-off, Kriminal. Written by Max Bunker and drawn by Magnus, Kriminal wore a skull mask as he committed extravagant acts of cruelty—until the same pressures that turned Fantômas into a charismatic hero

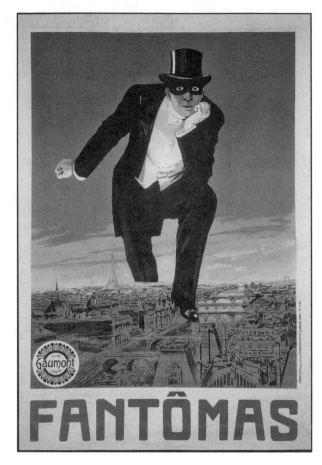

19.6 Fantômas.

wrought the same changes on Kriminal. We could go on and on with the various bastard children of Kriminal, but the point has been made.

Argentinean social critic Julio Cortazar wrote a multilayered and metaphysical fantasy in 1977 titled *Fantômas vs. the Multinational Vampires*. Cortazar was an expatriate living in Paris who had grown up exposed to both the Mexican and original French iterations of the character. *Fantômas vs. the Multinational Vampires* is an inspired and densely self-reflexive story within a story. In it, a fictional Julio Cortazar documents human rights abuses in Latin America. When the Cortazar in the story buys a Mexican *Fantômas* comic book, he finds his world increasingly reflected within it: Fantômas's fight against the evil forces that threaten the world's libraries starts to meld with Cortazar's "real-world" struggle against the forces of Latin American tyranny (Walz 2000).

Just as Magritte prescribed, to interact with Fantômas, one must enter into his dreamworld.

Independent filmmaker Howard Rodman is currently trolling his way through Hollywood's underground trying to drum up support for a new *Fantômas* film, *F*, starring Terrence Stamp. The better part of a decade has gone by with nothing much to show for Rodman's efforts, so the outcome of this venture is very much in question.

The band Fantômas has more to show for its fandom. Mike Patton, Buzz Osborne, Trevor Dunn, and Dave Lombardo are the musicians responsible for a heavy metal act named for the Lord of Terror. Nothing says "rock on" like the malevolent gaze of Jean Marais staring out at you from the CD store shelf.

Fantôfandom these days has dwindled from its mass-cultural peak of the early twentieth century, and the flame is now kept alive by a small coterie of devouts. Their passion is isolated but intense (antique copies of the books in English translations can fetch upward of $500 apiece). Fayard counted himself lucky to have a popular line of books in 1911; few could have suspected then that *Fantômas* would worm his way into a collective consciousness, and refuse to be uprooted by a century's worth of turmoil and change.

"Absence makes the heart grow fonder," as they say. Fantômas was ever an absence, a shadow, a mask concealing the facelessness beneath, the nobody who is yet somebody. It is easier to reinvent Fantômas for each new generation's needs because there is so little fixed in his universe; he is an empty void onto which the audience projects their own desires and fears. Since he was never here in the first place, he can never properly go away.

Notes

1. *The Backfire* (*Le Retour de Flamme*) is also commonly known as *The Flame Rekindled*.

2. See, for example, ⟨http://www.vidocq.org⟩.

3. See ⟨http://www.mtholyoke.edu/courses/rschwart/hist255/popcorn/lacenaire.html⟩.

4. See ⟨http://www.fantomas-lives.com⟩.

5. The 1909 serial thriller *Le Rour* by Allain and Souvestre marked the first-ever appearance of policeman Fuselier, a recurring character in the *Fantômas* universe. Juve and Fandor were introduced in this story's sequel, *The Print*.

References: Literature

Allain, Marcel (1925). *The Lord of Terror*. New York: David McKay Company. (Orig. trans. 1926.)

Allain, Marcel (1926). *Fantômas Captured*. New York: A. L. Burt Company. (Orig. trans. 1926.)

Allain, Marcel (1926). *Juve in the Dock*. New York: David McKay Company. (Orig. trans. 1926.)

Allain, Marcel, and Pierre Souvestre (1909). *Le Rour* [*Wheels*]. Paris: Union Générale D'Éditions. (Reprinted in 1974.)

Allain, Marcel, and Pierre Souvestre (1911). *The Daughter of Fantômas*. Encino, CA: Blackcoat Press. (New trans. 2006.)

Allain, Marcel, and Pierre Souvestre (1911). *Fantômas*. New York: William Morrow and Company. (New trans. 1986.)

Allain, Marcel, and Pierre Souvestre (1911). *The Long Arm of Fantômas*. New York: Macaulay Company. (Orig. trans. 1924.)

Allain, Marcel, and Pierre Souvestre (1911). *The Silent Executioner*. New York: William Morrow and Company. (New trans. 1987.)

Anonymous (2002). Friends of Fantômas Society. ⟨http://www.fantomas.org⟩ (accessed September 5, 2002).

Anonymous (2005). Vidocq Society. ⟨http://www.vidocq.org⟩ (accessed December 2005).

Appollinaire, Guillaume (1914). "Fantômas." *Mercure de France*, July 16.

Ashbery, John (1986). Introduction to *Fantômas*. New York: William Morrow and Company.

Berman, Tosh (1995). "Fantômas, My Love." ⟨http://www.altx.com/interzones/kino2/fantomas.html⟩ (accessed September 2002).

Breton, Andre (1924). "What Is Surrealism?" Pamphlet. ⟨http://www.popsubculture.com/pop/bio_project/sub/andre_breton.1.html⟩ (accessed September 2002).

Churchill, Ward (2004). "The Trajectory of Political Policing in the United States, 1870 to the Present." ⟨http://www.geocities.com/travbailey/index.html⟩ (accessed January 2007).

Desnos, Robert (1933). "The Lament of Fantômas." Broadcast. (November 1933).

Gablik, Suzy (1976). *Magritte*. Boston: New York Graphic Society.

Gillis, A. R. (1989). "Crime and State Surveillance in Nineteenth-Century France." *American Journal of Sociology* 95 (2): 307–341.

Gorey, Edward (1987). Introduction to *The Silent Executioner*. New York: William Morrow and Company.

Kalat, David (2002). "Lurking upon the Rooftops: Fantômas." *Scarlet Street* 44:56–63.

Kerr, Matthew (2000). "What's New with Pinkerton." International Foundation for Protection Officers. ⟨http://www.ifpo.org/articlebank/whats_new_pinkerton.html⟩ (accessed January 2007).

223

The Long Arm of Fantômas

Kohl, Leonard J. (2000). *Sinister Serials of Boris Karloff, Bela Lugosi, and Lon Chaney, Jr.* Baltimore, MD: Midnight Marquee Press.

Lacassin, Francis (1995). *Louis Feuillade: Master of Lions and Vampires*. Paris: Pierre Bordas and Sons.

Leblanc, Maurice (1906–1908). *Arsene Lupin versus Herlock Sholmes*. Holicong, PA: Wildside Press. (Reprinted in 2001.)

Lellis, George (1973). "Fantômas." *Cinema Texas Program Notes* 5, no. 10.

Leroux, Gaston (1907). *The Mystery of the Yellow Room*. ⟨http://www.blackmask.com⟩. (Reprinted in 1999.)

Leroux, Gaston (1913). *The Adventures of Rouletabille: The Secret of the Night*. Bordentown, NJ: Beltham House Press. (Reprinted in 2006.)

Lofficier, Jean-Marc, and Randy Lofficier (2003). *Shadowmen: Heroes and Villains of French Pulp Fiction*. Encino, CA: Blackcoat Press.

Macintyre, Ben (1997). *The Napoleon of Crime: The Life and Times of Adam Worth, Master Thief*. New York: Farrar, Straus and Giroux.

Meuris, Jacques (1992). *Rene Magritte*. Cologne, Germany: Taschen Verlag.

Schwartz, Robert, et al. (2006). "The France of Victor Hugo: The Dangerous Classes—Murderers." ⟨http://www.mtholyoke.edu/courses/rschwart/hist255/popcorn/lacenaire.html⟩ (accessed October 10, 2006).

Signoret, Simone (1976). *Nostalgia Isn't What It Used to Be*. New York: Penguin Books.

Smith, Elliott, and Robin Walz (2006). Fantômas Web site. ⟨http://www.fantomas-lives.com⟩ (accessed August 6, 2006).

Steele, Mark (2006). Introduction to *The Daughter of Fantômas*. Encino, CA: Blackcoat Press.

Torczyner, Harry (1979). *Magritte: The True Art of Painting*. New York: Abradale Press.

Walz, Robin (2000). *Pulp Surrealism: Insolent Popular Culture in Early Twentieth-Century Paris*. Berkeley: University of California Press.

Whitfield, Sarah (1992). *Magritte*. London: South Bank Centre.

References: Film

Dr. Mabuse der Spieler. Director Fritz Lang. Producer Erich Pommer. 1922.

Fantômas. Director Louis Feuillade. Producer Romeo Bosetti. 1913–1914. (Film serial in five parts.)

Fantômas. Director Pál Fejös. Producer Charles David. 1932.

Fantômas. Director André Hunebelle. Producers Paul Cadéac, Cyril Grize, and Allain Poiré. 1964.

Fantômas. Directors Claude Chabrol and Jean Luis Buñuel. Producers Claude Barma et al. 1980. (Television miniseries in four parts.)

Fantômas contre Scotland Yard. Director André Hunebelle. Producers Paul Cadéac and Allain Poiré. 1967.

Fantômas se Déchaîne. Directors André Hunebelle and Haroun Tazieff. Producers Paul Cadéac and Allain Poiré. 1965.

Judex. Director Louis Feuillade. Producer Léon Gaumont. 1916. (Film serial in twelve parts).

The Ministry of Fear. Director Fritz Lang. Producer Seton Miller. 1944.

Le Mort qui tue. Director Louis Feuillade. Producer Léon Gaumont. 1913.

Le Mystère de la Chambre Jaune. Director Bruno Podalydès. Producer Pascal Caucheteux. 2003.

Spione [aka *Spies*]. Director Fritz Lang. Producer Erich Pommer. 1926.

The 39 Steps. Director Alfred Hitchcock. Producer Michael Balcon. 1935.

Les Vampires. Director Louis Feuillade. Producer Léon Gaumont.. 1915. (Film serial in ten parts.)

224

David Kalat

With Strange Aeons: H. P. Lovecraft's Cthulhu Mythos as One Vast Narrative

Robert M. Price

H. P. Lovecraft created not only narrative worlds, but worlds within worlds, symbolized well by his description in "The Whisperer in Darkness" of a cosmology in which each universe is like a single atom in an unthinkably vast cosmic schema. He created not merely megatexts but mosaics of interlocking megatexts as well. This has its symbol too: the huge library of notebooks penned by captured minds from all past and future ages beneath the Australian desert in "The Shadow out of Time." We may trace the broad outlines of these arcs of world creation, and it may be that they will manifest more order than one might expect from the prototype of Lovecraftian world creation: the blind demiurge Azathoth who creates in mindless spasms, no two universes being alike.

Idol Types

Virtually all of Lovecraft's stories (and a number of his poems) can be assigned to one of four narrative cycles differentiated according to the predominance in each of three implicit myth cycles plus the reinterpretation of one of them. The fit is not exact, nor need it be. We find certain characters having adventures in one or more narrative universes, certain stories drawing in part on two different myth cycles.

The first narrative cycle is a set of stories that draw primarily on the most important lore system, which is usually called the Cthulhu Mythos or Yog-Sothoth Cycle of Myth (Mosig 1980, 106). That Mythos is a collection, possibly a system, of horrible, superhuman entities, aliens, or gods as well as cults devoted to them and secret books preserving their sacred lore. Lovecraft's chief influence in these stories

was, I think, Arthur Machen, who also wrote stories of hidden survivals of ancient pagan forces that occasionally make themselves known to foolish delvers. These Lovecraft stories are of course called "tales of the Cthulhu Mythos."

The second narrative cycle is that collection of tales set in a narrative universe modeled on that of Lord Dunsany, and making use of a Dunsanian cosmology and pantheon (Azathoth as a humanoid "daemon-sultan," Nyarlathotep as the Black Pharaoh or silk-masked hierophant of Leng, and the humble "gods of earth"). These are Lovecraft's "Dunsanian" tales that show either influence from or affinity with Lord Dunsany.

Third come the traditional tales of Gothic horror. Here, as Lovecraft himself put it, Edgar Allan Poe was his "god of fiction."[1] These stories involve elements of traditional supernaturalism (ghosts, crucifixes, vampires, race memory, and reincarnation), and have little to do with either Cthulhuvian or Dunsanian deities/demons.

Fourth are those stories in which Lovecraft strains at the bonds of his familiar Gothicism and Dunsanian fantasy, and heads in the direction of nearly pure science fiction. More specifically, he tries his hand at the lost race genre under the influence of John Taine, whose novellas *The Purple Sapphire*, *The Greatest Adventure*, and *The Time Stream* all left their mark on Lovecraft's own longest works.

These categories are ideal types. They do not match the phenomena of the actual texts perfectly, although they do on the whole. And it is the lack of complete conformity of the texts to the categories that makes ideal types useful: the distinctiveness of a particular story may be most clearly seen when we observe where, how, and why it varies from the prototype. All the stories will be seen as approximations, not as perfect instantiations, of the types just described. And that is good, because it is the story, and not the category, that is ultimately more important. We want to understand each story, not so much each category.

For example, "In the Vault," a creepy tale of a corner-cutting country mortician and the revenge taken on him by his shortchanged clients, is strict Gothic horror. So is "The Outsider," the "coming-to-awareness" tale of a long-buried ghoul who climbs up to alien daylight and horrifies witnesses, especially himself once he gets a glimpse in a mirror.

225

With Strange Aeons

20.1 Howard Phillips Lovecraft (1890–1937).

At the end of the story, we pick up cosmetic references to Egyptian lore that begin to remind us of the evocative language of the Mythos, but that is all it does. "Under the Pyramids" (aka "Imprisoned with the Pharaohs") blends such horror with Oriental adventure and intrigue, but it remains a specimen of more or less traditional horror, revealing the existence of living sphinxes and so on. It would have made a great Hammer Film. "The Horror at Red Hook" fits the pattern precisely, only this time it is a more ecumenical pantheon of traditional ghosts, ghouls, and gods—but no Cthulhu yet. "The Statement of Randolph Carter" delves into tombs and involves crumbling parchments in alien languages, but there is no Mythos element.

Straight Dunsanian tales breathe an atmosphere of dreamlike wonder, supported with a quasi-biblical prose-poetic style. Lovecraft's first such tale, "The White Ship," owes nothing to Dunsany, as he had not yet read him, but so great was Lovecraft's affinity in that direction that he had spontaneously produced something of a parallel to Dunsany's "Idle Days on the Yann." Soon he did discover the Irish baron and his work, and thenceforth Lovecraft

himself began referring to his tales in the same mood as Dunsanian. Occasionally there are names of divinities used in both the Mythos and Dunsanian tales, although it is as if the deities are not quite the same but rather more like counterparts whose distinctiveness is all the more striking for the expectation of similarity. Some of the Dunsanian tales are set in a collective dreamworld shared by sleepers of great depth and profundity. The mood varies from classical tragedy to lyrical wistfulness, yet we find ourselves in a world better than the waking one, not much worse than it, as in the Mythos and even the New England Gothic tales.

The boundaries blur when Carter stars in Dunsanian tales including *The Dream-Quest of Unknown Kadath* and "The Silver Key." And yet we still see Carter as the reclusive scholar characteristic of Lovecraft's tales of traditional Gothicism. He may venture out of those surroundings, but he does not become a naturalized Dunsanian character along the lines of Iranon or Barzai the Wise. Similarly, in the Gothic masterpiece "The Rats in the Walls," we are confined to eerie themes of ghosts and reincarnation, or racial memory. The story concerns a decadent ancestral cult related to the ancient mystery cults, not the worship of Cthulhu and the Great Old Ones. But at the end we do hear a bacchantic cry invoking Nyarlathotep, the screaming god of darkness. So the Mythos gets a toehold, just enough to bend our categories—but that's all. "The Dreams in the Witch-House" stands solidly within the group of New England horror tales, with its wicked witch and her familiar, who can be warned away with a Christian cross. Nyarlathotep appears as the New England satanic avatar, the Black Man. And the realms of magic turn out to be unsuspected dimensions of non-Euclidean geometry where one may encounter aliens like those who populate Lovecraft's latest tales of the Mythos, the ones that have become almost completely science fiction. The Lovecraftian Gothic tale par excellence is surely "The Hound," an adventure of a pair of tomb-robbing perverts. But suddenly we stumble on a reference to the corpse-eating cult of Leng—in the *Necronomicon*, the soul-blasting bible of the Cthulhu Mythos. The same is true in "The Festival," a story of degenerate Yule celebrations in which the *Necronomicon* appears, but

HOWARD PHILLIPS LOVECRAFT (1890-1937) belongs among America's most distinguished writers in the domain of the macabre. His letters reveal him to have been one of the nation's most interesting epistolarians.

Arkham House

Lovecraft

Selected Letters

Selected Letters

Selected Letters
H. P. Lovecraft

20.2 Cover of H. P. Lovecraft's *Selected Letters* (1965 ed.). (Courtesy of Arkham House)

Cthulhu and his brethren do not. These stories dip into the Cthulhu Mythos only marginally.

Yet there are Mythos tales pure and simple. "The Call of Cthulhu" (though inspired by Dunsany's "A Shop in Go-by Street") focuses on the emergence of an ancient secret cult of a monster-god in scattered corners of the world simultaneously, signaling an apocalyptic denouement. As one would expect, part of the mischief is set in New England, but just as much occurs in the Louisiana bayou country and the Arctic, with further references to Tibet and other places. The spotlight falls on the ancient lore of a forgotten and terrible religion. This is the seminal Cthulhu Mythos tale. Others confine themselves to New England, such as "The Haunter of the Dark" and "The Dunwich Horror." But one

feels that the main ideas and action could as easily be transplanted into other locales.

Again, there is significant overlap. *The Case of Charles Dexter Ward* and "The Shadow over Innsmouth" are really tales of New England in which the places described are the real protagonists, and the threatened eruption of a forbidden past into the present, or the invasion from alien cultures, constitutes the horror element.[2] Mythos elements obtrude in *Ward* and have a "supporting actor" role in "The Shadow over Innsmouth," but they do not take center stage. The Mythos is even more marginal in another Innsmouth tale, "The Thing on the Doorstep."

Lovecraft wrote very little that is strictly science fiction, as if consciously avoiding his familiar horror trappings, but there are a small number of examples. The early "From Beyond" and "Beyond the Wall of Sleep" are pure "scientifiction," as is the later "In the Walls of Eryx," although that one scarcely counts, being a collaboration with a young fan. Lovecraft's most significant science fiction tales are those in which he undertakes to demythologize the myths and magic of the Cthulhu Mythos and the *Necronomicon*, laying bare their secrets as those of modern and ultramodern science. Here the Gothic trappings are introduced and then cast aside like a veil. These stories include *At the Mountains of Madness* (whose title is yet a quote from Dunsany!), "The Shadow out of Time," "The Whisperer in Darkness," and "The Colour out of Space." These are really stories of alien invaders from space. They would all make good *X-Files* adaptations.

It is hard to categorize all the stories, but that is all right. The ideal types are only supposed to help us understand them, and in this case delineate the different elements that Lovecraft so potently combined.

It Will Cause Ye Thing to Breed in Ye Outer Spheres

I should say that Lovecraft began the development of his vast myth system in his early tales "Dagon" (1917) and "The Nameless City" (1921). The former briefly features the emergence from the exposed sea bottom of a giant fishman who worships an elaborately carven monolith depicting his own kind. The scene presages the hidden races of gigantic, monstrous beings with their antediluvian civilizations. The latter story contains the first mention of the mad Arab Abdul Alhazred, a name that Lovecraft adopted as a boy as part of his fantasy life, influenced by *One Thousand and One Arabian Nights*. In "The Nameless City," he credits the soothsayer Alhazred with an apparently well-known enigmatic verse: "That is not dead which can eternal lie/And with strange aeons, even death may die." It turns out that it refers to a subterranean city of ancient, intelligent crocodilians, inspired by Edgar Rice Burroughs's Mahars, the reptile rulers of underground Pellucidar.

The *Necronomicon*, a repository of ancient secrets, superstitions, and revelations, may be said to be the central prop of the Lovecraft Mythos, more than even Great Cthulhu

20.3 Cover of H. P. Lovecraft's *Dagon and Other Macabre Tales* (1965 ed.). (Courtesy of Arkham House)

himself, who will not enter the picture for another few years. But the *Necronomicon* makes its first appearance in 1922 in "The Hound," where it reveals the identity of an occult amulet discovered about the rotting neck of an exhumed corpse. It has nothing to say of primordial hordes of invisible whistling octopi from space, though. That comes later. The *Necronomicon*, it now appears, is the work of our friend Alhazred, to whom no book was previously credited. The same year, Lovecraft experimented with an envisioned Dunsanian novel to be called *Azathoth*, but he cast it aside. In it we would have encountered a nightmare "daemon-sultan" bearing little resemblance either to the "monstrous nuclear chaos" of Lovecraft's science fiction (a concept that

Brian Lumley would later carry further in the same direction, demythologizing Azathoth completely as nuclear power per se) or the mindless demiurge of the Cthulhu Mythos tales.

In 1923, there were two more incremental expansions of the Lovecraft Mythos. As already noted, he inserts the name Nyarlathotep into the denouement of "The Rats in the Walls," where it has neither weight nor much significance. And in "The Festival," he puts the *Necronomicon* into the dubious hands of his ex-human Kingsport Yule celebrants. All the book does is serve to warn the oblivious narrator of the corrupt, monstrous nature of the maggot men he is visiting. Three years later, in 1926, a major epiphany occurs with the writing of "The Call of Cthulhu," which unveils the unspeakably ancient and universal cult of the devil god Cthulhu, the high priest of the Great Old Ones, star-spawned entities of (implicitly) several types who once colonized the primeval earth, only to lapse into age-long slumber when certain astronomical and geologic changes forced them to retreat into hidden lairs, awaiting their half-clueless cultists' efforts to invoke them one day and return them to dominance. Here is the Cthulhu Mythos in a nutshell.[3] Cthulhu is the fountainhead of the whole subsequent flood.

Two years later, in 1928, Lovecraft the mythmaker was far from idle. Three more puzzle pieces fell into place. Lovecraft wrote up the fanciful "History of the *Necronomicon*," which supplied basic data about author biography, composition, translations, publications, attempts to suppress the text, and a list of modern institutions harboring copies. It was a straight-faced double hoax. In other words, as Lovecraft maintained the horror author must do, he poured into the pamphlet all the ingenuity required for a hoax, and yet he never meat to deceive anyone.[4] It was admittedly a snippet of fiction—like the *Necronomicon* itself. *Weird Tales* readers repeatedly badgered Lovecraft for information about the occult tome and admissions that it really existed somewhere. Few seemed to believe his disavowals, and even today, many fans are mistakenly convinced of the *Necronomicon*'s reality.

Besides this, Lovecraft first dropped two names that were to blossom from these seeds into major, albeit un-wholesome, growths in the flourishing garden of the Mythos: Yog-Sothoth appears merely as a name to conjure with, apparently from medieval sources, in *The Case of Charles Dexter Ward*, while Shub-Niggurath, the Black Goat of the Woods with a Thousand Young (as she would eventually be characterized) pops up without context in "Clarendon's Last Test" (aka "The Last Test"), a ghost rewrite of Adolphe Danziger de Castro's earlier published tale "A Sacrifice for Science."

Yog-Sothoth becomes more than a name in "The Dunwich Horror," a tale that bids fair to be considered the quintessential Lovecraft story. Composed of heavy doses of four Machen tales—namely, *The Terror*, "The Great God Pan," "The White People," and *The Novel of the Black Seal*—plus Harper Williams's *The Thing in the Woods*, "The Dunwich Horror" is the greatest proof of the claim that Lovecraft makes at the start of "The Picture in the House" that horror's most hideous lair is the backwoods of New England. At the same time, it is the perfect portrait of the confused but devout Mythos cultist, mixing chemicals that can bring down the created order. In this wonderful story, the threatened thing very nearly happens: the Gates to the Beyond are almost opened for ravenous Old Ones to pour through. But with exquisite irony, what saves the human race is the very thing that Lovecraft elsewhere says created it: a stupid mistake. The avatar of Yog-Sothoth—the Gate, the Key, and the Guardian of the Gate, the singularity where the spheres meet—is gored to death by a German shepherd in a bungled attempt to burglarize the *Necronomicon*. This is just perfect Lovecraft as well as perfect Mythos!

The sea change toward science fiction occurs two years later, in 1930, with "The Whisperer in Darkness." This one features all the props of the Mythos we have come to know and loathe so far. It even boasts an onstage appearance by Nyarlathotep himself. But this last is possible only because, as in the Dunsanian epic *The Dream-Quest of Unknown Kadath* (1926), Nyarlathotep does not appear as a shadow of the Transcendent, the horrific sublime. Rather, he is essentially humanoid, like the classical pagan-godlike Nyarlathotep of the Dunsanian dreamworld. In "The Whisperer in Darkness," he can appear as someone capable of sitting in a chair and simulating human speech, albeit heavily muffled and in dim light. The Mythos has yielded to science fiction.

The next year, 1931, Lovecraft penned (literally) two major works. The first, earlier in the year, *At the Mountains of Madness*, is pure science fiction. Again, Alhazred, the Old Ones, the *Necronomicon*, and so forth, all come in for mention, but only to be swept away as primitive attempts to convey the scientific truth of elder, outer entities from space whose antiquity and achievements dwarf those of humanity at their most advanced. It is the stunning implications of the sheer fact of an utterly superhuman race of starfish-headed, winged sea cucumbers (whom Lovecraft intimates were the real villains in Poe's *The Narrative of Arthur Gordon Pym of Nantucket*) that constitute the sanity-blasting truth discovered by modern delvers.

Later in the year Lovecraft shifted his weight to the other foot again, in his Gothic allegory of anti-immigration paranoia, "The Shadow over Innsmouth." While this one makes explicit reference to the scientifictional *At the Mountains of Madness*, its setting in the claustrophobic, crumbling wharves of old Essex County, Massachusetts, amid the cultic trappings of a local Cthulhu lodge, makes us feel we are again breathing the fetid, choking atmosphere of the Mythos in its pure state. And why not? It is all a matter of relative emphasis anyway, and it changes for greatest effect from one story to the next.

At any rate, "The Dreams in the Witch-House" (1932), as already mentioned, again combines the Gothic horror of the New England witch cult with the mind-twisting revelations of higher math, even letting us have a glimpse of an adjacent dimension where the star-headed Old Ones of *At the Mountains of Madness* appear to have taken up residence. The story—not exactly one of Lovecraft's best, though still mighty entertaining—endorses (for fiction's sake) the common notion that medieval witches were on to something, that they had precociously discovered modern science and were condemned as heretics for it. So far, that premise is pretty much the same as in *At the Mountains of Madness*, except that in "The Dreams in the Witch-House," witches still have demonic familiars and crosses still banish devils.

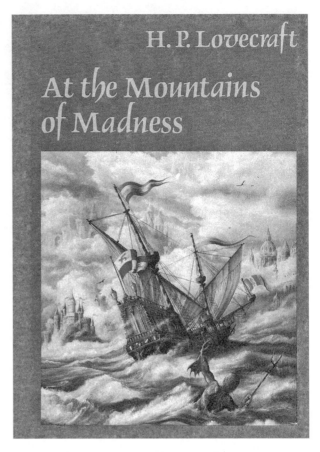

20.4 Cover of H. P. Lovecraft's *At the Mountains of Madness* (corrected 5th ed.). (Courtesy of Arkham House)

Lovecraft goes back to straight science fiction in his 1935 adventure in mind transfer and time travel, "The Shadow out of Time." Again, we have the notion that the *Necronomicon* was like the Book of Daniel or the Revelation of John as Hal Lindsey (*The Late, Great Planet Earth*) views them: what you would get if an ancient sage saw clairvoyantly some modern or ultramodern technology and had only primitive terms with which to describe it. The story owes a great debt to the pseudoscientific lore of the Theosophists, but remember, Theosophy and kindred movements claim that their occultism is advanced science, and that is the aspect Lovecraft is cashing in on. In "The Shadow out of Time," we discover that Alhazred gained his "revelations" by means of his encounters with time-voyaging minds from different eras—and planets. The means, then, was neither magic nor miracle but science. Lovecraft, as most know, was himself a devout naturalist, materialist, rationalist, and atheist. So fully did he believe in science that he felt the imagined contravention of natural law to be the most terrifying of horrors. And that was the effect he sought to simulate.

What, then, are the accoutrements of the Cthulhu Mythos as Lovecraft left it? For the moment, I restrict myself to listing the entities (gods?) and the scriptures of Lovecraft's own creation. Lovecraft created the Old Ones Azathoth, Great Cthulhu, Yog-Sothoth, Shub-Niggurath, and Nyarlathotep. His grimoires include the *Necronomicon* as well as a pair of writings originating in his Dunsanian cycle, relics of misty, forgotten civilizations: the *Pnakotic Manuscripts* and *The Seven Cryptical Books of Hsan*. On the whole, that is a rather more modest list than we might have expected.

Before turning to the contributions of Lovecraft's colleagues to the Mythos as a whole, it is important to raise the crucial question of a *synchronic* versus *diachronic* reading of the relevant Lovecraft texts. I have just surveyed the piece-by-piece accumulation of Mythos data in Lovecraft's writing. That, of course, is the diachronic reading, the tracing of the growth of the ideas *through time*. Once it has all been accumulated, readers (including writers, including Lovecraft himself) tend to look at the resultant system *synchronically*. That is what I mean when I call it a system. It has the dimension of *simultaneity*, and one can begin to ask how each part is related to the other parts. For instance, is Great Cthulhu one of the Old Ones? In "The Call of Cthulhu," he most definitely is, whereas in "The Dunwich Horror," he appears to be but a related entity: "Great Cthulhu is Their cousin, yet can he spy Them only dimly." Shall we seek to harmonize these texts, or shall we declare an *aporia*? I think the latter is in order, or is at any rate more in harmony with the effect that Lovecraft sought to achieve—namely, a likeness to genuine ancient mythology that exists in irreconcilable variants because it was not generated in any systematic manner. He left it to subsequent systematicians to lend artificial order to the thing. If anything, the error of Derleth, Lin Carter, and Lumley was to

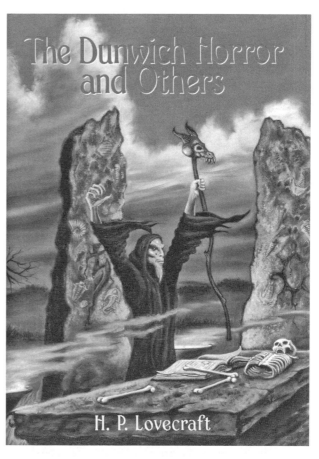

20.5 Cover of H. P. Lovecraft's *The Dunwich Horror and Others* (corrected 11th ed.). (Courtesy of Arkham House)

put such systems into the mouths of story characters instead of in nonfiction monographs where they belong (although they wrote those, too!).

The All-in-One and One-in-All

More important, I think, is the related question of how we are to read the stories in which the data of the Mythos occur. Some Lovecraft enthusiasts prefer to read early stories like "Dagon" and "The Hound" in light of the later, full-fledged Mythos stories, presupposing that the whole business of Cthulhu, the Old Ones, and so on, is in the background, and that we are being granted a glimpse of these in the earlier works.

Is this manner of reading fair to the texts? Is it realistic? Here is how I resolve the matter. It is entirely a question of which of the stories you consider any individual story to be a part of. If I am reading "The Nameless City" as part and parcel of "The Nameless City" by itself, I do not regard the story, despite its mention of Alhazred and the "unexplainable couplet," as having anything to do with a book called the *Necronomicon*, much less, God forbid, Cthulhu. But if I have read "The Call of Cthulhu" and then reread "The Nameless City" with a view to speculating where in the cosmic history outlined in "The Call of Cthulhu" the background history of the crocodilian race of "The Nameless City" fits into it, I am reading, so to speak, "The Nameless City" as a chapter of (intradiegetically with) "The Call of Cthulhu." Lovecraft invites such a reading when, in "The Call of Cthulhu," he says that not all the Old Ones were of the same kind, and that while some, like Cthulhu himself, were imprisoned beneath the water, others were under the earth. One cannot help thinking that he is retroactively reaching out to include "The Nameless City" within the orbit of "The Call of Cthulhu." Similarly, in "The Whisperer in Darkness," when he mentions Cthulhu, he is asking me as a reader to take "The Call of Cthulhu" as read. He is even asking me, when he mentions "Bran" and "L'mur-Kathulos," to consider Robert E. Howard's novel *Skull-Face* and his story "The Worms of the Earth" as, in effect, chapters of (intertextual with) "The Whisperer in Darkness."

When I read "Dagon," may I consider it "part of" the longer epic of "The Call of Cthulhu" and "The Shadow over Innsmouth," with their related themes of aquatic races and marine monsters? If I do, I shall be reading "Dagon" as a chapter of one of these other works. Keep in mind that by making explicit mention of features of "The Shadow over Innsmouth" in the subsequent "The Thing on the Doorstep," Lovecraft signals that he himself reads earlier stories retrospectively in light of later ones. In fact, it is evident that in "The Call of Cthulhu" he was retroactively appropriating "Dagon" into his growing Mythos, since he essentially rewrote "Dagon" into "The Madness from the Sea," the middle section of "The Call of Cthulhu." But does that mean he wanted readers of "Dagon" henceforth to consider it merely a precursor to "The Call of Cthulhu"? I doubt it.[5]

In terms of formal narratology, if we do choose to read earlier works as if they are part of later ones, as if they presuppose huge later events not in the writer's mind when he or she first wrote, what we are doing is treating the earlier work ("Dagon," *A New Hope*, etc.) as full of paraleipses, gaps we did not recognize as such at the time, but only in retrospect, once the paraleipses (hitherto-unknown omitted materials) are supplied to us. We hadn't known that so much, if anything, was missing at the time, and now that we know it, we can never read the original version in the same way. Jacques Derrida would call all such unanticipated sequels instances of "the dangerous supplement." In them, what appears to be an add-on to an original we once thought self-sufficient, turns out to subvert and undermine the original to the point of supplanting it as a new "original," since now the sequel dictates how the original is to be understood, transforming it retroactively into a mere "prequel."

The Unspeakable Spawning of the Proto-Shoggoths

It is not strictly accurate to say that Lovecraft left the Mythos in as compact a form as the previous section may have implied. Before Lovecraft's last story was finished, the Mythos had expanded pretty rapidly, just not only through Lovecraft. Numerous fans and friends tried their own hands at emulating Lovecraft's mythmaking. And whether or not they had the same success, they did have the same fun, and Lovecraft not only blessed their efforts in general (regarding them as the sincerest form of flattery) but also immortalized many of their new demon gods and magic books by mentioning them in his own stories, just as they dropped references to his own Cthulhu, Yog-Sothoth, and the *Necronomicon*.

Clark Ashton Smith is the most important outside contributor to the Lovecraftian mythology, not that he did it on purpose. As part of his quite different (more Dunsanian in flavor) Commoriom Myth-Cycle, centered on ancient Hyperborea, Smith created a quaint—even cute—deity named Tsathoggua, a bat-snouted badger of a god. Lovecraft loved the name and imported the creature. He began referring to Tsathoggua as black and furry but more toadlike, and sometimes as plastic, amorphous, and certainly more fearsome. His Tsathoggua, then, was quite different from Smith's, and played a different role in the Lovecraftian narrative universe (and Mythos) than the deity did in the Smith continuum. Likewise, Smith, who placed a number of tales in the fictive medieval kingdom of Averoigne, created a grimoire to enhance that setting. He called it the *Book of Eibon*, named for the ancient sorcerer who wrote it in metallic inks of various fiery colors on mastodon hide. Needless to say, Lovecraft loved this. And as Smith began dropping cosmetic (not cosmic) references to Lovecraft creations like Yog-Sothoth into his own stories, Lovecraft began employing the *Book of Eibon* in his own, usually as a bit of occult coloration, listed among many such tomes on a shelf. But *Eibon*, too, he developed in his own direction. The result was the adaptation as well as the adoption of a couple of "Smythemes" into the Lovecraft Mythos.

That bit of cross-pollination needn't imply that the reader, chancing on a reference to *Eibon*, need assume that henceforth Lovecraft's stories presupposed Smith's. Not necessarily, I say, except that further cross-references to Averoigne, Hyperborea, and so forth, seem to imply that Lovecraft *did* decide to absorb the whole fictive cosmos of Smith. But in this way, what would have been simple differences in the treatments of Tsathoggua, Eibon, and so on, became genuine contradictions, since at least for Lovecraft (but probably for Smith too), the stories had all become part of the same meganarrative.

Tangentially, Smith also invented Ubbo-Sathla (aka Abhoth the Unclean), a primordial lake of squirming protoplasm from which all life randomly evolved and to which it must one day be reduced again. There was also a spider deity called Atlach-Nacha as well as a string of unpronounceable letter jumbles that Smith jokingly supplied to fill gaps in the family tree of the Old Ones: Cxaxukluth, Ycnagnnisssz, and so on.

Robert E. Howard, famous as the creator of Conan the Cimmerian, was a great admirer of Lovecraft's work, and became a friend and correspondent. He, too, caught the Mythos bug and began creating his own versions of Lovecraftian props. Of dark gods, his addition to the pantheon was the obscure "Gol-Goroth," something of a double of

Lovecraft's version of Tsathoggua, toadlike but with no stable form. It had wings and hooves, though—maybe it was most like the Jersey Devil, part of Lovecraft's inspiration for the half-human Wilbur Whateley in "The Dunwich Horror." What really caught Lovecraft's imagination was Howard's counterpart to the *Necronomicon*—namely, *Nameless Cults*, an encyclopedic account of far-flung diabolisms and pagan survivals researched by the mysterious Friedrich Wilhelm von Junzt. Derleth suggested a German "original" for the title, and so it became *Unaussprechlichen Kulten*. Lovecraft mentioned the book, usually alongside the *Necronomicon* and the *Book of Eibon*, quite frequently in his stories. And it was Lovecraft who contributed von Junzt's first and middle names.

Frank Belknap Long Jr. was Lovecraft's best friend. He was a capable writer of weird fiction in his own right. As such, he pursued his own trajectory independent of Lovecraft, who respected and admired his work. But Long did occasionally give in to the temptation to play his friend's literary game. And the result was a pair of nightmare spawn. First were the Hounds of Tindalos, incorporeal preying beasts who range over hidden dimensions as long as they are kept at bay by curved space. Angles give them admission into our world, where they raven among fools who attract their attention by using the decadent, poisonous Liao Drug. "They are lean and athirst! The Hounds! The Hounds of Tindalos!" The other horror was one Chaugnar Faugn, Long's nightside version of the elephant-headed Hindu god Ganesha, a statue of whom gave young Long a jolting double take that he never forgot. Though Long contributed no new titles to the Mythos library, it was he who posited that Elizabethan magus John Dee had translated the *Necronomicon* into English—a suggestion that Lovecraft adopted readily.

Robert Bloch, later the famed author of *Psycho*, was a callow youth when he ventured to write to Lovecraft, who immediately saw the lad's great talent. Before he settled on his own characteristic style, Bloch wrote quite the bevy of Lovecraftian stories, all of which remain fiendishly charming to this day. He, too, contributed to the Mythos, and two of his best inventions were tomes of eldritch lore: *Cultes de Goules* as by the depraved Comte d'Erlette (obviously a

233

With Strange Aeons

tribute to Derleth) and *De Vermis Mysteriis* (the Latin title coined by Lovecraft for Bloch's English version, *Mysteries of the Worm*) as by the Flemish wizard Ludvig Prinn. These two titles usually accompanied the *Necronomicon*, the *Book of Eibon*, and *Unaussprechlichen Kulten* on the sagging library shelves of Lovecraft's protagonists. This blasphemous Pentateuch was the cream of the crop, and Lovecraft's favorites. But there would be many more, including young Bloch's *Cabala of Saboth*. Bloch's monster gods included Serpent-Bearded Byatis, Dark Han, and Byagoona the Faceless One.

Henry Kuttner was a teenage pal of Bloch, and emboldened by his buddy's easy approach to the Old Gent, Kuttner also began to correspond with Lovecraft. Here also, the youngster's talents were evident, and soon Kuttner began to publish in *Weird Tales* and *Strange Stories*. The Mythos stories of Kuttner are quite enjoyable and quite reminiscent of Bloch's, none of which is any criticism, but he, too, would find his own voice later as a fantasy and science fiction author. During his early Lovecraftian period, Kuttner created the *Book of Iod*, the secrets of which he never really got around to divulging, but that Lovecraft said he imagined must be an antediluvian source of secret lore like his own *Pnakotic Manuscripts*. Kuttner's divine monsters were three: Vorvadoss the Shining Hunter, Nyogtha the Thing That Should Not Be (an amorphous ooze of living tar dwelling in fissures deep beneath the earth), and Zuchequon (a swelling nebula of madness-inducing blackness swallowing all wholesome daylight).

Another young apprentice was Richard F. Searight, an imaginative fellow who, thanks to Lovecraft's coaching, had a few good tales turn up in *Weird Tales* and elsewhere. Searight made their friendship worthwhile to Lovecraft when he invented an ancient tome called *The Eltdown Shards*, which Lovecraft and Searight both went on to develop in different ways, each unaware of the other's efforts. In both cases, though, the *Shards* (whose title invoked the antiquity as well as perhaps the dubiety of the Piltdown man "discovery") turned out to be fabulously old, prehuman records of occult matters. Searight's version appeared in his "The Warder of Knowledge," which went unpublished until long after the author's death, while Lovecraft elaborated his vi-

sion of the text in his portion of the round-robin story "The Challenge from Beyond."

Duane W. Rimel was yet another capable amateur writer whom Lovecraft helped turn professional (indeed, Rimel had one of the longest-running writing careers of all the Lovecraft Circle). The best-forgotten history of elder aeons was set forth in Rudolf Yergler's *Chronicle of Nath*, which appeared in the Rimel-Lovecraft revision "The Tree on the Hill." Another young correspondent, the subsequently well-known Willis Conover, offered Lovecraft his own black book, the forbidding-sounding *Ghorl Nigräl*, which Lovecraft never wound up using in print—but he did write a single, shuddersome vignette in a letter to Conover featuring the book. (Carter would later employ the book in his own work, along with several other minor works dreamed up by the Lovecraft Circle.)

August Derleth, a prolific writer of historical, regional, and romantic fiction, and later cofounder (with Donald Wandrei) of Arkham House publishers, was ablaze with fannish enthusiasm about, first, his friend Lovecraft's writing, and second, the fascinating myth cycle he and the others had created. In a flood of stories, Derleth would not only systematize the Cthulhu Mythos (as he was the first to call it) but also considerably populate its ranks (with the help of fan editor Francis T. Laney, whose glossary of the Old Ones really lit Derleth's fuse). Before he was done, the fertile and indefatigable imagination of the real-life Comte d'Erlette had yielded *The R'lyeh Text*, *Confessions of the Mad Monk Clithanus*, the *Rituals of Yhe*, and the *Dhol Chants* along with and the gods Lloigor and Zhar, the flame elemental Cthugha, and (his version of the legendary Wendigo) Ithaqua. He shifted the theological focus of the Mythos somewhat (though not nearly so much as his latter-day detractors charged), adapting Lovecraft's notion of wars between interplanetary races into a more nearly conventional good versus evil contest between the benign Elder Gods and their rebellious onetime servants, the Great Old Ones. He also followed Laney in trying to squeeze the various Lovecraftian Old Ones into the pigeon holes of the ancient four-element schema—something not wholly without precedent in Lovecraft, who often created his monsters as embodiments of the evocative atmosphere of specific mysterious environments such as the Vermont hills, the Antarctican ice wastes, and the depths of the unplumbed ocean.

A Dweller on Two Planets

Beyond the hints and nods just summarized, there are two major stories in which Lovecraft mentions the creations of other writers, both predecessors and colleagues, in such a way as to suggest that they all share the same narrative universe. The revelatory speeches of the pseudo-Akeley alien in "The Whisperer in Darkness" make reference to various mythical items (Lovecraft related or not) created by Howard, Long, Dunsany, Robert W. Chambers, and others. Granted, the point is a "shout out" to his friends and favorites, but in the framework of the story we must surely understand that the alien voice knows about, among others, Howard's Bran Mak Morn and Long's Hounds of Tindalos. Similarly, in "The Shadow out of Time," when the displaced mind of narrator Nathaniel Wingate Peaslee, warehoused in the conical body of one of the time voyagers of Yith, tells of meeting captive intellects from ancient Cimmeria and Valusia, he is adding to the Lovecraftian narrative universe the Conan and Kull adventures of Lovecraft's friend Howard.

To borrow an analogy from comic books, what "The Shadow out of Time" gives us is a window between parallel narrative worlds, but not an unwieldy attempt to unify them in practice, such as we saw in DC Comics' 1985 series *Crisis on Infinite Earths*.[6] I am suggesting that Lovecraft, by mentioning Hyborian Age or Commoriom characters in his own stories, was doing a "crossover" between parallel narrative worlds, as DC did before the *Crisis*.

But that does not mean one couldn't go all the way and meld the worlds of Lovecraft, Howard, Smith, and others together in one grand vista, for it has already been done. Richard L. Tierney, in his stories and novels of Simon of Gitta, David Taggart, and Red Sonja, has done precisely this, and with great effect. He has also thrown in the Bible and Frank Herbert's *Dune* plus Karl Edward Wagner's Kane character.

A nonliterary analogy to what Tierney has done might be the case of certain would-be ecumenical religions that

view themselves as summing up all previous faiths and providing a new basis for their unity. Examples would be the Baha'i faith, the Ahmadiyya sect, and the Unification Church. What happens when such movements proclaim their message? They do produce a syncretism of elements derived from previous separate traditions. But few members of previous religions sign up. Thus one is left with each of the original continuities and communities intact, with a new option alongside them that consciously blends their emphases into its own new system. Even so, Tierney's "*Weird Tales* Cosmology," as I call it, combines Lovecraft's Cthulhu Mythos with the Hyborian Age of Howard and the Commoriom myth cycle of Smith, plus others. Most readers will know what came from where, but Tierney so expertly blends them that everything seems to have grown naturally together. And yet no reader turning back to the original stories of Lovecraft, Howard, or Smith need bother keeping Tierney in mind. Yet you could. It is, again, all a matter of whether you see the old story as "part of" itself or part of a new story written in light of it.

A whole generation of writers, whom Lin Carter, one of them, dubbed "the New Lovecraft Circle," kept the Mythos game going with new gods, new grimoires, and new haunted locales. The young Englishman Ramsey Campbell submitted a sheaf of Mythos tales to Derleth, who demanded considerable rewriting but accepted them for publication as an Arkham House book, called *The Inhabitant of the Lake and Less Welcome Tenants* (1964). Initially setting his stories in the overworked Lovecraftian territory of haunted New England, Campbell rewrote them, at Derleth's suggestion, as taking place in the Severn Valley in England, with his own sprinkling of dubious towns, such as Temphill, Goatswood, and Severnford. Instead of Lovecraft's Miskatonic University, Campbell opened his own Brichester University. Sure, it was derivative, but it worked quite well. He conjured monsters named Daoloth the Revealer and Y'golonac. His chief Mythos book title is the multivolume *Revelations of Glaaki*, which occasionally spawns new volumes like a paper Ubbo-Sathla.

Brian Lumley, one of the most ingenious and fantastically successful horror writers of all time, began as another Lovecraftian whelp in the post-Lovecraft generation. He, too, was a Derleth discovery. His many Mythos tales featured new characters (Titus Crow, Hank Silberhutte, etc.) and settings as well as numerous eldritch tomes (*Cthaat Aquadingen*, *Feery's Original Notes upon the Necronomicon*, and others borrowed by way of tribute to Carl Jacobi, such as *Unterzee Kulten* and *Hydrophinnae*). From his forehead burst forth gods like Ybb-Tstll, Bugg-Shash, and Shudde-M'ell. He expanded considerably on traditional Lovecraftian themes, cross-fertilizing Cthulhuvian horror with Dunsanian dreamworld themes in revolutionary ways.

Lin Carter, as big an enthusiast for the Mythos as Derleth ever was, and his natural heir, created his own Xothic Legend Cycle. His new deities include Zoth-Ommog and Ythogtha, sons of Great Cthulhu; Mnomquah, a crocodile-like titan imprisoned within the Moon; and Ubb, Father of Worms. His Mythos tomes include the *Ponape Scripture* and *The Xanthu Tablets*. His legend-shrouded locale was the Sanborne Institute for Pacific Antiquities in Santiago, California.

Such iterations of titles and unpronounceable names afford no real idea of the creative achievements of any of these writers. And space forbids my continuing the roll call of writers and their contributions to the Mythos, although I wish I could duly chronicle the relevant work of Gary Myers, James Wade, Colin Wilson, Walter C. de Bill Jr., Stefan B. Aletti, Stanley Sargent, Joseph S. Pulver Sr., Adam Niswander, James Ambuehl, and so on. The point is simply to indicate the continued growth of the Cthulhu Mythos.

And to raise one more intertextual question, if one enters the stream of Mythos writing, and plenty of intrepid souls still do, how much of the burgeoning supernarrative of these stories, and the supersystem of mythemes underlying them, is one obliged to hoist up and carry forward? The Cthulhu Mythos has grown so massive and complex, far more so than this brief survey suggests, that no writer can ever utilize enough of it for the reader to surmise the writer's principle of selection. But there is one important exception to this rule. As numerous scholarly articles, message board debates, and convention panel exchanges have revealed, fans tend to line up in at least five groups according to what they will include as genuine Mythos fiction.

First, some embrace the whole galaxy of creations and will consult ecumenical Mythos reference encyclopedias impartially. Second, others affirm a "back to Lovecraft" agenda, disclaiming every Mythos innovation since Lovecraft. Third, some go further still and repudiate everything that Lovecraft himself assimilated from his friends and colleagues. Fourth, some are happy to accept, mention, and elaborate the creations of post-Lovecraft writers, but only as long as they seem philosophically harmonious with Lovecraft's vision as they understand it. This stance means especially to eliminate from consideration the reinterpretations and inventions of Derleth, Carter, and Lumley. Fifth, still others will accept elements indiscriminately from any published Mythos stories and novels, while shunning the contributions of role-playing modules and other nonprint media. All of these stances represent different tellings or retellings of the composite Lovecraftian master narrative. I suspect one would find the same sort of categories among those who seek to write new Conan or *Star Trek* novels: which works are they willing to accept as the canon they hope to add to?

The Last and Least Likely Disciple

It is not often that we find someone being their own imitator. But one definite case is that of Lovecraft in his invention of a parallel Mythos for stories that he wrote for revision clients.[7] He seems to have wanted to create, simply for fun, the false impression that just as Smith and Howard invented their own Lovecraft Mythos analogues, so did his revision clients, who included Zealia Bishop, Hazel Heald, and de Castro. So he made up derivative versions of his own gods and mythemes that he virtually never referred to in stories he published under his own name, though he felt free to scatter them about in works written under the names of various ghostwriting clients, as if they were saluting one another!

In this manner, in "Out of the Aeons," written for Heald, Lovecraft described tentacled Ghatanothoa, a shapeless devil worshipped and feared on ancient Mu, a locale of which Lovecraft wrote only in revision tales, whether for Heald, Henry S. Whitehead, or anybody else. Anyone can recognize in Ghatanothoa a derivative version of Cthulhu.

Another monster deity he created for revisions and relegated there was Rhan-Tegoth, a gigantic creature combining portions of the anatomy of various phyla, rather like Whateley in "The Dunwich Horror." Still another was Yig, Father of Serpents. Nug and Yeb, the "twin obscenities," were born of Shub-Niggurath in the revisions. Shub-Niggurath herself originated in a revision tale, as we have seen, but Lovecraft liked the name (apparently derived from Lord Dunsany's Sheol-Nugganoth) so much that when he used her in his acknowledged tales, he let it be imagined he had borrowed her permanently from de Castro as he had borrowed Tsathoggua from Smith. Nug and Yeb barely appear even in revision tales, yet they never show up in his acknowledged fiction. Actually, most mentions of them occur in the frequent complex imaginative allusions in his letters to friends. In them he mentions "the Black Liturgy of Nug and Yeb" along with much more throwaway lore in a playful mood.

All this evidence suggests that in his parallel Mythos for his ghostwritten stories, where his good authorial name was not at stake, Lovecraft created a parody version of his own Mythos and never intended that both should stand side by side in a single story. He never used them so, but Carter did when he made Ghatanothoa a third son of Great Cthulhu alongside his own creations Ythogtha and Zoth-Ommog. The only reason not to do this sort of thing is that the "serious" and parodic/derivative versions each embody the same actantial role, and their characters are too powerful for them easily to share it. You just don't need more than one Cthulhu. The same incongruity arises in comic books. For instance, for DC Comics to import Fawcett's Captain Marvel into its own narrative continuity resulted in one Superman too many. It was more than business when DC had earlier sued Fawcett, claiming that Captain Marvel was a plagiarism of Superman. It was a literary insight: one of them had to go.[8]

Beneath the Curtain of Nephren-Ka

Another sense in which one may speak of a vast, extended narrative implicit in Lovecraft's works is that of an overarching cosmic history against which he set the events of his stories—most of it in the distant past. Lovecraft assembled this universal history piecemeal, and as a result it does not quite harmonize. But such as it is, it may be outlined as follows. In "The Call of Cthulhu" (1926), we learn that a prehistoric race of space beings, the Great Old Ones, arrived on earth. "The Great Old Ones...lived ages before there were any men, and...came to the young world out of the sky." They had already entered their great hibernation before the first humans appeared, but when they did, the Old Ones, in their "dreaming," communicated with the hominids telepathically, moving them to create the cult of the Old Ones, just as Jehovah spoke to Abraham. The narrator adds that some of the Old Ones wait on the sea bottom (octopoid Cthulhu and his brethren), while others sleep in pockets of the earth's crust, and this last must be a nod to the crocodilian race in "The Nameless City."

Things change quite a bit in "The Mound," ghostwritten for Bishop between December 1929 and early 1930. This time we read that "Great Tulu" touched down on the earth while it still cooled, bringing the Old Ones with him, but he is not one of them. Rather, they are extraterrestrial humanoids themselves and proceed to beget humanity of their own stock. At some point, most of the Old Ones retreat from the earth's surface to great caverns below in order to escape a great flood. There they build a vast city called K'n-yan. Somewhere along the line, an attack by an unnamed race of "space-devils" manages to sink the city of Relex (which equals R'lyeh in "The Call of Cthulhu"), Cthulhu's royal city. A good captain, Cthulhu goes down with his ship.

Lovecraft immediately went on to write "The Whisperer in Darkness" (between February and September 1930). In it we hear of another extraterrestrial race, the Outer Ones, who hail from a supercosmos in which our whole universe forms but an atom. Visiting earth from their previous outpost on Pluto (discovered while Lovecraft, an avid amateur astronomer, was writing this tale), they were mining some metal in the Vermont hills that they could not find elsewhere. These Outer Ones were something on the order of winged, human-sized lobsters with a neural knob of feelers instead of a head. These beings had visited K'n-yan. "They were here long before the fabulous epoch of Cthulhu was over, and remember all about sunken R'lyeh when it was above the waters." So are we to identify them with the space-devils mentioned in "The Mound"? It is tempting to do so, except for one consideration: the Outer Ones are said (or implied) simply to have outlasted R'lyeh and Cthulhu, since there is no suggestion of hostilities during which they might have torpedoed R'lyeh.

On the heels of "The Whisperer in Darkness" came *At the Mountains of Madness* (February–March 1931). This novella concerns yet another alien race of colonizers, again called the Old Ones. They are explicitly identified with the Old Ones of Alhazred and therefore might be expected to be Cthulhu's kindred, although they turn out not to be. In form, they are large barrels with five great membranous wings emerging from the middle of each of five segment panels. From their lower extremity sprouts a set of tentacles, while the other end issues in a starfish with five eye-stalks. Fantastic! Appearing on our planet about a billion years ago, they created human beings in their experimental labs. This point contradicts both "The Call of Cthulhu," which seems to envision a spontaneous evolution of human beings, and "The Mound," in which humanity is the offspring of humanoid alien Old Ones. Yet it is not only stories that collide. At some point there was war between the star-headed Old Ones and "a land race of beings shaped like octopi and probably corresponding to [the] fabulous prehuman spawn of Cthulhu," and this long before the star heads created humankind. But *At the Mountains of Madness* does not have R'lyeh sunk by its enemies. Rather, as in "The Call of Cthulhu," the island, along with much other inhabited Pacific real estate, goes down because of geologic instability. That's the end of the Cthulhu spawn in this account.

During the Jurassic period, the Outer Ones (plainly the same race as in "The Whisperer in Darkness") invade and drive the star-headed Old Ones into the sea. (They are easily able to live under water and build new cities there, later returning to the surface when the coast is clear.) Uh, didn't we read in "The Whisperer in Darkness" that the Outer Ones remembered the good old days when R'lyeh stood above the waves? In *At the Mountains of Madness*, alas, Cthulhu, his kin, and R'lyeh are long gone by the time the Outer Ones show up on the scene.

20.6 Cover of H. P. Lovecraft's *The Horror in the Museum and Other Revisions* (1970 ed.). (Courtesy of Arkham House)

In the 1933 revision tale "Out of the Aeons," it develops that the Outer Ones "had colonized the earth before the birth of terrestrial life" and perished "eons before" the first humans appeared on the vast continent of Mu in the Pacific. But this can't be if we take "The Whisperer in Darkness" seriously (or in terms I suggested above, if we want to read "The Whisperer in Darkness" as a chapter of "Out of the Aeons") because it has the Outer Ones still lurking in the Vermont forests in the early twentieth century.

"The Shadow Out of Time" (written between November 1934 and March 1935) forms almost a sequel to *At the Mountains of Madness*, making explicit reference to the events of that novella and even sharing one character in common. Thus, we can be pretty sure that Lovecraft wanted to fold the events and history of the one story into the other—but which way? Was he careful to make sure the history as represented in the new story fit comfortably into that of the old? Or was he, again, supplying paraleipses for hitherto-unguessed gaps in the previous story and hence reinterpreting it? In "The Shadow out of Time" we read of the appearance, via unaided evolution, on earth (Australia) of a race of beings shaped like great cones topped by a set of tentacles containing various sense organs and digits. They appeared a billion years ago, more or less coincident with the advent from space of the star-headed Old Ones in Antarctica. Then, about 600 million years ago, a new group of space creatures arrived on earth from some dark quarter where they had no need for sight. These "blind beings" dominated Australia until the arrival of the Great Race of Yith about 150 million years ago. Taking a page from Madame Blavatsky's cosmic history, Lovecraft therefore had a race of disincarnate minds from another world (Venus in Blavatsky and Yith in Lovecraft) project themselves into the rubbery cone forms, usurping the natural seat of the earthlings' primitive intellects. They proceeded to drive the blind beings underground from which they uneasily dreaded their eventual return to take revenge.

The Yith minds, embodied in the cone creatures, turned their attentions next to the star-headed Old Ones of Antarctica, making war on them at about the same time that the Antarctican Old Ones had their hands full trying to quell (ultimately without success) a rebellion by their Argus-eyed, shapeless slave creatures the shoggoths. Thus, this Australia versus Antarctica warfare must have followed that between the Old Ones and both the Outer Ones and the Cthulhu spawn. About fifty million years before the dawn of humankind, the Yith minds found themselves at bay from the returning blind beings, so they abandoned the cone bodies and projected into the forms of a far-future, posthuman beetle race.

Lovecraft's chapter of the round-robin "The Challenge from Beyond" was written only a few months after "The Shadow out of Time," and for it he decided to employ a simplified version of the Great Race and its history. This time the cone race does not derive its superintelligence from usurping extraterrestrial minds. It is homegrown on earth, though they do learn, by themselves, to project their minds through space and time. They are located not in Australia but at the South Pole, with no mention of the star-headed Old Ones. Again, they are engaged in warfare with another space race, but this time with a group of caterpillar-like beings from another planet.

"The Haunter of the Dark" (November 1935) centers around an otherworldly relic called the Shining Trapezohedron, a window on all time and space. The seer stone "was fashioned on Yuggoth [Pluto], before ever the Old Ones [are they the same as the Outer Ones?] brought it to earth. It was treasured and placed in its curious box by the crinoid things of Antarctica. How did it pass from the possession of the one race of aliens to that of the other? Perhaps it was a trophy of war.

In all this vast sweep of cosmic history, we find surprisingly little attempt by Lovecraft to keep things straight. It is almost as if he counted on the reader having only a vague recollection of the history as set forth in previous stories. He felt free to adjust the history according to the dictates and advantages of each particular story. The history of the Outer Ones is one thing when they are the stars of the show, but quite another when they appear only as second bananas and foils for new main characters like the Antarctican Old Ones. The conical Great Race may have originated on Earth or Yith depending on how technical Lovecraft wished to get in a single chapter of a round-robin story. The Outer Ones from Yuggoth are alive in "The Whisperer in Darkness" because they represent a fearsome invasion of Outsideness into our serene pond of a world. But they are long extinct in "Out of the Aeons" for the simple reason that there they are meant to function solely as an index for the antiquity of Ghatanothoa, the devil god they dropped off on Mu in ancient days.

There is no denying that Lovecraft was fashioning a common background for his narrative universe, but equally one cannot deny it is rife with contradictions. There is a limit to which one can read any one story as a chapter of some other. When we try to harmonize all the details, we are reading the story against the grain: we are taking what

239

With Strange Aeons

Deep Things Shared

In all this chronicling, one Lovecraftian race is conspicuous by its absence: where do the finny Deep Ones fit in? In "The Shadow over Innsmouth," Lovecraft says they were fish-men of the Pacific, something like the Creature from the Black Lagoon. They would make deals with human islanders to find them gold (artifacts of their own ancient civilization) and herd fish into the nets in return for interbreeding privileges. We almost get the impression that the Deep Ones cannot breed without human partners; their couplings eventuate not in half-and-half hybrids but in the complete genetic dominance of Deep One DNA. Deep One genes gradually become fully manifest when a human–Deep One offspring comes of age and undergoes "the change." If this is not the case, it is difficult to understand what benefit the Deep Ones gain from mating with human land dwellers.

Innsmouth shipping captain Obed Marsh encounters this sex-and-gold trade in the East Indies and brings it back to the North Atlantic with him. Eventually, we learn from local boozer Zadok Allen that the Deep Ones are making ready for a full-scale assault on the surface world. Among their allies are the shoggoths first mentioned in *At the Mountains of Madness*. The Deep Ones worship Cthulhu, but so do various fully human sailors and Eskimos. The Deep Ones, then, do not appear the same as the Cthulhu spawn of *At the Mountains of Madness*, for the latter were octopoid, unlike the Deep Ones. We can—indeed, we must—picture the shoggoths as surviving long after the slaughter of their masters and creators, the star-headed Old Ones. Lovecraft says that the Old Ones had cities at the North Pole as well, so presumably the shoggoths of "The Shadow over Innsmouth" could have gravitated there from either pole. Again, though, what of the Deep Ones?

Perhaps the mystery appears important only in retrospect—only, that is, if one has decided to read "The Shadow over Innsmouth" as a chapter of Derleth's *The Trail of Cthulhu*, or Lumley's "Dagon's Bell" or *The Return of the Deep Ones*. For the Deep Ones certainly do generate their own history after Lovecraft. Yet I suspect that Lovecraft does not work them into his table of inhuman nations for one reason: he does not really think of the Deep Ones as monsters. Their political-allegorical significance is too close to the surface for that. In "The Shadow over Innsmouth," Lovecraft's narrator Robert Olmstead (or so the notes and synopsis name him) recounts how Marsh brought home to New England a heavily veiled "Polynesian" bride. The clear implication is that she is a

Deep One for him to mate with, as part of the trade deal he has struck with "them fish-frog devils." But the tuned-in reader understands that for Lovecraft, the Deep Ones simply *are* Polynesians. He has the same racist disdain for them as he does for the half-castes, mestizos, mulattoes, Cubans, Portuguese sailors, and immigrants he rails about in "The Call of Cthulhu," "The Horror at Red Hook," and "He." The thick lips, bulging eyes, and greasy skins of the pre–Deep One Innsmouthers like Joe Sargent—well, you get the idea. The Deep Ones are ultimately more like the decadent Dunwich townies than they are the Old Ones with whom Wizard Whateley traffics.

was intended to be background and yanking it into the foreground. No wonder we see shortcomings and incongruities we would never see if we left the background where it belongs.

Let me put it another way. If one is determined to iron out Lovecraft's cosmic-historical notices into a unified, internally consistent narrative, one is following the example of L. Sprague de Camp when he tried to hammer the Conan adventures of Howard into a single "probable outline of the career of Conan the Cimmerian," and with the same perils. From internal clues, de Camp had little difficulty tracing a general chronology of Howard's Conan tales. There were plenty of adventures, more than a normal person might squeeze into a single lifetime. But Conan was a world traveler and a very busy man, so why not? The seams began to split, however, once de Camp went back to the drawing board to find appropriate niches for all the secondary Conan stories written by himself, Carter, and Bjorn Nyberg. It became an exercise in sheer absurdity once he endeavored to stuff in all the later novels by Robert Jordan, Leonard Carpenter, and many, many more. To fit them all in, one must almost imagine Conan living as long as Xena the Warrior Princess, who one week is patting the second-century physician Galen on the head and the next fighting alongside Hector in the Trojan War. I have always thought that de Camp made a fundamental mistake in the way he understood the Conan canon. It was not a piecemeal *epic* that had to be retroactively assembled like a puzzle. Rather, as Howard himself implied when he said he pictured Conan

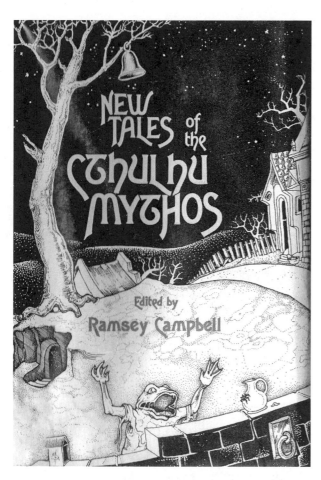

20.7 Cover of *New Tales of the Cthulhu Mythos* (edited by Ramsey Campbell, 1980 ed.). (Courtesy of Arkham House)

standing at his shoulder, recounting his tall tales, the various Conan adventures form a *legend cycle*. It is not that *all* of them *did* happen, but that *any* of them *might* have. And it is the same with Lovecraft's tales of the Cthulhu Mythos. If one assumes they all did happen, one invites the silly notion that some Lovecraft detractor has pointed out: numerous vastly superhuman alien races devoting grossly disproportionate attention to what Lovecraft himself considers our unimportant mud ball of a planet—and New England especially! Maybe they all favor clam chowder. (But probably not the crustacean Outer Ones, on second thought.)

To Correlate Its Contents

If Lovecraft thus created a narrative macrocosm, he does not seem to have created a narrative microcosm on the narrower band of history in which the events of his stories and the deeds of their human protagonists take place. Peter H. Cannon (1986) has taken the trouble to compile and examine the time references in the major stories in his *The Chronology out of Time*, but the result is entirely unremarkable. There are no important patterns such as to indicate Lovecraft was consciously coordinating the events of one story with another (except in the rare cases already mentioned), contra Dirk W. Mosig (1978): "Practically all of the stories written by H. P. Lovecraft can best be regarded as the loosely connected chapters of a gigantic novel."

But there does remain a sense in which the spans allotted the characters get coordinated with the cosmic panorama I have described. And that is the dawning realization on the protagonist that he belongs in the narrative universe to which he first thinks himself extradiegetic As Lovecraft's narrator or hero reads of the mythical epic of the Old Ones and the clashes of unknown prehuman civilizations, of the belittling creation of humanity as a mistake or a joke, he is bemused and disconcerted by the oddity of it all. Yet it is no worse than that, because the protagonist first keeps it at arm's length, thinking it an unaccustomed fiction, a preposterous fantasy. Then clues of genealogy, archaeology, and so on, begin to combine to convince him at last that his own life story is a small piece of that larger tapestry, for it is terribly and shockingly *real*. It is no fantasy after all; rather, it is his own hitherto-seemingly mundane life that has been the fantasy, lived in blissful ignorance of the true nature of the universe in which one is trapped. The protagonist realizes he is intradiegetical to the story, merely its latest momentary episode, and the outcome will not be a happy one.

Notes

1. Lovecraft so confesses his faith in a letter to Rheinhart Kleiner, February 2, 1916 (Derleth and Wandrei 1965, 20).
2. At some symposium (perhaps NecronomiCon 1993), I heard Donald R. Burleson suggest that the city of Providence is the real character in *The Case of Charles Dexter Ward*.

3. Lovecraft did not so denominate his growing mythology; his literary protégé August Derleth did, and he was right on target.

4. Writing to Clark Ashton Smith on October 17, 1930, Lovecraft says:

> My own rule is that no weird story can truly produce terror unless it is devised with all the care & verisimilitude of an actual *hoax*. The author must forget all about "'short story technique'", & build up a stark, simple account, full of homely corroborative details, just as if he were actually trying to "'put across'" a deception in real life—a deception clever enough to make adults believe it. My own attitude in writing is always that of the hoax-weaver. One part of my mind tries to concoct something realistic & coherent enough to fool the rest of my mind & make me swallow the marvel as the late Camille Flammarion used to swallow the ghost & revenant yarns unloaded on him by fakers & neurotics. For the time being I try to forget formal literature, & simply devise a lie as carefully as a crooked witness prepares a line of testimony with cross-examining lawyers in his mind.... This ideal became a conscious one with me about the "Cthulhu" period. (Derleth and Wandrei 1971, 193)

5. We may compare Lovecraft's treatment of "Dagon" and "The Call of Cthulhu" with George Lucas's apparent view on the *Star Wars* cycle. When we watched the original *Star Wars*, before it was renamed *Episode Four: A New Hope*, we knew that we were beginning in medias res. Much had already happened. We knew much was yet to occur after the end of the movie. Yet we didn't care, and we suspected that Lucas himself had virtually as little idea of the rest of the implied picture as we ourselves did. We really knew as much about Darth Vader, Obi-Wan Kenobi, Han Solo, and the others as we needed to—no further backstory was needed. There were various analapses (flashbacks, even if not shown as such) given in the discussion, as when Darth Vader several times refers to Obi-Wan as his old master and so on.

But when we later watch, for instance, *Episode Three: Revenge of the Sith*, we view a set of events that we are now asked to believe led to those of the original *Star Wars* movie. When next we watch *A New Hope* and come to the scene where Darth Vader confronts Obi-Wan, saying, "We meet again at last!" Lucas wants us to think of the last time they saw each other, during their duel on the lava planet in *Revenge of the Sith*. Shall we humor him? All I can say is that while watching *Revenge of the Sith*, I shall think, "Ah! These two will renew this fight aboard the Death Star some years hence!" But when I am watching the original *Star Wars*, however, I shall not think, "Oh, he is referring to their duel amid the lava." I know that nothing that specific was in Lucas's mind at the time, nor implicit in the script of the 1977 *Star Wars*. In other words, I have the choice of viewing the original 1977 film as either *Star Wars* or as part of *Revenge of the Sith*.

Lucas wanted everyone henceforth to view the 1977 movie as the sequel to *Revenge of the Sith*, and so to force us to do so, he issued one and then another version of the first *Star Wars* trilogy, editing them to eliminate narrative contradictions, trying to hide the fact that one script originally did not depend on another. He was winging it, lurching from movie to movie, completely reconceptualizing as he went. More recently, though, he has decided to reissue the original theatrical versions to allow older fans of those movies to watch them apart from the second trilogy. As readers, the choice is always up to us.

6. For years, superheroes from DC Comics' Golden Age (e.g., the Justice Society of America) had been pictured as living on an earth parallel to ours, Earth-2, while DC Comics's Silver Age heroes (the Justice League of America, etc.) dwelled on Earth-1. DC had also acquired the characters of Quality Comics, Charlton Comics, and Fawcett Comics. For years, there would be sporadic "crossovers" in which a hero from one parallel earth managed to make his or her way to one of the others and team up with its heroes for an adventure or two. But with *Crisis on Infinite Earths* all the heroes came to occupy the same earth, combining all the hitherto-distinct narrative universes.

7. One of Lovecraft's primary sources of income was the money he made from his "revisions." The level of work he performed on each client's story varied from case to case, but in many instances Lovecraft rewrote the original story in large part or almost entirely. "The Mound," for example, began as Zealia Bishop's one-sentence plot synopsis and ended as a fully ghostwritten, near-thirty-thousand-word Lovecraft story. The most elaborate of these revisions are published in H. P. Lovecraft, *The Horror in the Museum and Other Revisions* (1989).

8. And more than ever, this became clear when both inhabited the same comics continuity. This is why various DC writers keep pitting Superman against Captain Marvel, usually because the latter has lost his mind or memory. That's all they can think of to do with him. And it has never really grown beyond the dimensions of the first time that Wally Wood tried it in *Mad* magazine, having Superduperman fight Captain Marbles—a parody.

References

Cannon, Peter H. (1986). *The Chronology out of Time: Dates in the Fiction of H. P. Lovecraft*. West Warwick, RI: Necronomicon Press.

Derleth, August W., and Donald Wandrei (eds.) (1965). *H. P. Lovecraft, Selected Letters, Vol. I*. Sauk City, WI: Arkham House.

Derleth, August W., and Donald Wandrei (eds.) (1971). *H. P. Lovecraft, Selected Letters, Vol. III*. Sauk City, WI: Arkham House.

Lovecraft, H. P. (1985). *The Dunwich Horror and Others*. Sauk City, WI: Arkham House.

Lovecraft, H. P. (1985). *At the Mountains of Madness and Other Novels*. Sauk City, WI: Arkham House.

Lovecraft, H. P. (1986). *Dagon and Other Macabre Tales*. Sauk City, WI: Arkham House.

Lovecraft, H. P. (1989). *The Horror in the Museum and Other Revisions*. Sauk City, WI: Arkham House.

Mosig, Dirk W. (1978). "Innsmouth and the Lovecraft *Oeuvre*: A Wholistic Approach." *Nyctalops* 14:4–5.

Mosig, Dirk W. (1980). "H. P. Lovecraft: Myth-Maker." In *H. P. Lovecraft: Four Decades of Criticism*, edited by S. T. Joshi. Athens: Ohio University Press.

Robert M. Price

Deep Is the Well of the Past. Should We Not Call It Bottomless?: Thomas Mann's *Joseph and His Brothers*

William E. McDonald

I.

> O comfort-killing Night, image of hell!
> Dim register and notary of shame!
> Black stage for tragedies and murders fell!
> Vast sin-concealing chaos!
> —William Shakespeare, *The Rape of Lucrece*

> What is it all, if we all of us end but in being our own
> corpse-coffins at last,
> Swallow'd in Vastness, lost in Silence, drown'd in the
> deeps of a meaningless Past?
> —Alfred Lord Tennyson, "Vastness"

Vastness always seemed to sneak up on Thomas Mann (1875–1955). Despite a modest initial plan, his early smash hit from 1901, *Buddenbrooks* (Mann 1993), the one book mentioned in his 1929 Nobel Prize citation, took up 760 pages in the standard German edition. His publisher wanted to cut the enormous manuscript nearly in half, but the young writer bravely and wisely refused. *The Magic Mountain* came into being in 1913 as a brief "satyr play" to follow the tragic novella "Death in Venice." Thirteen years later an exhausted Mann wrote, in his crabbed longhand, *"finis operis"* on the last of its one thousand pages. He termed it a "triumph of obstinacy." In 1926, determined to undertake only smaller pieces, he decided on a trilogy of

historical novellas with religious subjects: the Joseph story in Genesis, the Reformation, and the Counter-Reformation.[1] More than sixteen years later, in early 1943, he ended his comic epic tetralogy with the words of its title, *Joseph und seine Brüder* (Mann 1967).[2] The four novels together run some fifteen hundred pages in John E. Woods's fine new translation (Mann 2005), and more than eighteen hundred in the German edition. The Reformation and Counter-Reformation stories were swallowed up in its vastness.

The physical girth of *Joseph and His Brothers* only starts, however, to describe its preoccupation with "bottomlessness": with the unfathomable beginnings of the West's archetypal stories, with the seemingly unconquerable distance between the "historical Joseph" and ourselves, and finally, with time itself. The time of its writing only multiplied this preoccupation. During these sixteen years Mann moved from a rooted, haute bourgeois family life in Munich appropriate to a Nobel laureate to a life of dislocation, daily uncertainty, and surprising political responsibility. He moved from halfhearted, self-protective resistance to the rising Nazi menace, to an aggressive attacker of Hitler's regime with a worldwide audience. Suddenly exiled from his beloved Germany in 1933—his daughter Erica had to smuggle the working *Joseph* manuscript out of his commandeered house—Mann wandered in Europe for a time before several trips to the United States led to a temporary appointment at Princeton University. He ended up in Pacific Palisades, dean of the great World War II expatriate community in Southern California, where the final words of the *Joseph* series were written on January 4, 1943. During all this time, interleaved with the tetralogy, he also wrote another major novel, *Lotte in Weimar*, a minor novel, several memorable short stories, and some fifteen major essays, and gave scores of radio talks and lectures together with hundreds of public readings of his work. In all of this the *Joseph* novels were at once his anchor—a steadying point against the vastation of his exile—and what Woods calls a "vast canvas" (Mann 2005, xiv), an oxymoronic phrase that captures the novels' seemingly unlimited scope and unfinishable demands together with their highly formal, meticulously framed structure.

II.

Thou god of this great vast, rebuke these surges
Which wash both heaven and hell.
—William Shakespeare, *Pericles*

Who like a late-sacked island vastly stood
Bare and unpeopled in this fearful flood.
—William Shakespeare, *The Rape of Lucrece*

I admire our ancestors, whoever they were. I think the
first self-conscious person must have shaken in his
boots. Because as he becomes self-conscious, he's no
longer part of nature. He sees himself against nature.
He looks at the vastness of the universe and it looks
hostile.
—John Shelby Spong

Vastness fascinates, attracting and repelling us at once. It's
an idea with a lengthy linguistic history beginning with the
Latin word *vastus*: waste, uncultivated, immense, desolate.
We English speakers have used the word since Shakespeare's day to denote empty space, and from Milton's day
to describe the heavens, and heaven itself, either literally or
figuratively. The weight has predominantly fallen on emptiness, however, on the "unpeopled" as Shakespeare has it in
my *Lucrece* epigraph. Deserts, seas, mountains, "Nature" itself (Blake's Los), and especially the cosmos are unpeopled
places, indifferent or inhospitable to our kind. In *In Memoriam*, Tennyson developed this usage, expressing succinctly
our need to contain and shape the inhuman immeasurable:
"A soul shall draw from out the vast/And strike his being
into bounds."

Tennyson's shaping "soul" here marks another traditional space that vastness names: the boundless territory of
our inner, buried life—memory, subliminal intuitions,
dream life, and the unconscious itself. From early religious
mystics and the Romantic poets to Freud and ourselves,
this inward territory has loomed as large as the empyrean
it mirrored. Expanding this repositioning, the word has
been, paradoxically, extended in our time to the small in nature, where "vast spaces" are now held to exist between the
nucleus of an atom and its electrons, or between quarks or

strings and the objects they compose. The positive qualities
of vastness mostly show up on this smaller scale; we speak
of individual artists or workmen with "vast skill," well beyond the norm but still within the human. This leads in
turn to the watered-down sense of the word as an intensi-
fier, like "extremely" or "very"; "vastly better," we say, or "a
vast improvement." Lord Chesterfield in the 1770s thought
so little of this usage that he complained about its popularity (*Letters* 195 and 196). The Latin derivation also picks
up a quality of vastness that may be obsolete or repressed
today, but that still figures, I believe, in the overtones of
the word: "uncultivated," beyond the range and capacity of
civilization, "desolate," "the waste-land." Thomas Mann drew
on every part of this catalog, in keeping with the encyclopedic nature of his four epic novels.

There are some early examples of vastness in Mann's
work before the *Joseph* tetralogy, but the most relevant
ones occur in the "Research" chapter of *The Magic Mountain*
(Mann 1995). There his young bildungsroman hero, Hans
Castorp, listens as a boy to his grandfather's hypnotic
stories—stories that recede into the past as the old man
chants "*Ur-Ur-Ur-Ur*," the "greats" mesmerizing "dreamily
thoughtless" Hans with the "somber sound of the crypt and
buried time" (Mann 2003, 36; 1995, 21). Later, as an adult,
he lies wrapped in blankets on the balcony of his tuberculosis sanitorium in Davos, Switzerland, and fortified by
cognac mixed in milk, reads deeply "in languor and excitement" into the sciences of his day (2003, 378ff; 1995,
267ff).

> While the moon followed its prescribed path across the
> high mountain valley glistening like crystal below, he
> read, in this vast setting, biology, then embryology, anat-
> omy and physiology, genetics, the study of organized
> matter, always pursuing the connections between the
> micro- and the macrocosm.[3] The atom was an energy-
> laden cosmic system, in which planets rotated frantically
> around a sun-like center, while comets raced through its
> ether at the speed of light, held in their eccentric orbits
> by the gravity of the core.... The innermost recesses of
> nature were repeated, mirrored on a vast scale, in the
> macrocosmic world of stars, whose swarms, clusters,

groupings, and constellations, pale against the moon, hovered above the valley glistening with frost and above the head of this master of muffled masquerade. Once the cosmic character of the "smallest" bits of matter became apparent, any objection about the "smallness" of these stars in the inner world would have been quite irrelevant—and concepts like inner and outer had now lost their foundation as well. The world of the atom was an outer world, just as it was highly probable that the earthly star on which we lived was a profoundly inner world when regarded organically then at the very moment when one thought one had reached the outermost edge, everything began all over again. (2003, 395–396; 1995, 279–280)

What holds us here is Mann's evocation of endlessly repeating vastnesses, extending the concept to infinity even as he affirms the ordering symmetries of the very large and very small. This seemingly contradictory drive to maintain form and order while extending vastness beyond all knowable boundaries in space and time ("Ur-Ur-Ur-Ur") comes under consideration again in the *Joseph* novels. Hans's solution may be somewhat incoherent here ("a profoundly inner world when regarded organically"), but will be sharpened and refined in the succeeding novels.

The "Prelude" to the *Joseph* tetralogy, titled "Descent into Hell," takes the reader on another vertiginous forty-page ride into the ungraspable origins of life and the cosmos. Mann's ostensible purpose is to transport us "down" to the *Ur*-time of Joseph, which for artistic purposes he makes contemporary with the eighteenth dynasty monotheistic Pharaoh Ikhnaton (c. 1372–1354 BCE).[4] But that date is only a provisional stopping point, for the archetypal tales that organize Joseph's world—paradise, the flood, the fall, and so on—have origins that long antedate Joseph's already-distant time. So we have a double vantage point: looking down to Joseph, and then with him looking even further into the obscure origins of our civilization's organizing narratives.

The Prelude shares with the "Research" chapter a musical form, presenting us again with an enormous theme and variations on the abysmal mythological accounts of our beginning. The Prelude itself has a prelude of its own: an introductory paragraph that states the composition's main theme forcefully, and then adds two central tropes that will provide richness and balance as the "totally unfathomable" is explored. The theme is clarion. Every claim for "the first foundations of humankind" quickly disappears from view, "for again and again they retreat farther into the bottomless depths, no matter to what extravagant lengths we may unreel our temporal plumb line. The salient words here are 'again' and 'farther,' because what is inscrutable has a way of teasing our zeal for placing it under scrutiny; it offers only illusory stations and goals, behind which, once we reach them, we discover new stretches of the past opening up" (Mann 1967, 9; 2005, 3).

"Again" and "farther": boundless time and space open under the reader's feet. The Prelude then complements its exploration of the vastness of time with a central spatial metaphor: the lone walker on the seashore.[5] The vastness of the sea (i.e., the past) strikes the stroller, but he is more taken by the endlessness of the shore before him: "behind each backdrop of loamy dunes [*Dünenkulisse*] that he strives to reach lie new expanses to lure him onward to another cape." Though Mann doesn't use the word, this vision of a fractal coast, endlessly repeating in space in tandem with our unbounded descent into time, gives us a double perspective that models our looking at and with Joseph. We walk with the stroller, immersed in a realistic world, but with the groundswell of myth opening ahead and beside us. From the beginning we are trained to read each scene stereoptically, dialogically, mindful of our present life, yet immersed in the journey toward the boundless.

Curiously, the third figure for vastness comes from the theater, *die Kulisse*, a "backdrop" or "façade" (Mann 1967, 9, 32, etc.; 2005, 3, 22), a word that appears some dozen times in various combinations throughout the Prelude. It gives us an artistic, performative trope to accompany our unbounded moving down and moving out. There is always something behind the backdrop, but we cannot see it; our awareness of that beyond, often subliminal yet always in play, reminds us that the boundaries we see are artificial, arbitrary; space and time always open out behind them. It leads to the old dilemma of fictionality: we know that we are witness to a representation, an unreality, and at the same time we prize the truth and the heightened sense of reality that the fraud of art puts before us. Moving beyond metaphor, Mann thematized his *Kulissen* in the character of Joseph, himself the performer par excellence, who embodies our pleasure in and anxieties with our own shape-shifting, unlocatable selves behind the artifice of our familiar narrative and dramatic self-presentations. Performance—ethical, artistic, political, and mythic—becomes a major theme of the *Joseph* novels. Nearly all the main characters are de facto playwrights, stage managers, and con artists who know how to serve their ancestors and their god by performing works. Further, performance was a major part of Mann's own artistic life. He loved to read his work aloud, and often did so at considerable personal sacrifice, thriving on the applause that the silence of the writing chamber denied him. The text of *Joseph* was written to be performed, and its comparatively short sections, frequently just the right length for a good public reading, made many appearances on the stage and lecture hall. Behind the *Kulisse* of Mann the performer, the audience could apperceive the living, fictional world of ancient Palestine. And behind that . . .

The Prelude climaxes with Mann's own mythic tale—one with identifiable roots in Gnosticism. The tale has two versions (Mann 1967, 39–49; 2005, 27–36). In the first, Adam *qadman*, "the youthful creature of pure light, . . . the prototype and epitome of humanity," falls in love with the beauty of "his own mirror-image in matter" and gives himself to it. In surrendering to this "narcissistic image of tragic loveliness," the youth's longing separates him from God, with the result that his desire becomes interwoven with guilt. This parable generalizes into the "romance of the adventurous soul," in which the youth's embrace of matter formed around his image becomes, allegorically, the union of form with unorganized matter. The soul suffers in its descent, both because it separates itself from God and because matter resists its attempts to give it beautiful form. God then sends "from his own substance" a second emissary, the reasonable "spirit," to rescue the soul from its love af-

fair. At this point an uncertainty about God's intent leads to the two versions of the tale. In the first, the spirit descends to show the soul that its embrace of matter was sinful and to recall it immediately to the upper world. In the second—the one preferred in the *Joseph* novels—the soul had not in fact "sinned," since God had not explicitly forbidden its congress with its own image—that is, with matter. So in this version the spirit comes not to woo the soul back to oneness with God but rather, as the well-known free shifting of tenses in mythic narratives suggests, to eventually become one with the soul, and produce a humanity blessed with both nature and spirit. The reasonable spirit too has its desires, but they point toward a new consummation, not a retrograde return. The soul's embrace of matter cannot and should not be undone, yet by itself it is "mindless" and therefore incapable of development. The spirit, however, signals a dynamic conception of creation and selfhood; it is both anchored and open to alteration. So the spirit is the "principle of the future," the soul is the holy "It was," and the spirit's role is essentially pedagogical: to save the soul for the future.

This is Mann's cosmic version of narcissism, that vast, ill-defined private universe of our earliest life.[6] Narcissism inaugurates creation just as it inaugurates personality, but cannot by itself complete it. Self-enamored youths like Joseph always fall into the blindness of the pit where his brothers cast him, and can only be rescued for the future by acknowledging the reality of the other and hearkening to a higher self-knowledge. This launches one of Mann's most interesting revisions of Freud. Mann will both endorse and swerve from his "scientific psychologist" mentor by working out the implications of the Prelude's allegory, eventually connecting his revision of identity to performance and even political action. We'll see shortly how this swerve enriches Mann's account of the vast.

III.

Owen Glendower: I can call spirits from the vasty deep.

Hotspur: Why, so can I, or so can any man. But will they come when you do call for them?
—William Shakespeare, *Henry IV*, Part 1

There is often a passage in even the most thoroughly interpreted dream which has to be left obscure; this is because we become aware during the work of interpretation that at that point there is a tangle of dream-thoughts which cannot be unraveled and which moreover adds nothing to our knowledge of the content of the dream. This is the dream's navel, the spot where it reaches down into the unknown. The dream-thoughts to which we are led by interpretation cannot, from the nature of things, have any definite endings; they are bound to branch out in every direction into the intricate network of our world of thought.

—Sigmund Freud, *The Interpretation of Dreams*

The scope of *Joseph and His Brothers* is not limited to the great depths of time and space that it enlists. It also, on analogy with the vastness of the very small in physics, gives us a model of the individual mind that, following Freud, is inexhaustible on the smallest, individual scale. This also empowers Mann's rare achievement in the history of vastness: comedy. Jacob's head servant, and Joseph's tutor in the ancient tales, is Mann's fictional Eliezer; a man of the same name also served Isaac and Abraham (Genesis 15:2), and the Isaacs and Abrahams that came before them. The current Eliezer does not draw any sharp lines between his predecessors and himself, and unself-consciously speaks of ancient events in the first, not the third, person. Mann's wonderful phrase is *"gleichsam nach hinten offenstand"*: his ego "as it were stood open at the back" and flows into those "Eliezers" that came before (1967, 122; 2005, 94). So Eliezer lives in the myth of being Eliezer, preserving a time before the claims of individuality and self-consciousness decisively set us apart from our ancestors. His unbounded ego refuses to stop with his skin, but extends itself deep into space and time: a destabilizing vastness of self that is also funny to encounter. The narrator campily complains about the difficulties this causes him—"We have no delusions about how difficult it is to speak of people who do not know precisely who they are" (1967, 128; 2005, 98–99: my translation)—but trades on this "fine discourse" and "moon grammar" to show how the spirits of his patriarchs developed out of the primal unity of soul and world (1967,

121; 2005, 93). Mann's Isaac is, comically, quite close to Eliezer, bleating at his death like the ram, the "saved sacrifice," he had always been, and even coming to resemble the animal physically, to the horror of his household (1967, 185–186; 2005, 147). Jacob, with all his cunning and cleverness, is also sometimes overtaken by the mythic in his dreamy associations. (He also uses this open-endedness, especially as an old man, to mystify and deflect.) Only Joseph is on the way to becoming the fully modern man, able to manipulate narratives of vastness to fulfill first his youthful narcissism, and later his loyal and loving rescue of Pharaoh's Egypt and his family. But he achieves his cosmopolitan secularism at a price; the deeply religious connectedness of his father, the lowest   and highest—layers of experience, are denied him.

In Jacob's dream life, no image is more famous than his vision of the heavens at Beth-el in Genesis 28:12: "He had a dream; a stairway [or ramp or ladder] was set on the ground and its top reached to the sky, and angels of God were going up and down on it."[7] God promised him the land on which he lay and to remain with him and his descendants. Mann predictably elaborates on this prototypical vision of vastness, but also offers a second image of "above and below" that sustains Jacob after his father Isaac's death. "And so Jacob's soul, though weighty and pondering, was raised up...for all the stories rose up again before him and were present in spirit, just as they had once been present in flesh molded according to their ancient archetype. And it seemed to him as if he were walking on transparent earth made up of countless, unfathomable layers of crystal descending into the depths and brightly lit by lamps hung in between. But here above them he walked in the stories of his own flesh" and sees his brother Esau likewise in the flesh, yet simultaneously as the archetype of "Edom, the Red One" (Mann 1967, 188; 2005, 149–150).[8] This reproduces Freud's account in my epigraph of the dream's taproot descending into the unconscious, but with an important and paradoxical difference: for Freud's darkness, Mann substitutes light and transparency. Jacob cannot see to the bottom of the crystal layers, yet they remain transparent all the way down. This brilliant image is but one of many ways in which Mann, well versed in Freud's writing, subtly shifted the stoic grimness of psychoanalysis to a broadly Dantesque comic vision. The archetypal stories are vast and limitless, yet light pervades their countless layers and casts light on the lives of the present, letting us see the past incarnate in the now.

One final note on comedy and the vast: in "The Grove of Adonis" section of *Young Joseph*, the seventeen-year-old lad, seeking to trump his father's famous ladder dream, forces his little brother Benjamin, a savvy eight year old, to hear his own self-consciously constructed "Dream of Heaven" that carries vastness to absurdity. The earthbound Jacob saw angels processing and an image of the divine; Joseph surpasses all the angels and flies right into heaven to present himself before a worshipful God, and declare himself "the Chosen One," the divine youth of sacrifice and resurrection. Jacob felt blessed to overhear the music of the spheres; Joseph puts himself at the center of the cosmos and hears the waves of sound rebound through heaven only to his own glory. Joseph chronicles himself as both hero and narrator, becomes everyone in his story (male and female), and sees his own greatness reflected in every face. The politely skeptical Benjamin asks "innocent" questions that deflate Joseph's narrative, but do not deter him; narcissism and vastness are cleverly linked, both in the over-the-top dream and in Joseph's mode of narration. There is never enough to satisfy narcissism or limit its stories: vastness in the service of a literary rather than psychoanalytic theory of character, and of a comic irony that keeps one kind of vastness in its place.

IV.

Isabella: Ay, just; perpetual durance, a restraint,
Though all the world's vastidity you had,
To a determined scope.
—William Shakespeare, *Measure for Measure*

For small creatures such as we the vastness is bearable only through love.
—Carl Sagan, *Contact*

Most readers who pick up the *Joseph* novels bring with them some knowledge of the Bible, Egypt and other ancient Near Eastern cultures, and perhaps some knowledge of the vast Midrash commentaries that have accumulated over the centuries. Others are more familiar with Mann's rich intellectual and artistic lineage (to mention a few: Goethe, Schopenhauer, Nietzsche, and especially for the *Joseph* novels, Freud and Wagner).[9] The intertextual wealth of associations produced by all this knowledge may well dwarf even the unbounded feeling of reading the text itself. Virtually every page can transport the reader along inexhaustible trails of associations. Just one structural example: Wagner's *Ring of the Nibelung*, with its preliminary evening of *Das Rheingold* followed by the three main operas of the cycle, matches exactly the preliminary novel "Stories of Jacob" and the three main novels focused on Joseph. On a smaller level, *Joseph and His Brothers'* opening note—"very deep is the well of the past"—directly echoes the low, sustained E-flat on the double basses that inaugurates *The Ring*, rising slowly from the invisible orchestra, itself "in the well" underneath the stage of Wagner's opera house at Bayreuth. Mann's self-conscious use of leitmotif technique, patiently building his enormous fiction out of small phrases, images, and objects, imitates—and sometimes parodies—Wagner's well-known practice of the same method. *The Ring* itself is famously a paragon of vastness, and Mann's thorough knowledge of its small intricacies and large, open-ended interpretation of human culture makes it an unending source of associations. As the reader comes to consider the parallels in story (e.g., Joseph and Siegfried) and theme (e.g., old religion's metamorphosis into a new humanism), the floor seems to open up beneath her. As a writer of "late epic," Mann's ever-increasing self-consciousness about his sources and his increasingly playful manipulation of them—for example, Joseph's economic policies in pharaonic Egypt mimic Franklin Delano Roosevelt's New Deal, which Mann much admired—adds a metafictional level for a reader already immersed in facts, history, and cultural conjugations. The book seems to extend beyond its covers in every direction and every scale.

Beyond this, as noted above, Mann undertook a number of related projects while the mammoth *Joseph* series gradually assembled itself. Each of these shorter works, especially the lecture-essays on Kleist, Lessing, Freud (two), Goethe (three), Wagner (two), Tolstoy, von Platen, Theodor Storm, Nietzsche, Schopenhauer, and *Don Quixote* have formative roles to play in the Joseph project; they shape, and are shaped by, the artistic gravity of the larger work. The reader who reads even a few of these essays in conjunction with the main text opens herself to yet more bottomless wells of intertextual association.

The actual reading of the *Joseph* novels brings on further experiences of the unbounded. The fantasy of losing oneself in a book, unaware of the pages as they fly by, can't sustain itself amid the vastness of the *Joseph* project: staying up all night just won't cut it. The conscientious reader, intent on remembering detail and the countless subtle variations on the novels' scores of motifs, reads more and more slowly as she moves through the work. At times hyperalert to these repetitions and elaborations, at times following them only half consciously, the reader enters labyrinthine corridors either way. A willed turning away from these seemingly unlimited associations may give a temporary sense of control, but it's hard to sustain; the text lures you back to its depths, and your involuntary memory refuses to sleep for long.[10] Like any great fiction, *Joseph and His Brothers* teaches us how to read it, and uncannily deters us from skipping or skimming; we come to realize that we are, among other things, reading for the experience of the unlimited that it so amply conjures.

Inevitably, the vastness of *Joseph and His Brothers* finally does come full circle, with the last words of the book repeating its title. The image of the revolving sphere is indeed the tetralogy's master trope, allowing Mann to contain vastness even as he insists on it. The sphere is at once a structural principle, thematic subject, and nascent theory of narrative. It appears more than sixty times over the course of the novels. The Prelude's master myth of the soul, spirit, and matter introduced, as we saw, the idea of descent and ascent between upper and lower worlds as well as the idea of a future of potential reunion and blessing. Pondering these revolutions, the narrator generalizes:

> And here, to be sure, what we have to say flows into a mystery in which our own information gets lost—the mystery, that is, of an endless past in which every origin

proves to be just an illusory stopping place, never the final goal of the journey, and its mystery is based on the fact that by its very nature the past is not a straight line, but a sphere. The line knows no mystery. Mystery lies in the sphere. But a sphere consists of complements and correspondences, a doubled half that closes to a unity; it consists of an upper and a lower, a heavenly and an earthly hemisphere in complement with one another as a whole, so that what is above is also below and whatever may happen in the earthly portion is repeated in the heavenly, the latter rediscovering itself in the former. This corresponding interchange of two halves that together build the whole of a closed sphere is analogous to another kind of objective change: rotation. The sphere rolls; that is the nature of a sphere. In an instant top is bottom and bottom top, if one may even speak of the generalities of bottom and top in such a case. It is not just that the heavenly and the earthly recognize themselves in each other, but thanks to spherical rotation the heavenly also turns into the earthly, the earthly into the heavenly, clearly revealing, indeed yielding the truth that gods can become human and that, on the other hand, human beings can become gods again. (Mann 1967, 189–190; 2005, 151)

The sphere provides a structure in which the infinite regress of the Prelude's descent and its own apparently endless revolutions can be contained. The sphere is finite and formed, yet unbounded. It operates independent of human knowledge, and has no beginning point; it has always already been there. Three-dimensional, the sphere encloses a vast archive "filled" with gods and men beyond count, and no one can know its totality. There is no place to stand outside all of its revolutions; the place of the observer within its many fields both enables and limits any understanding of its operation.

As it revolves men and gods ascend and descend, both as images and narrative dramas. They "behold" the images of one another and hear each other's stories. Perceived as narrative or drama, the sphere becomes a theater. Men and gods move across "stages" in every sense. Some are unknowing actors who mindlessly repeat the past—Isaac as the bleating sacrificial ram—but a talented, self-conscious performer such as Joseph can manipulate the scripts available to him. But no one in the novel, including its narrator, can master the mystery of the sphere. Its variations are endless, its shape enclosing and finite. Further, because it rolls through time—"men become gods, and gods men *again*"—it creates yet another set of patterns and indeterminacies. Time both moves and stays the same: we recognize this in the mystery of the annual feast—think of your annual family holidays—which both alters and stays the same. Indeed, the sphere's conception of meaning requires mystery, giving us the spherical sublime that echoes throughout Mann's project.

In addition to this, the sphere foregrounds intertextual reading. We do not simply absorb the text in a linear way but constantly move up and down, back and forth across its enormous tapestry. Every narrative requires this, of course, but most do not foreground or thematize the process; in this sense, reading *Joseph and His Brothers* necessitates and dramatizes self-conscious rereading. We come to see the dangers of monophonic or one-way reading: an uncritical projection of our own desire, a lazy or scattered memory, or the reductive perception of similarity that blinds us to the subtle changes in reincarnated archetypes. Intertextual threads weave our path, both in colors we can easily see and muted shades we can barely detect. In this way, Mann draws out the ethical entailments and responsibilities of reading. In sum, the dynamics of the sphere served him in many ways, making possible both encyclopedic inclusiveness and formal coherence.

V.

After the Warsaw premiere of Lutoslawski's First Symphony, one of the older listeners came over to the composer and while looking deeply into his eyes said, "What vastness of suffering!"
—Witold Lutoslawski, interview with Irena Nikolska

So where, then, has the experience of *Joseph and His Brothers'* vastness brought us? If we content ourselves solely with immersion in the endless intricacies of the text, we miss the "real-world" thrust of these seemingly unworldly narratives. Mann's fury at the rape of his country by the Nazis found direct expression in his letters, radio broadcasts, and generous aid to a number of fellow exiles trying to flee the continent. But he also used his great mythic project to expose the ancestors of Hitler's retrograde revolution in the ancient world. Just as the sphere revolves in the novels, turning gods into men and men into gods, so contemporary political figures resist or repeat the mindless indulgence in cultic irrationalism in ancient Egypt, imperial Rome, or medieval Florence. So in *Joseph in Egypt* and *Joseph the Provider*, Mann gives us a barely concealed allegory of contemporaneous events. In the conservative priests of Amun and their arche-fascist spokesperson Beknechons, Mann satirizes the Nazi Party organization, the Aryan rejection of all foreigners in the name of racial purity, and a masklike leader who puts the cult before any individual. More subtly, he showed how these debased ideas gradually possessed his remarkable female character Mut-em-enet, Potiphar's wife. Mann's self-declared mission was to rescue her from her sluttish reputation in Genesis, and he does so magnificently even as he traces the power of long-resisted passion to gradually destroy an innocent, loyal woman: fascism's cancer at work on the individual level. Joseph, the son of Israel, triumphs over them, and in ways that celebrate his humanity and knowledge of the sphere. His clever taxation schemes turn the priests' retrograde policies to democratic uses; his debasement in exile turns into a triumph in which he, like his author, rescues his people for the future.

Joseph and His Brothers, then, give us a kaleidoscopic account of vastness in its many shapes and colors: in the cosmos and the individual psyche, the labyrinths of intertextuality, religious and political allegory, and the inexhaustible time of reading and rereading. It closes with its title, completing the revolution of the sphere that brought it into being, and sustains the paradox of containing the vast without diminishing its unboundedness.

Notes

1. It was Goethe's offhand comment that the Genesis story of Joseph needed "filling out" that tempted Mann to revisit the original; forty-five times the original length certainly counts as a filling out.

2. The tetralogy is comprised of *The Stories of Jacob* (German publication in 1933; first English translation in 1934), *Young Joseph* (1934; 1935), *Joseph in Egypt* (1936; 1938), and *Joseph the Provider* (1943; 1944). The complete work in one volume first appeared in 1948. The cities of the German editions trace the flight of Mann's publisher, Samuel Fischer, from Nazi persecution: Berlin for the first and second editions, Vienna for the third, and Stockholm for the fourth.

3. Parts of Mann's science are, inevitably, dated even as Hans's descriptions are overblown, but "Research" could have happily accommodated contemporary discoveries; for example, had he known about Heisenberg, the much greater vastness of our universe today, or vector bosons and "charm" quarks, the chapter would have been longer and arguably even better, but not different in kind.

4. Scholars of the Bible locate the time of the patriarchs even earlier than this, circa 1900 BCE or even earlier. Mann was willing to give up a few centuries for the connection between the monotheisms of Jacob-Joseph and Ikhnaton.

5. This, too, has its precursor in the prelude to the seventh and final chapter of *The Magic Mountain*, "Strandspaziergang" ["A Stroll by the Shore"].

6. Put simply, Mann homogenizes Freud's account (1958, 75) of primary and secondary narcissism, blending the reductive account in the 1914 "On Narcissism" of a pre-Oedipal, universal Ur-narcissism and a secondary, more individual withdrawal of libido from persons in the world, in both reality and fantasy, after the initial choice of those objects.

7. Cited in Adele Berlin, Marc Zvi Brettler, and Michael Fishbane, eds., *The Jewish Study Bible* (New York: Oxford University Press, 1985).

8. Another name of Esau, and by extension, all the earth-bound "Esaus" that preceded him. See Genesis 25:30: "Feed me, I pray thee, with that same red pottage [Hebrew: *haadom, haadom*: "the red pottage"].... Therefore was his name called Edom"—that is, "red" or "red earth."

9. Mann scholar Herbert Lehnert compiled a sixty-two-page catalog of the principal works on ancient religion, history, and culture that Mann consulted during the making of his tetralogy: "Thomas Manns Vorstudien zur Josephstetralogie" (*Jahrbuch der Deutschen Schillergesellschaft* [Stuttgart: Kröner, 1963], 458–520). The page count dramatizes the scope of Mann's sources (and Lehnert's admirable thoroughness). The catalog naturally does not include the scores of later writers and thinkers from whom Mann discreetly borrowed.

10. I base these claims not only on my own reading experience but also the accounts of the hundred or so students that I have read the *Joseph* novels with over the years.

References

Freud, Sigmund (1958). *The Interpretation of Dreams*. London: Hogarth Press.

Mann, Thomas (1967). *Joseph und seine Brüder*. Frankfurt: S. Fischer. (Orig. pub. 1943.)

Mann, Thomas (1993). *Buddenbrooks*, translated by John E. Woods. New York: Knopf. (Orig. pub. 1901.)

Mann, Thomas (1995). *The Magic Mountain*, translated by John E. Woods. New York: Knopf. (Orig. pub. 1924.)

Mann, Thomas (2003). *Der Zauberberg*. Dresden: Staatsschauspiel.

Mann, Thomas (2005). *Joseph and His Brothers*, translated by John E. Woods. New York: Everyman's Library.

Milton, John (1998). *Paradise Lost*, edited by Alastair Fowler. New York: Longman.

Tennyson, Alfred (1902). *In Memoriam*, edited by Eugene Parsons. New York: T. Y. Crowell.

Deep Is the Well of the Past

Henry Darger's Search for the Grail in the Guise of a Celestial Child

Michael Bonesteel

Henry Darger was virtually unknown at the time of his death in 1973. But in the last quarter of the twentieth century, and particularly in the early years of the twenty-first, his name has become one that is recognized throughout the Western art world and Japan. This reclusive hospital janitor led the secret life of a monumental visual artist and epic novelist, despite his lack of formal training. When his cluttered, two-room apartment in Chicago was cleared out shortly before he died, a vast collection of creative work was discovered—most notably some two to three hundred watercolor, pencil, collage, and carbon-traced drawings as well as seven typewritten hand-bound tomes, thousands of bundled sheets of typewritten text, plus numerous journals, ledgers, and scrapbooks.

Much of Darger's visual art was so breathtaking that it established his growing reputation as arguably the greatest self-taught artist in the United States. What was less well-known was the unpublished fifteen-thousand-page epic fantasy novel on which these "illustrations" were based: *The Story of the Vivian Girls, in What Is Known as the Realms of the Unreal, of the Glandeco-Angelinian War Storm, Caused by the Child Slave Rebellion*—or for short, *In the Realms of the Unreal*—and its eighty-five-hundred-page sequel, *Further Adventures in Chicago*.

Darger's lack of formal training has presented little hindrance to the reception of his artwork as so-called outsider art (highly personal and idiosyncratic artwork with little or no connection to the mainstream art world, created by eccentrics, visionaries, outcasts, and the mentally ill, known in Europe as *l'art brut* or "raw art"). On the other hand, this same lack of training—in addition to the epic's enor-

mous length and physical inaccessibility—has been a major stumbling block to the recognition of Darger's writing within the literary world. Therefore, his novel has not received nearly the same attention as his visual art, except for relatively brief excerpts published to accompany discussions of his art in various books, catalogs, and periodicals.

The action of *In the Realms of the Unreal* is set on an imaginary planet "that is a thousand times as large as our own world, and with our earth as (its) moon." This planet is in the throes of a horrific world war fought between Christian and satanic nations over the practice, instituted by the latter, of child slavery. The saga was modeled on events transpiring during World War I, which was occurring at the time of its inception, and also incorporated aspects of the American Civil War along with borrowings from children's and adult literature—mainly L. Frank Baum's *The Wonderful Wizard of Oz* and Harriet Beecher Stowe's *Uncle Tom's Cabin*. Fictionalized autobiographical elements entered into the tale at periodic intervals as well.

The heroines of the story are the seven Vivian princesses, who lead an uprising against the child slaves' sadistic oppressors, known as Glandelinians. They are supported by their father, Robert Vivian, the emperor of Angelinia; Robert's brother, General Hanson Vivian; their guardian and protector, Colonel Jack Ambrose Evans; and their Christian armies and allies. The adventures of the Vivian girls (Violet, Jenny, Joice, Catherine, Hettie, Daisy, Evangeline, and Gertrude Angeline, their adopted sister), and those of their comrades, are played out in countless ways and in infinite detail over the course of some fifteen thousand pages. While never sexual in nature, the violence perpetrated on this war's victims, who are mostly children, is intense, culminating at times in graphic descriptions of mass strangulation, crucifixion, evisceration, dismemberment, and even cannibalism. Detailed depictions of this carnage are faithfully depicted in the visual art as well.

It is this story that is central to Darger's vision and on which the art depends for its existence. The visual art alone cannot relate the story, and taken by itself, remains a mysterious and enigmatic phenomenon. Unfortunately, the emergence of the visual art divorced from its literary heritage has resulted in premature negative reactions from

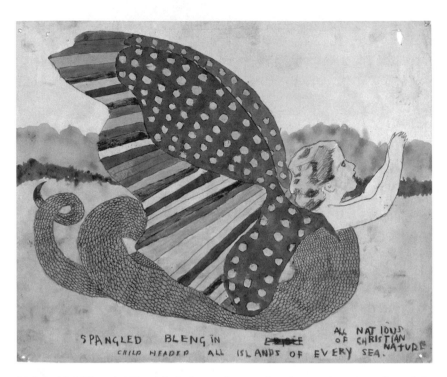

22.1 Untitled ("Spangled Blengin"). Carbon tracing, pencil, and watercolor, 14 × 17 in.; n.d. Image supplied by Kiyoko Lerner, courtesy Andrew Edlin Gallery, New York.

viewers who do not know the story underlying some of the more ghastly scenes depicted in the artworks.

Another part of the backstory that needs to be recognized is that the author, who writes himself into this saga as both a savior and betrayer of these child victims, was himself the real-life victim of a tragic and miserable childhood. At the age of four, Darger lost his mother when she gave birth to his baby sister, who was then put up for adoption. Not long afterward, his father became lame, could no longer take care of his son, and died several years later. Young Darger was brought up in a Catholic poorhouse in Chicago, then a Catholic boys' home, and finally an asylum for "Feeble-Minded Children" in Lincoln, Illinois, which held the notorious reputation of being one of the most abusive institutions of its time. Strangely, Darger's own recollections of the asylum in his autobiographical manuscript, *The History of My Life*, are fairly benign. Moreover, he even laments running away from the place. Apparently, in hindsight, the outside world was far more threatening to him.

Working Methods

The fictional development of his literary magnum opus was determined by and blended inextricably with real events in Darger's own personal life. The *Realms*, then, can be seen as a massive—and in some respects, brilliant—projection of Darger's own traumatized psyche, and his attempt to reconcile and heal the many parts of his wounded personality.

Darger is a passionate storyteller, and his work resonates as true on an emotional level because he put so much of himself and the dramatic experiences of his formative years into a story about the innocence of youth attempting to come to grips with the darker side of adulthood. It could be described as a coming-of-age novel, but Darger never really came of age emotionally. Although intellectually mature, he seems to have been emotionally arrested in adolescence, as one might expect of someone who has spent his childhood in institutions. The upside of this situation is that he never lost his ability to play. His work is an extension of the sort of spontaneous, playful imagination that rarely survives into adulthood. His subject matter can be quite adult, often disturbingly so, yet he handles it with the guilelessness of a child.

Although the original novel is presented in fourteen or fifteen volumes, each tome varies in length, from as few as 352 pages (volume 12) to as many as 1,689 pages (volume 4). Some volumes have a wealth of interesting material; others less so. The inconsistent numbering systems noted on many of the pages, the constant interspersing of 8.5 by 11 and 8.5 by 14 sheets of paper, and the frequent alternation of pica and elite type sizes from different typewriters all indicate that Darger was constantly revising and rearranging portions of the story throughout the more than twenty years he spent working on it.

It is impossible to know exactly how Darger's vast narrative proceeded before he began revising. Nevertheless, no matter how it may have been originally organized, the outcome would probably have been the same. Much of the *Realms* is composed of a repetitious succession of ripping yarns and talky interludes with the Vivian girls being chased by the enemy, countless adventures by their many comrades, and long-winded descriptions of battle scenes and cataclysms brought about by thunderstorms, forest fires, typhoons, and floods. In fact, there really is no sustaining plot.

Writing himself into the saga as the dashing and heroic Captain Henry Darger, the fictional development of his literary magnum opus echoed, was often determined by, and blended inextricably with real events and people in Darger's own personal life. These were embellished by numerous borrowings from historic newspaper accounts of the Civil War and World War I, silent film personalities and comic strip characters, Catholic prayers, liturgy and sacred hymns, and most conspicuously, classical and popular literary appropriations from L. Frank Baum, John Bunyan, Cervantes, Dante, Charles Dickens, William James, Henry Wadsworth Longfellow, Harriet Beecher Stowe, Robert Southey, Robert Louis Stevenson, Booth Tarkington, Francis Thompson, Mark Twain, Lewis Carroll, and Jules Verne, among others.

Viewed as a literary masterwork in the rough and the only U.S. literary epic of its type, the *Realms* has the poten-tial to become known beyond the field of folk/self-taught/outsider work, and to be viewed more as an idiosyncratic classic in the genre of adult fairy tales (known in Germany as *Kunstmarchen*) than a literary curiosity—a would-be U.S. *Lord of the Rings*. Having said that, however, it may be necessary to evaluate the literary merit or worth of the *Realms* by different literary criteria than those normally applied to the field of professional literature. Just as art by intuitive "outsiders" is not evaluated by the same set of formalist standards as the canvases of trained professionals working within the Western academic tradition, so too should we apply a different set of standards to a self-taught storyteller like Darger. Such standards would recognize the unique properties of self-taught work, which at its best glories in the communication of authentic personal experience, the innovative handling of unusual materials, subjects, or language, and the sometimes disturbing expression of unconventional or even taboo ideas; and at its worst is flawed by grammatical and structural problems, awkward constructions, unsophisticated modes of expression, and a meandering plot. All of these properties can be found in abundance in Darger's work.

Darger's writing is frequently marked by grammatical errors, usually having to do with subject/verb agreement, as well as typographic ones. Darger almost always corrected misspelled words on the spot by catching himself and stopping in the middle of a word, then starting over and retyping it correctly. Or else, if he didn't catch himself until he had already typed the full word, he might immediately type "or" or "I mean," and then type the correct word. As they often do in most self-taught work, even the unintentional mistakes, awkward constructions, grammatical errors, wrong or inconsistent spellings, inappropriate or missing punctuation marks, run-on sentences, and so-called happy accidents all convey a personal charm. His technical facility as a writer runs the gamut, from poor grammatical constructions to lofty flights of poetic description. Sometimes he states things clumsily, while at other times he writes dazzling and original prose. In the same manner as his visual art, individual components, which sometimes appear to be crude or unskilled when taken by themselves, often build to majestic and panoramic vistas.

22.2 Untitled ("At Jennie Richee"). Carbon tracing, pencil, and watercolor, 19 × 71 in.; n.d. Image supplied by Kiyoko Lerner, courtesy Andrew Edlin Gallery, New York.

Darger's visual art has a tangential relationship to events transpiring in the text—namely, portraits of the Vivian sisters and other protagonists of the story as well as scenes depicting specific incidents. They were probably originally conceived as illustrations to his story, much in the same fashion as illustrations found in both children's and adult books of fiction, popular literature, and poetry in the early twentieth century. He left a journal filled with notes for the *Realms* that includes a long list of scenes he intended to illustrate in separate works on paper. Some of these are marked as completed, while others are not. It appears that at some point, probably after he stopped writing the *Realms*, he continued to make improvisatory artworks that were no longer anchored to a particular text.

There are artifacts among Darger's oeuvre that show his early attempts to visually illustrate scenes from the *Realms* in a freehand fashion using crayons and graphite pencil. It would seem that his dissatisfaction with these rather crude pictures prompted him to experiment in collage and eventually invent a method to trace elements from other sources into his compositions. Almost every image in his visual art—figures, flowers, trees, foliage, houses, hills, and clouds—was appropriated from other sources, usually illustrations from catalogs, magazines, comics, and newspaper photographs, and then embellished with special appendages, clothing, patterns, and colors. The "glue" that holds his visual compositions together betrays his own attempts to tie disparate scenes together or fill in details in an obviously

"freehand" fashion. Such details appear to include the patterns in grass, contours on rocks, grooves in hair, scales on snake tails, designs on butterfly wings, and so on. Whatever he lacked in drawing technique is then overshadowed by the glorious color combinations of his painted scenes, and the organization of traced figures and forms into dramatic and surprisingly sophisticated compositions.

His literary approach, like his working methods for creating visual art, was to copy ideas as well as appropriate actual scenes, dialogue, poetry, and descriptions, but to a much lesser degree. It's possible that his ideas for borrowing from secondary sources in literature may have come before he applied the similar methods to his visual art. In his writing, the glue connecting his appropriated scenes would likely include the long lists of battle statistics or extensive descriptions of natural catastrophes. And yet, it appears that his original writing is far more prevalent in the novel than his original art is prevalent in his visual work. Rather than building his compositions around borrowed images as he does in his visual art, he reserves his literary borrowings for special moments in his story.

On certain occasions, his work appears suspiciously smooth and polished. Some of his chaste and yet emotionally overwrought love scenes, for example, seem lifted directly from early twentieth-century popular novels, newspaper serials, or story magazine romances. On the other hand, when it comes to hokey humor, silly wordplay, bad puns, and playful internal rhymes, he must be fully credited—or blamed, as the case may be. His dialogue, reflecting the vernacular of the time, is reminiscent of that used by stereotypical early twentieth-century paragons of wholesomeness—personifications of a brave, self-effacing, and pure-hearted U.S. ideal such as Bowery Billy, Fred Fearnot, and Diamond Dick. The inevitable obscurity and unfortunate disappearance of numerous vintage publications may prove to be an insurmountable problem in researching the popular literary influences on Darger's writing

Sometime between 1910 and 1912, when he was eighteen to twenty years old, Darger began writing his epic saga in longhand. He started typing it in 1916. In 1932, he embarked on the task of hand binding the first seven volumes. Clearly, Darger found the arrangement of his last volumes a daunting task, for the remaining seven or eight volumes were left unbound in separate bundled stacks, and the placement or order of several of them is somewhat questionable. He furnishes no clear ending to his saga, although a good case can be made for one of two probable conclusions. The choice of one conclusion over the other appears to have been entirely dependent on the hoped-for resolution of a real-life conflict that Darger imported into his fictional plot: the solving of the "Great Aronburg Mystery," which will be discussed shortly.

The text of Darger's *Realms* drew on three broad sources: historic events, children's and adult literature, and autobiographical elements. To a less conspicuous degree, he also borrowed from other forms: liturgical hymns and rituals of the Catholic Church, patriotic songs, the names of silent film movie actors, and newspaper comic strip characters.

Historic Events

The first *Realms* wars date back to the mid-1800s, leading one to suspect that Darger also was drawing parallels to the years preceding the Civil War. The Civil War certainly seems to inform the *Realms* to a great degree, from occasional references to "the Confederate States of Glandelinia," whose soldiers wear gray uniforms and defend the right to keep child slaves, to the names of battles, generals, war songs, and flag designs. Refreshing Darger's already-avid lifelong interest in the War between the States was the *Chi-*

cago Daily News series, "Civil War Story Told Day by Day," that began April 3, 1911, and continued for the next four years, no doubt providing him with an abundance of raw material.

Nevertheless, echoes of actual historic events seem to resound from the First World War as well. The beginnings of World War I, and certainly the Balkan Wars of 1912–1913, were reported in the newspapers that Darger read devotedly. Although the actual dates for World War I were from 1914 to 1918, Darger sets the main and final war in the *Realms* from 1910 to 1917. Curiously, however, Darger's Christian nations of Abbieannia, Angelinia, and Calverinia seem to be fictional stand-ins for Great Britain, France, and Belgium, correspondingly, while Glandelinia serves as a substitute for Germany. World War I began when Germany attacked what was then often described as "poor little Catholic Belgium." Catholic France came to Belgium's defense, followed by Great Britain. This is precisely how events transpire in the *Realms*. Glandelinia, acting like Germany, tries to take over Calverinia (Belgium). Angelinia (France) comes to Calverinia's defense, followed by Abbieannia (Great Britain).

The death of an Abbieannian king and queen recounted early on in Darger's story would seem to be thinly veiled retellings of the real-life assassination of Archduke Franz Ferdinand and his wife in 1914, combined with the torpedoing by Germany of the British passenger ship Lusitania in 1915. Here is an example from the *Realms*: "During the bloodiest war of eighteen forty-three, the Calverinian country succeeded to Angelinia, and Abbieannia, and this brought the first serious trouble between Glandelinia and Abbiennia, which led to the destruction of the ship loaded with children, and the Kings Wife and daughter and which caused the Kings death when he heard the news" (1:2).

Literary Sources

Darger used the persecution of African slaves in Stowe's *Uncle Tom's Cabin*—and the institution of slavery itself—as a social model for the phenomenon of child slavery in the *Realms*, and the rebellion that ensued because of it. Note this passage from Stowe's novel:

22.3 Untitled ("At McCalls Run Call Junction"). Collage, carbon tracing, pencil, and watercolor, 19 × 24 in.; n.d. Image supplied by Kiyoko Lerner, courtesy Andrew Edlin Gallery, New York.

Legree shook with anger; his greenish eyes glared fiercely, and his very whiskers seemed to curl with passion; but like some ferocious beast, that plays with its victim before he devours it, he kept back his strong impulse to proceed to immediate violence, and broke out into bitter raillery.

"Well, here's a pious dog, at last, let down among us sinners!—a saint, a gentleman, and no less, to talk to us sinners about our sins! Powerful holy critter, he must be! Here, you rascal, you make believe to be so pious,—didn't you ever hear, out of yer Bible, 'Servants, obey yer masters'? An't I yer master? Didn't I pay down twelve

hundred dollars, cash, for all there is inside yer old cussed black shell? An't yer mine, now, body and soul?" he said, giving Tom a violent kick with his heavy boot; "tell me!" (2001, 508)

Now here is Darger's almost-verbatim version from the *Realms*, substituting St. Clare for Legree and Jennie for Tom, and elaborating only slightly on the description:

St. Clare shook with anger as he stood over the little prostrate form, his eyes glaring fiercely, and his very whiskers seeming to curl with passion, but like some ferocious beast that plays with its victim before he

22.4 Untitled ("Overall Flowers"). Carbon tracing, pencil, and watercolor, 24 × 108 in.; n.d. Image supplied by Kiyoko Lerner, courtesy Andrew Edlin Gallery, New York.

devours it he kept back his strong impulse to proceed to immediate violence and broke out with bitter raillery.

"Well here is a pious dog at last, let down among us sinners. A saint, an angel and no less to talk to us sinners about our sins. Powerful holy critter she must be. Here you stripling, you make believe to be pious," he yelled, dragging Jennie to her feet. "Did you not ever read out of your own bible: 'SERVANTS OBEY YOUR MASTERS?' Ain't I your master? Did I not pay down ten thousand five hundred and sixty dollars cash for all there is in you, and inside you, you cussed shell? Ain't you mine body and soul?" he said giving Jennie several violent kicks with his heavy boot in her sides and even in her face and mouth, kicking out several of her teeth. "TELL ME?" (7:9 [bound], 7:97)

In volume 4 of the *Realms*, Darger lifts elements from both Carroll's *Alice's Adventures in Wonderland* (1865) as well as Baum's *Oz* books. Darger named "Jolly General Nick Chopper of the Angelinian Ninth Corps" after the Tin Woodman, who begins going by the name of Nick Chopper in the second book of Baum's series, *The Marvelous Land of Oz* (1904). Darger also utilizes Carroll's poem, "You Are Old, Father William," from *Wonderland*. Here is Carroll's original verse:

"You are old, Father William," the young man said
"And your hair has become very white;
And yet you incessantly stand on your head—
Do you think, at your age, it is right?" (1865)

And now the excerpt from Darger's *Realms*, in which the Vivian girls interact with a group of "kind Glandelinians" and their general, a Christian sympathizer:

"Tomorrow there won't be any more General Nick Chopper in the christian lines," wailed the little girls. "Oh dear, oh dear. Why did you have to be so foolish as to take this risk when you knew it would end this way?" And the little girls began to cry as if their little hearts would break.

"Stop, stop," begged the General, while the kind Glandelinians awkwardly patted the little girls to cheer them up. "I'd rather face a million guns than allow myself to face the firing squad anyday. I don't care a kinkajou for the rebel General Manley here, and neither do those friendly Glandelinians siding with me either. And as for the rest who suspect me, they are all unnatural villains who make my life miserable by telling me all sorts of lies about myself."

"Just like a song or poem I and my sisters once read in a school book," said Angeline as she and her sisters brightened up:

*You are very wicked Papa John, his young children said
and your face has become very white indeed, very white
And yet you incessantly curse and swear when on your last stand:
Do you think papa dear at your old age perditional punishment would readily serve you right?"*

"That's it, that is it exactly," exclaimed the General as the little girls finally finished repeating the verse. " 'You

are a treacherous christian dog, an imposter,' that's all I
hear. I could almost stand on my head in dismay and
fear. And, dear little princesses of Angelinia, I can't seem
to get used to being so long in the rebel encampments
either," added the General in a very melancholy voice.
"It's almost turning my hair gray."

He lowered his head and showed them his hair. (4:746)

Darger's variation plays fast and loose with Carroll's word-
ing, substituting his own somewhat mangled variation for
that in the original "You Are Old, Father William."

Meanwhile, in Carroll's *Wonderland*, the Caterpillar
criticizes Alice for not saying the verse correctly. Interestingly, Darger's version is not correct either. He substitutes
"Papa John"—a reference to General John Manley, leader
of the evil Glandelinian forces—for "Father William." And
it is not his hair that has turned white but his face. Papa
John does not stand on his head like Father William, either;
but the good Glandelinian general subsequently mentions
both standing on his head and his hair turning gray.

In another example, Darger uses Baum's description of
Princess Ozma in *The Road to Oz* (1909) as a springboard
for his description of the beauty of the Vivian princesses.
While Darger's text is by no means a direct paraphrase, the
source of the inspiration is unmistakable.

Here is Baum's original text:

The royal historians of Oz, who are fine writers and
know any number of big words, have often tried to describe the rare beauty of Ozma and failed because the
words were not good enough. So of course I can not
hope to tell you how great was the charm of this little
Princess, or how her loveliness put to shame all the
sparkling jewels and magnificent luxury that surrounded
her in this her royal palace. Whatever else was beautiful
or dainty or delightful of itself faded to dullness when
contrasted with Ozma's bewitching face, and it has often
been said by those who know that no other ruler in all
the world can ever hope to equal the gracious charm of
her manner. (1909)

Darger's more long-winded portrayal in the *Realms* uses
almost nothing from Baum's text, but rather he takes the

idea of being unable to describe the beauty of the Vivian
girls as well as the comparison of them to sparkling jewels
and how everything else pales in comparison.

Indeed for my part, human language is utterly inadequate to express the beauty of the Vivian girls. The su-
preme loveliness of the celestial spirits as it seems to me
can be compared with nothing like the Vivian girls who
far surpass everything that is pleasing to our mortal
eyes. How exquisitely beautiful is the blue vaulted heavens, when like so many sparkling gems it is studded
with so many stars. All natural beauty and grandeur
grows dim when compared to the charm and magnifi-
cence of the starry heavens on a tranquill summer night.
Beautiful is the sun which because of its wonderful
splendor and radiance was adored as a divine being by
so many pagan nations. Beautiful are the forms of the
Vivian girls ... the little girls were so attractive that people came flocking around to gaze at their lovely features
and the mere sight of them turned mere sadness into
joy and love. There is nothing yet that I have seen is far
more splendid and beautiful and sublime and excellent
than the angels and the little girls seemed next to them
in beauty. They seem to have angelic spirits about them
and all human beauty either of persons or things which
have ever existed from the beginning of creation or shall
yet be at the end of time is in comparison with the
beauty of the Vivian girls less similar than an ugly
worm compared with the charming face of youth.
(7:152)

Autobiographical Elements

Realms of the Unreal can be viewed as not only an alternative world but also an alternative life. In many respects, the
fantasy world that Darger created was more important and
ultimately more real to him than the day-to-day world in
which he lived and worked as a hospital janitor. His *Realms*
world was more vibrant and passionate than anything he
was involved with in his mundane existence. Darger could
create more, accomplish more, become more than he could
in real life; and so the *Realms*, its sequel, and the visual
interpretations of its inhabitants and terrain became very

22.5 Untitled ("Spangled Blengins, Boy King Islands"). Carbon tracing, pencil, and watercolor, 14 × 17 in.; n.d. Image supplied by Kiyoko Lerner, courtesy Andrew Edlin Gallery, New York.

much a substitute reality that preoccupied him for most of his adult life. In order to realize the *Realms*, he needed to put himself into it, to write himself into it in the guise of a heroic figure that could interact with not only the fantasy heroines of his tale but the thinly disguised characters from his real life too. Thus, he could remake his life and control his reality in a way that was never possible for him in the real world.

The heart and soul of the *Realms* is something that Darger refers to as the "Great Aronburg Mystery." Darger wrote his first draft of "Predictions and Threats" in his journal of notes for the *Realms* labeled *Time Book Monthly*. This is the first account of how Darger's loss of a picture of a little girl in real life took on a secondary life—and death—of its own, profoundly affected him as an author and a devout Catholic, and through a special feat of magical

thinking determined the fates of everyone and everything in the *Realms*.

In the mold of the great Catholic martyr, Saint Joan of Arc, Annie (also known as Anna or Annabelle) Aronburg led the first child-slave rebellion in Calverinia. She also is the sister of Angelinia Aronburg, better known as Gertrude Angeline, the adopted sister of the Vivian girls. In Darger's fictionalized account, Captain Henry Darger witnesses the brutal strangulation and slashing with a razor of Annie, who had given him a picture of herself that he later loses. The Angelinian traitor Phellinia Tamerline assassinates Annie—with the blessing of the villainous Glandelinian Raymond Richardson Federal (7:3 [unbound]).

In real life, Darger routinely cut out newspaper and magazine photos from articles about children as well as advertisements and catalog illustrations of children. He also collected storybooks and coloring books with children depicted in them. Darger would use these sources as models for the characters traced into his story, painting over them and altering their facial expressions, hairstyles, or styles of dress—and undress.

When Darger could not locate the newspaper photograph of the abducted and murdered five-year-old child Elsie Paroubek, which he had clipped from the May 9, 1911, edition of the *Chicago Daily News*, his anger and frustration mounted. He had intended to use the photograph as the model for Annie (with her last name, "Aronburg," being a variation on the word "Paroubek"). Darger began to threaten God. If the picture were not returned by a certain time (and he kept pushing the date farther and farther ahead), he threatened to turn the tide of the war against the Christian nations. He petitions God with prayer, offers novenas, says seven rosaries a day, and even erects an altar to Annie in his friend William Schloeder's barn. At one point, his identification with Annie becomes so intense that he takes her name.

In the earliest handwritten account of this in his *Time Book Monthly* journal, dated August 1912, Darger states:

The writing of the Glandco Angelinian war started in June, 1912 and still progressing up to January 1916 without change on account of the loss of said picture of little Miss Annie Aronburg taken from Chicago Daily News of June, May or July. In case of no return by March 1916 the Glandelinians will not be forced into submission, but shall progress better than before whipping the christians to the bitter end. Petition for return of same said picture was requested some time in March 1915 and a year from then only can give chance for christian success. (3)

The next apparent version of the text is the one that appeared in Darger's *Realms*:

PREDICTION AND THREAT.....................
AUGUST 1912

The main and terrible ferocity of the Glandco-Angelinian war started June 12, 1912, and is fearful in the unceasing battles. War progressed up to January,

1913 without any change, and it is blamed on account of the loss of the picture of little Annie Aronburg, taken from "The Chicago Daily Noise Paper" of May, June, or July, 1911.

It is reported that in case of no return to owner, by March, 1916, the wicked Glandelinians will not be forced into submission, but shall progress better than before, whipping the poor christians to the bitter end. Petitions for the return of same said picture was requested sometime in March, 1915, and it is reported that a year from then, only, can give chance for christian success. (1:295)

Darger writes in the *Realms* that his fictional alter ego had looked for the photo in newspapers in public libraries as well as in bound books and newspapers, but to no avail.

"How am I to recover it your excellency?" said General Darger sadly. "I have tried various means, invaded the Glandelinian Public Libraries, and so on, without success. As it is fair in war, I would have seized the book of newspapers the picture was in, but I could not trace it though I examined book after book. It was in some date of either June nineteen eleven or nineteen twelve." (7:3 [unbound])

It's unknown whether Darger actually attempted in real life to locate the photo by perusing the *Daily News* archive. For one thing, he had a different set of dates for the article in all three accounts. The most accurate was the second one, noted in volume 1: "May, June, or July, 1911."

Years go by. God did not answer his prayers. Feeling psychologically tortured and resentful, he responded as he always had whenever wronged: by dwelling on violent fantasies of revenge. Even at the risk of eternal damnation. Thus Darger, the author as well as his fictional counterpart in the *Realms*, Captain Henry Darger, went over to the dark side.

The Search for the Grail

At one point in the first volume of the *Realms*, Annie's celestial spirit appears before General Whilliamsburger. An earlier, handwritten draft of this episode penned by Darger in one of his journals—*Please Return This Book to Its Proper Place. This Means You. Henry D.*—was far more telling, because the celestial child does not appear to Whilliamsburger but to Darger himself.

Just as I reached Jennie's bridge, near Marcucian, I was suddenly aware of a person following me.

Drawing my pistol, I suddenly wheeled upon my follower intending to shoot without hesitation, as I expected no mercy from any Glandelinian who would suspect me of being an Angelinian spy. To my consternation, I beheld before me a little girl, the very likeness of the one in the picture I lost. I lost all my fear then, but said rather seriously:

"Little one, it ain't polite to scare a person like that. I thought you was a skulking Glandelinian following me. Who are you and what do you want?"

"My name is Annie Aronburg," she answered, to my further consternation. "Couldn't you for my sake withdraw the curse on the Christians because of your loss?"

I answered, "I don't know about that. It ain't my doing, and you ought to know it."

She begged me persistently, but the more she pleaded and teased, the more I refused. She then grew angry and told me that sticking up for the enemies of our Lord was an act of sacrilegious treason to God, that by doing that, I would never obtain the manuscript or picture that I lost, and that I was really a wicked man to refuse the request she begged of me.

Being aroused, I said, "Don't talk to me like that, you little winsome lamb," and attempted to seize her to give her a shaking up, but no one was there. As a large tree was standing just a foot from me, I quickly ran around it expecting that she had darted behind it, but she was not there. I looked everywhere but in vain.

She was gone! My, didn't I feel queer. I left the spot as quickly as possible, feeling the guilt of having insulted a celestial being. (382–392)

In the last book of the *Realms*, volume "B," Gertrude Angeline and Jennie Turmer (named after Darger's real-life childhood acquaintance, Jennie Turner) as well as Violet, Joice, and Catherine Vivian discuss the Aronburg Mystery and the aforementioned appearance of Annie to Whilliamsburger. Yet Gertrude's description of Annie imploring the general to cease prolonging the war because of the picture's loss is actually closer to the earlier journal draft for that episode.

"But it is strange about that Aronburg Mistery. It has not even been solved yet, and there was a report that if it could not be solved the war would be lost, and look where we are now." Said Gertrude Angeline.

"Yes it was funny," Said Jennie turning suddenly upon her, "But Gertrude dear was Anna Aronburg your only sister. We are wondering who the little girl was who was killed during that frightful battle of Erminie Run when she attempted to save the lives of the christian generals."

"No I had only one sister, and a little girl cousin by the name of Francis Aronburg." Said Gertrude Angeline. "And my cousin is still living   But then I think that was all humbug. How could the murder of a little girl cause the christian forces to lose the war? It seems a crazy thing to hear about it too."

"It may have been humbug but then she told that general herself who she appeared to her in celestial form that all of it was true and that the war would not be lost if he desisted in his efforts in recovering her picture. And she had not told a lie either. He has not recovered his picture and we are now besieging the Glandelinian capitol but God alone knows whether we will really capture it or not. Zimmerman may be killed in some battle during this siege, on him Evans depends all."

"Oh Josh." Said Jennie Turmer herself. "I don't believe he wants to recover it. Those notes you read before was a good evidence of his disloyalty to Angelinia and Abbieannia. You remember he stated once as you read that he had served in the Glandelinian army at Virginia Run and got injured during that battle, and so lost his command as he was unable to serve any longer. And that he threatened the christians all the more for it."

"Yes I remember it." Said Joice. "It does seem probable that he is really a secret Glandelinian officer and not a war correspondent as stated. You know we have two Dargers whom we know who have the very same looks and same names, and the only difference is they are taller than one another. Henry Joseph Darger on the side of the Christians the old time Geminie friend of ours, and general Henry Joseph Darger on the side of the Glandelinians. The one on the side of the enemy was equal in fury to our dreaded enemy general Raymond Richardson Federal whom we shot."

"And he was a dangerous raider too." Said Violet. "He was more dreaded by the christians than all of the Glandelinian generals put together. His brother general Decie Darger, and the other brother, Gallahan Darger died during their service in the war against us. But General Henry Darger just to used to ride his large cavalry forces around the rear of our christian armies and commit incalculable damage everywhere, and start forest fires, that burned hundreds of mile of forests in a few weeks. It is strange indeed that the little celestial sister of your Gertrude had the goodness to appear to him and try to change his wicked ways over the lost. He is not a born Glandelinian, at all his nationality is Abbieannian and so for his service in the Glandelinian army, he makes himself a treacherous traitor. It was mean of the one who made him suffer his heavy loss, but I do not see any reason of becoming such a bitter foe of God over it at all. And as he wrote in one of those notes he shot the one he accused in cold blood a regular assassination."

"Yes and it did not benefit him anything either." Said Catherine. "As it was later on found the man was not guilty of it at all. He did not do anything at all. His loss was through his own fault. He lived in a house which he never locked up when he went out, and some outsider came in when he was away and cleaned out everything he had. And it serves him right for his carelessness." (3507–3508)

There is not a lot of sympathy among the girls, it would seem, for Darger's ordeal.

As mentioned earlier, Darger wrote two "endings": one, apparently, to be used if the Aronburg/Paroubek newspaper photo were to be returned, and another if it was not

returned. In the former, the Christian forces are victorious; General Manley is forced to surrender and even asks the Vivian girls to pardon him ("B":3545 [unbound]).

In the alternative ending, Manley escapes, rallies his troops, and drives the Christian armies out of Glandelinia. The last sentence mentions that the "next volume" will relate the tale of "the bloody battle of Mc-Allster Run, which if it had not been a christian victory after such a series of disasters just past would have enabled the foe to win the entire war right then and there" ("B":n.p. [unbound]).

Which ending was Darger's intended one? Probably the first ending, since it is the one that actually follows the numbered sequence of pages. This last volume, provisionally titled volume "B," was initially labeled "Volume Four," and then crossed out by Darger. Perhaps he once anticipated that the Aronburg Mystery would be resolved by the end of volume 4, but when it wasn't, Darger shelved it and continued on for another eight volumes. And the fact that the alternative ending is on an unnumbered page and looks ahead to the next volume would indicate that even if he intended to use it, there would still be more to come and it would not be the final volume.

Some years after he finished work on the *Realms*, Darger began writing *The History of My Life*. But two hundred pages into it, at about the time he would have gotten around to explaining how he began writing the *Realms*, he launches into an imaginary account of witnessing a tornado, spends the next eight thousand pages describing the experience in obsessive detail, and never returns to take up where he left off. It is not only curious that the writing of his *Realms*—an event that occupied at least twenty years of his life—is never mentioned in his autobiography; its avoidance seems to be the catalyst for a monumental diversion into fiction. Why?

Was he so ashamed of having fallen away from God and the Church, of having tormented and butchered so many innocent children—albeit only on paper—that he couldn't face dredging up the memory of it? In Catholicism, after all, there is a thin line between bad thoughts and bad deeds, and Darger's profound emotional problems further prohibited him from always differentiating between the real world and the *Realms of the Unreal*.

Either the guilt of having separated himself from his faith weighed too heavily on him or the task of trying to organize the fifteen-thousand-page manuscript was simply beyond his abilities. He may have simply given up on trying to tie up all the loose ends. In the end, Darger chose to abandon the entire enterprise, packed the bound volumes and loose stacks of paper away in his trunk, and never looked at them again.

As painful as it all probably was for him, the crisis of faith endured by Darger sets into motion a strange and dramatic subplot that haunts the entire saga from beginning to end. The photo sought after by the author of the *Realms* was his holy grail. To risk finding it, the writer had to experience a loss of faith, a dark night of the soul. Darger's dark night of the soul was the Aronburg Mystery, and that mystery more than anything else drives the story to its uncertain conclusion.

References

Baum, L. Frank (1904). *The Marvelous Land of Oz*. Chicago: Reilly and Britton.

Baum, L. Frank (1909). *The Road to Oz*. Chicago: Reilly and Lee.

Carroll, Lewis (1865). *Alice's Adventures in Wonderland*. London: Macmillan.

Darger, Henry (n.d.). *The History of My Life*. Unpublished manuscript.

Darger, Henry (n.d.). *Please Return This Book to Its Proper Place. This Means You. Henry D*. Unpublished manuscript.

Darger, Henry (n.d.). *The Story of the Vivian Girls, in What Is Known as the Realms of the Unreal, of the Glandeco-Angelinian War Storm, Caused by the Child Slave Rebellion*. Unpublished manuscript.

Darger, Henry (n.d.). *Time Book Monthly*. Unpublished manuscript.

Edlin, Andrew, and Edward Madrid Gomez (2006). *Sound and Fury: The Art of Henry Darger*. New York: Andrew Edlin Gallery.

Stowe, Harriet Beecher (2001). *Uncle Tom's Cabin, or, Life among the Lowly*. New York: Modern Library.

Henry Darger's Search for the Grail

CHAPTER 11

Miss Fury and the Very Personal Universe of June Tarpe Mills

Trina Robbins

In 1941, when heiress Marla Drake donned a panther skin brought from Africa by her explorer uncle, she became Miss Fury, the heroine of a film noiresque adventure strip that ran in U.S. newspapers every Sunday for ten years. When cartoonist June Tarpe Mills (1915–1988) drew *Miss Fury*, she became her own masked and costumed action heroine whose life was filled with romance, danger, and stylish evening gowns. Writers and artists can play God. If you want a kid to attain superpowers as a result of being bitten by a radioactive spider, all you have to do is write and draw the story, and it's real. Like God, Mills created Miss Fury in her own image—literally—and was able to have, on paper, adventures she could never have in real life. Although Mills never went farther from her Manhattan apartment than Florida, she sent her alter ego, Miss Fury, to Brazil for four years, and lived her heroine's adventures vicariously. Lest readers think it was mere coincidence that Drake looked exactly like her creator, a newspaper article from the strip's first year included a photo of Mills and was head-lined "Meet the Real Miss Fury—It's All Done with Mirrors."[1]

Milton Caniff, creator of *Terry and the Pirates*, looked nothing like Terry or the more dashing Pat Ryan. Chester Gould bore no resemblance whatsoever to his creation, Dick Tracy. Although many comic strip creators must have iden-tified strongly with their characters—Dale Messick dyed her hair the same shade of red as her fictional reporter, Brenda Starr—no other cartoonists have as openly put themselves into their strips. Mills even gave her fictional creation the same white Persian cat that belonged to her flesh-and-blood creator, with the same name, Perri-Purr.

The fictional Perri-Purr is more than just another pretty face; he is a major character in the continuity of the strip. Twice he saves Drake from a bad guy by leaping onto the villain's head and digging in his claws. In a 1946 story arc, Drake is kidnapped, and an impostor takes her place. Nobody—not even her boyfriend or adopted son—can tell that the double is not Drake. But Perri-Purr knows, and follows the impostor around, hissing and spitting at her. The fluffy little guy himself is put in peril when the bald, monocled German general Bruno tapes an explosive to his fur, hoping to use the cat in an assassination attempt. Needless to say, the plot is discovered in time to save both the cat and the intended victim.

The universe of *Miss Fury* was a small world indeed, populated by a cast of memorable characters who were con-nected to each other by far less than six degrees of separa-tion and whose paths interwove like a complicated tapestry. One such was the aforementioned one-armed Bruno, a Rommelesque figure who is a German patriot, but plots to overthrow the Nazi Party. When he is introduced in the first story arc, Bruno still has both arms, but his assassina-tion attempt backfires and he loses an arm. He resurfaces in Brazil a year later, and Drake, unaware that this is the same man who tried to blow up her cat, appears on the scene just in time to save him from being lynched by an angry mob of Brazilian peasants. He thanks her by kidnap-ping her and holding her prisoner in his secret under-ground bunker. Bruno, who can safely be called Mills's favorite male villain, would reappear through the years until the strip's end in 1950.

Mills's favorite female villain was definitely Drake's nem-esis, the Baroness Erica Von Kampf, who, reports the artist in a 1944 interview, "at one time pulled in more fan mail than the heroine." The Baroness, her platinum blond bangs cut into a V shape to cover the swastika that was branded on her forehead, is what they used to call an "adventuress." My dictionary defines an adventuress as "a woman who schemes to get money, social position, etc.," but Erica is much more than that. Every noir movie of the 1940s had an adventuress, and she was always beautiful: the vamp, the Dragon Lady, or the Spider Woman. The scheming, deadly Baroness is one of those. But like the Dragon Lady of

23.1 Miss Fury.

Milton Caniff's *Terry and the Pirates*, who has a soft spot in her heart for Pat Ryan, the Baroness nurses a love-hate relationship with the equally memorable general Bruno. In a 1944 Sunday page, after the Baroness has blown up the general, along with his German army in their hidden Brazilian underground headquarters, she gloats, "Haha! How I *hated* that man!" But by the end of the same page, she has taken out his photo, and weeping over it, says "Oooh— *how* I loved that man!"

As for Drake, although she never knowingly meets the Baroness face-to-face, their fates are linked. The strip had only been running for two months when Drake, in her panther skin disguise, fleeing from police who think she's a criminal, finds herself in the Baroness's penthouse. The Baroness, emerging from her bath, confronts Drake in the act of stealing her clothes, and the two women have a cat-fight that lasts for an entire Sunday page. At the end, the Baroness, with one eye blacked by Drake, is tied up, and Drake escapes in the Baroness's clothing.

A year later, when the Baroness tricks Drake's weak-willed fiancé, Gary Hale, into marriage, Drake never knows that the woman who stole her boyfriend is the same woman whose clothes she stole. In 1944, Drake rescues a two-year-old boy from a mad scientist. She adopts the boy,

Meet the Real Miss Fury— It's All Done With Mirrors

By **JAMES ARONSON**

Girls, you'll have to get in line. Tarpe Mills, creator of "Miss Fury," is one of you, and she said today she isn't letting go of Dan Carey just like that. Recently she wrote one of Dan's more burning admirers:

"Listen, sister, put your name on the waiting list. I got here first!"

This fair warning is given because last month The New York Post received 533 letters from enthusiastic followers of "Miss Fury," the colored comic page that appears in the Week-End Edition. A lot of the letters were from girls who thought that Dan Carey, one of the heroes of the strip, was mighty brave and handsome, and if they ever met up with a type like him, well, their hearts would be faint and fluttery.

Tarpe Mills, Erasmus Hall High graduate, said that she literally stumbled into cartooning. She posed for portrait painters, photographers and sculptors to pay her way through Pratt Institute. She studied sculpture and was told that she showed promise; but the market for birdbaths was pretty dry, so she went into animated cartooning.

Among other things she created a few cat characters which were used in a series of pictures, and finally, she said, "I was carried out of the joint with a nervous breakdown." It was back to posing and free-lance drawing.

"Then," she said, "a foot injury kept me out of circulation and I started a serial called "Daredevil Barry Finn" for one of the children's comic books. I hated to drop Barry, so I went into the business whole hog and turned out such hair-raising thrillers as 'The Purple Zombie,' 'Devil's Dust' and 'The Cat Man.'"

Miss Mills dropped her first name (she won't say what it was because it was too feminine.

"It would have been a major let-down to the kids if they found

TARPE MILLS

out that the author of such virile and awesome characters was a gal," she said.

Miss Mills said she writes "Miss Fury" to provide amusement for kids and grownups alike. "Fashions, a hint of romance and human interest for the adults. Fantasy and action for the youngsters."

She admitted she doesn't know where she got her inspiration except that she was one of those imaginative kids "who hangs around the house reading books instead of running around outside playing hop-scotch."

Who poses for the girl characters in "Miss Fury," she was asked.

"It's all done with mirrors," she said. "I find it simpler to sketch from a mirror than to hire a model and explain just what himself."

23.2 The Real Miss Fury.

23.3 Tarpe Mills with Perri-Purr.

23.4 The Baroness with a swastika branded on her forehead.

never realizing that he is the child of her ex-fiancé and the Baroness. In this story arc the Baroness is last seen being dragged into a car by a vengeful Wolfram Von Prussia, another ex-lover whom she had left for dead, but Mills's favorite characters have a way of popping up again. Von Kampf would emerge, very much alive, in 1947.

Occasionally in the run of the strip, Mills appears to have grown so enamored of her villains that entire story arcs unwind featuring interaction between the villains, but without Drake. One such story takes place in 1944, with the Baroness and Bruno in his hidden fortress. Others take place in 1945 and 1950.

Other favorite characters resurface. In 1942, Drake finds herself first the prisoner and then the ally of Era, a Carmen Miranda look-alike who leads a band of guerrillas against the German army in Brazil. That same year she meets Albino Jo, a Harvard-educated, loincloth-wearing albino Indian, in the Brazilian jungle. In 1945, Albino Jo returns to the strip as a pipe-smoking criminologist dressed in a well-tailored suit. The next year Era returns as a nightclub dancer. And Bruno, apparently unkillable, returns again and again.

Miss Fury was by no means the only film noir–inspired adventure strip. Throughout the 1940s, the comics pages of newspapers in the United States featured strips like *Johnny Hazard*, *Kerry Drake*, and *Bruce Gentry*, all seemingly inspired by Caniff's *Terry and the Pirates*, starring hard-boiled guys who could usually be found fighting bad guys from the Axis, often in exotic foreign lands. Caniff favored China, and Mills favored Brazil. Neither artist ever actually traveled to their favorite countries.

For all its similarities to the Caniff-inspired adventure strips that were its contemporaries, *Miss Fury* differed in ways that pointed to the femininity of its creator. The strip's hero is Marla, not Kerry or Johnny or Bruce, and while the women in those other strips usually exist as decoration or victims to be rescued by the hero, Drake, though just as decorative, is as able as the men to take care of herself in a tight spot. Whereas at one point in Miss Fury's saga it does indeed take an entire platoon of marines to rescue her from the Germans, she is no slouch at the rescuing game herself. She gamely shinnies up vines and down

23.5 Miss Fury holds her own in a catfight with the villainess.

chains to rescue a boy from the clutches of a mad scientist, and carries an unconscious woman from a burning building. In catfights with villainesses, she emerges the victor, and when threatened by men, she kicks their guns away with one swipe of her high-heeled shoe and beans them on the noggin with whatever she has on hand—an ice bucket, a plate, or a telephone.

About that high-heeled shoe: Mills's entire run of *Miss Fury*, from wartime austerity's tailored suits to the New Look's longer skirts, can be read as a fashion history textbook, displaying a uniquely female sense of style. During the 1940s, while the average male comic artist put his heroines into featureless, but tight, short red dresses, Mills garbed her women in satin and lace evening gowns , and Joan Crawford–style shoulder-padded dresses. Drake brings an enormous steamer trunk full of clothes with her to the jungles of Brazil, and—in the jungle!—dresses up in frilly

lingerie, high heels, and a dress with a lace bodice, explaining as she sits at her mirror, "I always put on a bit of powder!" The only other cartoonist to pay as much attention to their female characters' wardrobe was Mills's contemporary, woman cartoonist Dale Messick.

And there were the men. While newspaper strips by the likes of Caniff, Frank Robbins, or Alfred Andriola all had their femmes fatales—dames in strapless gowns with cigarettes dangling from their scarlet lips—Miss Fury had her hommes fatales, exotic and attractive men from Bruno and Albino Jo to the slangy ex-hood "Fingers" Martin and handsome blond cop Dan Carey, Drake's main romantic interest after she breaks up with Hale.

The men of *Miss Fury* sprang from a woman's romantic fantasy, and a newspaper article from the period describes Mills receiving letters "from girls who thought that Dan Carey…was mighty brave and handsome, and if they ever met up with a type like him, well, their hearts would be faint and fluttery." Mills's classically hard-boiled tough gal answer illustrates how personally she took her characters: "Listen, sister, put your name on the waiting list. I got here first!"

Like Mills's other favorite characters, Carey appears and reappears throughout the ten-year run of the strip. He first meets Drake in the last panel of the first Sunday page, believing, as do most characters in the strip, that the mysterious masked woman must be a criminal. He returns to the strip later that year, when Drake has pneumonia. In her delirium, believing him to be her fiancé, she confesses to him that she is really the panther skin–clad Miss Fury. Carey never tells her that he knows her secret.

In 1944, Carey shows up in Brazil, now a Marine Corps captain, just in time to rescue Drake and Era from the clutches of Bruno, who is keeping them prisoner in his hidden fortress. Carey returns in 1946, finally as her love interest, which he remains until 1950.

There were no definitive endings to Miss Fury's adventures. As in today's television soap operas, plots and subplots twisted together like threads in that aforementioned tapestry. Just as one story arc tied up, Mills would introduce a new one, usually in the last few panels on the same page as the story that was ending. In a 1947 story arc, Drake has become involved with two handsome and seemingly young men, Thebold and Karvun, who are actually two hundred years old, and have been drinking an elixir to stay young. Meanwhile, unknown to Drake, the two men are hiding the aged Martin Von Lohmann, an escaped war criminal, in their mansion. Von Lohmann is blackmailing the two men, demanding that they make him young so that no one will be able to identify him as a wanted man. As Thebold and Karvun grow increasingly depressed with their situation—and perhaps, a little world-weary—Thebold convinces his friend Karvun that they should stop taking the elixir and let themselves die naturally.

At the same time, a mysterious stranger, whose face we do not see, visits Von Lohmann while he's still hiding in the mansion. The stranger strangles Von Lohmann, and the story arc ends with a house full of corpses: Von Lohmann strangled, and Thebold and Karvun dead of old age. As for

the mysterious strangler, the reader finally sees his face in the last four panels. He is none other than Bruno, who was not blown up in 1944 after all, but is back for a new story arc.

After the war, although Mills continued to resurrect her Nazi characters from time to time, she began using gangsters and gun molls as foils for Miss Fury. On August 31, 1947, she introduced two new intertwining threads. We meet a gangster named Gypsy Grigo, who is plotting against the recently returned Bruno. We also learn from his conversation that gang member Hammy "Trigger-man" Wexer is hiding out from the law on a cruise ship, and that he has "a new interest! There's a gorgeous brunette babe on the boat!" The last two panels of the page take us to the first threads of the next story arc on the cruise ship, where we discover that the "gorgeous brunette babe" is Drake, who complains to her maid, "There's the worst pest on board that I've ever come across! . . . Told me his name is Hamilton Wellington! But that his friends call him Hammy!"

On September 7, 1947, those threads that made up the Miss Fury tapestry broke. With no explanation, the strip disappeared from newspapers for sixteen months, returning on March 6, 1949. Mills's nephew Barry Finn was able to offer a possible reason for the strange hiatus. Mills's syndicate, Bell, was at that time suing a rival syndicate, which had started running a strip so similar to Miss Fury that it could claim plagiarism. Acting on the suggestion of the Bell syndicate's lawyers, Mills withdrew her strip until the suit was settled.

When the strip resumed, it picked up exactly where it had left off, with one important change. For the last two weeks before the strip took its mysterious vacation, the readers had seen Gypsy's red-haired girlfriend lounging in the background. On September 7, the sultry redhead, garbed in a low-cut evening gown, sits in a nightclub with Gypsy and his gang as they explain how Bruno escaped through an emergency shaft when his secret army was blown up. The redhead doesn't have a name yet, but Gypsy calls her "honey" and "baby," so the reader can guess their relationship.

Sixteen months later, when the strip returned, the redhead was still in it, but she had become a platinum blond. She also now uses German expressions like "Great Gott!"

Miss Fury

and leaves a note in German, warning Bruno that Gypsy's gang is after him. And now she has a name. She is none other than Erica Von Kampf Still in a love-hate relationship with Bruno, the Baroness wonders, "Ach—why *am* I so impetuous? Why *did* I want to save Bruno—the one man I fear most!"

Obviously, this nameless redhead did not start out as the platinum-haired Baroness. During the sixteen months that Mills had to ponder the path her strip would take, she must have decided to bring back her favorite villainess. Mills hints at how badly things have gone for the Baroness since we last saw her. Times grew tough for the lovely adventuress after the war, and she has been forced to ally herself with a gangster. Still a believer in the superiority of the "master race," she has only scorn for Gypsy, and thinks of him as "that mongrel-bred ruffian."

Fond as Mills seemed to be of the Baroness, perhaps by 1949 the time for film noir vamps had passed, along with the war. After this story arc, Von Kampf disappears, for good this time. Not so Mills's other favorite villain, Bruno, who becomes embroiled in a plot to bring back the Third Reich by use of a weapon stronger than the atom bomb: "dynasonic vibrations."

Bruno's tangled tale of dynasonic vibrations alternates with that of Drake on the cruise ship, where Hammy has

hidden diamonds inside her adopted son's teddy bear. Drake's thread tied up on August 21, 1949, while Bruno's story continued on through 1950, without a trace of Drake. Although Mills introduces a new character, pretty German peasant girl Lorelie, who is in love with Bruno, it is the villainous general himself who is the main character and protagonist of the story.

As for Drake, she returned for the next story arc with a new romantic interest, a handsome red-haired ventriloquist named "Red" Devlin, falsely accused of murder. But by this time, Miss Fury didn't have long to live. The strip had peaked in popularity during the war, when, along with the newspaper articles about her and even a 1943 article in *Time* magazine, the heroine's likeness was painted on the nose cone of a bomber. Eight issues of a *Miss Fury* comic book had been published, reprinting the newspaper strips, and had sold one million copies per issue. But Mills's health was deteriorating, and she was having trouble meeting deadlines. She suffered from arthritis and asthma, sometimes seriously enough to be hospitalized. Toward the end of the 1940s, she began resorting to an anonymous (and sadly untalented) ghost artist to help her meet deadlines. Her strips were more and more frequently ghosted through 1950, but *Miss Fury* staggered on for another year, finally ending in midstory, ingloriously, on December 23, 1951, leaving the readers hanging.

Mills's days of creating comics were not quite over, however. In 1979, inspired by a small press book that reprinted *Miss Fury*'s first year of continuity, she attempted a comeback. She began work on a graphic novel, returning to her favorite location, Brazil, and bringing back Jo, the Brazilian albino Indian, in a story she called *Albino Jo, the Man with Tigre Eyes*.

The graphic novel was never published and it remains unfinished. A look at the surviving pages shows that Mills had not lost a bit of her talent. The art is as beautiful as anything she drew in the 1940s, but it bears absolutely no resemblance to the popular comics style of the times, and would probably never have been published.

She died of emphysema in 1988, without ever having visited Brazil.

23.6 Miss Fury as nose cone art.

Timeline, 1941–1945

April–November 1941: Origin. Marla Drake dons panther costume and becomes Miss Fury. Dan Carey is introduced immediately. Story takes place in New York.

December 1941: Baroness Von Kampf is introduced.

January–March 1942: General Bruno enters the story line and promptly loses his arm in a botched assassination attempt. Von Kampf, on the verge of being deported as an undesirable alien, beans Carey on the noggin and escapes.

April–May 1942: Story line moves to Brazil, where it will stay through 1945. The Baroness, escaping to Brazil, meets Drake's fiancé, Hale, and tricks him into marriage. Drake flies down to Brazil in an unsuccessful attempt to prevent their marriage.

June–August 1942: Drake rescues Bruno from a lynch mob. He thanks her by kidnapping her and holding her captive in his underground fortress.

August 8, 1942: Drake escapes, and Era makes her first appearance in the last panel of this week's Sunday strip.

August 1942–October 1943: Albino Jo enters the plotline. Drake fights the Germans side by side with Era, Albino Jo, his Indian tribe, and her band of guerrillas. Drake and Era are recaptured by the Germans.

October 1943: Drake and Era are rescued by the Marines, led by Carey.

November–January 1944: The Baroness reenters the story, leaving death and destruction in her wake.

January 23, 1944: The baroness shows up at Bruno's underground fortress.

January–April 1944: All action takes place in Bruno's hidden fortress, as the baroness proceeds to vamp all the German officers and plot against Bruno. Drake is absent from this sequence.

April–May 14, 1944: The baroness blows up the German fortress, escapes with Von Prussia, then double-crosses him and leaves him for dead.

May 28, 1944: Drake enters the story again, still in Brazil, staying at a big hotel.

May–September 1944: Tangled romance at the big Brazilian hotel, when Drake discovers that both Carey and Hale are there, too. She chooses Carey. Reenter the Baroness, coincidentally also staying at the same hotel.

September 10, 1944: The reader learns that although Hale's marriage to the baroness was annulled, he is unaware that she gave birth to his son.

September–November 1944: We meet the handsome but mad doctor, Diman Sarif, who has raised the Baroness's son since birth. On realizing that she has no intention of marrying him, he plans to use the boy in his evil experiments.

November 12, 1944: In the last two panels of this page, Drake discovers that the little boy has wandered into her hotel room.

November–December 1944: Drake grows suspicious of the mad doctor, who passes himself off as the boy's father, and follows his car to his secret laboratory.

December 31, 1944: Meanwhile, the baroness gets dragged into a car by Von Prussia. We will not see her again until 1949.

January–April 1945: Sarif attempts to place the boy into his vat of chemicals, which dissolve human tissue and bone. The boy escapes and is rescued by Drake, in her Miss Fury disguise.

May 1, 1945: Never learning that he is the child of Hale and the Baroness, Drake adopts the boy—and finally leaves Brazil.

23.7 Tarpe Mills's last comic, 1979.

Note

1. The author of this article is the well-known journalist James Aronson, but I have been unable to find out exactly where or when it was published, although I suspect it was probably in the early 1940s, near the beginning of the strip, and possibly in the *New York Daily News*. The full article is reproduced on page 268.

References

Caniff, Milton (1934–1946). *Terry and the Pirates*. Chicago Tribune–New York News Syndicate.

Mills, June Tarpe (1941–1952). *Miss Fury*. Bell Syndicate.

Black Lightning's Story
Stanford Carpenter

Monday

The alarm rings. I wake up. Previous conversations with Phil Jimenez about African American superhero Black Lightning are on my mind. My wife and daughter have gone to work and day care, respectively. On the nightstand are books, comic books, and magazines. I run. On my return, I listen to the news as I eat breakfast and get caffeinated. My workday begins.

I am a cultural anthropologist. I interview and observe media makers to address the relationships between creative practices, production processes, identity construction, and the depiction community. I talk to a lot of people, but still, I have little firsthand knowledge of the world. I perceive myself, my identity, as part of a "matrix of relations" (Carpenter 2001) that reconciles my existence within a world, a history, and a story. My perceptions are based on my limited firsthand, a large set of secondhand, and an even larger set of mass-mediated experiences. And Black Lightning is a part of this process in which experiences, ideas, and things are a material resource, quite literally the means of imagining the world and my place within it (see Boyarin 1994).

My workday ends. My wife and daughter are home. The evening consists of conversation, food, play, reading, and television. Bedtime. The world goes dark. I dream. The alarm rings.

In his development of the concept of "bricolage," Claude Lévi-Strauss (1966) references Franz Boas's (1898) observation that mythological worlds are continually built up only to collapse, with the pieces being used to construct new mythological worlds. This is particularly true in a variety of media today, as ideas, images, and stories that reference identity and community are routinely deconstructed, transformed, recirculated, and recontextualized. Comic books are artifacts filled with ideas about the world that are embodied in characters created by creative teams with high labor turnover rates. As such, the characters and stories are more permanent than creative teams.

This is Black Lightning's story. It begins when one man's beliefs, ideas, and inspirations are transformed into DC Comics' corporately held property. DC Comics selected other comic creators—with different beliefs, ideas, and inspirations—to continue Black Lightning's story. And as the lists of creators, beliefs, ideas, inspirations, and story lines grew (cited below, to drive home the point), Black Lightning's story went from being the creation of one to the creation of many. This creative cycle involves the work of multiple generations. The DC Comics Universe (DCU) is a corporately owned mythological world consisting of thousands of characters with intertwining narratives or continuity. DCU characters and their stories are the means through which the metanarrative of the DCU is imagined. The relationship between a character and the DCU metanarrative is mitigated by a number of economic, editorial, and storytelling factors. DC Comics generates revenue by publishing comic books and licensing out its characters to create or add value to other products. Licensing generates more revenue. But it depends on publishing to create licensable products.

A solo comic book uses guest appearances by other characters as a means of imagining the main character. A group comic book uses its members as a means of imagining the group identity. Characters without books slip into an existence in which their primary purpose is to contribute to other characters' stories. Black Lightning's stories contribute to the DCU metanarrative and the DCU metanarrative contributes to Black Lightning's stories. These activities result in added value to existing properties as well as the creation of new properties. Essentially, creating good characters, maintaining character continuity, and telling good stories are forms of property management.

Paving the Way for Black Lightning

Tony Isabella created Black Lightning in 1977. Isabella was born in 1951 on the east side of Cleveland in what he describes as "an Italian enclave." His family moved to the west side of Cleveland to be closer to a good Catholic school. For Isabella (2006), the west side meant living in

275

the shadow of *The Untouchables* (1959–1963): "Everybody thought all Italians were criminals so I never felt like I was in the majority.... I never felt particularly white."[1] He was raised Roman Catholic, but drifted away from the church due to its treatment of women and gays, and its handling of recent scandals. Isabella believes in God, but "the Bible was written by men and men lie.... Things should be more fair to people."

Isabella argues that creating Black Lightning was a natural progression of his beliefs. He grew up relatively oblivious to the civil rights movement. He did not have African American friends until he went to comic book conventions. But as a young Italian American from west Cleveland, he understood African American desires for African American superheroes. It was about fairness.

Isabella entered the comic book industry as an assistant editor for Marvel Comics in the early 1970s, and went on to write for both Marvel and DC Comics shortly thereafter. There were three prominent black superheroes at the time: the Black Panther, created by Stan Lee and Jack Kirby (*Fantastic Four* 1, no. 52 [July 1966])[2]; the Falcon, created by Stan Lee and Gene Colon (*Captain America* 1, no. 117 [September 1969]); and Luke Cage, created by Archie Goodwin and John Romita Sr. (*Luke Cage, Hero for Hire* 1 [June 1972]). Isabella liked the characters, but they were small in number. The Black Panther was African. The two African American characters, the Falcon and Luke Cage, had criminal pasts. With the emergence of "African American leaders" throughout the country, he thought that there had to be more African American superheroes with different backgrounds. In response, Isabella transformed two existing African American characters into superheroes in their own right.

Isabella transformed an unnamed black female detective created by Roy Thomas and Ross Andru in *Marvel Team-Up* (no. 1 [March 1972]) into Misty Knight, detective with a bionic arm, in *Marvel Premiere* (no. 20 [January 1975]). Stan Lee and Don Heck introduced Dr. Bill Foster, an African American colleague of Dr. Henry Pym (aka Giant-Man) in *The Avengers* (no. 32 [September 1966]). Isabella, along with George Tuska, transformed Foster into Black Goliath in *Luke Cage, Powerman* (no. 24 [April 1975]). In February 1976, Black Goliath had his own self-titled book.

While Isabella was a driving force behind Black Goliath, he still had to contend with his fellow creators' ideas about what an African American character should be. According to Isabella, the initial concept included the name Goliath and a leopard skin–patterned costume. The costume was changed when Isabella argued that he "never really thought of this guy as being that akin to the jungle. He's a scientist. You know, he's smarter than any of us." Isabella also did not like naming him after a biblical villain. At the time, blaxploitation films were influential among white creators, and "black" was seen as more than a racial designation—it denoted hip and cool—so as a compromise he changed the name to Black Goliath.

Creating Black Lightning

Isabella regards Black Lightning as his greatest achievement. In 1976, he was approached by DC Comics to develop a concept they had purchased, titled "The Black Bomber." When Isabella read the scripts he was taken aback: "The Black Bomber was a racist [white] Vietnam vet who had undergone chemical camouflage experiment in Vietnam to allow him to blend into the jungle. [The experiments] didn't seem to have any effect. But when he got home, in times of stress he would turn into a black superhero." He retained no memory of his actions as the Black Bomber and continued to be a racist when he transformed back into his normal white self. Isabella's response was explicit: Black Bomber was offensive and a poor choice to be DC Comics' first high-profile black superhero with his own book. He figured this would end his relationship with DC Comics. Instead, it commissioned him to create a new black character. Black Lightning was a former athlete, a teacher by day and a crime fighter by night. The name came from a dialogue on the cover of a *Wonder Woman* comic book, which Isabella thought sounded cool: "I had everything created except his secret identity and saw a *Wonder Woman* cover that had her lassoing a black lightning bolt. And in those days, of course, we had to spell this stuff out so she's saying on the cover something like, 'Hera, help me lasso this black lightning bolt.'"

He wanted Black Lightning (aka Jefferson Pierce) to be African American, an accessible and attainable role model, and a man who had fallen from grace, but still had a sense of law, politics, religiosity, and righteousness. He did not want him to be "ultrapowered," motivated by revenge or angry, or to have a criminal past. Two inspirations came together. The first inspiration was the television program *Welcome Back Kotter* (1975–1979): "The idea of a teacher coming back to his old neighborhood…every kid has a teacher," explains Isabella. The same thing could not be said for a private detective or a scientist. The second inspiration was the 1968 Olympics, during which African American athletes raised the Black Power salute on the winners' podium as a sign of political protest. As a result they were stripped of their medals. Unfortunately, this part of Pierce's backstory—his fall from grace—was not fully explained until the second *Black Lightning* series in the 1990s.

According to Isabella, an editor came up with the idea of attaching an afro wig to Black Lightning's mask because he, and some of the other editors, thought it looked cool. Another editor successfully lobbied to have Black Light-

ning's shirt open to his waist to show that the character was unmistakably black. Isabella liked Black Lightning's afro because it signaled Black Power, Black Pride, and radical politics while maintaining Pierce's short hair and a conservative veneer in his civilian identity. Isabella did not like the open shirt.

Black Lightning was canceled after the eleventh issue. The character later appeared in *Cancelled Comics Cavalcade* (1978), *World's Finest Comics* (nos. 256–259 [April–May 1979 through October–November 1979]), and *Justice League of America* (1, nos. 173–174 [December 1979–January 1980]). The *Justice League of America* story was more about affirmative action than Black Lightning's merits as a superhero. In it, Green Arrow advocates recruiting Black Lightning to diversify the all-white Justice League. They agree to consider Black Lightning only if he passes a series of unprecedented initiation tests. Black Lightning passes the tests, but refuses membership because he did not want to be a token or distracted from local crime fighting.

24.1 Covers to *Black Lightning* 1 (no. 1, April 1977) and *Black Lightning* 1 (no. 2, February 1995). © 1977 and 1995 DC Comics. All Rights Reserved. Used with permission.

Black Lightning in the 1980s

Black Lightning's adventures continued during the 1980s, though not under Isabella. Batman, created by Bob Kane and Bill Finger in *Detective Comics* (no. 27 [May 1939]), formed the Outsiders in *Brave and the Bold* (no. 200 [July 1983]) to face threats too politically sensitive for the Justice League. Black Lightning and Metamorpho—a multicolored, formerly white male created by Bob Haney and Ramona Fradon (*Brave and the Bold* [no. 57. December 1964–January 1965])—were the only existing DCU characters recruited for the team. The other recruits, Geo-Force (an Eastern European white male), Halo (a white woman), and Katana (a Japanese woman), first appeared in *Brave and the Bold* (no. 200, 1983). The Outsiders' adventures continued throughout the 1980s in *Batman and the Outsiders* (nos. 1–32 [August 1983–April 1986]), *Adventures of the Outsiders* (nos. 33–38 [May 1986–October 1986]), and *Outsiders* (nos. 1–28 [November 1985–February 1988]).

The DCU has many characters, so comic book creators often consult previous artists, editors, and writers of the characters they are using for their own stories. This was the case when *Outsiders* writer/cocreator Mike Barr consulted Isabella about Black Lightning. "[He] changed a few things," says Isabella. "He played down Black Lightning's super strength for *Outsiders* because he had Geo-Force on the team." Consulting past creators also contributes to an informal sense of ownership of characters by creators. Isabella still makes references to "my Black Lightning," even though he knows that the character is owned by DC Comics.

Black Lightning in the 1990s

In 1995, Isabella was tapped to write a second *Black Lightning* series. He was excited to have the chance to do what he could not do in the first series and bring the character up to date. The afro mask and the open shirt had to go; he thought the costume was dated and no longer politically significant. Isabella took inspiration from "a news article about a bank robber who used [makeup to create fake] boils and scars" to thwart attempts at identification. He worked with Eddie Newell to create a new look that included a costume that covered Black Lightning's chin and featured lightning bolts shooting from his eyes.

Before he wrote the script for the first issue, Isabella started off with a two-year plan that he shared with his editor. The plan consisted of one-year cycles, with each year incorporating a change in focus. Isabella wanted to "constantly [shake] things up [while maintaining the sense that Pierce] was an incredibly good man in an incredibly bad world." This would give the book an overall sense of direction, but leave the door open to alter elements along the way. For example, as Isabella notes, "I didn't originally figure on Black Lightning getting back with his ex-wife but then after he was shot and she came to his side the chemistry between them was just so great that I knew I had to go in that direction."

The second series took place in Brick City, named after a section of Isabella's hometown of Cleveland. Isabella established that Pierce was an only child raised by his widowed mother. As a result, Isabella says that "he builds a family wherever he goes…he's a very religious man [and] he's very liberal in his outlook." Isabella's take on Black Lightning in the 1980s was that the Outsiders were the family he built and watched fall apart. "He had a failed marriage [and] people he couldn't save. [His confidence was shaken,] but when we started out the second series there he was in his neighborhood confident that he could turn that around."

Isabella was replaced as the writer of the second *Black Lightning* series by a new editor assigned to the project before the first issue hit the stands. "I had written nine issues of the book when they fired me. The official reason given for firing me was lateness," explains Isabella. All nine of Isabella's issues were published and "sold really well." If there had been a second year, "we would have had him fighting the political elements of that crime. He would have ended up eventually as mayor of Cleveland and eventually 'Black Lightning' would have referred to an organization that he headed rather than just him. He would have gotten remarried to his ex-wife. They would have had a kid…every year the book would be something different from what it was the previous year."

Isabella describes Black Lightning as the "the soul" of the DCU. He planned to show how age and experience would change the hero's methods. Black Lightning was a reminder that doing the right thing "is a hard road to go, that it doesn't happen easily." But the consequences for doing the right thing merely strengthened Black Lightning's resolve.

Black Lightning in the 2000s

Judd Winick was born in a middle-class enclave of Long Island, New York, in 1970. He describes himself as a "white guy" whose culture is Judaism. Winick (incidentally, a participant in MTV's 1994 *The Real World* television series) became a writer for DC Comics in the late 1990s. His experiences with fellow *Real World* participants, HIV-positive Cuban American Pedro Zamora and Chinese American Pam Ling, had a lasting effect on his writing. During an offscreen conversation about childhood superheroes, Ling remarked that as a Chinese American girl she did not have a superhero.

Zamora died of AIDS in 1994. Winick and Ling married in 2001. Winick's interactions with Zamora and Ling have led him to explicitly consider the identities and sexual orientations of characters, emphasize a variety of familial relationships, and incorporate HIV awareness into his writing (Winick 2006).

Winick began writing *Green Arrow* (vol. 3, starting with no. 26 [July 2003]) and cocreated a new version of *Outsiders* (no. 3 [August 2003]). Winick's *Green Arrow* featured a nontraditional superhero family setting: Green Arrow lived with and shared his superhero name with his multiracial illegitimate son, Conor Hawke, created by Kelley Puckett and Jim Aparo in *Green Arrow* (vol. 2, no. 0 [October 1994]); the two took in Mia Dearden, a former child prostitute, in another issue of *Green Arrow* (vol. 3, no. 2 [2001]).

In *Green Arrow* (no. 27 [2003]) tensions are running high over a development project managed by the Everlast Corporation that will displace residents of one of Star City's poor neighborhoods. Green Arrow, a DCU character with an established left-leaning political perspective, is in the ironic position of having to fight off a group of kids trying to sabotage construction equipment in the dead of night.

During the melee, a lightning bolt stuns one of the kids. Green Arrow turns around to face an African American man, standing tall in a business suit crackling with residual electricity. Green Arrow looks up and says, "JEFFERSON PIERCE. BLACK LIGHTNING."

Pierce had gone through some changes since the 1990s. Longtime Superman foe Lex Luthor, created by Jerry Siegel and Joe Shuster in *Action Comics* (no. 23 [April 1940]), was elected president of the United States in 2000 as part of a companywide crossover. President Luthor appointed Pierce to be his secretary of education. Unbeknownst to most of the DCU characters, Pierce accepted the position in order to keep tabs on Luthor.[3]

Later in *Green Arrow* (vol. 3, no. 27 [August 2003]), Black Lightning and Green Arrow meet for drinks (in their respective secret identities, Pierce and Oliver Queen). Pierce reveals that his daughter, Anissa, has superpowers. He does not want her to become a superhero, and has convinced her to finish college first. The conversation is interrupted by the arrival of Pierce's niece, Joanna Pierce. Joanna Pierce is the attorney representing the impoverished residents facing displacement. Over the course of the next five issues, Queen becomes romantically involved with Joanna Pierce and, as Green Arrow, takes on the cause of the residents.

In addition to former residents, monsters terrorize the Star Center construction site. Everlast hires Draken, a paid assassin. Draken kills Joanna Pierce in *Green Arrow* (vol. 3, no. 30 [November 2003]) when he discovers that there is a connection between her and Green Arrow. Then he goes after Hawke and Dearden in *Green Arrow* (vol. 3, no. 31 [December 2003]. Green Arrow brings down the Everlast Corporation when he proves that the monsters are construction workers mutated by exposure to toxins created by one of Everlast's subsidiaries.

Pierce meets up with Queen in a hospital waiting room at the end of the final installment of the story line (*Green Arrow* (vol. 3, no. 31 [December 2003]). Dearden is recovering from her injuries. In the background a television news anchor reports the mysterious death of the CEO of Everlast, the result of being struck by lightning. Queen tries to apologize to Pierce for his niece's death. Pierce replies:

WHAT DO YOU HAVE TO BE SORRY FOR? I INTRODUCED HER TO YOU. I SHOULD HAVE KEPT HER OUT OF THIS LIFE. SHE WAS FAMILY. WE'RE SUPPOSED TO PROTECT FAMILY. NOT PUT THEM IN THE CROSSHAIRS. NOT MAKE THEM SUFFER FOR MY BAD JUDGMENT . . . GOODBYE OLIVER.

The next time we see Black Lightning is in *Outsiders* (vol. 3, no. 3 [2003]), also written by Winick. According to Winick, the lineup of the Outsiders was intentionally diverse, and played on notions of legacy and family. Winick's version of the Outsiders was composed of Arsenal, Grace, Indigo, Jade, Nightwing, Shift, and Thunder. In *Outsiders* (vol. 3, no. 1 [August 2003]), written by Judd Winick and illustrated by Tom Raney, the Outsiders were reformed by former Green Arrow sidekick Roy Harper (aka Speedy, Arsenal, and later, Red Arrow). Harper's first appearance was in *More Fun Comics* (no. 73 [November 1941]), by Mort Weisinger and Paul Norris. He was a white male raised on a Navajo reservation. Former Batman sidekick Nightwing was originally introduced as Robin in *Detective Comics* (no. 38 [May 1940]) and as Nightwing in *Tales of the New Teen Titans* (no. 44 [July 1984]). Jade, introduced in *All-Star Squadron* (no. 25 [September 1983]), by Roy Thomas and Jerry Ordway, was the green-skinned daughter of the original Green Lantern, white male Alan Scott. Indigo, introduced in *Teen Titans/Young Justice: Graduation Day* (no. 1 [July 2003]), by Judd Winick and Ale Garza, was an android descendant of Superman villain Braniac. Grace, an Asian woman; Shift, a multicolored male grown from a remnant of Metamorpho; and Thunder, Black Lightning's daughter, were all introduced in *Outsiders* (vol. 3, no. 1 [August 2003]).

Winick used the scene between Queen and Pierce in *Green Arrow* (no. 27) to establish that Black Lightning had a daughter with superpowers; the death of Joanna Pierce also serves to underscore Black Lightning's reservations about his daughter becoming a superhero. This issue is put center stage when Black Lightning shows up in *Outsiders* (vol. 3, no. 3 [October 2003]) to try to convince Thunder to quit the latest incarnation of his former team.

Under Winick, Pierce isn't the only patriarch struggling to protect family members who lead risky lives. Arsenal is nearly shot to death in *Outsiders* (vol. 3, no. 5 [December 2003]). Both Green Arrows (Queen and Hawke) appear at his bedside in *Outsiders* (vol. 3, no. 6 [January 2004]) and help the Outsiders to bring Arsenal's assailants to justice. News of these events prompts Pierce to show up in *Outsiders* (vol. 3, no. 9 [April 2004]) to demand that his daughter leave the team. Instead he finds himself teaming up with the Outsiders to bring down a demon in *Outsiders* (vol. 3, no. 10 [May 2004]). Much to Black Lightning's chagrin, Thunder is so impressed with her father's skills in battle that she redoubles her efforts to be a better superhero.

The issue ends in the White House where President Ross confronts Pierce both for his culpability in the Everlast CEO's death and the controversy surrounding his exploits as Black Lightning, which Ross describes as the "worst-kept secret in Washington." Pierce explains that he did not mean to kill the Everlast CEO and offers to turn himself in. Ross orders Pierce to keep the incident a secret for the good of the nation and demands his resignation as secretary of education.

Green Arrow faces his own challenges as a father figure. In *Green Arrow* (vol. 3, no. 43 [December 2004]), Dearden learned she was HIV-positive, and she appropriated Green Arrow's former sidekick's name, Speedy, in *Green Arrow* (vol. 3, no. 45 [February 2005]). Black Lightning returned to the pages of *Green Arrow* in issues 54–59 (November 2005–April 2006). The rift between Black Lightning and Green Arrow is healed as they fight to save Star City from Dr. Light just before the advent of the "Infinite Crisis."

Black Lightning and *Infinite Crisis*

Over time, the unified history created by the *Crisis on Infinite Earths* unraveled, necessitating additional crossover events and retroactive continuity (or "retcon," a term used to describe the rewriting of a character's history). *Infinite Crisis* (2005–2006) was a DCU crossover event that served as a sequel to *Crisis*. As part of the event, DC Comics compelled all of its comic book creative teams to bring their current story lines to a close during the same month. Many of the comic books' creative teams were changed, some comic books were canceled, and some new comic books were introduced. The following month, all of the DCU books' story lines were restarted, jumping forward one year

Crisis on Infinite Earths

Infinite Crisis was a sequel to *Crisis on Infinite Earths* (April 1985–March 1986) (hereafter *Crisis*), a twelve-issue miniseries that radically restructured the DCU. Both series occurred when the DCU's corporate mythological universe begins to collapse under the weight of its accumulated narratives—a process that echoes my previous references to Boas and Lévi-Strauss. The *Crisis* story line crossed over into all of the DC Comics superhero books, and served multiple editorial, economic, and narrative purposes. The pre-*Crisis* DCU consisted of multiple parallel universes, each with different histories and alternate versions of many of the more popular DCU characters. This provided greater story-telling flexibility and an easy way for DC Comics to publish characters it had purchased from other companies. If a story or character did not make sense in light of what had happened years before, it was explained away as happening on a different Earth. But it was confusing. Creators, editors, and fans had trouble keeping track of what story happened when, and where. Many editors and executives regarded this as a barrier to entry for new readers.

Crisis offered a solution to this problem: an interdimensional battle in which all of the universes were destroyed in whole or part, with the pieces being knit back together into one coherent DCU. *Crisis* also served as an opportunity to revamp existing characters, introduce new characters, and establish one single DCU history. The series was a commercial success, but quickly began to generate its own creative problems. Many comic book creators felt constrained by the necessity of having to contribute to a single history that included thousands of characters, each with their own individual histories. Discrepancies (including many created by the events of the *Crisis* itself) that would once have been explained away as the product of multiple Earths were now brushed aside by references to "pre-*Crisis*" and "post-*Crisis*" continuity.

(this is hereafter referred to as the one-year gap). A new title, *52* (2006–2007), debuted as a weekly comic book, and told the story of the one-year gap. The conclusion of *52* reestablished the multiple Earths concept, but limited the number of universes to fifty-two. Essentially, post-*52* DCU continuity is a compromise between the pre-*Crisis* infinite number of universes and the post-*Crisis* single universe. How it works out remains to be seen.

Black Lightning, Cyborg, and the John Stewart Green Lantern were DC Comics' highest-profile pre-*Crisis* African American male superheroes. The post-*Crisis* continuity saw the addition of Mr. Terrific and Steel to the list. Denny O'Neil and Neal Adams created the John Stewart Green Lantern in *Green Lantern* (vol. 2, no. 87 [December 1971]). The Guardians of the Universe selected him to fill the shoes of Earth's white male Green Lantern—created by John Broome and Gil Kane (*Showcase*, no. 22 [October 1959])—in time of need. Much like Black Lightning, John Stewart appeared in solo comic books, group comic books, and guest roles. Cyborg, created by Marv Wolfman and George Perez (*DC Comics Presents*, no. 26 [October 1980]), was a founding member of the New Teen Titans, one of DC's most popular comic books throughout the 1980s. Steel, created by Louise Simonson and Jon Bogdanove (*Adventures of Superman*, no. 500 [June 1993]), became the "Black Superman" as part of the "Death of Superman" DCU crossover event. The new Mr. Terrific, created by John Ostrander and Tom Mandrake in *Spectre* (vol. 3, no. 54 [June 1997]), replaced the original Mr. Terrific, created by Charles Reizenstein and Hal Sharp in *Sensation Comics* (no. 1 [January 1942]), a white male superhero murdered in *Justice League of America* (vol. 1, no. 171 [October 1979]). The new Mr. Terrific joined the Justice Society of America in issue 11 of its title (*JSA*, no. 11 [December 1999]) and was elected chair of the Justice Society in *Justice Society of America* (no. 27 [October 2001]). Both Mr. Terrifics are motivated by a desire to be role models. The original Mr. Terrific was a socially conscious member of the idle rich. The new Mr. Terrific is a former Olympic athlete and recognized corporate leader with a genius-level intellect. He is haunted by the tragic death of his wife, and in spite of the wonders that he has seen, questions the existence of God (for more details,

BOYS...SO DAMN PREDICTABLE.

OKAY, NEXT. BLACK LIGHTNING.

I KNOW HE HAS ALLEGIANCE TO YOU, BRUCE. A) WILL HE SAY "NO" AGAIN? AND 2) WILL HE WORK WELL IN THE GROUP?

HE NEVER SAID NO.

AND HE DID GREAT WORK AGAINST LUTHOR.

HE'S STILL DOING IT NOW.

BRUCE, YOU KNOW HIM BEST...

24.2 Black Lightning in his most recent costume in *Justice League of America* 3 (no. 3, December 2006). While his initial refusal to join is mentioned, the racial undertones are omitted. © 2006 DC Comics. All Rights Reserved. Used with permission.

see Carpenter 2005). Since becoming the chair, Mr. Terrific is arguably the highest-profile African American DCU superhero.[4]

Black Lightning and the new Mr. Terrific first meet when Batman calls on them to infiltrate and disable an evil artificial intelligence satellite in *Infinite Crisis* (no. 6 [May 2006]). Batman believes that they are the best at what they do and that their combined abilities (electric manipulation and invisibility to technology) are ideal for the task. Their meeting is significant because, according to *Infinite Crisis* writer Johns (2006), they are high-profile African American DCU superheroes, have similar motivations, and have faced criticism over their costumes and names, but still represent different African American perspectives. Johns used their interaction during the mission to affirm Black Lightning's and Mr. Terrific's mutual sense of pride and awareness of their respective positions in the DCU metanarrative and comic book history:

Black Lightning: SO YOU **REALLY** CALL YOURSELF MR. TERRIFIC?

Mr. Terrific: YOU REALLY CALL YOURSELF **BLACK** LIGHTNING?

Black Lightning: HEY, BACK WHEN I STARTED IN THIS BUSINESS, I WAS THE ONLY OF **US** AROUND. I WANTED TO MAKE SURE EVERYONE **KNEW** WHO THEY WERE DEALING. WITH GUESS THAT'S WHY YOU'VE GOT YOUR **NAME** STITCHED ON TO THE BACK OF YOUR JACKET.

Mr. Terrific: ACTUALLY, IT'S **EXACTLY** WHY.

Toward the end of *Infinite Crisis*, all of DC Comics' story lines were moved ahead one year, allowing for significant character and story changes. The Justice Society and the Justice League disbanded after *Infinite Crisis*, and reformed during *52*. Mr. Terrific emerged as the codirector/White King of the reformed international intelligence organization, Checkmate. He is also a member, though no longer chair, of a revamped Justice Society of America.

Black Lightning was conspicuously absent in the wake of the one-year gap, but *Outsiders* (vol. 3, no. 45 [April 2007]) contained a flashback that explained his absence since the events of *Infinite Crisis*. *Outsiders* (vol. 3, no. 44 [March 2007]) had ended with the revelation that Black Lightning had been tricked by an assassin into believing that his lightning bolt had been responsible for the death of the CEO of Everlast. *Outsiders* (no. 45) explained that during the one-year gap, Pierce had turned himself in to Checkmate for murdering the Everlast CEO. Fearing the ramifications of a public trial that would endanger the U.S. government and the superhero community, Checkmate altered Pierce's appearance, fabricated equivalent charges, and imprisoned him under an assumed name. The Outsiders then had to break him out of jail in *Outsiders* (vol. 3, annual 1 [2007]) because the circumstances of his incarceration rendered him unpardonable.

In *Justice League of America* (vol. 3, no. 7 [May 2007]), the newly revamped Justice League of America recruits Black Lightning—with no mention of his skin color.

Saturday

"So what do you think?" asked Phil Jimenez as he showed me a series of sketches that he had done of Black Lightning. I liked the drawing with the beard, glowing eyes that emitted tiny bolts of energy, and a logo on his chest with a black hand emitting a lightning bolt.

Born in 1970, Jimenez is an openly gay Hispanic comic book artist/writer. He grew up in Southern California and moved to New York City to pursue a career in comic books. I met him in 1999 while conducting ethnographic fieldwork among comic book creators. Jimenez was contracted to redesign Black Lightning's costume in advance of the character's recruitment by the Justice League of America (mentioned above). He jumped at the chance. Jimenez's interest in identity, politics, and popular culture has led him to incorporate ethnic, gender, racial, and sexual diversity in his work. During his critically acclaimed two-year run on *Wonder Woman* (vol. 2, nos. 164–188 [2001–2003]), he stirred controversy among fans by giving Wonder Woman an African American male love interest.

When he solicited my thoughts on the character and the costume during a phone conversation several weeks before Wizard World Philadelphia 2007, I was overcome by a sense of anticipation, flattery, and irony. After all, it was quite the turnabout to be interviewed by someone who I had interviewed on multiple occasions.

I recounted purchasing *Black Lightning* (vol. 1, no. 1 [April 1977]). I liked the afro wig because of its association with masculinity as well as such slogans as Black Power and Black is Beautiful. But living in a mostly white suburb meant that much to do with black empowerment was considered "radical" in a pejorative sense. I also liked that Black Lightning was middle class, had no criminal past, and was nobody's partner or sidekick. I did not like his exposed chest and overwhelmingly urban locale. I bought every issue. And I was pissed when it was canceled.

Jimenez was surprised to hear my take on the afro. Jimenez's first reading of Black Lightning was in the 1980s, at a time when Black Power and Black is Beautiful were ancient history. But he sympathized with my feelings about the afro once I explained them. We both agreed that a twenty-first-century Black Lightning with an afro would be read as anything but political. Maybe dreadlocks might have a similar effect, yet as Jimenez remarked, the people at DC were leaning toward having him be bald—maybe with a goatee.[5]

As for making Black Lightning more explicitly political, Jimenez was not optimistic. It had been established that Black Lightning was an Olympic gold medalist and that his politics had prevented him from cashing in on his fame. While a reference to the 1968 Olympics would have made the character too old, it did not rule out a reference to apartheid, civil war in Africa, or some other more recent event. Since DCU characters age slowly, if at all, tying characters to historical events creates continuity problems over time. Jimenez was interested in playing up Black Lightning's politics, but the reality was that his job was to revamp Black Lightning's costume, not his continuity. He pushed for a logo with a black fist holding a lightning bolt as a nod to Black Power, but was unsuccessful. Once Jimenez's task was complete, Black Lightning was turned over to other writers and artists with different visions.

Black Lightning's story is the embodiment of the beliefs, ideas, and inspirations of creators of different backgrounds and generations. He is property. His two solo comic book series lasted roughly a year each. Throughout much of his existence, his publication has depended on his appeal to the creators of other comic books. His comic book narratives emphasize faith, family, and generational change in ways that reflect the creators' lives. He started as *the DCU African American superhero* and his adventures focused on his *being African American*. As he became *one of a few DCU African American superheroes*, his adventures came to emphasize *his African American perspective*. For example, as an African American superhero who sires another African American superhero, he puts family and legacy into an African American context.

Isabella, a baby boomer Italian American Roman Catholic, came of age when black characters were underrepresented in popular culture. He sought to right this wrong within a moral framework influenced by his minority experiences. Jimenez, Johns, and Winick are of the post-soul generation —a generation that saw black culture as a part of popular culture (Neal 2002). They altered, revamped, and tweaked Black Lightning to usher the character into the next age.

A generational cycle contributes to a metanarrative. One generation looks at its reality and imagines something better. That generation's dreams and struggles are transformed into the reality of the next generation. And this next generation looks at the reality bequeathed them, imagines something better, and continues the cycle. The DCU metanarrative is cyclical. It advances gradually until its corporate mythological universe collapses under the weight of its accumulated narratives (see Boas 1898; Lévi-Strauss 1966), creating an opportunity for a new generation to radically alter the status quo in accordance with their beliefs, ideas, and inspirations.

This is the story of all of DC Comics' characters that contribute to the DCU metanarrative. This is the story of Black Lightning.

Notes

1. Hereafter in the text, all Isabella quotes are also from his 2006 interview with the author.

2. This was no surprise. Since the mid-1980s, bald heads and goatees have replaced the afro as symbols of black masculinity in television and film. Avery Brooks led the trend with roles in *Spenser: For Hire* (1985–1988), *A Man Called Hawk* (1989), and *Star Trek: Deep Space Nine* (1993–1999). In the 2000 remake of the 1971 film *Shaft*, Samuel L. Jackson replaced Richard Roundtree's afro with a bald head and goatee. Laurence Fishburne's Morpheus in *The Matrix* (1999), *The Matrix Reloaded* (2003), and *The Matrix Revolutions* (2003) was black and bald as well. Black and bald superhero makeovers (as well as the addition of goatees) are a trend among comic book superheroes. It began in the 1990s and has continued into the present, encompassing Black Lightning, Black Panther, the Falcon, and Steel.

One notable instance showing the relationship between film and comic books occurred in Marvel Comics' Ultimate Universe, an ongoing line of comic books that reimagines Marvel's established characters. In the Ultimate Universe, white male colonel Nick Fury, commander of the international spy organization S.H.I.E.L.D., was re-created as an African American general explicitly modeled after bald-headed, goateed Samuel L. Jackson.

3. Luthor is forced out of office in *Superman/Batman* (no. 6 [March 2004]) and succeeded by his vice president, Pete Ross, a childhood friend of Superman's.

4. Mr. Terrific rose to prominence under comic, television, and film writer Geoff Johns. Johns was born in 1973 in Detroit and grew up in suburban Detroit. When asked about his identity, he is quick to acknowledge that he is half Lebanese: he grew up in a Lebanese household, and people made fun of his Lebanese name until he switched to his "American" name. Since then he has been "regarded as a white guy" (Johns 2006). Still, his immediate existence is much more diverse than people might assume. His wife is African American. Family gatherings are multicultural affairs, affecting both his outlook on life and work. When he sees an African American or Middle Easterner he does not see an "other," he sees someone who could be family.

5. The comic book references use the publication date listed in the comic book. The norm is for comic books to be released two to three months before the publication date listed in the actual comic books.

References

Boas, Franz (1898). "Introduction to: James Teit, 'Traditions of the Thompson Indians of British Columbia.'" *Memoirs of the American Folklore Society* 6.

Boyarin, Jonathan (1994). "Space, Time, and the Politics of Memory." In *Remapping Memory*, edited by Jonathan Boyarin, 1–39. Minneapolis: University of Minnesota Press.

Carpenter, Stanford W. (2001). "What We Bring to the Table: The Means of Imagination in an African-American Family." In *The Ethics of Kinship*, edited by James D. Faubion, 194–214. Lanham, MD: Rowman and Littlefield Publishers.

Carpenter, Stanford W. (2005). "Imagining Just Them, Just Us, or a Just Society: Creating Black Characters for the Justice Society of America." In *Africa and the African Diaspora: Cultural Adaptation and Resistance*, edited by E. Kofi Agorsah and G. Tucker Childs. Bloomington, IN: AuthorHouse.

Isabella, Tony (2006). Recorded phone interview with author, Baltimore, MD.

Isabella, Tony (creator and writer), Trevor Von Eeden (artist), F. Springer (artist), Liz Berube (colorist), P. G. Lisa (colorist), Jack C. Harris (story edits); DC Comics (1977). *Black Lightning* 1, no. 1 (April).

Johns, Geoff (2006). In-person recorded interview with author, Rosemont, IL.

Johns, Geoff (writer), Phil Jimenez, Jerry Ordway (penciller), Ivan Reis (penciller), Andy Lanning (inker), Jerry Ordway (inker), Art Thibert (inker), Jeromy Cox (colorist), Guy Major (colorist), Rod Reis (colorist), Nick J. Napolitano (letterer), Jeanine Schaefer (assistant editor), Eddie Berganza (editor); DC Comics (2006a). "Faith." *Infinite Crisis* 5 (April).

Johns, Geoff (writer), Phil Jimenez (penciller), Jerry Ordway (penciller), George Perez (penciller), Ivan Reis (penciller), Andy Lanning (inks/finishes), Jerry Ordway (inks/finishes), George Perez (inks/finishes), Ivan Reis (inks/finishes), Oclair Albert (inks/finishes), Marc Campos (inks/finishes), Drew Geraci (inks/finishes), Sean Parsons (inks/finishes), Norm Rapmund (inks/finishes), Art Thibert (inks/finishes), Jeromy Cox (colorist), Guy Major (colorist), Rod Reis (colorist), Rob Liegh (letterer), Jeanine Schaefer (assistant editor), Eddie Berganza (editor); DC Comics (2006b). "Touchdown." *Infinite Crisis* 6 (May).

Lévi-Strauss, Claude (1966). *The Savage Mind*. Chicago: University of Chicago Press.

Neal, Mark Anthony (2002). Soul Babies: Black Popular Culture and the Post-Soul Aesthetic. New York: Routledge.

Puckett, Kelley (writer), and Jim Aparo (artist); DC Comics (1994). *Green Arrow* 2, no. 0.

Smith, Kevin (writer), Phil Hester (penciller), Ande Parks (inker), Sean Konot (letterer), Guy Major (colorist/separations), Michael Wright (associate editor), Bob Schreck (editor); DC Comics (2001). *Green Arrow* 3, no. 2 (May).

Winick, Judd (2006). Recorded phone interview with author, Baltimore, MD.

Winick, Judd (writer), Carlo Barberi (penciller), John J. Hill (letterer), Guy Major (colorist), Art Thiebert (inker), Rachel Gluckstern (associate editor), Joan Hilty (editor); DC Comics (2007). *Outsiders* 3, no. 44 (March).

Winick, Judd (writer), and Ale Garza (artist); DC Comics (2003). *Teen Titans/Young Justice: Graduation Day* 1 (July).

Winick, Judd (writer), Phil Hester (penciller), Ande Parks (inker), Sean Konot (letterer), Guy Major (colorist), Michael Wright (associate editor), Bob Schreck (editor); DC Comics (2003a). "Straight Shooter Part One: Hired Guns." *Green Arrow* 3, no. 26 (July).

Winick, Judd (writer), Phil Hester (penciller), Ande Parks (inker), Sean Konot (letterer), Guy Major (colorist), Michael Wright (associate editor), Bob Schreck (editor); DC Comics (2003b). "Straight Shooter Part Five: Loose Ends." *Green Arrow* 3, no. 30 (November).

Winick, Judd (writer), Phil Hester (penciller), Ande Parks (inker), Sean Konot (letterer), Guy Major (colorist), Michael Wright (associate editor), Bob Schreck (editor); DC Comics (2003c). "Straight Shooter Part Six." *Green Arrow* 3, no. 31 (December).

Winick, Judd (writer), Tom Raney (penciller), Scott Hanna (inker), John Workman (letterer), Gina Going (colorist), Lysa Hawkins (associate editor), Eddie Berganza (editor); DC Comics (2003d). "Role Call Part One: Opening Offers." *Outsiders* 3, no. 1 (August).

Winick, Judd (writer), Tom Raney (penciller), Scott Hanna (inker), John Workman (letterer), Gina Going (colorist), Lysa Hawkins (associate editor), Eddie Berganza (editor); DC Comics (2003e). "Role Call Part Three: Jokes on You." *Outsiders* 3, no. 3 (October).

Winick, Judd (writer), Tom Raney (artist), Scott Hanna (artist), Gina Going (colorist), Comicraft (letterer), Lysa Hawkins (associate editor), Eddie Berganza (editor); DC Comics (2004a). "Devil's Work Part Two: Lightning from Above and Below." *Outsiders* 3, no. 9 (April).

Winick, Judd (writer), Tom Raney (artist), Scott Hanna (artist), Gina Going (colorist), Comicraft (letterer), Lysa Hawkins (associate editor), Eddie Berganza (editor); DC Comics (2004b). "Devil's Work Part Three: A Family Matter." *Outsiders* 3, no. 10 (April).

Black Lightning's Story

See the Strings: *Watchmen* and the Under-Language of Media

Stuart Moulthrop

High Magic

Comics belong to an interstitial form, occupying a privileged place between the dominant media of word and image. They are enough like long-form prose narrative for some to be known as *graphic novels*, and they are first cousins to storyboards, important genetic material for most films. Indeed, as Scott McCloud (1999, 8) suggests, a comic is a bit like a film reel with a slow playback rate. Yet we should also mark a crucial difference between comics and film: the separation of visual units by a gap or gutter, so that arrangement and disposition strongly influence interpretation. Unlike film frames, comics panels are presented not singly but in groups, one page—or in book form, one bifold spread—at a time. Turning the page of a comic book presents a simultaneous array of images and words, which readers break down into the conventional, right-left-top-bottom reading sequence inculcated by print. This scheme is often discarded by readers and comics creators alike, but exceptions tend to reinforce the basic rule. Reading comics generally involves dual modes: scanning the page grid, and then focusing attention on a particular region within it (McCloud 1999, 95).

McCloud rightly insists that a comic is not a hybrid or synthesis of two modes but something more like a suspension, where combined elements remain distinct. To some extent, this duality reflects the history of media and culture. As Lev Manovich (2001, 322–323) points out, the "logic of industrial production" that emerged in the last two centuries promoted a sequential way of thinking about the world, and to express that worldview, it encouraged convenient forms of narrative, from journalism and novels to movies and television shows:

> This type of narrative turned out to be particularly incompatible with the spatial narrative that had played a prominent role in European visual culture for centuries. From Giotto's fresco cycle at Capella degli Scrovegni in Padua to Courbet's *A Burial at Ornans*, artists presented a multitude of separate events within a single space, whether the fictional space of a painting or the physical space that can be taken in by the viewer all at once.... [S]patial narrative did not disappear completely in the 20th century, but rather, like animation, came to be delegated to a minor form of Western culture—comics.

The historical nonconformity of comics may have more than academic interest. Keepers of the great traditions, as opposed to true critics like Manovich, have little time for "minor" practices. Meanwhile, those less attached to the cultural center find value at the margins. Take, for instance, Jimi Hendrix's or Neil Young's distortion-rich guitar styles from the late 1960s, or Grand Wizard Theodore's invention of record scratching a decade later. The market masters have generally dismissed these techniques as gimmicks that define at best a limited niche—until those niches grow large enough to exploit. Meanwhile, a generation of grunge players and hip-hop artists hear possibilities for musical deconstruction, ways to fold back the conformations of media history. By flaunting outmoded, analog technologies like vacuum tubes and vinyl records, they expose and complicate the prevailing aesthetic of digital synthesis. Noise becomes interpretation.

"Minor forms" thus hold the seeds of major critique, especially when they play deliberately with ambiguity or doubleness. As Thomas Pynchon (1966, 129) realized, there can be "high magic to low puns." At any liminal point, or along an interface, value assignments tend to reverse: "everything bad is good for you," as Steven Johnson (2005, 9) polemically indicates. *Watchmen* offers an excellent case in point. By manipulating the interstices and invisible art of a medium that comes from the gutter, Alan Moore and Dave Gibbons have produced a work that reflects profoundly on space and sequence, and that, if read carefully, affords an important perspective on modern media.

Beyond Your Wildest Imagining

Watchmen was published in 1986–1987 as a twelve-issue series by DC Comics. Reissued as a trade paperback during the graphic-novel boom of the late 1980s, it has remained in print for twenty years, winning multiple awards and the praise of Marvel founder Stan Lee, who called it a milestone in the evolution of comics (*Wikipedia*). Moore, who conceived and scripted the project, originally thought about a multipart superhero story involving the Mighty Crusaders, characters developed in the 1950s and 1960s by MLJ-Archie Comics. He later adapted this concept to another defunct superhero line from the Charlton Comics house, which had been acquired by DC.[1] In the end, Moore was not able to use the Charlton characters, probably because DC planned to feature them in new comics, while Moore envisioned a closed story arc where some major figures would die. The result was an original world with its own dramatis personae (see notes in Moore and Gibbons 2005).

Moore has said he wanted to create "a superhero *Moby-Dick*" (*Wikipedia*), and indeed the work has been treated as a contemporary classic by both fans and scholars. As its substantial entry in the Internet's open encyclopedia attests, *Watchmen* blurs distinctions between popular and polite cultures, offering broadly accessible entertainment whose intricacy and technical sophistication invite careful study. *Wikipedia* cites four Web sites offering analysis of the work as well as a reconstruction of *Tales of the Black Freighter*, *Watchmen*'s comic within a comic.

These projects demonstrate a strong affinity between *Watchmen* and what Yochai Benkler calls the emerging "folk culture" of the Internet. Steven Johnson argues that technologies for easy access and repetition, such as DVD players and video on demand, have led television producers to more complex narrative forms, from the ensemble style of *Hill Street Blues* to the epic story arc of *Babylon 5*. Johnson sees a developing trend from "least objectionable" to "most repeatable" programming. (Johnson 2005, 160–162). Graphic novels certainly fit this pattern, especially those as rich and demanding as *Watchmen*. We might then propose

yet another interstitial placement for this work, not between print and cinema, but between the old regimes of cinema and press and the electronic frontiers of the Net.

Watchmen offers an attractive framework or seedbed for Internet culture. Taking up this cue, in the early days of the World Wide Web, I deployed a reader's guide or "digital companion" to the comic, noting that its narrative structure seemed well served by hyperlinked, multithreaded commentary (*Watching the Detectives*). Five years later, as contributions from readers of the site accumulated, colleagues of mine reengineered the original site as a protowiki, streamlining the process of textual expansion. As we will see, this convergence of *Watchmen* with what Michael Joyce calls "constructive hypertext" is far more than a coincidence of structural features and literary tastes. By illuminating the boundary zone between dominant and nonconforming media, *Watchmen* offers a great deal to those concerned with emerging textual practices.

Themes and design aside, however, the relationship between this artifact of the 1980s and the twenty-first century is not straightforward. Set in a fictional 1985 that contains several costumed crime fighters and one genuine superhuman, the story tracks an elaborate conspiracy to eliminate masked heroes, ushering in a new world order where problems must be addressed by more ordinary means.[2] The analogy to nuclear weapons seems clear enough, and the Moore and Gibbons emphasize it by identifying their superman as a walking "H-bomb" (II.8.5) and excerpting a tract called *Super Powers and the Superpowers*.[3] *Watchmen* is rooted in the waning days of the cold war, caricaturing the Reagan-Thatcher axis with a Nixon administration that survives Vietnam, Watergate, and the Twenty-second Amendment to rule for seventeen years. In one of many ironic flourishes, political speculations concerning a presidential bid by "RR" point to Robert Redford; Ronald Reagan is dismissed as a washed-up cowboy actor (XII.32.3–4).

Most of its satiric targets have drifted from history's shooting gallery, but *Watchmen* remains powerfully resonant with recent times. The Bush gang of Washington "humanoids" (XI.Doc.1) learned deceit and subversion under Richard Nixon, giving their geopolitics of oil and terror a clear line of descent from the cold war. *Watchmen*'s visions of hovering airships and free electricity cut the other way, ironically counterpointing our Götterdämmerung of fossil fuels and the general decline of our not-so-superpowers There is a passing resemblance between Tony Blair and *Watchmen*'s arch-antivillain, Adrian Veidt—in features, political philosophy, and some would say, morals. This seems either prophetic (Blair was after all an important political actor in the 1980s) or in the strict sense *weird*.

Yet such direct comparisons can only go so far. *Watchmen* presents an alternative history, diverging deliberately from the world we know. Tilting the prism another way, keen students of comics might thus try a different sort of thought experiment. What if our universe is the cartoon, and *Watchmen*'s four-color fantasy an image of higher reality? In this scheme, our recent governmental bungling might represent a Bizarro-world inversion of *Watchmen*'s elegant, sinister intrigues. Veidt then would not be a type of Blair but rather an antitype of George W. Bush, who seems born to the part of Bizarro Superman.

These readings are admittedly fanciful, but there is at least one point of clear convergence between *Watchmen*'s universe and ours. Global warming, Middle Eastern conflict, and suicide bombers do not feature in this nightmare of more innocent times, but *Watchmen* does include one scene of chilling currency: a tableau of New York streets strewn with bleeding corpses (XII.6.1). Within the story, this moment horribly realizes a promotion for a fitness method invented by the conspirator Veidt: "I WILL GIVE YOU BODIES BEYOND YOUR WILDEST IMAGINING" (X.13.1). Indeed he does. The bodies in question include both a cyclopean monster, purportedly an invader from another dimension, and thousands of civilians killed by a psychic blast when the phantom appears. The giant alien remains a figment of comics—or television, since its origins trace to an episode of the *Outer Limits* series from the 1960s (XII.28.4). The heaps of victims, terrible to say, are not beyond anyone's imagining these days. Moore and Gibbons place their ground zero some blocks north of ours, but it is still impossible to read the final chapter of *Watchmen* without remembering that its lurid, apocalyptic fantasy came true, in some sense, fifteen years later.

If we are living on the Bizarro planet, it is possible to die there. Indeed, an especially dark resonance between *Watchmen* and real life arrived during the writing of this chapter. Brewing up their atmosphere of crisis, Moore and Gibbons make passing reference to the Doomsday Clock of the *Bulletin of the Atomic Scientists*, part of the obsession with time and timepieces that serves as *Watchmen*'s white whale. In the first chapter, a newspaper headline reports that the clock "stands at 5 to 12" after the "American superman" suddenly vanishes, leaving the United States vulnerable to Soviet attack (I.18.4). Meanwhile, back in Bizarro reality, our own atomic scientists, including global warming for the first time in their deliberations, reset the clock on January 20, 2007, from 11:53 to, yes, 5 minutes before midnight (see ⟨http://www.thebulletin.org⟩).

These days we all watch the clock, when we are not watching the watchmen; but how can we truly understand the tenor and the terror of these times? Perhaps as Pynchon (1973, 760) says, we have "always been at the movies," but then again, if our world is largely a mechanical projection, the sequential narrative of cinema may not be the best way of seeing our predicament. Comics and spatial narrative may shed more useful light.

Under Language

The medium of comics provides a powerful way to interrogate a reality abundant with signs, symptoms, and synchronicities. As noted, comics are always inherently dualistic, playing off space and simultaneity against succession and sequence. In most cases, the panel of a comic does not fill the visual field but rather coexists with others in the structure of the page. Likewise, the various verbal elements of comics (word balloons, text boxes that simulate a voiceover, and such) impinge on the graphical surface of every panel. In developing the script for *Watchmen*, Moore was acutely aware of these basic properties. He notes in a 1992 interview:

> What it comes down to in comics is that you have complete control of both the verbal track and the image track, which you don't have in any other medium, including film. So a lot of effects are possible which simply

25.1 *Watchmen* panel I.1.1. © 1986 DC Comics. All Rights Reserved. Used with permission.

cannot be achieved anywhere else. You control the words and the pictures—and more importantly—you control the *interplay* between those two elements in a way which not even film can achieve. There's a sort of "under-language" at work there, that is, neither the "visuals" nor the "verbals," but a unique effect caused by a combination of the two. (Wiater and Bissette 1997, 163)

Happily, Moore is an artist, not an academic theorist, so his concept of under-language offers a possible guide for interpretation rather than a formula for composition. As indications go, however, the idea of an under-language in *Watchmen* seems enormously valuable. Looking closely at the interplay of visual and verbal, and the logical and figurative structures through which it operates, can reveal a great deal about the work.

Take, for example, the first panel of *Watchmen*. The text box at the top contains an excerpt from the diary of Walter

Kovacs, the borderline personality behind the costumed vigilante Rorschach: "Dog carcass in alley this morning, tire tread on burst stomach. This city is afraid of me. I have seen its true face."

The phrase "true face" delivers our first taste of the under-language by way of a characteristic visual-verbal pun. The words appear above a channel of bloody water that flows (appropriately enough) into a gutter, washing past a bloodstained lapel button. The button is an instance of that familiar pop culture flotsam called the *happy face* or *smiley*, and it initiates the series of significant faces—human, symbolic, and horological—that forms the main symbolic register of *Watchmen*. This under-language juxtaposition implicitly frames a question: Does the bloody button represent the true face of which Rorschach speaks? Various answers are possible.

Like irony, Moore's other favorite trope, puns superimpose identity and nonidentity, setting up an array of simultaneous, contradictory readings. The face in this picture is both true and false, or a truth based on a lie. Strictly speaking, the image does not show a true face: first, because it is a minimal representation, an icon that reduces a human face to three simple marks (McCloud 1999, 29); and second, because this particular button was the sardonic emblem of Edward Morgan Blake, a costumed thug known as the Comedian, a figure whose true face (or identity, motives, or allegiances) usually stayed hidden. Then again, the moments to which this object graphically connect— Blake's collapse just before Veidt hurls him to his death (I.3.3), and his anguished appeal to a former enemy a week before the murder (II.23.8)—may indeed add up to a moment of truth. Read more figuratively, the bloody button may be a true face after all. Marked with Blake's blood, the object does echo his actual face, slashed by a scorned woman in Vietnam, the cut approximating the angle of spatter on the button (II.14.6).[4] In a larger sense, a bloodstained leftover from some mindless fad, turned into the calling card of a government assassin, finally a token of his violent death, might indeed represent the true face of *Watchmen*'s Pax Americana: a brittle, false prosperity built on brutality and lies.

Clockwork

The search for a true face, or the face of truth, runs throughout *Watchmen*. Moore and Gibbons construct a densely interwoven gallery of human faces, often drawn in one-third view, dead on, looking straight at the reader, as if in intimate address—or framed for a mug shot. Nonhuman faces also matter a great deal. As we might expect from something called *Watch-men*, dials, clock faces, and other timepieces proliferate. Every chapter closes with the story's own Doomsday Clock, each image placing the hands closer to midnight. Jon Osterman, the atomic scientist accidentally made superman, starts on his path when his father, a jeweler, scatters watch parts into the street, declaring the end of the Newtonian universe after reading about the theory of relativity (IV.3.6–7).

In the fatal event, Osterman is betrayed by a pair of timepieces. In 1959, he enters an experimental chamber to retrieve a wristwatch he has repaired for his fiancée, Janie Slater, becoming trapped by a time lock on the door, thus dooming him to disintegration (IV.8.2). Albert Einstein, or the collateral result of his physics, is still very much to blame. Slater's wristwatch is smashed by a "fat man" (IV.6.5), connecting it by allusion to the image of a blasted watch on the cover of *Time* magazine in 1985, commemorating the fortieth anniversary of the Hiroshima bombing (IV.24.7).[5]

The under-language is strong in this chain of references, and indeed throughout the fourth chapter, "Watchmaker." Many major themes converge here: symmetry and reciprocation (the tick and tock of clockwork); desire and fatality (Osterman offers to repair Slater's watch after they first make love); submission and dominance (Osterman's destruction and transfiguration); and finally, time itself—or rather, a particular critique of time.

The superbeing that Osterman becomes, named Doctor Manhattan by his government handlers, exists outside mortal categories. Somehow his will and consciousness survive the destruction of his original body, enabling him to reassemble a new, heroic body by directly manipulating fundamental particles and forces. The reborn Osterman is apparently indestructible: Veidt immolates him a second

time in the final chapter (XII.14.4), but he simply reconstitutes on a larger scale (XII.17.4). Along with death, Doctor Manhattan has also escaped the human experience of time. As he explains to Laurie Juspeczyk, his estranged partner: "Time is simultaneous, an intricately structured jewel that humans insist on viewing one edge at a time, when the whole design is visible in every facet" (IX.6.6).

Even without the benefit of Moore's hints about an under-language, it should be apparent that Doctor Manhattan's jewellike conception of time also describes the architecture of *Watchmen*. All the examples we have discussed above exhibit this spatial or fractal quality in some degree. While each panel of *Watchmen* may not display "the whole design," most seem to fold back against other moments in the story, making distinctions of time and sequence seem arbitrary. Chapter IV, which lays out the autobiography of Osterman, presents a series of flashes back and forward, punctuated by something like jump cuts. The under-language of comics thus works to simulate Doctor Manhattan's unique awareness, his post-Newtonian, relativistic being in time.

This convergence of narrative and medium begs an important question: How are we to understand a story operating in jeweled or prismatic time? To recur to Manovich's comments on comics and the logic of industrialism, what is gained by deconstructing the over-language of film and prose, reaching beyond the two dimensions available to screen and page? This peculiar way of storytelling gives access to a simultaneous, parallelistic conception that would be much harder to express in conventionally sequential media; but radical moves always imply skepticism, if not resistance. Pynchon, whose work reaches in its own way toward spatial narrative (and comics), has given us a useful parable. In *Gravity's Rainbow* we meet a misallied couple, Leni and Franz Pökler, similar in some ways to Moore's Juspeczyk and Osterman, though with different fates. Leni is given to mystical thinking, while engineer Franz prefers more linear solutions:

> He was the cause-and-effect man: he kept at her astrology without mercy, telling her what she was supposed to believe, then denying it. "Tides, radio interference,

damned little else. There is no way for changes out there to produce changes here."

"Not produce," she tried, "not cause. It all goes together. Parallel, not series. Metaphor. Signs and symptoms. Mapping on to different coordinate systems, I don't know..." She didn't know, all she was trying to do was reach.

But he said: "Try to design anything that way and have it work."
(Pynchon 1973, 159)

In many ways, *Watchmen* seems the true child of Leni's mystical understanding, shot through with coincidences, parallels, and what Pynchon calls "Kute Korrespondences," connections that point to ominous or fatal design. In reading *Watchmen* we always seem to be "mapping on to different coordinate systems," through visual and verbal puns, analogies, or other agencies of association. Yet as the insistent duality of *Watchmen* reminds us, every Leni has her Franz, an idiot questioner who will ask what the clockwork does when we engage its mainspring—whether, once we have designed a model of jewel time, we can somehow "have it work." Foolish though it may be, this question deserves consideration, if not a direct answer. To do this, we need to examine more closely some features of *Watchmen*'s remarkable construction.

Who Makes the World?

Shortly before Doctor Manhattan delivers his jewel theory to Juspeczyk, she asks why, if he is able to foresee everything that will ever happen to him, he is constrained to behave in any particular way. The superman replies that he is still a puppet of the universe, but "a puppet who can see the *strings*" (IX.5.4). Ever the atomic scientist, Manhattan/Osterman refers to those higher-dimensional structures that cosmologists have postulated as the basis for post-Einsteinian physics. Yet since this phrase invokes another magical pun, we are reminded of puppets and puppeteers, watches and watchmakers, and other more mechanical structures. Reaching further, as *Watchmen* always encourages us to do, we might also think of "the strings" as a fig-

ure for those threads or skeins of meaning that network the text, and thus of the basic geometry of *Watchmen* itself. What does it mean to "see the strings" in this sense?

To begin with, this point of view implies the ability to change scale or perspective, the better to appreciate local structures in a larger context. An excellent illustration of this principle comes at the end of Osterman's interview with Juspeczyk in chapter IX, "The Darkness of Mere Being." Disillusioned by the breakdown of his marriage and insinuations that he has caused cancer in those close to him, Doctor Manhattan removes himself to Mars, the better to contemplate the difference between a sterile, red planet and a blue one teeming with life (IX.9.1). He raises an elaborate building from the Martian sands, meaning to put humanity on trial in the person of his estranged lover. This fortress of solitude or palace of justice is a gigantic, abstract sculpture suggesting a deconstructed clockwork (IV.27.3, IX.4.4). At the climax of their interview, just as Juspeczyk passes the test that redeems the human race, she throws a bottle into the structure (fantastic or not, this is still a domestic incident), shattering it into a shower of fragments.

What follows is perhaps the second most impressive technical maneuver in *Watchmen*. As Doctor Manhattan walks out of the ruined palace to return with Juspeczyk to Earth, the perspective begins to shift, panel by panel, from a few meters above the scene (IX.26.1–3) to a distant point in interstellar space (IX.28.3). This ambitious crane shot is reminiscent of the Charles and Ray Eames's *Powers of Ten*, and even more closely, the astronomical pullback in Andrei Tarkovsky's *Solaris*, where the camera zooms out like a rocket to reveal that an apparently domestic scene actually belongs to an alien world.[6] The sequence is more than just homage, however. It is shot through with crucial details, most significantly the image reproduced on this page.

After its tour of the planet, Doctor Manhattan's clockwork palace has come to rest within a crater in the Argyre Planitia. This formation has a secondary impact ridge and two large boulders or outcroppings—elements that form the ubiquitous happy face. The magical quotient of this visual pun is very high indeed, as it turns out that this curious spot is an *actual feature* of the planet Mars, a crater

25.2 *Watchmen* panel IX.27.1. © 1987 DC Comics. All Rights Reserved. Used with permission.

called Galle, first photographed by Viking Orbiter 1 in 1976, revisited by the Mars Global Observer in 1999 (Malin Space Science Systems).[7] It is easy to imagine Moore and Gibbons's delight in discovering this piece of areology. If a circle with two dots and a curve is the simplest, iconic representation of a face, and if this icon is in a sense a primitive element of comics art, then the Galle crater is a cosmic comic. The artist is unknown, perhaps nonexistent—and for *Watchmen* at least, this uncertainty is very much the point. As Doctor Manhattan muses, watching his Martian palace rise from the sands, "Who makes the world?" (IV.27.3). We might also frame a slightly different question: If a pattern forms on a dead planet, when does it become a face?

Leaving theology and metaphysics aside, we should notice an important difference between astronomical data and artistic rendering. Moore and Gibbons have fiddled the proportions: crater Galle is 215 kilometers across, or about the distance from Washington, DC, to Philadelphia, at which scale we would not be able to resolve both human figures and the boulders that form the eyes (IX.26.5). More significantly, they have added the smashed remains of Doctor Manhattan's flying palace, which does not correspond to anything in the actual crater. In their depiction, the wreckage lies just southeast of the right-eye boulder (at left in

the panel above), thus echoing with only slight variation the Comedian's bloodstained button.

The first resonance of this image is local, climactically closing the ninth chapter with a visual power chord. Doctor Manhattan decides to avert a possible nuclear holocaust after Juspeczyk unwittingly reminds him of the miraculous improbability of human life. The crater beautifully symbolizes this primal accident: a highly unlikely arrangement of inert matter into an echo of that other sublime accident (or if you prefer, divine design), the human face. In an odd way, the dead, red world has produced an image of life—or an emoticon, at least.

At the same time, though, the discovery of this image resonates in other ways as well. As an ordinary human, Juspeczyk cannot see the larger pattern of which she is a part, even though she determines at least its final stroke, first by refusing to fly further, causing Doctor Manhattan to land at Galle (IX.22.1), and then by smashing the palace where it stands. Both actions are impulsive and entirely unplanned —"thermodynamic miracles," to echo Doctor Manhattan's description of humanity (IX.21.9). As a superman, he is capable of both astronomical views and grand architectural gestures, but there is no indication of either in this moment. When he and Juspeczyk vanish from Mars, they reappear on Earth, so the cosmic crane shot on the chapter's final

See the Strings

pages does not represent their point of view. (It probably prefigures Doctor Manhattan's departure at the end of the story, but this is mapping to another system, in every sense.) In effect, the perspective of the final sequence belongs only to the reader and the authors. Reading the under-language of comics, we see what the characters do not or cannot; but what exactly do we see?

Taking the Galle tableau at (unavoidably) face value, the scene would seem to signify completeness or perfection of symmetry. As the characters agonize about the possibility of meaning, they walk through a gigantic design that is both highly significant and entirely accidental. Watching the watchmen, we close the circuit of irony between authors and reader. We also witness an act of inscription: Juspeczyk's destruction of the palace has quite literally *graphic* consequences. In terms of its own semiotics or under-language, *Watchmen* thus inscribes its primary icon on itself, setting up a resonant, self-referential sign system, a kind of standing wave or feedback loop. This episode of visual noise rings true. Even accident produces pattern, and when humans come on the scene, pattern becomes meaning. Delivering this message, art confirms its function. Beauty is truth, and life goes on. The pendulum of uncertainty, oscillating between extinction and survival, red Mars and blue Earth, ticks back again, duly reciprocal. Even the planet smiles.

This all-too-easy reading, however, neglects at least one crucial detail. To complete the grand design, Juspeczyk must shatter the crystal palace, reducing its elegant architecture of cups, wands, and wheels, with its meticulous fourfold balance, to a jumbled heap of fragments. In creating the larger, unseen pattern, she destroys the one at hand, wrecking its harmonic arrangement. Notably, she must also disrupt the larger symmetry of the original scene: by adding a fifth stroke to the design, the fallen palace defaces the face on Mars. This more complicated reading reminds us that noise or entropy are as important in *Watchmen* as integrity of signal. The under-language of this work contains more than puns, ironies, echoes, and other reciprocating structures. It also encompasses flaws, fissures, gaps, gutters, and other limits to design.

Everything Balances

We can find the most compelling demonstration of this fact in the remarkable chapter V, "Fearful Symmetry," structurally speaking the most impressive part of *Watchmen*.[8] As the title suggests, the chapter is filled with doubles, mirrorings, echoes, and dichotomies. Its main subject is Rorschach, a masked marauder whose costumed face is an ever-changing inkblot. Like many comic book heroes, Rorschach leads a double life, maintaining a secret identity as Walter Kovacs, a sometime mental patient and self-appointed prophet of doom (I.1.3). In much more than name, Rorschach is deeply linked to *Watchmen*'s symbology. At one point we watch him idly deface a menu in a diner, pouring ketchup on to a page, and then folding it over to create a symmetrical stain (V.11.7–9). As we will see, this reference to patterns on folded pages has more than momentary or local significance.

Chapter V abounds with indications of doubleness. The main narrative begins and ends outside a bar called Rumrunners, whose emblem, a pair of mirrored *R*s integrated into a stylized skull and crossbones, constitutes a double visual echo (V.1.1). It recalls the traditional flag of piracy, and hence the comic-within-a-comic *Tales of the Black Freighter*, introduced in chapter III and further developed here. At the same time, the mirrored *R*s of the bar sign echo Rorschach's signature (V.3.9). Since Moore and Gibbons never do their doubling by half, we first see this emblem as a reflection in a puddle, taking us deeper into the hall of mirrors.

Both the theme and the structure of chapter V participate in this system of echoes. As he hauls Rorschach away at the end of the episode, a police officer notes that the "terror of the underworld" will be locked up with the men he hunted: "Everything balances," the detective says (V.28.8). This statement may not be entirely accurate but is certainly salient on many levels—including, for chapter V, the material structure of the text itself. The 220 panels and twenty-eight numbered pages of chapter V form a graphic palindrome, a kind of comic as inkblot. On each side of the chapter's seven signatures, the division of panels on the left-hand page mirrors the arrangement on the right. Page one mirrors page twenty-eight, page two mirrors page

25.3 *Watchmen* pages V.14–15. © 1986 DC Comics. All Rights Reserved. Used with permission.

twenty-seven, and so forth.[9] The effect is literally half-concealed. Fourteen pages use a regular, three-by-three grid, and so offer no immediate clue to the scheme. Interspersed throughout the chapter, the other fourteen pages vary the regular grid, revealing their relationships more readily. On page nine, for instance, the basic nine-panel page is cut down to six by stretching panels one, four, and five to double width. Page nine is eight pages from the beginning $(1 + 8)$, so its mirror correspondent is eight pages from the end, page twenty $(28 - 8)$. On that page, the doubled panels are two, three, and six, reversing the geometry of page

nine. Of course, the most striking evidence of the palindrome falls at the center, as seen in the accompanying image.

Any palindrome implies a crossing point or chiasmus where orientation reverses. The center spread of chapter V constitutes this structure, especially the cardinal panels (V.14.2 and V.15.1). *Chiasmus* comes from the Greek letter *chi*, which gives us the Roman *X*. *X* indeed marks the spot where opposites converge and "everything balances," ostensibly at least. The *X* is formed by the golden *V* from Veidt's corporate logo and the two clashing bodies, Veidt at the left, and his hapless would-be assassin at the right. Veidt's leg makes up his side of the X pattern, while the assassin's upper body provides the opposite. Veidt swings his improvised weapon in an arc traversing the upper three-quarters of the image, while the assassin falls in a complementary arc below. The object, evidently an ashtray in the style of an Egyptian urn, is convex at the left, and concave at the right. In the lower quarter of the image, an upright golden head at the left (a dead king) mirrors the inverted face of the killer at the right (a doomed fool), and both are reflected in the fountain pool below, yet another plane of symmetry.

In more than one sense, these panels represent the heart of a hall of mirrors, since what we seem to witness here—Veidt's miraculous escape from a murder attempt, evidently part of the conspiracy against costumed heroes—is an elaborate falsehood, a piece of brutal theater concocted by Veidt to hide his true purpose. The crossing point consummates a double-cross. It would follow, then, that the apparent perfection of symmetrical design is deeply suspicious, and in fact, there is something wrong with this picture. A duly sensitized reader might notice at least one asymmetry, with two horrified onlookers standing at the left and only one on the right. The right-hand figure is a letter carrier (again, in several senses), and on his bag we can make out the characters "US" and "AIL"—suggesting perhaps that something in this scene reveals what in *Watchmen*'s world might *ail us*.[10] Those who have seen the ending know the culprit is Veidt, but his megalomania might raise concern even for an obediently serial, first-time reader. On the next page we see him apparently find (actually plant) a poison capsule in the mouth of the stunned assassin, and then at the end of all the carnage calmly ask an employee to "call the toy people" and cancel a line of action figures (V.16.9). To Veidt, the genius antivillain, humanity is made up of "toy people" who need his attentions. Like the duped assassin in the central scene, or like Rorschach, framed for Edward Jacobi's murder at the climax of chapter V, everyone is caught in the elaborate structures of Veidt's plot.

At a later point in the story, Veidt will tell Dan Dreiberg, the hapless Nite Owl, that he is "not a Republic serial villain" (XI.27.1). He means that he has revealed his master-stroke only after it is complete, and the costumed crusaders actually are, as Pynchon (1973, 751) says, "My God...too late." But another sense of *serial* also operates here: Leni Pökler's dyad, "parallel, not series." Veidt is indeed a non-serial villain. He bases his heroic identity partly on Alexander of Macedon, whose "lateral thinking" defeated the Gordian knot (XI.10.2). He uses a method of planning derived from William S. Burroughs's cut-up technique (XI.1.1–6) and takes as his oracle an array of television screens (visually, of course, an analogue of the comics page, and thus of spatial narrative: XI.2.4).

Though Veidt is a meticulous cause-and-effect man and a hell of an engineer, his conspiracy ultimately owes as much to Leni as to Franz. The plot is an elegant, nefarious arrangement of "signs and symptoms." Nonetheless, it would appear that he does "have it work"—or as Moore and Gibbons quote Shelley: "Look on my works, ye mighty, and despair" (XII.28.14). At least on first inspection, the irony of Shelley's poem, where the boast is inscribed on ruins and emptiness, seems reversed. Veidt is successful, and his works reshape the world. By the final chapter, he has managed to outwit his human adversaries, Dreiberg, Juspeczyk, and the resurgent Rorschach. He tries first to deceive, then to destroy Doctor Manhattan, and though he fails, he does force their contest to a draw. "What's that in your hand, Veidt," the reintegrated Doctor Manhattan asks derisively, "another ultimate weapon?" (XII.8.4). The object in question is the remote control for Veidt's video wall, now showing news accounts of his deadly attack on New York. Evidently his phony alien invasion has forced the United States and the USSR to retreat from the nuclear brink—hence the little gadget does stop the superman in his tracks.

Veidt creates an artifice of meaning that becomes the true face of *Watchmen*, an image of official happiness stained with blood. The "ultimate weapon" is information or persuasion, an appeal to map the world situation on to new coordinate systems, and recognize the necessity of that arrangement. Facing the end of the end of the world, yet apparently still committed to humanity's survival, Doctor Manhattan must enlist in the deception, even to the point of homicide; so he confronts the implacable Rorschach, who intends to reveal Veidt's murderous fraud. "Evil must be punished," Rorschach insists (XII.23.4). Doctor Manhattan levels his omnipotent hand, Rorschach urges, "Do it!" (XII.24.3), and the "judge of all the earth" blasts him to bits, leaving one last smear of blood (XII.24.4–5).[11]

It would appear, then, that everything balances. Americans and Russians stand down from Armageddon. Veidt is left like a happy spider at the center of his new world order. Having silently blessed the union of Juspeczyk and Dreiberg, Doctor Manhattan removes himself to a distant planetary system, evidently planning to create life—this after facing Rorschach, his final adversary, and granting his wish for death. Tick, tock.

Five to Twelve

On closer inspection, though, this great clockwork displays a suspicious hitch or wobble. Just as Doctor Manhattan's will defies disintegration, Rorschach leaves a testament that survives his messy death. Before he and Dreiberg set off to confront Veidt in Antarctica, Rorschach mails his journal to the "only people [he] can trust" (X.22.5), a reactionary, anti-Semitic rag ironically named the *New Frontiersman*. A few pages later, we see Rorschach's book arrive, at which point the editor, Hector Godfrey, tells his plodding assistant Seymour to add it to the "crank file," where it is buried in an "avalanche of drivel" (X.24.4–9). The term *avalanche* is telling, since such structures tend to collapse, smashing everything in their path, and the metaphor may be apt. At the time he dispatches his journal, Rorschach and Dreiberg have accumulated enough evidence, particularly financial and business records, to raise serious, perhaps fatal questions about Veidt. True, Dreiberg and Juspeczyk, the only living witnesses to Veidt's confession, have absconded under new identities at the end of the story; but mention in Rorschach's journal would presumably make them subjects of speculation and maybe even pursuit. In short, Rorschach's posthumous testimony can at least potentially unweave all Veidt's machinations.

These possibilities converge in the final panel of *Watchmen*, which we will consider presently. First, however, we need to explore one more crucial feature of the underlanguage in chapter V, an essential precondition for that final stroke. We have discussed in some detail the internal structure of the chapter, but something needs to be said as well about the way that structure relates to the larger scheme of the work.

Viewed from outside the chapter (from orbit, as it were), the double-crosser's cross at the middle of chapter V seems oddly placed. As a matter of fact, the entire chapter may be mislocated, if we assume that a palindromic comic makes a natural pivot or bearing for a structure of bilateral symmetry. The midpoint of a twelve-part epic falls in the gap between the end of the sixth part and the beginning of the seventh. Of course, this makes the graphical chiasmus of chapter V formally impossible, so clearly Moore and Gibbons had to break some rules to accommodate their ingenious design. Other decisions seem possible, though, such as locating the palindromic chapter in the sixth or seventh position, or creating a matched set of mirror chapters in both positions. Why choose the fifth chapter for a tour de force of symmetry?

For the author of *V for Vendetta*, and a keen reader of Pynchon's *V*, the temptation to play some variations on the fifth Roman numeral may have been too hard to resist. The development from the *V* of *Vendetta* to Veidt, the Mr. X of *Watchmen*, does seem resonant. One careful reader points out that chapter V constitutes the midpoint of the ten-chapter sequence where Rorschach compiles his journal, detailing the events leading up to the cataclysm in New York (J. S. Brogee, quoted in Furé 1999). This interpretation makes some sense, especially considering the *V*-into-*X* symbolism, which invites attention to the numbers five and ten. Yet as Jessica Furé (1999) points out, the middle of a ten-part series comes between five and six, not midway through five. If we insist on reading with scientific precision (not the only way to read, of course), it seems clear that the strongest image of centrality and symmetry in *Watchmen* is out of alignment. The chiastic center spread of chapter V sits at an awkward point in the timeline, throwing the entire structure of *Watchmen* off balance. To paraphrase Pynchon: *My God, we are too early!*

On the other hand, perhaps the fateful symmetry of chapter V is right where it belongs, in precisely the wrong place. The brilliant artifice of the palindrome chapter does

25.4 *Watchmen* panel XII.32.7. © 1987 DC Comics. All Rights Reserved. Used with permission.

not integrate into a grand design but rather disintegrates, or in the strict sense deconstructs that design, opening up its artifice for critical understanding. Chapter V might be understood as an image of Veidt's plot, an attempt to create a universal balance that cannot succeed because it is subsumed by a larger principle of chaotic flow. Thus we refute Franz Pökler: it is less important to see how the clockwork operates than to know how it fails.

See the Strings?

At the end, then, we have to wonder whether the underlanguage of *Watchmen* can truly deliver an image of Doctor Manhattan's jewel time. Perhaps we are left less with an image than a model, a structure subject to testing or experiment, and perhaps the point of this experiment is to observe that model's failure. Like Doctor Manhattan's crystalline judgment seat, smashed into signifying wreckage in the Galle crater, Veidt's plot also seems poised for collapse in the last panel of *Watchmen*.

Predictably enough, a work that started with a visual-verbal pun ends on the same note: Godfrey's exasperated outburst, "I leave it entirely in your hands." As it is in the beginning, the under-language here is deeply ambiguous. Literally, Godfrey's statement is true enough. He tells Seymour to choose something from the crank file to fill a hole

in the upcoming issue. Since the truly ultimate information weapon is now on top of the stack, Godfrey has placed the fate of Veidt's illusion, on which humanity entirely depends, in Seymour's unwashed hands.

At the same time, though, there is a strain of inversion or irony in this final line of *Watchmen*. Though the sequence implied here is formally incomplete—we never see where Seymour's hand comes down—the deck is stacked (or the stack is decked out) for revelation. Rorschach's notebook is rendered in full color and detail, so that we can see the book tape inserted two-thirds through, presumably marking the last journal entry. Other elements of the pile are sketched in, suggesting they are not in focus, and inked in blue to indicate they lie in shade. In the near background, the inevitable stain on Seymour's smiley-bedecked jersey also points decisively toward the book, or if you read its arrow shape the other way, over Seymour's shoulder into the unwary world. Finally, if we consider the name of our numinous decider, the public can probably expect to See More than it does at present—perhaps more than is good for it.

Reading the last panel as overdetermined in this way reasserts at least one aspect of reciprocation, if not balance: the swinging pendulum of sequential time. Perhaps what we have here, though, is not so much the ticking of a clock (*tick-tock*) as of a bomb (*tick-tock-BOOM*). This reading is inescapably fatalistic, nihilistic, or perhaps in a terrible way, realistic. Veidt's plot staves off an imminent nuclear war, so dismantling its artificial détente raises the likelihood of renewed conflict and perhaps the end of civilization. Read in this way, *Watchmen* is an enormously tragic comic.

Consider its ultimate symbol or icon. The stain on Seymour's jersey, ketchup now, not blood, concludes and summarizes a series of repetitions, from the blotched button of the first panel through various coy echoes of the stain shape (e.g., XI.1.2, XI.28.12) to the defaced face on Mars. This is, finally, the true face of *Watchmen*'s city of heroes: a bright circle of devious contrivance, blotted with blood, trauma, and the emergent catastrophes that beset all complex systems. It is the emblem of a clockwork that slips a gear, a broken symmetry that fails to encompass its world.

Yet as we have seen, most signs and statements in *Watchmen* have two or more senses, infused by the essential field of allusion and irony that permeates the work. So the signature image or true face of *Watchmen* also stands for the miraculous catastrophe by which order, consciousness, and meaning emerge from chaotic flux. Bending the light this way through *Watchmen*'s intricate prism brings a different view of the last panel. If the entire structure of this epic comic is in some way experimental, then we can take the final panel as an ultimate observation. As the second-person address in the last line hints, the subject of this test is the reader, or "you."

Read as final exam, the last panel poses a deceptively simple question: *Can you see the strings?* That is, can you understand the under-language of this comic, and of comics generally, sufficiently to recognize the artifices at work here? More crucially, can you also hold those artifices in suspension? Learning from chapter IX about the enlightening effects of scale change, and from chapter V about the relationship of local structures to global, we might remember that every panel belongs to a larger pattern, and that it may not complete that pattern but rather disrupt it. Even though so much in *Watchmen*'s final measure points toward apocalyptic unveiling, it does after all fail to conclude the act.[12] Seymour's hand has not come down. Strictly speaking, it never does. Looking with educated eyes, we may detect details and arrangements that foreordain an outcome —cosmological strings, puppet strings, or chains of under-language—but we who watch the watchmen stand outside them.

Read this way, the iconography of the final panel depends not so much on the ominously illuminated book, the final evocation of the world's true face, or even Seymour's fatally outstretched hand. What signifies most is the emptiness of that hand, and the fact that the book of final judgment remains shut. *Watchmen* ends with an image of its own medium, a bound volume, *seen from outside*, arrested at the moment before irrevocable conception, in spite of all strings visibly attached. It thus gives a symbolic signature for a liminal or interstitial relationship to objects of communication, a way of seeing and reading that does not hide the strings.

In Your Hands

Interstices are inherently awkward places. Those who haunt the gutters tend to look toward the stars or those places where stars gather. As sequentially time-bound animals, denizens of a postindustrial culture still heavily conditioned by linear processes, we do not take easily to spatial narrative. Seeing the strings comes hard, and sometimes you just want to watch something.

We do not lack for choices. The television series *Heroes* is now well into its second season, weaving tropes and themes of *Watchmen* into a new context that speaks particularly to these post-traumatic times. The Trade Center site of actual disaster is now flanked symbolically not just by *Watchmen*'s Institute for Extraspatial Studies, but by Kirby Plaza as well, another gathering point of pattern and coincidence, not coincidentally named for the great comics master. Tim Kring has even shown us his own version of the strings, in the three-dimensional model of convergences found in Isaac Mendez's apartment.

Meanwhile, a film version of *Watchmen* is once again in preproduction, the most recent of several attempts to bring Moore and Gibbons's work to the screen. Moore is notoriously disdainful of Hollywood, refusing to let his name be used in connection with film versions of his comics. He reputedly told the director Terry Gilliam that the best cinematic treatment of *Watchmen* would be none at all (*Wikipedia*). The reasons for this antipathy are best known to the author, though seeing a work with the scope and nuance of *From Hell* turned into megaplex fodder certainly does not help. When you read this, you may be able to judge whether the film version of *Watchmen* fell closer to genuinely interesting inventions like *Batman Begins* or to vapid star vehicles like *The League of Extraordinary Gentlemen*. Then again, history may record yet another failed project, leaving *Watchmen* among cinema's greatest stories never told.

In some ways, that last outcome would be appropriate, however it might diminish the canon of comics films. No sequential medium—not cinema, not print, and certainly not the sort of print that makes up a scholarly essay—can do full justice to the under-language of *Watchmen*. As indicated, this comic delivers not a working timepiece but something more like a catastrophe simulator, an open-ended experiment that the reader is invited or expected to perform. Understanding *Watchmen* in this light makes it seem distinctly avant la lettre, something impossible to describe in traditional terms. More than the relic of an older, spatial way of seeing, it prefigures and perhaps inaugurates the next thing in sign systems.

In this century we are beginning to build on our technologies of recording and inscription new media and new language that operate by systematic simulation. We deal less in simple arrays of signs than in sign systems that do not simply store but actively produce and modify meaning. Thanks to instrumentalities like the Web and Google, this change increasingly affects even the most traditional communications. These innovations demand many changes of mind. To acquire the new language, we need an ability to map across multiple coordinate systems, an awareness of contingent or emergent forms, and a keen appreciation of the limits to any neat, self-enclosing order. We must *see the strings* in many senses: as patterns of association, multilinear paths, and the under-language of database structures, lines of code, and visual presentations. This is by no means easy work, and the magnitude of the change is so great that we tend to engage it only at the limits of awareness, in odd cases and ostensibly minor forms.

As a masterpiece of its particular, invisible art, *Watchmen* bears in a major way on our moment. Its nightmare of bodies beyond imagining may have come true in post-9/11 history, but at the same time, so has at least one analogue of its hyperconnected, deeply intertwingled worldview—as every Web site devoted to Moore and Gibbons's work attests. Living as much in the future as on Bizarro World, we pass naturally enough from the pages of a self-deconstructing comic to hypertexts, wikis, and other forms that both reveal the strings and make them ready to hand. If *Watchmen* did not literally anticipate Internet culture, it provides a structure, and some crucial lessons in structural inquiry, that may be of great help in understanding its underlying media. In an important sense, we must make our world, and reading *Watchmen* may help us live up to the task.

Notes

1. Traces of these origins survive as grace notes in *Watchmen*: Nite Owl's airship is called Archie, and Walter Kovacs (Rorschach) spends his childhood in the Charlton Home for orphans. These may be "fanboy" details, as Moore calls them, but they also indicate how deep the texturing of allusion runs in his work.

2. This theme is a recurrent concern for Moore. An email from editor Pat Harrigan notes its appearance at the end of Moore's *Swamp Thing* as well as in the unproduced *Twilight of the Superheroes* outline.

3. Citations from *Watchmen* refer to the trade paperback edition (Moore and Gibbons 1987), which preserves the pagination of each monthly issue. References are given by chapter, page, and panel number, using the top-bottom, left-right graph order: II.8.5 thus refers to the fifth panel on page 8 of chapter 2. Each chapter of *Watchmen* closes with an excerpt from a fictional document. Citations for these sections are given as chapter, "Doc," and local pagination of the document, not the chapter: XII.Doc.1 thus refers to the first page of the document included at the end of chapter XII.

4. In the attack (II.14.6), we see Blake from behind, with a spray of blood running across his face, projecting above the left temple, forming an angle that is similar to the blood on the smiley button (about 11:00 in clock terms). In subsequent panels (II.15.3–6), Blake's hand is raised to his face at about the same position. Yet the scar from the wound is more ambiguous. In II.23.8, it runs across the lower part of Blake's face, pointing to about 9:00, while in IX.23.8 it runs from mouth to eye socket, angled toward 10:00. Moral of the story: though *Watchmen* seems to invite an obsessive attention to visual detail, it is not after all a clockwork device. As we will see, the fact that Blake's face carries a scar and thus lacks perfect symmetry matters more than the exact conformation of the scar.

5. "Fat Man" was the nickname for the plutonium bomb dropped on Nagasaki. The Hiroshima device was called "Little Boy." For what it's

worth, the panel preceding the fat man's tread (IV.6.4) shows a young boy in tears.

6. At the end of *Watchmen*, we see an advertisement for a Tarkovsky film festival, evidently a sign of U.S.-Russian concord.

7. I am indebted to Dennette Harrod Jr., a contributor to my *Watchmen* commentary site, for bringing this fact to my attention. See ⟨http://www.waterholes.com/~dennette/comix/watchmen/mars.htm⟩. The Galle crater is not to be confused with the more debatable structure in the Cydonia region, more or less debunked by the Mars Global Surveyor. See ⟨http://mars.jpl.nasa.gov/mgs/msss/camera/images/4_6_face_release/index.html⟩.

8. My treatment of chapter V owes a great deal to Jessica Furé's reading, which she developed in a research project undertaken with me in 1999. Her essay "Why Five?" is available as part of *Watching the Detectives*: ⟨iat.ubalt.edu/moulthrop/hypertexts/wm/readings/fearSym/comments.htm⟩.

9. This scheme implies relationships between the panels of corresponding pages. Jessica Furé and I developed a browser for juxtaposing paired panels, and notes on some of the more interesting correspondences. See ⟨iat.ubalt.edu/moulthrop/hypertexts/wm/readings/fearSym/sp0128.htm⟩.

10. Admittedly, another reading is possible: what ails us microscopic analysts may be a strange compulsion to read comic books with a 3× lens. In our defense, Harrigan wisely points out that Moore seems to encourage, if not require, this sort of paranoiac view. *Watchmen* contains a vast number of minute but significant details, and anyone who doubts their intentionality should glance at one of Moore's scripts, where he often takes several paragraphs to specify a single panel. See, for instance, the excerpted script for chapter I included in the *Absolute Watchmen* (Moore and Gibbons 2005), or *From Hell Book One: The Compleat Scripts* (Moore 1994).

11. In another email note from Harrigan, he writes,: "I can't resist mentioning issue 17 of Denny O'Neill's *The Question* (1988) where the Question (on whom the character of Rorschach was based, of course), picks up a copy of *Watchmen* and reads it on a flight across the country. He falls asleep and has nightmares about dying in the snow, like Rorschach. Naturally, at the end of the issue he finds himself at the mercy of some killers in the middle of a snowstorm, and flashes back to *Watchmen*, before Green Arrow arrives to save him."

12. If McCloud (1999) is right about visual closure, then the grammar of comics depends on our ability to infer context from fragmentary images of actions, so here we have one final case of Moore and Gibbons running around with their under-language on display. At the same time, there is a literary reference here, to the unfinished business at the end of *The Crying of Lot 49*, which leaves the status of the Tristero system permanently unresolved.

References

Furé, Jessica (1999). "Why Five?" ⟨iat.ubalt.edu/moulthrop/hypertexts/wm/readings/fearSym/comments.htm⟩.

Johnson, Steven (2005). *Everything Bad Is Good for You*. New York: Riverhead.

Manovich, Lev (2001). *The Language of New Media*. Cambridge, MA: MIT Press.

McCloud, Scott (1999). *Understanding Comics*. New York: DC Comics.

Moore, Alan (1994). *From Hell Book One: The Compleat Scripts*. Baltimore, MD: Borderlands Press.

Moore, Alan, and Dave Gibbons (1987). *Watchmen*. New York: DC Comics.

Moore, Alan, and Dave Gibbons (2005). *Absolute Watchmen*. New York: DC Comics.

Pynchon, Thomas (1966). *The Crying of Lot 49*. New York: Harper.

Pynchon, Thomas (1973). *Gravity's Rainbow*. New York: Penguin.

Wiater, Stanley, and Stephen R. Bissette (1997). *Comic Book Rebels: Conversations with the Creators of the New Comics*. Nevada City, CA: Underwood Books.

Managing Multiplicity in Superhero Comics: An Interview with Henry Jenkins

Sam Ford and Henry Jenkins

A lifelong comics fan, Henry Jenkins has increasingly turned his attention to the permutation and experimentation that is shaping the contemporary superhero comic book, suggesting that this niche site of cultural production may be an important indicator of trends that will soon impact the entertainment industry as a whole. In this interview with Sam Ford, he discusses some of the things that we can learn about transmedia entertainment by studying how DC and Marvel Comics manage their long-standing stable of men and women in capes.

Sam Ford: Henry, you address some of your personal history with comic books as a reader and a scholar in your essay "Death-Defying Heroes" (Jenkins 2006c). While that essay discusses some of the personal roles comics have played in your life, let's start here by briefly addressing the impact comic books have had on your work—superhero comics in particular. What do you see as the impact of superhero comics both in your own life and on popular culture more broadly?

Henry Jenkins: Scott Bukatman (2007) recently remarked on the autobiographical imperative that runs through comics criticism. Because most of us are comics fans before we are comics scholars, we return to our own childhoods when we assert our authority to speak on this topic. And so, yes, I have written an autobiographical essay, tracing my interests back to early elementary school and Adam West's *Batman*, describing an era when comics were pulled randomly from spin racks in drugstores, and linking my memories of comics to the process of mourning the death of my mother.

I returned to comics with real intensity about six or seven years ago. I went from reading a few comics a year to reading thirty or forty titles a month. Some of this was no doubt personal. I was feeling some great responsibilities in my life and figured I could use some great powers about now. These superhero stories functioned, as Sherry Turkle (2007) might suggest, as "evocative objects," providing me with metaphors for working through issues about leadership and adult responsibilities, aging and mourning, the relationship between our past and present selves. I am someone who never does anything for fun without turning it into work. So I now read comics and graphic novels as a medium for rapid prototyping for new content strategies that will soon shape the rest of the entertainment industry. They are relatively cheap to produce by comparison with a computer game, television series, or feature film. Their content is mined for both mainstream and independent films. Their aesthetic gets tapped for games. And superheroes spill over into television as well—witness *Heroes*. The turnaround from conception to production is rapid: trends impact comics first. Comics are somewhat mainstream (if we are talking about DC or Marvel), but also niche. Comics are fighting for survival and so are taking risks that more stable media would avoid. They are constantly testing new markets, putting a new twist on familiar genre conventions.

Ford: For some scholars, superhero comics have traditionally held less interest than independent and more avant-garde comic books. Yet should even those focused on comics outside the mainstream superhero genre acknowledge some creative influence from superhero comics on other genres? And in particular, do you think some independent comics have built on the classic archetypes created by superhero comics for their work?

Jenkins: It's hard to think of any other medium so thoroughly dominated by a single genre. At any given point in time, almost all of the top hundred selling comics belong to this genre.

Given this, it is scarcely surprising that experimental or independent comics have defined themselves in opposition to superhero comics. They don't just choose to tell other stories or explore other themes. They consistently define themselves, consciously or unconsciously, as "*not* superhero comics," often self-consciously parodying or negating the values found there. After all, the majority of comics creators, at least in the U.S. context, first got interested in comics by reading about men in capes. It is not hard to find memory traces of superheroes running through works that operate largely outside that tradition.

Take, for example, Justin Green's *Binky Brown Meets the Holy Virgin Mary* (1995)—a landmark of the 1960s' underground comics scene. On one level, *Binky Brown* couldn't be further removed from superhero comics— an autobiographical story about obsessive-compulsive disorder with a controversial mixing of sexual and religious imagery. Yet on another level, the book's protagonist has constructed his personal narrative from the basic building blocks of the superhero genre, including an origin story, superpowers (he imagines rays shooting out of all of the protuberances of his body) and ways to manage them, secret identities, and hidden weaknesses, all of which become the stuff of his obsession. He gets these powers through masturbating while thinking about the Virgin Mary, not by getting bitten by a radioactive spider, but still, he sees himself in pretty much the same terms as Peter Parker does.

In other cases, the references are much more overt. Superman appears from time to time in Chris Ware's *Jimmy Corrigan* book (2004), and more recently, Ware has incorporated a young boy's erotic fantasies about Supergirl into *Rusty Brown* (2006). In Daniel Clowes's "The Death Ray" (2004), the protagonist sees himself as a superhero, though readers are more likely to see him as a sociopath.

Project Superior (various authors 2005) allowed independent comics creators to try their hands at superhero stories—abstracting them to their basic visual archetypes or rubbing superhero fantasy against the narratives of failure that characterize so much indie comics work. At the same time, the mainstream comics industry is recruiting independent comics creators to provide a new burst of innovation to their long-standing franchises. DC published a series of *Bizarro* (various authors 2003, 2006) books that feature takes of independent comics creators on the *Justice League* characters. These two projects are breaking down the lines between independent and mainstream comics genres from both directions.

Ford: I have written about comic book universes in relation to the immersive storyworlds they create (Ford 2007), which are characterized by such things as seriality, multiple creators, long-term continuity, a character backlog, contemporary ties to a deep history, and a sense of permanence. Such characteristics have a meaningful impact on the current interest in transmedia storytelling more broadly. How have comic books demonstrated storytelling techniques that in many ways, act as a precursor for these transmedia stories?

Jenkins: Many of the earliest media franchises drew on comics material—going back at least as far as Buster Brown in the early part of the twentieth century (Gordon 1998). Within just a few years of his conception, Superman was appearing in comic books, comic strips, live-action serials, animated cartoons, and radio dramas. Each of these media contributed to his evolution—as did television a few decades later. From day one, one of the superhero's powers was to be able to leap across different media channels in a single bound. The superhero genre anticipates the focus on expansive and immersive storyworlds. As I suggest in *Convergence Culture* (2006b), world building is part of the structuring logic of the new transmedia franchises. For decades, DC and Marvel treated all of their titles as interconnected: characters move across different series, and universe-wide events periodically require readers to buy titles that they were not otherwise reading to understand their full ramifications. Each book adds new information, looks at the situation from a different perspective; each book has to satisfy the hard-core fan's mastery over a complex mythology while trying to remain accessible to first-time readers.

Today, we are seeing comics play an important role in a growing number of transmedia franchises. Because the cost of comics production is relatively low, comics are being used to expand on universes created for other media into directions that might be cost-prohibitive in film or television. Joss Whedon is an important figure to watch in this regard. Around his *Buffy the Vampire Slayer* (Whedon 2007–ongoing) franchise, he developed *Tales of the Slayers* (Whedon 2002) and *Tales of the Vampires* (Whedon et al. 2004), which dealt with the world's prehistory, and *Fray* (Whedon 2003), which dealt with its future. Around *Firefly*, Whedon published a miniseries to bridge the gap between the television series and the *Serenity* theatrical film (Whedon, Matthews, and Conrad 2006). He has even described a recent series of *Buffy* comics as the "eighth season": he contends that they are the definitive version of what happened after the televised series ends. Comics focused on film or television franchises aren't new; I used to read Jerry Lewis or *Star Trek* comics in grade school. Nobody would consider those titles to be canonical. But the Whedon comics are absolutely canonical in the views of many fans.

Ford: One of the most heralded of these crossover stories has been *Civil War* (Millar 2007), the 2006–2007 Marvel series that pits contemporary concerns of national security against civil liberties. How has this series capitalized on the cross-title strengths of these types of superhero crossovers, and the strengths of a superhero immersive storyworld as a whole, in tackling issues so important to our current society?

Jenkins: *Civil War* demonstrates the power of this mode of expanded storytelling. The *Civil War* series dealt with the politics surrounding a decision by the U.S. government to require all superheroes to register, thus forfeiting their secret identities and accepting the control of civilian governments. This is a referendum about the future of the superhero genre—at least within the Marvel universe—with different characters aligning on opposing sides. The story was framed, implicitly and sometimes explicitly, as a comment about the Patriot Act and Gitmo. The issues raised were big, and they demanded large-scale development if they were not going to be dismissed with some simplistic swat of the hand. Marvel explored them across more than a hundred issues, crisscrossing every major title it publishes. No other medium could have done a story with this scope and intensity, with several new stories appearing every week for more than a six-month period.

Civil War exploited this transmedia system's ability to show the same events from multiple characters' points of view and conflicting (and self-conflicted) political perspectives. In one book, we may see what an incident means for those, such as Iron Man or Mr. Fantastic, who are supporting registration. In another, we may see it from the perspective of Captain America and the others who are resisting it; the X-Men, who are trying to remain neutral; the Thing, who is watching Marvel's First Family disintegrate around him; Spider-Man, who develops a greater political consciousness and shifts sides during the series; or the Black Panther, who brings a non-U.S. perspective to the fracas.

New titles such as *Civil War* and *Frontline* were created to bring together the conflicting perspectives within a single issue. *Frontline* showed the story from the perspective of two reporters—Ben Urich, whose editor wants him to improve the publication's readership by stirring up anger against unregistered superheroes, and Sally Floyd, whose publisher sees the act as the latest intrusion of the state into the lives of its citizens. This ability to spread the story across all of these different vantage points also increases the likelihood that for at least some readers, their favorite hero ends up on an ideological side different from their own, opening them to listening more closely to the arguments being formed out of sympathy for a character they have invested in for years and years. All of this used the potential of a publisher-wide event to intensify debate and discussion about core issues, such as liberty, privacy, civil disobedience, and the power of the state, which could not be timelier in our current political context.

305

Managing Multiplicity in Superhero Comics

The *Civil War* series was largely successful at realizing all of these goals, generating large readerships, transforming the rules of the genre (through events such as Spider-Man's unmasking or Captain America's death, which will have a lasting impact), and raising political awareness—all through tapping the deep investments that fans have made in the Marvel universe. Like many previous attempts at transmedia storytelling, though, *Civil War* was most compelling in the middle—when fans could still speculate about what directions the story line would take, debate its core ideological issues, and argue about the protagonist's motivations—whereas the ending frustrated almost everyone. Despite the scale of the project, the final chapters felt abrupt and arbitrary. The wrap-up required a number of the heroes to act out of character (and thus may have done damage to all of the franchises involved). The weight of the book's political contention (especially when read through the lens of contemporary real-world politics) was opposed to registration, but in the end we are asked to believe that Iron Man and his allies were doing the right thing, that the end justified what many of us saw as unacceptable means. We can learn a tremendous amount about the aesthetics and reception of transmedia stories by dissecting what worked and what went wrong with *Civil War* (Austin 2007).

Ford: The permanence and long-term continuity may be one of the greatest strengths of these comic book universes, but some also see this history as limiting, especially as characters, and the continuity attempted to maintain their stories, stretch past hundreds of issues. How do generations of creative teams struggle with maintaining interest in these characters over time, and respecting and acknowledging the long histories of these characters while adding their own creative direction?

Jenkins: Since the 1960s, comics fans have demanded continuity across not only the installments of the same superhero narratives but also all of the superhero franchises published by the same company. Fans talk about the DC Universe and the Marvel Universe, seeing these stories as connected in complex ways. Publishers have become adept at distributing information relevant to one story line across multiple titles, increasing the number of books that the average fan reads in a given month. This system is worth exploring at a time when the most successful media franchises—*Lost*, for example—depend on complexity rather than simplicity (Mittell 2006). No matter how complicated the superhero narratives may feel to the uninitiated, they are not nearly complex enough to satisfy their most demanding readers.

Indeed, this is the most common complaint of those who don't read comics. They can't jump into any of the most established titles because they don't know the backstory taken for granted by their writers. I feel sympathy for this perspective. I have more or less given up ever understanding what goes on in the *X-Men* titles. The series simply has so many different characters and subplots that unless you grew up reading it, you are going to remain perpetually lost. Finding that balance between complexity and accessibility is a problem that television producers are just starting to confront. Comics don't always get it right. But there are several decades worth of experiments to study.

Moreover, the comics publishers face the challenge of keeping us engaged with these characters, when the sagas of Superman, Batman, Wonder Woman, and some of the others have had a shelf life that is double or triple that of the longest-running film or television franchises. Historically, writers assumed that their readers discovered comics, read for a few years, and then abandoned them at puberty. They could thus "refresh" the series every few years to reflect new cultural trends. On the lesser titles, this is still possible. We see, for example, radical revampings across the history of Aquaman that makes it impossible to situate that character into the DC continuity. But hard-core fans now remain true to the most popular characters for decades; most or all of the back issues are continuously reprinted. Writers have to avoid contradicting that complex and multigenerational continuity when it is clear that the collective intelligence of the fan community will always far outstrip the memory of any given creator.

Ford: This question of continuity has traditionally been an important one within comics, but initiatives over the past several years have moved comic book universes toward multiplicity—with several versions of the same comic book title running simultaneously. Of course, these two concepts are not mutually exclusive, so even as a comic book character may have alternate worlds running at the same time, continuity must still play a significant part. How do contemporary comic book creative teams manage and juxtapose multiplicity with continuity?

Jenkins: Television and film producers often express the need to maintain absolute fidelity to one definitive version of a media franchise, fearing audience confusion. Comics, on the other hand, are discovering that readers take great pleasure in encountering and comparing multiple versions of the same characters. There are multiple versions of, say, the Spider-Man character in publication at once: in some, Peter Parker is still a teen, while in others he is an adult; in some he is married to Mary Jane and living at the Avengers Mansion, while in others he is still courting her. Some emphasize action elements, and others stress romantic entanglements. But this is just the start. Further on the fringes, comics publishers experiment with books that are told from the perspective of long-term villains (stories centered on Lex Luthor, the Kingpin, and Doctor Doom have surfaced in recent years), stories that situate the protagonists in radically different time periods (see Paul Pope's *Batman Year 100*), experiments where the characters are reconceptualized from the ground up (DC ran a *Just Imagine* series a few years ago allowing longtime rival Stan Lee [2004] to develop totally different conceptualizations of Batman et al.), or characters are placed in different generic or historical contexts (the DC Elseworlds series). The closest we have seen in other media to this kind of radical repositioning of characters might be the Year One story in *Batman Begins* or the prehistory in *Smallville*, both of which have enjoyed considerable success.

Multiplicity seems to coexist with continuity at the present moment: fans are expected to know which interpretive frame should be applied to any given title. Marvel's Ultimate series was created to wipe the slate clean of continuity and reintroduce some of the core characters—Spider-Man, the Fantastic Four, the X-Men, and the Avengers—to a new generation. We are now more than a hundred issues into some of the Ultimate titles, and they have developed their own complex, parallel continuities. All along, much of the pleasure of reading them—for older fans—has come in seeing how the new authors revisit classic moments, sometimes taking radically different directions from the same choice point.

We might see Year One stories as a classic example of how comics publishers balance continuity with multiplicity. The Year One story takes us back to that time when the superhero was still struggling to define his or her identity, first encountering key allies or enemies. This returns us to a moment when the conventions surrounding a particular book were not as rigidly defined, and thus enables new kinds of experiences with these characters without destroying the core continuity. *JLA Year One* (Waid and Augustyn 1999), for example, plays around with the possibility of a romance between Black Canary and the Flash that would never be possible in the established comics because these two characters are within long-standing relationships. These Year One stories are often seen as ideal jumping-on points for new readers because they reintroduce core mythology; but they also reward the expertise of long-standing fans because they depend on our recognition of the later significance of these first-time meetings.

Ford: How has this sense of multiplicity impacted the development of alternate realities in superhero comics universes such as the Elseworlds?

Jenkins: There have long been "imaginary stories" within the superhero genre—stories understood by readers and writers alike as romps in alternative universes. Much like Vegas, what happens in an imaginary story stays in the imaginary story and doesn't impact the main continuity. Most such stories took the established continuity as their starting point—they operated in a similar world where one or two aspects of the character's relationships were altered to see what would happen. We have the pleasure of seeing how the world might have proceeded differently if Superman married Lois Lane, Batman became a father, Jimmy Olsen got a clue, and so forth. Increasingly, some of these once-unthinkable elements have found their way into the main continuity: Lex Luthor was elected president, Bruce Wayne became a fugitive, Gotham City suffered a cataclysm, and Clark and Lois finally tied the knot.

By contrast, the Elseworlds series goes meta, inviting us to think about the genre elements, the ideological logic, or the representational conventions that go into the construction of these worlds in the first place. Here's how DC describes the series on the back of every issue: "In Elseworlds, heroes are taken from their usual settings and put into strange times and places—some that have existed or might have existed and others that can't, couldn't, or shouldn't exist. The results are stories that make characters who are as familiar as yesterday seem as fresh as tomorrow."

The Elseworlds series is being produced for readers who have fully embraced the multiplicity principles we are talking about here.

When I first stumbled on the Elseworlds series, I was struck by how much it felt like a commercial version of the fan fiction I had studied—an attempt to radically rewrite the stories of familiar media icons in ways that could not fit comfortably within the rules and conventions of commercial entertainment. The first issue I bought was called *Superman's Metropolis* (Lofficier et al. 1997); it basically mashed up the Superman origin story with the plot and visual style of Fritz Lang's German expressionist classic. Rather than exploring other aspects of the DC continuity, this title examined what a German expressionist superhero story might have looked like. The ideal reader has dual competencies: able to recognize references to silent cinema and minor DC characters.

Something similar can be said of *Gotham by Gaslight* (Augustyn 2006), which puts Batman into a Victorian universe closer to the world of Sherlock Holmes. The *Red Son* series imagines what would happen if the space-

ship carrying the infant Kal-El had landed in Russia rather than the United States. As the back cover explains: "It's a bird! It's a plane! It's Superman! Strange visitor from another world who can change the course of mighty rivers, bend steel in his bare hands, and who, as the champion of the common worker, fights a never-ending battle for Stalin, Socialism, and the International expansion of the Warsaw Pact!" (Millar 2004).

In some cases, the Elseworlds are designed to introduce historical consciousness: *The Kents* (Ostrander, Truman, and Mandrake 2000) is basically a Western where Pa Kent's ancestors (who are only dubiously related to the adopted Clark) aid Kansas's move to statehood; *Evil's Might* (Chaykin and Tischman 2002) uses the Green Lantern to explore the Irish immigrant experience during the period depicted in *The Gangs of New York*. In other cases, these books embrace alternative genre traditions (as when Batman takes on the role of the Phantom of the Opera in the lushly romantic *Masques* (Grell 1997), or when the Joker and Batman are rival captains of pirate ships in "Leatherwing" [Dickson 1996]).

In some ways, then, the Elseworlds books represent the most radical edge of the multiplicity that is defining contemporary superhero comics—they literally rewrite everything about these characters, their worlds, and their genre conventions. Yet the Elseworlds books can also be deeply conservative. For one thing, they really are hermetically sealed from the main continuity: we can experiment this radically with the mythos because these things can't spill over. For another, many of these stories reaffirm the underlying logic to these characters. Batman would have behaved more or less the same in another time and place. Superman and Lex Luthor were destined to be archrivals. The more we change, the more it is clear that the world depicted in the normal continuity had to be what it is because of the core integrity of these characters.

Ford: This multiplicity has also affected comic books in terms of "pop cosmopolitanism," to borrow one of your phrases (Jenkins 2006d). How is globalization shaping the content of contemporary superhero comics?

Jenkins: The kinds of multiplicity we have discussed so far depend on the reader's heightened consciousness of authorial style, the series history (First Year stories) and generic traditions (Elseworlds stories). Multiplicity also plays on a growing awareness of the ways comics operate within a global marketplace. On the one hand, consumers around the world are often encountering these superheroes for the first time when they reach the big screen. And DC and Marvel are trying to move the comics into these newly opened markets. Something like *Spider-Man: India* (Kang 2005), produced by a South Asian team of writers and artists, represents a form of localization, which factors in the Indian consumer's interest in mythological elements (Green Goblin is a Hindu demon in this version) or incorporating in local geographic references (a Mumbai setting).

Yet these books often do better in the United States than elsewhere because of the U.S. fan's greater investment in the characters, but also because of the fan's growing global consciousness (what I call pop cosmopolitanism). These products can also be seen as part of the U.S. publisher's attempts to hold off foreign imports. By some accounts, manga outsell U.S. comics by as much as four to one in the U.S. market. Just check out the shelf at your local Borders or Barnes and Noble and see how much shelf space is devoted to Japanese comics. This is a unique situation for a U.S. media industry—to be outsold in its domestic market by a foreign competitor. The sting is even greater: manga is attracting younger readers who shun the comics specialty shops and reaching more female readers than comics have seen in three or four decades. The U.S. publishers crave a share of that readership and they are trying to attract it through collaborations with Asian artists. There have been other attempts to rework their superheroes as they might have been conceptualized within the genres that dominate manga production (the *Marvel Mangaverse* [Dunn 2002]). We can also see them taking a preemptive strike at competition from other Asian countries—China, India, and Korea—before they can get too much traction in our market. (Virgin recently created a comics publisher that specializes in adopting South Asian comics content for the U.S. market.)

Ford: In your chapter in Alan McKee's *Beautiful Things in Popular Culture*, you write about Brian Michael Bendis as "the best contemporary mainstream superhero comics writer" (Jenkins 2006a). In the process, you raise interesting points about creative control, the artist, and the writer. How do the industry, critics, and fans negotiate authorship in relation to comic book texts?

Jenkins: Contemporary mainstream comics are now defined as much around the personalities of the authors as they are around the personalities of their protagonists. This focus on authorship—at least among the most knowledgeable comics fans—has been hard-won. For decades, comics contained little or no information about their creators, though this did not prevent fans from distinguishing "the good duck artist" (as Carl Barks used to be called) from the rest of those working for Disney (Andrae 2006). As the comics collector market grew and the readership matured, identifying key creative personnel added economic value: collectors want the complete works of particular writers or artists, and that helped to fuel comics collecting and speculative investment. As their value increased in the marketplace, artists and authors pushed for greater creative control. There were various attempts to frame a comics creators' Bill of Rights; there was the push to create an independent comics market where creators could control the rights to their own books. Today, many of the best comics authors move back and forth between work-for-hire and creator-controlled, if not creator-owned, comics. Trying to hold on to top talent, DC and Marvel have began to carve out distinctive corners of their superhero universe for specific creators.

Spider-Man stories created by Bendis operate in a different conceptual space from those produced by J. Michael Straczynski, even though they are both technically under the same franchise. This becomes simply one of a series of factors pushing comics toward a logic of multiplicity.

Bendis is a good illustration of this process at work: he has moved from fairly experimental early work to the center of Marvel's publishing strategies for the past decade, becoming the company's most acclaimed and commercially successful author, even as he has kept a few creator-controlled titles in production. And yet, he has maintained some distinctive personality traits—especially surrounding his use of naturalistic and pop culture–inflected dialogue—which allow fans to recognize his work in all of these different contexts. Bendis is only one of many contemporary writers who are being encouraged to develop distinctive voices that encourage readers to follow them from the most commercial titles into some of the back corners of the publisher's rosters.

Ford: The history of superhero comics is tied up with genre play from the origins of many of these characters. What is your sense of "superhero comics" as a genre and genre play within superhero comics as a tradition? What are some of the ways contemporary comic book creators are playing with these concepts of genre within superhero comics?

Jenkins: One can debate whether superhero comics represent a coherent and self-contained genre (as we often discuss them), or whether they represent a character type that plays across a range of different genres. The superhero figure emerges from the different story types and genres of the pulp magazine tradition. Many early publishers of the first comic books drew on the full spectrum of genre traditions they inherited from the pulp magazines; the superhero genre itself took definition slowly, building off a range of related genre traditions—the detective story (Batman), the science fiction saga (the Fantastic Four), the spy genre (Iron Man and Black Widow), the soap opera (Spider-Man), horror (the Hulk), the supernatural (Doctor Strange), and so forth. We can see these older genre traditions as latent possibilities within the different superhero franchises. So all the comics need to do is introduce a secondary character—Black Panther, say, who introduces African and geopolitical themes into the mix—and the story lines are pulled into another genre direction altogether.

And the balance between comedy and melodrama in the Fantastic Four comics shifts from author to author.

This mixed-genre strategy allows these franchises to refresh themselves on a regular basis, but it is also one more force pushing toward multiplicity within comics publishing right now. Robert Kirkman, who writes one of the best contemporary horror comics, *The Walking Dead* (2006b), carried some of these genre elements over with him as he was recruited to work for Marvel. Kirkman's best contribution to mainstream comics so far was the invention of a kind of parallel world where the Marvel superheroes live as zombies. Kirkman is playing here with an inside joke: the company's fans have been called "Marvel Zombies" as far back as the 1960s. He is also creating a unique way of looking at the familiar characters: the covers of the *Marvel Zombies* (2006a) series are pastiches of classic Marvel covers given a particular macabre twist (restaging through rotting and dismembered bodies). The *Marvel Zombies* walk the edge between splatterpunk horror (full of grisly details) and black comedy (full of inside jokes.) These monstrous versions of the Marvel protagonists do things that would be inconceivable within continuity: Spider-Man munching on Aunt May, or Captain America accidentally cutting off the top of his head when his mighty shield boomerangs. This is a Marvel continuity—it exists in parallel with the characters and worlds we already know. In some issues of the *Fantastic Four* books, the zombies have spilled over into the main continuity, facing off with their more established counterparts. This series plays on the seemingly infinite capacity of superhero comics to absorb other genre traditions and the openness of readers to explore possibilities that would once have seemed out of bounds. While experimental in tone and controversial in content, these books have enjoyed enormous market success, with the initial miniseries spawning a succession of sequels, including one set that crosses over the *Marvel Zombies* and the *Evil Dead* franchise.

Ford: What do you believe will be the continued impact of superhero comics on your work, and do you have future projects planned that will deal with super-hero storyworlds explicitly?

Jenkins: I am still trying to figure that out. I write regularly about comics—superheroes and otherwise—through my blog at ⟨http://www.henryjenkins.org⟩. Comics are informing pretty much everything I do right now. They have become my preferred recreational medium. But I have certainly been giving serious thought to writing a book that would explore the various forms of multiplicity that are shaping contemporary comics publishing and suggest ways that they might inform our understanding of transmedia entertainment more generally. We will see.

References

Andrae, Thomas (2006). *Carl Barks and the Disney Comic Book: Unmasking the Myth of Modernity*. Jackson: University Press of Mississippi.

Augustyn, Brian (2006). *Batman: Gotham by Gaslight*. New York: DC Comics.

Austin, Alec (2007). "Expectations across Entertainment." Master's thesis, MIT.

Bukatman, Scott (2007). "Secret Identity Politics." Paper presented at Comics and the City: Urban Space in Print, Pictures, and Sequence, Berlin, June 7–9, 2007.

Chaykin, Howard, and David Tischman (2002). *Green Lantern: Evil's Might*. New York: DC Comics.

Clowes, Daniel (2004). "The Death-Ray." *Eightball*, no. 23.

Dickson, Chuck (1996). "Leatherwing." In *Superman/Batman: Alternate Histories*, 9–66. New York: DC Comics.

Dunn, Ben (2002). *Marvel Mangaverse*. New York: Marvel Comics.

Ford, Sam (2007). "As the World Turns in a Convergence Environment." Master's thesis, MIT. ⟨http://cms.mit.edu/research/theses/SamFord2007.pdf⟩.

Gordon, Ian (1998). *Comic Strips and Consumer Culture, 1890–1940*. Washington, DC: Smithsonian.

Green, Justin (1995). *Binky Brown Meets the Holy Virgin Mary*. Reprinted in *Green's Binky Brown Sampler*, 9–53. San Francisco: Last Gasp.

Grell, Mike (1997). *Batman: Masques*. New York: DC Comics.

Jenkins, Henry (2006a). "Best Contemporary Mainstream Superhero Comics Writer: Brian Michael Bendis." In *Beautiful Things in Popular Culture*, edited by Alan McKee, 15–32. London: Blackwell.

Jenkins, Henry (2006b). *Convergence Culture: Where Old and New Media Collide*. New York: New York University Press.

Jenkins, Henry (2006c). "Death-Defying Heroes." In *The Wow Climax: Tracing the Emotional Impact of Popular Culture*, 65–74. New York: New York University Press.

Jenkins, Henry (2006d). "Pop Cosmopolitanism." In *Fans, Bloggers, and Gamers: Exploring Participatory Culture*. New York: New York University Press.

Kang, Jeevan (2005). *Spider-Man: India*. New York: Marvel Comics.

Kirkman, Robert (2006a). *Marvel Zombies*. New York: Marvel Comics.

Kirkman, Robert (2006b). *The Walking Dead*. New York: Image Comics.

Lee, Stan (2004). *Just Imagine Stan Lee Creating the DC Universe*. New York: DC Comics.

Lofficier, Jean-Marc, Randy Lofficier, Roy Thomas, and Ted McKeever (1997). *Superman's Metropolis*. New York: DC Comics.

Millar, Mark (2004). *Superman: Red Son*. New York: DC Comics.

Millar, Mark (2007). *Civil War*. New York: Marvel Comics.

Mittell, Jason (2006). "Narrative Complexity in Contemporary Television." *Velvet Light Trap* 58, no. 1. ⟨http://muse.jhu.edu/journals/the_velvet_light_trap/v058/58.1mittell.html⟩.

Ostrander, John, Timothy Truman, and Tom Mandrake (2000). *Superman: The Kents*. New York: DC Comics.

Pope, Paul (2007). *Batman Year One Hundred*. New York: DC Comics.

Pustz, Matthew J. (2000). *Comic Book Culture: Fan Boys and True Believers*. Jackson: University Press of Mississippi.

Turkle, Sherry (ed.) (2007). *Evocative Objects: Things We Think With*. Cambridge, MA: MIT Press.

Various authors (2003). *Bizarro Comics*. New York: DC Comics.

Various authors (2005). *Project: Superior*. New York: AdHouse.

Various authors (2006). *Bizarro World*. New York: DC Comics.

Waid, Mark, and Brian Augustyn (1999). *JLA: Year One*. New York: DC Comics.

Ware, Chris (2004). *Jimmy Corrigan: The Smartest Kid on Earth*. New York: Jonathan Cape.

Ware, Chris (2006). *Acme Novelty Library*, no. 17. (November).

Whedon, Joss (2002). *Tales of the Slayers*. New York: Dark Horse.

Whedon, Joss (2003). *Fray*. New York: Dark Horse.

Whedon, Joss (2007–ongoing). *Buffy the Vampire Slayer*. New York: Dark Horse.

Whedon, Joss, Ben Edlund, Jane Espenson, and Brett Matthews (2004). *Tales of the Vampires*. New York: Dark Horse.

Whedon, Joss, Brett Matthews, and Will Conrad (2006). *Serenity: Those Left Behind*. New York: Dark Horse.

Managing Multiplicity in Superhero Comics

Lost and Long-Term Television Narrative

David Lavery

Prologue: *Life on Mars*

> Narratives that require that their viewers fill in crucial elements take...complexity to a new level. To follow the narrative, you aren't just asked to remember. You're asked to analyze. This is the difference between *intelligent shows, and shows that force you to be intelligent.* (italics added)
> —Steven Johnson, *Everything Bad Is Good for You*

In episode one of the BBC police drama *Life on Mars* (2006–2007), our hero, Sam Tyler, walking through a busy street in Manchester, England, the Who's "Baba O'Reilly" playing on the sound track, contemplates the show's central mystery: Is he really in 1973, teleported back in time after being hit by a car in 2006, finding himself trapped in a *Starsky and Hutch* world, or is he still in a coma, or possibly insane, in the series' present tense?[1]

Strolling alongside "CID Girl" Annie Cartwright, the only one in the past to whom he has confessed his "true" situation, Sam insists that a "mind can only invent so much detail" and announces his intention to walk—following the "Yellow Brick Road"—until he "can't think up any more faces or streets," until he escapes the "madness" in which he finds himself. It is a transcendent television moment, linking Sam with cinematic heirs like John Murdoch in *Dark City* (directed by Alex Proyas, 1998) and Truman Burbank in *The Truman Show* (directed by Peter Weir, 1998), both of whom succeed in surpassing the artifice of their constructed worlds.

At this point in the narrative—as I write, fourteen of sixteen episodes have aired—Sam has not walked out of the cave, though his "life on Mars," his existence in a world of the past that, as the opening voice-over of each episode tells us, might as well be "another planet," is of course full

of cracks—the Test Card Girl's performances, the many messages from radios and televisions and telephones that bombard him from his supposed future, his uncanny encounters with his mother, his father, and himself as a child—through which he can glimpse the nature of his delusion.

At the end of the first episode of the second series, Sam answers the phone only to learn something of great importance. The voice on the other end of the line—for the first time a message our hero receives isn't one way: the voice on the phone actually responds to Sam—tells him his mission is almost complete, and he must be patient and not disclose his situation to anyone. Soon, it assures him, he will be able to go home.

As a richly intertextual, open-ended, serialized, enigmatic mystery that may or may not be science fiction, the series calls to mind ABC's *Lost* (2004–).[2] But unlike its U.S. contemporary, now sixty-plus episodes in, *Mars*' life span will be short: the current series will be its last; Sam indeed will, as the voice on the phone tells him, be going home soon. The narrative skein, the "yellow brick road," of *Life on Mars* will not be long enough for Sam to outpace illusion, or in what amounts to the same perturbation, for the writing team of Matthew Graham, Ashley Pharaoh, and Tony Jordan to exhaust their powers of invention.

Typically British in duration, *Life on Mars* is *not*, for all its brilliance, a long-term television narrative (hereafter LTTVN).[3] On the other hand, the exemplary *Lost* may well be, in keeping with the tradition of the form, an LTTVN in trouble, though it, and LTTVNs in general, do lay claim to a British forebear. For LTTVNs in this "era of television complexity" (Mittell 2006b, 29), it would seem *the* precursor, the patriarch, with whom they must come to terms is the seemingly unlikely figure of a Victorian novelist.

Dickensian Television

Master Sergeant: Set of keys; one pocket watch, gold plated; one photograph; one book, *Our Mutual Friend.* Why didn't you bring that inside?

Desmond: To avoid temptation, brother. I've read everything Mr. Charles Dickens has ever written—every

27.1 Sam Tyler (John Simm) finds himself abruptly in 1973 in the first episode of *Life on Mars* (2006).

wonderful word. Every book except this one. I'm saving it so it will be the last thing I ever read before I die.
—"Live Together, Die Alone," *Lost*

Everywhere we turn these days, Charles Dickens seems an influential figure on and behind our television screens, and not because *Masterpiece Theatre* is rerunning one of its Dickensian adaptations or the BBC is airing its more recent *Bleak House* miniseries.[4] On *Lost*, one of his books, *Our Mutual Friend*, puts in an appearance and even becomes one of the island's literary denizens.[5] We also hear the prime movers of that enigmatic series speaking of Dickens as an admired ancestral serial storyteller. Tim Kring, the creator of "this year's *Lost*," the NBC series *Heroes*, likewise acknowledges Dickens as an inspiration.[6] The creator of *Buffy the Vampire Slayer*, *Angel*, and *Firefly*, Joss Whedon, names the Victorian novelist his favorite writer (Whedon 2000; Wilcox 2005). In "Scene in a Mall," a season four episode of the supremely literary *Gilmore Girls*, Lorelai explains (complete with an affected British accent) that while emailing, she likes to imagine Dickens writing letters, with his dog and pipe and "fancy feathered pen," exclaiming "Cheerio old bean!" and asking "How's Big Ben?"[7] A soap opera scholar draws on Dickens in order to illustrate the usefulness of reader-response criticism for understanding television.[8] A critic, contemplating HBO's *Deadwood*'s seriality, draws extensive comparisons with Dickens's work and, in particular, the novel *Lost*'s Desmond saved for last.[9]

And in a controversial book, a cognitive science popularizer argues that "mass culture," including television, reveals

not the end of the world as we know it, as its adversaries so often insist, but a "progressive story" in which our entertainments are "growing more sophisticated, demanding more cognitive engagement with each passing year" (Johnson 2005, xiii).[10] And of course he finds Dickens to be "the classic case of highbrow erudition matched with popular success, . . . who for a stretch of time in the middle of the nineteenth century was the most popular author writing in the English language, and also . . . the most innovative" (133), central to his considerations.

Lost as LTTVN

> *Carlton Cuse*:   [Dickens]'s getting a lot of play on *Lost*, isn't he?
>
> *Damon Lindelof*:   He is indeed. He's a favorite writer of ours. He wrote serialized stories just like we did. He was accused of making it up as he went along, just like we are.
>
> *Cuse*:   That's right. . . . He didn't even have a word processor.
> —Official *Lost* Podcast, October 3, 2006

The above exchange between the executive producers of *Lost* concerning serial fiction's founding father took place in fall 2006, just after the airing of the first of a six-episode miniseries that would launch its third season prior to a two-month, *Lost*less hiatus during which the network would launch (unsuccessfully) *Daybreak*, a new serial drama in *Lost*'s time slot.[11] Reruns of *Lost* in season two had not done well in the ratings (the show's avid fandom, it seemed, wanted only new shows to watch and found reruns a turnoff). Hence the new scheduling strategy: after the miniseries and the hiatus, the remainder of season three would air uninterrupted, a new episode each week, February to May.[12]

In Lindelof and Cuse's simpatico bond with the ancestral father of modern seriality—both are charged with the "serial crime" of narrative contrivance—we can detect a hint of the difficult situation in which *Lost*, for most of its first two seasons a fan (and media) darling, now finds itself. Despite *Lost*'s creators' insistence that they had, even at the outset, five years of stories to tell, they are now frequently accused of having lost their way. In a March 2007 interview on National Public Radio, Lindelof acknowledges that the beginning and the end of the show have never been a problem; the "middle," however, remains a challenge (Ashbrook 2007). When "Not in Portland" aired in February 2007, a month after the media was filled with stories that Lindelof and Cuse were in negotiation with ABC to set an agreed-on-in-advance duration for the series, three million viewers in the United States did not return with it.[13]

The challenges, the "peaks and valleys," as Marc Dolan (1994) deems them, facing the creators of today's long-term television narratives are unprecedented. Of indeterminate length (they may have multiseason runs or could be peremptorily terminated); the product of multiple authors (who may or may not be there for the duration); required to sustain suspense and audience interest not only within an episode but between episodes; susceptible to diegetic and nondiegetic, internal and external, artistic and commercial, industry and fan pressure; and obligated to supply temporary satisfactions and yet promise continuing dramatic developments—it is amazing that so many television series have maintained their excellence for so long.

Lost, in this regard, is especially miraculous. The story of its birth—its metamorphosis from banal "plane crashes on desert island" into fantastic, perplexing serial mystery—has been told elsewhere (Porter and Lavery 2007). No LTTVN has been more cognizant of its failed predecessors.[14] Yet none has taken larger risks, posed more challenges to its viewers or itself, or given us a greater "cognitive workout" (Johnson 2005, 77).

In its first season a *Lost* champion (and influence), Stephen King (2005) had pleaded in *Entertainment Weekly* for the series to end when it needed to end—when its story had naturally run its course, and not in subservience to "the Prime Network Directive: Thou Shalt Not Kill the Cash Cow." Lindelof and Cuse's seeming readiness to commit preemptive narrative euthanasia on their story in the hopes of maintaining quality of life for *Lost*'s remaining days would seem to indicate their acquiescence with King's entreaty.[15]

How did it come to this? Why have even successful LTTVNs become imperiled?

LTTVNs: A Brief History

> U.S. television has devoted increased attention in the past two decades to crafting and maintaining ever more complex narratives, a form of "world building" that has allowed for wholly new modes of narration and that suggests new forms of audience engagement.
> —Jeff Sconce, "What If?"

The LTTVNs at which the medium has excelled have taken on many forms in television's relatively short history.[16] Prime time was dominated until the 1960s by the *episodic series*, in which individual episodes stood for the most part alone, discrete, with the story line of any particular hour (or half hour) almost never escaping its own frame, seldom spilling over into episodes to come. "To a certain extent," Dolan (1994, 33) observes, "viewers of an episodic series watched in the secure knowledge that, whenever something drastic happened to a regular character like Lucy Ricardo or James T. Kirk in the middle of an episode, it would be reversed by the end of the episode and the characters would end up in the same general narrative situation that they began in." In such series, "narrative change is minimized."

Existing contemporaneously with the episodic series but ghettoized in the different mediacosmos of daytime television, *continuous serials* told stories that "were by contrast, deliberately left hanging at the end of each episode; nearly all plots initiated in a continuous serial were designed to be infinitely continued and extended" (ibid.).[17] Linear, as opposed to the episodic series' inherent circularity, the continuous serial makes narrative change its raison d'être.[18]

Once the continuous serial broke free from its daytime prison, migrating to prime time first in the form of nighttime soaps like *Dallas*, the *sequential series* was born.[19] Television schedules were quickly populated by shows that "had they been made a decade earlier, would almost certainly have been constructed in almost purely episodic terms," series that "could very often not be shown in an order other than their original one, since events in one episode clearly led to events in another" (ibid.).[20]

The last two decades of television have seen the spread of what Robin Nelson (2006, 82) terms *flexi-narratives*, a "hybrid mix of serial and series forms...mixtures of the series and the serial form, involving the closure of one story arc within an episode (like a series) but with other, ongoing story arcs involving the regular characters (like a serial)." The widespread appeal of the flexi-narrative is not difficult to understand, for it "maximises the pleasures of both regular viewers who watch from week to week and get hooked by the serial narratives and the occasional viewers who happen to tune into one episode seeking the satisfaction of narrative closure within that episode" (ibid.).

Drawing on the ideas of Umberto Eco's (1989) call in *The Open Work* for a "poetics of serial thought" and Gilles Deleuze's (1993) notion of individual narratives as incarnations of the "infinite work in progress," Angela Ndalianis (2004, 86–87) has described the advent of the latest generation of LTTVN as "neo-baroque." The defining trait of neo-baroque, she argues, is not, as is traditionally thought, the visual or the spectacular, but "lack of respect for the frame." The "madness of vision" of the neo-baroque manifests itself in narrative—in what Henri Focillon once deemed "an undulating continuity, where both beginning and end are carefully hidden."

Exemplary LTTVNs

This narrative system has permutated a wide variety of LTTVNs over the last three decades. *Dallas* (CBS, 1978–1991), a nighttime soap/sequential series, which gave us perhaps the mother of all cliff-hangers (1980's "Who Shot J. R.?"); begat the manically inventive and intertextual *St. Elsewhere* (NBC, 1982–1988), a medical drama episodic serial; which begat *Twin Peaks* (ABC, 1990–1991), a splendid postmodernist failure of an episodic serial, which peremptorily ended with its hero, Special Agent Dale Cooper, possessed by the supernatural parasitic being named BOB;[21] which begat *The X-Files* (FOX, 1993–2002), a flexi-narrative, which mixed monster-of-the-week episodes with a multiseason "mythology" arc about an alien invasion of Earth; which begat *Babylon 5* (PTEN, 1994–1997; TNT, 1998), an unprecedented series conceived in advance by J. Michael Straczynski, its mastermind, as a five-year narrative arc; which begat *Buffy the Vampire Slayer* (1997–2003), another flexi-narrative that each year combined a self-contained, season-

long story arc, in which the Scooby Gang battled and defeated a "Big Bad" threat, with multiseason character development and a repeated famous line in its final episode (Giles's "The earth is doomed") that had ended its first installment, 144 episodes and seven years before;[22] which begat *24* (FOX, 2001–), an episodic serial in which each season tells the "real time," "by the clock" story of one day in which Jack Bauer (Kiefer Sutherland) must save the world from enemies of the United States; which begat *The Sopranos* (HBO, 1999–2007), a flexi-narrative mob drama, which put similar demands on its audience's memory; and all the quality "not television" HBO dramas that followed in its wake, including series such as *Six Feet Under* (2000–2005), *The Wire* (2002–2008), and *Deadwood* (2004–2006).

Signs of the neo-baroque can be found throughout these series as the era of television complexity dawns and comes into its own. One season of *Dallas* (its eighth) turned out to be Pam Ewing's nightmare while her husband Bobby was in the shower (thus permitting Patrick Duffy, who had quit the series, to return after his character had seemingly been killed in the seventh season's finale). *St. Elsewhere's* final shot—a snow globe containing the series' eponymous hospital—suggested that its entire story had been the dream of an autistic boy. *Twin Peaks* regularly showed no respect for the frame: to cite but one example, after his landmark dream in the second episode, Agent Cooper impossibly snaps his fingers in sync with the extradiegetic score on the sound track. In a famous season three episode, "Jose Chung's 'From Outer Space,'" *The X-Files* self-consciously spoofed its own conventions, and in season seven's "Hollywood AD," agents Mulder and Scully serve as consultants for a hyperreflexive Hollywood version of their story. *Buffy the Vampire Slayer* often deconstructed itself, and season four's "Superstar" gave us an episode in which a minor character hijacks the diegesis, making himself, with the assistance of a magic spell, the show's hero. *The Sopranos* has regularly given dreams significant roles in the ongoing story; in season two's "Funhouse," for instance, a talking fish reveals to Tony the identity of the traitor in their midst.

But none of these series, for all their playfulness, for all their willingness to engage in what Sconce (2004, 107) calls "conjectural narrative," for all their self-conscious creation of verses primed for audience exploration and habitation, could be said to be so ardently neo-baroque as *Lost*.[23]

Lost as Neo-Baroque

Certainly, chief among *Lost*'s pleasures is the show's ability to create sincere emotional connections to characters who are immersed in an outlandish situation that, as of this writing, is unclassifiable as science fiction, paranormal mystery, or religious allegory, all constructed by an elaborate narrational structure far more complex than anything seen before in American television.

—Jason Mittell, "Narrative Complexity in Contemporary American Television"

The "madness of vision" of *Lost*, its "undulating continuity, where both beginning and end are carefully hidden," is both its blessing and its curse. Conscious as no LTTVN before it of the potential of the "collective intelligence" (Mittell 2006b, 31) of its hyperactivated audience, *Lost*'s creators have stoked the fires through a number of strategies.

At heart the story of a plane crash on a mysterious South Pacific island and the struggle of its survivors in its aftermath, *Lost* also opted to tell the backstories, in flashbacks, of each of its key characters, in which we learn, in a series saturated by dramatic irony, of the many ways in which the lives of Oceanic 815's perfect strangers have actually intersected before they boarded the plane ("*Lost* crosses," Lindelof and Cuse call them in a podcast).

Consciously modeled on/inspired by video games (Porter and Lavery 2007), *Lost* teases both the characters within the diegesis and the fandom with Easter eggs to reward their diligent obsession.[24] It even offers its own painstaking alternative reality game, the *Lost* Experience, from which discoveries made might be imported back into the narrative (see Mittell 2006a).[25]

Lost has also been wildly intertextual. Cinematic ancestors—disaster films, *Castaway*, *Jurassic Park*, and *The Wizard of Oz*—and television series—*The Adventures of Brisco County, Jr.*, *Buffy the Vampire Slayer*, *Gilligan's Island*, *Survivor*, *The Twilight Zone*, *Twin Peaks*, and *The X-Files*—have all influenced *Lost*'s themes, mise-en-scène, character-

27.2 *Lost*'s Desmond (Henry Ian Cusick) and his copy of *Our Mutual Friend* in the season 2 episode "Live Together, Die Alone" (2006).

ization, and narrative style. And no series has made actual texts more a part of its own text than *Lost*. I have already noted above Dickens's *Our Mutual Friend*'s guest appearance, but a list of book cameos would need to include as well Dostoyevsky's *The Brothers Karamazov*, Nabokov's *Laughter in the Dark*, Stephen King's *Carrie*, Stephen Hawking's *A Brief History of Time*, Richard Adams's *Watership Down*, Madeline L'Engle's *A Wrinkle in Time*, Judy Blume's *Are You There, God? It's Me, Margaret*, Walker Percy's *Lancelot*, Ayn Rand's *The Fountainhead* (the last five all read by Sawyer), Henry James's *The Turn of the Screw*, Ambrose Bierce's *An Occurrence at Owl Creek Bridge*, and most notoriously, Flann O'Brien's *The Third Policeman* (the last three found in the hatch), and *Bad Twin*, a *Lost* tie-in novel supposedly written by the late Oceanic 815 passenger Gary Troup. To paraphrase a question that Stanley Fish (1980) once famously asked in the title of a book: "Is there a text on this island?" Many, many texts is the answer, each of them inviting additional reading and rereading, research, and speculation.

And *Lost* piles mystery on mystery. What do Hurley's lottery-winning numbers (4, 8, 15, 16, 23, and 42) really mean? What is the monster that terrorizes the island? How/why was Rose's cancer cured and Locke made to walk again on the island? Who exactly are the Others? What is the significance of that four-toed statue? Why did a shark have a Dharma logo on its fin? Did that bird call out Hurley's name? Can Desmond see the future? Satisfying answers have yet to be provided.

At the beginning of the last decade audiences were so impatient to learn, finally, who killed Laura Palmer that they began to jump ship en masse after only eight episodes. Visitors to *Mars* have only been asked to wait for sixteen episodes to learn the truth about Sam's conundrum. The core *Lost* audience has to date waited patiently, enjoying speculation, engaging in their own "amateur narratology" (Mittell 2006b, 38) in lieu of answers, but many are now becoming increasingly irritated and annoyed.

"Tap dancing," Lindelof tells Tom Ashbrook (2007), using that nuanced, virtuoso, yet strangely immobile art as the vehicle for his metaphor, is interesting for a limited period but ultimately boring. And yet an LTTVN as ambitious as *Lost*—especially one as ambitious as *Lost*—must perform in place, must stay for a time in the diegetic middle, before it can head for the exits. Series like *Life on Mars* or *Grey's Anatomy* need not tap: a run of sixteen episodes does not require time in idle, nor for a different reason, does a "franchise" show (as Cuse deems *Grey's* [ibid.]) with no discernible end point.

The Future of LTTVNs

> We don't own *Lost*. While the network is committed to the show creatively, their job is to develop shows and hope that they become hits and then support them so that they stay hits. When we pitched *Lost*, part of it was convincing ABC we could keep it on the air for as long as they wanted. If we told them we could only do the show if we ended it after 100 episodes, they never would've agreed to it. And who could blame them?
> —Damon Lindelof, quoted in "When Stephen King Met the 'Lost' Boys"

Jason Mittell (2006b, 35) detects evidence in the sort of narrative moves *Lost* makes—he speaks of "narrative pyrotechnics" and "the narrative special effect"—of a growing tendency to "push the operational aesthetic to the foreground, calling attention to the constructed nature of the narration and asking us to marvel at how the writers pulled it off; often these instances forgo realism in exchange for a formally aware baroque quality in which we watch the pro-

cess of narration as a machine rather than engaging in its diegesis."

Mittell's choice of the word "machine" is perhaps unfortunate. The behind-the-scenes processes that fans of LTTVNs now follow as avidly as any 'shipper follows mating patterns on a favorite show are not being executed by a computer or ground out by an industry engine. They are born in the neurons of a Whedon, Lindelof, or Kring.

If Johnson and Mittell are right, if today's television viewer is becoming smarter—and must become smarter—to keep up with today's series, then it goes without saying that the creators of these series must be smarter too. Consider the hit series du jour, NBC's *Heroes* (2006–), created by Tim Kring, best known previously as the creator of *Crossing Jordan* (2001–), an episodic serial about a Boston medical examiner (played by Jill Hennessey). While *Lost*, whose inspiration Kring readily acknowledges, is indebted to video games, *Heroes* draws on the conventions and look of comic books. From its opening sequence—in which (unlike most television shows) we actually get to see the episode title and chapter number on-screen ("Chapter Seventeen: Company Man")—to Issac's paintings (rendered by comic book artist Tim Sale) to its episode-closing "To be continued," *Heroes* embraces the comic book aesthetic, splicing it together with the LTTVN. Will *Heroes* and *Lost* succeed where *Twin Peaks* and *The X-Files* failed?

For several years now I have been speaking of "rooting for television" (Lavery 2004), a scholar-fan tendency I find in myself as well as others (McKee 2007), to identify with television creativity, finding myself happy, thrilled in fact, at brilliant character developments, ingenious narratological developments, tour de force action sequences and special effects, delicious subversions of broadcasting codes, getting-away-with-murder wickedly risqué verbal and visual double entendres, and perfect, fertile, closureless endings. Mittell's notion of the foregrounding of operational aesthetics and mine are not in opposition. I root for creative achievement in all its forms and spheres, and nowhere does it amaze me more at present than in television's splendidly imaginative engagement with long-term television narratives. If *Lost* or *Heroes* pulls it off, makes it to the finish line with its integrity and sense of wonder still intact, still believing with Whedon (2001) that there is "a religion in narrative," and their audiences still reasonably devout, the human imagination will be the victor.

Postscript

Since I wrote the above, season two (and with it the series itself) of *Life on Mars*, season one of *Heroes*, and season three of *Lost* all came to an end. Prior to its final episode, word got out that *Mars* would have a sequel, *Ashes to Ashes*, set now in early 1980s' London, with Sam replaced by another cop from the future, a woman it was rumored (correctly) to be partnered with Gene Hunt.

So not surprisingly, the series finale was ambiguous, since it needed to require narrative space for *Ashes*. Sam returns to the present. The 1973 cop who had involved Sam in a conspiracy to expose Hunt's criminality turns out to be his twenty-first-century surgeon, and Sam awakens in the here and now in the middle of a life-and-death situation in the past. But he finds the present lifeless and soulless, and jumps off a roof, finding himself, of course, back in 1973, where he heroically saves his friends and pledges himself to Annie—"forever." In the episode's final moment, the Test Card Girl, who turns out to be a neighborhood child, looks directly into the camera, and then reaches out and turns off *our* sets, calling attention to *Mars*' exuberant televisuality.

Heroes ended its first season with a superficially extraordinary three-part episode that for the most part disappointed fans because of its predictability and heavy-handedness.

Lost's "Through the Looking Glass," however, saved its season and rewrote all of its, and LTTVN's, rules. In the final moment of a Jack-intensive episode (in which war breaks out between the castaways and the Others, Locke comes back from the grave, Charlie dies, and escape seems imminent, or if Ben speaks the truth, everyone will soon be killed by outside forces anxious to take possession of the island), we learn that what we thought were flashbacks are, in fact, flash-forwards to the present day, in which a suicidal Jack and a happily married, Volvo-driving Kate are off the island, back in Los Angeles. (We should have known

27.3 The little girl from the television (Harriet Rogers) switches us off in the final episode of *Life on Mars* (2007).

from the name of that funeral home, Hoffs/Drawlar—an anagram of "flash-forward"—that things were not what they seemed.)

The negotiations mentioned above for a predetermined end to *Lost* proved successful. Darlton (the new slash name fans have given *Damon* Lindelof and *Carlton* Cuse) secured an ABC commitment to three more dramatically shorter seasons (sixteen episodes instead of twenty-two or more), each starting, *24*-style, early in the new year, with the series ending in May 2010. In the meantime, *Lost* will combine, in an unprecented LTTVN experiment, flashbacks and flash-forwards, taking the neo-baroque to another level.

Notes

1. The British would say *The Sweeney* (1975–1978), a *Starsky and Hutch* contemporary, which aired on Thames Television.

2. *Mars* regularly evokes not just *The Sweeney* but a wide range of British television from the early 1970s. For example, in an episode in the first series, asked by Annie whether he has come to terms with his time traveling, Sam replies that he has "seen Doctor Who, who prescribed some pills," and in a second series episode Sam has a dream in which he has become one of the figures in the stop-motion children's show *Camberwick Green* (1966). On *Lost*'s problematic SFness, see Lavery (2007).

3. A few years ago, I appeared on the BBC's *Front Row* to speak with television critic Mark Lawson about the astonishing difference in length—the number of episodes per season/series; the total number of years on air—between British and U.S. series. Famously, John Cleese called a halt to the brilliant *Fawlty Towers* (1975, 1979) after only two series and twelve episodes (with a four-year hiatus between the series). *The Office* (2001–2003), Ricky Gervais's and Stephen Merchant's virtuoso comedy, ran for only twelve episodes (plus a two-part Christmas special); the U.S. version (2005–) has already aired forty-two. Even *Prime Suspect*, the groundbreaking police procedural starring Helen Mirren in the role of DCI/DCS Jane

Tennison and airing on ITV periodically from 1991 to 2006, only consisted of seven total "series" (really miniseries, none longer than 200 minutes), and its total running time of 1,525 minutes/25-plus hours hardly compares to any hour-long U.S. series with a five-year run (on average approximately 4,620 minutes, or 77 hours of narrative). (The narrative duration of Dick Wolf's *Law and Order* [NBC], on air continuously since 1990, is approximately 14,784 minutes/246-plus hours.)

British television does have its long-term narratives of course. Soap operas like *Coronation Street* (ITV, 1960–) and *EastEnders* (BBC1, 1985–), both less than a half hour per episode, like their U.S. contemporaries *General Hospital* (ABC, 1963–), *Days of Our Lives* (NBC, 1965–), and *One Life to Live* (ABC, 1968–)—all now hour dramas—have had exceedingly long hauls. And the incomparable, oft-reincarnated story of *Doctor Who* (BBC1, 1963–1989, 2005–) has now been told in 723 episodes (as of July 2006).

4. Although all the examples that follow are from the United States, Dickens, I should note, does put in an occasional television appearance in his native land. On a 2005 episode of *Doctor Who*, "The Unquiet Dead," Dickens assists the ninth Doctor and Rose's investigation of a zombie outbreak in 1869 Cardiff. My thanks to Leon Hunt for calling my attention to this episode.

5. *Lost*'s executive producers Damon Lindelof and Carlton Cuse got the idea for Desmond's choice of deathbed book from U.S. novelist John Irving, who has similar plans for Dickens's own last completed work. The first episode of *Lost*'s third season, "A Tale of Two Cities," also evokes Dickens.

6. In an interview with the Superhero Hype Web site, Kring admits that "one of the things that we talked about early on when doing a big saga was Charles Dickens. Most of his novels were written in one-chapter segments from the newspaper, so that's why they have that big serialized feel to them. He never knew quite where they were going. He was just writing them one chapter at a time. We're doing obviously a very similar thing here, so the art of the coincidence becomes a big part of the show, how people cross, how people's lives come together, and it's a very fun way to tell stories." (Kring 2006a)

7. Gilmorisms commonly make reference to Dickens. The following episodes all evoke/mention him: "The Lorelais' First Day at Chilton" (1.2), "Christopher Returns" (1.15), "Girls in Bikinis, Boys Doin' the Twist" (4.17), "Tippecanoe and Taylor, Too" (5.4), "Pulp Friction" (5.17), and "A House Is Not a Home" (5.22). Thanks to Scott Diffrient for the catalog.

8. "During Dickens's lifetime," Robert C. Allen (1987, 84) writes in a seminal essay called "Reader-Oriented Criticism and Television,"

> Most of his readers read his novels in weekly magazine installments, rather than as chapters of a single book. In fact, says [Wolfgang] Iser, they frequently reported enjoying the serialized version of *The Old Curiosity Shop* or *Martin Chuzzlewit* more than the same work as a book. Their heightened enjoyment was a result of the protensive tension occasioned by every textual gap (What's going to happen next?) being increased by the "strategic interruption" of the narrative at crucial moments, while the delay in satisfying the reader's curiosity was prolonged. By structuring the text around the gaps between installments and by making those gaps literally days in length, the serial novel supercharged the reader's imagination and made him or her a more active reader.

9. With *Our Mutual Friend*, "a serial fiction about seriality," in mind, Sean O'Sullivan (2006, 117) observes that

> Dickens understood how the serial, by its nature, exists at the crossroads of the old and the new. Unlike the stand-alone novel, or a feature film, which presents itself to us *in toto*, the serial offers constantly the promise of the new—the new installment next week or next month, often bringing with it a new plotline or character that will change everything. Given its leisurely unfolding, however, the serial also draws us into the past, as old characters appear and disappear, as old green covers pile up by our nightstand, or old episodes of a program burrow into our memory, creating a history commensurate with our lifespan, unlike the merely posited past and present of a text we can consume in a few hours or days. Every reading, or every watching, requires a reconnection of old and new, an iteration of past and present; and within a week or a month, what was new will get funneled into the old.

10. According to Steven Johnson (2005, 9), popular culture, video games, television, and movies are "getting more intellectually demanding, not less." He has particularly interesting things to say about LTTVNs, which as he demonstrates, "have also increased the cognitive work they demand from their audience, exercising the mind in ways that would have been unheard of thirty years" ago (62). Now "another kind of televised intelligence is on the rise," demanding the same kind of "mental faculties" normally associated with reading: "attention, patience, retention, the parsing of narrative threads" (64).

11. The following exchange, on a later official *Lost* podcast (November 6, 2006), is likewise noteworthy:

> *Cuse*: And Charles Dickens was also a wonderful inspiration, because here he was, writing these great, wonderful, sprawling, serialized books . . .
>
> *Lindelof*: Also, Dickens, the master of coincidence. Y'know. . . . His stories always hinged on the idea of interconnectedness . . . in a very strange and inexplicable way.

12. The usual gaps that punctuate a typical U.S. television season are the result of the necessities of production. It is impossible to have enough episodes for uninterrupted airing throughout a season "in the can" beginning in September of each year; the gaps allow a series' creative team, working under a time-intensive schedule, to eventually catch up, turning out the (customary) twenty-two episodes needed to complete a season. A series like *24*, which in keeping with its time-sensitive nature, now (since season four) airs all its episodes without interruption, can only do so by delaying the start of its season (or "day," in *24* parlance) until January, a strategy that was implemented by *Lost* for 2007 on.

13. In the Ashbrook interview, Cuse is quick to dispute the commonly held notion that *Lost*'s audience is dwindling rapidly, reminding listeners that the "Live Plus 7" numbers, which measure the number of people using such other platforms as Web streaming, TiVo, and iTunes downloads, show the drop in viewers to be much smaller than reported.

14. In an *Entertainment Weekly*–arranged colloquy (Jensen 2006) between *Lost*'s prime movers and their hero Stephen King, we find the following revealing exchange:

> *J. J. Abrams*: I'm saying that the reason [ABC] would want the show to continue isn't because they care about the characters.

It's because there's an economic model that says the show must go on for five years. *Twin Peaks* did not make them money. We love it because it was cool...

Carlton Cuse: ...but it was a cult thing.

Abrams: And a cult doesn't pay for it.

15. For more on the struggle between art and commerce on *Lost*, see Jensen (2006).

16. Here and throughout this section, I have relied extensively on the superb examinations of television's narrative forms by Marc Dolan and Jimmie Reeves. The work of John Ellis, Jane Feuer, John Tulloch, Manuel Alvarado, Robin Nelson, Jeffrey Sconce, and of course, Jason Mittell has also been influential.

17. Until the 1970s, Dolan (1994, 33) explains, "the episodic series and the continuous serial were almost inevitably segregated into separate areas of viewing time, the former dominating the prime time hours, the latter dominating the mornings and afternoons. This gave network television a remarkably split personality, with happy love affairs and marriages ruling by night, for example, and infidelity and divorce ruling by day."

18. As Tulloch and Alvarado (1983, ix) note, the continuous serial is "characterized by the fact that it can run infinitely and that it possesses multiple narrative strands which are introduced and concluded in different temporal periods."

19. Tulloch and Alvarado identify a closely related narrative form that they deem the *episodic serial*. Episodic serials exhibit continuity between episodes, but only for "a limited and specified number" (Tulloch and Alvarado 1983, ix). The subject of their study, *Doctor Who*, serves as an example, as does another famous British series, *The Prisoner*.

20. Horace Newcomb (1985) uses a different designation for essentially the same narrative manifestation: "cumulative narrative."

Like the traditional series and unlike the traditional "open-ended" serial, each installment of a cumulative narrative has a distinct beginning, middle, and end. However, unlike the traditional series and like the traditional serial, one episode's events can greatly affect later episodes. As Newcomb puts it, "Each week's program is distinct, yet each is grafted onto the body of the series, its characters' pasts." (Reeves, Rodgers, and Epstein 1996, 30)

21. Tulloch and Alvarado (1983, ix) raise the intriguing question "whether a continuous serial which 'fails'...becomes, through its failure, an episodic serial!" What does a failed episodic serial then become?

22. For more on *Buffy*'s narrative form, see Lavery (2002, 2003).

23. Sconce's (2004, 105–109) essay offers a superb overview of such playful experiments.

24. In the *On Point* NPR interview, Lindelof takes the metaphor one step further, reminding us that kids on a real Easter egg hunt sometimes find things the parents didn't actually hide. In other words: at least some of the discoveries of *Lost*'s voracious fandom were not intended (Ashbrook 2007).

25. In a startling admission, Lindelof and Cuse answering a listener question about why the revelations of the alternative reality game have not yet been incorporated into the narrative proper, acknowledge that the Web seems to them the perfect venue for disseminating information about the series' deep mythology for the "hard-core fan." For the characters on the island, fighting for survival, are not concerned with the identity of Alvar Hanso or the Dharma Initiative (Ashbrook 2007).

References

Adams, Guy, and Lee Thompson (2006). Life on Mars: *The Official Companion*. New York: Pocket Books.

Allen, Robert C. (1987). "Reader-Oriented Criticism and Television." In *Channels of Discourse: Television and Contemporary Criticism*. Chapel Hill: University of North Carolina Press.

Ashbroook, Tom (2007). "ABC's 'Lost' TV Drama" (interview with Carlton Cuse and Damon Lindelof). *On Point*. WBUR Boston, March 28. ⟨http://www.onpointradio.org/shows/2007/03/20070328_b_main.asp⟩.

Deleuze, Gilles (1993). *The Fold: Leibniz and the Baroque,* translated by Tom Conley. Minneapolis: University of Minnesota Press.

Dolan, Marc (1994). "The Peaks and Valleys of Serial Creativity: What Happened to/on *Twin Peaks*." In *Full of Secrets: Critical Approaches to* Twin Peaks, edited by David Lavery, 30–50. Detroit: Wayne State University Press.

Eco, Umberto (1989). *The Open Work*. Cambridge, MA: Harvard University Press.

Feuer, Jane (1986). "Narrative Form in American Network Television." In *High Theory, Low Culture: Analysing Popular Television and Film*, edited by Colin McCabe, 101–114. Manchester: University of Manchester Press.

Fish, Stanley E. (1980). *Is There a Text in This Class? The Authority of Interpretive Communities*. Cambridge, MA: Harvard University Press.

Jensen, Jeff (2006). "When Stephen King Met the 'Lost' Boys." *Entertainment Weekly* 1, September. ⟨http://www.ew.com/ew/article/0,,1562722,00.html⟩.

Johnson, Steven (2005). *Everything Bad Is Good for You: How Today's Popular Culture Is Actually Making Us Smarter*. New York: Riverhead Books.

King, Stephen (2005). *"Lost's Soul." Entertainment Weekly* 9, September.

Kring, Tim (2006a). Interview (with Edward Douglas). Superhero Hype. (August 30). ⟨http://www.superherohype.com/news.php?id=4685⟩.

Kring, Tim (2006b). Interview with Josh Weiland." Comic Reel. (September 21). ⟨http://www.comicbookresources.com/?page=article&id=8146⟩

Lavery, David (2002). "A Religion in Narrative: Joss Whedon and Television Creativity." *Slayage: The Online International Journal of Buffy Studies* 7. ⟨http://www.slayage.tv/essays/slayage7/Lavery.htm⟩.

Lavery, David (2003). "Apocalyptic Apocalypses: The Narrative Eschatology of *Buffy the Vampire Slayer*." *Slayage: The Online International Journal of Buffy Studies* 9. ⟨http://www.slayage.tv/essays/slayage9/Lavery.htm⟩.

Lavery, David (2004). "'I Only Had a Week': TV Creativity and Quality Television." Keynote address at Contemporary American Quality Television: An International Conference, Trinity College, Dublin.

Lavery, David (2007). "The Island's Greatest Mystery: Is *Lost* Science Fiction?" In *The Essential Science Fictional Television Reader*, edited by J. P. Telotte. Lexington: University Press of Kentucky.

Lindelof, Damon (2006). Heroic Origins: An Interview with Tim Kring." 9th Wonders. ⟨http://www.9thwonders.com/interviews/tim.php⟩.

McKee, Alan (2007). "Why Do I Love Television So Much?" *Flow* 5, no. 9. ⟨http://flowtv.org/?p=107⟩.

Mittell, Jason (2006a). "*Lost* in an Alternative Reality." *Flow* 4, no. 7. ⟨http://jot.communication.utexas.edu/flow/?jot=view&id=1927⟩.

Mittell, Jason (2006b). "Narrative Complexity in Contemporary American Television." *Velvet Light Trap* 58, 29–40.

Ndalianis, Angela (2004). *Neo-Baroque Aesthetics and Contemporary Entertainment*. Cambridge, MA: MIT Press.

Nadalianis, Angela (2005). "Television and the Neo-Baroque." In *The Contemporary Television Series*, edited by Michael Hammond and Lucy Mazdon, 83–101. Edinburgh: Edinburgh University Press.

Nelson, Robin (2006). "Analysing TV Fiction: How to Study Television Drama." In *Tele-Visions: An Introduction to Studying Television*, edited by Glen Creeber, 74–86. London: BFI.

Newcomb, Horace (1985). "*Magnum*: The Champagne of TV." *Channels of Communication* (May–June): 23–26.

O'Sullivan, Sean (2006). "Old, New, Borrowed, Blue: *Deadwood* and Serial Fiction." In *Reading* Deadwood, edited by David Lavery, 115–129. London: I. B. Tauris.

Porter, Lynnette, and David Lavery (2007). *Unlocking the Meaning of* Lost: *An Unauthorized Guide*. 2nd ed. Napierville, IL: Sourcebooks.

Reeves, Jimmie L., Mark C. Rodgers, and Michael Epstein (1996). "Re-Writing Popularity: The Cult Files." In *Deny All Knowledge: Reading* The X-Files, edited by David Lavery, Angela Hague, and Maria Cartwright, 22–35. Syracuse, NY: Syracuse University Press.

Sconce, Jeffrey (2004). "What If?: Charting Television's New Textual Boundaries." In *Television after TV: Essays on a Medium in Transition*, edited by Lynn Spigel and Jan Olsson, 93–112. Durham, NC: Duke University Press.

Tulloch, John, and Manuel Alvarado (1983). Doctor Who: *The Unfolding Text*. London: Macmillan Press.

Whedon, Joss (2000). Interview with David Bianculli. *Fresh Air*, May 9. ⟨http://www.npr.org/templates/story/story.php?storyId=835108⟩.

Whedon, Joss (2001). "Interview with Tasha Robinson." *Onion AV Club*, September 5. ⟨http://www.avclub.com/content/node/24240⟩.

Whedon, Joss (2002). Interview. In *The Tenacity of the Cockroach: Conversations with Entertainment's Most Enduring Outsiders*, edited by Stephen Thompson, 369–377. New York: Three Rivers Press.

Wilcox, Rhonda V. (2005). *Why Buffy Matters: The Art of Buffy the Vampire Slayer*. London: I. B. Tauris.

David Lavery

Reconnoitering the Rim: Thoughts on *Deadwood* and Third Seasons

Sean O'Sullivan

Narrative, we might say, comprises three elements: the possible, the necessary, and the possible disguised as the necessary. The possible offers the originating conditions for watching or reading a story, the promise of infinite directions in which a particular character or situation might develop. The possible is particularly crucial to serial narrative, which by its structures of storytelling and necessities of production must keep the possible omnipresent, and constantly changing.

The HBO series *Deadwood* (2004–2006) makes the possible its thematic core and essential premises, as it begins with the settlement of a camp in the Black Hills of South Dakota at the onset of the 1876 gold rush. The possible is the promise of Deadwood to its settlers, the desired story of sudden wealth, material transformation, or more simply beginning anew, shedding the fixed conditions of an earlier existence. Such a narrative of transformation encloses not only prospectors like the veteran, rough-hewn Ellsworth or the neophyte, city slicker Brom Garret but practical businessmen like Seth Bullock and Sol Star, who see in Deadwood not so much possibility-as-magic but possibility-as-investment—a sound enactment of the narrative of what-might-be—through the establishment of a hardware store for miners, the possibility of transformation rendered through hip boots and pickaxes.

The genre of the Western, of course, uses a certain version of the possible as its template—the sense of a world stripped of certainty, where each day offers the promise of unknowable and perilous adventure, where artful improvisation is necessary for survival. *Deadwood*, through its creator David Milch, takes that rubric of artful improvisation be-yond the one-on-one clashes between civilization and the wild, or between the known and unknown, which the Western puts front and center. The series' main interest lies in the creation of community, or the organization of the possible, the metamorphosis, from the mud of the main thoroughfare that is the town's chief medium, of a scattering of possibilities (of people, ambitions, and ideas) into a collection of possibilities.

The second element of narrative, the necessary, must operate in possibility's wake. We want, as viewers and readers, to enter a world suffused with the possible, so that we can guess, or be mystified by, what a certain character might do, what direction the plot may take, or simply what the tease of another installment might contain. But if the possible, or certain aspects of the possible in the particular world of the narrative, do not assume the character of the necessary—a direction or resolution toward which the narrative must be tending—then the narrative remains caught in the sphere of potential.

One immediately recognizable avatar of the necessary, especially in serial drama, is sexual tension between two central characters. Here we have a basic illustration of the give-and-take between possible and necessary: an unconsummated attraction, both in life and art, represents the thrill of the possible, the imagined collision of the speculative and the physical, but oriented toward a particular, necessary goal. The aim of a serial drama, in respect to sexual tension, is to stay in the realm of the possible for as long as feasible, all the while recognizing that this realm of the possible must hint at the necessity of resolution.

The first season of *Deadwood* dutifully offers such a scenario in the figures of Bullock, the sheriff turned hardware retailer turned sheriff, and Alma Garret, widow of the neophyte prospector Brom Garret. They meet in the fifth episode, are hampered by familiar narrative impediments (he is married, and she is supposedly in mourning), and then consummate their affections in the twelfth and final episode of the year.

But the series shows itself alert to the necessary not just in terms of basic strategies (sex) for keeping viewers interested but as a force both to be acknowledged and feared. That force is represented, in part, by Yankton, the capital of the Dakota Territory that exists in *Deadwood*'s narrative infrastructure as the incarnation of the necessary, the camp's eventual transition from infinite possibility to the grid of laws and conventions.

Al Swearengen, saloon keeper and presiding spirit of the camp, practices the improvisational methods of the possible while recognizing the necessity of the necessary. Late in the first season, when Swearengen and oleaginous hotelier E. B. Farnum are parceling out bribes for Yankton politicians, Farnum complains that the ad hoc government the camp's fathers have created may have to fund projects other than the administration of graft, such as an infirmary and a garbage dump. Swearengen shows himself attuned to narrative's accommodation of the necessary with a breezy acknowledgment: "That type shit's inevitable" ("Mr. Wu," 1.10).

The programmed clash between possible and necessary will continue to drive the series until it reaches a terrifying embodiment in the third season in the figure of George Hearst. His success as a miner derives precisely from his nose for the possible, as the "Boy the Earth Talks To" (2.12), who is able to address the mishmash of potential embedded in an array of claims. Hearst sees himself as a narrative both fabulously successful and utterly predictable.

The fixed mechanics of that narrative are apparent midway through the third season, when Cy Tolliver, a rival saloon keeper and whoremonger to Swearengen, arrives to take direction from Hearst in the plot to induce Alma Garret to sell the property bought by her late husband, the only property standing between Hearst and his total ownership of the camp. "My instructions," Hearst tells Tolliver, "would have to do with bringing the inevitable about." Now the inevitable refers not to the basic elements of solidified community—an infirmary or a garbage dump— but to one man's absorption of a narrative requirement into himself.

Just as *Deadwood* thematizes the possible as a subject and danger in its first season, the series thematizes the necessary as a subject and danger in its third season. Hearst's ingestion of the camp offers a kind of critique of a viewer's desire for the necessary, for shape, for amalgamation and consolidation.

And here we reach that third narrative element, the possible disguised as the necessary, the element most critical to serial drama in particular. I should pause here, and distinguish between that vein of narrative known as soap opera and the vein of narrative that goes by the name of *Deadwood*, or *The Sopranos*, or *Six Feet Under*.

The most relevant distinction has nothing to do with perceptions of "quality" or degrees of melodrama; it has everything to do with the fact that soap opera—and here I mean those serials that run and run on daytime television, or in comic strips of the daily newspaper—operates outside the requirement of conclusion. Beyond the rhythm of the hour or the week, which imposes some kind of shape to what might otherwise be molten plot, soap opera traffics in the possible and the necessary, but with no need to synthesize those forces into destination or result. There is no such thing as the end of a "season" of *All My Children*, and certainly not of the overall arc of *All My Children* itself. *All My Children* may stop at some point, but no one will interpret such a cessation as anything other than an unforeseen exhaustion on the part of the makers or viewers, or both. What *All My Children* lacks is any sense of "the between."

As I have argued elsewhere, in the context of *Deadwood*'s second season, close-ended serial drama has, since its rise in popularity at the hands, initially, of Charles Dickens, negotiated between the old and new, between the compact of earlier episodes and the promise of new ones, and we navigate such a territory conscious that we are between one thing and another, between a beginning and an end (O'Sullivan 2006, 121).

In Dickens's case, this beginning and end frequently were expressed in terms of twenty monthly installments, beginning with *The Pickwick Papers* in 1836. That template operated vestigially even with his weekly serials (such as *A Tale of Two Cities* and *Great Expectations*), where the total number of episodes was not advertised in advance but where the assurance of imminent terminus—the knowledge that the end would arrive within a few months of the beginning—shaped the readers' response to the narrative.

I would suggest here that another way of thinking about the "between" is as the possible disguised as the necessary. By this I mean the way in which, out of the array of possible stories and interests presented in the start-up operations of a narrative, some get selected and acquire the force of necessity without having ever really been necessary all along. This force of necessity accrues from the existence of a terminus, which asks that the possible acquire some short of shape over the course of the regular production of episodes.

I exclude from the possible disguised as the necessary such story lines as the one pursued by Bullock and Alma, since they are introduced to the narrative from the beginning as love interests, as an inevitable necessity of the drama—an inevitability underscored by the facts of the actors themselves: their physical attractiveness, degree of fame (especially in regard to other actors in the series), and prominent position in the opening credits. I mean then the specific directions and consequences—the ends that look necessary only in retrospect—that we might not automatically expect, given the field of possibilities at the start of a serial drama.

To watch such a drama is to want two things at the same time; namely, a multiplication of potential directions and consequences—to keep us guessing and active, eager for the terminus—and a deferral of those potential directions and consequences—to delay the inevitable disappointment of selection, the extinguishment of the imagined in favor of the actual.

To some degree, the possible disguised as the necessary haunts the very making of serial drama, since frequently the authors do not know how exactly the narrative will end until that end is reached, or, even if some plot resolutions have been predetermined, the specific execution of the narrative, the details that make it more than a series of arcs and arrows, invariably occurs midstream. Again, Dickens's career offers a spectrum of models, from the wholly improvised, barely sustained narrative of *The Pickwick Papers* to the carefully mapped-out trajectories of his last novels, which were nevertheless always vulnerable to alterations and redirections.

Milch's scrambling approach to *Deadwood* offers an extreme example within the schedule-driven world of cinema and television of the last-minute style; as Sean Bridgers, who played Swearengen's lackey Johnny Burns, says, "Every

actor who works with David struggles with the fact that you have to have faith in the way he works, that you might not get your lines until you are about to shoot the scene.... When it feels like there's a gap in the story, we know that David will put something in there" (Milch 2006, 160).

Milch's strategy emphasizes dwelling in the realm of the possible for as long as he can, fending off the necessity of finished dialogue, images, and plot threads—an approach that illustrates just how contingent its narrative circumstances are—so that what in hindsight appears to be the fixed trajectory of a character (what she or he did, or said, or chose on-screen in front of the viewer) retains the aspect of being one possibility among many. The disguise of the necessary looks deliberately thin in cases like these.

As always with *Deadwood*, things that are true of its narrative infrastructure are also true of its subjects and events. Milch provides an illustration of this in discussing the ritual of canned peaches, which Swearengen offers, to the mystification of his fellows, at the camp's first semiofficial meeting of elders ("Plague," 1.6) and then at subsequent gatherings:

> Now it happens that Swearengen remembers that food was served at a meeting he once saw. He has some canned peaches, and so he puts the peaches out on the table. And in the electrical force field created within that meeting, the presence of the peaches has a significance as a gesture. The symbol becomes separate from the specific moment that generated it. So from then on, you don't fuck with the peaches.... Watching these accidental accretions of meaning, we realize how provisional order is, how mystical and superstitious it is. (Milch 2006, 137)

Milch's sense of the "electrical force field"—that is, the combination of aleatory and planned elements that shape all of experience—and the provisional nature of order argues for a kind of resistance to narrative itself, or at least a resistance to an interpretation of narrative where the inevitable effaces the possible.[1]

The popular convention, used often to explain narrative circumstances of real life, that "everything happens for a reason," would seem to represent the exact opposite of

Milch's attitude toward narrative, where everything happens for no single reason at all, or for a collision of reasons that is beyond any being's control. Hence character George Hearst's role as an anti-Milch, as an author of events who might indeed agree that everything happens for a reason—the reason, in this case, being Hearst, the god of the totalizing narrative system of capital.[2]

For the remainder of this argument, I would like to examine the intersections of the possible, the necessary, and the possible disguised as the necessary in light of the third season of *Deadwood*—but also in light of third seasons more generally. The topic of this collection is vast narratives, and I would suggest that the third season of a television serial marks the point when that narrative becomes vast, when it threatens to sprawl out beyond what we might have conceived of as the recognized and perhaps necessary limits of that narrative.

In conceptual terms, we can see the scheme of this evolution. The first season of a serial creates its universe, populates it with possibilities, and frequently reaches a crescendo of necessary storytelling termini, while keeping other storytelling possibilities open. The second season inevitably operates as a sequel, speaking in direct dialogue with the first season—as either an explicit continuation, explicit reversal, or some combination thereof. This dialectic tension between the old and the new, that which makes a serial world familiar to us, and those foreign elements that are introduced into that serial world, is explicitly explored in *Deadwood*'s second season (O'Sullivan 2006, 119). However fraught that dialectic might become, its very presence suggests a kind of continuity, an explicit connection that marries the first two seasons.

We might look to two of *Deadwood*'s sister narratives, under the HBO umbrella, for evidence of such connection. *The Sopranos* offered linkage within the narrative frame, as the story of Tony Soprano's betrayal by his best friend, Pussy Bonpensiero, bridges the gap, moving from open-ended question at the end of season one to the final narrative terminus of season two. *Six Feet Under* offered linkage within the frame of viewership, as HBO announced, before the first episode aired in June 2001, that the network had decided to order a second season, instantly providing for the audience a narrative space that would extend through twenty-six, instead of only thirteen, episodes.

When faced with two seasons, we might feel that we can still contain the shape of the series, to enclose it either as a collective experience extending over little more than a year of our lives, or as a tennis match between one narrative cluster and another.

Three, though, is a crowd. Since television serials that have survived as long as three seasons threaten to survive considerably longer—in part due to economic reasons involving syndication and built-in audiences for DVD sales—viewers may realize just how deep their commitment may have to be, not only to keep the series' history in their heads, but to prepare for a narrative future of uncertain length. We have moved past sequel and into franchise, a franchise predicated not on a single biennial update—as may be typical for a series of novels or feature films—but on a weekly schedule, accumulating gradually to many more hours than can easily be squeezed simultaneously within a continuous spectatorial perspective.

While it would be impossible to pinpoint exactly when we lose containment, either in terms of an individual series or in terms of individual viewers of individual series, third seasons would seem likely candidates for such an event. This potential trauma of narrative consumption may explain the predictable declarations, around this time in the life cycle of a series, that a show has jumped the shark, loosely defined as the point where it has stopped being itself—stopped behaving as the essential, the true, and the faithful version of the show that each viewer contains in his or her mind—or as the point where it starts to parody itself by exaggerating its eccentricities, or repeating behavioral or narrative tendencies beyond some acceptable limit.

While it is difficult to calculate the precise validity of such laments, it is less difficult to posit that there is some correspondence between third seasons and the laments' volume and violence.[3] Partly, we can attribute this phenomenon to the weight of nostalgia, which kicks in once we are distanced enough in time and have fetishized enough memories to provide a powerful counterweight to the latest generation of material. On a broader scale, this postlapsarian backlash once again finds a parallel in Dickens, since

Pickwick—a picaresque anomaly in a career defined by fictions of grand architecture—was always his most beloved novel, and since the public readings he gave at the end of his life, in deference to the assumed inclinations of his audience, were never drawn from his most recent work (Collins 1975, lxvi).[4]

The violation of norms in the third season may not simply be a matter of spectatorial perception but rather a manifest rupture within the narrative, such as the death of Livia in *The Sopranos* or the absence, for the first four episodes, of Brenda in *Six Feet Under*.[5] Or the third season may offer a violation-in-waiting, like the famous missing Russian from the "Pine Barrens" episode of *The Sopranos*, whose complete disappearance from the narrative became emblematic, many seasons later, of the series' persistent rejection of the possible disguised as the necessary.

The existence of a third season means that the first season—the beloved object—is now officially outnumbered, and will get increasingly outnumbered as the seasons increase; so the beloved object must either be rescued from the increasing sprawl (by mourning the first season's diminishment), or the sprawl must be allowed to recontextualize the meanings—the possibilities and necessities—of the first season.

The peculiar situation of *Deadwood* is that its third season does not quite fit the model adumbrated above in that this season represents not simply the transformation from sequel to franchise but also the cessation of the series; in a reversal of the immediate-renewal scenario of *Six Feet Under*, *Deadwood*'s cancellation was announced before the third season began.[6] So instead of a sense of expansion stretching to a distant point on the horizon, the third season arrived suffused with the spirit of elegy. And yet everyone associated with the show during the making of that third season assumed that the show was closer to the middle of its run than to its end.

Milch, in *Deadwood: Stories of the Black Hills*, a book written during but released subsequent to the third season, explains that Tolliver "will wind up becoming, over the course of five seasons, the great philanthropist and feminist of Deadwood" (2006, 91), and that "the true test for Trixie is gonna come when Star proposes to her" (111)—a proposal still in the offing at the end of the last season. The show's sudden death complicates our response to its narrative, thwarting our impulse to see the possible disguised as the necessary, to read this season as the inevitable, as an outcome, even as, faced with cessation, we cannot resist such an impulse.

The third season, then, is both a between point and an end point, an oxymoron italicized by the season's reluctance to conclude. Both the first and second seasons of *Deadwood* finished with some version of comic conclusion. In the first case, this conclusion arrives not simply through the long-delayed sexual congress of Alma and Bullock but a kind of marriage between Bullock and Swearengen—who reach a long-delayed understanding of sorts, a fusing of interests— and the spectacle of grumpy Doc Cochran and Jewel "the gimp" dancing merrily in Swearengen's Gem Saloon. In the second case, we have a literal matrimony, the wedding of convenience between Alma and Ellsworth, designed to legitimize her pregnancy—a scene that for all its fictions, gives us another moment of festival, of the camp asserting its existence through rituals of courtship and camaraderie, and once more the spectacle of Cochran and Jewel dancing awkwardly but happily.

The iteration of the Cochran-Jewel pairing—two characters who normally have little business with one another— serves to bring together not only scattered inhabitants of the community but also the first two seasons, to affirm a kind of narrative unity. In both cases, Swearengen looks benevolently on from a balcony, containing, we might say, the narrative below him.

The third season, by stark contrast, concludes with Swearengen scrubbing blood off the floor of his office, alone, talking to himself, between a coffin and a safe. This is, at the very least, a violation of the norm established by *Deadwood* in its first two seasons—coming-together replaced by isolation—and most certainly a violation of any kind of protocol of valediction. This is a rejection of containment, by any standards. It's evidence of a third season looking for trouble rather than for solace.

To assist our investigation of the looking for trouble that we might say describes the ending and the business of the third season, we might look back to the early stages of the first season, and one of *Deadwood*'s initial moments of trouble searching—certainly, the first moment of trouble searching involving a character who might resemble a member of the audience of *Deadwood*. That character is Brom Garret, the arrogant, clueless New Yorker who has come to Deadwood with his wife for what she calls "an adventure," a brush with the forbidden and the strange—much as spectators in the twenty-first century, wholly unfamiliar with the realities of Deadwood and largely familiar with the urban, cultured, meekly thrill-seeking milieu of Brom, watch *Deadwood* for a brush with the forbidden and the strange.[7]

Brom realizes that he has been duped into buying a claim that all the colluding parties deem to be worthless, at the cost of $20,000. He confronts Swearengen, the chief colluder, and threatens to bring the Pinkertons to town unless restitution is made. Swearengen asks Dan Dority—his henchman, who has been assisting Brom in his efforts—if Brom has asked Dan to "reconnoiter the rims" of the claim. Brom, like all newcomers to Deadwood the camp, and like all newcomers to *Deadwood* the narrative, is confronted with a term or a construction of language that he doesn't understand but that seems readily understood by the natives, or at least by Swearengen.

> *Garret*: What are you talking about, specifically?
>
> *Swearengen*: The gold you found washed down from somewhere—that's the law of gravity. And your claim runs rim to rim the width of the fucking gulch. So the original deposit, the gold you found, washed down from is likely, on your claim, above, near one of the rims.
>
> *Garret*: And that's what you feel I should reconnoiter?
>
> *Swearengen*: First place the Pinkertons would look. Unless I'm fucking wrong.
> ("Reconnoitering the Rim," 1.3)

"Reconnoitering the rim," a phrase that also provides the title of the episode, is an archetypal *Deadwood* neologism, a collection of words that may or may not mean something, yet that when assembled, create an electric force field, an accretion of meaning, that gives it the status of epiphany.

28.1 Brom and Alma Garrett (Timothy Omundson and Molly Parker) in "Reconnoitering the Rim."

Brom returns to Alma and tells her of his plan to reconnoiter the rim of the gulch with Dority, since this is the kind of "due diligence" (another near-meaningless phrase, from another field of language making) that his father would require. When Brom and Dority arrive at the rim at night, Dority throws Brom to his death, following Swearengen's instructions—only to discover that the site of Brom's landing also proves the immense value of the claim.

I take this incident as a fable illustrating the perils of mapping this territory as a narrative space, specifically the perils of sketching that space that runs rim to rim the width of the gulch; it is a warning against, while also an invitation toward, the viewer's quest to contain the narrative. That this warning/invitation should be issued near the beginning of the series does not make us any more adept at containment or reconnoitering the rims as we go along —so tricky are *Deadwood*'s labyrinths of diction and design.

The additional complication of the third season is that Swearengen, for the first time, found a gulch that he is unable to reconnoiter successfully—the gulch that goes by the name of George Hearst. Not only does Hearst, with the help of his own henchman, chop off Swearengen's middle finger early in the season, but Hearst's maneuvers continue to baffle the one character who, until this point in the series, has successfully reconnoitered all that came before him. If the third season does not exactly turn Swearengen into Brom Garret, it nonetheless makes him similarly endangered by the rims of his environment—the rims as those places where one thing abuts another and therefore becomes defined, becomes knowable.

The connection between the site of Brom's demise and the disorientations of the third season go beyond the allegory I have been drawing. As I have argued elsewhere, each of the first two seasons are governed by a controlling figure who controls as much by absence as by presence. In the first season that figure is Wild Bill Hickok, whose death early on signals a crisis for the itinerant, pioneer flavor of the camp. In the second season that figure is Hearst, who while represented only by his deputy Francis Wolcott until the final episode, is the force behind the corporate interests and territorial acquisition that drive Deadwood's transition from tribe to system (O'Sullivan 2006, 127). In the third season that figure is another absent presence: the very gulch that doomed Brom and made his wife rich.

The only obstacle to Hearst's mastery of the camp, his containment of it, is the property that Alma owns but refuses to sell, at least on Hearst's terms, until the end of the season. Hearst champions, early in the season, "the virtue of consolidating purposes" to Swearengen, but his antagonist sees it otherwise: "purposes butt up against each other, and the strong call 'consolidating' bending the weak to their will" ("I Am Not the Fine Man You Take Me For," 3.2).

Is Hearst's consolidation so different from Swearengen's containment? Those closing tableaux of seasons one and two, when Swearengen seemed to contain the camp, provide an answer here: not only are those images of containment plainly temporary, they represent the illusion of the organic, of a feral world ruled by a creature (Swearengen) who nonetheless belongs to that world. Jack Langrishe, the theatrical impresario and old friend of Swearengen's who descends on Deadwood with his troupe in the third season, calls Hearst a "murderous engine," a vision of Hearst as machine that dovetails with Swearengen's awareness, in the same episode, that he is limited by his technological primitivism: "I should have fuckin' learned to use a gun, but I'm too fuckin' entrenched in my ways" ("Tell Him Something Pretty," 3.12).

Langrishe and his company connect to another way in which the third season resists containment, by either echoing the known ground of the series or cloaking the possible as the necessary. The second season began with the arrival of a coach in camp—a coach whose inhabitants would all soon be dead or traumatized by death. Most of the inhabitants were prostitutes headed to Joanie Stubbs' new bordello, the Chez Amis, where Wolcott eventually murders three of them. Early in the third season, another coach full of the possible arrives, this time bearing Langrishe and two actresses in his employ; their form of entertainment is only slightly more proper than that of Stubb's prostitutes, and they too will end up at the Chez Amis. Langrishe's remakes the brothel (lately used as a schoolhouse) into a theater, bringing high-minded drama to a low spot of infamy.

In some ways, Langrishe is another version of Brom— the sophisticated outsider who fits in awkwardly in the rough-and-tumble of Deadwood, though certainly a more adaptable one. We see the scattered members of the troupe rejoining in Deadwood—two actors arrive by a later conveyance—arranging a new schoolhouse to serve the children, attracting public interest through an amateur night…and then never putting on a play. In a season far more replete with loose ends than its predecessors, the entire subplot of these newcomers sits around, waiting to "develop," in some conventional sense, a plot. The actors exist almost exclusively in the realm of the possible, untethered from the necessary.

This is largely true of the two most prominent characters on the coach that immediately precedes the Langrishe group's arrival: Aunt Lou Marchbanks, Hearst's cook, and Mr. Wu, the leader of the camp's Chinese population, both from San Francisco. Aunt Lou, we will learn, merely plays the submissive mammy role for her employer; in her free time, she smokes cigars while playing rowdy mah-jongg and has a scheming son, Odell, who soon arrives with a scam for Hearst. But her role diminishes greatly over the final episodes, once Odell has died offstage, on his way out of town. Again, she remains a cluster of possibilities more than a compelling necessity.

The same, in even sharper relief, is true for Wu, whose main narrative function in the season is to gather 150 Chinese fighters, in alliance with Swearengen, to confront Hearst and his Pinkertons. Those would-be troops never come into play, as a result of Swearengen's hesitancy and Hearst's superior numbers. Rather than serving as a literal vehicle of plot or the possible disguised as the necessary, as the coach did in season two, here the coach serves as a vehicle for the possible tout court. Milch counterbalances in the third season the hypertrophy of necessity, of bending things to one's will in the figure of Hearst, with the hypertrophy of the unnecessary, of characters and possibilities that refuse to be reconnoitered, at least not by the industrial methods represented by Hearst's consolidating force.

We do get one thespian moment in the third season, but it is a private performance. One of the two late-arriving actors in the troupe is on the verge of death, but not through the plot-infested means that dominate the second season; rather, he suffers from an illness that resembles tuberculosis, or even more proximately, old age—an unheard-of condition in Deadwood. His name is Chesterton, and Langrishe arranges for him to be brought to the renovated bordello in anticipation of the theater's opening and the actor's demise.

As they sit in the darkness, looking in the direction of the stage, they exchange words about the muses of comedy and tragedy, and the configurations of the rake. Langrishe, sensing this to be his last opportunity, then asks: "Dost thou know Dover?" He and Chesterton haltingly exchange dialogue from the play that Langrishe has quoted, until Chesterton, barely sentient, asks "Line?" of an imagined prompter and dies. Langrishe then calls the other members of the company, whom we have not seen, in from the darkness to see to their colleague's remains.

This is a moving scene, though radically free of context, since we really know nothing about Chesterton, and little more about the amiable but buffoonish Langrishe; it seems to belong to another narrative, another mood. But the source of the final exchange between Langrishe and Chesterton opens up an array of issues, one that shows Deadwood's third season to be embedded with seeds of ideas that have been deliberately kept undernourished. "Dost thou know Dover" cites the fourth act of King Lear, and specifically the blind Gloucester's question to a man who calls himself Poor Tom, who is in fact Gloucester's disinherited son. Gloucester asks to be taken to the cliffs of Dover,

so that he may end his misery with a suicidal fall. Edgar pretends to lead him to the place. After the addled Gloucester slumps to the ground in the belief that he is plummeting to his death, Edgar, adopting another guise, tells Gloucester that he indeed fell from a cliff, and that the man leading him appeared to be a fiend. Gloucester, amazed to have suffered no injuries in his descent, agrees to take this miracle as a sign that the gods have deliberately spared his life.

The invocation of King Lear fits the pattern of reversal that infects the third season of Deadwood. These two narratives are in many ways stories moving in opposite but contiguous directions. If Deadwood is a story of creating community, laws, and social relations out of nothing, then Lear is a story of destroying community, laws, and social relations, ending in nothing, the play's signature word. If Deadwood's third season is about consolidation, the systematic alignment of many properties into a single property, and the fiefdom of Hearst, Lear is about dissolution, the disastrous carving up of the single kingdom of Britain into several parts.

There is a gruesome act of eye gouging, midway through the third season, which echoes the blinding of Gloucester. In this case the victim is Captain Turner, Hearst's deputy, in muddy hand-to-hand combat with Dority, a brutal struggle that, as Milch explicitly writes, recalls Lear's characterization of man as a "poor, bare, forked animal" (Milch 2006, 169)—a spectacle of mere biology, in contradistinction with the pathos and familial crisis resultant from Gloucester's injury, and the scene with Edgar that Langrishe and Chesterton summon. And while the positions and strengths of the town are hardening, each warring faction more entrenched in its position, there is a touching fragility to the way in which Langrishe and Chesterton switch roles imperceptibly during their scene, with Langrishe swapping Gloucester for Edgar, and Chesterton swapping Edgar for Gloucester—again, a suppleness that bespeaks a desire to linger in the possible, and avoid the necessary.

Most telling, however, are the words themselves, specifically Gloucester's words of instruction, as recited by Langrishe: "There is a cliff whose high unbending head / Looks fearfully on the confined deep; / Bring me but to the brim

of it, / And…from that place / I shall no leading need."
Then, picking up Edgar's role, at the pretended arrival at
the cliff, Langrishe marvels, "How fearful / And dizzy it is
to cast one's eyes so low," and finally says, "You are now
within a foot." It is at this point that Chesterton asks for a
line, and perishes.

We have here a rendering, by completely different participants, in a completely different space, through recitation
and imagination, of the death of Brom. Once again a perilous cliff that instills fear, once again an act of deception,
and most important a fatal rim, or in this case a brim. If
Langrishe is a revisitation of Brom—and Langrishe is given
a tour of the camp, a reconnoiter of its rim, on his arrival,
which is a favor bestowed on no other character on the
show—then he is manifestly a reversal of Brom, a person
who seeks the immediate gratification of plot, of the necessary (the Pinkertons, an extraordinary gold strike) at its
most predictable, turned into a person who is all possibility
and no action, a theory and not an enactment of narrative.

This theatrical interlude serves to illuminate how curious and full of accidental accretions of meaning is the
world of a serial drama like *Deadwood*, especially in middle
age. The fragment from *King Lear* points to an immediately
recognizable foundation of facts—facts that we call
words—to which actors on the stage can return again and
again. Live theater, as a medium, could not be more different from television drama: the compression of time, the
stress on imagination over imitation, the performance's control over the space and context of reception, and the knowledge (on the audience's part) that what is begun will be
finished.

Milch, by infusing his narrative with a pinch of this
alien narrative mode, seems to be resisting seriality's dictates and conventions. He offers another form of resistance,
if we can call it that, in his use of narrative time. As he
notes in the afterword to his book, each of *Deadwood*'s episodes "took an Aristotelian approach to dramatic structure
—more-or-less, each story took place in twenty-four hours"
(Milch 2006, 217). That internal constriction already pushes
against some of the conventions of television serials by
denying the very principle of expansiveness, of stretching
out, inherently endorsed by a narrative that cannot be con-

tained, whose sum exceeds our capacity to remember it.
Milch pushes the constriction further in the third season,
as seven episodes—the fifth through the eleventh—appear
to unfold on consecutive days. This pattern is not unusual
for *Deadwood*, or Milch more generally.[8] But the intensity
of this onrush of story is particularly acute here, as he
works to eliminate the gaps, the spaces between emphasized by Dickens, that define serial narrative.

At times, it seems that he is trying to film a twelve-hour
play, to make the genre continuous, rather than exploit the
gaps and shifts, as did Alan Ball with *Six Feet Under* and
David Chase with *The Sopranos*. The effect, in the last half
of the last season of *Deadwood*, is of a narrative that cannot
quite be contained by its rims and brims, that sloshes over
from one hour to the next, and that threatens to slosh on
past the final episode.

As I have argued earlier, that last bit of sloshing offers
a new maneuver, refusing to pause for a scene of reunion,
eager to get to the next season, or perhaps to dismiss seasons altogether and simply keep rushing.

The blood that Swearengen is cleaning, in that final
shot, is the blood of Jen, a prostitute he has killed to sate
Hearst's requirement for revenge. In the ultimate stages of
the season, Hearst arranges to kill Ellsworth, whom he
rightly sees as the last impediment to Alma's cession of her
property, of the gulch with the perilous rims. This murder
outrages Trixie, Swearengen's lead prostitute and Star's love
interest, who shoots Hearst in turn, succeeding only in
wounding his shoulder. As a last gesture of submission,
Hearst requires that Trixie forfeit her life for her attempt
on his—although Trixie's stratagem, in baring her breasts
and genitals to Hearst as she shot, succeeds in making him
uncertain as to her facial appearance.

The unwitting Jen, who looks enough like Trixie to fool
Hearst, is dispatched instead, to the consternation of Burns,
who is made distraught by the unfairness of it all. This unexpected switched-at-death prestidigitation differs strikingly
from the culminating and necessary deaths of season one
(Reverend Smith, whose fatal disease had been a prominent
story for most of the season) and season two (Wolcott,
whose dark adventures always seemed headed for a dark
end).

28.2 George Hearst (Gerald McRaney) and Al Swearengen (Ian McShane) meet for the last time in the final episode of *Deadwood*'s third season ("Tell Him Something Pretty" [2006]).

The improvised solution closes off the third season in yet another struggle against the necessary, or what might look like grand design. Jen is a character, unlike Smith or Wolcott, who is barely known to us, and who has not reached any kind of discernible narrative destination as her predecessors did. Johnny is particularly saddened by the fact that she is just learning to read. In the world of narrative, she is possibility itself.

Deadwood, like Edgar with Gloucester, goes out of its way to stage a kind of suicide at the end of its third season, killing off a narrative that has not even begun. It is a crime entirely appropriate to a season more interested in pursuing failed stories than successful ones, in pushing past the rims of its own claim.

Notes

1. The most famous instance of a refusal to disguise the possible as the necessary would be the instantly notorious conclusion of *The Sopranos*, which also pointed to the disjunction between, in Milch's terms, symbols and the specific moments that generate them.

2. Authorship and plotting are frequently recurring phrases in season three, especially in regard to Hearst.

3. These laments are followed, occasionally, with later recantations when the series succeeds in reprogramming its audience's expectations, or when what was seen as tediously iterative or annoyingly inappropriate is understood and valorized. Examples of this reversal abound. Virginia Heffernan's initial negative verdict on *Six Feet Under*—"the ties that tangled up the Fishers and the Chenowiths, internally and then with each other, during the first two seasons have simply come undone" (2003a)—was followed, exactly ten months later, by her declaration that the third season proved the show to be the best program on television (2003b). More recently, see the excoriation of *Lost*, which was attacked furiously in its third

season until its finale, when it was perceived to have gloriously redeemed itself (see the sine curve of reaction on the Television Without Pity discussion boards: ⟨http://forums.televisionwithoutpity.com/index.php?showforum=708⟩). The fact that such redemption often depends, narratively, on much of the material that was earlier vilified appears to be a predictable feature of this ritual.

4. "In confining his Readings to the earlier novels ... Dickens was—whether to please them, or himself, or both—giving his public what he rightly guessed they would most want" (Collins 1975).

5. Livia's death on *The Sopranos* was written in due to the unexpected death of actress Nancy Marchand in 2000. Similarly, actress Rachel Griffith's real-life pregnancy led to the character of Brenda being written out of the first four episodes of *Six Feet Under*'s third season.

6. The reasons for this cancellation remain somewhat murky; for a murky explanation of these murky reasons, see Milch (2006, 217). With the significant exception of *Deadwood*, HBO's glamour serials—those that garnered critical acclaim, and that the network made synonymous with its brand name—have always had their final season announced prospectively, so that the structure of valediction could be built into both the making and reception of that narrative. These "glamour serials" would include *The Sopranos*, *Six Feet Under*, *Sex and the City*, *The Wire*, and (perhaps less prominently) *Oz*—all of which aired for at least five seasons.

7. Such characters—the bourgeois sophisticates who get jazzed by watching others kill and cuss—are also lampooned mercilessly in *The Sopranos*, most prominently in the second-season episode "Bust Out."

8. For further evidence of this tendency, see the names of the first four episodes of Milch's successor series to *Deadwood*, *John from Cincinnati*: "His Visit: Day One," "His Visit: Day Two," "His Visit: Day Two, Continued," and "His Visit: Day Three."

References: Literature

Collins, Phillip (ed.) (1975). *Charles Dickens: The Public Readings*. Oxford: Clarendon Press.

Heffernan, Virginia (2003a). "The Living End of *Six Feet Under*." *Slate*, February 28. ⟨http://www.slate.com/id/2079490/⟩.

Heffernan, Virginia (2003b). "Television: The Highs." *New York Times*, December 28, sec. 2, 26.

Milch, David (2006). Deadwood: *Stories of the Black Hills*. New York: Melcher Media.

O'Sullivan, Sean (2006). "Old, New, Borrowed, Blue: *Deadwood* and Serial Fiction." In *Reading* Deadwood: *A Western to Swear By*, edited by David Lavery. New York: I. B. Tauris.

Shakespeare, William (1623). *King Lear*. Complete Works of William Shakespeare Online. ⟨http://shakespeare.mit.edu/lear/index.html⟩.

References: Television

Deadwood (2004–2006). Creator David Milch. HBO.

The Sopranos (1999–2007). Creator David Chase. HBO.

Six Feet Under (2001–2005). Creator Allan Ball. HBO.

Absent Epic, Implied Story Arcs, and Variation on a Narrative Theme: *Doctor Who* (2005–2008) as Cult/ Mainstream Television

Matt Hills

Prior to its 2005 regeneration, the BBC television series *Doctor Who* ran from 1963 to 1989, returning briefly as a one-off television movie in 1996. Alongside this primary text of television episodes, *Doctor Who* has existed in comic strip form, short stories, stage plays, radio plays, novelizations, and original novels. The BBC Wales reinvention of the show has also been no stranger to this narrative proliferation, featuring not only book and magazine extensions of its diegesis but also "TARDISodes" available online or as cell phone downloads. These augmented television episodes of the 2006 series by showing some aspect of the backstory of each (see Arnopp 2006; Russell 2006, 243–244). Despite the fact that it can no longer be assumed that fans will have consumed every *Doctor Who* narrative linked into its unfolding diegesis (Sandvoss 2005, 132–133), "there are fanzines and Web sites that demonstrate the ability of at least some fans to keep track of the entire range of narratives belonging to a single saga" (Thompson 2003, 102). All in all, *Doctor Who*'s narratives can lay claim to having generated guidebooks' worth of continuity. As Sara Gwenllian Jones (2004, 85) has noted, "Cult fictions extend themselves beyond the bounds of their primary texts … morphing into countless versions … that together constitute vast … metatexts."

Kristin Thompson (2003, 102) has argued that this scenario of cult media franchises and their transmedia intertexts might indicate that narrative is becoming "so dispersed [across cultural sites] as to slip away from the possibility of traditional academic analysis." I want to resist this idea, however. Narratives that are vaster than ever before, and more insistently stretched and serialized across different media, call for analysis that does not equate narrative with a singular, symbolically bounded artwork or media text. And though I will focus here predominantly on *Doctor Who* (2005–) as televised, my contentions and examples also refer to the likes of podcast commentaries, making-of books, *Doctor Who* annuals, original novels, and so on.

Given this mass of material, fans of *Doctor Who* have sought to plot its immense skein of narratives on a single timeline, as in Lance Parkin's playful but scholarly *Ahistory: An Unauthorised History of the Doctor Who Universe*: "This … seeks to place every event referred to in *Doctor Who* into a consistent timeline. Yet this is *a* history of the *Doctor Who* universe, not the 'definitive' or 'official' version.… [It is] one attempt to *retroactively* create a consistent framework.… It is essentially a game, not a scientific endeavour" (2006, 13).

I want to consider what's at stake in this fan "game," given that the 2005 incarnation of *Doctor Who* has been positioned as continuing the ongoing narrative of the original (now dubbed "classic") series. But how have episodic narratives been altered in this latest version? And how has the "continuity" so beloved by fans been managed and dealt with textually so as not to alienate new viewers unfamiliar with massive backlogs of story and character information? I will argue that although the show has been narratively redesigned in line with contemporary U.S. and UK television series norms that stress that "stand-alone" tales should be threaded through into ongoing "story arcs," it has also adopted a number of unusual strategies to avoid losing an imagined audience of "mainstream" or more casual viewers ("followers" rather than "fans" in the terminology of Tulloch and Jenkins [1995, 23]).

These narrative strategies include: the creation of "absent epic," whereby highly significant and presumably spectacular narrative events are only verbally alluded to by characters rather than being depicted; "implied story arcs" that work as much through the ludic accumulation of minor, background details as through the new development of detailed continuity; and perhaps the most important narrative strategy of the latest series—parallelism or "variations on a theme." Here, motifs and moments of narrative business are replayed in different ways across episodes, thus rewarding loyal audiences who can appreciate the difference-within-similarity of these parallels, without their resonances wrong-footing mainstream audiences or assuming that they will necessarily share the detailed story knowledge built up by fans.

I will focus on each of these narrative devices in turn. *The* defining feature of the new *Who*, I would say, is the deft way in which it satisfies cult fans' interests in diegetic continuity and coherence while at the same time reconfiguring continuity such that it becomes inclusive rather than a barrier to new mainstream audiences. *Doctor Who* (2005–) may be notable for other reasons (Hills forthcoming), but in narrative terms it successfully establishes a *fully inclusive continuity*, and hence bridges cult and mainstream television status.

Absent Epic: "A War so Big That Humanity Doesn't Even See It"

The Time War between the Daleks and Time Lords is undoubtedly one of the new series' major additions to *Doctor Who*'s established lore.[1] Despite its obvious potential for visual and special effects spectacle, however, the war has not yet been fully represented on-screen (as of the end of series three). Instead, it has been used as a backstory, working to underpin the altered characterization of the Doctor as supposedly the Last of the Time Lords. As a result of this creative decision, the latest series is marked by the war's structuring absence, with a "steady drip of revelations" (Newman 2005, 115) emerging across episodes. For example, when the Time War is first introduced, in "Rose," it isn't at all clear exactly who and what it involves: "while the story is very much self-contained, there are many hints

29.1 The Ninth Doctor (Christopher Eccleston) with companions Rose Tyler (Billie Piper) and Captain Jack Harkness (John Barrowman) in "The Doctor Dances" (2005).

and references throughout to an ongoing storyline involving many alien species in a war" (Lyon 2005, 220). And even after three series, and the transition from ninth Doctor (Christopher Eccleston) to tenth Doctor (David Tennant), the details of the Time War remain somewhat sketchy.

Semiotician Umberto Eco (1995, 198) has argued that for texts to attain cult status, they should "provide a completely furnished world"; a detailed and expansive diegesis from which "fans can quote characters and episodes…a world about which one can make up quizzes and play trivia games so that the adepts of the sect recognize…a shared expertise." And yet, the narrative absence-presence of the Time War—cumulatively referred to but also visually and narratively withheld—suggests that this "completeness" may not define cultification:

> Television series achieve cult status not because they present "completely furnished" worlds but rather because…their fantastic imaginaries draw the audience's attention to the fact that their diegetic worlds are invariably incompletely furnished…. There is always a deficit between what is (or can be) shown and what the avid audience wants to see, explore, develop, and know. (Gwenllian Jones 2000, 12–13)

Directly countering Eco's argument, Gwenllian Jones highlights the fact that though cult fans may appreciate displaying their knowledge of series' continuity—via such things as Eco's "quizzes and trivia games"—so too do they appreciate speculating about elusive narrative details.[2] Whether or not a narrative world is "completely" or "incompletely" furnished, then, perhaps the more important point is that cult narratives tend to both support fans' interests in accumulating detailed knowledge *and* structurally incite their desire to know more. The inclusion of the Time War strongly positioned new *Who* on the side of enigma and fan incitement, rather than knowledge and fan expertise: "The Time Lords had to go, it was a programme coming back with an awful lot of mythology and backstory and I wanted to give it a background in which fans and brand-new viewers would be on a level playing field. You didn't have to know about the Death Zone on Gallifrey and the Master and the Rani" (Russell T. Davies, cited in Russell 2006, 29).

The war's present-absence reduces the show's emphasis on fan knowledge, making it more accessible to those who don't have a detailed grasp of continuity established across years of prior narrative. But it also partly returns the series to its roots by introducing a new level of mystery to the exploits of its central character. This has been called *Doctor Who*'s "originating hermeneutic" (Tulloch and Alvarado 1983, 65): just who is the Doctor, what is he capable of, and in this instance, how exactly did he survive the war and contribute to its resolution?

Show-runner Russell T. Davies recognizes that these sorts of questions are likely to especially appeal to established fans of the series. As such, Davies downplayed the importance of this narrative strand when initially pitching his more inclusive vision to the BBC: "To have described it [the Time War] would have made this pitch too sci-fi...and frankly too fannish" (2005, 40). By remaining an offscreen backstory, the Time War lends *Doctor Who* a veneer of large-scale space opera while actually functioning more as an emotional, character-driven hook for old and new fans alike. Both the removal of the Time Lords' home planet/society and the manner of their narrative displacement work to address dedicated fans as well as more casual followers of the show by creating an "endlessly deferred narrative" (Hills 2002, 135), which provides character motivation and an ongoing sense of mystery. Though it may be assumed that new *Who*'s debts to soap opera come primarily

in the form of its emotionalism, and Rose Tyler (Billie Piper) and her family, I would argue that it is actually more significantly indebted to soap via its inclusion of the largely untold Time War. For as Robin Nelson (1997, 23) has claimed of "multi-narrative series": "The interweaving of different narrative strands developed in soaps has become TV drama's model form.... [I]t can afford the satisfaction of the occasional closure of narrative strands, while perpetually deferring the final satisfaction of ultimate closure overall."

And one way in which *Doctor Who* now perpetually defers this final satisfaction is by including a long-term narrative puzzle such as the war that remains in play, despite other episodic resolutions (as in most stories), series resolutions (as in "Parting of the Ways"), multiseries resolutions ("Doomsday" and its reuniting of Jackie Tyler played by Camille Coduri and alt–Pete Tyler, Shaun Dingwall), and even the reintroduction of the Doctor's Time Lord nemesis, the Master, in series three. If the "insistent demand of the hermeneutic code, the desire to resolve narrative mysteries, loses its grip on the reader once the story's resolution becomes fully known" (Jenkins 1992, 67), then by endlessly deferring full resolution in relation to the Time War, the hold of the hermeneutic code can be sustained.

Davies (2006b, 21) has toyed with the fan audiences' desire to know more about the Time War by penning an introduction to the Doctor in the *Doctor Who Annual 2006* that includes the following:

> Across the universe, on the planet Crafe Tec Hydra, one side of a mountain carries carvings and hieroglyphs, crude representations of an invisible War. The artwork shows two races clashing, one metal, one flesh; a fearsome explosion; and a solitary survivor walking from the wreckage. Solitary? Perhaps not. Under this figure, a phrase has been scratched in the stone, which translates as: you are not alone.

Even prior to the events of "Gridlock" in series three, this was arguably canonical narrative information, penned by the series' executive producer and lead writer. It forms part of a game of hints and implications—one that fully recognizes the ludic nature of fans' intertextual and metatextual speculations, acting as an example of what John Caldwell

(2002, 259) terms "backstory elaboration." Caldwell emphasizes how official online texts can supplement television narratives by "[fleshing] out character biographies in far more detail than a broadcast episode ever could—and mak[ing]...the users better narrative decoders of the series as well.... [N]arrativised elaboration of the text works by allowing the narrative arc of the show (and the narrative reception of the show) to 'continue' outside of the show itself."

This exterior "continuation" of the television show was, of course, eventually brought back into its televised story lines by the Face of Boe's message to the Doctor in "Gridlock": "You Are Not Alone." Online and cell-phone-downloadable "TARDISodes" also worked as further "narrativised elaborations" for series two (Jenkins 2006), despite backstory elaboration and character biography evidently not being restricted to new media narrative add-ons. As well as playing with the Time War, Davies (2006a) also contributed a biography of Rose to the *Doctor Who Annual 2006*, indicating that Rose's decision to dump Mickey (Noel Clarke) and travel with the Doctor was fully in character, since she had previously done something at least broadly analogous by leaving Mickey to move in with a man older than herself whom she hardly knew, but had fallen in love with. Though the televised episode "Rose" does not exhibit this depth of character psychology, Davies's narrative elaboration converts the character's on-screen decision to join the Doctor into one moment in a larger pattern of behavior.

Along with the "overall grand narrative design" (Chapman 2006, 194) of the Time War, the new *Who* has offered up other candidates for story arc status, such as the Tyler family, Mickey, and their relationships (across series one and two), Bad Wolf (across series one), Torchwood (series two), and the Saxon story line of series three. Story arcs, or ongoing serialized story lines threaded across numbers of episodes, surely presume and reward loyal viewer knowledge and fan engagement. It can also be assumed that story arcs may threaten to alienate casual followers of the show who may have missed certain episodes or narrative details. How, then, has the BBC Wales reinvention of *Doctor Who* sought to create innovative story arcs that, like the Time War's status as "absent epic," keep the show equally accessible and

narratively pleasurable to cult fan and mainstream audiences alike?

Implied Story Arcs: "You Need to Welcome the Reader of This Thing, Not Throw Up Barriers"

The rise of the story arc, and increase in "series memory," has been traced as one of the key developments in contemporary television drama seriality (see Hagedorn 1995; Nelson 1997; Ndalianis 2005).[3] Although the "classic" series of *Doctor Who* was frequently marked by continuity references and a sense of its own past, and though it occasionally featured seasons that had ongoing "umbrella" narratives, the new *Who* is nevertheless somewhat distinct in terms of its reliance on stand-alone stories placed within overall story arcs: "New *Doctor Who*...bears affinities with American series such as *Babylon 5* at the level of narrative. While the series itself is episodic...individual segments are linked by a 'story arc.'...The presence of a story arc, even only a partial one, is evidence that the series was conceived as an integrated whole rather than as a series of discrete episodes" (Chapman 2006, 194).

And yet, James Chapman's comparison with U.S. cult television series *Babylon 5* doesn't quite capture the distinctiveness of *Doctor Who*'s story arcs. Though there is a sense of unity to the new *Doctor Who*, this is not always a tightly organized linear narrative drive. Davies (2005, 40) offers "some sort of linking element, for the devoted viewer," across each series. But rather than this being a central element of the narrative it is more of a "continuing thread...mentioned in almost every story" (Kim Newman, cited in Lyon 2006, 326) in series one and two.

It is not even clear that "story arc" is quite the right term for the approach to narrative developed by Davies. For instead of layering plot development on plot development, and so assuming cumulative audience knowledge, Davies instead tends to repeat a specific signifier, seeding it relatively unobtrusively into the background details or dialogue of episodes for fans to spot. Mainstream audiences—imagined as being less likely to rewatch episodes and study these mentions—can thus enjoy *Doctor Who* without even noticing, or prioritizing, mentions of "Bad Wolf," "Torchwood," or "Saxon." This type of narrative game and puzzle hence does not alienate mainstream audiences who might otherwise feel they are lacking in story knowledge, as it is sufficiently peripheral and marginal throughout its "build-up" phase (episodes one to eleven of both the 2005 and 2006 series, and the first half of series three) to potentially not even register for casual viewers. And when the eventual payoff arrives in each series—for example, the episodes "Bad Wolf"/"Parting of the Ways," "Army of Ghosts"/ "Doomsday," and "The Sound of Drums"/"Last of the Time Lords"—then cult fans can enjoy the game-playing speculation they've engaged in, while followers of the show can still appreciate the more episodic narrative aspects of the series without being excluded.

Rather than indicating a tightly plotted narrative "plan," the unity of Davies's *Doctor Who* appears, on the whole, to be more organic and improvised in tone. As the show runner himself freely admits, he hadn't carefully mapped out exactly how "Bad Wolf" and "Torchwood" would crop up in the series, so that the pitch for the 2006 series, for example, was "missing...the Torchwood strand, cos I fed that in as I went along" (Davies 2006c, 4). Thus, though it may be tempting to discuss the new *Who* in terms of story arcs, I would argue that Chapman's hesitation in fully applying the term is instructive (note that he refers, in the quote above, to "only a partial" arc appearing in the Eccleston series).

What the 2005 and 2006 series of *Doctor Who* succeeded in doing was creating the impression or sense of a story arc *without* requiring viewers to remember swathes of cause-and-effect narrative information. These "arcs" were not event based so much as purely signifier based. In 2005, the phrase "Bad Wolf" variously turned up—among other places—as graffiti on the side of the TARDIS; as the Welsh name of a nuclear power plant in Cardiff; as a helicopter call sign; and as a future media corporation. Mentions of it were also integrated into various spin-off original novels, so the fannish game of Bad Wolf spotting was not restricted to the "primary" television text (see Lyon 2005, 396–398).

Addressing these iterations of Bad Wolf as a story arc would involve reproducing the common notion of different narrative "levels"—that is, that there are analytically sepa-

rable elements of the purely "episodic" and the unfolding "arc": "The idea of narrative levels is an excellent example of the narratological imaginary.... The geometry of levels has a comforting clarity and simplicity. With narrative levels, you know where you are" (Gibson 1996, 216). Yet the more inclusive "implied story arcs" of the new *Who*—which like the Time War backstory, offer a leveled-out playing field for fans' intensely ludic speculation and mainstream viewers' relative downplaying—surely confuse such concepts of diagrammatic narrative. Rather than being able to "map" the Bad Wolf arc, it is a matter of random repetition, of the dispersal of one phrase through all of time and space. Indeed, Davies makes the diegetic, narrative-world explanation of its recurrence one that mirrors his own practice as writer of randomly inserting the phrase into different background details. Its appearance is both motivated (Rose sending a message to herself; Davies sending a message to fan audiences) and entirely arbitrary (scattered through time; scattered throughout the text). There is something almost rhizomatic or transversal about these implied story arcs: they work nonlinearly through an accretion of references, with the repeated mentions or appearances of Bad Wolf and Torchwood cutting across each other, not seeming to fully cohere or add up. They are portents; pure narrative lures that refer only to the promise of their own deferred and dispersed meaning within the diegetic game.

The Saxon story line of series three was, by contrast, a little more conventionally arclike, possibly as a result of the production team's increased confidence at this stage that it could carry an audience with it without alienating more casual viewers. This time it was not merely one signifier's iteration across episodes that set up the events of the series finale. Instead, stronger connections were made to the events of preceding stories, but again these links were not so much cumulative cause-and-effect sequences as the reiteration of plot elements; the Lazarus Experiment's tampering with age is drawn on in "The Sound of Drums"/"Last of the Time Lords," while an important plot device from "Human Nature" also reappears later in series three, along with a reiteration of Boe's "Gridlock" message. This is certainly the closest the show has come to a conventional arc, yet anxiety with regard to losing mainstream viewers

29.2 The Master (John Simm) and Lucy Saxon (Alexandra Moen) gloat over their domination of the Earth, as an unnaturally aged Tenth Doctor (David Tennant) watches helplessly in "The Sound of Drums" (2007).

remains evident in the program's structure, which repeatedly relies on "flashbacks"—essentially, montage-style iterations of key scenes from earlier stories—to make sure that anyone who might have missed narrative information is presented with it (or re-presented, if they haven't been sufficiently attentive and fanlike). Hence moments from "Gridlock" and "Human Nature" are replayed in "Utopia," while "Last of the Time Lords" also replays material from "Utopia," "The Sound of Drums," and really getting into the swing of directing audience attention to key narrative information, also iterates several of its own earlier moments.

Cybertheorist Janet H. Murray (1997, 85) argues that one of the key developments of television seriality in the Internet age is that cult fans' attention to narrative continuity will start to become a more generalized feature of audience activity: "In the past this kind of attention was limited to shows with cult followings.... But as the Internet becomes a standard adjunct of broadcast television, all program writers and producers will be aware of a more sophisticated audience, one that can keep track of the story in greater detail and over longer periods of time."

Murray suggests that television serial viewers will be "able to keep track of longer plot arcs and a greater number of interconnected story threads" (256) as a result of using the Web to debate plot details. The revival of *Doctor Who*, however, certainly does not indicate this mainstreaming of cult television audiences' styles and modes of interpretation.

On the contrary, its narrative design seems to be generally marked by a fear of audience alienation; a fear that the imagined mainstream audience it courts will precisely *not* want to keep up with the detailed narrative information of a full story arc, or at the very least, will need to be reminded of earlier narrative events at key moments. It could be argued that these concerns are related to the show's targeting of a young audience. Yet given that many child fans do, in fact, follow the show's continuity avidly—as witnessed by the "Who-Ru" feature in the 2006 series of *Totally Doctor Who*, a BBC1 spin-off broadcast aimed squarely at kids and shown as part of the channel's children's schedule—I would argue that anxiety over audience alienation is less a product of the expected age of viewers, and far more a result of the courting of non-cult-fan and mainstream audiences.

Hence one imaginative solution arrived at by Davies— to splinter and prestructure cult fan and mainstream interpretations by using a partial, implied story arc that incites fan speculation without being too distracting (or even especially evident) for mainstream and more casual audiences. I would contend that the undoubted mainstream media success of *Doctor Who* (2005–), particularly in the United Kingdom, doesn't mean that it is no longer a cult television show nor that its cult status has been definitively mainstreamed. Instead, its narrative design works to manage the vast backstories, transmedia metatexts, and fan speculations it generates, containing these within symbolic boundaries of the "absent epic" and "implied story arc." This careful semiotic containment enables the show to appeal differentially (but nonhierarchically and inclusively) to new and old fans, and fans and followers alike. There is one further element of this inclusive "grand...design" (Chapman 2006, 194) that I want to explore in the final section. It is perhaps the most important diegetic device in the show's new format: the use of narrative parallels across stories.

Variations on a Theme: "Narrative Similarity and Difference"

Similarity and difference are part of any established television series, since all shows are required to both vary and at the same time draw on their particular narrative forms and structures.[4] Having said that, *Doctor Who* has always taken a specific route into narrative sameness and difference. When, in *Doctor Who: The Unfolding Text*, John Tulloch and Manuel Alvarado broach this topic, it is the Doctor's regeneration that preoccupies them. For narrative similarity and difference are, unusually, played out across the Doctor's character via its embodiment in a range of different actors. Though there is a "sameness" or Doctorish series of attributes to the titular figure, different actors have also introduced significant twists. Eccleston's portrayal was undoubtedly the most intense of the television Doctors to date, while Tennant's more humanized and empathetic representation deliberately contrasted with this.

Although the classic series made use of changes to the Doctor himself to somewhat vary its narrative possibilities, the new series takes this idea and relates it not just to parallels between regenerations but also between narrative moments, settings, and even specific camera shots. It is as if the text itself has been regenerated—repeated with a difference—along with the Doctor's change from Eccleston to Tennant. For instance, the introductory shot of "Rose," an FX shot swooping down from outer space to Rose's home, is repeated at the start of "The Christmas Invasion" (TCI), the first full-length episode featuring Tennant. And this same shot appears again at the beginning of "Army of Ghosts," the two-part story that writes Rose out of the show. As a reiterated motif, this shot is linked to key developments in Rose's tale.

Other narrative moments are reiterated and paralleled across the show; in the "Children in Need Special," we see the tenth Doctor take Rose's hand just as the ninth Doctor did when he first met her: "just one word, one word I said—run!" And though this moment represents the program self-consciously recalling its own recent past, narrative parallels are consistently threaded through series one to three. This mirroring is perhaps most pronounced at moments of change in the show, so that TCI recalls "Rose" not just in its opening but also in Rose's reenactment of the Doctor's "shadow proclamation" speech to the Nestene Consciousness. And the following year's Christmas special, "The Runaway Bride" (TRB), also then parallels TCI by including a robot Santa raising a tuba as if to fire at the

Doctor—this event, similarly filmed, was exactly what happened to Rose the year before, and was featured widely in promotional trails for TCI. By reiterating such a moment, the show is able to draw attention to narrative similarity and difference—this time it's the Doctor confronting robot Santas—but again without assuming audience knowledge or confronting casual audiences with material that could alienate them by implying that they lack narrative information. TRB also parallels TCI by introducing menacing Christmas trees—this time around their baubles are grenade-type devices—and concluding with a science-fantasy snow scene. TCI ends with what looks like snow, but is explained away as the falling ash of an incinerated spaceship; TRB rounds up with the Doctor using the TARDIS to artificially create snow. As Tennant has pointed out in the podcast for TRB —⟨http://www.bbc.co.uk/doctorwho/sounds/⟩ (accessed January 15, 2007)—this allows the Christmas specials to include iconic snow scenes without falling back on the standardized clichés of more realist Christmas television.

The show's second Christmas episode also parallels its predecessor by introducing a bit of comedy business about pockets: the bride, Donna (Catherine Tate), has no pockets in her wedding dress, and so can't carry anything important such as a cell phone. By contrast, the Doctor possesses magically large pockets, allowing him to store a remote control for the killer Christmas tree baubles and use it against the villain of the day. This is a variation on the resolution of TCI (both episodes were written by Davies). Here, the Doctor uses a satsuma—earlier comedically set up as being in his dressing gown pocket—to defeat the Sycorax leader. In each case the essential, improvisational energy of the character is depicted (he'll use whatever's in his pockets to defeat alien menaces), while each also revolves around a seemingly throwaway bit of banter that sets up a vital plot point. Just as with the Time War backstory and the Bad Wolf arc, these narrative parallels reward loyal fan audiences who can play spot-the-difference across episodes without detrimentally affecting the enjoyment of less committed or narratively knowledgeable audiences. Such parallels run constantly across different stories: a full list of them would fill several pages at the very least. To take a few more examples, the introduction of Adam as a traveling companion in "The Long Game" visually parallels Rose's first journey in the TARDIS in "The End of the World," as both look out into space (like the audience at home) via a widescreen-television-like viewing platform. In exaggerated contrast to Rose's appreciation of this spectacular vista, Adam faints. And these parallels are themselves again mirrored by Donna's introduction as a temporary companion to the Doctor, though this time she looks out of the TARDIS doors at the cosmos. Furthermore, Donna's abrupt appearance inside the TARDIS at the close of series two (the final moments of "Doomsday") is itself directly paralleled by another disruptive entry to the time machine at the end of series three. The Doctor's accompanying dialogue—"What? What!? *What*?!!?"—is also reiterated, reperformed, and recontextualized as the show delights in differentially replaying its own earlier series finale.

Such parallels do not just concern the Doctor and his companions: series two's "The Age of Steel" offers up a number of narrative parallels to "Father's Day," as Rose again meets her dead father, though on this occasion by entering a parallel universe rather than time travelling. Indeed, the device of a parallel world enables a whole series of narrative differences-within-similarities, thereby condensing one of show's overarching narrative logics into a specific story line (Lyon 2006, 227).

Scholar of media narrative Angela Ndalianis has explored this kind of narrative parallelism in depth (2004), pointing out that it primarily "relies on the technique of 'variation on a theme' and on the personality of the main character…. There is no overall series story that closes the show's form…and the series could continue indefinitely…. Episodes build upon the model established in previous episodes" (2005, 94).

Given this reliance on the central character as a point of stability, Ndalianis (2005, 95) suggests that this type of seriality is most often linked to crime series, referring to the likes of *Columbo*, *Monk*, and *CSI*. She goes on to argue that this narrative form

> suggests a multi-layered structure that resembles a palimpsest. Each additional episode lays itself over prior episodes in an attempt to perfect on its predecessors and, partially at least, erase their presence through

outperformance…. Integral to the strategy of "variation of a theme" is the…principle of virtuosity. Virtuosity and variation on a theme rely on the active engagement of an audience familiar with prior episodes in the series. (ibid.)

This "outperformance" also tends to be linked to crime series: the investigator has a different case to crack each week, but instead of constantly referring back to previous crimes, such shows instead invoke their previous episodes by attempting to outdo them. If this makes *Doctor Who* closely akin to crime series then perhaps that should come as no surprise; just as *Monk* involves a quirky detective figure thinking his way idiosyncratically to a solution each week, then *Who* involves a quirky Time Lord thoughtfully improvising salvation from an alien crime of the week. Repetition and the layering of palimpsest-like narrative gives rise to "rich dramatic parallels" where loyal viewers can "juxtapose events told months or even years apart" (Murray 1997, 256).

It is just such juxtapositions that the new *Who* repeatedly offers up as a reward to fan audiences. Unlike continuity rendered in dialogue or strongly dependent on cause-and-effect information, parallels of the kind that Davies has seeded into the text will simply not be noticeable for nonfan, follower, or casual audiences. The motif of regeneration—self-aware difference within repetition— that gave *Doctor Who* one of its most distinctive narrative devices has, I would say, therefore been generalized and dispersed across its narrative moments. As Davies himself has noted, in the podcast commentary for "Last of the Time Lords": "I love the fact we've killed the Prime Minister [character] every year…. It's those repetitions within the format of *Doctor Who*…. In a series that's different every week, you build in rhythms that are constant. And I like Number Ten as one of them" (⟨http://www.bbc.co.uk/doctorwho/sounds/⟩ [accessed July 1, 2007]).

And though fans may more vocally celebrate and debate backstory such as the Time War or implied story arcs such as Bad Wolf, I would argue that it is this generalized regeneration—this generalized narrative similarity and difference—that has most significantly brought *Doctor*

Who (2005–) cult *and* mainstream success. It represents a kind of "series memory" and self-consciousness that is thoroughly inclusive by virtue of not discriminating between continuity-loving fans and more continuity-indifferent audiences. And though mainstream audiences may not get hung up on what the Time War could mean for the Doctor Who mythos or what Bad Wolf would turn out to be, they can nevertheless start to spot and appreciate parallels and resonances across episodes, reading these for what they say about different characters, and what they say about the show's bid to "outperform" its own earlier special effects, spectacle, and narrative threats. Narrative parallelism therefore rewards new fans as much as old, and mainstream as much as cult audiences. Absent epic and implied story arcs tend to split audiences into imagined cult and mainstream components. This tendency is somewhat less pronounced with regard to narrative parallelism, making this a textual quality that ranges of different audiences can appreciate together, even if it may still pass unnoticed by the most casual of audiences dipping into the show from time to time.

BBC Wales' *Doctor Who* has succeeded in bridging cult and mainstream audiences, meeting the expectations of different interpretive communities without alienating either new viewers or long-established fans. If series three has perhaps been the most continuity-heavy and story-arc dependent at the time of this writing (July 2007), it has nevertheless still been scrupulously careful not to assume narrative knowledge on the part of its audience, making the links between its stories dependent more on major plot devices rather than minor narrative details, as well as incorporating the direct repetition of key narrative information. Continuity may have become more important in the narrative mix as the latest incarnation of the program has accumulated and consolidated its own mythology, but this remains a fully inclusive continuity, crafted so that its resonances for long-term fans are not at the expense of newer fans or casual viewers. In short, *Doctor Who* (2005–) offers theorists of narrative a vast transmedia, metatextual "saga," now approaching forty-five years of backstory, which has nonetheless found a series of narrative strategies to manage its own continuity and become, once again, an accessible, successful, crossover media franchise.

Notes

1. The phrase in the subtitle is a quote from J. Shaun Lyon's review of "Rose," contained in *Back to the Vortex* (2005, 220). It should be noted that a war between the Time Lords and an unnamed "Enemy" had previously been introduced in the BBC Books' Eighth Doctor range beginning with Lawrence Miles's *Alien Bodies* (1997). The "Time War" of the 2005 television series hence explores territory, in its own way, that had previously been developed in the spin-off, original novels.

2. On "hyperdiegesis," see also Hills (2002, 134).

3. The phrase in the subtitle is taken from Russell T. Davies's commentary on his pitch document for the 2005 series of *Doctor Who* (2005, 40).

4. The phrase in the subtitle is John Tulloch and Manuel Alvarado's chapter heading when they deal with the topic of the Doctor's regeneration (1983, 61).

References

Arnopp, Jason (2006). "TARDISodes!" In *Doctor Who Magazine* 368: 30–32.

Caldwell, John (2002). "New Media/Old Augmentations: Television, the Internet, and Interactivity" In *Realism and "Reality" in Film and Media*, edited by Anne Jerslev, 253–274. Copenhagen: Museum Tusculanum Press.

Chapman, James (2006). *Inside the TARDIS: The Worlds of Doctor Who*. London: I. B. Tauris.

Davies, Russell T. (2005). "Pitch Perfect." In *Doctor Who Magazine Special Edition: The Series One Companion*, 40–49.

Davies, Russell T. (2006a). "Meet Rose." In *Doctor Who Annual 2006*, 38–39. Tunbridge Wells, UK: Panini Books.

Davies, Russell T. (2006b). "Meet the Doctor." In *Doctor Who Annual 2006*, 20–21. Tunbridge Wells, UK: Panini Books.

Davies, Russell T. (2006c). "Second Sight." In *Doctor Who Magazine Special Edition: The Series Two Companion*, 4–10.

Eco, Umberto (1995). *Faith in Fakes: Travels in Hyperreality*. London: Minerva.

Gibson, Andrew (1996). *Towards a Postmodern Theory of Narrative*. Edinburgh: Edinburgh University Press.

Gwenllian Jones, Sara (2000). "Starring Lucy Lawless?" *Continuum* 14 (1): 9–22.

Gwenllian Jones, Sara (2004). "Virtual Reality and Cult Television." In *Cult Television*, edited by Sara Gwenllian-Jones and Roberta E. Pearson, 83–97. Minneapolis: University of Minnesota Press.

Hagedorn, Roger (1995). "Doubtless to Be Continued: A Brief History of Serial Narrative." In *To Be Continued . . . Soap Operas around the World*, edited by Robert C. Allen, 27–48. London: Routledge.

Hills, Matt (2002). *Fan Cultures*. London: Routledge.

Hills, Matt (forthcoming). *Triumph of a Time Lord: Regenerating Doctor Who in the 21st Century*. London: I. B. Tauris.

Jenkins, Henry (1992). *Textual Poachers*. New York: Routledge.

Jenkins, Henry (2006). *Convergence Culture*. New York: New York University Press.

Lyon, J. Shaun (2005). *Back to the Vortex*. Tolworth, UK: Telos Press.

Lyon, J. Shaun (2006). *Second Flight: Back to the Vortex*. Tolworth, UK: Telos Press.

Miles, Lawrence (1997). *Alien Bodies*. London: BBC Books.

Murray, Janet H. (1997). *Hamlet on the Holodeck: The Future of Narrative in Cyberspace*. Cambridge, MA: MIT Press.

Ndalianis, Angela (2004). *Neo-Baroque Aesthetics and Contemporary Entertainment*. Cambridge, MA: MIT Press.

Ndalianis, Angela (2005). "Television and the Neo-Baroque." In *The Contemporary Television Series*, edited by Michael Hammond and Lucy Mazdon, 83–101. Edinburgh: Edinburgh University Press.

Nelson, Robin (1997). *TV Drama in Transition*. London: Macmillan.

Newman, Kim (2005). *BFI TV Classics: Doctor Who*. London: BFI.

Parkin, Lance (2006). *Ahistory: An Unauthorised History of the Doctor Who Universe*. Des Moines: Mad Norwegian Press.

Russell, Gary (2006). *Doctor Who: The Inside Story*. London: BBC Books.

Sandvoss, Cornel (2005). *Fans: The Mirror of Consumption*. Cambridge, UK: Polity Press.

Thompson, Kristin (2003). *Storytelling in Film and Television*. Cambridge, MA: Harvard University Press.

Tulloch, John, and Manuel Alvarado (1983). *Doctor Who: The Unfolding Text*. London: Macmillan.

Tulloch, John, and Henry Jenkins (1995). *Science Fiction Audiences: Watching Doctor Who and Star Trek*. London: Routledge.

Matt Hills

Vaster Than Empire(s), and More Slow: The Politics and Economics of Embodiment in *Doctor Who*

Anne Cranny-Francis and John Tulloch

The *Who*scape is vast, with the Doctor and his companions traversing time and space for over four decades. This makes *Doctor Who*, which first aired in 1963, the longest-running science fiction series in television history.

One referent for this chapter is thus the actual historical extent of *Doctor Who*, and in particular the way in which specific eras of production—always seeking new audiences—locate themselves in history and context. Our concern here is two recent series of *Doctor Who* (2005 and 2006), and how they speak from within the social and political context of our time.

In its opening years, *Doctor Who* worked, like other new BBC genres of the period (Tulloch 2000, 372), strongly within the dominant BBC metaphor for its state broadcaster function as a "theatre in the middle of town," presenting voices from the "Right" and the "Left" without ever standing *for* the positions of "militant" unionism or "unscrupulous" big business (Tulloch and Alvarado 1983, 50–52). This was in contrast to the earlier BBC consensus of cultural and class leadership, following the guiding philosophy of Lord John Reith, and replacing that leadership role with a "standing back" professionalism within the consensus of state welfarism (Tulloch 2000, 374).

Thus, when in 1972, in "The Curse of Peladon" episodes (9.5–8), the Doctor faced an alien/human, modernity/ feudalism political conflict (and a miner's strike) on the planet of Peladon—in the same year as the British miners' strike against the Heath government—actor Jon Pertwee effortlessly combined the James Bond–style meritocractic national imaginary with the values of "welfare statism" and the "neutral" professional values of the BBC at this time (Tulloch 2000, 376). But three decades later, in 2005, *Doctor Who* emerged out of a different national imaginary: the emergent populist nationalism called "Thatcherism" that had crushed the 1983–1984 miners' strike, and at the BBC, dominated what television dramatist Trevor Griffiths (1990) described as the "vicious if undeclared *Kulturkampf* still being waged by the British state against independent thought and belief [that] has left its mark on almost every aspect of civil society."

The other referent for this chapter is Ursula K. Le Guin's story "Vaster Than Empires, and More Slow" (1975), which tells of a group of visitors to an apparently uninhabited planet. They discover, through the perceptions of one of the party who is an empath, that the sentient life-form on the planet is arboreal. The trees around them are the major life-form and are, in fact, in shock at encountering life that this collective life-form does not recognize as sentient. The central concern of the story is the nature and meaning of difference; whether these disparate life-forms can recognize each other's validity and right to exist. The right to exist—and exist well—is a major focus of this chapter, as it is of contemporary political debates.

Consequently the technologies by which we, as citizens, encounter and engage with these debates are the focus for this chapter—the television program as a social technology, and the material, economic, and political technologies that characterize life in early twenty-first century Western society. This leads us to current debates about the nature of the human that emphasize the role of the emotions and the senses as well as the mind in human thinking and being. And with the new episodes, for the first time *Doctor Who* acknowledges the Doctor as a sexual being! This recognition of the nonrational is also an essential component of the Doctor's encounters with those hyperrational entities, the Daleks and the Cybers.

The chapter begins by describing the political and economic context when two new series of *Doctor Who*—the 2005 series starring Christopher Eccleston as the Doctor, and the 2006 series starring David Tennant—were produced. It then explores the ways in which the series responds to this context through events and characters that have direct referents in contemporary Western society.

Vast Narratives, Particular Histories

Doctor Who's historical and political context spans the last years of welfare consensus as well as the early, triumphalist years of Tory and New Labour neoliberalism in Britain. Neoliberal governance is grounded in neoclassical economics, which Alan Finlayson and his colleagues (2005, 519) describe as "a technological system producing a particular form of social order and social relations—a society constructed and animated in accordance with the logic, rules, and values of the neoclassical narrative." In policy terms, this led governments (both Tory and New Labour) to divest themselves of state-owned enterprises and excise underprivileged citizens from social welfare (Krueger 1997), as either a Thatcherite, radical individualist repudiation of the very notion of "society" or to eschew welfare dependence. As Finlayson and his colleagues (2005, 526) explain it:

> Structural adjustment programs (SAPs) imposed by the International Monetary Fund (IMF) seek to stabilize national currencies through the restructuring of the economies of debtor nations. The goal of SAPs is to increase investment and stabilize currency by demanding national economic austerity (largely meaning cuts in social programs). The result of this emphasis on debt repayment, currency stability, and national economic capacity for external investment means that many countries have had to cut back on social services and privatize key functions of the state, all with the aim of increasing the financial liberalization of the economies of the countries in question.... When the IMF mandates that states cut subsidies to their citizens, this mandate comes from an interest rooted in an ideology based primarily on a neoclassical economic calculation.

So increasingly, citizens are isolated and individuated, and at the same time situated within a narrative that positions them as without agency. Agency, by contrast, belongs to the policymakers who determine the lives of millions of disenfranchised people with decisions made at a remove from those lives. Joseph Stiglitz (2002) has compared the policy of international economic managers who mandate government policy from a distance with the "smart bombs" that kill from a distance, since the military, the financiers, and those for whom they supposedly act (the pacified citizenry) do not experience the devastation they cause.

As Stiglitz notes, linking neoliberal politics with "new wars" rationalism, "One should not see unemployment as just a statistic, an economic 'body count,' the unintended casualties in the fight against inflation or to ensure that Western banks get repaid. The unemployed people are people, with families, whole lives are affected—sometimes devastated—by the economic policies that outsiders recommend, and in the case of the IMF, effectively impose" (cited in Finlayson et al. 2005, 526–527). The distance of these international policymakers is denying people the right to live well, or even to live at all.

Many academic commentators (Barber 1996; Weintraub 1999; Green and Huey 2005; Finlayson et al. 2005) have also remarked that this economic rationalism has been translated across a scholarly profession's boundary of classical economics "into communities of administrators and policy makers...and a whole range of journalistic practices and news-reporting strategies" (Weintraub 1999, 148). Drawing on philosophers Jean-François Lyotard and Michel Foucault, Finlayson and his colleagues (2005, 522) note this process "of transference of discipline from society to the individual—a process of internalizing the order of things including prevailing systems of power.... Socialization is...impersonal and indirect via the media of mass communication—television, radio, newspapers, and movies," telling us "not only how to think and act but who we are."

The 2005 *Doctor Who* episode "Bad Wolf" (1.12) addresses this type of social organization with this kind of media. For example, when the Doctor comments on the social inequality of Earth by saying, "So the population just sits there. Half the world's too fat, half the world's too thin and you just sit there watching telly," his words refer not only to the narrative role of the media in that particular episode but also more generally to the notion of media pacifying the population.

This exchange between the Doctor and the character Lynda takes place on a media station constructed in space (at fifty thousand feet) by world banks interested in "long-term investment." This distance between prospective investors and the world can certainly be read as a physical analogue of the metaphoric distance between neoclassical economics and the citizenry. Ironically, there is little left to invest in, as the Doctor and Lynda stare down at a planet covered by pollution storms, and as the people, as Lynda tells him, "get news flashes telling us when it's safe to breathe outside."

But then, the machinelike and dehumanized discourse-based social technology of neoclassical economics, while successfully dominating cultures around the world, "does not offer a solution for the many environmental problems associated with industrial and post-industrial society, nor does it offer hope for the many environmental problems evident in a globalizing world" (Finlayson et al. 2005, 531).

Not all is quite as controlled as this notion of a systemic alliance between media and political governance seems to suggest, however. Neoliberal economics (and its post-9/11 neoconservative political inflection) has, in fact, generated its own opposition, especially through its foreign policy and "new wars" in Kosovo, Afghanistan, and Iraq. The Iraq invasion in particular, and its "War on Terror" human rights abuses—Guantanamo Bay, Abu Ghraib, the torture flights of "special rendition," the killing of countless (and uncounted) thousands of Iraq citizens as "collateral damage," and the visual disappearance of these citizen-victims—created the largest and most visible opposition within British civil society in decades, at the same time that the new *Doctor Who* series was being planned, produced, circulated, and received by television viewers.

A wide range of British media critiqued the outcomes, if not always the ideology, of neoliberal imperialism in the Middle East, together with its human rights abuses. In art journalism, writers like John Berger (2004) spoke of a new retrospective of Francis Bacon's work speaking in a new

way to "today's pitilessness," which "is perhaps more unremitting, pervasive and continuous. It spares neither the planet itself, nor anyone living on it anywhere. Abstract because deriving from the sole logic of the pursuit of profit (as cold as the freezer), it threatens to make obsolete all other sets of belief, along with their traditions of facing the cruelty of life with dignity and some flashes of hope."

In theaters around the United Kingdom, in the British liberal/left press, and even in conservative newspapers like the *Times*, the *Daily Telegraph*, and the *Daily Mail*, voices were to be heard—and cartoons were to be seen—strongly challenging the politics, economics, and human "othering" generated by the Iraq invasion.

For example, in the *Times* in May 2005, a cartoon labeled "Abu Ghraib," which drew directly on two of Bacon's paintings ("Three Studies for Figures at the Base of a Crucifixion" and "Painting") sat prominently in the newspaper next to the day's editorial on Abu Ghraib. It translated from "Painting" the horrifying, male-suited beast, his black umbrella and hidden gaze shielding him from the animalistically flayed, crucified body behind. The crucifixion in "Painting" is also reproduced in the cartoon, arms outstretched, vertebrae bared, sinews unraveling. But in the cartoon, this human crucifixion is resignified as "Abu Ghraib" by transferring to the Bacon image the torturing electric cables attached to the hands, also outstretched, of the hooded civilian-prisoner standing on a box at Abu Ghraib prison—one of the defining photographic icons of the Iraq invasion. A rejection of this tortured othering—reseen via Bacon, of abused Muslim civilians by way of neo-imperial and neoliberal foreign policies—is the central point of the *Times* cartoon.

Thus, when the 2005 *Doctor Who* episode "Dalek" (1.6) imaged the pitiless torturing of a jailed Dalek as "other" (which British newspaper reviewers, cued by the orange overalls worn by workers in the episode, read as "political" and "about Guantanamo" (see, for example, Morris 2005), and narratively located this torture overtly within the "rational self-interest" business economy of the United States; when it translated aliens into fake 10 Downing Street politicians frightening television audiences with nonexistent "massive weapons of destruction" ("Aliens of London" [1.4] and "World War Three" [1.5]); when an Eccleston episode in 2005 ("World War Three") has a new people's prime minister rejecting preemptive attack (though the same prime minister later falls in line with this policy in the series two opener, "The Christmas Invasion") along with the craven notion of blindly following U.S. policy; and when two whole episodes of the 2005 *Doctor Who* series present chilling media empires that promote cultures of fear and a deliberate construction of borders between "us" and the migrant Other, the new *Doctor Who* series was not operating in a critical media vacuum for its UK audiences.

In the 2005 *Doctor Who* episode "The Long Game" (1.7) —the first of two episodes about the media ("Bad Wolf" [1.12] is the other)—we see another Baconesque image, derived this time from the snarling, ripping-mouthed, and long-necked monsters from his painting "Three Studies." This is the Jagrafess, an alien beast who is editor in chief, "overviewing literally everything" of the Satellite 5 space station that transmits all the Earth's news. The Doctor recognizes that "every single fact in the Empire beams out of this place—now that's what I call power"—and he is quick to resist its protocol journalism, challenging Cathica for not asking reflexive questions about her own profession.

Doctor: Don't you ever ask? . . . You're a *journalist*! Why are all the crew human? No aliens on board, why?

Cathica: . . . I suppose immigration has tightened. It's bound to, what with all the threat.

Doctor: What threat?

Cathica: I dunno. Borders and usual stuff.

Later, in the process of torturing the Doctor, the human Editor gives him a clearer answer, saying that "to create a climate of fear you need to keep the borders closed. It's just a matter of emphasis. The right word in the right broadcast, repeated often enough, can destabilize an economy, invent an enemy, change a vote."

This exchange succinctly captures the political strategy described by many critics of neoliberal Western governments, as they create fear through the creation of otherness—a strategy in which they are often abetted by unreflexive, cooperative media.

By the time the Doctor returns to Satellite 5 in the second 2005 media story "Bad Wolf," one hundred years have passed. In the earlier episode, the Doctor had destroyed the Editor's control over the news channels but did not replace them with any kind of critical faculty. As Lynda explains:

Lynda: That's when it first went wrong, 100 years ago like you said. All the news channels just went down overnight.

Doctor: That was me. I did that!

Lynda: There was nothing left in their place, no information. The whole planet just froze. The government, the economy, they collapsed. That was the start of it. A hundred years of hell.

Doctor: Oh my g. . . I *made* this world!

In the place of news and current affairs are game shows and makeover programs, the "reality television" that constitutes much of our current programming. In "Bad Wolf" they take on a particularly negative character as game show contestants become biological matter for the regeneration of the Daleks, whose emperor is the show's hidden sponsor.

The Emperor Dalek claims to be a creator god (of the new, "humanly" engineered race of Daleks), and he calls the Doctor a destroyer god, as he assembles a machine that will kill not only the Daleks but all life on Earth. Like Tom Baker's Doctor in the 1975 "Genesis of the Daleks" (12.11– 16), Eccleston's Doctor holds in his hands the technological means to kill all future Daleks. In both cases the Doctor declines to do so, and in "Bad Wolf," the Emperor Dalek then taunts the Doctor for his cowardice and lack of active will.

But what is noticeably different in the 2005 episode is that whereas the 1975 intertextual reference when the Doctor makes his choice is high cultural—Dostoyevsky's legend of the Grand Inquisitor—the intertexts in "Bad Wolf" are from popular culture. The new *Doctor Who* celebrates at every turn its own popular cultural status—in its production values, star charisma, narratives, and audiences; and it regularly draws intertextually on popular film and television (from *Sex and the City* and *Buffy the Vampire Slayer* to *High Noon*). The new *Doctor Who* is pulsatingly successful popu-

30.1 Sarah Jane Smith (Elizabeth Sladen) and Harry Sullivan (Ian Marter) watch in disbelief as the Fourth Doctor (Tom Baker) hesitates to destroy the Dalek race in "Genesis of the Daleks" (1975).

30.2 A furious Ninth Doctor (Christopher Eccleston), via hologram, threatens to "wipe every stinking Dalek out of the sky" to save Rose in "Bad Wolf" (2005). He will not make good on this threat.

lar culture: in its intertexts, in its reviews and television awards, and for its audiences. Yet the new series also, professionally, works within a neoliberal economy and politics, within which, as both program creators and (diegetically) the Doctor know, creation and destruction both depend on mediated knowledge and affect.

This knowledge is dramatized in the 2005 episode "World War Three," which lampoons the first-strike prerogative claimed by the United States and its allies. In the episode, an alien masquerading as the British prime minister announces to the British media (via the real-life Channel 4 news presenter) that "our inspectors have searched the sky above our heads and they have found massive weapons of destruction capable of being deployed within forty-five seconds.… We are facing extinction unless we strike first. I beg the United Nations, pass an emergency measure." The horrified Doctor, speaking to Harriet Jones, a popular back-bench member of Parliament, responds to the television broadcast: "He's making it up. There's no weapons up there. There's no threat. He's just invented it.… They want the whole world panicking because you lot, you get scared. You lash out."

The relationship between a mediated culture of fear, human emotions, and violence runs as another key theme through the new *Doctor Who*. *This* is the long media game that the Doctor describes in the two media episodes. "Going way back…[s]omeone's been playing a long game, controlling the human race behind the scenes for generations." But there is also a continuing challenge from the Doctor.

Jones will go on to become a people's prime minister, with three terms that the Doctor describes as a new golden age of governance—though the Doctor's approval later comes to an end when Jones, too, engages in this first-strike action. In "World War Three," he sees she already has the right qualities for this new kind of leadership, as she responds to Rose's indirect reference to Britain's Iraq invasion.

Harriet Jones: The British Isles can't gain access to atomic weapons without a special resolution from the UN.

Rose: That's never stopped them!

Harriet: Exactly. Given our past record—and I voted against that, thank you very much—the code's been taken out of the government's hands and given to the UN.… If only we knew what the Slovenes wanted.

Doctor: …They're out to make money. That means they want to use something…some kind of asset.

Rose: Like what?

Harriet: Gold? Oil? Water?

Doctor: You're very good at this!

We might presume that when Jones becomes prime minister, gold, oil, and water will be reconfigured in a new legitimating "socio-natural narrative that takes as its primary concern principles of social equity and environmental integrity" (Finlayson et al. 2005, 553). Yet once placed in this role, with the neoliberal logic still in place, Jones succumbs to the same complex of fear and xenophobia that motivated her predecessors.

"It's Pure Emotion..."

The new *Doctor Who* addresses this concern about neoliberal rationalism in another way also; it deals with emotion —with sexuality and relationships—as it explores political and social concerns. In so doing, it acknowledges that mind and body, idea and emotion, are not separate but intertwined—nowhere more obvious than in the fear-generating polemic of many current Western governments.

The later-hour scheduling of *Doctor Who* in 2005 was also the scheduling of sexuality. Throughout the years of *Doctor Who*'s longest-serving producer, John Nathan-Turner, production mores were dominated by Nathan-Turner's regular "note": "there's no hanky-panky in the TARDIS" (Grieves 1984). But the chemistry between Eccleston and Billie Piper, who played Rose, was all about sexuality, loving, and the steady growth of a mutual intimacy. Building up to the deep kiss between them in "Bad Wolf," signifying Rose's saving of humanity and the Doctor's saving of her, the 2005 and 2006 series were marked by a series of flirting relationships—Rose with Mickey; Rose, sexually, with Captain Jack; Rose with Adam; and the Doctor with other women too, such as Lynda in "Bad Wolf" and Reinette/Pompadour in "The Girl in the Fireplace" (2.4).

These come-ons and "dances" are sexual as performed, but they also signal the development of intimacy between the Doctor and Rose. So that when the Doctor triumphantly says, "I can dance," and does a long, slow movement with Rose to the music of Glenn Miller—replicating the sexual passion between Rose and Captain Jack as they dance, also to Miller, on the outside of his ship next to the top of Big Ben in "The Doctor Dances" (1.10)—this is an overt metaphor for intimacy beyond their sexual coupling. "No hanky-panky in the TARDIS" is clearly dead and buried,

as the series shifts from a distancing voyeurism to all kinds of emotional and sexual engagement; for example, Captain Jack also kisses the Doctor full on the mouth as he says his good-byes.

The narrative of the new *Doctor Who* plays with the equivalent possibilities of hetero-, metro-, and bisexuality, and with the muddled nature of the experiences, needs, desires, and emotions of seeking and finding love. This is enacted particularly through the alien embodiment of the Doctor, his regenerative ability meaning that he will live on long after any human companions have aged and died. Diegetically, this provides a reason for the constant parade of attractive female companions, though politically it has been an issue since at least the 1970s that the Doctor thereby acts as male hero with disposable female companions.

The 2006 Tennant/Piper episode "School Reunion" (2.3) directly addressed this gender politics with the reintroduction, after twenty-seven years, of the fans' favorite female companion, Elizabeth Sladen as Sarah Jane Smith. Jealousy bursts out immediately when Rose realizes that the Doctor has had intimate relationships before—and Mickey gets his own back for his constant put-downs from the Doctor (itself a sign of his own jealousy of Mickey). Mickey claps him on the back, with "Welcome to every man's worst nightmare," as Rose and Sarah Jane bitch competitively over their remembered experiences with the Doctor.

Executive producer Russell T. Davies gave writers and cast the advice that this relationship in "School Reunion" is "a bit *Sex and the City*. Write it like it's Samantha and Cassie fighting over one man" (quoted in *Doctor Who Confidential*: "School Reunion" 2006). Sarah Jane and Rose resolve their differences when they share their "fan" memories of the Doctor's every foible. They laugh together about him and then embrace.

So the question of the heroic man dumping his woman assistant is explored for the first time in forty years of *Doctor Who* narratives. Sarah Jane says, "I waited for you. You didn't come back. I thought you'd died.... Did I do something wrong? You never came back for me. You just dumped me.... You could have come back." When the Doctor tells her that it was OK because she just got on with her life, Sarah Jane replies, "I waited for you. I missed you.... You *were* my life."

Davies describes this as an especially emotional story, "beautiful, funny, romantic and gorgeous," where "the electric sentiments of the scene absolutely come to the surface.... It's pure emotion. All of that has been pent up for Sarah Jane for *decades*, absolute decades. She gets her chance to say goodbye properly." And the episode director James Hawes says, "She needs closure.... She needs to move on. It's all very well for him to say 'everything will be fine.' But it can't always for a human, and she *is* going to age and die. And she needs the end of that part of her life, *especially* having seen he's carried on with her replacement" (*Doctor Who Confidential*: "School Reunion" 2006).

Rose herself recognizes for the first time that "I'm just the latest in a long line.... You just leave us behind. Is that what you're going to do with me? With Sarah Jane you were that close to her once, and you never even mention her." Yet the Doctor's reply is equally disturbing: "You can spend the rest of your life with me. But I can't spend the rest of my life with you. I must live on alone; that's the curse of a Time Lord" (ibid.).

This intense association of the Time Lord/hero/other with the most empathetic of human emotions, loneliness, and isolation is one of the strongest emotional investments in the new *Doctor Who*, as we see clearly throughout the first Tennant series (where Pompadour describes the Doctor as her "lonely angel"), and especially in the final series two episode, "Doomsday" (2.13), which concludes with the departure of Rose. "Dead" on her own planet, Rose is trapped forever on the alternative Earth with Mickey, her mother, and her "parallel" father. But she knows she will never see the Doctor again, and knows he will go on alone.

Doctor: Here you are, living a life day after day—one adventure I can never have.

Rose: (cries) I'm never going to see you again.

Doctor: (gently) You can't.

Rose: (crying) What will you do?

Doctor: (trying to be a bit upbeat) I've got the TARDIS. Same old life, last of the Time Lords.

Rose: (sobbing) On your own?

Doctor: (nods seriously, eyes looking down bleakly)

Rose: I...(struggling for breath through her tears) I *love* you.

Doctor: ...And I suppose it's my last chance to say it. (with emotion) Rose Tyler...

The image link ends, Rose's head collapses into her hands on a beautiful Norwegian beach. The Doctor, in his TARDIS, tears staining his cheek, also drops his head into his hands and then wearily moves to the TARDIS controls.

But loneliness also identifies the Doctor with the Daleks. In the 2005 episode "Dalek," the Doctor tells the last remaining Dalek that he has wiped out all the others in a war that also killed the other Time Lords. Henry van Statten, the capitalist entrepreneur who holds and tortures both the Dalek and the Doctor, equates them with each other, as having equivalent commodity value, as each the last "assets" of their race. The program's equation of Dalek and Doctor is different, exploring the overlaps and contradictions between pitiless violence and empathetic pity (which is what led to Rose touching the Dalek and generating its "human" mutation), between loneliness and social solidarity. As Finlayson and his colleagues (2005, 532) say, in critiquing the rationalist narrative of neoclassical economics,

> People do not live their lives as disembodied rational minds processing complete information, making decisive choices among clear alternatives. Quite to the contrary, we are embodied, contextualized muddlers moving through our lives enmeshed in an infinitely complex and ever-changing web of relations, experiences, emotions, needs, wants and desires. Not only are our alternatives seldom clear to us; we seldom make clear and conscious choices among them. Instead, we continuously experience our life as an ebb and flow of inchoate aggregate emotional states in which we seek to maintain some sense of generalized well-being. Each choice and action is not in pursuit of some preexisting, clearly perceived, disembodied goal, but is a more or less consciously embodied reactive adjustment to a subjectively experienced context.

They go on to argue that "the institutional response to growing economic inequality, social disruptions, and terrorism has been the loss of democratic rights and civil liberties at all levels of all societies. However...many...have demonstrated that the potential for paradigmatic challenge and social change is evident at all times and in all places" (ibid.).

Exploring emotional and sexual intimacy is one of the ways in which the new *Doctor Who* not only invigorates and updates its own narrative; it also enables the program to challenge neoclassical rationalism at its very base, which is the individuation and isolation of all social subjects, and the maintenance of a split between thought and embodied experience (mind and body).

"Modern Paranoias and Modern Obsessions..."

We find this same address to mainstream attitudes and values in the program's address to contemporary biopolitics, the ways in which our understandings of embodiment and being are affected by the material technologies (digital and biological) in which we are immersed. We are challenged to consider what it is that makes us viable social subjects, and how we draw the boundaries of being; whom we consider nonviable (other), and how we justify that stance ethically. This is another way of exploring the foreign policy implications of neoliberalism, with its disregard for human rights and associated othering strategy, and combines this with the kind of intimate politics we see in the program's exploration of gender relationships.

The most recent series of *Doctor Who*, starring Tennant, make particular use of this focus on embodiment, building on some of the issues already explored in the previous Eccleston season. These include the explicit sexualizing of the relationship between the Doctor and Rose, and the exploration of difference through encounters with alien life-forms, including the Daleks and another old foe, the Cybermen.

The first of the "traditional enemies" encountered by the Tennant version Doctor are the Cybermen. Their double episode, "Rise of the Cybermen" (2.5)/"The Age of Steel" (2.6), is set on a parallel Earth, where Rose's father (killed in the previous Eccleston season) is still alive and has prospered—though he and Jackie have no daughter, just a dog called "Rose" (much to the Doctor's amusement). As in the case of "Bad Wolf," the game show episode of the previous series, this world is symptomatically similar to our own, and one of the earliest markers of this is the ubiquitous mobile/cellular communication technology. Seemingly everyone in parallel London permanently wears two Bluetooth-style earphones to which are transmitted news and entertainment from the Cybus Corporation.

Commentary from actor Tennant and producer Davies puts it this way:

Tennant: It is using things that *are* happening in the modern world, and maybe that we have a slight paranoid fear about as well—this whole idea that we get information downloaded. We download it into our computer, we download it into our phones. It's just a short hop to downloading it straight into your head.

Davies: People *want* to relate to technology, that's... what they're after. And, you know, how many people do you see walking around with the Bluetooth attachment now.... Tapping into modern paranoias and modern obsessions, things that people get joyous about as well—upgrading, that notion of upgrading, that notion that every year you can change your phone, you can change your FE3 player, and if you don't keep up with the technology, then you're going to be left behind.

Tennant: I think it's always good to just tap into those slight worries that people have about modern life—mobile phones that people are now absolutely reliant on and yet at the same time I think we're all slightly nervous about. We don't really understand them, most of us. We don't really know how this information comes into this little plastic thing that we carry about.... That's where all the Cybermen come from anyway, this whole idea that the modern technology will slowly replace us, and that modern technology is out to get us.... That's what we see throughout that episode, just this whole idea that it will slowly creep up on us and we won't quite notice it happening, which just makes it that worrying bit closer. (*Doctor Who Confidential*: "The Rise of the Cybermen" 2006)

It is also easy to see this as a metaphor for the Rupert Murdoch–dominated Western media world—especially when, during a download, everyone stops and listens, then obediently laughs on cue to the same joke. This is Foucault's disciplinary regime writ large, with media technologies as the pervasive apparatus of that control. The Cybermen story focuses on the Cybus Corporation, run by the Dr. Strangelove-esque character John Lumic. Confined to a wheelchair by a debilitating illness, he is determined to develop a new form of embodiment that will enable him to live on beyond the death of his physical body. The episode opens with an exchange between Lumic and the scientist in charge of the Cyber program:

Scientist: The prototype has passed every test, sir; it's working.

Lumic: I hardly think "working" is the correct word. (audibly moves wheelchair forward) That would apply only to machines.

Scientist: I'm sorry. I should say, "It's alive."

This echoes the famous words of Victor Frankenstein announcing the vivification of his "creature," the first cyborg—a being composed of parts of dead bodies. Lumic later describes the Cybermen as brains sustained "within a cradle of copyrighted chemicals" welded to an exoskeleton: "The latest advances from synapse research allow the cyberkinetic impulses to be bonded to a metal exoskeleton. This is the ultimate upgrading. Our greatest step into cyberspace." Lumic's depiction recalls the mind-in-a-vat thinking abhorred by Bruno Latour (2003), among others; that is, the very notion that any kind of being can be sustained when the brain is separated from its physical embodiment. As Latour argues, the mind is an organic brain. Separated from its body, it does not exist; any other suggestion is a dystopian nightmare. Of course, we might assert that the Cybermen are a dystopian nightmare, and that this is the point of the episode. Latour's contention, however, is not that this concept is unpleasant or unethical but that it is impossible. In Latour's terms, the Cybermen could not march—as they palpably do—through the streets of parallel London.

The marching of the Cybermen is a curious feature of these episodes, and demarcates them from the Cybers of previous Doctors and series. Their heavy, rhythmic march draws attention to the physicality of the Cybers in a different way from their earlier appearances, which focused more on their alienness or strangeness. The horrific thing about these Cybers is not their inhumanness but rather the fact that they are (also) human—or were. Soon after their first public appearance, the Doctor describes the Cybers to Rose: "They were [people]. They've had all their humanity taken away. It's a living brain inside a cybernetic body—a heart of steel, with all emotions removed."

If we follow this logic, then the Cybers are the result of separating mind and body, rather than acknowledging embodied consciousness as the interrelation of mind and body. In a sense, they are the apotheosis of neoclassical economics' "rational man." Again, this accords essentially with Latour's argument when he notes that the problem with modern science is its separation of science from what he calls "the social world": that the artificial separation of the organic brain from its sensory and social context creates a decontextualized and asocial science that can be used in ways inimical to human being.

The Doctor's gloss on this identifies the humanity of the Cybers specifically with their emotions, which is a familiar trope in science fiction. The dehumanization of the Cybers is achieved through the excision of their emotions. The central horror of the Cybers in the new Doctor Who, then, might be described as not their simple difference (or otherness)—as it was for the earlier Cybermen—but as the vision of humans who are effectively devoid of all that we characterize as human. These "dehumanized" humans are capable of actions that emotionally and sensorially engaged humans are not, like the dispassionate destruction of human beings. The assumption here is that this emotional and sensory engagement creates an empathetic connection (between people or "beings") that prevents such callous destruction. In other words, ethics is not a reasoned set of practices and beliefs but an embodied practice based in the ability to feel and perceive as others do.

Again, returning to Latour, we might argue that it is not possible to simply remove a human being's "emotion chip," to dehumanize someone by removing their ability to feel—so that the Cybers are not readable as a possible future for humanity. But the more horrifying reality embedded in many episodes of the new *Doctor Who* is that human beings already behave this way, with their empathetic responses disengaged. So what do the new Cybers figure for us?

In having the members of this society connected together by the ubiquitous Bluetooth device, the episodes also suggests that the Cybers are the logical end of that relationship between embodiment and technology—in which the embodied humans allow themselves to be subject to the technology, and controlled by it. When the Doctor and Rose find themselves among a crowd of humans all stopped in their tracks, preoccupied by a download, they witness the genesis of the Cybermen.

In the early twenty-first century, electromechanical and information technologies are ubiquitous. And the horror of this time is not that the technology physically destroys workers—such as when unsafe machines killed nineteenth-century workers—but that they dehumanize them. Like the disciplined subjects of Foucault's (and philosopher Jeremy Bentham's) panopticon, modern workers allow themselves to be told what to think (the news) *and* what to feel (the joke). Not only their thoughts but also their emotions and senses are dictated by the information technology to which they are connected—and which thereby also determines their empathetic responses, or lack thereof.

In other words, we might read the wired-in citizens of parallel Earth, and the Cybers they become, as a figure for and consequence of the uncritical consumption of contemporary technologies. Again, the problem identified with this embodiment is not only that the workers themselves are harmed but that they are thereby rendered capable of harming others. As, for example, through the delivery of massive firepower on an unprotected civilian populace (in Iraq), the deployment of smart bombs and the attendant collateral damage (dead civilians), the sexual and/or psychological abuse of prisoners in Abu Ghraib and Guantanamo Bay. Or the stagnation of critical thinking generated by the celebrity culture that pervades the Western media in "Bad Wolf."

The Doctor's interactions with the Cybers are readable, therefore, as his rejection of this dehumanizing potential in contemporary technologies. He seems to kill Cybers without mercy at times, though at other times he expresses pity for their plight. And we might note that in "Age of Steel," he destroys the Cybers by switching their emotions back on—so that they collapse in horror at the monsters they have become. Their monstrosity lies, we might argue, not in their changed bodies but in their changed embodiment through which they are constituted as capable of horrific acts of murder without pity, without empathy; they are inhuman, not alien—a category that simultaneously acknowledges the humanity of their being as well as its malignant practice.

The ethical problem posed by the Cybers is effectively voided by having the Cybers judge themselves. The Doctor does not have to destroy them; they destroy themselves. Their answer to the ethical question of whether they have the right to destroy others in order to propagate their kind is not answered in this episode by the Cybers or the Doctor but by the human component of the Cyber—the sensing, feeling part—and the answer is "No."

The other "traditional foes" with whom the Doctor faces the same dilemma are the Daleks. As noted earlier, the Daleks are different from the Cybermen in that they are not human (though the emperor has begun to integrate human physical material into the Dalek matrix); both are an amalgam of organic and technological components, however, and in this form they embody contemporary concerns about technology. The Dalek episodes of the first Tennant series are "Army of Ghosts" and "Doomsday," which end series two and result in the "death" of Rose, the Doctor's companion. This story features both the Cybermen and the Daleks as well as the ongoing story of Torchwood, the weapons institute founded in 1879 by Queen Victoria. Here the Doctor finds out he is regarded as "the enemy...an enemy of the Crown."

The story of Torchwood, as it unfolds in these episodes, is that of the ideology that underlies the use of weapons technologies against those who are perceived as potentially threatening the state. As Torchwood director Yvonne Hartman explains to the Doctor, the institute was founded by

Queen Victoria with the two related aims of "keeping Britain great and fighting the alien horde." Its motto, she has explained previously, is: "If it's alien, it's ours—for the good of the British empire." The key terms are "alien" and "empire," with Britain identified as deeply, fundamentally colonialist and xenophobic so that even the Doctor is classified as dangerous, because he's alien (or other). Torchwood embodies the combination of social and material technologies that are typical of colonialist powers, and that can result in aggressive political actions, including the preemptive strike action that we see in the Western attack on Iraq.

The Cybermen and Daleks in this episode are written with broad brushstrokes, and at times border on the ludicrous—as when Mickey describes their confrontation as "like Stephen Hawking versus the Speaking Clock." Perhaps the most interesting statement from the Cybermen comes with their declaration of intention to humankind: "This broadcast is for humankind. Cybermen now occupy every landmass on this planet. But you need not fear. Cybermen will remove fear. Cybermen will remove sex and class and color and creed. You will become identical. You will become like us."

The equation of fear with difference identifies the Cybermen with Torchwood, which has a similarly xenophobic ideology. All of the social markers that are used to understand human differences and different human embodiments will be neutralized by the Cybermen, whose metallic exoskeletons conceal any differences between the humans they once were. In this way, the story clarifies what it is that constitutes difference and alienness—"sex and class and color and creed." The episode also briefly explores the relationship between the sensory, the emotional, and embodiment, again by comparison with the unemotional and sensorially inert cyborg characters. For example, the Cyberleader tells the Doctor that he is proof that "emotions destroy you"—just before he is himself destroyed by allies of the Doctor. In this situation, the Doctor's recourse to the emotion of hope—"I quite like hope; hope's a good emotion"—immediately precedes his rescue. Combined with the Cyberleader's destruction, this constitutes a rejection of the Cyberleader's position.

And in another exchange, when the Daleks attempt to force the Doctor to open the Genesis Ark, explaining that it is Time Lord technology, he relates their inability to sense to a kind of madness: "Technology using the one thing a Dalek can't do—touch. Sealed inside your casing, not feeling anything, ever. From birth to death, locked inside a cold metal cage, completely alone. That explains your voice; no wonder you scream."

Implicit in the Doctor's statement is a claim that viable embodiment involves the integration of the sensory ("sealed inside") and the emotional ("completely alone") with the intellectual or conceptual.

The modern Cybers and Daleks seem to be based in different technologies, even if, as the Cyberleader claims, they are "compatible." The Daleks are based in a kind of biotechnology; the Cybers in a version of information technology—a difference emblematized in their different war cries: "Exterminate!" (Dalek); "Delete!" (Cyber). Both are unemotional, kill with compunction, and have no empathy or compassion. Again, we might argue that both cyborg creatures can be seen as configuring the dangers for embodied human subjects who are subsumed by their technology; that this technology effectively overrides or excises the sensory-emotional complex that characterizes human being. It is this complex that the Doctor repeatedly describes—gleefully—as the essence of the human. For example, in the episode "The Impossible Planet" (2.8), the Doctor challenges the humans in a space station orbiting a black hole about why they are there, in such an extraordinarily dangerous situation, and then answers his own question: "So when it comes down to it, why did you come here? Why did you do that? Why? I'll tell you why: because it was there! Brilliant!" And the Doctor then hugs the mission commander, Zac, who responds with a smile. The Doctor's analysis and Zac's wry response acknowledge that a human being is not simply rational (the Cartesian subject). As the Doctor then concludes: "Human beings, you are amazing—but apart from that you're completely mad." It is this ability—or not—to move outside the mechanical dictates of rationalist thinking that defines both human and cyborg being.

The exceptions are the converted Cyber-version of Hartman in "Doomsday" and the four Daleks who comprise the Cult of Skaro. Cyber-Hartman turns on the other Cybers: as she shoots them down, she intones, "I did my duty for

Queen and country," and oily tears flow from the eyeholes in her exoskeleton. She is a dysfunctional Cyber, precisely because she makes her own judgment about this situation and acts to protect humanity—and the signifier of this residual humanness in Hartman is not the (intellectual) decision to fire on the other Cybers but her emotional response embodied as tears.

The Cult of Skaro Daleks differ from their fellows in that they have names: Dalek Thay, Dalek Sec, and so on. The Doctor explains that these Daleks are different because they have to "imagine" that they are their enemies in order to work out how to kill them more efficiently. The equation of this nonrational imaginative capability with individuated names—another marker of the difference between human beings (individual embodied human subjects) and cyborg collectives such as the Cybermen and the Daleks—once again characterizes humanness. In this case, the human is identified not specifically with emotion but with nonrationalism; humans are not simply "rational man." It is not the ability to think rationally that characterizes humanity but the combination of rationality with imagination, with an emotionally and sensorially engaged response to the world.

Vaster Than Empire...

The broad sweep of the *Doctor Who* narrative emblematizes the imperial, colonialist, neoliberal ideology that the first Eccleston and Tennant series identify as mobilizing British institutional politics. And this ideology is located through an exploration of forms of embodiment, and the politics they generate and reveal. Through the Cybermen and the Daleks, and through both interpersonal and mediated experiences, the series explores the nature of embodied human subjectivity as a mixed and muddled sensory, emotional, and intellectual complex, not a simple linear Cartesian monad (rational man). It also explores the ways in which technology and human embodiment are interrelated—and the potential dangers for humanity in creating a purely rationalist, nonsocial (in Latour's terms) science, economics, and politics.

The series' exploration of embodiment in interpersonal, mediated, and technological terms also generates an analysis of what constitutes the ethical—and again it is the rejec-

tion of simple rationalism that is most striking. Ethical judgment in these two series of *Doctor Who* is not based on intellectual or rationalist judgments but on a fully embodied, emotional, sensory, and intellectual engagement with the context of the judgment. The Cybermen and the Daleks make rational judgments, freed of emotional complexity, and the results are not only simplistic and unsatisfactory for human beings; they fail.

Most strikingly, the series uses these structuring narratives to reflect on a number of contemporary social and political concerns, including the Blair government's involvement in the Iraq War, and its collusion with the United States in preemptive strike practices; Western involvement in the torture of prisoners; the role of the media in promoting an uncritical acceptance of mainstream values; and the homogenizing effect of information technologies and its products. Like the Le Guin story that was a catalyst for this analysis, the series uses perceptions of embodied difference to explore the problems that arise when we fail to perceive others as viable beings with as much right to exist as ourselves—and that relates as much to the dumped female companions of the Doctor as it does to the human victims of the series' more overt politics.

For Le Guin, writing in the 1970s, "Vaster Than Empires, and More Slow" engaged with the politics of the United States and the Vietnam War, the civil rights movement, and the women's movement. In this context, its ethical endeavor is to explore how difference can be understood and respected, without being othered. One of Le Guin's characters muses on the empath's decision to join with the collective consciousness of the planet: "He had given up his self to the alien, an unreserved surrender, that left no place for evil. He had learned the love of the Other, and thereby had been given his whole self.—But this is not the vocabulary of reason" (1975, 216). As Le Guin's character acknowledges, such a recognition of difference is not possible for a rationalist subject.

In the Britain of 2005 and 2006, the text of *Doctor Who* articulates different concerns and problems, but shares with Le Guin's story an engagement with ethical questions and a concern about the status of embodied being as a marker of difference. And it introduces into this interrogation a specific concern with the relationship between the senses, the emotions, and embodied being, which is also an articulation of contemporary concerns about the impact of new technologies and old economics on human embodiment.

References: Literature

Barber, Benjamin (1996). *Jihad vs. McWorld: How Globalism and Tribalism Are Reshaping the World*. New York: Ballantine Books.

Berger, John (2004). "Prophet of a Pitiless World." *Guardian*, Saturday, May 29.

Finlayson, Alan, Thomas Lyson, Andrew Pleasant, Kai Schafft, and Robert Torres (2005). "The 'Invisible Hand': Neoclassical Economics and the Ordering of Society." *Critical Sociology* 31 (4): 515–536.

Green, Brian, and Laura Huey (2005). "The Politics of Economic Restructuring: Class Antagonism and the Neoliberal Agenda." *Critical Sociology* 31 (4): 639–650.

Griffiths, Trevor (1990). Foreword to *Television Drama: Agency, Audience, and Myth*, by John Tulloch, ix–x. London: Routledge.

Grieves, Robert T. (1984). "Who's Who in Outer Space." *Time*, Monday, January 9. ⟨http://www.time.com/time/magazine/article/0,9171,952321-2,00.html⟩ (accessed July 19, 2007).

Krueger, L. W. (1997). "The End of Social Work." *Journal of Social Work Education* 33 (1): 19–27.

Latour, Bruno (2003). "Do You Believe in Reality? News from the Trenches of the Science Wars?" In *Philosophy of Technology: The Technological Condition. An Anthology*, edited by Robert C. Scharff and Val Dusek, 126–137. Oxford: Blackwell.

Le Guin, Ursula K. (1975). "Vaster Than Empires, and More Slow." In *The Wind's Twelve Quarters*. New York: Harper and Row.

Morris, Mike (2005). "Love and Hate; A Frightening Feeling." Posted on the Doctor Who Rating Guide: By Fans, For Fans, September 5. ⟨http://pagefillers.com/dwrg/dalek.htm⟩ (accessed July 19, 2007).

Stiglitz, Joseph (2002). *Globalization and Its Discontents*. New York: W. W. Norton.

Tulloch, John (2000). "Producing the National Imaginary: *Doctor Who*, Text, and Genre." In *A Necessary Fantasy? The Heroic Figures in Children's Popular Culture*, edited by Dudley Jones and Tony Watkins, 363–394. London: Garland Publishing.

Tulloch, John, and Manuel Alvarado (1983). *Doctor Who: The Unfolding Text*. Basingstoke, UK: Macmillan.

Weintraub, E. R. (1999). "How Should We Write the History of Twentieth Century Economics?" *Oxford Review of Economic Policy* 15, no. 4 (Winter): 139–152.

References: Television

Doctor Who (1963–1989). BBC. Creator Sidney Newman.

Doctor Who (2005–present). BBC Wales. Creator Sidney Newman and executive producer Russell T. Davies.

Doctor Who Confidential. "The Rise of the Cybermen" (2006). BBC Wales. Creator Russell T. Davies.

Doctor Who Confidential. "School Reunion" (2006). BBC Wales. Creator Russell T. Davies.

War Stories: Board Wargames and (Vast) Procedural Narratives

Matthew Kirschenbaum

In an old note-book, soiled and dog-eared by much traveling, yellow and musty with the long years it had lain in a Samoan chest, the present writer came across the mimic war correspondence here presented to the public. The stirring story of these tin-soldier campaigns occupies the greater share of the book, though interspersed with many pages of scattered verse, not a little Gaelic idiom and verb, a half-made will and the chaptering of a novel.... Nothing is more eloquent of the man than the particularity and care with which this mimic war correspondence was compiled; the author of the "Child's Garden" has never outgrown his love for childish things, and it is typical of him that though he mocks us at every turn and loses no occasion to deride the puppets in the play, he is everywhere faithful to the least detail of fact.
—Lloyd Osbourne, "Stevenson at Play"

I.

In the lead chapter in *Second Person: Role-Playing and Story in Games and Playable Media*, Greg Costikyan (2007, 5) flatly declares: "There is no story in chess, bridge, *Monopoly*, or *Afrika Korps*." The last of these is a board wargame published by the Avalon Hill Game Company in 1964. It places the player in the shoes of either Field Marshall Erwin Rommel or the British general Bernard Law Montgomery, recreating the fighting in North Africa from 1941 to 1943. The box cover offers a direct appeal to the second-person player perspective: "Now **YOU** Command in this realistic Desert Campaign GAME by Avalon Hill."[1]

In addition to being an influential designer and critic on the contemporary scene, Costikyan got his start working at SPI (the most prolific wargame publisher in the business

before it folded), so it would seem he knows whereof he speaks.[2] Costikyan's argument is that games and storytelling are natural antagonists, and that despite early and unsatisfying experimentation in both the literary avant-garde (Julio Cortazar's *Hopscotch* and hypertext fiction) and the commercial marketplace (*Choose Your Own Adventure* and *Dragon's Lair*), the potential for game-story hybrids really only begins to emerge out of the tabletop role-playing game tradition (he is pessimistic that these techniques can be successfully ported to digital platforms any time soon).

Yet other contributors to *Second Person* contest this genealogy. Kevin Wilson writes lucidly about transliterating the "story" of *Doom* from screen to tabletop board game, and Bruno Faidutti (2007, 95) asserts that "you can easily retell a game of chess or Go with the same tension and suspense of a whodunit." Eric Lang, Pat Harrigan, and James Wallis also offer various counterexamples, documenting non- or quasi-tabletop games that support and sustain activities we can recognize as "storytelling."

Costikyan (2007, 9) notes that role-playing games often generate so-called expedition reports, which are narrative retellings of events that unfolded during the gameplay. Board wargames, however, have spawned an equivalent genre, the after-action report (named after a military document type), which are *also* narrative retellings of events that unfolded during gameplay. Sometimes after-action reports have enough detail that nowadays, when posted online, they are preceded by a disclaimer lest an unwary Web surfer, Googling for grist for a term paper, mistake a wargame after-action report for an authentic account of a victorious Japanese navy at Midway or a triumphant Napoleon at Waterloo.[3] Yet they are not an especially recent phenomenon. An early nineteenth-century instance comes from the memoirs of a lieutenant in the British Forty-third Light Infantry who, with a fellow officer, played out an elaborate wargame involving a castle under siege. The regimental paymaster followed the game closely: "When he heard that the [toy] sergeant had at last fallen, he burst out of the room in a fit of despair at the unfair way he had been treated. For days afterwards he would enter the room and say,

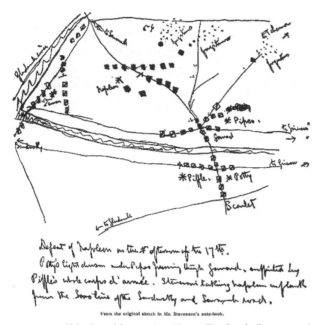

From the original sketch in Mr. Stevenson's note-book.

movement at Yolo, General Stevenson's long inactivity in Sandusky, and his advance at last, the one right movement and in the one possible direction.

YALLOBALLY RECORD.—" The humbug who had the folly and indecency to pick up the name of Napoleon second-hand at a sale of old pledges, has been thrashed and is a prisoner. Except the Army of the West, and the division on the Mar road, which is commanded by an old woman, we have nothing on foot but scattered, ragamuffin regiments. Savannah is under fire; that will teach Osbourne to skulk in cities instead of going to the front with the poor devils whom he butchers by his ignorance and starves with his peculations. What we want to know is, when is Osbourne to be shot?"

NOTE.—The *Record* editor, a man of the name of McGuffog, was subsequently hanged by order of General Osbourne. Public opinion indorsed this act of severity. My great uncle, Mr. Phelim Settle, was present and saw him with the nightcap on and a file of his journals around his neck; when he was turned off, the applause, according to Mr. Settle, was deafening. He was a man, as the extracts prove, not without a kind of vulgar talent.

YALLOBALLY EVENING HERALD.—" It would be idle to disguise the fact that the retreat of our Army of the Centre and the accidental capture of the accomplished soldier, whose modesty conceals itself under the pseudonym of Napoleon, have created a slight though baseless feeling of alarm in this city. Nearer the field the

717

31.1 Page from "Stevenson at Play" in *Scribner's* (1898), showing a portion of his after-action report and a sketch of the strategic situation from his notebook.

'Really I cannot forget that poor sergeant'" (Pearson 2007, 132). Likewise, the novelist Robert Louis Stevenson produced an extensive written fiction based on a series of campaigns with toy soldiers in his attic (the "mimic war correspondence" of my epigraph).

In addition to the actual battles and maneuvers recounted in this "correspondence," Stevenson created a host of fictional reporters and journalistic outlets in which to "report" all the news from the front, resulting in a text with a high degree of narrative self-consciousness.

There is, then, ample evidence that the proposition that there is no story "in" a game like *Afrika Korps* is simply wrong.[4] Costikyan's blind spot here, however, also suggests we need to do more to understand exactly how game systems actually produce narrative (what Marie-Laure Ryan has dubbed "narrativity").[5] In particular, I want to suggest that while we may or may not be able to tell a compelling story about a game of chess or *Monopoly* (we can argue about this), board wargames incorporate distinctive *formal* elements that make them qualitatively different kinds of storytelling systems, and that the kind of storytelling they encourage is much closer to that of role-playing games than Faidutti's *Mystery of the Abbey* (even despite the fact that it is based on a novel) or the *Doom* board game. I will contend that board wargames demonstrate that storytelling is dependent on *procedural granularity* and that extremely complex rule systems actually encourage rather than discourage the act of storytelling.

II.

Let me begin by being precise about what I mean by a board wargame. While games with abstract martial themes date to antiquity (Go and chess), and while the world's militaries have taken tabletop wargaming (*Kriegspiel*) seriously since the early nineteenth century, historically focused board wargames represent a distinct genre of twentieth-century commercial entertainment board game publishing. Their origins are typically traced to Charles S. Roberts, who published the games *Tactics* and *Gettysburg* out of his basement in the mid-1950s, and went on to found the Avalon Hill Game Company in Baltimore, which produced a number of wargames, including the above-mentioned *Afrika Korps*. Board wargames are not to be confused with miniatures rules, which apply to painted figures and models in three-dimensional terrain, though there are obvious antecedents and crossovers. Instead, board wargames use (mostly) two-dimensional paper components to replicate a particular historical battle, campaign, or conflict. The hex-based map and the cardboard counter (unit token) are the genre's most recognizable icons. Dice, usually a d6 or d10, introduce the element of chance that always accompanies warfare (there is no certainty on a battlefield), but players attempt to manage the situation and make their own luck by amassing superior numbers, occupying the right terrain, and leveraging special units such as airpower or artillery to their advantage. In short, players learn to apply principles of real-world military strategy to create the most favorable conditions they can for success.

Wargames have to manifest some degree of historical specificity to be differentiated from generic conflict games like *Stratego* or *Risk*. The popular *Axis and Allies* franchise (Hasbro) or more recently *Memoir '44* (Days of Wonder) represent about the minimum acceptable in this regard. Unlike many Euro games, where the nominal historical subject is nothing but a thematic skin for the underlying game engine, board wargames try to capture some salient aspect of the events they depict, be it a particular strategic dilemma, operational opportunity or challenge, or battlefield dynamic. Unit strengths and capabilities are usually based on quantitative models derived from what is known historically and technically about the combatants and their weaponry. Game topics range from ancient warfare to contemporary and hypothetical conflicts, with Napoleon's campaigns, the American Civil War, and World War II the most popular eras.

The heyday of such games in North America and to a lesser extent elsewhere (notably Europe and Japan) extended from the 1960s through the early 1980s, when SPI's *Strategy and Tactics*, the hobby's premier magazine, enjoyed a subscriber base numbering as high as thirty thousand; since then, role-playing games, computer games, collectible card games, and Euro- or German-style games have all but eclipsed this market share. Yet board wargaming still persists with pockets of enthusiasts around the world, supported and sustained by dozens of new game releases every year in cottage industry print runs of three or five thousand copies. Designers continue to innovate, and production values can rival all but the most elaborate Euro titles.[6]

Board wargames ought to be of interest to the contemporary ludologist for at least the following reasons:

- Several thousand titles have been published. Collectively these represent a distinct commercial and design genre for the board game hobby, one that enjoyed considerable popularity and market penetration. For example, Avalon Hill's *Squad Leader* (1977), earnestly glossed as "the

game of infantry combat in World War II," sold two hundred thousand copies. In obvious ways, such games are essential context for the current crop of military- and conflict-themed computer games as well as ongoing debates about violence, militarism, and gaming ethics. Yet a recent book-length survey of exactly that subject (Halter 2006) makes no mention of board wargames anywhere in its 350-plus pages—the kind of oversight that suggests their existence and popularity remains unknown to many now working in the field of ludology.[7]

- The sheer size, scale, and scope of many wargames places the genre at the formal, physical, and ergonomic limits of board gaming. Here is the back-of-box description for SPI's *The Campaign for North Africa* (1978), on the desert war 1940–1942:

CNA has (almost) everything: 1800 counters, over 1000 of them representing land combat units are provided. Five 23″ × 34″ four-color maps cover the sands of North Africa from the Nile to Nofilia, with off-map boxes representing Tripoli, Malta, Crete, Italy, and Sicily. And last, but not least, over 100 pages of rules and supporting charts and tables.... From individually rated pilots and types of aircraft to the higher consumption of water by Italian units because of the fact they were supplied with spaghetti to the decided superiority of the German 88's—*CNA* has it all!...The complete campaign game runs well over 1000 hours of playing time.[8]

Sometimes called monster games, a wargame of such magnitude exhibits a materiality distinct from any other ludic artifact by virtue of its formal and physical extremes.

- Board wargames function as paper computers. The abstraction of combat, movement, supply, morale, and other basic military considerations into a numerically expressed spectrum of outcomes, randomized by die rolls within the parameters of a situation, makes the genre a rich source for anyone interested in the formal and procedural representation of dynamic, often ambiguous, literally contested experience.[9] Moreover, because wargames are embodied in cardboard and charts rather than algorithms and code, they are by their nature "open source." That is, the quantitative model underpinning

31.2 *Europa*, a "monster" game covering World War II in its entirety in Europe and the Middle East, in play at Origins 2006. Each hex represents sixteen miles, each game turn represents two weeks, and units (the individual counter tokens) are typically divisions. (Michael Dye)

the game system is materially exposed for inspection and analysis, frequently by way of innovative graphic and information design.

It is not uncommon for enthusiasts to collect a number of different games on the same battle or campaign in order to explore what different designers have chosen to emphasize in their models, and how successfully historical events are depicted by the competing game systems. (As Costikyan points out, the occupational title "game designer" was used for the first time in conjunction with board wargames.[10] Moreover, wargames often include extensive "designer's notes," which explain the designer's intentions and often explicitly reference other games on the same subject.) Likewise, many players tinker with game systems, employing house rules and modifications to implement their own interpretation of the

history. To the extent that wargames aspire to instruct us in specific historical outcomes, such as "why Napoleon lost at Waterloo" and the like, they also represent a significant corpus of what many now call "serious games," and what Ian Bogost has lately termed "persuasive games."

• Finally, while most often understood in terms related to either gaming or simulation, board wargames can also function as powerful narrative agents. As already noted, the after-action report is the most literal manifestation of this behavior, but wargamers routinely discuss their games' capacities for narrative, meaning whether the discrete die rolls and events allow them to suspend disbelief and create a believable storyworld that accords with their sense of historical plausibility.[11]

Given the specific focus of *Third Person* on vast narratives, this chapter will primarily address the last of these

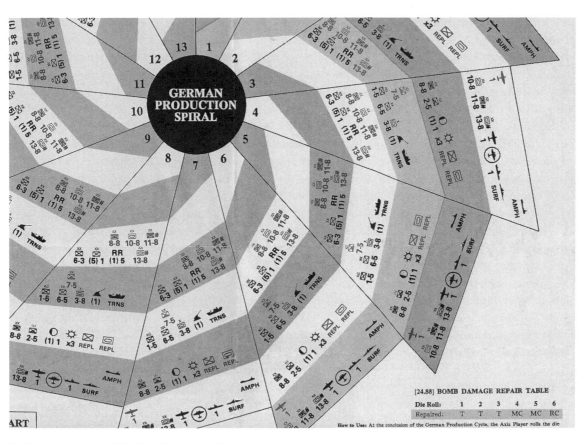

31.3 Component from SPI's *War in Europe* (1976).

areas and tackle the question of narrative agency (or narrativity) in board wargames, literally vast in their physical components and formal complexity. Specific questions to be considered include: How does narrative emerge from the procedural mechanisms of the game? What is the relationship between the physical components (map, unit tokens, charts, etc.) and the storyworld? How do the formal and physical extremes of board wargames give rise to narrative detail and nuance? How do we think about after-action reports in relation to alternative history and military historiography? What is the role of the player in the game, and are wargames second- or third-person player experiences?

III.

Why is war such a popular subject for toys and games? Partly, of course, because both war and games share elements of conflict, competition, and conquest. A more complete answer to this question is beyond the scope of this chapter, but in the same way that Jesper Juul (2005, 5) asks why play games with computers rather than devices like microwave ovens, one might also ask why play games about war as opposed to games about cooking. I would much rather be in a kitchen than in a battle, but warfare and gameplay have a long, deep, intertwined history with one another, much as the world's militaries have a deep and intertwined history with computers and computing.

Wargaming and the literary imagination also have a long history. Playing with toy soldiers encouraged the making of rules, and the rules seemed to encourage stories about the unfolding action, by definition the stuff of high drama. H. G. Wells wrote two books on the subject, *Floor Games* (1911) and *Little Wars* (1913). The Brontë sisters were captivated by toy soldiers, and their whole family played games with them using rules they collectively devised. So did Robert Louis Stevenson, as we have seen, as well as Hans Christian Andersen and the modern fantasist Fletcher Pratt (who authored a set of naval wargame rules). Games like chess have been written down and recorded for centuries, but this kind of documentation should be understood as occupying the minimalist end of a spectrum or continuum of game-based writing. At the other end are the fully realized narratives inspired by gameplay. Tom Clancy and Larry Bond cowrote the best-selling techno-thriller *Red Storm Rising* (1986) based in part on sessions with Bond's modern naval wargame *Harpoon*. The practice is more prevalent in the role-playing game world, with the most successful example probably being Margaret Weis and Tracy Hickman's *Dragonlance* books, mature fantasy novels whose episodes are based, again in part, on actual *Advanced Dungeons & Dragons* campaigns. The German board game *Settlers of Catan* has spawned a novel, and popular video games increasingly include novelizations in their franchise.

My basic thesis in what follows is that the narrative impulse often stimulated by wargames is a function of the games' procedural granularity. (I prefer granularity to a term like complexity because it better captures the particularity of details—so important to Stevenson's mimic war correspondence, for example—as narrative stimuli.) All games are procedural systems, by definition. Wargames, however, have denser and more interdependent procedures than most games, and it is precisely the density and interconnectedness of these procedures that stimulates narrative agency, or contributes to Ryan's narrativity. If games are digital constructs—digital in the sense that they are composed of discrete units and rules for their manipulation—then wargames are perhaps the highest-resolution games yet created—certainly higher than any other class of board game. The higher the resolution of the game system, the richer the narratives it can support and sustain.

Chess is capable of an extraordinary range of permutations in its gameplay, and hence the interest it has sustained over the centuries. It is the epitome of the ludic ideal of easy to learn, difficult to master. (While chess is not as easy to learn as, say, checkers, the basics—how the

pieces move, and how the game is won—are readily assimilated, and a novice player can obtain the requisite level of procedural competency—that is, they can play the game without breaking the rules—in short order.) Wargames, by contrast, have much more procedurally granular rules, and it is not uncommon for even an experienced player to discover, on reviewing the rule book, that they have been playing some aspect of a particular game's rules wrong for many years. *Advanced Squad Leader* (1985), a World War II game that sports a legalistic rules manual approaching two hundred pages, has as its second rule ("case") the stipulation that any erroneous application of the rules must stand once gameplay has passed beyond the point of correction. This would be the equivalent of telling a chess player that if a rook is inadvertently moved diagonally and the other player offers a countermove without having first spotted the mistake, then the rook's diagonal move, in that singular instance, is *formally legitimated* by the rules of the game. Such a scenario is improbable in chess, but not uncommon in *Advanced Squad Leader*.[12] Not coincidently, *Advanced Squad Leader* is also capable of generating some extraordinary narratives.

It is time to look at how this actually works. Let's take chess first. Here, knight is about to take pawn:

31.4 Knight takes pawn.

In algebraic chess notation, this move would be recorded as Nxe5 (Knight *captures* the piece on grid square e5). But what kind of *story* can we tell about what has just transpired? The narrative details licensed by the game's formal procedures are scarce. The most obvious response is to suggest that what we have is a martial episode, with the cavalry riding down the infantry, though even these basic troop types are suggested only by the names and shapes of the pieces.[13] "Cavalry" and "infantry" are identities at best obliquely authorized by the game's actual procedures and mechanics—for while knights in chess are indeed more freewheeling in their movement patterns than pawns, neither piece's movement is particularly realistic. Historically, a charge formation was an unwieldy one, and the pawn's irreversible forward motion ironically provides a better model for the behavior of heavy cavalry on the battlefield than the knight's hopscotching. And surely the "pawns," for their part, ought to be able to retreat (move backward) in the face of overwhelming force or turn to face a threat from the flank? (Such maneuvers were well rehearsed by professional men-at-arms.) In any case, while one can tell whatever story one likes here, little of it will be anchored by procedural details, and any narrative details will be merely contrived. Did the infantry break ranks and get ridden down, or did they attempt a defensive formation? Did they surrender en masse or were they butchered to the last man? Did the horses charge home or execute the caracole? What kind of ground did the fighting take place on? What orders were given? The very plurality of potential narratives is a strong indicator of the ultimate arbitrariness of any single one of them. Since one story is just as good as any other, there is little incentive to go to the trouble of actually telling one.

A similar encounter in even the simplest of wargames offers considerably more procedural granularity. Here is a typical situation from SPI's *Napoleon at Waterloo* (1971), a classic wargame once given out for free to promote the hobby.[14]

The first thing to note is that we are looking at a historically specific situation. The counters are distinguished by nationality, corresponding to those of the actual combatants. Moreover, each counter is labeled with the military designation of the historical formation it is intended to represent. These labels have no procedural impact on the gameplay, but do serve to individuate the tokens. The numbers on the counters denote combat strength and movement allowances, respectively, and these are anchored in what is known about the formation's actual troop strength and movement capabilities. The different troop types are infantry, cavalry, and artillery, designated using so-called

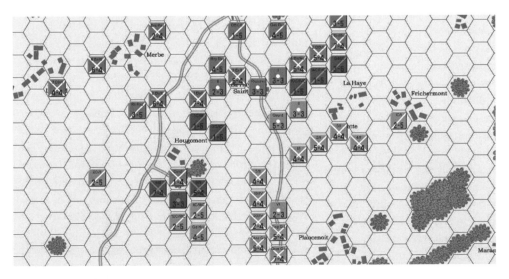

31.5 *Napoleon at Waterloo* (SPI).

NATO symbology (X for infantry, / for cavalry, and • for artillery). The map on which the battle is fought is a hex-grained abstraction of the actual terrain (students of the battle will recognize landmarks), and the forces are set up in their historical dispositions and deployments. Victory will be determined by the same tactical objectives that governed the actions of the historical commanders. Thus, we see that narrative detail is already being licensed by a combination of representational particularity as well as the close correspondence between the game's formal devices and abstracted elements of the historical situation—what Katie Salen and Eric Zimmerman (2004, 427–431) would call "procedural representation," and what Ryan (2006, 193–195) might call "narrative design."[15]

In chess, the combat model is deterministic: one piece challenging another piece will always do so with a known outcome. A heroic pawn will never fend off an attacking bishop through good fortune or stoutness of heart. In *Napoleon at Waterloo*, the combat is resolved by deriving a ratio from the combat strengths of the opposing pieces (quantitative abstractions of historical capabilities) and rolling a six-sided die. The result of the die roll is cross-indexed with the appropriate ratio on the Combat Results Table, and modified for the presence of the terrain (the defender's combat strength is doubled in woods and towns). Failure for the attacker is possible even at two-to-one odds, and the Exchange result (Ee) means that both sides may be bloodied at up to five-to-one odds.

A few additional notes: the game is played in turns, and at each turn each player may, in sequence, move any or all of his or her pieces, and attack with any or all that are eligible. This in itself is strikingly different from chess or checkers, where a player moves one token per turn. Combat is mandated when pieces are adjacent, occupying one another's "zone of control." The zone of control, however, does not apply to all terrain types uniformly; for example, a unit occupying a fortified defensive position in a château hex is not required to attack any adjacent enemy units. In the actual battle of Waterloo, British infantry held just such a fortified château against repeated French attacks throughout the day, fighting a disciplined defensive battle within

Combat Ratios (Attacker to Defender Strength)										
DIE	**1-5**	**1-4**	**1-3**	**1-2**	**1-1**	**2-1**	**3-1**	**4-1**	**5-1**	**6-1**
1	Ae	Ar	Ar	Dr	Dr	Dr	De	De	De	De
2	Ae	Ae	Ar	Ar	Dr	Dr	Dr	De	De	De
3	Ae	Ae	Ae	Ar	Dr	Dr	Dr	Dr	De	De
4	Ae	Ae	Ae	Ar	Ar	Dr	Dr	Dr	De	De
5	Ae	Ae	Ae	Ar	Ar	Ee	Dr	Ee	Ee	De
6	Ae	Ae	Ae	Ae	Ar	Ar	Ee	Ee	Ee	De

Attacks executed at worse than "1 to 5" are treated as "1 to 5"; attacks executed at greater than "6 to 1" are treated as "6 to 1".

31.6 The *Napoleon at Waterloo* Combat Results Table. Results are Attacker or Defender Retreat, Attacker or Defender Eliminated, or Exchange (Ee).

the walled gardens and buildings of Hougoumont. A combat model that forced these units in the game to take the offensive and attack neighboring French would be unrealistic.

Yet even here, the procedural granularity is limited and the "resolution" comparatively low. Outcomes are mostly binary, affecting one side or the other exclusively, and each unit is affected as a whole. In the situation depicted above, we see French cavalry closing unsupported with the British lines, much as happened at the height of the historical battle. Historically, the British and allied infantry adopted a square formation, and the cavalry attacks were ineffectual. Here too these attacks are unlikely to succeed, given the low odds ratios. One can well imagine a colorful after-action report that would describe the foolish French gambit as well as the heroic charge by the individual cavalry brigades and their inevitable repulse. But there is nothing in the game's procedures to license more particular narrative elements, such as whether an attack fails because the infantry has formed square, or because it has stood in line and delivered a withering fusillade of musketry. Similarly, we won't know if the cavalry retreated from casualties or if it simply wheeled about the squares ineffectually before retiring. Ben Hull's *This Accursed Civil War* from the *Musket and Pike Battles Series* (2002), by contrast, tracks individual unit integrity along three separate vectors: morale, formation, and casualties (mechanically, this is accomplished by placing markers above or below the unit). Thus, narrative detail as to whether a given unit sustains too many casualties to

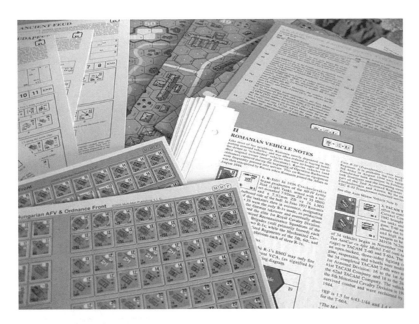

31.7 *Advanced Squad Leader* rules and components.

fight on, or has its ranks in disarray or simply loses its collective nerve—or some combination thereof—is licensed by explicit procedural representations.

The limit case in board wargaming is almost certainly *Advanced Squad Leader*, which was Avalon Hill's 1985 upgrade to its tremendously successful *Squad Leader* series. The game (more properly, game system, as one acquires it as a series of modules) focuses on Word War II small unit combat, with counters representing infantry squads and individual leaders, vehicles, and heavy weapons. Here is not the place to go into detail about *Advanced Squad Leader* itself, which in theory allows a player to re-create any small unit action from any theater or phase of the war. The game system is capable not only of accommodating movement and attacks but a vast array of other actions. A building struck by an artillery shell may "rubble," in turn collapsing other buildings around it. Underbrush may be set on fire. A tank can throw a tread as it crashes through a wall, rotating its turret to fire at a target glimpsed for a moment through a narrow village street. Squads may generate heroes, who can become wounded, but nonetheless survive to scrounge an abandoned machine gun that might

then malfunction only to be repaired and then lost when the wounded hero is captured (he may then escape).

Everything I have just been describing is actionable via the specific gameplay procedures that are documented in the game's formidable rules manual (which comes in a loose-leaf binder), complete with seemingly acres of foldout charts and flowcharts (putting even the most involved role-playing games to shame).

Advanced Squad Leader has become infamous in board gaming circles for its excesses (like the "Sewer Emergence Chart"), yet if one thinks of the game as a form of vast world building—in Juul's terms, *Advanced Squad Leader* is much more incomplete than incoherent—it becomes less risible. World War II saw more urban combat than any other conflict in history, and not a few cities boasted extensive sewer systems. These were, predictably, utilized by the combatants, and *Advanced Squad Leader*, as a game, incorporates procedures for entering the sewer system, navigating it (you can get lost), and emerging from the sewers (you may be spotted, you are more vulnerable to enemy fire if you are, and you are less capable of firing effectively in return). Once these procedures are set in motion, it is not hard to see how a rather vivid and satisfying story might emerge about a squad that attempts to use the sewers to infiltrate the enemy's positions, gets lost, turns up in the wrong place, is spotted by the enemy, but then manages to escape back to its own lines, guns blazing. A typical *Advanced Squad Leader* scenario will generate dozens of comparable episodes. Playing a game of *Advanced Squad Leader* means a lot of die rolling, chart flipping, and rules lookups. Yet players generally find these activities unobtrusive and often cite "narrative" as the single most compelling aspect of the gameplay, suggesting that both narrative and immersion can arise from procedural extremes as well as procedural economy.

IV.

The above examples serve to demonstrate the correspondence between procedural granularity and narrativity that I believe is at the base of a ludic genre like an after-action report as well as more impressionistic appreciations of a game's narrative. Tellingly, its aficionados will frequently say that for all its complexity, *Advanced Squad Leader* is less a simulation of actual World War II small unit tactics than it is an imitation of World War II seen through the lens of a Hollywood movie camera. Meaning that its narrative elements are no less culturally determined than narratives originating in nonludic genres and settings. While I believe the correspondence between procedural granularity and narrative detail is fundamental, and therefore serves to challenge the kind of thesis James Wallis (2007) puts forward—that narrative arises from rules that don't get in the way—there are also other factors to consider. I will discuss two of them here briefly.[16]

First, let's look at a game's visuals. In the *Napoleon at Waterloo* example above, unit types are designated by generic symbols. These are functional, but lacking in atmosphere. Moreover, they do not convey any particular point of view, other than perhaps that of a general studying a map. Compare this to the *Advanced Squad Leader* counter art—vehicles and tanks are depicted using overhead views, in keeping with the aerial perspective of the map boards themselves. The squads and leaders deviate from this, but

the result is a compromise between information design and atmospherics. Wargamers will squabble endlessly over the virtues of abstract symbology versus "sprites" (miniature depictions of soldiers or vehicles), or overhead views that bring the game as a whole closer to a miniatures experience. What is at stake here is often precisely narrative, where the functional ergonomics of the situation contribute to creating a particular point of view, essential for any narrative. Is the player on a hilltop overlooking the battlefield, in a bunker that is miles behind the front, or in a foxhole? Graphic design always implies a point of view, and good game designers know how to take advantage of this.[17]

The second additional consideration is player identity. As we have seen, in ways that anticipated *Choose Your Own Adventure* novels, interactive fiction, and other second-person ludic devices, the wargames often appealed to players' desires for a participatory experience: "Now YOU Command." In truth, however, board wargames are hybrid second-person/third-person experiences. Almost from the start, wargames incorporated representations of actual historical military formations and commanders, allowing players to move not just a generic tank formation but Rommel's Twenty-First Panzer. This alone is an enormously powerful narrative element, and its effects run the gamut from allowing a player to push around a cardboard Rommel or Napoleon to an ordinary dogface, as is the case with the individually named fictitious leader counters in *Advanced Squad Leader*. Many are the after-action reports that have revolved around the exploits of a heroic Sergeant Stahler or Sergeant Kibler, each an "8–1" who came with the original *Squad Leader* game.[18]

Indeed, the original *Squad Leader* even incorporated a simple role-playing module, where players could adopt the identity of one of the cardboard personae and follow its career from scenario to scenario, earning promotion until an (almost inevitable) demise in some geomorphic village or hilltop. While this particular aspect of the game never really caught on and was subsequently dropped from *Advanced Squad Leader*, it would have been difficult to conceive of at all had not the game system incorporated the mechanisms for sophisticated storytelling.

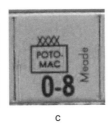
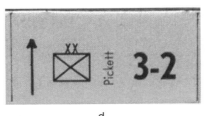

a   b   c   d   e

31.8 Counters. Rommel and the Twenty-first Panzer Regiment (*Afrika Korps*), George Meade's Army of the Potomac HQ, and Pickett's ill-fated division (*Gettysburg*), and a battle-scarred Sergeant Kibler (*Squad Leader*). The double-sized Pickett counter helps re-create the American Civil War's linear formations on the game board.

In fact, the "YOU Are in Command" motif of the box cover belies the often ambiguous role that a player actually takes. Who *is* the player in *Afrika Korps*? Are we adopting the identity of a theater commander like Rommel or Montgomery? This is what the box cover would have us believe. Yet wargames routinely slide between macro- and micro-decision making, and the player's role is further complicated by the presence of counters that embody the historical identities he or she is putatively assuming. So is the *player* Rommel, or is "Rommel" the counter one is moving across the map? In actuality the player is called on to assume a composite identity, one that sometimes coincides with the counter on the map, but that is possessed of other kinds of knowledge and perspectives besides. (The player in a game of *Advanced Squad Leader* sees a good deal more than Sergeant Stahler ever would from inside his foxhole.) Thus, while the games appeal to YOU, *you* are also a fluid and mobile identity, dispersed into third-person representations that are concretized in the game pieces as "Rommel" or "Sergeant Stahler." Once a player finds him- or herself manipulating units with discrete identities (either "Napoleon" or the "Twenty-first Panzer Regiment") on a historical map, the stage is clearly set for narrative: *Rommel and the Twenty-first Panzer swept into Tobruk, just behind the Desert Rats of the Eighth Army as they withdrew from the city . . .*

This seems qualitatively different from both role-playing games with figurines (where the player's identity is always tightly coupled to the figure on the tabletop) and most Euro-style games, which employ generic pawns (usually distinguished from one another only by color coding) to represent the player's interests on the board.

V.

So what kind of war stories are we actually making? First, wargames are emergent game systems par excellence. While the number of positions in chess is vast, that number is dwarfed by even the simplest wargame, where there are dozens (if not hundreds) of units in play, multiple units can be moved in any turn, the playing area has hundreds (if not thousands) of partitions, and conflict resolution is generally probabilistic rather than deterministic. As agents of procedural narratives, then, wargames are also agents of emergent narratives, and the number of narrative permutations is truly vast, or for all practical purposes infinite.

Here is an excerpt from an after-action report about the Battle of Edgehill from the English Civil War (1642), played using GMT's *Musket and Pike Battles Series* rules:

Parliament, meanwhile, switched over to Make Ready orders and refused its flanks, strengthening its right flank with the reserve cavalry of the center wing while deploying a solid line of musketeers and cavalry on its left. All this took place over 45 minutes (3 turns), while the threat from Rupert developed and the artillery of the two sides boomed more or less uselessly, though Astley became concerned by the way shot tracked his position and attempted to retire behind his troops, only to be damned as a coward and placed back at the front.

Aries, however, would not be cheated of his sport and soon enough, the armies came together. Rupert's wing plowed into Ramsey's—Parliament, rather than intercepting, chose to stand its ground and trust to its muskets. However (as later events would reinforce), it was not a day for musketry and the Royal cavalry rapidly plowed Ramsey's boys under (with the exception of Ramsey himself, who rode off the battlefield after a couple of fleeing Royal horse). Essex, during the long retreat after the battle, was heard uttering the most unkind comments about Ramsey for this decision. Even more amazingly, none of Rupert's well-disciplined troops pursued their opponents off the map. (3 consecutive cavalry pursuit rolls of 1 or less.)

However, as is so often the case, this affair produced an opportunity for heroism and Balfour seized it. With a cry of "Charge," he launched the Parliament brigades at the Royal center, without the courtesy of announcing his intentions by slowing to fire. Originally, Charles was heard to mutter, "We have them where we want them," but as the smoke began to disperse, it became clear that the opposite had occurred. One brigade had simply vanished and two more were cut down by pursuing infantry as they scattered from the field. Worse yet, Astley had disappeared at the critical moment, apparently slain. Two royal brigades remained on the right of the center, one on the left, but all of them had felt the sting of the attack and their formations stood ragged, their morale low. Parliament's cavalry reserve, however, had not come through the fighting unscathed.[19]

While after-action reports run the gamut from stark procedural records of moves and die rolls to elaborate fictionalizations, it's not uncommon to witness shifts in discursive modality.[20] The preceding example does this self-consciously, using its rhetorical wit to oscillate between the player's experience (die rolls or "Make Ready" orders) and that of his or her fictional counterparts, with the result being a narrative construct that is a hybrid of fiction and the real world—precisely "half real," as Juul would say. The incident involving the cowardly Astley, for instance, is the redaction of the "gamey" tactic of deliberately sniping at leaders in hopes of eliminating them with a lucky die roll. Or else brave Balfour's cry of "Charge!" in which a fictional element and a gameplay mechanic are seamlessly superimposed (there is an explicit procedure for issuing orders to charge).[21]

While anecdotal evidence suggests that wargame after-action reports, when posted online, are enjoyed by the fan communities who frequent online forums, it is safe to assume that in and of themselves they will never find a mass-market audience (Clancy and Bond's *Red Storm Rising* is an extreme exception). Most after-action reports resemble the type of military historiography that John Keegan (1976) has termed the "battle piece," a spectacle-laden accounting of maneuvers and positions, charge and countercharge, absent any interrogation of human motive or emotion, any of the stuff of the lived experience of the battlefield: what a British line soldier saw—and heard and smelled and felt—at Waterloo, for instance, as opposed to at what hour Michael Ney ordered the cavalry to go in. Not surprisingly, the battle piece corresponds to the omniscient view of the battlefield enjoyed by wargame players, where the player has a perspective that would have been the envy of any historical commander, and that is perhaps only now being realized in the form of Predator drones, battlefield LANs, and individual soldiers outfitted with GPS. As alternative history, then, wargame after-action reports hew to the most pedestrian habits of military genre writing, with little opportunity for exploring the emotions and intensity of experience that warfare elicits. As such, their narrative range is ultimately limited. Keegan's thesis is that the battle piece is a distinctly British and Victorian construct— one that emerged in the wake of Sir Edward Creasy's enormously influential *The Fifteen Decisive Battles of the World* (1851). The pervasive influence of the narrative artifact of a "battle" as a decisive turning point has gone unacknowledged by professional military historians, Keegan argues; it has certainly influenced the wargame industry as well— indeed, as of this writing, a publisher called Turning Point Simulations has just announced plans for a series of twenty games, each based on one of the "decisive" battles in Lieutenant Colonel Joseph B. Mitchell's 1964 update to Creasy (which added another five to the list).[22] If board wargames are to offer different kinds of narrative experiences then some or all of their fundamentals, both rules systems and physical presentation will need to be rethought.

This chapter has focused on board wargames, not computer games. This is partly because board wargaming represents an underacknowledged tradition, the scant critical attention disproportionate, I believe, to its actual significance for contemporary ludology. Certainly computer games have embraced military and militaristic simulations of all types, from the ubiquitous "shooters" (one company, Kuma, specializes in excruciatingly topical shooters based on firefights in Fallujah and the like) to throwback hex and counter simulations transposed to the computational environment, complete with sequential turn sequences.[23] In *Second Person*, editors Pat Harrigan and Noah Wardrip-Fruin (2007) claim that computers are inherently better suited to vast or extensive proceduralism than tabletop games, since computers mask all of the mechanical overhead. They cite the specific example of *Squad Leader*, and suggest that *Brothers in Arms*, a computer-based World War II squad game, offers both a better simulation and more enjoyable gameplay (107).

I disagree. By exposing the players to rules and procedure, *Squad Leader* also exposes the formal and quantitative modeling that underlies the game system. This does not in and of itself make it a better game or a better simulation but it does make it a qualitatively different *kind* of ludic artifact than an electronic game whose world model is black boxed, or accessible only by prescribed Preferences. Attending to procedure is sometimes tedious, but wargamers also experience a "flow" not unlike that enjoyed by computer programmers or others engaged in intense procedural activities. From this flow, or immersion, comes a narrative experience that is licensed by both participatory decision making and vastly unpredictable rules interactions (not to mention luck). Of course too much procedure is distracting, and no player enjoys a "fiddly" game that consists of endless dicing and chart lookups. But one thing that board wargames might have to teach designers of electronic games is that more thought needs to go into when and where process is exposed, and when and how it is kept under wraps. Board wargames help us understand the role of process and procedure in stories and games, and as such remain a unique and relevant example of the game designer's art.

Peace.

Notes

I am grateful to Peter Bogdasarian, Steve Jones, Henry Lowood, Jason Rhody, Marc Ruppel, and Markus Stumptner as well as Pat Harrigan and Noah Wardrip-Fruin for comments and feedback on this chapter.

1. For further discussion of the *Afrika Korps* box cover, which also included a rebus-writing introduction to the historical situation, see Lowood (2007). Henry Lowood writes: "It was the player's role to venture into a ludic possibility space of counterfactual moves and *change* history" (email to author, July 23, 2006).

2. Costikyan offers his take on what happened to the hobby in "A Farewell to Hexes," available at ⟨http://www.costik.com/spisins.html⟩.

3. Here's an example from an after-action report on Wake Island: "DISCLAIMER: I have been informed that multiple people have complained . . . about the 'lies' being spread in this document. To those who engaged in such behaviors, folks, this is a REPLAY of a GAME. It's not a history of the REAL THING. Thank you for understanding this important distinction in the future." See ⟨http://www.dbai.tuwien.ac.at/user/mst/games/sol/repwake.html⟩.

4. Here, Costikyan might object he intends a much more literal meaning of the key preposition *in* than I am apparently willing to give him credit for. We can tell stories *about* almost any game, certainly including board wargames, but that is not the same as demonstrating that storytelling mechanisms are actually built into a particular game system, he might say. Role-playing games, Costikyan might insist, incorporate such mechanisms, whereas a board wargame like *Afrika Korps* simply does not, however alluring the prospect of crafting an after-action report out of its gameplay. This is a reasonable objection, yet I would argue that the kind of procedural granularity I will be discussing in this chapter, coupled with the representational specificity that is characteristic of board wargames as a genre, serves to inject always at least latent storytelling impulses into the gameplay, so much so that it is all but impossible to play a board wargame and *not* allow it to furnish some kind of narrative experience—thereby rendering the objection that there is no story actually *in* the game trivial at best. See also notes 15 and 21, below.

5. See Ryan (2006, esp. 181–203).

6. Current board wargame publishers of note include GMT, MultiMan Publishing, Clash of Arms, Decision Games, Compass Games, Columbia Games, Worthington Games, Avalanche Press, L2 Design Group, Australian Design Group, and the Operational Studies Group. In addition to Web sites for each of the publishers named above, the online hubs for board wargaming are ConsimWorld, available at ⟨http://www.consimworld.com⟩, and Web Grognards, available at ⟨http://www.grognard.com⟩. BoardGameGeek maintains a more pluralistic focus on all types of board games, but is still a useful community for board wargamers; available at ⟨http://www.boardgamegeek.com⟩.

7. One encouraging exception is Katie Salen and Eric Zimmerman's *Rules of Play* (2004), which devotes several pages to "Learning from Wargames" in its section on "Games as the Play of Simulation" (442–446).

8. Richard Berg, the game's designer, often says that the business about the pasta was always intended as a joke, a bit of self-mockery about the game's level of detail.

9. Frank Davis's comments in the designer's notes to one of his games are exemplary in this regard: "I will begin by saying that I cannot claim that *Wellington's Victory* [1976] is an accurate simulation of the Battle of Waterloo. Like Wellington, I believe that an accurate account (much less a game) never has or will be produced on the subject of Waterloo. No soldier, historian, or game designer knows or fully understands exactly what occurred that Sunday afternoon more than a century and a half ago. All I can therefore claim is that the game accurately reflects my own carefully constructed interpretation of the events of June 18, 1815. I am grateful that our exhaustive playtesting indicates that when the game is played effectively, it does in fact resemble a reasonably accurate working model of the actual battle."

10. See ⟨http://www.costik.com/weblog/2005_03_01_blogchive .html#111070130229508681⟩.

11. Charles Vasey refers to this as "experience gaming":

> Experience Gamers are not interested in an intellectual puzzle. They want to see a story unfold as they play. To this end they may accept a complete lack of opportunity to influence the game providing it generates the required experience. The most famous class of Experience Gamers are the sports replay gamers (and we have all done it, so no sneering) who enjoy recreating an entire season or game where the two sides react in the same way as their real-life counterparts. Of course Experience Games do not preclude skill choices, but I do not think they depend on them. We all enjoy the Experience Game (even if vicariously) because one can amble up to the gamer and say, "How are the Steelers doing?" and read the results (and yes, you do find yourself saying, "Goodness, they beat the Oilers").

See Vasey's essay on "Chaos Gaming," available at ⟨http://www .gamecabinet.com/sumo/Issue7/Chaos.html⟩.

12. Nevertheless, *Advanced Squad Leader* is not to be mistaken for free-form role-playing, or a metagame like *Nomic*, where gameplay proceeds through an emendation of the rules. Nothing could be further from the truth. *Advanced Squad Leader* players get rules wrong not because they are inattentive or impish but because the numbers of procedures and their potential interactions is so vast. That being said, a competent *Advanced Squad Leader* player is unlikely to make a major rules error (and/or the opponent is unlikely not to notice) when working within the game's most commonly used rules sections. See my *Zone of Influence* blog for more discussion on this point, available at ⟨http://www.zoi.wordherders.net/?cat=3⟩.

13. Actually, as Jason Rhody pointed out to me, there is an even simpler story one could tell about this situation—namely, "Jane just moved her knight to capture Joe's pawn."

14. The complete rules and components to *Napoleon at Waterloo* are available for free download and assembly at ⟨http://www .alanemrich.com/PGD/Week_03/PGD_NAW_rules.htm⟩.

15. One of Ryan's key points in her chapter on games and narrative is that computer games have the distinction of being the first games to effectively combine *ludus* and *paidia*—that is, competitive, rule-based play versus free-form, imaginative play (the distinction was originally introduced by Roger Caillois). Video games, by virtue of their fully realized virtual worlds, routinely accommodate both these forms of play. Yet wargames, I would argue (and as Ryan acknowledges in a note [244–245] inspired by a comment of mine originally posted on the GrandTextAuto blog, available at ⟨http://

grandtextauto.gatech.edu/2004/04/25/computer-games-at-ssnls-narrative-conference/#comment-1200⟩), are a significant precursor to computer games. The historically specific terrain of a wargame map furnishes a storyworld that predisposes certain stories to being told while discouraging others. A good Gettysburg game, for example, will often see fighting at Culp's Hill, Cemetery Ridge, and Little Round Top, not because players are slavishly intent on mimicking the history, but because those are the best defensive positions on the map, and the game system will reward a Union player who chooses to fight there as opposed to in the Peach Orchard. Other game maps might be dominated by a river, thus ensuring that a dramatic river crossing will be part of the narrative as the gameplay proceeds. In general, the historical specificity of a wargame map also entails asymmetry (compared to a uniform chess grid or the game board for *Scrabble*), and asymmetry is a powerful agent of narrativity. (Wargames also manifest other forms of asymmetry that heighten narrativity: compared to chess, say, where both players have equal forces, quality versus quantity on the battlefield is a classic wargame dynamic, from Alexander the Great's battles against the Persians to hypothetical NATO versus Warsaw Pact conflicts.)

16. I'm thinking in particular of Wallis's comments in his *Second Person* essay: "No game can exist without rules, at least implicit ones. . . . But in story-making games, too great a density of rules or a single rule in the wrong place can destroy the cohesion or the effect of the story" (79).

17. I have also written about this in more detail on *Zone of Influence*, available at ⟨http://www.zoi.wordherders.net/?p=16⟩.

18. *Advanced Squad Leader* leader names often function as insider jokes, using the names of game designers, playtesters, and hobby celebrities; getting one's own "vanity counter" is the highest sign of achievement in the *Advanced Squad Leader* world, except perhaps for winning the annual *ASLOK* tournament.

19. The after-action report is written by Peter Bogdasarian, who was the Royalist player (I was the Parliamentarian). See ⟨http:// www.boardgamegeek.com/thread/33943⟩ for the AAR in its entirety.

20. In terms of structural procedural records, software utilities for remote electronic play—for example, VASSAL—automatically record log files of the gameplay, meaning that each session spawns a basic computer-generated after-action report.

21. By way of contrast, here is a "session report" of *Carcassonne* (2001), a popular Euro-style game:

> Right from the start many farmers were put on the tiles. It's sad we couldn't take a picture because there was so many meeples for this start. Martin again was able to place 3 farmers on what developed as a big field. Even if there was [sic] a lot of people in this big field Martin planned a long term strategy and connected the field and his 3 farmers. Pierre didn't make any big castles as he picked several road tiles but he was able to make some interesting scoring specially with some bonus road tiles. Sophie and Martin had a tough blow when Nathalie put a cathedral on their big castle and they weren't able to complete it. We thought Martin would win the game easily with his 3 farmers in the big field but Mario had a great comeback when he was able to put his 4th farmer to pass ahead of Martin for this big scoring and he finally won the game. (Available at ⟨http://www .boardgamegeek.com/thread/151109⟩)

There is little in the way of "game fiction" here (to use a term employed by both Jason Rhody and Juul), only a lucid but mechanical accounting of how the gameplay unfolded.

22. The argument, of course, is not that battles are never important or even "decisive" but that military history is a narrative genre (much as Hayden White has contended that all history is narrative discourse) and that the pride of place battles occupy in military historiography represents an always interested interpretation of the past. It is no accident, for instance, that the culminating example in Creasy's Victorian volume is Waterloo, which set the stage for the Pax Britannica. Likewise, in his update, Mitchell makes the controversial choice of selecting Vicksburg and not Gettysburg (both fought in 1863) as the decisive battle of the American Civil War, since it secured the Mississippi and the West, and led to Ulysses S. Grant's elevation as the top Union commander.

23. HPS Simulations is probably the current state of the art; see ⟨http://www.hpssims.com/⟩.

References: Literature

Costikyan, Grey (2007). "Games, Storytelling, and Breaking the String." In *Second Person: Role-Playing and Story in Games and Playable Media*, edited by Pat Harrigan and Noah Wardrip-Fruin, 5–13. Cambridge, MA: MIT Press.

Creasy, Sir Edward (1851). *The Fifteen Decisive Battles of the World From Marathon to Waterloo*. Whitefish, MT: Kessinger Publishing. (Reprinted in 2004.)

Faidutti, Bruno (2007). "On *Mystery of the Abbey*." In *Second Person: Role-Playing and Story in Games and Playable Media*, edited by Pat Harrigan and Noah Wardrip-Fruin, 95–97. Cambridge, MA: MIT Press.

Halter, Ed (2006). *From Sun Tzu to Xbox: War and Video Games*. New York: Thunder's Mouth Press.

Harrigan, Pat, and Noah Wardrip-Fruin (eds.) (2007). *Second Person: Role-Playing and Story in Games and Playable Media*. Cambridge, MA: MIT Press.

Juul, Jesper (2005). *Half Real: Video Games between Real Rules and Fictional Worlds*. Cambridge, MA: MIT Press.

Keegan, John (1976). *The Face of Battle*. New York: Penguin.

Lowood, Henry (2007). "It's Not Easy Being Green": Real-Time Game Performance in *Warcraft*." In *Videogame/Player/Text*, edited by Barry Atkins and Tanya Krzywinska Manchester: Manchester University Press.

Osbourne, Lloyd (1898). "Stevenson at Play." *Scribner's Magazine* 24:709–719.

Pearson, Harry (2007). *Achtung Schweinhund! A Boy's Own Story of Imaginary Combat*. London: Little, Brown and Company.

Ryan, Marie-Laure (2006). *Avatars of Story*. Minneapolis: University of Minnesota Press.

Salen, Katie, and Eric Zimmerman (2004). *Rules of Play: Game Design Fundamentals*. Cambridge, MA: MIT Press.

Wallis, James (2007). "Making Games That Make Stories." In *Second Person: Role-Playing and Story in Games and Playable Media*, edited by Pat Harrigan and Noah Wardrip-Fruin, 69–80. Cambridge, MA: MIT Press.

Wilson, Kevin (2007). "One Story, Many Media." In *Second Person: Role-Playing and Story in Games and Playable Media*, edited by Pat Harrigan and Noah Wardrip-Fruin, 91–93. Cambridge, MA: MIT Press.

References: Games

Advanced Squad Leader. Don Greenwood; Avalon Hill Game Company. 1985.

Afrika Korps. Charles S. Roberts; Avalon Hill Game Company. 1964.

The Campaign for North Africa. Richard H. Berg; Simulations Publications Incorporated. 1978.

Carcassonne. Klaus-Jürgen Wrede; Rio Grande Games. 2000.

Napoleon at Waterloo. James F. Dunnigan; Simulations Publications Incorporated. 1971.

Squad Leader. John Hill; Avalon Hill Game Company. 1977.

This Accursed Civil War (Musket and Pike Battles Series). Ben Hull; GMT Games. 2002.

Wellington's Victory. Frank Davis; Simulations Publications Incorporated. 1976.

Epic Spatialities: The Production of Space in *Final Fantasy* Games

William H. Huber

When first asked to write about "vast narratives" for this book, I was inclined to discuss the *Final Fantasy* games as *Gesamtkunstwerk*: the epic themes, the exhaustive dramatis personae, and the fantastic cosmological preoccupations of the game franchise that seem so rich for such interpretive study. I have taken something of a "spatial turn," however, that brings me through the question of the epic narrative to the modifier "vast," which is at the very least a spatial metaphor (mapping time as space, and duration as expanse). Rather than dwell on surface narrative epic aspects that are consistent with other, noncomputational representational practices (particularly anime and manga in the case of Japanese games), I was drawn to the elements of these objects that produced the experience of the vast in a distinctive fashion.

Video games have been described as "play spaces" (Jenkins 1998), partially to distinguish them from other screen-based representational practices by emphasizing that their spaces are not simply represented but also experienced, understood, and navigated. Yet there has been little to suggest a critical inquiry into the production of space in the authoring and playing of video games in general, much less within genre- and title-specific terms. Space is not a straightforward category in the physical world. The design and authorship of video game space is no less a complex practice.

A relationship between spatiality and narrative is alluded to by Henry Jenkins (2004) in his essay "Game Design as Narrative Architecture." The essay is a general defense of attention to narrative aspects within video games, rather than a theory of spatiality itself. It might be more productive to see both play and story elements as temporal orderings, and then to understand the relationship between those temporal orderings along with the spatialities created by game design and game experience.

An undifferentiated hermeneutics of video game space cannot manage an analysis of these spatialities with adequate granularity. It is within genres, franchises, and titles that we can unwind strategies and methods by which space is produced, represented, and engaged (outside the categorical observation that video game space is, materially, software-generated space). The *Final Fantasy* franchise is one such framework for conceiving the practices of spatiality within the authorship and play of video games, particularly insofar as it utilizes techniques of telescoping scale and acceleration through space in the service of the creation of what is still an expansive, epic *Gesamtkunstwerk*.

Space and spatiality are fraught, elusive categories. An excellent conceptual model for the production of space is proffered by David Harvey (2006) in his chapter "Space as a Keyword." He intersects a tripartite model of space with another tripartite model, described by Henri Lefebvre (1991), to produce a matrix of concepts for understanding space and spatiotemporality.

The first of these concepts is that of absolute space, typically characterized as Newtonian or Cartesian space. This is space as a fixed system of coordinates that exists without reference to the objects that are then conceived as populating or traversing it. This exists in a dialectical tension with relative space, most powerfully expressed as Einsteinian space. It is in temporal terms that the most basic distinction between absolute and relative space is drawn; as Harvey (2006) writes, "The idea of simultaneity in the physical universe, [Einstein] taught us, has to be abandoned." Relative space might be seen as the spatiality that relies on spatial framings that can be brought into some friction with other spatial framings—for example, the internal space of a train coach, which is both a static frame of spatial reference for the inhabitants of the coach even as it is traversing the space on land.

The third of Harvey's concepts is that of relational space, which he associates with Leibniz's critique of Newton. Harvey (2006) observes that "there is no such thing as

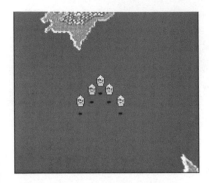

32.1 Airships in *Final Fantasy IV*: Relative "material" (experienced) space.

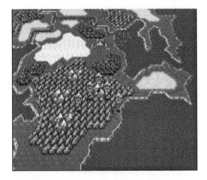

32.2 *Final Fantasy IV*: Authored material on the Super Famicom.

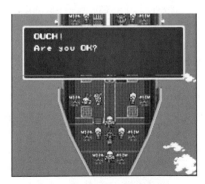

32.3 Airship deck, *Final Fantasy IV*: A relational material space. The "moving" space of the airship becomes a containing space of interaction between characters, until an encounter with a hostile creature moves the player...

32.4 ...into battle space. The emergent conventions of the console (particularly Japanese) role-playing game during this period (roughly 1987 to the mid-1990s) used shifts of perspective to visually cue the transformation of space, from isometric to top-down to stylized side view.

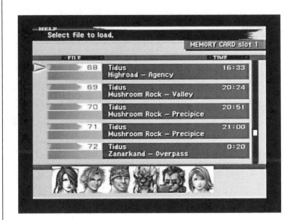

32.5 *Final Fantasy X*: Saved games loading menu. Place marks play, and flags an instant in a temporal progression, creating an intersection between fictional space/time and playtime.

32.6 Combat *in Final Fantasy X*. The overlays convey operational information. The visual display of space is unchanged: the transformation of space once performed by shifts in angle is now served by the heads-up display and the cues of the sound track. Operational spatial deixis remains stylized in keeping with the traditions of the genre, a practice that would only change with *Final Fantasy XI* and *XII*.

32.7 A relational space of representation, from *Final Fantasy X-2*: The sphere theater allows players to play back movies and music from earlier in the game. To be added to the player's library, each "memory" (media file) must be purchased using the game's currency.

32.8 Relational spaces of representation: The ruins of Zanarkand in *Final Fantasy X*. In the preapocalyptic milieu of the game, Zanarkand is a desolate place of spiritual portent and traumatic memory. The place is revisited early in the play of the sequel, *Final Fantasy X-2* . . .

32.9 . . . where it becomes a space of public memory, and (as one of the player's characters notes) "a tourist attraction." The episteme of the sequel is that of postwar levity: the often melancholic piano trills of the first game are replaced with jazz funk and pop songs, and even the game mechanics reflect the emergence of a euphoric commodity culture. This shift in the character of place is reinforced by dialogue between player and non-player characters, before the place is again recast . . .

32.10 . . . as an operational space. The interface then foregrounds the omnipresent representation of space (the map on the heads-up display), and the player stance shifts from reflection to active and instrumental navigation.

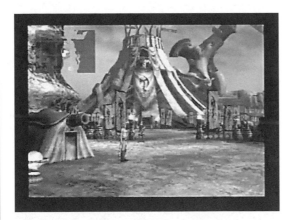

32.11 The "Youth League Headquarters" represented in material space in the game, and . . .

32.12 . . . within a space of representation within the options menu.

space or time outside of the processes that define them," which, for Leibniz, connotes the freedom of a creator to produce any one or another spatiotemporality. "Processes do not occur *in* space," adds Harvey, "but define their own spatial frame. The concept of space is embedded in or internal to process." While Harvey, as a geographer of urban spaces and differential global development, understands "process" mostly in historical, economic, and sociopolitical

terms, we can exploit a different idea of process in this regard to foreground the authorial and programmatic aspects of the production of video game space.) Among the operations that embed relational spaces within it are those of collective memory: the idea of Hiroshima, the "Orient" and the "West," Ground Zero, Nanking, and Abu Ghraib.

Harvey is interested not in determining whether space is absolute, relative, or relational but seeing how all these conceptualizations are implicit in human social practice. In his recent work, he extends his three conceptions of space by transecting them with one that foregrounds experiential (rather than conceptual) categories, drawn from a phenomenological (rather than analytic) reflective tradition. According to Lefebvre, space can be analyzed as a phenomenon produced in three different modes of human activity. Harvey describes material (or experienced) space as "the world of tactile and sensual interaction with matter," as produced and traversed by the immediate actions of bodies and objects. This mode of spatial phenomena includes a range of practices, from our immediate, bodily interactions with stairs, bridges, walking surfaces, and so forth, to environmental and microscopic experiences of space.

There exist also what Lefebvre (1991) calls "representations of space" and "spaces of representation." The first of

William H. Huber

these are spaces produced by human representational practices, including cartography (especially administrative and cadastral), narratives of landscape, simulated space, scientific models of space, spatial metaphors, painterly spaces, and (according to Harvey) cyberspace. Aesthetic practice generally produces representations of space, often in readings of the experience of material space (and I will be able to trouble Harvey's assignation of cyberspace to this mode accordingly).

Spaces of representation are the various affective, interior, and situational conditions under which humans represent space, including memory, imagination, anxiety, fantasy, loss, shame, nostalgia, trauma, and desire. The practice of representing space is drawn as much from these internal states as from the experience of material space. While at first this seems like the most elusive of the phenomenological categories, one can recall what it is like to revisit, after a long absence, the place of one's childhood, or a place of personal or collective trauma, to capture how distinct this mode of spatial production is from those that are either material or simply representational, and how it determines much of the perceptual and navigational experience of these spaces.

Harvey (2006) creates a three-by-three matrix, transposing his original conceptual modes of space with Lefebvre's phenomenological ones. The resulting grid allows us to speak, for example, of "absolute material (or experienced) space," such as that created by walls, bridges, and other physical, body-navigable features; "relative spaces of representation," such as that produced by the frustrations and anxieties of a commute through dense traffic; and "relational spaces of representation," which includes, in his words, "surrealism; existentialism; psychogeographies; cyberspace," and the spatial modes characterized by Leibniz and Gilles Deleuze. It is through this matrix of spatial categories that I will parse the spatial elements of the Japanese console role-playing game, *Final Fantasy X*, with reference to previous and subsequent games in the series.

The *Final Fantasy* series of games spans four primary platforms in its mainline history (with other platforms targeted for ports, adaptations, and the like.) Within these games, platform differences account for the broadest diver-

gences in the material experience of space. The series began with a title released in Japan in 1987 by a then-struggling Square, Inc., which had already released a handful of unsuccessful titles for the Nintendo Famicom. The title reflected the belief of the game's director and original creator, Hironobu Sakaguchi, that it would be the company's last release before being forced to close; hence "Final." While the game has become the representative title for the Japanese role-playing game genre, its predecessor, Enix's *Dragon Quest* (1986), was released a year earlier (Berardini 2006). The genre produced by these two titles was both a continuation of and a response to the Western computer-based role-playing genre, and particularly the *Ultima* series, first produced in the early 1980s for desktop personal computers (especially the Apple II). In particular, the third title of the series, *Ultima III: Exodus*, had a strong influence on the developer of *Dragon Quest* (Barton 2007).

Richard Garriott's *Ultima* games, and other Western computer-based role-playing games, were adaptations of the nondigital practice of pen-and-paper role-playing games such as *Dungeons & Dragons*, which had become popular in the late 1970s. Pen-and-paper role-playing games emerged from miniature wargaming hobbyists, who grafted a narrative and fantastic sensibility on to a medieval-themed, one-to-one scale military simulation.[1] Within this relatively brief history—though military simulation as both a hobby and an element in military practice has a history dating at least as far back as the late eighteenth century, the passage through *Dungeons & Dragons* to *Final Fantasy* encompasses less than fifteen years—the migrations of the space of practice accompany a transformation in the practice of space. Pen-and-paper games often relied on grid paper to generate adventure maps. The grid space is then used in conjunction with game rules that dictate rates of traversal, effective ranges for weapons, line of sight, and the like. The representation of space mandated by these games is motivated by the need to create a material object on which to perform the calculations that constitute the simulation. When these calculations are performed on a computer, players no longer directly perform this representational practice.[2] Instead, the representation of space is constrained by technological considerations, and the perception of space becomes a matter worked out through the computer interface.

The Japanese reception of role-playing games includes a discontinuity: there is little sign of a culture of tabletop fantasy role-playing games in Japan before the production of computer-based games. *Dungeons & Dragons* was translated into Japanese in 1985, the same year that *Dragon Quest* was released. The *Ultima* and *Wizardry* games were already in widespread Japanese distribution by this time. While the acronym RPG signifies pen-and-paper role-playing games in the United States and other Anglophone regions, it signifies computer-based games in Japan, and the pen-and-paper games are referred to as TRPG, (テーブルトーク RPG) (a transliteration of "Table-Talk RPG") (TRPG.net 2003). Thus, the temporal framework for the role-playing game in Japan has been primarily computer based from the outset; the evolution of role-playing game mechanics as a practice performed by a collaborating group of players does not exist in Japan. The "roles" of role-playing are categories of character function, and the player-driven theatrical aspects of pen-and-paper role-playing are instead replaced by story practices that owe as much to cinema and television as they do to military simulation. This is the historical context for the creation of the *Final Fantasy* games.

Using Harvey's and Lefebvre's categories for the production of space, the platform produces, first, absolute and relative material space. It also contributes considerably to the structuring of material relational space; genre and story conventions and patterns, however, also contribute to this conceptual mode. That it does so with a symbolic, representational system (programming as well as digital and digitized artwork) is an inversion of the typical characteristics of spatial relationships, but this is the nature of the production of spatial phenomenon authored by computer software.

Material Space and the Production of Bodies

Video games create space by first materially representing it within specific material constraints created by the hardware and software platforms on which the games run. The initial

Final Fantasy games produced material space within the constraints and affordances determined by their target platforms (broadly speaking, of course, this could be said to be true of any game). The Nintendo Famicom was an eight-bit video game console system, developed by Nintendo Japan and released in 1985. It was capable of producing a video display of 256 pixels by 240, and displaying fifty-three colors (Diskin 2004). The Nintendo platforms lacked true 3-D display capabilities (except by isometric projection).

Final Fantasy X was the first of the franchise's titles to be produced for the Sony Playstation 2. The platform afforded the designers increases in storage capacity (Playstation titles were shipped on compact discs; a single title required as many as four compact discs), processing power, and most important, video resolution, particularly for 3-D models. The Playstation 2's computational architecture revolves around the "Emotion Engine," described as "a combination CPU and DSP Processor, whose main function is simulating 3D worlds" (Stokes 2000).

These platforms, and to a lesser extent the regimes of controllers and inputs associated with them, created broad limits on the relationships between body and space. The Nintendo games had three primary spatial displays: city/dungeon-scaled space, in which the display screen bounded a scaled region analogous to one or two city blocks; battle space, in which the characters would be depicted individually; and countryside/landscape space. The transitions between them were well marked. The player would move their avatar on to an icon marking either a town or, often, a cave entrance. Some event would usually presage the transition to the battle space, such as dramatic music. Within any given scale, the navigation of spaces on Nintendo platforms is generally continuous.

The world spaces of the Playstation 2 (and to a somewhat lesser extent, Playstation) games are implemented as a series of zones, characteristic spaces that frequently also have an architectural, aesthetic unity. The focus on display technologies and the use of read-only discs, rather than cartridges, as delivery media would make it impossible to have extensive spatial continuity within a given scale on the Sony platforms. Instead, as a spatial transition occurs, the

William H. Huber

required data is loaded into the working memory of the Playstation. As these transition load times could be noticeable (the disks would spin), it was more effective to turn these transitions into temporal and narratological ones as well as to turn places into "chapters" of sorts.

While zone transitions became less continuous, transitions from travel to battle would become more continuous, as the representations of characters in the navigational screens increased in resolution and scale. Beginning with *Final Fantasy XII* (2006), the transition from navigation interface to conflict interface was effaced (except for the drawing of lines of hostile force, indicating that a combatant was targeting a character).[3] We can characterize two trends in the history of the game: the convergence of relative spaces (active/battle space and travel space), and the division of space along geographic (zones as aesthetic and landscape ideas) and temporal (zones as chapters) lines.

Representations of Space (and Place): Producing Worlds

At least four of the worlds of the *Final Fantasy* games are named, and in the naming of the worlds, subfranchises have been created. The world of Ivalice, for example, was introduced in the game *Final Fantasy Tactics* (1997). The world would be revised and reused for a number of other games, culminating in the recent *Final Fantasy XII* (2006) and a series of related products, called the *Ivalice Alliance*, for handheld platforms.

The authorship of the fictional world included a process of aesthetic sampling of our own world. *Final Fantasy XI* (2002), a massively multiplayer role-playing game, is set in a world called Vana'diel, divided into loosely Western-styled nations.[4] In re-creating Ivalice for *Final Fantasy XII*, teams of world designers traveled through Turkey and India (IGN staff 2003). The fictional setting of *Final Fantasy X* was a departure from the preceding titles. *Final Fantasy VI* (1994), *VII* (1997), and *VIII* (1999) in particular, and to a lesser extent *Final Fantasy IX* (2000), featured worlds of fantastic technology and "steampunk," retro-futurist aesthetics. They were also identified as having architectures that evoked a European sensibility. The designers of *Final Fantasy X*—

especially producer Yoshinori Kitase and character designer Tetua Nomura (Squaresoft 2001)—wedded a move to a more traditional fantasy ambience to an aesthetic turn away from Western tropes of place.[5]

Final Fantasy X is set in a world called Spira, which is dominated by a religious institution called Yevon. Spira endured a cyclical cataclysm: the destruction of any center of population greater than a village by Sin, a huge, armored monstrosity that came from the ocean. The doctrines of Yevon taught that Sin was punishment for technological ambitions. It would later be revealed that this was not the case, and that the religious institution itself was complicit with the destruction wrought by Sin.

Final Fantasy X begins in the city of Zanarkand, a fantastic, technological metropolis. The avatar controlled by the player is soon identified as Tidus, an up-and-coming sports superstar, on his way to a professional Blitzball match. The spatial representations are on a local, urban scale (although somewhat constrained: there are few open urban spaces in *Final Fantasy* games, and instead, there are interconnected zones of passage, resembling the Situationist topographies of Paris as a system of nodes).

This scale of player-space relationships persists—that is, a broader geographic representation of space is not yet presented—when the initial apocalyptic event, the destruction of the city of Zanarkand, destroys this space before it can be explored or understood. Transported to another time-place, the player is left with an unsatisfied curiosity about the space of initial play. From this new place, the player begins a process of narrative and spatial traversal that resembles and reflects that of the genre within the franchise: "forward" progression through space (that is, from the known and "cleared" region to the unknown; to another place directed by the conditions of the game), which is slow and fraught with challenges.[6]

The game is divided into zones, the initial entry into which is experienced as a chapter; the temporal dimension is managed by the navigation of space. On entering a new zone for the first time, the name of the zone ("Besaid," "Kilika," or "Zanarkand Ruins") is flashed across the screen, along with a panning shot of the zone's typical landscape.

These markers serve to indicate to the player that they are, indeed, making progress through the story line.

Players need not make this progress immediately. Most *Final Fantasy* games adhere to role-playing game conventions originating in *Dungeons & Dragons*.[7] Characters are a bundle of statistics that simulate traits and abilities, and these statistics are modified by the experience of the character. In practice, every battle that a character fights provides the character with "experience points." By earning experience points, a character will "level up," becoming stronger, more difficult to destroy, and capable of various previously inaccessible feats of combat, magic, and the like. The result is a kind of statistical bildungsroman. It is possible, although time-consuming, to repetitively kill weaker opponents in the game to increase one's level in such a way as to make the traversal of zones trivial. The "experience points/level" mechanic is nearly ubiquitous to this genre of games, and exceptions to this mechanic are often notable for just this reason.[8]

Also, *Final Fantasy* games are known for their inclusion of minigames: mise en abymes that occur in fictional spaces of their own. *Final Fantasy XI* features "Tetra Master," a collectible card game (with a separate in-game interface) popular on the continent throughout which the characters travel.[9] In-game tournament-level play occurs in a specialized arena. The minigame in *Final Fantasy X* plays a central role in the plot: the lead character is a professional athlete (as was his father, whose fate is connected to that of Sin). It is possible to play Blitzball as a stand-alone sports game, along with league management mechanics that involve recruiting players throughout the world of Spira. The practice of building, managing, and playing a Blitzball team becomes a possibility during the indefinitely extensible period before the game's denouement.

The tactic of "leveling up," of seeking out story-irrelevant combat in order to improve the statistics of the players' avatars is, ironically, outside the fictional temporality of the game, which is generally only driven forward by the passage into new zones.[10] Inverting the customary relationship between time and space, it is the passage through geographic space that creates the tempo for the passage of fictional/historical time.

Final Fantasy X's lead character, Tidus, finds himself displaced several times before being given agency over his own navigation.[11] After the first cataclysmic displacement, he finds himself swimming and wandering through half-submerged ruins. He is later picked up by a ship over which he has no control, and is eventually again thrown ashore. In time, he meets the other members of what will become his band of friends and companions for the rest of the game. His primary love interest, Yuna, is a summoner, a figure of destiny with the power to call on powerful, primordial beings, and who has the ability and responsibility to bring about a twenty-year period of calm from the destructive power of Sin, through an event called the Final Summoning.[12] Before this can take place, she—escorted by Tidus and other companions—must make a pilgrimage to a series of temples throughout Spira. Each temple visit requires the party to solve puzzles and battle opponents, and this pilgrimage provides the dominant (though by no means only) fiction that orders the temporal progression through the zones of the game. As the party progresses, epiphanies and expositions disclose more of the nature of the world of Spira—including the discovery that the Final Summoning involves the martyrdom of the summoner, and the phantasmal nature of Tidus's own existence (DigiCube Company 2001).

As play and story progress, the player develops multiple and layered perceptions of the spatialities of the game. Common to many of the games are modes of transportation that become available to the player at critical junctures. These modes of transportation have become brand icons of their own. One is the chocobo, a large, flightless yellow bird that is ridden as a mount, which appears in most *Final Fantasy* games since *Final Fantasy II*. In most games, players who have access to a chocobo are able to navigate spaces more quickly. Riding a chocobo also avoids the random combat that otherwise besets players moving on foot through the games' terrain. Another of these iconic modes of transportation is the airship, which constructs space as a network of disparate, connected nodes (just as real air travel does).

Each mode of transportation presents certain landscapes as navigable and impassable. In *Final Fantasy III*, the player will get access to different airships that may allow access undersea, yet be unable to cross over a mountain. Toward the end of the game, the player has access to a flotilla of airships that account for every possible terrain. These modes of transportation occur with the relative modes of the representation of space. Velocity compresses the experience of place and creates the passing landscape, or spaces of transition. There can be affective shifts associated with moving through a space quickly through which one once moved slowly—even without conflict, a kind of mastery is produced, and the satisfaction of this telescoping mobility is a significant element in the aesthetics of the play of these games.

Final Fantasy X culminates in a series of epic battles against primordial forces and figures within Sin. Before taking the steps that trigger this series of battles, the player enjoys almost complete freedom over the world of Spira. This is when the Blitzball tournament minigame becomes available. It is also during this time that the ancillary quests, which unlock valuable items and resolve side narratives, can be undertaken. A completionist approach to the game is possible at this point, collecting sets of various types of items, weapons, and the like. When the final narrative sequence is launched, however, the world is "closed," unless the player opens a saved game, participating again in this penultimate moment of maximal liberty.

Spaces of Representation: Spira Revisited

As frequently occurs in successful franchises and entertainment commodities, the popularity and lingering narrative tension of *Final Fantasy X* motivated the production of a sequel, *Final Fantasy X-2*. Much of the software and many of the resources of the original game were repurposed for the sequel. The world in which the game occurs remains the same, and the protagonists of the sequel are three young women, two of whom were lead characters (though neither the lead protagonist) of the original game.

A short film, created as bonus content for one of the later editions of the game, acts as a narrative bridge between the two titles and provides the internal impetus for producing the sequel (Dunham 2003).[13] The two titles are set in the same world, and largely feature the same charac-

ters, yet are starkly distinct in the experience of play. Whereas *Final Fantasy X* begins with a mysterious world that is slowly, painstakingly uncovered through pilgrimage, the sequel, set two years after the end of the events of the first game, immediately places the protagonists in control of an airship, with full access to a world that is, for the most part, completely familiar to players of the first game. The space of representation has changed from one created by foreboding, expectation, and cataclysm to one dominated, mostly, by a lighter sense of play. The lead character, Yuna, has survived what was meant to be her moment of world-saving self-sacrifice, and now is faced with a kind of existential crisis: what to do with the rest of her life, after her world-historical moment.

The music of the sequel, too, dramatizes the shift in mood. Whereas the first title favored orchestral program music, the sequel tends toward popular, jazz, and even funk-inflected sounds. In light of the conscious "turn to Asia" that motivated the directorial team of these titles, it is easy to see allegorical references to the experience of Japan during and after the Pacific War.[14] If the turns of complicity, ironies of memory, and slow construction of spaces through travel in *Final Fantasy X* evoke the national memory up to and through the war period, the sequel suggests the giddy consumerism and conflicted identities of the postwar period. Two of the playable characters of the first game, Wakka and Lulu, are now expecting their first child (and are thus removed from the cast of playable characters for the sequel).

The three female protagonists begin the game as neither sports heroes (as Tidus was in the first game) nor as traditional epic heroes, but as pop stars. Their efficacy within the game mechanics is managed by a system of costume changes, accompanied by animations that resemble music videos. Whereas the first game portrays a traumatized world suffering disastrous paroxysms, the sequel suggests a postmillennial world of giddy consumerism and optimism.

While there are differences in mechanics between the first game and the sequel, it is in the mood and the framing of space that the sequel diverges most clearly from the original. What occurs as discovery and epiphany in the first game becomes nostalgia, revision, and a struggle to frame

Table 32.1

	Material space (experienced space)	Representation of space (conceptualized space)	Space of representation (lived/ played space)
Absolute space	Rendered 3-D space; physics; buildings, trees, grass, road; barriers, walls, and rivers that effect navigation	Map displays; intertitles; landscape features; textured spaces; city layouts; reference to spaces in FAQs, walk-throughs, and guides	The game world and its fiction as an object of contemplation; literacy of game space and ability to interact with it confidently—the space created by mastery; the learned map, becoming traversable with minimal attention
Relative space	Modes of transportation and acceleration: chocobo space, airship space; scaled space (from overhead map to walking space to battle space)	Airship destination menus; nodes and linkages; zone transitions; hidden and revealed spaces (secret doors, corridors); minigame (Blitzball) spaces	Affective play spaces: melancholy, anxiety/tension—sense of threat/ excitement in high-risk zones and boss fights; shifts of attention motivated by changes in level of threat and comfort; cutscene spaces[1]
Relational space	"Battle space" versus "traversing space"; transitions in scale; blockages and transitions between zones and modes	Narrated space;[2] the fictional accounting of fictional space; aestheticized space, rendered architectures, and landscapes	Collective and personal memory; pre- and postcataclysmic spaces; zones of return; sublime spaces

Notes:
1. This kind of space is thematized within *Final Fantasy* X through various tropes: the "dreaming" of Zanarkand by the disembodied spirits of its former residents, the space of the massive "Sin," and so on. Since much of this is revealed through expository—some of it extragame—it remains otherwise outside the scope of this work.
2. Within *Final Fantasy* X and *X-2*, one of the nonplayer characters, a wandering scholar named Maechen, periodically meets the party, and reveals various historical and "scientific" aspects of Spira. Several *Final Fantasy* games have characters who generate authoritative, expository knowledge.

the events and places of the original title: in the wake of the institutional discrediting of the religion Yevon through the events of the first game, a cultural civil war brews between two major factions, embroiling places and characters familiar to players of the first game.

When a space of experience becomes represented through interiority, through memory or desire, it becomes a space of representation. Players return to a known world—a world that is much like that which they remember, as an experienced (material) space. The fictional historical change in these materially unchanged spaces produces experiences such as nostalgia, mourning, and expectation, through a fictive collective memory, abetted by the player.

The Matrix of Spatialities Revisited

It is now possible to locate these various spatial modes in Harvey's grid. This matrix works at a specific scale. For example, it does not include the living room or desktop of

the player, or the environmental context of play. Such a scale of inquiry would dilute our analysis by becoming a general theory of video game spaces, obscuring the ways in which the game as an authored system produces these spatial effects. We see character/avatar/player relations as a deictic displacement across multiple modes (that is, as the way in which the "as if" of the game fictions can recruit the player into space–production rather than just a representational strategy. Attention to only the fictive space of the game would diminish the materiality of the spaces produced.

Rethinking Space and Game Narrative

A more exhaustive conceptual approach to space affords us a better way to discuss the aesthetic and textual aspects of games. While it may seem somewhat arbitrary to adapt a theory of spatialities originally developed by geographers and urban studies theorists, such an environmental and architectural approach to game spaces overcomes an approach that omits the spatial, navigation, and deictic elements that are part of the mode of attention that screen-based video games demand, especially those that feature 3-D graphics and spatialized player-avatar relations. Japanese role-playing games have generally been treated simply as linear stories driven by various role-playing mechanics. Such a criticism implicitly eclipses spatiality by its emphasis on temporal organization. If we attend to these spatial aspects, particularly to the production of spaces of representation, we can identify the relationship between game structures and affective experiences of space in these games—a relationship driven by play in which narrative performs a distinctive supporting role. Some impasses in critical approaches to video games might be resolved by taking a spatial turn.

Notes

1. In terms of "one-on-one," one game unit represented one simulated combatant, rather than a group or organized unit of combatants.

2. There are interstitial practices, by which computer systems are used to perform calculations within the context of pen-and-paper games, or—particularly for text-based role-playing games such as the early *Zork* games—in which players produce their own hand-drawn cartographies of the game spaces as mnemonic and tactical aids.

3. The temporalities of battle in the games would go through various changes as well, and would act as a differentiator between titles. Nevertheless, these design differences were less dependent on platform considerations.

4. An expansion, *Final Fantasy XI Online: Treasures of Aht Urghan* (2006), added a Near Eastern "Orient" as a newly discovered continent.

5. Tensions between magical/religious and technological ideologies are common themes of *Final Fantasy* narratives. Other common tropes are memory and trauma, friendship and isolation, and complicity. Addressing these issues exhaustively is far beyond the scope of this piece; one monograph in Italian (Calamosca 2003) has attempted to deal with them at greater length. Many of these tropes are well-represented in other forms of Japanese cultural production, including literature, film, television, and manga.

6. The fiction of the game makes the relative status of these new spaces rather elusive. Far later in the game, it is revealed that while the initial space did exist in the historical past, the instance of it that the player, as the character, Tidus, experienced, was a phantasmal space generated by the collective memory of those destroyed in the original cataclysm.

7. An exception is *Final Fantasy* II (1988).

8. The *Legend of Zelda* series of games published by Nintendo, among others, does not use this mechanic, relying instead on changes in player inventory to differentiate abilities and constraints.

9. As is now often the case with fantasy franchises, an actual (paper) version of Tetra Master was produced and marketed in Europe; it was not particularly successful. An online version of the game is now part of Square Enix's PlayOnline service, which primarily delivers *Final Fantasy XI Online* (2002).

10. Many Japanese role-playing games differ from most Western role-playing games by representing a group, rather than an individual, as the unit of play. This could be interpreted broadly as a cultural difference—the well-worn and, in my view, overstated observation of the importance of the group over the individual in Japanese culture (the observation leaves too many questions about the construction of the self and subjectivity unanswered)—but it is also an adaptation of the dynamics of the tabletop role-playing game, which foregrounds group tactics and coordination, to the computer/console. Representing a party of characters, rather than a single character, as the unit of play is truer to the origins of the role-playing game, also creating tactical play options that do not arise in an action/adventure game with a one-to-one-to-one player/avatar/character relationship.

11. The names of the male and female leads, Tidus and Yuna, are the Okinawan terms for "Sun" and "Night," respectively, reflecting the association of Spira with the Asia-Pacific region (Khosla 2003).

12. *Final Fantasy* games have an extensive secondary literature in Japanese, published by Square Enix, that includes strategic, tactical, and fictional data unavailable in English. While most of this work is redundant of information available in game, the *Ultimania* series of books, published by DigiCube (and later Square Enix Publishing), includes interviews with directors, developers, and designers describing their processes and extending the fictions of the world.

13. Interestingly, one narrative motivation for the sequel was to offer the possibility of overcoming the tragic overtones of the conclusion of the first game with the possibility of a nontragic ending; the use of the sequel to overcome the tragic would be repeated by the producers of the *Final Fantasy* series when they released a number of products that continued the story of *Final Fantasy VII*.

14. The naming of this conflict is not a straightforward task: referring to it simply as "World War II" places it on the periphery of the European conflict, even though the hostilities in the Pacific began earlier. In Japan, it is usually referred to as the Pacific War (太平洋戦争), or sometimes (often by defenders of Japan's actions during this period) as the Greater East Asian War (大東亜戦争). I choose to use the more neutral Japanese nomenclature when discussing a Japanese cultural production.

References: Literature

Barton, Matt (2007). *The History of Computer Role-Playing Games*, Part 1: The Early Years (1980–1983). ⟨http://www.gamasutra.com/features/20070223a/barton_01.shtml⟩.

Berardini, César A. (2006). *An Introduction to Square-Enix. TeamXBox.com*. ⟨http://features.teamxbox.com/xbox/1554/An-Introduction-to-SquareEnix/p1/⟩.

Calamosca, Fabio (2003). "Final Fantasy: vivere tra gli indigeni del cyberspace." *Ludologica* 5 (1).

DigiCube Company, Limited (2001). *Final Fantasy X Ultimania Ω*. Tokyo: DigiCube Company, Limited.

Diskin, Patrick (2004). *Nintendo Entertainment System Documentation*. Tokyo: Nintendo.

Dunham, Jeremy (2003). *Final Fantasy X-2 Developer Interview*. ⟨http://ps2.ign.com/articles/442/442025p1.html⟩.

Harvey, David (2006). *Spaces of Global Capitalism: Towards a Theory of Uneven Geographical Development*. London: Verso.

IGN staff (2003). *IGN: Final Fantasy XII Q&A*. ⟨http://ps2.ign.com/articles/441/441293p1.html⟩.

Jenkins, Henry (1998). "'Complete Freedom of Movement': Video Games as Gendered Play Spaces." In *From Barbie to Mortal Kombat: Gender and Computer Games*, edited by Justine Cassell and Henry Jenkins, 262–297. Cambridge, MA: MIT Press.

Jenkins, Henry (2004). "Game Design as Narrative Architecture." In *First Person: New Media as Story, Performance, and Game*, edited by Noah Wardrip-Fruin and Pat Harrigan. Cambridge, MA: MIT Press.

Khosla, Sheila (2003). *FLAREgamer | Tetsuya Nomura's 20s*. ⟨http://flaregamer.com/b2article.php?p=81&more=1⟩.

Lefebvre, Henri (1991). *The Production of Space*. Oxford: Blackwell.

Squaresoft, Inc. (2001). *The Creators (Final Fantasy X: Behind the Game)*. ⟨http://www.square-enix-usa.com/games/FFX/btg/creators.html#1⟩.

Stokes, John (2000). *Sound and Vision: A Technical Overview of the Emotion Engine*. ⟨http://arstechnica.com/reviews/hardware/ee.ars/1⟩.

TRPG.net (2003). *TRPG.net*. ⟨http://www.trpg.net/WhatisTRPG.html⟩.

References: Games

Dragon Quest. Chunsoft, Yuji Horii, Akira Toriyama, and Koichi Sugiyama; Enix Corporation. 1986.

Final Fantasy. Hironobu Sakaguchi, Masafumi Miyamoto, Yoshitaka Amano, Kenji Terada, Nobuo Uematsu, and Nasir Gebelli; Squaresoft. 1987.

Final Fantasy II. Hironobu Sakaguchi, Akitoshi Kawazu, Masafumi Miyamoto, Kenji Terada, Yoshitaka Amano, and Nobuo Uematsu; Squaresoft. 1988.

Final Fantasy IV. Hironobu Sakaguchi, Takashi Tokia, Nobuo Uematsu, and Yoshitaka Amano; Squaresoft. 1991.

Final Fantasy VI. Hironobu Sakaguchi, Yoshinori Kitase, Hiroyuki Ito, Tetsuya Nomura, Yoshitaka Amano, and Nobuo Uematsu; Square Company, Limited. 1994.

Final Fantasy VIII. Hironobu Sakaguchi, Shinji Hashimoto, Yoshinori Kitase, Yoshitaka Amano, Tetsuya Nomura, Kazushige Nojima, and Nobuo Uematsu; Square Company, Limited. 1999.

Final Fantasy IX. Hironobu Sakaguchi, Shinji Hashimoto, Shuko Murase, Kazuhiko Aoki, Yoshitaka Amano, Nobuo Uematsu, and Hideo Minaba; Square Company, Limited. 2000.

Final Fantasy XI Online. Hiromichi Tanaka, Hironobu Sakaguchi, Koichi Ishii, Yoshitaka Amano, Ryosuke Aiba, Nobuo Uematsu, Naoshi Mizuta, and Kumi Tanioka; Square Enix Company, Limited. 2002.

Final Fantasy XI Online: Treasures of Aht Urghan. Square Enix Company, Limited. 2006.

Final Fantasy XII. Yasumi Matsuno, Akitoshi Kawazu, Hiroshi Minagawa, Hiroyuki Ito, Daisuke Watanabe, Hitoshi Sakimoto, Yoshitaka Amano, and Akihiko Yoshida; Square Enix Company, Limited. 2006.

Final Fantasy Tactics. Hironobu Sakaguchi, Yasumi Matsuno, Hiroyuki Ito, Hiroshi Minagawa, Akihiko Yoshida, Masaharu Iwata, and Hitoshi Sakimoto; Squaresoft. 1997.

William H. Huber

Arachne Challenges Minerva: The Spinning Out of Long Narrative in *World of Warcraft* and *Buffy the Vampire Slayer*

Tanya Krzywinska

In Ovid's epic poem *Metamorphoses* (completed around AD 8), a mortal woman named Arachne challenges Minerva, the goddess of warriors, crafts, and wisdom, to a duel. Fueled by hubris, Arachne proclaims that she can weave a tapestry of far superior quality than any produced by the proud goddess. The two set about the task, their "labor lightened by pleasure" (Ovid 2004, 212). Minerva depicts her defeat of Neptune in a dispute over a claim on a city.[1] The other gods "look on in amazement" while she is crowned by victory (213). Surrounding the central image are four smaller vignettes showing contests between mortals and gods; in each, the mortal is punished for their audacity. Arachne's tapestry takes as its main subject matter the seduction of Europa by Jove in the guise of a bull; "the bull and the sea were convincingly real" (215). Other mortal women seduced by the gods are also shown (Leda, Asterie, Antiope, Danae, and Erigon, plus others—the list of seductions depicted is long). Such was Arachne's skill, "not even the goddess of Envy could criticize weaving like that" (216). Minerva is thrown into a furious rage: she "ripped up the picture betraying the gods' misdemeanors" (216), struck Arachne several times on the head, and transformed her into a spider, condemned forever to weave.

This story can be regarded as expressing two opposing approaches to conceiving long narrative in epic poetry. Minerva's approach characterizes through her tapestry the heroic epic mode where violence is masked by derring-do, and the gods are noble and majestic, and their behavior predictable, making for a fixed and rule-based world order. Because of its structured simplicity, it is easy to imagine what her work looks like. Arachne's depiction, by contrast, is distinctly "unepic." Her treatment of the gods is disdainful, and they appear feckless; the subject matter provides a critical comment on the lack of agency afforded to mortals who become playthings for the gods. The tapestry itself is chaotic, with transformative elements; indeed, so much so that it becomes difficult to picture her tapestry, as it is so complex and multithreaded. Woven into Arachne's tapestry is the view of Ovid's poetic contemporaries that the classical heroic epic form was stultified, had an outmoded view of the gods as forcefully real rather than personifications, and that diminished human agency (in fact, it has been claimed that *Metamorphoses* marks the transition from myth as religious in function to myth as literature). And as suits my purpose in this chapter, it may be said that Arachne's tapestry emblemizes the way that *Metamorphoses* itself transforms the values, conventions, and concomitant worldview of the established epic form.

Using the duel between Arachne and Minerva as an interpretational frame, the object of this chapter is to explore the ways in which two recent "epic" texts, the television series *Buffy the Vampire Slayer* (1997–2003) and the massively multiplayer online role-playing game *World of Warcraft* (2005–present), weave their particular long narratives. Resulting perhaps from the way that contemporary popular culture's romance with the heroic is often tempered by a relativized and liberal worldview, each can be said to have both Arachnean and Minervan qualities. Read within these terms, it becomes possible to identify how these epic texts share certain formal and structural characteristics. Yet some significant differences also emerge. It is important to account for both. The long narratives of these texts are shaped and engage us differently in a number of respects in accord with the specific properties of their media platforms (television and computer-based game).

Tanya Krzywinska

Weaving World, Form, and Narrative

Long narrative is not a new phenomenon: epic poetry is one of the oldest literary forms, with ancient examples such as the *Epic of Gilgamesh*, of which twelve stone tablets written between 669–653 BC comprise the fullest existing example; and *The Odyssey*, said to have been written down in 800–600 BC. Both these examples appear to be a collection of products of an oral tradition rationalized through single authorship into a unified and linear story (the latter is not the case with *Metamorphoses*, which can be described as episodic in form). The epic format has stood the test of time, demonstrating continued cultural value: *Nibelungenlied* is a widely known medieval example, as is *Beowulf*; later ones include John Milton's *Paradise Lost* (1667) and its sequel *Paradise Regained* (1671) and John Keats's *Hyperion* (1818). Each deliberately uses the scope, meter, and length of the traditional epic form to lend gravity to their subject matter (if rejecting in some cases their pagan grounding). Prose-based epics appeared during the medieval period, and in this category we might include, as recent entries into the canon, J. R. R. Tolkien's *The Lord of the Rings* (originally published in three volumes in 1954 and 1955) and, through a modernist frame, James Joyce's *Ulysses* (1922). Long narrative is not the sole preserve of "high" myth-based literature, however. Aspects of the epic—thematic and structural—find their way into fantasy-based long narratives that populate recent CGI-informed media. In *World of Warcraft* and *Buffy the Vampire Slayer*, the heroic aspects of the epic are nonetheless copresent and often juxtaposed with the quotidian, sometimes to dramatic and/or comic effect.

Beginning with the serialized fiction in magazines and newspapers of the nineteenth century, consolidated later in comic books and the "new" popular media of cinema, radio, and television, and after shedding its ties in many cases with the heroic and archaic myth, the long narrative accrued a new lease of vigorous life in the domain of the popular. In what might seem distant from the epic poem, soap operas and serials provide perhaps the most widely consumed long narratives—the trend extending into literary series like J. K. Rowling's *Harry Potter* (the first of which was published in 1997). It is pertinent here to understand something of the serial form as it will inform my investigation of the similarities and differences between the structure, delivery, and use of long narrative in *Buffy the Vampire Slayer* and *World of Warcraft*. Glen Creeber (2004) argues that the television series has moved from the tendency to have one coherent story within any one episode to a mode that resembles the practice established in soap operas, where story arcs stretch across multiple episodes. Michael Z. Newman (2006) has said that the practice of retaining some story coherence within an episode has not disappeared, however, because it works to retain a more casual audience for shows, which is important for advertising revenues. As such, *Buffy the Vampire Slayer* uses a combination of both. There are long story arcs, spanning a whole season or even beyond, but many episodes have discrete, self-contained story lines. This show spanned seven seasons, with most seasons running to twenty-two episodes. As the show became assured of a committed audience, and to encourage loyalty, increasingly longer story arcs appeared that gave greater scope for character and "world" development. The shift becomes apparent in season three with developments arising from the increasingly conflicted relationship between the good and bad slayers: Buffy and Faith, respectively.

The transition to character-based long narrative in television series did not occur in isolation, and should be regarded in the context of a more widespread trend to embrace long narrative in popular culture (the reasons for which are discussed below). Included within this trend is the emergence of long narrative in fantasy-based role-playing video games as well as examples from other genres of video games. Unlike soap operas, many video games and *Buffy the Vampire Slayer* draw on some core aspects of the epic form, which inform their particular engagement with long narrative. Dovetailing with the more obvious presence of heroic deeds and supernatural entities, the invocation in those ancient tales of a fantasy "world" provides a key for unlocking the way these later texts construct, deliver, and make use of long narrative.

It is a common attribute of fantasy fiction that story events take place in a developed world rather than simply in a setting. For fans, "world" needs no definition, which probably means that its collective meaning accumulates as an individual becomes more knowledgeable about the genre.[2] A fictional world is governed frequently by a set of organizing features that afford it a specific character and coherence (world as "gestalt," because of its unifying function). These organizing features might be geographic, temporal, social, political, cultural, technological (magic included, where it is used in the practical and agentic senses), metaphysical, historical, or "racial" (meaning the categories of living beings found in the world).

Buffy the Vampire Slayer is set in the real world, but augments it on the basis that magic and the supernatural exist.[3] Various hell dimensions, of which most humans are happily unaware, are copresent with the seemingly "normal" real world. As such, the show's world is defined primarily by its fantastic metaphysics, much in the manner of classical myth. Other worlds are far less wedded to the real world, at least in visual terms. While there are seas and continents, lakes and forests, towns and villages, *World of Warcraft*'s cartoonish graphical qualities and pervasive fantastic mise-en-scène means that it is not meant to be taken as the world that we inhabit in everyday life. The particular character of these two screen-based worlds is a composite of a range of defining fantastic and familiar features that are underpinned by the different ways these are realized in formal and media-specific terms.

Within fantasy-based fiction, the character of a "world" is bound intimately to long narrative. This is the case with both *Buffy the Vampire Slayer* and *World of Warcraft*, although the delivery and structure of their narratives are rendered quite differently. Central to this is the fact that *Buffy the Vampire Slayer* is designed to be consumed as television, and *World of Warcraft* as an online game (with rules and a set of winning conditions) and social space in which players have agency and presence. *Buffy the Vampire Slayer* is set in Sunnydale, a midsize Californian town, and the (then) present day. As well as the usual features one would expect of a town of this type—a mall, a club where the gang hangs out, a school, suburbs, and so forth—Sunnydale is situated on a "Hellmouth," a portal to a hell

dimension that although mostly closed, attracts all manner of demonic beings, vampires, magic–users, and supernatural events. (There are other Hellmouths around the world, including one in Cleveland, and there are any number of hell dimensions; *World of Warcraft* also has hell dimensions—the Twisting Nether and Outland.) In using a type of magical realism as the basis for its world (magic exists in what viewers are asked to take as the real world), *Buffy the Vampire Slayer* is able to mix together elements that are strongly coded generically as fantasy (Gothic set pieces, heroic "to the death" battles, vampires, etc.) with aspects of the real, quotidian world (everyday problems of being a high school teenager, particularly relationships with others and the frequent use of distinctly unepic, humorous speech; e.g., "I'm totally her archnemesis"). This mixture emblematizes the Arachnean way that this show transforms and hybridizes diverse genres (soap, horror, and serial), and the way that supernatural forces transform and change the world along with its characters. The weaving of the supernatural, the epic, and the quotidian supplements this, defining the world and generating potentialities for a range of possible story lines and dramatic tensions. There are two main, if interrelated, aspects that propagate the show's longer and more complex story arcs: the development of characters as they go through life changes, and their participation in the battle against evil forces (which at times bring about all kinds of moral and social dilemmas).

Due to its serial, televisual format, and in an attempt to garner prime-time status, narrative is core to the structure of *Buffy the Vampire Slayer*, and it is delivered in a mainly linear fashion (although there are techniques of repetition employed to cue new or casual watchers into the current state of affairs, such as the "previously on *Buffy the Vampire Slayer*" sequence that appears at the start of some episodes). As I have already noted, each episode usually has some kind of self-contained story line; usually Buffy—the "chosen one"—and her friends have to deal with some kind of supernatural threat to the human world. In "Phases," from season two, a werewolf has appeared in Sunnydale. The "Scooby gang"—Buffy and her close friends—set about discovering the human identity of the werewolf.

It turns out that this threat to humanity is the otherwise benign new boyfriend (Oz) of one of the central characters (Willow). There is resolution at the end of the episode as we discover the identity of the werewolf, and along the way Buffy manages to get the better of a thoughtless rogue werewolf hunter; but the events that occur are nonetheless stitched into a much longer story arc around interpersonal relationships and personal transformation. The latter constitutes a primary overarching thematic concern: the experience of life changes on identity and relationships. The presence of werewolves and vampires emblemize the transformation theme, couched as they are within a horror-genre frame where exaggerated bodily changes are rendered as horrifyingly extreme and spectacular. In placing character development so centrally in the show's long story arcs, the type of long narrative found in soap operas is co-opted. Also, the werewolf transformation is supported and given logical credence by the particular metaphysics of the show's world.

As a game within which players can make choices about what they do, narrative does not take center stage in *World of Warcraft* as it does in *Buffy the Vampire Slayer*. But as a world with a well-developed, multithreaded history, there are a number of ways in which the game makes use of long narrative. These are bound intimately into the state of affairs of the game's world as experienced by the player, and in turn tied into core gameplay activities.

Within the burgeoning field of academic-based games studies there has been much debate about the credence of regarding games in terms of story. Various critics have argued that narrative in digital games is secondary to gameplay.[4] While the story context of many games is faint or indistinct, the *Warcraft* franchise has an expansive, epic-scaled story line that has accumulated across a number of games. Long, thick narratives are common in role-playing games, while in other game genres story lines are simply expositional, with the emphasis placed far more on ratcheting-up scores or kills.

Even with its provision of a complex and expansive story line, players of *World of Warcraft* may choose not to engage with it any closer than is absolutely necessary. Even for those invested in piecing it together, engagement with localized tasks at hand—perhaps concentrating their ef-

forts on getting a sequence of key presses in the right order or on organizing their team—may well overshadow, at least temporarily, all else (see King and Krzywinska 2006). Nevertheless, a great deal of story is available to *World of Warcraft* players, even if it is delivered in often fragmented ways. This is evident in the "making-of" DVD that came with the *Burning Crusade* "collectors" expansion set (2007). In it, the team of designers spoke of the story line of the game, and how this informed the design of the game's world and gameplay features. On the team is a "historian" of the world who is responsible for maintaining the *Warcraft* "bible," which documents the narratives that underlie each of the game's races as well as the overarching game story and substories. Whether a player chooses to engage with the game's story or not, the development of the game story provides the guiding logic for the design. This includes the gameplay tasks offered. One of the game's designers spoke of the way that they had to check the content of quests given in the *Burning Crusade*'s Hellfire region with the game's creative director to ensure that they dovetailed with the main story. As we can see, story lines generated in this fashion become more than simply a style guide.

Unlike *Buffy the Vampire Slayer*, where viewers might miss episodes or begin watching somewhere other than episode one, season one, the player of *World of Warcraft* always begins at the beginning of the game—a factor that affects the structure and delivery of narrative. When a player loads the game software on to their computer for the first time, some background to the world's state of affairs is imparted through voice-over. It begins, "Four years have passed since the mortal races stood together against the might of the Burning Legion. The tenuous peace forged in a time of desperation is fading."[5] This exposition works with material developed in the previous *Warcraft* games and contextualizes what players are to do in the world. It helps to define their character and locates them within a matrix of competing claims, on an epic scale, that have led up to the current state of affairs. Story, presented as history and realized using what some players may recognize to be the rhetorical style of classical myth, offers *potential* meanings to the activities with which players must engage if they are to progress through and within the game.

In addition to the initial exposition, the creation of every new character by a player is accompanied on first entry into the game world by a further voice-over that broadly outlines something of the history of their race. When creating a Blood Elf, for instance, the player is told that the Blood Elves are an ancient race that five years ago lost their connection to powerful arcane magics because of an invasion into their lands by the Undead scourge and its leader, Arthas, who destroyed the Sunwell (the power source of much of their magic). Once the expositionary cutscene ends, the player receives a quest, delivered as scripted text, that tells them something about the power that has been lost and the effect of this on the creatures of the land—who are now no longer under Blood Elf control. Further information about the race and their fight to regain power is given through the preprogrammed speech assigned to characters, the quests a player encounters in their homelands, overheard conversations—often happened on while exploring the land and doing quests—and importantly, inscribed into geographic features of the game (more on this later). A vast array of narrative threads make up the world and its history.[6] These are presented in multiple ways: some tie obviously to the overarching narrative arc, but others are more localized (a lost trinket perhaps that must be found to kick-start a stalled romance), and some give more information about aspects of a player's race (there are ten in the game) or class (mage, rogue, priest, etc., which dictates the abilities assigned to a character). The game's overarching *given* narrative knits the condition of the world with the tasks afforded to, and abilities of, the player character.

If we are to gain a fuller picture of the complex and Arachnean ways that long narrative is present in the game and experienced through gameplay, it is also important to take into account what Lisabeth Klastrup (2003) calls the player's *lived-story*. The experience of playing the game is, she argues, "tellable" in story terms (and there are Web sites devoted to player stories). This story is composed of what player characters have done in the game world, and unlike the given narrative, is emergent through what player characters do in the game and what players bring to that. We might extend this notion to become the *player character's story*. The players' activities are framed by the game itself in narrative terms—quests operate in this way particularly. The items collected and worn by players are also testimony to the player character's story, as these are important signifiers to other players and shape their regard of those they meet. Items won in difficult situations when players have reached the higher levels of the game, termed "epic" (or "epixx," as it is often written), tell a tale to onlookers and speak thereby of the player character's long personal story arc.

It is in the commercial interest of this subscriber-based game to keep players playing for long periods of time; expansion packs that give long-term players new things to do is part of this strategy, and thereby extends the length of both the game's given narrative and, potentially, the emergent player character narrative.

Narrative and generic context, the chains of cause and effect, and the way that gameplay is designed around progression are likely to lead to players understanding their experience as a story. The longer a player sticks with the game, becoming increasingly knowledgeable about the state of affairs of the world, the more likely they are to experience the game and their own experience of being-in-the-game-world as a form of long narrative (indeed, playing the game might also become part of a player's own life story).[7] For those people who choose to actively role-play (there are servers available dedicated to role-play), it is common for them to have worked out their own backstory: where they come from, and what experiences they have had that shape their character's identity and status. Player-made backstories are in most cases generated through contextual cues provided by the game world, and role-players are perhaps the players most likely to understand their experience of playing (in) the game as a long narrative. Not all players will exhibit such levels of engagement with the game story, however, and the game is designed to accommodate a whole range of playing styles and interests.

As a massively multiplayer game, this is a highly social world. Here, "worldness" is not just what is programmed into the game; it is also propagated through the interaction of players with each other, which is encouraged in various ways. Given the length of time that many people play the game, strong bonds are often formed through the friend and guild system (player-run subcommunities that frequently stay in close contact and have community Web sites). High-level epic items, for example, are only won in group raids in "instances" that can involve up to forty players.[8] Instances are dotted across the game world and function as locations cut off from the persistent world (although tied explicitly into the game's given narrative). Within these, players are offered what the game's Web site describes as "a more personal experience exploring, adventuring, or completing quests in your own private dungeon."[9] Organizing large groups of players of diverse ages and backgrounds so that they each know what to do in an instance is a managerial challenge, and therefore often undertaken in guilds. It is likely that it will take at least several attempts to complete the instance successfully. Sharing such strong experiences and the added sense of agency afforded by group action helps knit players together as a community. The collective experience of achieving success for the first time in a high-level instance is likely to be remembered, becoming part of a guild's hi/story.

As a virtual world within which players have agency and interact with the game and each other, *World of Warcraft* is more complex technically, and has more work to do to create a sense of world than the noninteractive and augmented real world of *Buffy the Vampire Slayer*. This has an impact on the structure and delivery of long narrative. Viewers of *Buffy the Vampire Slayer* do not have to act (and act with increasing skill competency) in the world to uncover the story line, nor do they have to go about the quotidian business of chatting to friends or "grinding" gold and items to be able to increase agency. In the show, story is paramount. It is delivered in a transparent and mainly linear manner, and in this the show can be deemed Minervan. The given, predetermined long narrative of *World of Warcraft*, by contrast, is delivered in a more piecemeal and nonlinear fashion, many components of which have to be read into the organization and content of the world. The given long narrative is not intended to be easily grasped; instead, it is designed to be pieced together through the course of multiple activities and close readings of quests and other textual features. As with Arachne's tapestry, long narrative in *World of Warcraft* is more than simply the story of heroic

deeds; it is multidimensional with complex chains of cause and effect that resonate through the world on an epic scale. Player characters are born into a preexisting historical framework that determines who they are in terms of their race and, importantly, frames what they are impelled by the game to do in order to progress. Players can choose whether or not to engage and pay close heed to the given story. This may depend on what the players bring to the game. They can remain uninterested in the given story yet nonetheless play in an extremely engaged way. Even if players ignore hi/story, their characters are still highly determined by it. This demonstrates a significant difference between the way that television serials and games are structured and engaged with in terms of their stories: it is extremely unlikely that viewers uninterested in the story lines of *Buffy the Vampire Slayer* would remain viewers for long.

Geography and Long Narrative

The geography of the world is much less important to the construction and delivery of long narrative in *Buffy the Vampire Slayer* than it is in *World of Warcraft*. The latter is far more obviously a "world" in geographic terms than the former. There are, though, some aspects of the show's geography that contribute to the generation of narrative. The presence of a Hellmouth, located beneath the school's library, is core to the generation of sustained story lines (proximity to the Hellmouth is the reason why the Master, an übervampire, is resident in Sunnydale, thus providing the main story arc for season one, for example). The juxtaposition of othered, liminal spaces (often presented in Gothic terms: crypts, hell dimensions, and the graveyard as well as those episodes that look back to the past of vampires like Spike, Drusilla, and Angel, or the ex-demon turned teenager Anya) with familiar domestic spaces (the Scooby gang's homes, the school, and later the university) provides the impetus for some of the story lines relating to events and character arcs. Such geographic juxtapositions tie into the tensions that inform the long narrative of the show and supply the means of counterposing for dramatic effect epic qualities—heroic deeds, saving the world, Manichaeanism—with those of a more quotidian nature. The hell dimensions remain offscreen and are largely implied, lending room for the viewer's imagination to come into play.

Reference to ancient books to gain knowledge of such spaces is a neat device to get around the expense of realizing such realms in visual terms. Such devices enable the show to stay in both the present and the "real" world, but still divulge information that allows viewers to piece together the logic of the Buffyverse, including its framing metaphysical dimensions (deliberately and appropriately left "occulted," creating enigmas and affording a dramatic atmosphere of uncertainty). We learn that demons once ruled the earth and some of these who have not quite adjusted to a quieter existence once again seek dominion.[10] In terms of narrative, this has obvious Minervan qualities as it leads to heroic deeds. This is also the case with *World of Warcraft*, and in both, fights have a structural integrity—a formulaic quality—of their own that sets them somewhat aside from the main narrative (even though they are contextualized by it, which is a property of epic and action narratives generally). But for *Buffy the Vampire Slayer*, it is character development rather than fighting and defeating evil that is core to the making of the show's long narrative. Through their encounters with the supernatural the characters struggle with agency, personal relationships, power (and the lack thereof), identity, moral relativity, and ambiguity. These are Arachnean qualities. What we see of the "world" of *Buffy the Vampire Slayer* in geographic terms is economical rather than extravagant. It is not designed to be "read" closely—as is the case in *World of Warcraft*, which has stronger narrative-imparting properties and where you must read terrain to be successful in combat—but instead to support the core narrative focus on the dramatic interplay between supernatural metaphysics and everyday life.

The geography of *World of Warcraft* makes a strong contribution to the sense of the game space as a world and is closely connected to the world's history as long narrative. This is partly because the landscape itself is one of the primary ways that the game communicates the state of affairs to players. In order to progress through the game, players must travel through the game's geography. The game's quest system is designed to promote travel to new areas by

33.1 A map of the zones that make up Outland, the continent that expands the "world" of *Warcraft* to three continents, made available with the *Burning Crusade* expansion.

directing the player toward certain tasks. The game's geographic features of the world carry aspects of narrative. These features percolate down into a given zone's nonplayer character population and the style of its landscape, player versus player objectives, the types of story arcs offered, and the language of the text used to deliver quests.

The world's map shows three continents each divided into zones. Each zone has specific characteristics: Stranglethorn Vale is a jungle populated with tigers, panthers, and aggressive trolls; Gadgetzan is a desert region with a goblin-run town; The Barrens is savannah with an Orc encampment; and Felwood is a dank, moss-shrouded forest where the trees themselves have become corrupted and aggressive. These are just a few of the many zones that make up the world, yet the game's varied landscapes do more than provide visual pleasure. They speak of culture and history. Ruined temples and decaying forests once loved and nurtured signify the fall of the Night Elf race due to overweening ambition. Silvermoon City, the home of the Blood Elves, is partly in ruin after the race was decimated by the demonic Scourge and they lost the magic that held up their buildings. The other part of the city is left intact. Its opulent architecture and red and gold color scheme speaks of the Blood Elves' love of material luxury, justifying thereby the race's affinity with the profession of jewel crafting (figure 33.2). Every race in the game has suffered, either

Arachne Challenges Minerva

33.2 Silvermoon City: The opulent home of the power-hungry, vain, and materialist Blood Elves.

Tanya Krzywinska

through its own folly, or in the case of the Orcs, due to being enslaved by demons of the Burning Legion from which they are now free. This story line informs the differences between the triumphalist architecture of the Orcs' territory on Hellfire Peninsula in their original homeland of Draenar, now known as Outland, and the more humble and makeshift architecture of the Orc city Orgimmar, their new capital. More generally, the factional or racial ownership of zones is established in some cases, and contested in others, and this is an example of the way that the long story of the game provides impetus for gameplay, while also further rationalizing the player versus player component of the game that players can choose to take up.[11] A strong example of the way that story and geography are tied together explicitly is found when players are offered a quest in the city of Shattrath in Outland: a guide shows the player around the city, explaining the historical events that lead to the city being divided into hostile factions.

The narrative dimensions inherent in the game's geography and architecture lend greater depth of meaning to the experience of being in the world. As with Arachne's tapestry, narrative is not delivered linearly but in fragmented, diffused, multiple, and at times, subtle ways. Narrative may not always be to the fore for players, however. Engagement varies depending on the task at hand, the player's tastes and investments in the game, and even mood. While players can choose to rush their way through *World of Warcraft*, focused intently on gaining levels and skills, this was not possible with *Buffy the Vampire Slayer* when it appeared on television. Viewers of the show had to wait for new seasons and episodes to be made and aired. It is also likely that some viewers of comparable ages to the characters "grew up" with the show over its seven-year run. *Buffy the Vampire Slayer* often dovetailed fantasy elements with more realistic and potent ones, including, for example, the move from school to university, the making and breaking of romantic relationships and friendships, and the death of Buffy's mother. In this sense, the show is potentially able to mesh with viewers' life events in a way that *World of Warcraft* cannot.

While both falling into the category of epic-based fantasy fiction, the worlds of *Buffy the Vampire Slayer* and *World of Warcraft* are realized and structured in quite different ways. In the latter, worldness is very much in the foreground, and there is a strong sense of synergy between world (in the fullest sense), audiovisual presentation, social interaction, and long narrative. Here, the world makes stories, and the stories make the world. Representations tell stories, and stories guide the logic of representations. This mode of constructing long narrative can be considered Arachnean—with each plane working together, which places a strong emphasis on transformation, refractivity, and the intricacies of Web world making. Worldness is important to *Buffy the Vampire Slayer*, but because of the character-centered narrative, it is more about setting or premise than generative of narrative.

Persistence versus Seriality

One of the primary distinctions between *Buffy the Vampire Slayer* and *World of Warcraft* that affects the structure and delivery of long narrative lies between persistence and seriality. *World of Warcraft*, like most massively multiplayer games, is persistent and real-time. This means that the world continues to exist when a player leaves the game and it is a feature that is particular to online games. That the game is delivered in real time does not mean, however, that the game is linear, nor that it has complete temporal continuity; for instance, players can kill the dragon Onyxia over and over again—and killing her once doesn't alter the game world itself other than temporarily. Onyxia respawns according to a set pattern, and because she is found in an "instance," several groups can kill her independently without competing. In this, the temporal pattern of the game is at times recursive. Persistence is also an ideal state, and there are often interruptions due to technical issues.

Serial formats are structured episodically, which promotes the presence of certain temporal and linear conventions. Due to the constraints of televisual scheduling, series like *Buffy the Vampire Slayer* are limited to forty-minute episodes, and various strategies are used to accommodate this. A viewer may watch the show back-to-back on DVD or video, but this does not affect the imposition of a forty-

minute episode duration and a range of other features connected to its televisual context that shape the formal structure of each episode. Newman (2006, 20) argues that "a strong dose of episodic unity mitigates any textual instability caused by serialized aperture. Without this unity, casual viewers are less likely to watch." A commercial imperative drives this: maximizing the audience means that casual and committed viewers must be catered to. *World of Warcraft* is also designed to cater to both casual and committed players (it is the MMO that is credited with making the format friendly for casual players—testified to, perhaps, by the fact it has drawn more players than any other such game), but it is not limited to structuring events into regular-length episodes.

The episodic nature of *Buffy the Vampire Slayer*, along with the use of frequent ellipses, might appear to create temporal disjunctions. Instead these become integral to the show's structural grammar, to which regular television series viewers have become habituated. This means that all the events that occur are tailored to suit best the economical and apparently seamless delivery of story lines. *World of Warcraft* uses no ellipses whatever, as this would disrupt the player's sense of "being" in a real-time persistent world. The episode and season format of *Buffy the Vampire Slayer* affects profoundly the shape of the narrative: each builds up and ends with a climax, even though some threads might be left hanging to be taken up in the new season. This sets up the narrative-based expectation that Buffy and the gang will defeat the "Big Bad" (a term equating to the "boss" that appears frequently in games), even if it takes a whole season to do so. The resolution of tension and conflict provides one of the pleasures offered by most popular narratives, although the time that is afforded by the length of a season enables pleasures relating to character development and the build up to resolution. By contrast, while players of *World of Warcraft* might expect to be successful in a raid, quest, or fight, there is no guarantee that this will happen. The conditions must be right, and the player is expected to judge those conditions, aided by interface statistics and by reading the world's terrain. If a player judges badly, then they will "lose" in that situation. Players are invited to learn from that experience. This underlies the

Arachne Challenges Minerva

quality of agency that is instrumental to *World of Warcraft* as a game. Resolution has to be won and is not a given as it often is in *Buffy the Vampire Slayer*. This also offers a clue to the way that the game is structured, which informs gameplay as well as the design and delivery of long narrative.

Newman (2006) says that television serials "parcel" the delivery of story in ways that encourage viewer interest. Serials "organize their stories into rather short segments, often less than two minutes in length. Viewers might call these scenes, but writers call them 'beats' and they are television's most basic storytelling unit" (17). This makes for a fast pace, which is thought to keep viewers hooked into events and that specific channel. The beat format is largely evident in *Buffy the Vampire Slayer*, although longer scenes do occur particularly in the later seasons. Ellipses and cross-cutting result from the (in part industrial) requirement to speed up events, thereby creating a strong sense of drama and forward movement. Advertising breaks also affect the pacing of the show—with high points preceding breaks to encourage the return of viewers (the break points are most apparent when the show is watched on DVD).

World of Warcraft has rather different modes of keeping players' interest, although story elements and gameplay are certainly "parceled" and have episodic features. Gaining levels, items, and money are clear forms of positive feedback that encourage a player to stay in the world. The desire to view more content as it is added and to fulfill the stipulations attached to gaining success are also motivators. "Grinding" for items or levels can prove an exhausting, repetitive business, however. Such laborious and usually time-consuming activities conducted in real time often retard the delivery of the given narrative, although they can be regarded as forming part of the player character story. This makes for different pacing than the lively beat structure of *Buffy the Vampire Slayer*, where ellipses are generally in play. The given narrative of the game operates more as a context for action than a core motivation for play, which allows it to be stretched out over a longer timescale. Because narrative is not the primary driver to keeping the player hooked, as it is with the show, the game needs to reward play by creating a strong sense of progression.

To retain the interest of players, there are therefore a number of ways that the game structures the player's experience that have some equivalence to the beats and episodes of television serials. Each time a player gains experience from killing a monster, it is shown incrementally in the user interface. This can be regarded as a type of beat. Also, every hit a player lands on a monster is shown: the beating given to a monster, and vice versa, is segmented into a beat. This is also the case with increases to certain skills through acts performed. Each time a level is gained, new quests, use of items, and skills become available. This structure can be regarded as episodic. These examples do not relate directly to the given narrative but instead resonate with the player character's story. Quest chains can also be regarded in terms of episodic segmentation. In this case, they do frequently deliver incrementally given narrative content. Fights or quests can also be regarded in themselves as mininarratives that provide a sense of rhythm and expectation (will you prevail over your enemy, or find that required item?). Fights are longer in many cases than in the show, tailored to level and situation, but they too have some structural similarity as they can be regarded as being parceled into beats: knots of hostiles are often spaced out to allow players to take on only what they can manage to defeat with relative comfort.

Repetition is also found in both texts—meaning that narrative isn't fully progressive—although to different degrees. In the show, repetition is used in various ways to cue viewers into events and character developments. This might be through references in dialogue to past events that have led up to the current situation, or through less narratively cued dialogue that encapsulates a character's state of mind. The use of montage sequences at the start of each show acts as a reminder of events that lead up to that current situation. Repetition in *World of Warcraft* is more pervasive, though. It is centered on acquisition and gaining skills, rather than better acquainting players with the given narrative. It might mean going back and again fighting the monsters that just got the better of you, or going back multiple times to the same instance with a group or raid to gain useful items for party or guild members.

Retaining the interest of players relies at least in part on setting clear goals for the player; narrative coherence plays second fiddle, unlike with the show. The reinforcement of progression and agency in the game is one of the ways that this world can be said to be Minervan. As Minerva shows in her tapestry, there are rules that must be obeyed, rules that govern the condition of being in the world of gods and heroes. Judge those conditions, work with them, and success will be had. Perhaps this gets to the root of how games like this provide pleasure. In *World of Warcraft*, skill and good judgment always lead to just rewards. It is a highly predictable, statistically based world in a technical sense (luck is factored into the internal dice system when hitting mobs, for example, but plays a relatively small role). Social interaction helps ameliorate this—human behavior being less predictable than computers. This is unlike the capricious and uncertain nature of the real world. Player characters and monsters all have levels, and, say, if a player's character is of a substantially higher level than the monster they are fighting and they are careful not to attract the interest of other monsters in error, they are highly likely in most circumstances to win out. In *Buffy the Vampire Slayer*, as in the real world, no such predictable and transparent conditions exist. This gives room for more complex, situation-based, and problematic issues to come to the fore (even if we expect Buffy to triumph eventually, which accords with the "laws" of prime-time television narrative). In *World of Warcraft*, character transformation is mechanical and is signified ludically through predetermined increases in the progress bar (although it might be the case that encounters with other players might lead to personal transformation). In *Buffy the Vampire Slayer*, character transformation is far deeper and multifaceted, and thereby Arachnean. A player might gain a sense of agency through winning an epic sword, which might get the approval of guild friends and help the player character to progress more quickly, but it is not a transformation that speaks very deeply of existential matters. It is in essence something that seems more related to the limited satisfactions of acquisition-based consumer culture than deep personal change or struggle between conflicting desires, as can be said to be the case with the main characters at the core of the long narrative in *Buffy the Vampire Slayer*.

Player-centered choices are present in *World of Warcraft*, however. Some of these are hardwired into the game mechanics. The player can chose to assign their character's "Talent" points (gained when you achieve a new level) to shape the abilities of the character. More profoundly, a player is asked to make moral choices in their dealings with other players, and it is here that more complex aspects emerge. But the nature of a persistent world means a player is likely to reap as they sow: if you choose not to play in a group-friendly way, then others are unlikely to want to play with you again.

While the persistent real-time, game format of *World of Warcraft* lends room to build given narrative complexity on a truly epic scale and provides the context for the player character long narrative, the statistic-based features of the game along with the fact that the given story arc is dispersed temporally and structurally means that the type of emotional and psychological complexity that we gain through the narrative of *Buffy the Vampire Slayer* is only achieved via the investments and choices made by the player in their character. In this sense, emotional and psychological complexity is potential and emergent rather than inherent in the given narrative. While a viewer also has to have some investment in the show to make its stories and character arcs meaningful, the show demands less work and time on the part of the viewer. The show's televisual format—the demand to make the story "pacey," and the demands of episodic form and coherency—does mean that there is less room for narrative to become truly epic in scale. Here, the narrative is not woven through multiple perspectives as it is in *World of Warcraft*. In the latter case, playing only one character will only achieve a partial view of the whole story, which can encourage players to create differently raced characters if they are to gain a broader view of the expansive and multithreaded narrative scope inherent in the game.

Convergence

The entertainment industries have of late embraced world-based fiction, and this is because the format lends itself extremely well to multiauthored, cross-media franchises. Worlds like *Warcraft* and *Buffy the Vampire Slayer* become, as Henry Jenkins (2006) has said, playgrounds for numerous artists and writers. Worlds offer up a recognizable brand that can be used to produce a whole range of different products. *World of Warcraft* comes as an addition to a previously established world found in the real-time strategy games *Warcraft* (the first appearing in 1994), and there are now multiple spin-off products, including collectors items, novels, a card game, board games and other related merchandise. The television serial *Buffy the Vampire Slayer* has canonical status within a whole range of spin-off products, and since the much-lamented demise of the show, such material has kept the Buffyverse spinning for fans. These include the television show *Angel*—which by running concurrently with *Buffy* from *Buffy* season four on, often keyed into narrative events in the "parent" show—plus three video games, a board game, a "Top Trumps" card game, two tabletop role-playing systems, a host of novellas and comics, a huge number of fan and slash fictions published on the Web, and a range of merchandising (bags, T-shirts, plastic figures, etc.). Each of these ties into and broadens the scope of the world that was set up in the "parent" television show. World-based long narratives encourage fan-type consumption that goes beyond the canonical text.

While shows that encouraged this type of consumption used to be considered "cultish" and marginal to mainstream popular culture, they are now becoming central (*Doctor Who* and *The Lord of the Rings*, for example). This dovetails all too neatly with greater industrial and technological convergence, which depends increasingly on formulating devices to create long-stay audiences/consumers who will spend money to remain in contact with their preferred world. Long narrative is, within the context of a world, made in the mold of much older types of epic texts, and has therefore found a renewed and diverse lease on life.

Conclusion: From Epic to Epixx

I want to end with an overview of the Minervan and Arachnean features of these two epic texts. *World of Warcraft* is mainly Minervan in its world. It is rule based, and has predictable sets of cause and effect that are well suited to generating compelling and contextualized gameplay. At base it is a fixed and programmed world, albeit that the social dimension of the game and the choices that players make lend a sense of agency as well as presence to it. Player characters are set up as heroes doing what will benefit their race and faction. They undertake heroic deeds with predictable outcomes, if conditions are well judged. The predetermined rhetoric that informs the game is mythological and thereby epic (even if players fail to achieve tasks, or rail against their heroic status through speech or action).

Buffy the Vampire Slayer is largely Arachnean through the obscured and enigmatic metaphysics that define its world. As such, this is a highly unpredictable world in which emotions, identities, relationships, and moral meanings are thematically in flux. Fluidity and relativity are symptomatic and generational of long narrative, even if temporary resolutions are found. While Buffy herself is made somewhat in the mold of hero and is the prime enactor within the show, it is the fallout and problems of this heroic status on her life and relationships with others that provides the show with much of its (melo)dramatic tension. The interlacing of these elements is Arachnean. The way that the show uses yet undermines the heroics of classical epics by addressing power relations and transformation bears thematic comparison to Ovid's *Metamorphoses*.

World of Warcraft is mainly Arachnean at the level of narrative. Narrative is dispersed, perspectival, multileveled, and nonlinear. What the player does in the world does not affect the base level of events, and as such, a recursive temporality is often in play. In this, the game story does not have a structure that compares with the forward progression of most mainstream narratives (although various techniques are employed to help mask the recursive and static nature of the world and its story). What is perhaps most Arachnean is the way that micronarratives (player character stories, quests, localized race-based stories, etc.) are set within an overarching, relativized, multithreaded historical situation. Lastly, the fact that the given long story arc is optional, dispersed, and demands work and interest to uncover it, suggests a different mode of handling narrative than has occurred in any other fiction-based media form. In

Tanya Krzywinska

this sense the game can be compared with Ovid's *Metamorphoses*, which in its highly episodic and multithreaded form, offered a new way of telling and structuring long narrative.

Buffy the Vampire Slayer is largely Minervan at the level of narrative structure. It is delivered in linear form. Even though people do come back from the dead, bosses tend to stay dead once killed with due diligence. Buffy and the gang don't kill enemies multiple times, for example, like some players of *World of Warcraft* are likely to do, say, with the dragon Onyxia. Each season has an end boss who is instrumental in organizing the trajectory of that season's narrative arc. The show largely takes the viewpoint of the Buffy gang, with Buffy at the center of most things. It does not offer multiple, relativized viewpoints of the world and its history, depending on the class and race of the character played, as is the case with *World of Warcraft*. You can't choose to take the view of one of the vampires, for instance, unless the show chooses to depict that for a core narrative purpose. Narrative rules all the show's events, which is part and parcel of the particularities, constraints, and opportunities offered by the televisual, formal, and industrial context in which the show appears. The payoff for the Minervan and centralized narrative structure of *Buffy the Vampire Slayer* is that oppositions and resolutions are played through in coherent and tight-knit ways. This is not the case with the sprawling and disparate narrative structure of *World of Warcraft*.

Long narrative plays an important, if scaled, role in both *World of Warcraft* and *Buffy the Vampire Slayer*. Although there are some generic, thematic, and structural points of convergence, and both make use of features that can be regarded as Arachnean and Minervan, long narrative is nonetheless spun in accordance with the specific affordances and expectations offered by their foundational media.

Notes

1. What would become known as Athens, after Minerva's Greek name Athena.

2. In science fiction and role-playing circles, a fictional "world" is often termed the "verse," short for universe.

3. The "real world" is perhaps too uncomplicated a term to use here in an unqualified way, given that our experience of the real world

can be considered "virtual" and fantasmatic (because of the way that "seeing" the world is mediated by the brain and eye). I refer the reader to Michel Foucault's essay "Heterotopia," where he makes this point. I use the term here, however, in a structuralist sense, with the real world being marked off from "fictional" worlds that are meant, at least ostensibly, to be consumed as entertaining fancy. At the same time, it is crucial to acknowledge that virtual worlds like *World of Warcraft* or *Second Life* have real social and economic dimensions.

4. For a fuller account of the nature of this debate, see Wardrip-Fruin and Harrigan (2004); King and Krzywinska (2006); and Ryan (2006).

5. This cinematic is also available to be played at any time via the sign-in screen, and a further cinematic was added with the addition of the *Burning Crusade* expansion in January 2007.

6. While the game's history should be regarded as a long narrative arc, it is also important to acknowledge that it has some characteristics of a simulation, in the sense that the game's history is composed of complex, webbed interactions as well as through the emergent social interactions and economies of the game. The player's story, however, is exempt from the canonical story line material. Story provides the "bones" of the world, and simulation might be understood as the "live" experience. The combination of narrative with simulation, in a broad sense, is what contributes to the game's epic qualities: the presence of a *given* long narrative and the fact that players can't affect the game world other than in a superficial way means that this game is not a simulation in a pure sense, as might be said of *EVE Online*, where there are few rules and restrictions, and that provides supported opportunities for players to create and grow their own stories on top of the basic material. (My thanks to Douglas Brown for suggesting this example.)

7. For a discussion of being-in-the-game-world, see King and Krzywinska (2006).

8. In *World of Warcraft*, thousands of people play on the same server at the same time. Instances or dungeons permit a party of players to quest or raid in a designated, limited space that is replicated on servers so that multiple groups can do the quests in an instance without hindrance from others.

9. See ⟨http://www.wow-europe.com/en/info/basics/instancing.html⟩.

10. I have explored the mythological rhetoric of the game elsewhere (Krzywinska 2006).

11. Players can elect to fight and "kill" player characters of the opposite faction rather than non-player characters or monsters controlled by the game. Some servers are dedicated to such play (known as PvP servers), whereas players have to elect to participate in fighting another on player versus environment or role-play servers.

References: Literature

Creeber, Glen (2004). *Serial Television: Big Drama on the Small Screen*. London: BFI Publishing.

Jenkins, Henry (2006). *Convergence Culture: Where Old and New Media Collide*. New York: New York University Press.

King, Geoff, and Tanya Krzywinska (2006). *Tomb Raiders and Space Invaders: Video Game Forms and Contexts*. London: Wallflower Press.

Klastrup, Lisabeth (2003). "A Poetics of Virtual Worlds." ⟨http://hypertext.rmit.edu.au/dac/papers/Klastrup.pdf⟩.

Krzywinska, Tanya (2006). "Blood Scythes, Festivals, Quests, and Backstories: World Creation and Rhetorics of Myth in *World of Warcraft*." *Games and Culture* 1 (4): 383–396.

Newman, Michael Z. (2006). "From Beats to Arcs: Toward a Poetics of Television Narrative." *Velvet Light Trap* (Fall): 16–28.

Ovid (2004). *Metamorphoses: A New Version Translation*, translated by David Raeburn. London: Penguin Books.

Ryan, Marie-Laure (2006). *Avatars of Story*. Minneapolis: University of Minnesota Press.

Wardrip-Fruin, Noah, and Pat Harrigan (eds.) (2004). *First Person: New Media as Story, Performance, and Game*. Cambridge, MA: MIT Press.

Reference: Games

World of Warcraft. Blizzard. 2005–present.

Reference: Television

Buffy the Vampire Slayer (1997–2003). 20th Century Fox; Mutant Enemy; Kuzui Enterprises; Sandollar Television.

Tanya Krzywinska

Competing Narratives in Virtual Worlds

Ren Reynolds

One approach to investigating the philosophical implications of virtual worlds is to inquire into what kinds of meaning we attribute to them as artifacts and social practices that become associated with them.

As science and technology studies suggest, the processes by which new technologies take on accepted cultural values are often complex and contested. One way to trace how meanings evolve is to look at the narratives that various actors apply to the technology at hand. Hence, the approach taken here will be one that examines dominant narratives, and is informed by notions of social construction (Searle 1995), the power of metaphor (Lakoff and Johnson 1980), and the mutual shaping of technology, practices, and values as encapsulated in actor-network theory (see, for example, Latour 1987; Law and Hassard 1999).

There are many narratives associated with virtual worlds, ranging from the vast to the minute. Every day in virtual worlds such as *Second Life* and *World of Warcraft* these narratives are played out and challenged. Virtual worlds and their associated narratives are an important topic of philosophical analysis, not simply as a matter of semantics, but for at least two socially significant reasons.

First, as increased numbers of people spend more time in virtual worlds, the role of virtual spaces in debates over issues such as free speech and privacy rights increases in significance, simply by virtue of the number of people potentially impacted. The way we understand virtual worlds determines at a theoretical and practical level whether issues such as these are even accepted as a valid topic of debate. If, for example, virtual worlds are property, aspects of the debate over privacy may have no meaning; whereas if they are public spaces, the debate is central.

Second, virtual worlds seem to act like a warped mirror of the physical world, a mental tool where groups of people can interact with a simultaneously imagined possible world (Ryan 2001) that refracts meaning through the virtual, allowing us to reevaluate the most deep-rooted of contingent values. A good example of this is the way that debates over virtual money such as *EverQuest* gold tend to quickly turn into a debate over what money means anyway.

In this sense virtual worlds are potentially a highly disruptive force. Whether this disruption cashes out as social goods or not depends, in part, on the narratives that come to dominate our understanding of them.

In the rest of this chapter I will look at a few of the narratives that are dominating the current debate over virtual worlds, and examine both how the narratives are being constructed and how they are being challenged.

Background

Before looking at individual narratives, we need to recognize that they sit in a technological and critical continuum.

Technologically, today's virtual worlds grew out of the combination of single-player computer games and multiuser computer systems, which in turn grew out of the playful use of computing and electronics that stretches back at least to the 1950s.[1] All of this is informed by the rich cultural history of play and games, and the competing notions that society places on them (Sutton-Smith 1997; Harris and Park 1983; Huizinga 1949).

Similarly, the terms "virtual" and "world" have rich histories of their own. The word virtual, as Marie-Laure Ryan (2001) has discussed at length, has "Two (and Thousand) Faces." Ryan traces the debate over the value of the virtual to the schism between Aristotle and Plato over the value of arts and the imagination. Where Plato saw much of the arts as false (see the *Republic*, etc.), Aristotle imagined them as essential and full of potential and possibility (see *Nicomachean Ethics*, *Poetics*, etc.).

As we will see, this potential dichotomy is just one of the interplays of grand narratives that center on virtual worlds. As the use of virtual worlds expands, the controversies and competing concepts about what virtual worlds "really are" have spiraled in many directions, and taken on more cultural weight. The question that seems to be at the heart of many of the key current debates is, Who's in control?

This is sometimes explicit, such as in the case of arguments over who controls the processes of actual governance (Mnookin 1996); often a feature of the debate, such as in cases of arguments over property rights and law (Lastowka and Hunter 2004), and related debates over speech (Balkin 2004) and privacy; and sometimes implicit, such as in popular debates about the reality of virtual worlds (Siklos 2006).

Blizzard's GLBT Debacle

One of the most famous examples of negotiated meaning in virtual world history is the so-called GLBT-friendly (gay, lesbian, bisexual, and transgender) guild debate in *World of Warcraft*.

In late 2006, Sara Andrews posted a message (see below) to the in-game general chat channel of *World of Warcraft*, advertising for members of a GLBT-friendly guild. The response from Blizzard was that this was "inappropriate"; the email from Blizzard to Andrews reads, in part, as follows:

> Account Action: Warning
> Offense: Harassment—Sexual Orientation
> This category includes both clear and masked language which: ... [I]nsultingly refers to any aspect of sexual orientation pertaining to themselves or other players.
> Details (Note—Times are listed in Greenwich Mean Time, GMT): 1/12/2006 8:50 (GMT)
> Shimmre General—Stormwind City "OZ is recruiting all levels, but especially 50–60s! We are working on our Onyxia Chains and will be doing UBRS and hopefully Onyxia soon! We are not 'glbt only,' but we are 'glbt friendly'! http://guilduniverse.com/oz."
> The actions detailed above have been deemed inappropriate for *World of Warcraft* by the In-Game Support staff of Blizzard Entertainment. For further information, please view the *World of Warcraft* Policies and Terms of Use Agreement.
> (⟨http://www.worldofwar.net/articles/glbt.php⟩)

We can see here that a number of things are going on, and we need to start to trace through legal documents to unpack the multilayered story that Blizzard is asserting about *World of Warcraft*.

Like most publishers of virtual worlds, Blizzard tells two stories about what virtual worlds are. Through much of the Web site—⟨http://www.worldofwarcraft.com⟩—one finds language about "game" and "community"; even the browser title for the home page is "*World of Warcraft* Community Site." Much of the language is friendly, and the images are playful. Yet as one can see by the forum post above (which is typical), if there is conflict, Blizzard, like other publishers, gives primacy to a set of legal documents on the site and the tortuous definitions of the virtual space that they contain.

The grand narrative here is a detailed one that starts in typical fashion for virtual worlds: not a "a long long time ago in a land far far away" but rather):

> this software program, and any files that are delivered to you by Blizzard Entertainment, Inc. (via online transmission or otherwise) to "patch," update, or otherwise modify the software program, as well as any printed materials and any online or electronic documentation (the "Manual"), and any and all copies and derivative works of such software program and Manual (collectively, with the "Game Client" defined below, the "Game") is the copyrighted work of Blizzard Entertainment, Inc. or its licensors (collectively referred to herein as "Blizzard"). Any and all uses of the Game are governed by the terms of this End User License Agreement. (⟨http://www.worldofwarcraft.com/legal/eula.html⟩)

What is being said here and further detailed in the rest of the three thousand words or so of the agreement is that the virtual world is in fact and essence a piece of intellectual property, which by virtue of Blizzard's ownership of said property gives it rights through contract to define what can and cannot be done in the virtual world.

Primacy of Property

Property is the dominant narrative among virtual world publishers. The associated origin story rests on John Locke (i.e., we made it, so we own it [Reynolds 2002]), and the grand narrative of property encompasses everyone that uses virtual spaces. Property is a story of control; property laws tend to focus on what others cannot do, as the post from the Blizzard staffer above says, in rather empowered tones: "actions detailed above have been deemed inappropriate."

The "Offense" quote in Blizzard's reply is a reference to, and extract from, its "Harassment Policy." Blizzard opens the description of this policy by stating: "To ensure your time spent in *World of Warcraft* is safe and enjoyable, we have broken down what types of language and behavior are inappropriate and the penalties associated with each type of infraction (⟨http://www.blizzard.com/support/wowgm/?id=agm01719p⟩).

Here, Blizzard seems to be adopting a Hobbesian role of some form of duty-bound guardian preserving the safety and pleasures associated with the virtual world that is at the same time beyond the rules. The virtual world is here assumed to be something both "safe" and "enjoyable"; these are, however, certainly not necessary aspects of games (Malaby 2006).

This stance seems to fit well with the "Strict Father" explanatory metaphor advanced by George Lakoff (1996) for the conservative political outlook in contemporary U.S. politics. Even if not an exact fit, the Lakoff model of conservative versus liberal outlooks can help to explain how a worldview resting on property-based control can include notions of game, both to encompass a broader range of acts within the legitimate sphere of control and lend more weight to the control argument. That is, "game" is defined in legal terms (see above), and when evoked more broadly, the connotations that are given primacy are those that emphasize rules and control (for a theoretical basis for this, see, for instance, elements of the definitions of game in Suits [1978]).

Stories of property, at least in the context of virtual worlds, tend to be told as fairly straight-line affairs. There is a clear object, a clear owner, and a clear user. What's more, they are powerful narratives not only because they can be backed up by the control that publishers have over virtual worlds in virtue of the power asymmetries supported by the technical affordances that the artifacts give them but also because of the coherence of the narrative and its resonance with at least one notion of game.

Despite the power of the property narrative put forward by Blizzard and many other designers of virtual worlds, there remains room for alternative narratives or narrative interpretations. That is, disagreements tend to operate within the scope of the grand narrative or assert a counternarrative. In current debates over virtual worlds we often find users arguing for the basis of their rights in property, or within the social and technical affordances defined by the publisher. As we will see in the Blizzard GLBT case, Andrews first argued within an interpretation of the rules of *World of Warcraft* and then presented an alternative grand narrative—one inspired by civil rights.

Civil Rights

The initial debate between Andrews and Blizzard occurred via a range of electronic media, and were based on Andrews's assumption that Blizzard had simply made an error in interpreting the rules (⟨http://www.1up.com/do/feature?cId=3149452⟩). Failing this, and as the disagreement between Andrews and Blizzard drew wide media attention, the contention from Andrews within the context of Blizzard's forums and within the frame of a warning/appeal system was supplemented by: debates on gamer sites such as Kotaku "geek" sites such as Boing Boing (Doctorow 2006); the BBC (Ward 2006); open letters jointly posted on blogs (Hunter et al. 2006); an open letter to the Stonewall Champions and the Spreading Taint guilds sent to Blizzard (Ward 2006); and in-world protests such as a Pride march and "gay cruise" (Davidson 2006).[2] Andrews herself joined in this extraworld debate by being party to a letter on behalf of herself and Greg Wu from Lambda Legal (Chase 2006)—a move that introduced a civil rights counternarrative.

As the debate moved outside the *World of Warcraft* forums into broader game discussion boards, and out further into spaces such as blogs, general media, and the law, the hold of Blizzard's primary narrative seemed to diminish and the power of the alternative narrative of civil rights gained popular appeal.

In Dan Hunter and his colleagues's analysis of the situation (2006), attention is drawn to the way that Blizzard appears to draw equivalence between the fact of a reference to homosexuality and offense. This rhetorical move brings with it the grand narrative of civil rights, and one that certainly in the U.S. context, might be seen as equally strong as the property story.

The civil rights narrative is made more explicit in Lambda Legal's explanation of its actions (Chase 2006): "Lambda Legal stepped in to help Sara by drafting an advocacy letter to Blizzard. We outlined the company's mistake in seeing the honest presence of LGBT people as harassing to anyone else, and stated that relevant antidiscrimination laws forbid such a company-imposed cloak of invisibility."

This is an interesting text, as not only does it bring in the language of rights, it also reintroduces the playful elements of *World of Warcraft* as a game. The letter opens with the line, "Over the past several weeks, I have had the pleasure of representing two gnomes." In what might be seen as highly ironic, we have a game company, which may for all we know be staffed by left-leaning liberals, issuing statements based on contract, and a legal firm using playful references to gnomes.

Looking at this case in a broader context, we can understand what is occurring as a historic interplay of narratives being replayed in the virtual sphere. That is, even if we look only at the twentieth-century history of civil rights in the United States, we can see instance after instance of a tension between actors asserting and imposing norms through the power they have by virtue of being property owners, and resistance to this, often using property as site, catalyst, or target of action. For example, we might read both *Brown v. Board of Education* and Rosa Parks's civil disobedience as focusing on whether control over property legitimizes control over people.[3] Of course things are not this simple, as many civil rights campaigners also used their access to property or related power to fight for rights, but at the level of grand narratives, the parallels seem striking.

In this case the civil rights narrative won out. Blizzard publicly stated that it had made a "mistake" (Chase 2006). Yet this public outcome leaves the status of virtual worlds and speech rights in particular in an unresolved state. What we have is a specific incident in a specific virtual space; it would be wrong to believe that the scope of civil rights now extends into virtual spaces or that the narrative of property-based control now accommodates such rights.

Public Spaces

The narrative of civil rights when associated with virtual worlds brings up a whole range of problematic issues that the Blizzard GLBT case above only briefly touches on. The first of these issues is the application of the notion of space to virtual worlds.

So far I have left the "world" part of virtual worlds relatively unexamined. At one level the narrative of virtual worlds relies on their worldness. *Second Life* (⟨http://www.secondlife.com⟩) proclaims on its home page, "Your World. Your Imagination." *Lord of the Rings Online* (⟨http://www.lotro.com/index.php?page_id=51&siid=2⟩) states, "Players can experience the most famous fantasy world of all time."

When we think of what one does in virtual worlds, one thinks of "in-ness," travel, and space. The visual representation is a moving 2-D image that reacts to us and gives a sense of 3-D space.

While this idea of space (one might almost call it diegetic pace) is essential to the internal narrative of virtual worlds as we know them, it remains a metaphor. In a physical sense there is no "there" there. But this does not mean that the metaphor is without wide and powerful application. Indeed, some advocates—for instance, Julian Oliver (2002)—call for virtual worlds to be viewed as a "new publics and new places."

Here, the idea of space is starting to be conjoined with narratives of rights. We have gone from the ludic utility of the virtual space to one that has civic connotations. While for many, this is just how the story goes when you have spaces and people, for virtual world publishers, ideas of space that connote the potential of a civic discourse do not necessarily sit well with concepts such as property and control.

Even within the spatial metaphor there are competing similes and stories to back them up. Peter Jenkins (2004), for instance, suggests that we think of virtual worlds as being like the U.S. notion of a company town. This is a compelling idea, as it includes the idea of a virtual world as a space, the rhetoric of ownership, and virtual worlds as places where there are civil rights and a duty on the owner to maintain those rights (or at the very least, in its role as a pseudostate actor, not to interfere with them).

As Jack M. Balkin (2004) discusses, however, one can also apply the model of a shopping mall to virtual worlds. After all, shopping malls are consistent with many of the same metaphors as the company town idea; one might also add that shopping malls are a better reflection of social practices due to the voluntary nature of one's entry into them. What's more, the shopping mall idea is one that is much more sympathetic to the idea of controlling speech (at least under current U.S. law, where in some cases First Amendment rights have been held not to pertain).

As one can see, extending the spatial metaphor beyond its use within the context of a virtual world rapidly becomes problematic. Given the history of the relationship between "cyberspace" and the extended use of the spatial metaphor, this should not come as a surprise. Hunter (2003), for example, has written, "Initial discussions of cyberspace as place have mistaken the idea of how we think about cyberspace, with the normative question of how we should regulate cyberspace." He goes on to comment on the almost-pernicious power of the spatial metaphor that has an "unacknowledged, and unrecognized, influence," and ultimately that the "conception of 'cyberspace as place' leads to the implication that there is property online, and that this property should be privately owned, parceled out, and exploited."

While writers such as David McGowan (2004) reject the idea that the spatial metaphor causes judicial confusion, I think that the history of cyberlaw, both old and new, is testament to the unstable nature of the concept of space when applied to the virtual, even a virtual as concrete as a virtual world.

Social Capital and Identity

A radically alternative narrative to those of property, control, and space that we have discussed so far is that of society or community. This narrative gives primacy to the social relations between individuals that use a virtual world.

For some, such as Sal Humphreys (2003), a social relation–based narrative can counteract what is hidden by the sometimes-dominant property-based rhetoric. Indeed, Humphreys argues further that by imposing a property regime (that is, by going along with property as a domi-nant narrative), we are giving property an "illegitimate foothold in social and community relations." These points are also touched on by T. L. Taylor (2002), who, focusing on arguments over property in *EverQuest*, notes that the broadening of specifically intellectual property rights is problematizing both collaborative efforts and the resulting cultural and symbolic artifacts.

The narrative of society is every bit as polymorphous as that of space or property. A specific concept that researchers have begun to adopt in an attempt to define certain aspects of the social is that of "social capital." The concept is now strongly associated, especially in a normative form, with Robert Putnam's work *Bowling Alone* (2000). In this work, Putnam identifies two useful concepts: bridging and bonding. Bridging refers to individuals from different backgrounds making links between social networks, and bonding is the process of providing a substantive form of support to each other.

Now while it might seem that the social narrative removes us from the more spatiotechnical aspects of the space, property, and control metaphors, some maintain that the elements of the physical are necessarily related to the social. Indeed, Putnam seems to see at least some form of technology as a thing that isolates us in physical space, thus reducing social capital.

The undercurrent in much of the rhetoric here returns us to the idea of the virtual as fake. For example, trust seems to be essential for forming social bonds—a number of writers including Helen Nissenbaum suggest that critical elements in the formation of trust are missing in the nonphysical; that is, the virtual. Three such elements are a lack of identity, a lack of personal characteristics, and an inscrutable social setting and a lack of clear roles (Nissenbaum 2001; see also the work of Philip Pettit). The implication here is that any trust we may think we have or any social relations we believe we have built up in a virtual space are not genuine in some way or other.

In the specific case of trust, though, people such as P. B. De Laat (2005) have directly challenged these assertions through empirical study. Looking at virtual worlds, Dmitri Williams (2003) conducted a study using *Asheron's Call 2* that examined Putnam's bridging and bonding factors, demonstrating that they indeed can exist online. More generally, both Williams (2003) and Taylor (2002) have noted that the almost exclusive focus given to the physical, and the simple binary distinctions between it and the virtual, mask the intermedial ways that people in practice form and negotiate relationships.

This recent research gives theoretical backing to elements of the social narrative, and provides good reason to separate it from many of the necessary bonds that the physically and property-based narratives often attempt to claim.

Protest

Where the ideas of society versus property/control come into direct interaction is when users of virtual worlds protest. Typically at some point in every virtual world, the tensions between groups of users and virtual world creators break down to the point that there is an in-world protest. These now have a tradition of their own: they typically involve a large number of player characters converging on one area of a virtual world to the point that the software ceases to function. Often the player characters are created especially for the event, are low-level, and usually have some aspect to them that is intended to be humorous. Examples include the vomiting avatars in *Ultima Online*, the call to arms in *EverQuest*, and the credit dupe debacle in *Star Wars Galaxies*—which one group covered live on its own forums, role-playing as journalists:

Allehe: This is Allehe signing off from somewhere on Dathomir awaiting death.

Avalie: And this is Avalie reporting live (but frozen) on Endor.

Back to you, Dan . . .

Dan: A sad conclusion to an otherwise fantastic news day. Allehe, may your unfurtunate [*sic*] trip to the cloners be quick and painless.
(⟨http://www.intrepid.galaxyforums.com/index.php?showtopic=7190&st=40⟩).

Similarly, in *Second Life* in 2003, there were protests over the "tax" system levied on users of the space by Linden Lab. It should be noted that *Second Life* is a virtual space where the in-world currency is freely traded with U.S. dollars (more recently Linden Lab has created a bid-matching system for users who want to trade in and out of the virtual currency). In this case, users (calling themselves "Americana") in an area of *Second Life* created virtual tea crates and even role-played aspects of the Boston Tea Party, as demonstrated in this dialogue reported by Wagner James Au (aka Hamlet Linden, aka Hamlet Au), at the time an "embedded reporter" for Linden Lab):

> "Redcoat spy!" Bosozoku Kato shouted.
> "Please please please," Ryen Jade interjected, "let me shoot him!"
> (⟨http://www.nwn.blogs.com/nwn/2003/09/tax_revolt_in_a.html⟩)

As can be seen from the two brief dialogue extracts, protests in virtual worlds tend to be knowing performances. They borrow tropes from historic forms of protest and adapt them for the environment. They also carry with them the narratives of civil disobedience and the implications of civil rights, and thus a notion of civic identity and society that embodies those rights.

Conclusion

The aim of this chapter was not to provide persuasive arguments for one grand narrative of virtual worlds over another. Rather, it was to show that there are a range of competing narratives, some of which are wholly or partially compatible, and others that are directly contradictory. What's more, in many of the important debates over virtual worlds, there is no essential definition of what a virtual world is, however powerful a given narrative happens to be.

The narratives that come to dominate the debate are those that resonate most with cultures in which practices of virtual world development and use are most embedded. Given the global nature of virtual worlds (the United States, Korea, and China are currently the dominant forces in virtual world creation and use) and their ability to enable us to rethink cultural assumptions, their semantic status might eventually be settled—but their power as a culturally disruptive force may well remain. Publishers, users, and policymakers will still be left with the question of where we will go next, being led by those able to harness the power of the virtual for social change.

Notes

1. The Brookhaven National Laboratory in the United States suggests that the first "video game" may be *Tennis for Two*, a game created from basic components and an oscilloscope display by William Higinbotham, and reported in the *Brookhaven Bulletin* of 1958.

2. In the interests of full disclosure, it should be noted that the blog on which I post published an open letter to Blizzard, though I was not a signatory to this letter, having not been engaged or fully conversant with the debate at the time.

3. *Brown v. Board of Education of Topeka*, 347 U.S. 483 (1954).

References

Balkin, Jack M. (2004). "Virtual Liberty: Freedom to Design and Freedom to Play in Virtual Worlds." *Virginia Law Review* 90, no. 8 (December).

Chase, Brian (2006). "When the Pen Is Mightier Than the (Magic) Sword." ⟨http://www.lambdalegal.org/our-work/publications/page.jsp?itemID-32007393⟩ (accessed on January 1, 2007).

Davidson, Neil (2006). "Canada No. 1 in Hard-core Sex Video Gaming; Title is 'State of the Art.'" ⟨http://www.ctv.ca/servlet/ArticleNews/story/CTVNews/20061113/adult_gaming_061113/20061113?hub=Entertainment⟩ (accessed on January 1, 2007).

De Laat, P. B. (2005). "Trusting Virtual Trust." *Ethics and Information Technology* 7: 167–180.

Doctorow, Cory (2006). "*World of Warcraft*: Don't Tell Anyone You're Queer." Boing Boing. January 27. ⟨http://www.boingboing.net/2006/01/27/world_of_warcraft_do.html⟩ (accessed on January 7, 2007).

Harris, J. C., and J. Park (eds.) (1983). *Play, Games, and Sports in Cultural Contexts*. Champaign, IL: Human Kinetics.

Huizinga, Johan (1949). *Homo Ludens: A Study of the Play-element in Culture*. London: Routledge.

Humphreys, Sal (2003) "Online Multiuser Games: Playing for Real." *Australian Journal of Communication* 30, no. 1: 79–91.

Hunter, Dan (2003). "Cyberspace as Place and the Tragedy of the Digital Anticommons." *California Law Review* 91, no. 2 (March): 439–519.

Hunter, Dan, et al. (2006). "Open Letter to Blizzard Entertainment." TerraNova blog. February 8. ⟨http://terranova.blogs.com/terra_nova/2006/02/open_letter_to_.html⟩ (accessed on January 7, 2007).

Jenkins, Peter (2004). "The Virtual World as a Company Town—Freedom of Speech in Massively Multiple Online Role Playing Games." *Journal of Internet Law* 8, no. 1 (July).

Lakoff, George (1996). *Moral Politics*. Chicago: University of Chicago Press.

Lakoff, George, and Mark Johnson (1980). *Metaphors We Live By*. Chicago: University of Chicago Press.

Lastowka, Greg, and Dan Hunter (2004). "The Laws of the Virtual Worlds." *California Law Review* 92 (1).

Latour, Bruno (1987). *Science in Action: How to Follow Scientists and Engineers through Society*. Milton Keynes, UK: Open University Press.

Law, John, and John Hassard (eds.) (1999). *Actor Network Theory and After*. Boston: Blackwell.

Malaby, Thomas (2006). "Beyond Play: A New Approach to Games." ⟨http://ssrn.com/abstract=922456⟩ (accessed on January 7, 2007).

McGowan, David (2004). "The Trespass Trouble and the Metaphor Muddle." *Minnesota Legal Studies* Research Paper No. 04–5. ⟨http://ssrn.com/abstract=521982⟩ (accessed on January 7, 2007).

Mnookin, Jennifer (1996). "Virtual(ly) Law: The Emergence of Law in Lambda MOO." *Journal of Computer-Mediated Communication* 2. ⟨http://jcmc.indiana.edu/vol2/issue1/lambda.html⟩ (accessed on January 7, 2007).

Nissenbaum, Helen (2001). "Securing Trust Online: Wisdom or Oxymoron." *Boston University Law Review* 81, no. 3 (June): 635–664.

Oliver, Julian (2002). "The Similar Eye: Proxy Life and Public Space in the MMORPG." In *Christian Game Developers Conference Proceedings*, edited by Frans Mayra. Tampere, Finald: Tampere University Press.

Putnam, Robert D. (2000). *Bowling Alone: The Collapse and Revival of American Community*. New York: Simon & Schuster.

Reynolds, Ren (2002). "Intellectual Property Rights in Community Based Video Games." In *The Transformation of Organisation in the Information Age: Social and Ethical Implications*, edited by Isabel Alvarez et al. Lisbon: Lusiada University.

Ryan, Marie-Laure (2001). *Narrative as Virtual Reality*. Baltimore: Johns Hopkins University Press.

Searle, John (1995). *The Construction of Social Reality*. New York: Free Press.

Sicart, Miguel (2005). "Game, Player, Ethics: A Virtue Ethics Approach to Computer Games." *International Review of Information Ethics* 4.

Siklos, Richard (2006). "A Virtual World but Real Money." *New York Times*, October 19.

Sommer, Joseph H. (2001). "Against Cyberlaw." *Berkeley Technology Law Journal* 15.

Suits, Bernard (1978). *The Grasshopper: Games, Life, and Utopia*. Toronto: University of Toronto Press.

Sutton-Smith, Brian (1997). *Ambiguity of Play*. Cambridge, MA: Harvard University Press.

Taylor, T. L. (2002). "'Whose Game Is This Anyway?': Negotiating Corporate Ownership in a Virtual World." In *Christian Game Developers Conference Proceedings*, edited by Frans Mayra. Tampere, Finland: Tampere University Press.

Ward, Mark (2006). "Gay Rights Win in *Warcraft* World." BBC news online. February 13. ⟨http://news.bbc.co.uk/1/hi/technology/4700754.stm⟩ (accessed on January 7, 2007).

Williams, Dmitri (2003). "Bridging, Bonding and Slaying the Evil Foo: Social Capital in an Online Game." Presentation at the Association of Internet Researchers Annual Conference 4.0, Toronto, Ontario, October 18.

Competing Narratives in Virtual Worlds

Warcraft Adventures: Texts, Replay, and Machinima in a Game-Based Storyworld

Henry Lowood

In October 2004, the fourth World Cyber Games were held in San Francisco. Contestants competed in this international tournament, the "video game Olympics," for championship titles in each of seven competitive games. The prize money was substantial: $20,000 for first place to each of the individual winners in games such as the popular real-time strategy title *Warcraft III*. More than seventy players from forty-four countries arrived to compete for this championship alone. Few spectators were present at the Bill Graham Civic Auditorium to see the *Warcraft III* finals between the favored player, WelcomeTo (real name: Hwang Tae-Min) from Korea, and the underdog, Grubby (real name: Manuel Schenkhuizen) from the Netherlands. Many more observers would view the game by other means, via Webcast or replays, eyes glued not on the human contestants but on the player-controlled units, interface, and contested terrain depicted in the game.

Relatively little attention has been given in game studies to digital game spectatorship, though players especially of multiplayer and competitive games frequently watch other players play. Replays of played games such as these *Warcraft III* finals have become one of the most popular forms of game-based "video." Web sites such as ⟨http://www.wcreplays.com⟩ or ⟨http://www.warcraftmovies.com⟩, and viral video sites such as YouTube, offer literally tens of thousands of competitive replays and video captures in various formats. Of course, every replay tells a story, and such stories extend the experience of playing games such as *War-*

craft III, both for the creator and the viewer. As replay documents played games, the stories associated with them have to do with cyberathletic performance in a competitive arena. Spectators who watch replays are usually intimately familiar with the spaces and player actions depicted in them. In order to understand the popularity of digital game spaces as "sets" for animated movies that their creators use to tell fictional stories rather than document played games, we must start by trying to understand what player-spectators see—in both senses of the term—in replays.

One way to tell the story of the *Warcraft III* finals match revolves around a pivotal moment: a stunning reversal that led to Grubby's upset win. What did spectators see? After losing the first match in the best-of-three finals competition, they observed roughly six minutes into the second match that units controlled by the two players were skirmishing near Grubby's main base. WelcomeTo was perhaps threatening to end the match, but after the battle intensified, his army fell back. His critically important main hero character (a "Farseer") had suffered quite a bit of damage, and so he decided to use a portal scroll to teleport his army back to the safety of his home base. To this point the game action was easy for spectators to follow, but suddenly something unexpected happened: as soon as his army teleported into his base, WelcomeTo's Farseer toppled over dead. The disastrous setback led to Grubby's win in the match, accompanied by wild cheers from the small, largely European crowd in the auditorium. Clearly rattled, WelcomeTo played poorly in the third match, and Grubby won the championship. But what had happened to the Farseer? What caused his demise? Only experienced players could quickly understand the sequence of events.[1] Players looking carefully at replays, with access to the game's interface and both players' view of the action, could eventually translate the crucial ten seconds or so of action into Grubby's rapidly executed player actions. Here is what they then saw:

Grubby's own Farseer hero had earlier in the game taken a "wand of lightning" from a gnoll assassin while "creeping," and for most of the game it had stayed unused in his inventory. When WelcomeTo activated the portal

35.1 Grubby defeats WelcomeTo, World Cyber Games 2004.

scroll, his Farseer was invincible, but Grubby instantly clicked on his wand (or hit a key selecting it), moused his cursor over WelcomeTo's *second* hero, a Firelord, and clicked the mouse to cast a lightning shield on *him*, not the Farseer. This shield would do damage over time to any unit standing *next* to the Firelord. Grubby knew instinctively what would happen and executed his idea in an instant: WelcomeTo's heroes landed together in their base; instead of finding safety, the wounded Farseer died simply from standing next to his charged ally. I have shown the replay of these pivotal moments to academic audiences and players on several occasions. Only one or two viewers have been able to explain what Grubby did to win. If you don't play the game, you can't translate the on-screen action into Grubby's mastery of *Warcraft* tactics and interface skills. For those who understood it, Grubby's masterful performance became a story about the match, a subjective version of what happened during the game. A story that directly

translated into game syntax, with beginning and end at an arbitrary point in the game, was a *chronicle* of that game. *Warcraft* Web sites and forums offered chronicles of Grubby's victory, with a fair amount of enunciation and commentary by knowledgeable players. Others *emplotted* the game action by explaining or giving dramatic structure to what transpired.[2] A one-sentence example of such a text might be, "Grubby's brilliant use of the lightning shield to kill Zacard's hero was the turning point of their match, brought about a shocking comeback against the favored player, and led him to the 2004 championship in the World Cyber Games *Warcraft III* tournament." At this level of narrative there is greater latitude for the description; it is no longer a derivative of the sequence of game actions. Some spectators might miss the brilliance in Grubby's move altogether, others might prefer to see this game as a morality tale about an overly confident Korean favorite or the triumph of a lesser-known, hardworking European opponent

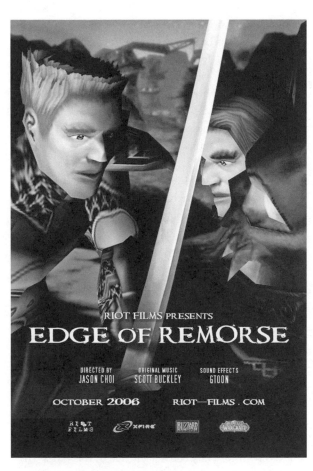

35.2 Poster for Riot Films' *Edge of Remorse*.

for their gameplay. Roughly ten percent of the videos based on the massively multiplayer online game *World of Warcraft* and hosted by the most popular site for downloading them, ⟨http://www.warcraftmovies.com⟩, have been categorized as "story line" movies. These are machinima projects that present linear narratives through the recording and editing of in-game performances.

An example of such a *World of Warcraft* movie is the award-winning *Edge of Remorse*, produced by Riot Films and directed by Jason Choi.[5] The story recounts how two brothers choose different sides in the war ravaging Azeroth (the world in which the game is set) and reveals the origins of their split as love for the same girl, with whom they grew up as an inseparable trio. In the end, rivalry and betrayal results in the tragic death of all three. Choi's telling of the story in machinima form never makes direct reference to events of the game's storyworld, nor does it present unadorned gameplay or settings from the game as a player would typically see them. *Edge of Remorse* does not name its protagonists or setting, or use spoken dialogue to bring the viewer back to reference points from the game on which it is based. It relies instead on the skillful use of a variety of filmmaking and video editing techniques (montage, foreshadowing, flashback, sound effects, musical scoring, compositing, and chroma keying) to focus on the universal aspects of the story: the intertwined fate of three characters and the revealing moments leading to their demise. Lasting roughly eight minutes, with some 120 cuts and fades, *Edge of Remorse* is no replay or continuous recording of gameplay, but an intricately composed piece of visual storytelling. Nonetheless, players recognize it unmistakably as a story set in the world depicted by the *World of Warcraft*. The plot's logic is determined by the eternal conflict between Horde and Alliance; the twist in *Edge of Remorse* is to explore the destructive nature of this world in the form of a vignette, a small, precise piece that comments on the tragic nature of warfare by showing the impact of specific events on ordinary characters. Choi's work thus engages players while moving beyond the self-referentiality of much machinima, and viewers unfamiliar with the *World of Warcraft* or the *Warcraft* series of games can easily grasp its message.

who has since taken over the throne, and so on. What many players see as the value of these replays is not just the training they provide but the capacity for telling stories as fans of their games and its players.

Not all game videos are replays, however.[3] A new narrative medium, called machinima, has sprung out of computer game technology and play since the mid-1990s. Machinima has been defined as "filmmaking within a real-time, 3D virtual environment," and it means using game software and gameplay to create animated videos (Marino 2005).[4] The growth of machinima has provided an outlet for players to work in a story-driven medium. Machinima also extends their engagement with games that they enjoy playing as well as the storyworlds that can provide a narrative context

35.3 Screenshot, *Edge of Remorse*.

Introduction

This chapter will focus on a particular meeting point of game developers and players in the cocreation of a storyworld: movies made with the software used to develop and play computer games. It will consider the full range of game-based productions, from game replays that document actual matches, to story line movies through which players seek to tell stories about game worlds or completely unrelated topics. In particular, I will concentrate on the ways in which game-based replays and machinima have extended player engagement with a specific game series and associated storyworld: that of Blizzard Entertainment's *Warcraft* series, including its extension to the massively multiplayer *World of Warcraft*.

The subject of this chapter is the community player; that is, the player who performs for other players and spectators. Like other activities, such as modifying games or posting opinions about games, recording and showing gameplay or using games to make a movie are forms of performance dominated by players. How do these projects extend both player engagement with the storyworld created by Blizzard's developers and the narrative space itself through the works created by these players?

In considering this question, an important aspect is the relationship of two forms of creative expression—those of the developer and the player—and an important issue is whether their relationship is characterized more accurately as one of conflict or cooperation (or perhaps as something in between?). Another critical set of issues circulates around the nature of game-based moviemaking as storytelling. As a developer, Blizzard has expended great effort to create prerendered and in-game videos, particularly "cutscenes," that

establish strong story lines and motivate players to follow lengthy campaigns organized as a series of single-player "missions." Players, for their part, have created tens of thousands of their own videos, ranging from saved replays and remixed screen captures of competitive games to story-based machinima pieces.

Spectatorship, multiplayer competition, and player communities have been crucial to the success of the *Warcraft* series of games as well as providing a context and culture for player-created replays and videos. At the same time, many machinima projects have focused on stories, characters, and events drawn from the "world of *Warcraft*" that might be described as textual production. Is it more useful to think of the storytelling possibilities of these projects in terms of textual production or as community play taking place in performance spaces? In short, what do we learn by paying more attention to the modes of performance available to the player, and the ways in which such performances are viewed, enunciated, and reworked by a community of players?

The *Warcraft* Series: A Brief History

The first *Warcraft* computer game, published in 1994, was called *Warcraft: Orcs and Humans*. Blizzard Entertainment, founded as Silicon and Synapse in 1990, was the developer, as it has been for every subsequent title in this series. The *Warcraft* series played a significant role in defining a new game form or genre that became known as real-time strategy.[6] *Warcraft: Orcs and Humans*, along with Westwood Studios' *Dune II* (1992) and Westwood's *Command and Conquer* (1995), are generally recognized as the founding trio of the real-time strategy genre, though of course there were numerous antecedents for various aspects of these games.[7] The notion of a "real-time" game stands in contrast to the turn-based game. In the latter, players take turns in sequence, one player moving his or her units while the other waits or watches, existing for all intents and purposes in a world for which time stands still. The difference in real time is not so much about what happens computationally as it is that the states of the game occur at specific times in a continuous stream—time flows in an uninterrupted (generally) and synchronous way for both players. Turns

35.4 The original *Warcraft: Orcs and Humans* interface (1994).

no longer freeze the passage of time for one player while the other contemplates the perfect move. Instead, time becomes a constant source of pressure and stress. Players multitask, meaning that they observe, think, plot, micromanage, manipulate the interface, and attempt to control their units, all while their opponent is moving and countermoving at the same time. Writing about the first game in the *Warcraft* series, the editor of *Computer Gaming World* described a "panicked pace," "split-second decisions," and a "mad-dash juggling of resources and demands." He advised that "if you can't manage the carpal calisthenics to right and left mouse click in rapid succession, you can forget about *Warcraft*" (Lombardi 1995).

The first *Warcraft* game offered an early version of this stressful multitasking as the basis for strategy play, but one that a decade later, *Warcraft III* players would certainly find quaint and slow paced. For this reason, it is necessary to consider *Warcraft* as an evolving series of games. There were many crucial refinements of game mechanics, technology, and interface. Especially important for performance and the creation of a viable storyworld, each version of the game introduced narrative elements, ranging from new information and content (maps, dates, characters, etc.) about

the history of Azeroth, the fictional world in which events take place, to ways of telling the story through real-time strategy play and online role-playing in *World of Warcraft* (the association of audio with characters, skills, and spells associated with heroic characters, lavish cutscenes, game-based moviemaking, etc.). Moreover, both developers and players were engaged by the continuity and accumulating details of the storyworld as the basis for what Henry Jenkins (2003) has called "transmedia storytelling." As Jenkins has often pointed out, the intriguing issue with respect to narratives and digital games is not whether these games present us with self-contained stories worked out by playing them; instead, they provide elements for telling stories across media. In the case of digital games like *Warcraft* and *World of Warcraft*, these elements were not limited to characters and settings that could serve as seeds for stories in other media such as short stories or card games. It was also the case that the game technology itself could be used as a narrative medium, as was the case with game-based moviemaking such as machinima. Before turning to the ways in which this occurred, it is worth taking a moment to compile a brief history of the *Warcraft* series, along with the other game formats and media that it spawned, as a first

35.5 The *Warcraft II* interface (1996).

indicator of the sheer mass of the material available to players and fans of the series.

The two major revisions of *Warcraft* were the appropriately named *Warcraft II: Tides of Darkness* (December 1995) and *Warcraft III: Reign of Chaos* (2002). These versions also spawned expansions, patches, and projects that brought the *Warcraft* settings to different game systems and media. Two conventional add-on titles, *Warcraft II: Beyond the Dark Portal* (May 1996) and *Warcraft III: The Frozen Throne* (2003), primarily added new content (such as maps, campaigns, new units, etc.). *Warcraft II: Battle.net Edition* (1999) was an update that modified a few of *Warcraft II*'s features (including its expansion) and made it compatible with battle.net, Blizzard's network for competitive play.

Blizzard also published "battle chests," anthologies, soundtrack CDs, DVDs of high-resolution cutscenes, cinematic trailers (including a theatrical release), collector's editions, and gift sets that included versions of the game, expansions, and more, such as strategy guides, art books, or soundtrack CDs. Other companies provided new content as well. Tewi Verlag's *Levels and Add-ons for Warcraft II* in 1995, Sunstone Interactive's *W!Zone* (1996), and Aztech New Media's *Aztech's Armory: Campaigns for Warcraft II* (1997) were examples of independently developed levels, maps, and campaigns for *Warcraft II*, while Electronic Arts published a version of *Warcraft II* for the Sony Playstation and Sega Saturn consoles, called *Warcraft II: The Dark Saga*, in 1997. And still that was not all. *Warcraft* also spawned *Warcraft: The Board Game* (Fantasy Flight Games, 2003) and *Warcraft: The Role-Playing Game* (Sword and Sorcery, 2003), based on the *Dungeons & Dragons* system, and that in turn has generated several books providing details about the characters, monsters, magic spells, and items that can be found in the world.

In late 2004, Blizzard released the eagerly anticipated *World of Warcraft*, a massively multiplayer online role-playing game that incorporated elements of these previous projects in presenting a digital version of the storyworld in which players could act as individual characters. An enormous success, *World of Warcraft* in turn became the basis

35.6 Interface mastery and competitive play: *Warcraft III* (2002).

for *World of Warcraft: The Role-Playing Game* (Sword and Sorcery, 2005), a revision of the *Warcraft*-based game *World of Warcraft: The Board Game* (Fantasy Flight Games, 2005) and the *World of Warcraft Trading Card Game* (Upper Deck, 2006). Writers such as Richard Knaak, Christie Golden, Jeff Grubb, and Chris Metzen have produced novels, stories, and comic fiction based on stories drawn from *Warcraft* or *World of Warcraft*. And finally, players of games in the *Warcraft* series and *World of Warcraft* have generated thousands of replays, dance movies, story line machinima, and player versus player movies.

High-Performance Play: Textual Production or Performance Space?

This lineage of games and other media testifies to the fact that *Warcraft* is not only a successful game franchise but also has generated story settings capable of being revisited through various media; some are other kinds of games, and others are what we more conventionally take to be (gener-

ally linear) narrative forms. It is important to be clear about this claim. Gameplay need not necessarily constitute a narrative medium for it to be the case that stories set in a game world extend engagement with games. Digital games such as *Warcraft* or *World of Warcraft* provide elements for storytelling that can extend the game experience in various ways, for both designers and players. It is clearly the case that these games supply what Greg Costikyan (2007, 9) has with respect to massively multiplayer online games called "story settings." Players are not obligated to care about these settings or the possibility of some sort of story arc that is enacted through them, but it is almost impossible to play inside game worlds and learn absolutely nothing about the characters, locations, and events that occur there. For those who do notice or perhaps even desire to learn about these settings while playing, knowledge about game worlds is readily portable to other media forms; settings can be elaborated or connected to each other. Sometimes developers do this in a way that tends to focus on the historical continuity and consistency of game worlds, but just as often players are the ones eager to compile details about characters and elaborate on them by creating stories that occur in these worlds. The result—over a time period of roughly a dozen years, through numerous tellings and retellings of stories set in the world of *Warcraft*—has been the piecewise construction of a robust storyworld. Of course, this process can feed back to game development. The world of *Warcraft* might be thought of as a series of game settings, many of which have been borrowed from various media through which stories about the world *of Warcraft* have been told. They are cited and depicted in several different ways, including the actions of non-player characters, design of quests, or architecture and game objects found at various locations.

In addition to game settings, developers also create the game engines (software) that make it possible to play digital games such *as Warcraft* and *World of Warcraft*. One way of describing the history of machinima during a three-floor elevator ride is to summarize it as the transformation of game engines into narrative engines, in the sense that players learn how to use this game technology to create linear stories, generally game-based movies. As machinima matured from its origins as *Quake* movies, ambitious players (some with backgrounds in film, television, or improvisational comedy) decided that game-based moviemaking could move beyond a self-reflexive game culture, and they began to tell stories that no longer referred back to the particular storyworlds associated with the game engines used to make movies (Lowood 2007a).

Game-based storytelling embedded in established storyworlds and machinima offer players two game-derived story production options that can either be linked together or remain quite independent. In other words, the fact that stories told across media have been set in game-based storyworlds is not the whole story about how games have functioned as narrative engines. Some players are inspired by gameplay to tell stories about games, and others find more appeal in the idea of performing in game spaces. In order to address these forms of game-based storytelling and their relationship to each other, it is time to focus on the nature of performance in *Warcraft*.

Warcraft—along with other real-time strategy games—redefined the strategy game as a performance arena in several ways. As it evolved, the real-time strategy genre highlighted a key aspect in the transition from turn-based, tabletop strategy play (board games, miniatures, and chess) to multiplayer, real-time games: *interface mastery*. To play *Warcraft* well, players must demonstrate rapid performance of interface skills, principally the interpretation of on-screen data as well as the manipulation of control devices such as the keyboard and mouse. Winning depends at least as much on interface mastery as the contemplative problem-solving and decision-making skills traditionally associated with the strategy game. In real time, hand-eye coordination became one of the salient qualities of successful players. Popular strategy game formats such as historical simulations (board games), tabletop miniatures, and even military wargames were transmuted into real-time game systems that redefined player skill and performance in terms of the rapid execution and mastery of computer interface and control. Though perhaps surprising to those who think of digital play as sedentary, *Warcraft* as a real-time game made possible by computer technology thus introduced an element of embodiment and physicality into "brain games." Put another way, player skill, especially in competitive multiplayer real-time strategy games, took a step toward a notion related to athletic performance. Since players often describe fast-paced digital games as "twitchy," the impact of real-time strategy as a genre can be characterized as taking the digital strategy game into a zone of competitive performance somewhere between thoughtful strategy and twitchy skill. The significance of interface mastery for game-based performance was that it provided a basis for spectatorship, skills demonstration, and learning through replay movies. Learning about the production, editing, and postproduction of demos and replays was the historical foundation for story-driven machinima based on game technology (Lowood 2006a).

Having established real-time strategy gameplay as performative, it is easier to think of the *Warcraft* player as creative. James Naismith may well be the "author" of basketball as a game form, but Michael Jordan was indisputably a creative genius through his gameplay. Ask any basketball fan if they would rather read the original rules of basketball, or watch clips of Jordan's dunks and clutch shots. Still, the structure of the game system (text) and creativity in play (performance) work together to produce a context for skillful play as performance.[8] Of course, athletic competition and digital play are not the same thing, either with respect to performance or spectatorship, but noting this interplay of text and performance as part of competitive play can help us think about two important ways in which game-based moviemaking contributes to the extension of games as narrative spaces. The first emphasizes the use of game elements as *libraries* of texts available to moviemaking players, and the second involves the *archival* use that game-based movies can serve in recording performance in digital games as performance spaces.

While the foregrounding of interface mastery emphasized play performance as skills demonstration and the competitive game as a form of e-sports, in the *Warcraft* series the same play dynamics also propelled a relatively linear story arc built from the mission structure of the single-player campaign game. In this mode, players enacted stories grounded in the player's particular performance, but bounded by a linear structure developed—one might say, authored—by Blizzard's talented game designers. This does not mean that playing *Warcraft* is equivalent to simply enacting a text.[9] As already noted, however, the narrative aspects and threads found throughout *Warcraft* games do provide pieces for the construction of a storyworld— pieces that then can individually or collectively be elaborated through fan fiction or player-created machinima. So rather than portraying gameplay as interacting with some sort of text, it makes more sense at least for *Warcraft* to think in terms of players encountering a multitude of small texts during the course of gameplay. They may ignore the texts, simply notice them, remember them as part of the experience or the culture around the game, or choose to work on the further construction of a storyworld that can be constructed from these texts as building materials.[10]

Players, of course, are not the only ones who engage in the addition and extension of story elements. As the *Warcraft* series continued, each version of *Warcraft* grew more ambitious by this measure, as developers built out the storyworld and its history, added episodes to a gradually filled-in chronology of the world's history, and produced cinematic cutscenes that not only marked and rewarded the attainment of stages in the campaign but also presented key moments in the lives and lore of characters. It may be objected here that I am letting a "game as story" argument in through the back door of incremental contributions to a vast storyworld. Yet it bears repeating that in *Warcraft*, these story elements are activated in the course of gameplay; players are not compelled to view themselves as "reading" or even enacting a story, as opposed to simply playing a game.

The main point here is that a library of texts or story elements was deployed by *Warcraft* developers as an aspect of game design that only incidentally had anything to do with these games being read as texts. In this sense, despite the temptation to think of these texts as being like a library of books, they have just as much in common with a library of software routines or tools (which of course, at a level less obvious to players, they are). Consider examples of two kinds of story elements. The first is a *narrative touch*. It is a small, idiosyncratic part of *Warcraft* that nonetheless played a huge role in its player culture: the race-specific "pissed quotes" emitted when a player clicks on one of the characters in his or her army (e.g., Orc Grunt: "It's not easy being green"). Players quickly discovered that these characters could be made to say something new by mouse clicking on them repeatedly; this induced the in-game character to speak characteristic lines, deliver jokes, or otherwise amuse the player. Just as important as what the characters said, the characters' voices (many provided by *Warcraft*'s producer, Bill Roper) gave players a sense of their personal characteristics—dull-witted, idle Orc Peons, for instance. What began as a simple interface device, providing feedback to the player when selecting a unit, became a vital part of the game's lore. Players poked every avatar on the screen to find out what they said, or used utilities to search inside the game software for the corresponding sound files; FAQs and Web sites transcribed and cataloged quotes from each unit type in the game. Before long, pissed quotes became part of the shared experience of the player community;

Voice Acting
Jay Hathaway, Kyle Harrison, Jason Hayes, Tiffany Hayes, Eric Henze,
Harley Huggins, Thomas Jung, Matthew King, Monte Krol, Rob
McNaughton, Chris Metzen, Lani Minella, Micky Neilson, Bill Roper, Lisa
Schoner, Glenn Stafford, Ted Whitney

35.7 An example of a narrative touch from *Warcraft III*'s *Frozen Throne* expansion: Heavy metal characters, music, and images reappeared in *World of Warcraft* character dances and machinima as well as the band featured at Blizzard's Blizzcon convention.

every *Warcraft* player appreciated jokes and references to them.

The second example of a story element in the *Warcraft* library is a *narrative structure*. Roper and other members of the Blizzard development team realized that one problem with the notion of the game as story is that stories seldom provide much replay value. Few people watch the same film over and over. From the beginning, *Warcraft: Orcs and Humans* was essentially a competitive, multiplayer game; during the original rounds of testing, the game was balanced, in Blizzard parlance, for "sentient versus sentient" play, in part because the limited computing power available in the mid-1990s was not capable of producing adequate computer-controlled players in real time.[11] The essential unit of play was therefore the competitive round, player versus player, which in the single-player game became the "mission," a single round of play devoted to the accomplishment of a specific objective.

Since neither playing the same skirmish scenario on the same map over and over nor a strictly linear story development provided attractive options for a single-player game structure, Blizzard focused on a method for stringing together a series of missions in a compelling "campaign," a notion readily available from wargames or role-playing games. In order to accomplish this, the *Warcraft* designers gradually came to think in terms of "story nodes."[12] They aligned the game's skeletal story line in synchronization with a player's progress through the game by determining "nodes" in gameplay appropriate for the introduction of significant story elements. This technique reached maturity in another Blizzard title, *Starcraft* (1998), then was further refined during the lengthy development of *Warcraft III*. Player strategies and actions during a mission were usually open-ended, at least within the constraints of the game system; if a player defeated a computer opponent, he or she progressed to the next mission and eventually reached a story

"Why Don't You Bother Someone Else with Your Incessant Clicking?"

"Pissed sounds" (also known as "poke quotes" or "unit quotes") are short audio files buried inside the vast library of *Warcraft* game assets. They have played a major role in the shared player culture around the game. Each of these bits of spoken dialogue is associated with a specific character type or character in the real-time strategy game; when an on-screen unit is "poked" by clicking on it more than once, the poked character says something different from the normal confirmation sound. Poke it again, and it might say something different again; poke it many times, and you may get an infrequently heard bit of dialogue from the unit as it becomes more irritated. For example, the Blood Elf peasant unit introduced in the Frozen Throne expansion of *Warcraft III* will say, "Why don't you bother someone else with your incessant clicking."

As Bill Roper explained in a conversation at Stanford University on March 1, 2005, he and Glenn Stafford at Blizzard produced the first group of pissed sounds after testing the concept with the first quotations for Orc units. As the game series became more popular, especially after the publication of *Warcraft II*, players began to poke characters even more incessantly or dig into the game software to find them. The quotations became part of the fan culture around the game, so it is hardly surprising that player-fans began to produce texts to document what they learned.

MunikBleedsGreen's "*Warcraft III*: Pissed Off Unit Quote Collection" provided a comprehensive list; it also supplied information submitted by other players that traced sources for the references and jokes that Blizzard's developers cited in many of the quotations. For example, the Orc Farseer says, "I see dead people," and this quotation is traced to the movie *The Sixth Sense* as well as to an in-game cheat code. Easy enough. His second quotation, "Touch your tongue to mine," leads to a more complicated interpretation comparing two possible sources before deciding in favor of *Thumb Wars*. It is too easy for nonplayers to dismiss narrative touches such as *Warcraft*'s unit quotes and players' attention to them as trivial. In fact, such forms of fan engagement demonstrated by the players' shared knowledge of these quotations and commentary on them is an important aspect of the cultural economy around the game.

Orc Grunt

From MunkiBleedsGreen's "Pissed Off Unit Quote Collection":

—"Why you poking me again?"
>*Other: Thanks to Bo Koch for pointing out that this is indeed a follow-up to the Grunt's "Stop poking me!" in* WC2.
—"Why don't you lead an army instead of touching me?"
—"Poke poke poke. Is that all you do?"
—"Ooh, that was kind of nice."
—"Me so horned. Me hurt you long time."
>*Movie: Play on the prostitute's line in* Full Metal Jacket. *Much thanks to Chris Hall for the correction, your ears are working fine.*
—"Me no sound like Yoda. . . . Do I?"
—"It's not easy being green."
>*Other: Kermit the Frog's signature song.*

node. These nodes were usually marked by dramatic, pre-scripted cutscenes that functioned as rewards ("eye candy"), a kind of break in the fast-paced action, and taken together, a telling of the events of the storyworld's history in a chronological sequence.[13] Occasionally, and exceptionally, the designers would even pause a mission for a "major story point" (Pardo 2000).

Narrative touches and structure are elements of game design, first and foremost. Every player enacts or experiences the results during gameplay. Those interested in these moments find that despite variations in their strategies, capabilities, and successes as players, elements such as quotations from characters or story nodes are capable of supporting a common player culture and a fairly consistent storyworld. Despite the wild variability of in-game performance, players thus share the same (or at least a similar) vast, overarching narrative and storyworld. Blizzard's library of game texts were important for *World of Warcraft* machinima projects as story elements that could be retold, reworked, and remixed through player-created productions such as these movies.

Competitive performance in multiplayer games such as *Warcraft* offers a narrative potential that differs from projects based on the library of game texts. Stories based on competition are, generally speaking, chronicles or emplotments of gameplay. They are *historical*. Replays and other game-based movies (speedruns, player versus player movies, clan demos, etc.) are *archival*, because they record and hence document performance in the agonistic arena of digital games. Game archives are created by and for players; at least in the first instance, the developers create the game libraries. In multiplayer, competitive *Warcraft*, gameplay rather than narrative elements provides the starting point, as syntax, tactics, and strategy of play are presented, studied, and supplemented by subsequent enunciation and interpretation.

The crucial roles played by spectatorship, multiplayer competition, and player communities in extending real-time strategy games in this fashion suggest that *Warcraft* can indeed be understood (even if metaphorically) as a performance space rather than as a text. The worn contrast of game versus narrative helps us little to sort out the complex intermixture of traditional strategic game form, the narrative unfolding of single-player campaigns, and competitive e-sports within a single package. In exploring relationships among gameplay, competition, narrative, and virtual world, it is a mistake to see the player merely as a kind of reader, or even enactor, when a huge community of *Warcraft* players has learned to see the player as *performer*. We need to pay more attention to modes of performance available to players and the ways in which their play performances are captured, viewed, interpreted, and narrated within this community of players.

The shift from the calculated decision making of turn-based games to the quick reactions, interface mastery, and micromanagement of units became a hallmark of *Warcraft*. While retaining much of the core gameplay from previous turn-based wargames focused on the strategy and tactics of battle, it emphasized not only understanding what to do but also rapid execution of the syntax of gameplay through mastery of the computer interface. By "syntax" I mean the sequence of coordinated mouse, keyboard, strategy, and reflexes in real time that correspond to a series of player actions during the course of a game.[14] These actions can be described as basic elements of gameplay, such as selecting units or having a hero unit cast a spell, but in terms of the

player's activity they correspond to sequences of mouse and keyboard activity. An important aspect of player skill is understanding and rapidly executing this syntax. As mundane as they may seem, these actions play a crucial role in the archival recording of gameplay and forms of spectatorship based on the making and sharing of replay movies. First, recording these basic actions (keystrokes and mouse clicks) in the sequence of a played game has been the basis for most systems of replay capture. Leaving aside technical issues, in *Warcraft III* this might mean that rather than devising some arcane code for "the grunt attacked the dryad," the replay file essentially records each player's actions with a time-marking system to keep everything in synchronization. So the grunt's attack might be read as, "Moved cursor over Grunt—clicked left mouse button—depressed A—moved cursor over Dryad—clicked left button." These are two equivalent ways to chronicle gameplay. The viewer views avatars battling on the screen. Based on knowledge of the game system, the viewer can interpret this view as "something happened," "one unit attacked another," or "the grunt attacked the dryad." We might describe this straightforward, sequential depiction of gameplay as a chronicle of events based on the archival record (the replay file). It is not until players enunciate what happened during a competitive game that they begin to rework the chronicle into a narrative form, which we might call a *historical text* about the game.

Thinking about *Warcraft* in terms of player performance sets the stage for a discussion of the role of game-based movies in the cocreation by developers and players of two distinctive kinds of storyworlds. Movies made with *Warcraft* and *World of Warcraft* can be used to add to the *library of texts* or the *historical archives* associated with the game. In some cases, they may be able to do both.

The most viewed of all *World of Warcraft* movies, *Leeroy Jenkins*, tells a story about a player and an in-game event, whether staged or not.[15] One of the players recounts their plans, laying out elements of syntax and tactics, while another carefully calculates the probability of success. These are familiar moments for *World of Warcraft* players. The video can be read as an ordinary, if humorously disastrous replay. *Leeroy Jenkins* has also become a player-created nar-

35.8 The setup for *Leeroy Jenkins*.

rative touch in the game's storyworld, such as by the inclusion of a card named after the protagonist in the collectible card game. Indeed, it has even infested *other* storyworlds; for example, a non-player character named Kilroy Stoneskin in *Guild Wars* is clearly derivative of Leeroy Jenkins. It is time to turn to more examples of how game-based movies both extend and work within the vast narratives of *Warcraft*'s game space. What are the important connections and differences between game-based movies as player-generated *archives* that replay the performance of competitive skills (and stories about those performances), and player-created *texts* that extend Blizzard's library of textual elements and extend the *Warcraft* storyworld?

Moviemaking and *Warcraft*

The first point I want to make about game-based moviemaking is historical. The brief history of demo movies, replays, speedruns, *Quake* movies, machinima, and other formats has included nearly every game genre, from first-person shooters and massively multiplayer online games to

console games. As a historical rule, *archival* production has preceded *textual* production. That is to say, players have first documented gameplay and then turned to story line projects. Note that in the previous section of this chapter I presented textual and archival modes of game-based storytelling in the opposite order. My intention was to deflate the temptation to engage in a kind whiggish reasoning that would portray this as a necessary progression from lower to higher forms of narrative—say, from chronicles to histories. Noting the historical progression is nonetheless critical for at least three reasons. First, it reiterates the main difference between movies made in *Warcraft* (the earlier real-time strategy series) and *World of Warcraft* (the later massively multiplayer online game). *Warcraft* moviemaking is founded on replay, and thus is primarily archival and historical. Nearly all of the player-created texts contributing to *Warcraft* as a storyworld have been made using *World of Warcraft*. I will return to this point below. Second, *World of Warcraft* can be played as a competitive game (player versus player or speed leveling, for example), and even in single-player or cooperative modes of play, player skills can be demonstrated and learned through replays. *World of Warcraft* movies are therefore inextricably connected to *Warcraft*'s replay culture, and in fact, *World of Warcraft* has been introduced to players through replay movies, from the beta period (e.g., JuniorX's replay of every moment in the first ten levels of his dwarf hunter) to the present (e.g., the movies accompanying Joana's Horde leveling guide). Third, as I have argued elsewhere, *Warcraft* was at the center of a virtual community of real-time strategy players and fans built on the foundation of competitive play as a mode of performance. It makes sense that the existence of this community as *World of Warcraft* was tested and launched goes a long way to explain the voracious appetite of its players, many of whom also play *Warcraft*, for game-based movies right from the beginning. Still, the question remains: Has the performance-oriented culture around replay movies had any impact on *Warcraft* as a storyworld, or indeed as any form of vast narrative?

Demo movies, spectator modes, machinima, and other modes of game-based moviemaking to document performances by "worthy gamers" (id Software) were introduced by players of first-person action games such as *Doom* (1993) and *Quake* (1996). *Warcraft II* (1994) was the first game in the *Warcraft* series to support matching services (Kali) and multiplayer competition via commercial networks (TEN, Mpath, and Engage Games Online). Within a few years, Blizzard had launched its own client-server network for multiplayer competition, ⟨http://www.battle.net⟩. Network support not only made it easier to play with others but also to watch others play, and of course the community of players also took advantage of network technology to share and discuss replays. Tournaments and a laddered ranking system, the matchmaking of players for pickup team games, team versus team skirmishes, and other ways to play against other players online were offered for *Starcraft* initially, and then to *Warcraft II* players. Player-created software tools such as War2BNE captured replays of battle.net and other games.

The release of *Warcraft III: Reign of Chaos* in 2002 intensified the player community built around competitive, networked play. Multiplayer competition became the primary basis for player discussion, commentary, and performance. In *Warcraft III*, built-in spectator modes and replay capture, Web sites for distributing replays and video on demand, reports and interviews from tournaments such as the World Cyber Games, and SHOUTcast commentaries of games contributed to the creation of a player-spectator relationship around competitive game performance and replays. Clan Web sites and Web sites such as ⟨http://www .wcreplays.com⟩ offered replays, audio commentaries, videos, interviews, and game news. These media outlets played a major role in creating a shared culture of stories about champion players, strategies, exploits of interface mastery (better known as "micro" for micromanagement), and the like. Take the previously mentioned Grubby, a premier player from the 4 Kings clan based in Europe. Replays showing his mastery of the Orc side in *Warcraft* are readily available: a few dozen videos at YouTube or Google Video; an entire page with articles, interviews, and features at ⟨http://www.wcreplays.com⟩, with nearly thirty replay files for the current patch of the game alone; more demos and replays at his clan site; and so on.

Competition in *Warcraft* has thus clearly produced archival production and demand for movies, and the vast amount of textual production devoted to star players, leading clans, and noteworthy performances has contributed to a shared culture around memories and stories derived from competition. The relationship between visual media and cultures of sports fandom is familiar; important examples include the impact of television on the Olympics or U.S. football, or heavily produced advertising shorts on the presentation of National Basketball Association stars such as Michael Jordan or Lebron James.[16] As we have already seen, multiplayer gaming and spectatorship were foundations for *Warcraft* as a performance space rather than as a text. It was especially key that unlike professional sports, *Warcraft* spectators were also players. This explains the crucial role that recorded replays have played as a media object in these communities. Repetition is OK. Without the dramatic tension of an unknown outcome, spectators who are not players are just not interested in watching replays; players (and coaches), on the other hand, watch them incessantly, mining this "game film" for the slightest edge in improving their own skills and strategies. Despite the importance of the player culture built around replay movies, however, it is a dubious proposition that replay movies have provided significant texts to augment the narrative touches and structure provided by Blizzard in the packaged games. Put another way, we can credit the replay archives with providing a foundation for histories based on the chronicles of gameplay and for creating a large community of spectators. Unlike other genres, though, real-time strategy games have not offered a particularly lively platform for a story line library.

For *Warcraft* game movies as story texts, we must consider a kind of transgenre storytelling as we move from the *Warcraft* real-time strategy to the online role-playing game *World of Warcraft*. By considering these games together, a more familiar story about the emergence of storytelling from replay in game-based moviemaking emerges. The first indications of this transition occurred already during the beta version of *World of Warcraft*. Many early players knew all about *Warcraft* and were experienced players of the real-time strategy game. As a result, it was no surprise that some aspects of *Warcraft*'s replay culture of player-created game movies carried over as an outlet for performance in game movies by *World of Warcraft* players. Players such as the aforementioned JuniorX recorded gameplay as player biography, documenting every moment in the creation and leveling of a new character, the familiar archival mode of replay. These movies eased players from the mind-set of competitive real-time strategy games, took them to familiar settings from the *Warcraft* narrative arc or reminiscent of multiplayer maps (e.g., Booty Bay or Duskwood), and moved onward into the new game form played as an individual character in the world of *Warcraft*.[17]

We can track elements of the transition from competitive replay movies to engagement with the *World of Warcraft* storyworld in several ways. Consider the breakdown of *World of Warcraft* movies at the leading site for their distribution, ⟨http://www.warcraftmovies.com⟩. As of early March 2007, this site offered more than 5,500 player versus player movies and nearly 400 "instance" movies; both categories are essentially archival replays or demos. This compares to about 675 story line movies and 442 dance/music

movies. Thus, it is clear that *Warcraft*'s tradition of replay documentation has carried over to the community of *World of Warcraft* players. At the same time, few, if any, digital games have produced so many machinima projects for storytelling or mediated performance as *World of Warcraft*. Many of these movies are focused on the development of characters, known and unknown, and their exploits in the storyworld. A good example of a transitional movie between replay and story is Daddar's *The Ironforge Bank Robbery* (*Ironforge Bankers* on ⟨http://www.warcraftmovies⟩). It documents a dramatic and unexpected in-game exploit that functions as a sort of skill demonstration for this particularly character type and player. At the same time, Daddar's massacre of the Ironforge bankers became a part of the world's lore through its telling in the movie. Players commenting on the piece noted their desire to roll a new rogue character like Daddar's and see if they could experience a similar moment for themselves; for a while, the replay movie certainly influenced attitudes among players about Horde, Undead, or Rogue characters When players thought about imitating Daddar, they meant to test out their own skills against a now legendary, if shadowy, figure, but at the same time, the spectacle of Daddar's video also became part of the player community's shared sense of the history of the online game world. This documented moment from the history of the digital world thus helped to shape both the fictional world of Azeroth and its player-created counterpart.

Examples such as Daddar and Leeroy Jenkins suggest that character development has been an important characteristic of *World of Warcraft* textual production by players making story line machinima movies. Clearly, players are fans of the games that they play, and as in other kinds of fan production, they are eager to delve into characters encountered in games such as *World of Warcraft*, or to create new ones as part of their engagement with the game and its storyworld. They can accomplish these goals by setting both developer-authored and original characters in familiar locations, with hooks grappling into narrative structure or elements that might be from Blizzard's games, novels, or the role-playing game. In turn, the stories told through these movies add new narrative elements or even

35.9 Daddar escapes Ironforge in the *Ironforge Bank Robbery*.

entire story arcs to the world. Riot Films' *Edge of Remorse*, Sleeping Dogs Productions' (Clara/J. Joshua Diltz) *Rise of the Living Dead* trilogy, Bannerman Productions' (Corey Bannerman) *My Life for the Horde: The Legend of Seemos*, and the AFK Pl@yers' (John Hsu, Epla Hsieh, and Outy Yang) *Thrall's Christmas Tree* are examples of such projects.

I have already taken a look at *Edge of Remorse* and will be examining *Rise of the Living Dead* in a moment. *The Legend of Seemos* is the second of a trilogy of movies, in progress, closely tied to an important story arc introduced in *Warcraft III*, the betrayal of the unsteady Orc-Human pact on Kalimdor by Admiral Proudmoore, a key character in both *Warcraft II* and *Warcraft III*. As the ten-minute movie begins, it is announced as "a tale inspired by the history of *Warcraft*." The focus is "one hero that stands above the others"; this hero, Seemos, is an entirely new character introduced in the movie, though characters from *Warcraft*, such as the Orc leader Thrall (in the narration) and Proudmoore, appear in it. A conventional story about a hero's impact on Azeroth's history, the creators show how machi-

nima can provide new textual elements to fill in previously unexplored aspects of the gameworld's history.

The Taiwanese group's *Thrall's Christmas Tree* takes the rather different tack of introducing new minor characters to reveal aspects of established characters from the Blizzard's *Warcraft* library, such as Jaina Proudmoore, Rexxar, and Thrall himself. They accomplish this by inventing a young character named Sirloin Bloodhoof, whose unremarkable party sets out to locate a unique Christmas tree to satisfy Warchief Thrall's reputation and impress Lady Proudmoore. Nothing quite satisfies the great Thrall, of course. This comedic machinima movie takes Bloodhoof's group to locations throughout Azeroth, which are recast through the various compositing and editing techniques employed by AFK Pl@yers; ultimately they arrive at the World Tree, a location of special significance to the storyworld's history explored in *Warcraft III*, and bring it to Theramore to satisfy Thrall's need to impress. The juxtaposition of *My Life for the Horde* and *Thrall's Christmas Tree* shows us that the players who create machinima works

35.10 Thrall makes an appearance in a scene from AFK Pl@yers' *Thrall's Christmas Tree*.

can operate along a range of character and story elements, from the heroic to the ordinary, and the familiar to the unexpected.

Diltz's *Rise of the Living Dead* trilogy is one of the most ambitious machinima projects set in the *World of Warcraft*, running nearly eighty minutes in length altogether. It also builds on the narrative structure established by the *Warcraft* series, and develops borrowed and new characters to create an original story. *Rise of the Living Dead* is an eerie, heavily atmospheric movie that tells a new story about the prophesied "end of days" in Azeroth, as the dead rise everywhere to overcome the living. It uses distinctive cinematography, postproduction editing, voice acting, and sound effects to follow two story lines: the sacrificial attack by Captain Bernandette's troops against the massed Undead in Andorhal, and the efforts of a smaller band led by the Elven General Tal to pass through the Unholy Gates and destroy the source of this threat to their world. It is a light versus darkness story focused on a possible end of the storyworld. Diltz and his collaborators build on both the library of story elements provided by the game and familiar aspects of gameplay while moving their original story forward. Narrative touches from the Blizzard library mix in familiar quotations, non-player characters, and other elements from *World of Warcraft*, and scenes are set in well-traveled locations from the game.

These connections to the game resonate as part of an experienced storyworld; viewers who have played the game are drawn in by these subtle touches, as when a character says "beware the living" (a common utterance of Undead non-player characters in the game) or a "mob" ("mobile" or AI-controlled opponent) previously encountered in the game, such as Araj the Summoner, is given a speaking part that fleshes out his role—insofar as this can be said of an Undead character. Araj presides over Andorhal, a human town overrun by ghouls and skeletons in both the game world and the machinima trilogy; even though his appearance in *Rise of the Living Dead* is brief, players who have dealt with him immediately touch back to the game as a narrative context for what transpires in the video. Narrative elements in the game and machinima story work reciprocally as the new story line unfolds, reinforcing the engagement of viewers who have played the game. Indeed, more stories set in the campaigns established by the trilogy can easily be imagined, for example, to provide backstories and biographies of the characters. In effect, *Rise of the Living Dead* demonstrates the possibility of presenting new vast narratives within *Warcraft* as an established storyworld.

The *Rise of the Living Dead* trilogy does not only rely on the library of story elements provided by the game, however; it also presents gameplay such that players can hardly refrain from dissecting its key action scenes as they would a replay or player versus player video. Diltz does this primarily in two ways. First, he reflects on moments, actions, or conversations that players frequently experience in *World of Warcraft*. For example, in *Rise of the Living Dead II*, the small party under General Tal discusses how it will cut through enemy lines to reach its goal, the Unholy Gates of Hell. Significantly, the small group is made up of five members, the canonical size for in-game parties before the larger endgame raids, and like many such parties, they begin to plan their attack by discussing strategy. Until this point in the story, the characters have spoken entirely in keeping with their characters. Now they reveal their tactics in the language of players, speaking in terms typical of in-game parties—Tal cautions to "stay clear of mobs," the troll Tourach advises his sister, a rogue, to "sap the bears," and

35.11 Jane of Blades in Sleeping Dogs Productions' *Rise of the Living Dead III: The Turning*.

35.12 The beach scene from Myndflame's *Illegal Danish: Super Snacks*. The scene was composited and constructed from various game elements, including the *Escape from Orgrimmar* trailer.

Henry Lowood

the human soldier Dartric proclaims, "I'll tank the ghostly knight." In a humorous transition back to the atmosphere and roles of the story, Tal begins what players now understand as a climactic "instance crawl" by saying to Councilor Keltwyn, "My Lord, will you do the honors of pulling the first mob?" This scene subtly recalls the narrative structure of games in the *Warcraft* series and *World of Warcraft*; by briefly portraying the characters as players, it suggests that the party will move the story forward by successfully concluding the impending skirmish.

The second way in which this and other machinima movies build on the player's experience of the game is through actual gameplay. A lengthy fight scene in part two of the trilogy plays a crucial role in the story. The antagonists are two groups of characters, one Horde, and the other Alliance; in the backstory provided by knowledge of the game, these are natural enemies. After fighting, though, they realize, as Tourach points out, that "our worlds are one and the same," and they must unite to fight the same enemy. Still, the preceding fight draws players into the action by focusing on the various abilities, spells, and tactics used by the combatants; during the fight, the diegetic context for the characters' actions is less that of in-story roles than of in-game player classes and skills. And yet, the camera angles, editing, and voiced dialogue show these "moves" as players would never see them during their own gameplay, resulting in a carefully scripted replay.

The content of machinima is often completely independent of the games used to make them, even when artistic assets and character models are used virtually without alteration. Even so, players are acutely aware of gameplay, and carefully "read" the skills, tricks, and decisions on view as a crucial aspect of their appreciation of these projects. Even when machinima creators tell stories based on games that can be appreciated and enjoyed by anyone, players are in a sense incapable of not seeing them differently from nonplayers. This is perhaps a quality that machinima shares with other forms of "transmedia storytelling." As Jenkins (2007) has put it, producers of such stories "have found it difficult to achieve the delicate balance between creating stories which make sense to first-time viewers and building in elements which enhance the experience of people reading across multiple media."[18]

Story line machinima movies made with *World of Warcraft* raise an important question: How much narrative freedom can movies created inside a game world have from texts presented in those games; that is, from the content created by the game developers? This question is at the heart of what differentiates the relationship of machinima to game from, say, fan fiction to the novels or films that inspire them. In a nutshell, any response to this question must take into account, as I have already noted, that game developers produce both narrative *texts* and narrative *engines*. Fan fiction based on *The Lord of the Rings* or *Star Wars* cites these texts (even remix is a form of citation, rather than copying), but short of plagiarism it does not *use* them. Machinima creators use the games they cite as movie production technology at a minimum, but often for sets, artwork, and animation as well.

Much of the most recent history of *World of Warcraft*–based machinima, in particular, revolves around efforts to open up a dependence that machinima artist Tristan Pope described with respect to the making of his "Not Just Another Love Story" as, "I only executed what the pixels in *WoW* suggest."[19] In Pope's case, this statement was a defense of the depiction of sexual imagery in his movie by half-jokingly arguing that he had merely showed "what *WoW*'s pixels imply." Another take on this theme was offered by Deeprun Goldwin Michler's *The Man Who Can*, which depicts a character who escapes the limitations imposed by Blizzard's pixels by dancing with new moves animated by Michler. Later machinima projects such as Rufus Cubed's (Terran Gregory and Ezra Ferguson) *Return: A Warcraft Saga*, Mike Spiff Booth's *Code Monkey*, or Myndflame's (Clint and Derek Hackleman) insanely fast-paced *Zinwrath: The Movie* and *Illegal Danish: Super Snacks* used model viewers, compositing, and postproduction editing in ways that broke open creative (but not necessarily legal) constraints on the use of server-based online games and their artistic assets to make independent movies. As Gregory has put it:

> The power of the modelviewer lies far beyond its individual features: It is what I would deem the "Key" to unlocking *WoW* Machinima as a whole. As its enthusiasts would claim, Machinima is supposed to be an empowering art form that delivers you from the typical restrictions and limitations of real-world filmmaking, allowing you to realize your vision irrespective of your resources.... Modelviewer was the great virtual socioeconomic equalizer, that truly allowed *WoW* movie makers to experience all of the freedoms that are inherent to Machinima.[20]

35.13 The party scene at the conclusion of Myndflame's *Illegal Danish: Super Snacks*.

The storyworld of *Warcraft* was constructed as an accumulation of text elements from games, and then accumulated across several games and other media; a piecewise rather than a unified notion of story production has resulted from this process. When Gregory writes about the Model Viewer as the key to unlocking the independent production of machinima made in *World of Warcraft*, he suggests that machinima makers have opened up access to both the text library and the narrative engine in a way that lends them status as coproducers of the *Warcraft* storyworld.

Conclusion: Conflict or Cooperation?

Most game research depicts the game designer as auteur and development teams as offering the primary creative impulses in game culture. How have the replay and machinima projects described in this chapter extended player engagement with the storyworld created by Blizzard's developers? And is the relationship of these two forms of creative expression—those of developers and players—characterized more accurately as one of conflict or cooperation? I would answer this question differently with respect to archival and textual production. In the case of game-based movies based on *Warcraft* and *World of Warcraft*, even supplementing the notion of developer as author by allowing that players have elaborated stories created by Blizzard seems inadequate. In the case of replay, it is clearly the case that we are dealing with the player not only as performer but also as creator of the medium of presentation as well as the new forms of spectatorship associated with it. Archival replay also produces stories, which I have described as historical accounts of documented players and games. In short, replay is the domain of the player as performer, though as I have argued, just as gameplay may ignore lovingly created in-game narrative texts, replay has had little to say about *Warcraft*'s storyworld. Even though games can incorporate texts and be used to tell stories, playing *Warcraft* no more requires taking note of these stories than playing basketball requires knowledge of the history of that game.

With so-called story line machinima, however, the situation is more nuanced and the results are different. Even if developers created texts and textual elements that players may or may not choose to have "read" or even noticed during gameplay, these texts nonetheless have added up to a consistent storyworld proven capable of supporting many new texts and games in a variety of media. Some players are eager to add their own texts set inside the storyworld or extend their deep commitment to *Warcraft* as a game by figuring out how to use it in new ways. These players work out projects that combine their skill as players, technical chops, and storytelling verve. They create game-based texts that for the thousands of players who download and view their movies, extend engagement with both the game and the storyworld.

Let me say clearly that critical attention to game design, to the game developer as author, is important. It is certainly true that players would not be using games to make movies if game developers had not given them compelling games. That said, the creativity of players is often just as compelling as game design. This creativity, as well as the forms of performance and spectatorship it has spawned, certainly deserves more attention than it has thus far received from game studies. Like Michael Jordan painting on James Naismith's canvas, players are the experts on using digital games as performance space, and showing off their own moves as players and storytellers.

Henry Lowood

Notes

1. My account of this match is partly based on my observations as head referee of this event, supplemented by viewing the replay, and reading commentary on clan and replay Web sites.

2. These ideas about narratives based on gameplay are influenced, of course, by Hayden White's writing on "metahistory" (1975, 7–11) as well as John Fiske's work on enunciative fan production (1992, 30–49).

3. Strictly speaking, most replays are viewed not in video formats but as demo or replay files executed by the game. This distinction is significant both for spectatorship and machinima production, but it does not affect my argument about the relationship between watching replays and watching story line machinima.

4. For the history of machinima, see Lowood (2006a).

5. The awards that *Edge of Remorse* has received include "best overall film" of the Xfire Summer Movie Contest 2006 as well as "best direction" and "best visual design" at the 2006 Machinima Film Festival.

6. Henceforth, I will use *Warcraft* to refer to the *Warcraft* real-time strategy game series, including its revisions and expansions. Game titles will be named individually—for example, *Warcraft III*, when necessary. *World of Warcraft* is not included when I refer to *Warcraft* as a game title.

7. For details on the history of the real-time strategy genre, see Lowood (2007b).

8. Naismith's original thirteen rules are available quite literally as a text, published originally in January 1892 in the Springfield College newspaper, the *Triangle*.

9. The best guide to thinking about issues related to this notion remains Murray (1997).

10. These choices are compatible with the modes of fan production offered by Fiske (1992).

11. The balance for sentient versus sentient play was largely because "humans" were an in-game race.

12. Conversation with Bill Roper, Stanford University, March 1, 2004.

13. This structure resembles the "beads-on-a-string" model proposed by Costikyan (2007, 8) for combining games and stories.

14. I am indebted to former student Rene Patnode for this notion of game syntax.

15. This video was created by the Pals for Life guild (⟨http://www.thepalsforlife.com⟩) in May 2005, perhaps under the title *A Rough Go*. The original video is available at ⟨http://www.warcraftmovies.com/movieview.php?id=1666⟩.

16. On media and sports, see Crawford (2004, 130–153).

17. This perhaps is one way in which the multiplayer game heightened engagement with *World of Warcraft* as a compilation not just of *Warcraft* story settings but also of its competitive game settings.

18. Jenkins has written widely on this topic.

19. Quoted in "Videos," available at ⟨http://www.craftingworlds.com/videos.html⟩ (accessed April 2005). On the controversy unleashed by Pope's movie, see Lowood (2006b).

20. Email communication, December 11, 2006. Gregory is referring to the Model Viewer authored by John Steele.

References

Costikyan, Greg (2007). "Games, Storytelling, and Breaking the String." In *Second Person: Role-Playing and Story in Games and Playable Media*, edited by Pat Harrigan and Noah Wardrip-Fruin, 5–13. Cambridge, MA: MIT Press.

Crawford, Garry (2004). *Consuming Sport: Fans, Sport, and Culture*. London: Routledge.

Fiske, John (1992). "The Cultural Economy of Fandom." In *The Adoring Audience: Fan Culture and Popular Media*, edited by Lisa A. Lewis, 30–49. London: Routledge.

Jenkins, Henry (2003). "Transmedia Storytelling." *Technology Review*, January 15. ⟨http://www.technologyreview.com/Biotech/13052/⟩ (accessed July 2007).

Jenkins, Henry (2007). "Transmedia Storytelling 101." Confessions of an Aca-Fan Weblog, March 22. ⟨http://www.henryjenkins.org/2007/03/transmedia_storytelling_101.html⟩ (accessed June 2007).

Lombardi, Chris (1995). "War Crime in Real Time." *Computer Gaming World* 126:229.

Lowood, Henry (2006a). "High-Performance Play: The Making of Machinima." In *Videogames and Art: Intersections and Interactions*, edited by Andy Clarke and Grethe Mitchell, 59–79. Bristol: Intellect.

Lowood, Henry (2006b). "Storyline, Dance/Music, or PvP? Game Movies and Community Players in *World of Warcraft*." *Games and Culture* 1 (October): 362–382.

Lowood, Henry (2007a). "Found Technology: Players as Innovators in the Making of Machinima." In *Innovative Uses and Unexpected Outcomes* (MacArthur Foundation Series on Digital Media and Learning), edited by Tara McPherson. Chicago: Macarthur Foundation.

Lowood, Henry (2007b). "'It's Not Easy Being Green': Real-Time Game Performance in *Warcraft*." In *Videogame/Player/Text*, edited by Barry Atkins and Tanya Krzywinska. Manchester: Manchester University Press.

Marino, Paul (2005). "The Machinima FAQ (Updated 8.03.2005)." Academy of Machinima Arts and Sciences. ⟨http://machinima.org/machinima-faq.html⟩ (accessed October 2006).

MunkiBleedsGreen (2003). "*Warcraft* III | Pissed Off Unit Quote Collection." ⟨http://www.gamefaqs.com/computer/doswin/file/589475/18136⟩ (accessed July 2007).

Murray, Janet (1997). *Hamlet on the Holodeck*. Cambridge, MA: MIT Press.

Pardo, Rob (2000). "Stages of *Starcraft*: *Brood War* Campaign Design." In *Game Design: Secrets of the Sages*, edited by Marc Saltzmann, 141–142. 2nd ed. Indianapolis: Brady Games.

White, Hayden V. (1975). *Metahistory: The Historical Imagination in Nineteenth-Century Europe*. Baltimore: Johns Hopkins University Press.

Warcraft Adventures

All in the Game: *The Wire*, Serial Storytelling, and Procedural Logic

Jason Mittell

The Wire (2002–2008) is paradigmatic of a critical darling —few people watch it (at least in the numbers typical of commercial television), but it generates adoration and evangelism by nearly all who do. Television critics have taken it on themselves to lobby their readers to give the show a chance, asking reluctant viewers to overlook its dark and cynical worldview to see the truth and beauty offered by its searing vision into the bleak heart of the U.S. city. Thankfully for us scattered fans, HBO has allowed the show to continue for five seasons, even without a clear sense that the show's dedicated fandom leads to overt profitability.[1]

What is most interesting to me about the critical praise deservedly lavished on *The Wire* is not how it may or may not yield an increase in viewership but how the critical consensus seems to situate the show distinctly within the frame of another medium. For many critics, bloggers, fans, and even creator David Simon himself, *The Wire* is best understood not as a television series but as a "visual novel." As a television scholar, this cross-media metaphor bristles—not because I don't like novels but because I love television. And I believe that television at its best shouldn't be understood simply as emulating another older and more culturally valued medium. *The Wire* is a masterpiece of television, not a novel that happens to be televised, and thus should be understood, analyzed, and celebrated on its own medium's terms.

Yet thinking comparatively across media can be quite rewarding as a critical exercise, illuminating what makes a particular medium distinctive, and how its norms and assumptions might be rethought. So before considering how the show operates televisually, what does thinking of *The Wire* as a novel teach us about the show? And might other cross-media metaphors yield other insights?

From the Literary to the Ludic

The Wire's novelistic qualities are most directly linked to its storytelling structure and ambitions. As Simon attests in frequent interviews and commentary tracks, he is looking to tell a large sweeping story that has traditionally been the purview of the novel, at least within the realm of culturally legitimate formats. He highlights how each season offers its own structural integrity, much like a specific book within a larger epic novel, and each episode stands as a distinct chapter in that book. The model, modestly left unspoken, might be *War and Peace*, a vast narrative containing fifteen "books," each subdivided into at least a dozen chapters and released serially over five years—Simon has less modestly mentioned *Moby-Dick* as another point of comparison, although that epic novel was neither serialized nor subdivided into books.

In *The Wire*, each season focuses on a particular facet of Baltimore and slowly builds into a cohesive whole. An episode typically does not follow the self-contained logic of most television programming, as story lines are introduced gradually and major characters might take weeks to appear. "Novelistic" is an apt term for describing this storytelling structure, as we rarely dive into a novel expecting the first chapter to typify the whole work as a television pilot is designed to do. Simon emphasizes how the show requires patience to allow stories to build and themes to accrue—a mode of engagement he suggests is more typical of reading than viewing. Enhancing the show's novelistic claims is the presence of well-regarded crime fiction writers like George Pelecanos, Richard Price, and Dennis Lehane on the staff, and Price's novel *Clockers* is surely an influence with its dual focus on a criminal and a cop in the urban drug war.

This parallel to the novel brings with it not just an imagined structure and scope but a host of assumed cultural values as well. While the novel's history in the eighteenth and nineteenth centuries featured numerous contestations over the form's aesthetic and cultural merits, by the time television emerged in the mid-twentieth century, the literary novel's cultural role was firmly ensconced

36.1 "I'm a free born man of the USA." The Baltimore police, including Lester Freamon (Clarke Peters) sing along with The Pogues' "The Body of an American" at an officer's wake in the third season *Wire* episode "Dead Soldiers" (2004).

as one of the most elite and privileged storytelling formats. As the most popular and culturally influential form of storytelling, television has usurped the role that the early novel played as a lowbrow mass medium threatening to corrupt its readers and demean cultural standards.

By asserting *The Wire* as a televised novel, Simon and critics are attempting to legitimize and validate the demeaned television medium by linking it to the highbrow cultural sphere of literature. The phrase "televised novel" functions as an oxymoron in its assumed cultural values, much like the term "soap opera" juxtaposes the extremities of art and commerce into a cultural contradiction. For *The Wire*, especially in its context of HBO's slogan "It's Not TV, It's HBO," the link to the novel rescues the show from the stigmas of its televised form, raising it above the commercialized swamp of ephemera imagined by many as typical television. But I would contend that emphasizing the literary facets of *The Wire* obscures many of its virtues and qualities, setting it up to fail when measured by some of the aesthetic aims of the novel.

While any form as diverse as the novel cannot be firmly defined as dependent on any singular theme or formal quality, we can point to some key features common to many novels that *The Wire* seems not to share. Novels typically

probe the interior lives of their characters, both through plots that center on character growth and transformations, and through the scope of narration that accesses characters' thoughts and beliefs. Even novels about a broad range of people and institutions often ground their vision of the world through the experiences of one or two central characters who transform through the narrative drive—for instance, a Charles Dickens novel like *Bleak House* examines institutions like the legal system, but does so primarily through the experiences and perspective of a central character. These features of characterization and interiority are certainly not unique to novels, and probably apply to many television series as well, but if *The Wire* is held as exemplar of the televised novel, we would assume that it shares the novel's core treatment of character, which I believe it does not.

Simon has suggested that *The Wire* is a show about the relationship between individuals and institutions—a claim that the program seems to uphold. But I would argue that the point of emphasis is much more clearly on institutions rather than individuals, as within each of the social systems that the show explores—the police, the drug trade, the docks, city government, and the educational system—the institution is brought into focus through the lens of numerous characters. Certainly Jimmy McNulty is a central point of access to understand police bureaucracy and functions nominally as the show's main character, but by season four he is in the margins while characters like Cedric Daniels, "Bunny" Colvin, and Bunk Moreland provide alternate entry points to explore the police system. Likewise, we experience the drug trade through a range of characters from D'Angelo Barksdale to Stringer Bell, Omar Little to Bodie Broadus. While all of these characters have depth and complexity, we rarely see much of their existence beyond how they fit into their institutional roles. Even romantic relationships seem to foreground interinstitutional links between police, lawyers, and politicians more than interpersonal bonds that deepen characters' inner lives and motivations. The chronic alcoholism and infidelity of *The Wire*'s police officers offers a portrait less of flawed personalities than of a flawed institution; for instance, the police admire the systematic discipline and coordination of Barksdale's crew, which is distinctly lacking in the Baltimore Police Department.

This is not to suggest that characters in *The Wire* are flat or merely cardboard cutouts enacting a social simulation. One of the show's most masterful features is its ability to create achingly human characters out of the tiniest moments and subtle gestures, such as Lester Freamon silently sanding doll furniture, Barksdale D'Angelo picking out his clothes, or Bubbles walking through "Hamsterdam" in a daze trying to find himself. But the way *The Wire* portrays its characters seems distinctly not novelistic: we get no internal monologues or speeches articulating characters' deep thoughts, and few senses of deep character goals or transformations motivating the dramatic actions. Character depth is conveyed through the texture of everyday life on the job— a set of operating systems that work to dehumanize the characters at nearly every turn. As Simon notes,

> *The Wire* has … resisted the idea that, in this post-modern America, individuals triumph over institutions. The institution is always bigger. It doesn't tolerate that degree of individuality on any level for any length of time. These moments of epic characterization are inherently false. They're all rooted in, like, old Westerns or something. Guy rides into town, cleans up the town, rides out of town. There's no cleaning it up anymore. There's no riding in, there's no riding out. The town is what it is. (Quoted in Mills 2007)

In the show's character logic, the institution is the defining element in a character's life, externalized through practices, behaviors, and choices that deny individuality and agency—a storytelling structure that seems contrary to principles typical of most literary novels.

There are clearly aspects of the novel that have inspired *The Wire*—the sweeping storytelling scope, the attention to details of systems and characters, and the social issue probing of works like *The Jungle*. Additionally, literary developments in recent decades have opened up the formal and stylistic possibilities of the genre, and thus there are certainly fictional trends that *The Wire* taps into. Ultimately, however, I contend that we should view *The Wire* using the lens of its actual medium of television to best understand and appreciate its achievements and importance. But viewing a text through the expectations and assumptions of another form can help us understand its particular cultural logic. Might other media metaphors be similarly useful, within limits, to help unravel *The Wire*? Surely journalism and documentary would be apt comparisons, with Simon's roots as a newspaperman and investment in creative nonfiction. Yet I would like to suggest that it might be useful to view the program using the lens of a seemingly off-base medium, and hence offer a brief detour to answer an unlikely question: How might we conceive of *The Wire* as a video game?

Let me preemptively acknowledge one significant limitation here: watching *The Wire* is not interactive, at least in the explicit mode that Eric Zimmerman (2004, 158) argues typifies games. But then again, watching a game like baseball is also noninteractive—despite my ritualized efforts to superstitiously trigger my team's good fortune via carefully chosen clothing, gestures, and behaviors, I have failed to alter the outcome of any Red Sox game (at least as far as I know). In thinking about a filmed series like *The Wire* as a game, we need to think of the ludic elements within the show's diegesis, not the interactive play that we expect when booting up a video game. Thus *The Wire* might be thought of as a spectatorial game, being played on-screen for the benefit of an audience.

Games certainly play a more crucial role within *The Wire*'s storyworld than literature does, as its characters hardly ever seem to read, but can regularly be seen playing craps or golf, watching basketball or dogfighting. More centrally, nearly every episode has at least one reference to "the game," a slang term for the urban drug trade that extends to all of the show's institutional settings. Within the show's portrait of Baltimore, the game is played in all venues—the corners, City Hall, the police station, and the union hall—and by a range of players—street-level junkies looking to score, corrupt politicians filling campaign coffers, cops bucking for promotion, stevedores trying to maintain the docks. "The game" is the overarching metaphor for urban struggle, as everyone must play or get played—as Marla Daniels tries to warn her husband, Cedric, "The game is rigged—you can't lose if you don't play" (episode 1.2). Sometimes characters are playing the same game, as the chase between the cops and Barksdale's crew develops into a series of moves and countermoves, but some institutions engage in a different game altogether—in season one, the cops go to the FBI for help busting Barksdale's drug and money-laundering system, but the feds are only playing the terrorism and political corruption game. Ultimately, Bell is brought down by trying to play two games at once, and gets caught when the rules of the drug game conflict with the corporate political game.

Simon has suggested that the show's goal is to "portray systems and institutions and be honest with ourselves and viewers about how complex these problems are" (quoted in Zurawik 2006). While Simon imagines that the televised novel is the form best suited to accomplish such goals, in today's media environment, video games are the go-to medium for portraying complex systems. As Janet Murray writes, "The more we see life in terms of systems, the more we need a system-modeling medium to represent it—and the less we can dismiss such organized rule systems as mere games" (quoted in Moulthrop 2004, 64). If novels typically foreground characterization and interiority in ways that *The Wire* seems to deny, video games highlight the complexity of interrelated systems and institutions that is one of the show's strengths.

Many video games are predicated on the logic of simulating complex systems, modeling an interrelated set of practices and protocols to explore how one choice ripples through an immersive world. Ian Bogost (2006, 98) defines a simulation as "a representation of a source system via a less complex system that informs the user's understanding of the source system in a subjective way"—a formulation that certainly captures the essence of *The Wire* as a dramatic distillation of Baltimore's institutional systems viewed through the critical perspective of Simon and his cowriters. We might imagine the show as a televisual adaptation of Will Wright's landmark game *SimCity* (1989): an array of systems are dramatized, each with changing variables that ripple across the larger simulation model in unpredictable and often counterintuitive ways. *SimCity* functions as a "God game" at a macrolevel of control over the microdeci-

sions of urban existence. But *The Wire* dramatizes its institutions more through the actions of characters in relation to the institution, blending the urban scope of *SimCity* with the personal focus typifying *The Sims* (2000), Wright's most popular iteration of the simulation game genre. Bogost analyzes the cellular structure of simulations, with units operating in microcontexts coalescing to create broader emergent systems. Such is often the case in *The Wire*'s Baltimore; in the first episode, for instance, a chance violent encounter between Johnny Weeks and Bodie leads Bubbles to seek revenge on Barksdale's organization, a small-scale unit operation that leads to major institutional transformations for both the police and drug dealers. Such small occurrences and changes at the levels of both character and institution are followed throughout the series to model how institutions operate and infiltrate the lives of their employees and members—a mode of representation blending the logics of *SimCity* and *The Sims*.

One of the central elements of games, especially those centered on simulations, is replayability; for a game to be embraced by its players, it typically must allow enough experiential variation to invite multiple passes through its ludic journey. Instead of viewing each of *The Wire*'s seasons as a singular book within an epic novel, we could view them as one play through its simulation game. In the first season, we walk through the police's attempt to take down Barksdale's drug operation, concluding seemingly in a "checkmate" scene where Avon Barksdale and Stringer Bell yield to the police's final moves (1.12). Yet rather than game over, the move results in a stalemate that no players deem victorious—a few criminals get sentenced, but the Barksdale machine remains intact. Season three offers a replay with some changed variables and strategies for all sides: What if drugs are decriminalized? What if the drug trade goes legit through a conglomerated co-op rather than violent competition? What if a former soldier repents and tries to give back to his community? Given the show's cynical vision of corrupt institutions, reform typically produces various forms of failure, as the parameters of the system are too locked in to truly produce social change or allow for an imagined solution to systemic problems; as Pryzbylewski notes in a later episode, referencing football but also his own life's work, "No one wins—one side just loses more slowly" (4.4). Yet the ludic joy of the third season is the ability to replay the first season's narrative through the imagination of new rules and ways to play the game—a mode of engagement offered with less imaginative vision and more amoral brutality in season four's replay of the drug game under the leadership of Marlo Stanfield.

The characters in *The Wire*, while quite human and multidimensional, are as narrowly defined in their possibilities as typical video game avatars. They each do what they do because that is the way the game is played—Bubbles can't get clean, McNulty can't follow orders, Avon can't stop fighting for his corners, and Frank Sobotka can't let go of the glory days of the docks. The characters with both the will and opportunity to change, like Bell, D'Angelo, or Colvin, find the systems too resistant, the "boss levels" too difficult, to overcome the status quo. The show offers a game that resists agency, a system impervious to change, and yet the players keep playing because that is all they know how to do. The opening scene in the series shows McNulty interviewing a witness to a murder, killed after trying to rob a craps game; even though the victim tried to "snatch and run" every Friday night, the witness says that they had to let him play, because "it's America, man" (1.1). The game must be played, no matter the cost. Throughout the series, the moments of greatest conflict are where a player steps over the line and breaks the unwritten rules of his or her institution—shooting Omar on Sunday morning, Carver leaking information about Daniels, Nick Sobotka going beyond smuggling to enter the drug trade. In the show's representation of Baltimore, the game is more than a metaphor; it is the social contract that just barely holds the world together.

Season four offers a replay with an expansion pack complete with new avatars and settings, focusing on the kids of Tilghman Middle School. The introduction of this new system triggers emotional distress—the rules of *The Wire*'s simulation logic all but ensure that most of the children will end up broken and damaged, as that's the way the game is played. As we watch the season progress, the choices that the kids make and the actions that are enacted on them all function as unit operations, microinstances

that begin to coalesce into larger systemic forces. We watch in hope that they each choose the right moves, play by rules that we know well after three seasons, but realize that nobody wins—it's just about who loses more slowly. It is a tribute to the efficacy of the show's logic of emergent systems that the end result of each child's fate is both entirely unpredictable from the outset and completely inevitable given the way each played—and was played by—the game. As viewers, we also play along in rooting for particular players, tracking the near misses that could have changed each of their lives along the way, and learning the lessons of the show's simulation rhetoric. As Bogost (2006) observes, simulations make arguments and reinforce ideologies through their underlying rules and assumptions; *The Wire* serves as a prototype of a persuasive game, making arguments about the inefficacy of the drug war, the class politics of urban America, and the failure of U.S. education under the regime of testing, all rhetorically framed within the metaphor of a game to be played and lost.

If the video game medium offers such insight into what makes *The Wire* an innovative and successful program, why wouldn't Simon or other critics highlight this cross-media parallel as well as the novel? One answer is obvious: it helps legitimize the show by comparing it to the highbrow, respectable literary form rather than the more derided and marginalized medium. And of course, I do believe that Simon and his cowriters do conceive of their practices as fitting with their conceptions of what the novel can do, with "the game" serving as mostly a metaphor for the desolate lives of their characters and institutions. But through my own little game here, reading *The Wire* for the anthology *Third Person* through the analytic lens of its previous game studies iteration of *First Person*, we can see both the possibilities and limitations of analyzing a text through the framework of what it is not. Ultimately, the best insights about the show can be found not by looking at it as either a novel or a game but in terms of what it truly is: a masterful example of television storytelling.

The Serialized Procedural

Placing *The Wire* in the context of television storytelling helps us understand why Simon felt compelled to frame his

36.2 "Makes me sick, motherfucker, how far we done fell." Bunk Moreland (Wendell Pierce) has a heart-to-heart with stickup artist Omar Little (Michael K. Williams), in *The Wire* episode "Homecoming" (2004).

series as atypical of television beyond the implied cultural hierarchies. On the show's debut in 2002, television was in the midst of a distinctive shift in its storytelling strategies and possibilities, exploring a mode of narrative complexity that I have analyzed elsewhere (Mittell 2006). Simon's previous work in television was primarily on the NBC series *Homicide: Life on the Street*, which was based on his journalistic book; *Homicide*'s producers were constantly battling network requests to make plots more conclusive and uplifting, adding hopeful resolution to its bleak vision of urban murder. But in the decade between *Homicide*'s 1993 premiere and *The Wire*'s debut, many programs offered innovations in complex long-form television storytelling, including *The X-Files*, *Buffy the Vampire Slayer*, *The West Wing*, *Alias*, *24*, and most important for Simon's own program, HBO's critically acclaimed offerings of *Oz*, *The Sopranos* (1999–2007), and *Six Feet Under* (2001–2005) as well as his own miniseries *The Corner*. Thus, while Simon frames his series primarily in novelistic terms in opposition to his frustrations working on *Homicide*, there were many key televised precedents for long-form gradual storytelling for him to draw on.

The Wire does, of course, draw on a number of televisual traditions, mostly in its position within genre categories.

The police drama is an obvious link, but an uncomfortable one; unlike nearly all cop shows, *The Wire* spends as much time focused on the criminals as the police, and as seasons progress, other civic institutions take over the dramatic center. The show belongs more to a nonexistent category of "urban drama," documenting a city's systemic decay; thematically, police dramas are nearly always about fighting the tide of decay, rather than contributing to its demise. In spirit, if not in execution, *The Wire* harks back to the critically hailed yet little seen social issue dramas of the early 1960s, like *East Side/West Side* and *The Defenders*, but given the new industrial framework of premium cable television, *The Wire* can survive (if only barely) as a bleak social statement without reaching a mass audience—a luxury that its 1960s' network counterparts could not afford.

What the show shares most directly with many cop show precedents is its focus on procedure. *Dragnet* (1951–1970) pioneered the television cop show in the 1950s, inventing both the formal and cultural vocabulary of the police procedural. Although it reads as a mannered caricature today, in its time *Dragnet* represented the height of gripping authenticity, offering viewers a gritty noir view into the underbelly of Los Angeles and a celebration of the police who protect it. The show's narrative scope focused on the functional machinery of the police world, presenting a form of "systemic realism" that sublimated character depth to institutional logic (Mittell 2004, 137). While *Dragnet* did distill the larger institution into the perspective of Detective Joe Friday and his assorted partners, creator/producer/star Jack Webb designed the show for Friday to be viewed as "just one little cog in a great enforcement machine" (quoted in ibid., 126), and downplayed the character to generate a level of emotional engagement appropriate for a cog, redirecting viewer focus on to the minute details of police procedures. The legacy of *Dragnet*'s procedural tone lives on in the long-running *Law and Order* and *CSI* franchises, each of which offer just enough emotional investment in their institutional workers to engage viewers, but hook them with twisty mysteries each week to be solved by effective forensic detection or prosecution.

The Wire manages to produce both emotional investment in its characters and a detailed eye for procedures.

The opening credits of each season typify the show's focus. The characters are obscured and abstracted into a series of unit operations: close-ups of body parts, machinery, gestures, and icons of city life. What matters in the credits, and arguably the series as a whole, is less who is doing the actions, but more the practices of institutional urban life themselves: the policing, drug slinging, political bribing, and bureaucratic buck-passing that comprise the essence of the show's portrait of Baltimore in decay. *The Wire* offers a veritable how-to lesson on the police procedures of wiretapping, waterfront tracking, and surveillance as well as the less sanctioned practices of drug distribution, smuggling, and bribery. A real New York drug ring even modeled their strategy of dumping cell phones after the practices of Barksdale's crew—a connection that police learned about while listening to dealers recap the previous episode via a wiretap (Rashbaum 2005). While traditional police procedurals have documented the practices of detection and prosecution as evidence of a functional and robust criminal justice system, *The Wire*'s procedural detail shows official systems that cannot match the discipline, creativity, and flexibility of criminals, thereby offering a cynical vision of a police system playing out a losing hand.

The show's formal style supports its claims to authenticity. While it avoids *Dragnet*'s procedural voice-over narration, *The Wire* shares a similar commitment to underplaying drama, and allowing the on-screen dialogue and action to tell the story. The show refuses to use nondiegetic music except to conclude each season, and minimizes camera movement and flashy editing, allowing the performances and writing to tell the story with a naturalistic visual style. Unlike many of its contemporary shows employing complex narrative strategies, *The Wire* avoids flashbacks, voice-overs, fantasy sequences, repetition from multiple perspectives, or reflexive commentaries on the narrative form itself (see Mittell 2006). In terms of how the show stylistically tells its story, *The Wire* appears more akin to conventional procedurals like *Law and Order* than contemporary innovators like *The Sopranos* or *24*, sharing a commitment to authenticity and realism typified by a minimized documentary-style aesthetic that Simon (2006) summarizes: "Less is more. Explaining everything to the slowest or lazi-

est member of the audience destroys verisimilitude and reveals the movie itself, rather than the reality that the movie is trying to convey."

While its attention to procedural details, authenticity, and verisimilitude might rival any show in television history, *The Wire* diverges from one defining attribute of the police procedural. Typically procedurals, whether focusing on police precincts, medical practices, or private detectives, are devoutly episodic in structure—each week, one or more cases gets discovered, processed, and resolved, rarely to reappear or even be remembered in subsequent episodes. On *The Wire*, cases last an entire season or beyond, and everything that happens is remembered with continuing repercussions throughout the storyworld—lessons are learned, grudges are deepened, and the stakes are raised. The show demands audiences to invest in their diegetic memories by rewarding detailed consumption with narrative payoffs; for instance, a first season bust of an aide to Senator Clay Davis adds little to that season's arc, but it sets up a major plotline of seasons three and four. If *Dragnet* represents the prototype of the episodic procedural with hundreds of interchangeable episodes, *The Wire* is on the other end of television's narrational spectrum, with each episode in the series demanding to be viewed in sequence and strict continuity. Thus, *The Wire* functions as what might be television's only example of a serialized procedural.[2]

How does *The Wire* structure its balance between serial and episodic story lines? In many examples of television's contemporary narrative complexity, individual episodes maintain a coherent and steady structure, even when they primarily function as part of a larger storytelling arc (Mittell 2006; Newman 2006). Individual episodes typically offer one self-contained plotline to be resolved while others function primarily within larger season arcs; for example, each episode of *Veronica Mars* typically introduces and resolves one new mystery, while longer character and investigative arcs proceed alongside that week's self-contained plot. Other shows use structural devices to identify distinct episodes, such as *Lost*'s designation of a specific character's flashbacks each week or *Six Feet Under*'s "death-of-the-week" structure. *The Wire* offers little episodic unity. Although each episode is certainly structured to deliver narrative engagement and payoffs in specific beats and threads, it is hard to isolate any identifying characteristics of a single episode in the way that a show like *The Sopranos* has particular markers, such as "the college trip" or "the Russian in the woods." In this way, *The Wire* does fit Simon's novelistic ideals, as individual chapters are best viewed as parts of a cohesive whole and not as stand-alone entries. *The Wire* is therefore at once one of television's most serialized programs, yet also uniquely focused more on institutional procedures and actions than character relationships and emotional struggles that typify most serialized dramas.

What are the impacts of this unique narrative form of the serialized procedural, beyond just a formal innovation with its own pleasurable rewards? *Dragnet* and subsequent police procedurals represent law enforcement as an efficient machine—a perspective that the narrative form reinforces; by offering a weekly glimpse of how cases are solved and justice is served, the genre supports an underlying ideology of support for the status quo to reassure viewers about a functional state system able to protect and serve. Even *Homicide*'s cynical and downbeat vision of law enforcement offers resolution, if not reassurance, through its closed narrative structures.[3] On *The Wire*, the ongoing investigations rarely close and never resolve with any ideological certainties or reassurances, heroic victories or emotional releases. When McNulty allows his pride to swell in recognition that their detail is made up of elite "natural police," Freamon knocks him down, pointing out that even if they do close a big case, there will be no "parade, a gold watch, a shining Jimmy McNulty Day moment" (3.9). Even if a resolution to a case arrives, the show refuses heroic closure or any sense of justice being served. By refusing ideological closure or easy answers to solving the complex systemic problems documented in *The Wire*, the show reminds us that in the end, it's all just a game with another hand waiting to be played.

The Wire's game logic returns to the fore here. Many of television's complex narratives employ a puzzle structure to motivate viewer interest, inspiring fans to watch shows like *Lost*, *Veronica Mars*, and *Heroes* with a forensic eye for details to piece together the mysteries and enigmas encoded

within their serial structures. Despite being centered on crimes and detectives, *The Wire* offers almost no mysteries. We typically know who the criminals are and what they did. Even though the second season begins with an unsolved murder of a shipping container full of Eastern European prostitutes, the whodunit is downplayed in the narrative drive, with the final revelation becoming almost an afterthought as the focus is shifted to the larger systems of corruption, smuggling, and the disintegration of labor— the only closure offered by discovering the name of the already-dead murderer is the ability to remove the "red names" from the board in the homicide squad room. Instead of mysteries, the show's narrative is focused on the game between competing systems, with suspense and tension generated through anticipation of what procedures will pay off for each side, and how the various sides will end up before the next round is played. In season four, we watch in anticipation of the twists and turns it will take before the police discover the bodies entombed by Chris and Snoop as potential leads and connections are missed until chance encounters point Freamon toward the significance of a nailed-up board. The payoff is not justice being served, as the case remains unsolved at the season's end, but the procedural journey toward the discovery. The cultural logic of traditional mysteries is based on a belief in functional institutions of justice being able to solve and punish crime; in *The Wire*'s cynical vision, mysteries are only obstacles to improving clearance rates for homicide detectives or disruptions in the functioning machinery of a criminal operation.

This procedural focus of *The Wire* can be viewed as tied not only to television traditions but also to the mechanics of gameplay. Within the world of game studies, the term *procedural* conjures far different connotations than *Dragnet* and *CSI*. Some game scholars see procedural authorship as the essence of coding gameplay or "procedural narrative," outlining the unit operations that render the storyworld and enable player agency (Mateas and Stern 2007). For Murray (1997, 274), the procedural nature of games and digital narrative is unique in "its ability to capture experience as systems of interrelated actions"—a description seemingly capturing *The Wire*'s narrative mode. Bogost (2006, 46) builds on Murray's model to extend a critical

36.3 No Jimmy McNulty Day moment (Dominic West in *The Wire* episode "Slapstick" [2004]).

eye to "both technology-based and non-technologically based works from the single perspective of their shared procedurality." Although *The Wire*'s procedural language is not written in binary, each Baltimore institution has an underlying code, from the rules of the drug game's parlay to the racial rotation in electing union leaders. The series frequently highlights what happens when conflicting codes overlap, as with Bell's attempt to bring Robert's Rules of Order to the meetings of drug dealers, or Colvin's détente in the drug war to create Hamsterdam; such procedural conflicts trigger the complex social simulation needed to represent the urban environment as "systems of interrelated actions." In both *The Wire* and the realm of digital games, procedures are the essential building blocks of narrative, character, and rhetoric, the actions that are undertaken within the parameters of the simulation, the rules of the game.

Ultimately it is through its focus on procedure, at the levels of action, play, and code, that *The Wire* generates its verisimilitude, creating a ludic engagement with the *SimCity* of twenty-first-century Baltimore. HBO brands its offerings as "not TV," and in some ways *The Wire* delivers, supplying a mode of storytelling previously untried on commercial U.S. television, with a tone and outlook antithetical to the medium's perceived cultural role as a consensus-building ve-

hicle for selling products and ideologies. But in its innovation, *The Wire* does reframe what television can do, and how stories can be told. Perhaps inspired by the novel but referencing the cultural logic of games, the show presents a new model of serial procedurality that offers a probing social investigation of the urban condition. And as the players remind us, "it's all in the game."

Notes

1. This chapter was composed in the interim between seasons four and five, and thus only refers to the show's first four seasons. The author would like to thank the readers of his blog, Just TV, for the thoughtful feedback posted about a draft of this chapter as well as the comments by this volume's editors.

2. Also debuting in 2002, *The Shield* blends the procedural with the serial by mixing ongoing conflicts into its focus on the workings of a corrupt branch of the Los Angeles Police Department. *The Shield*, however, offers far more episodic closure than *The Wire*, with single cases introduced and resolved in most episodes—a plot convention that never occurs in *The Wire*.

3. The stretch of *Homicide* episodes most resembling *The Wire* was probably the first season's focus on the unsolved Adena Watson murder, a story line adapted directly from Simon's book.

References: Literature

Bogost, Ian (2006). *Unit Operations: An Approach to Videogame Criticism*. Cambridge, MA: MIT Press.

Mateas, Michael, and Andrew Stern (2007). "Writing *Façade*: A Case Study in Procedural Authorship." In *Second Person: Role-Playing and Story in Games and Playable Media*, edited by Pat Harrigan and Noah Wardrip-Fruin, 183–207. Cambridge, MA: MIT Press.

Mills, David (2007). Undercover Black Man: "Q&A: David Simon (Pt. 1)." January 22. ⟨http://undercoverblackman.blogspot.com/2007/01/q-david-simon-pt-1.html⟩.

Mittell, Jason (2004). *Genre and Television: From Cop Shows to Cartoons in American Culture*. New York: Routledge.

Mittell, Jason (2006). "Narrative Complexity in Contemporary American Television." *Velvet Light Trap* 58:29–40.

Moulthrop, Stuart (2004). "From Work to Play: Molecular Culture in the Time of Deadly Games." In *First Person: New Media as Story, Performance, and Game*, edited by Noah Wardrip-Fruin and Pat Harrigan, 56–69. Cambridge, MA: MIT Press.

Murray, Janet H. (1997). *Hamlet on the Holodeck: The Future of Narrative in Cyberspace*. New York: Free Press.

Newman, Michael Z. (2006). "From Beats to Arcs: Toward a Poetics of Television Narrative." *Velvet Light Trap* 58:16–28.

Rashbaum, William K. (2005). "Police Say a Queens Drug Ring Watched Too Much Television." *New York Times*, January 15.

Simon, David (2006). "*The Wire* on HBO: Play or Get Played | Exclusive Q&A with David Simon." August 16. ⟨http://members.aol.com/TheWireHBO/exclusive-1.html⟩.

Zimmerman, Eric (2004). "Narrative, Interactivity, Play, and Games: Four Naughty Concepts in Need of Discipline." In *First Person: New Media as Story, Performance, and Game*, edited by Noah Wardrip-Fruin and Pat Harrigan, 154–164. Cambridge, MA: MIT Press.

Zurawik, David (2006). "David Simon Has Novel Ideas about *Wire*." *Baltimore Sun*, September 10.

References: Games

SimCity. Will Wright; Maxis. 1989.

The Sims. Will Wright; Maxis. 2000.

References: Television

Dragnet (1951–1970). NBC. Creator Jack Webb.

Six Feet Under (2001–2005). HBO. Creator Alan Ball.

The Sopranos (1999–2007). HBO. Creator David Chase.

The Wire (2002–2008). HBO. Creator David Simon.

Jason Mittell

Contributor Biographies

Rafael Alvarez

Rafael Alvarez is a short story writer who spent twenty years as a City Desk reporter for the *Baltimore Sun*. In 2007–2008, he worked as a writer/producer for the NBC police drama *Life*, starring Damian Lewis and Adam Arkin. The author of *Orlo and Leini*, a collection of short stories published in 2000, Alvarez lives in Baltimore and Los Angeles.

Richard Bartle

Dr. Richard A. Bartle cowrote the first virtual world, MUD ("Multi-User Dungeon") in 1978, and so has been at the forefront of the online games industry from its inception. He is an influential writer on all aspects of virtual world design, development, and management; his 2003 book, *Designing Virtual Worlds*, has established itself as a foundation text for researchers and developers of virtual worlds alike. Bartle lives in Colchester, England, where he teaches computer game design at the University of Essex.

Michael Bonesteel

Michael Bonesteel is an art history instructor at the School of the Art Institute of Chicago, and an arts and entertainment editor for Pioneer Press Newspapers in Chicago. His books include *Henry Darger: Art and Selected Writings* (Rizzoli International Publications, 2000) and a catalogue raisonné of the prints of John Himmelfarb (Hudson Hills Press, 2005). He has published art criticism and feature articles in *Art in America*, *Artforum*, and *Raw Vision*. Bonesteel has also curated exhibitions at the American Visionary Art Museum and the Chicago Cultural Center. Reviews and articles regarding his publishing and curatorial work have appeared in the *New York Times*, *Bookforum*, *U.S. News and World Report*, the *Washington Post*, the *Baltimore Sun*, the *Chicago Tribune*, and the *Chicago Sun-Times*.

Stanford Carpenter

Stanford W. Carpenter is a cultural anthropologist and an assistant professor of visual and critical studies of the School of the Art Institute of Chicago. He conducts ethnographic research among media makers to address the relationships between creative practices, production processes, identity construction, and the depiction community. Carpenter uses his ethnographic research both for scholarly manuscripts and arts-based projects. As Brother-Story, he is a founding member of Critical Front, an arts-based project in which academics use superhero alter egos as a means of cultural criticism and research into cultural production. He is currently finishing a book for Duke University Press on identity in comic books from the perspective of comic book creators.

Monte Cook

Monte Cook has worked in the gaming industry since 1989. He was one of the three principal designers of the third edition of *Dungeons & Dragons* and the d20 system, and was the primary author of the *Dungeon Master's Guide*. In 2001, Cook created Malhavoc Press, his own design studio, and has produced many award-winning game products. He lives in Wisconsin with his wife, Sue, and their Welsh Corgi, Marley. Cook has published two novels and numerous short stories, and is a graduate of the Clarion West Writer's Workshop.

Paul Cornell

Paul Cornell is a novelist, television writer, and comics writer. He has written for shows like *Doctor Who* and *Primeval*, and the Marvel Comics miniseries *Wisdom*. His novels include *Something More* and *British Summertime*.

Anne Cranny-Francis

Anne Cranny-Francis is an associate professor in English and cultural studies at Macquarie University in Sydney, Australia. She has published widely on feminist fiction, media, cultural theory, and literacy. Her books include *Feminist Fiction: Feminist Uses of Generic Fiction* (1990), *Engendered Fiction* (1992), *Popular Culture* (1994), *The Body in the Text* (1995), *Gender Studies: Terms and Debates* (2003), and *Multimedia: Texts and Contexts* (2005). See also ⟨http://www.ccs.mq.edu.au/staff_afrancis.php⟩.

Sam Ford

Sam Ford is an affiliate of the Convergence Culture Consortium in the comparative media studies program at MIT and director of customer insights for Peppercom. He received a master's degree from MIT in 2007, focusing his thesis on how soap operas and their fan communities are adapting and should adapt in the future to new technologies and new configurations of producer/consumer relationships. Ford has published and taught courses at MIT on American professional wrestling, soap operas, and journalism, and he served as project manager for the Consortium from 2007 to 2008. His work focuses on fan proselytism, fan archiving, and narrative worlds that foster a deep engagement. Ford is also a professional journalist, writing a weekly column for the *Ohio County Times-News* in Hartford, Ky., and won a Kentucky Press Association award for his 2006 work for the *Greenville Leader-News* in Greenville, Ky.

Chaim Gingold

Chaim Gingold is the design lead for *Spore's* player creativity tools and has done extensive prototyping across the project. Prior to joining Maxis/Electronic Arts, he studied at Georgia Institute of Technology, where he wrote a master's thesis about player creativity and game aesthetics. He has lectured around the world on prototyping, game design, and player creativity. Growing up, his favorite toys were Transformers and Legos.

A. Scott Glancy

Adam Scott Glancy was born on the same day that *Star Trek* premiered on NBC, a propitious beginning to a lifelong love of science fiction and fantasy. He is a recovering attorney who currently operates Pagan Publishing, a small press publisher specializing in publishing supplements and fiction for the *Call of Cthulhu* role-playing game. Glancy is one of the three authors of the award-winning *Delta Green* role-playing and fiction franchise. He values his two Origins Awards almost as much as his LebowskiFest "Best Walter 2007" trophy.

Richard Grossman

Richard Grossman was born in Lubbock, Texas, in 1943. The son of a Chevrolet dealer, he was raised in Minneapolis, Minnesota, attending public schools and then Stanford University, where he graduated with a BA in English literature in 1965. For many years, Grossman has been concentrating his efforts on creating a vast work titled *American Letters*. The first book in the trilogy, *The Alphabet Man*, won the FC2 National Fiction Competition in 1993, and was nominated for a Pen West award. *Breeze Avenue*, a compilation of thirty-seven works that occupy three million pages, is the product of over thirty-five years of literary labor. It is slated for publication in 2009. He currently lives in Los Angeles with his wife, Lisa Lyons.

Pat Harrigan

Patrick Harrigan is a Minneapolis-based writer and editor. He has worked on new media projects with Improv Technologies, Weatherwood Company, and Wrecking Ball Productions, and as marketing director and creative developer for Fantasy Flight Games. He is the coeditor of Fantasy Flight's *The Art of H.P. Lovecraft's Cthulhu Mythos* (2006, with Brian Wood), and the MIT Press volumes *Second Person: Role-Playing and Story in Games and Playable Media* (2007) and *First Person: New Media as Story, Performance, and Game* (2004), both with Noah Wardrip-Fruin. He has also written a novel, *Lost Clusters* (2005).

Matt Hills

Dr. Matt Hills is a reader in media and cultural studies at Cardiff University. He is the author of *Fan Cultures* (Routledge, 2002), *The Pleasures of Horror* (Continuum, 2005), and *How to Do Things with Cultural Theory* (Hodder-Arnold, 2005). Hills has contributed work on *Doctor Who* to a number of publications, and is currently working on *Triumph of a Time Lord: Regenerating Doctor Who in the 21st Century* (I. B. Tauris, 2008).

Kenneth Hite

Kenneth Hite is the author or coauthor of over fifty role-playing games games and supplements, including the Origins Award–winning *GURPS Infinite Worlds* and *Star Trek: The Next Generation RPG*. In addition to *GURPS Infinite Worlds* and *GURPS Cabal*, he has created campaign settings for Elsewhere Entertainment's *Totems* console game, and *GURPS Horror* and *GURPS WWII: Weird War II*. He has also created game material for preexisting settings, including *Star Trek*, *Lord of the Rings*, World of Darkness, *Unknown Armies*, and *In Nomine*. Since 1997, he has written "Out of the Box," a role-playing game industry news and review column currently available at ⟨http://www .gamingreport.com⟩.

William Huber

William H. Huber is a doctoral student researching video games, software, and media theory at the University of California at San Diego, in the art and media history, theory, and criticism program. He has taught video game theory and practice courses at a number of institutions, including the University of Southern California and California State University at Fullerton, and has also worked for several years in the software industry. Huber has published articles and book chapters on Japanese video game aesthetics and the critical study of games as texts. His current research interests include game aesthetics as well as the relationship between software and authorship.

Adriene Jenik

Adriene Jenik is a telecommunications media artist who lives in Southern California. Her works, including *El Naftazteca* (with Guillermo Gómez-Peña), *Mauve Desert: A CD-ROM Translation*, *Desktop Theater* (with Lisa Brenneis and the DT troupe), and SPECFLIC harness the collision of "high" technology and human desire to propose new forms of literature, cinema, and performance. Jenik is an associate professor of computer and media arts in the Visual Arts Department at the University of California at San Diego.

Henry Jenkins

Henry Jenkins is the director of the MIT Comparative Media Studies Program and the Peter de Florez Professor of Humanities. He is the author and/or editor of nine books on various aspects of media and popular culture, including *Textual Poachers: Television Fans and Participatory Culture*, *Hop on Pop: The Politics and Pleasures of Popular Culture*, and *From Barbie to Mortal Kombat: Gender and Computer Games*. His newest books include *Convergence Culture: Where Old and New Media Collide* and *Fans, Bloggers, and Gamers: Exploring Participatory Culture*. He recently developed a white paper on the future of media literacy education for the MacArthur Foundation that is leading to a three-year project to develop curricular materials to help teachers and parents better prepare young people for full participation in contemporary culture. Jenkins is one of the principal investigators for the Education Arcade, a consortium of educators and business leaders working to promote the educational use of computer and video games, and is one of the leaders of the Convergence Culture Consortium, which consults with leading players in the branded entertainment sector in hopes of helping them adjust to shifts in the media environment.

David Kalat

David Kalat is a film historian and DVD producer living in La Grange Park, Illinois, with his wife and two children. He has written several books on movies, including *J-Horror*, *The Strange Case of Dr. Mabuse*, and *A Critical History of Toho's Godzilla Series*, and presides over the specialist DVD label All Day Entertainment.

Matt Kirschenbaum

Matthew G. Kirschenbaum is an assistant professor of English at the University of Maryland, where he specializes in digital studies, applied humanities computing, images and visual culture, and postmodern/experimental literature. His book *Mechanisms: New Media and Forensic Textuality* was published by the MIT Press in fall 2007. He is the associate director of the Maryland Institute for Technology in the Humanities (MITH). Kirschenbaum has played board wargames off and on since he was a teenager.

Norman M. Klein

A historian in the fields of architecture, media, and culture, Norman M. Klein was born in Brooklyn in 1945, and has been a professor of critical studies at the California Institute of the Arts for over thirty years. He is the author of *Seven Minutes: The Life and Death of the American Animated Cartoon* (1993), *The History of Forgetting: Los Angeles and the Erasure of Memory* (1997), *The Vatican to Vegas: The History of Special Effects* (2003), and a fictionalized memoir, *Freud in Coney Island and Other Tales* (2006). Klein's exhibition, Scripted Spaces: The Chase and the Labyrinth, was presented at the Rotterdam Centre for Modern Art, Witte de With, and in the Künstlerhaus in Stuttgart. His 2003 work *Bleeding Through: Layers of Los Angeles, 1920–86* is an interactive compact disc with an accompanying book, developed in association with the Karlsruhe Centre for Art and Media. Another DVD-ROM database novel, *The Imaginary Twentieth Century*, appeared in 2007. He lives in Los Angeles.

Tanya Krzywinska

Tanya Krzywinska is a professor in screen studies at Brunel University in London. She is coauthor of *Tomb Raiders and Space Invaders: Videogame Forms and Contexts* (I. B. Tauris, 2006), coeditor of *Videogame, Player, Text* (Melbourne University Press, 2007), coeditor of *ScreenPlay: Cinema/videogames/interfaces* (Wallflower, 2002), and author of *Sex and the Cinema* (Wallflower Press, 2006) and *A Skin for Dancing In: Possession, Witchcraft, and Voodoo in Film* (Wallflower Press, 2002). Krzywinska convenes a master's program, Digital Games: Theory and Design, and is president of the Digital Games Research Association (⟨http://www.digra.org⟩). She is currently playing *Lord of the Rings Online* and working on a monograph titled *Imaginary Worlds*.

David Lavery

Dr. David Lavery is an American, now chair in film and television at Brunel University in London. The author of numerous essays and reviews, and the author/coauthor/editor/coeditor of over a dozen books on television, he coedits the e-journal *Slayage: The Online International Journal of Buffy Studies*, edits *Intensities: The Journal of Cult Media*, and is one of the founding editors of the new journal *Critical Studies in Television: Scholarly Studies of Small Screen Fictions*.

Robin Laws

Robin D. Laws is a writer and game designer. His role-playing game designs include *Feng Shui*, *The Dying Earth*, *Rune*, *HeroQuest*, and *The Esoterrorists*. Among his six novels are *Pierced Heart*, *The Rough and the Smooth*, and *Freedom Phalanx*, a book set in the universe of the *City of Heroes* computer game. His nonfiction work includes *40 Years of Gen Con*, an oral history of the hobby games industry's biggest convention. Always ready to take an intriguing career detour, his other past projects include collectible card games, computer games, and comic books.

Sarah Lewison

Sarah Lewison is a media producer, artist, and writer whose work examines power, economics, and political subjectivity. Her teaching and research areas include media and social change, ecological pedagogy and experimental performance. Her video work includes the documentary collaboration *Fat of the Land*, which screened on PBS and in museums, festivals, and community spaces worldwide, and is noted for stimulating the do-it-yourself waste-grease biodiesel movement. Lewison is corresponding editor for the *Journal of Aesthetics and Protest*, and her writing about media aesthetics, social history, sustainability, and culture has been published in *Tema* (Denmark), *Journal of Northeast Studies* (Hamburg), *Area* (Chicago), and *Failure! Experiments in Aesthetics and Social Practices* (Los Angeles). She is an assistant professor of radio-television at Southern Illinois University Carbondale.

Henry Lowood

Henry Lowood is curator for the History of Science and Technology Collections at Stanford University, and a lecturer in the History and Philosophy of Science Program and in the Science and Technology Studies Program. He has written widely on the history of science and technology and game studies. Currently, he is the coprincipal investigator of "How They Got Game: The History and Culture of Interactive Simulations and Videogames," a research project sponsored by the Stanford Humanities Laboratory.

William E. McDonald

William E. McDonald taught at the University of Redlands' Johnston Center from 1969 until his retirement in 2005; he was a professor of English and held the Virginia Hunsaker Chair in Teaching. He has coauthored two volumes on the Johnston Center (1989, 2004) and published a book on Thomas Mann (1999). McDonald is now working on a book-length study of J. M. Coetzee's *Disgrace* with some twenty of his former colleagues and students. His other academic fields include international modernism, literary theory, ancient Greece, and interdisciplinary studies in the humanities. He was privileged to work with this volume's two editors during their undergraduate years, and now vastly beyond.

Matthew P. Miller

Matthew P. Miller started in the computer games industry at the age of twenty working for Domark Software (which eventually became Eidos Interactive) as a tester and doing phone support for its virtual reality program and flight simulator. He worked as a designer on flight simulators for the company as well as the science fiction game *Absolute Zero*. Miller eventually became an associate producer for Eidos, and worked on titles such as *Thief: The Dark Project*, *JSF*, *Terracide*, and *Revenant*. After Eidos, he worked for Prolific Publishing as a producer on such titles as *Shrek's Fairy Tale Freakdown* and *Shrek Kart Racing* as well as the *Serene Screen* screen saver. Finally, Miller moved back to the Bay Area and began working for Cryptic Studios as a designer on *City of Heroes*. With the release of *City of Villains*, he became the lead designer on *City of Heroes* and *City of Villains*, driving the creative team into outputting new content for the games on the order of three times per calendar year. He is married and has a son.

Jason Mittell

Jason Mittell is an assistant professor of American studies and film and media culture at Middlebury College. He is the author of *Genre and Television: From Cop Shows to Cartoons in American Culture* (Routledge, 2004), numerous essays in a number of journals and anthologies, and the blog Just TV. Mittell is currently writing a textbook on television and U.S. culture, and a book on narrative complexity in contemporary U.S. television.

Stuart Moulthrop

Stuart Moulthrop is a professor of information arts and technologies at the University of Baltimore, where he teaches a number of courses in new media, including occasional classes on comics. He is a well-known writer and designer, author of *Victory Garden* (1991), "Reagan Library" (1999), and other works of electronic literature. His critical essays have been reprinted in several anthologies, including the *Norton Anthology of Theory and Criticism* and *The New Media Reader*.

Kate Orman

Kate Orman has written and cowritten over a dozen *Doctor Who*–related novels, many with her husband and collaborator, Jon Blum. Their novella *Fallen Gods* won the 2003 Aurealis Award for best Australian science fiction novel. Kate and Jon live in Sydney, Australia.

Sean O'Sullivan

Sean O'Sullivan is an assistant professor of English at Ohio State University. He is the author of *Mike Leigh* (a volume in the Contemporary Film Directors series published by the University of Illinois Press). His work addresses British cinema and television, serial fiction across media, and narrative connections between the visual and verbal arts. O'Sullivan's next book project will examine serial narrative of the nineteenth and twenty-first centuries.

Lance Parkin

Lance Parkin has written a couple dozen books, including the science fiction novel *Warlords of Utopia*, a critical biography of Alan Moore, and (with Mark Jones) *Dark Matters*, a guide to Philip Pullman's *His Dark Materials* trilogy. He worked on the British soap opera *Emmerdale*, and wrote four books about the show. Parkin has written seven *Doctor Who* novels and *Ahistory: An Unauthorized History of the Doctor Who Universe*, a survey of the series' convoluted continuity. He is currently working on a novel and a number of Web comics.

Robert M. Price

Robert M. Price discovered the work of H. P. Lovecraft, along with that of Robert E. Howard, J. R. R. Tolkien, Edgar Rice Burroughs, Lin Carter, and so many others, at age thirteen, during the great paperback revival of pulp fiction in the late 1960s. He has never been the same. His short stories in a Cthulhu Mythos vein have appeared in numerous small press anthologies and magazines. He has edited Lovecraftian fiction anthologies for Del Rey, Chaosium, Fedogan and Bremer, Arkham House, and others. His Mythos fanzine *Crypt of Cthulhu* reached its 109th issue, and after strange aeons, just may come back again.

Ren Reynolds

Ren Reynolds is a consultant, philosopher, and writer based in the United Kingdom and numerous virtual worlds. Academically, he writes about the ethics of technology, computer games, and virtual worlds. He has published papers on topics such as massively multiplayer online games and digital identity, virtual property, sexuality and video games, and the ethics of cheating. Reynolds writes on the TerraNova blog (⟨http://terranova.blogs.com⟩) as well as for Gamasutra and the IGDA (⟨http://www.igda.org/articles/rreynolds_ethics.php⟩), where he is a member of the Sex in Games (⟨http://www.igda.org/sex⟩) and Intellectual Property (⟨http://www.igda.org/ipr/about.html⟩) special interest groups. He is the ex-head of global strategy for Internet, mobile, and applications for Cable and Wireless, where he developed a digital media service portfolio. Reynolds has also consulted in marketing and product strategy/development for British Airways, BBC, Sky, Publicis, the UK government, virtual world start-ups, and charities; and has written extensively for IBM on the business application of emerging technologies for strategic advantage. He has numerous media credits, including MTV, G4 TV, BBC World Service, NY Public Radio, and Radio Sweden,

and has been interviewed by *New Scientist*, *Popular Science*, the *Guardian*, and many other periodicals.

Trina Robbins

Historian and writer Trina Robbins has been writing graphic novels, comics, and books for over thirty years. Her subjects have ranged from Wonder Woman and the Powerpuff Girls to her own teenage superheroine, GoGirl!, and from women cartoonists and superheroines to women who kill. She has written over a dozen educational graphic novels for three different publishers, provided English-language rewrites for shojo manga graphic novels, and lectured on comics and graphic novels throughout the United States and Europe. Robbins lives in San Francisco, in a moldering 102-year-old house with her cats, shoes, and books.

Ken Rolston

Ken Rolston designs really big computer role-playing games. Currently the lead designer on an unannounced project for Big Huge Games in Timonium, Maryland, Rolston was lead designer for Bethesda's award-winning *The Elder Scrolls IV: Oblivion* and *The Elder Scrolls III: Morrowind*. Previously, Rolston was an award-winning designer of paper-and-pencil role-playing games, including games and supplements for *Paranoia*, *Runequest*, *Warhammer Fantasy Roleplay*, *Advanced Dungeons & Dragons*, *Dungeons & Dragons*, *Star Wars*, *Ghostbusters*, and *Stormbringer*. A winner of the H. G. Wells Award for Best Role-Playing Game (*Paranoia*, 1985), he served as role-playing director for West End Games, Games Workshop, and Avalon Hill Game Company. Author of the novel *Nobody Knows the Trouble I've Shot*, Rolston is a member of the Science Fiction Writers Association, holds a master's degree from New York University, and has been a professional games designer since 1982.

Dave Sim

Dave Sim is the illustrator (with Gerhard) and writer of the six-thousand-page graphic novel *Cerebus*, published in single-issue form from 1977 to 2004. He is the founder of Aardvark-Vanaheim Press and the winner of multiple awards, including the Eisner, Harvey, Ignatz, and Kirby awards. He lives in Kitchener, Ontario.

Greg Stafford

Greg Stafford is one of the founders of the adventure game industry, working as a publisher and author since his first professional game, *White Bear and Red Moon*, was released in 1975. He founded Chaosium, publishing *Thieves World*, *Call of Cthulhu*, and many other notable games. Stafford is the designer or codesigner of five role-playing games (*RuneQuest*, *King Arthur Pendragon*, *Prince Valiant*, *Ghostbusters*, and *HeroQuest*), four board games (*White Bear and Red Moon/Dragon Pass*, *Nomad Gods*, *Elric*, and *King Arthur's Knights*), one miniatures game (*Merlin*), and one computer game (*King of Dragon Pass*), plus numerous campaigns, scenarios, and game aids. He is currently working on a Gloranthan novel and a book of Oaxacan legends.

Tamiko Thiel

Tamiko Thiel (⟨http://www.mission-base.com/tamiko⟩) is developing the dramatic and narrative capabilities of interactive 3-D virtual reality as a medium for addressing social, cultural, and political issues. Her online virtual play space for seriously ill children, *Starbright World*, designed with Steven Spielberg, won numerous awards, including the Global Information Infrastructure Next Generation Award. Thiel's virtual reality installation *Beyond Manzanar* is discussed in Whitney Museum media art curator Christiane Paul's reference work *Digital Art*, and in Boston University professor Matthew Smith's book *The Total Work of Art: From Bayreuth to Cyberspace*. To create her newest work, *The Travels of Mariko Horo*, she received a Japan Foundation Fellowship for the Kyoto Art Center in 2003, and a Research Fellowship at the Center for Advanced Visual Studies in 2004 at MIT.

John Tulloch

John Tulloch is a research professor in sociology and communication at Brunel University, the deputy head of school (research) in the School of Social Sciences, and the director of the University Interdisciplinary Research Centre in Media, Globalization, and Risk. He is the author (with Manuel Alvarado) of *Doctor Who: The Unfolding Text* (1983) and (with Henry Jenkins) *Science Fiction Audiences: Watching Doctor Who and Star Trek* (1995). His recent books, *Trevor Griffiths* (2006), *Shakespeare and Chekhov in Production and Reception* (2005), and (with Deborah Lupton) *Risk and Everyday Life* (2003), combine his long-term background in television studies, audience research, risk sociology, and popular and high cultural studies. On July 7, 2005, he had a very close encounter with the suicide bomber Mohammad Sidique Khan in a London underground train and was seriously injured. His book *One Day in July: Experiencing 7/7* (2006) is an account of the experiential and media reconstruction of his identities after that event.

Noah Wardrip-Fruin

Noah Wardrip-Fruin is a digital media writer, artist, and scholar with a particular interest in fiction and playability. His writing/art has been presented by galleries, arts festivals, scientific conferences, DVD magazines, and the Whitney and Guggenheim museums. He has recently edited three books for the MIT Press: *Second Person: Role-Playing and Story in Games and Playable Media* (2007), *First Person: New Media as Story, Performance, and Game* (2004), both with Pat Harrigan, and *The New Media Reader* (2003, with Nick Montfort). Now at the University of California at Santa Cruz, he has previously taught in Brown University's literary arts program, the University of Baltimore's School of Information Arts and Technologies, New York University's graduate film and television program, and the University of California at San Diego. He is a vice president of the Electronic Literature Organization and blogs at ⟨http://grandtextauto.org⟩.

Walter Jon Williams

Walter Jon Williams is the author of *Hardwired*, *Aristoi*, and the forthcoming *Implied Spaces*. He has won two Nebula Awards for his writing, and has appeared on the *New York Times* best-seller list. Williams has also written for film and television. He is a scuba diver, small-boat sailor, fourth-degree black belt in Kenpo Karate, and consultant to the Department of Homeland Security.

Permissions

The editors wish to thank the following people and organizations for their permission to reproduce material in this volume. Most images not listed here are by permission of the author of the associated chapter, or are reprinted under fair use practice. In a small number of cases it was not possible to locate the copyright holder.

Aardvark-Vanaheim Press:
Images of *High Society*, *Jaka's Story*, and *The Last Day* appear courtesy of Aardvark-Vanaheim Press.

Arkham House:
Images of Arkham House publications appear courtesy of April Derleth and Arkham House.

BBC Books:
Images of *The Infinity Doctors*, *Trading Futures*, and *The Year of Intelligent Tigers* © BBC Books. Used with permission. All rights reserved.

Kirsten Beckerman:
Image of Jay Tinker appears courtesy of Kirsten Beckerman.

Blizzard Entertainment:
World of Warcraft® images provided courtesy of Blizzard Entertainmnent, Inc.

Jim Burger:
Image of David Simon and Rafael Alvarez appears courtesy of Jim Burger.

Monte Cook:
Image of *Ptolus: City by the Spire* appears courtesy of Monte Cook.

Cryptic Studios:
Image of *City of Heroes* appears courtesy of Cryptic Studios.

DC Comics:
Images from *Black Lightning*, vols. 1 and 2, *Justice League of America*, vol. 3, and *Watchmen* © DC Comics. Used with permission. All rights reserved.

William Donohoe:
Image of Virgin Books' *Human Nature* appears courtesy of William Donohoe.

Bill Finn:
Images of *Miss Fury* appear courtesy of Bill Finn.

Peter Graf:
Images of *The Travels of Mariko Horo* appears courtesy of Peter Graf.

David Kalat:
Fantômas images appear courtesy of the collection of David Kalat.

Matt Kirschenbaum:
Images of wargames appear courtesy of the collection of Matt Kirschenbaum.

Norman Klein:
Images of *Bleeding Through* and *The Imaginary Twentieth Century* appear courtesy of Norman Klein.

Kiyoko Lerner and Andrew Edlin Gallery:
Images of the works of Henry Darger appear courtesy of Kiyoko Lerner and the Andrew Edlin Gallery, New York.

Maxis Entertainment:
Images of *Spore* appear courtesy of Maxis Entertainment.

Eric John Mithen:
Image of Minas Konsolas's mural of Leini appears courtesy of Eric John Mithen.

Mount Sinai Hospital:
Images of *Starbright World* appear courtesy of Mount Sinai Hospital.

Pagan Publishing:
Images of *Delta Green: Countdown*, *Delta Green: The Rules of Engagement*, and *Delta Green: Denied to the Enemy* appear courtesy of Pagan Publishing.

Lee Sullivan:
Image of Virgin Books' *Love and War* appears courtesy of Lee Sullivan.

Philip Thiel:
Images of the "forward isovist" and "Space / Place / Occasion / Scene" appear courtesy of Philip Thiel.

Tamiko Thiel and Zara Houshmand:
Images of *Beyond Manzanar* appear courtesy of Tamiko Thiel and Zara Houshmand.

Pete Wallbank:
Image of Virgin Books' *The Left-Handed Hummingbird* appears courtesy of Pete Wallbank.

White Wolf Publishing, Inc.:
Images of *King Arthur Pendragon* and *The Great Pendragon Campaign* appear courtesy of White Wolf Publishing, Inc.

Index